P9-DXZ-174 (5)

D0010574

Index to

The Modern Theatre

THE MODERN THEATRE

A collection of plays

selected by

MRS. ELIZABETH INCHBALD

First published London, 1811

in ten volumes

Reissued in 1968
in five volumes
by Benjamin Blom, Inc.

Benjamin Blom, Inc.

New York

THE

MODERN THEATRE;

A COLLECTION OF

SUCCESSFUL MODERN PLAYS,

AS ACTED AT

THE THEATRES ROYAL, LONDON.

PRINTED FROM THE PROMPT BOOKS UNDER THE AU-
THORITY OF THE MANAGERS.

SELECTED BY

MRS INCHBALD.

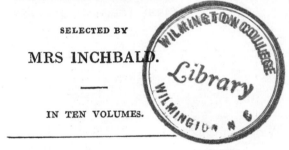

IN TEN VOLUMES.

VOL. IX.

LONDON:

PRINTED FOR LONGMAN, HURST, REES, ORME, AND BROWN,
PATERNOSTER-ROW.

1811.

First published London, 1811
Reissued 1968,
by Benjamin Blom, Inc. Bx 10452

Library of Congress Catalog Card No. 67-13004

Manufactured in the United States of America

THE

BANK NOTE;

OR

LESSONS FOR LADIES.

A COMEDY,

IN FIVE ACTS.

AS PERFORMED AT THE

THEATRE-ROYAL, COVENT-GARDEN.

BY

WILLIAM MACREADY

VOL. IX. A

DRAMATIS PERSONÆ.

Sir Charles Leslie,	Mr Holman.
Mr Bloomfield,	Mr Middleton.
Father,	Mr Hull.
Lieutenant Selby,	Mr Macready.
Ned Dash,	Mr Fawcett.
Mr Hale,	Mr Quick.
Killeavy,	Mr Johnstone.
Tim (*Servant to Dash*),	Mr Townsend.
Careful (*a Steward*),	Mr Powell.
Young Bloomfield,	Miss Standen.
Mr Bloomfield's *Servant*,	Mr Abbot.
Porter,	Mr Coombs.
Gentleman,	Mr Platt.
Cook,	Mr Ledger.
Butler,	Mr Williamson.
Lady Supple,	Mrs Davenport.
Mrs Bloomfield,	Mrs Mattocks.
Miss Russel,	Miss Wallis.
Miss Emma Hale,	Miss Hopkins.
Sally Flounce,	Mrs Lee.
Maid,	Mrs Norton.
Gentlewoman,	Mrs Follett.

Visitors,—Gentlemen, Ladies, &c. &c.

BANK NOTE.

ACT THE FIRST.

SCENE I.

The Park.

Enter MR BLOOMFIELD *and Servant.*

Bloom. Well, I am coming; there's no occasion for all this bustle.

Serv. Lord, sir, he's gone, I'm afraid.

Bloom. No, that he is not, if you left him with Emma—a lover and his mistress are not so easily separated—I knew I was right—here they come.

Enter SELBY *and* EMMA.

So, Selby, the hour's arrived.   [*Exit Servant.*

Sel. It is; that hour which calls me from friends, from home, from my love.

Em. Oh! heavens! must you, will you leave me?

Bloom. Will he? most assuredly, therefore think not of his going, but console yourself with the pleasing hope of his return.

Em. Ah, sir, 'tis easier far to counsel than to act, and every one's provided with wisdom that has not a share in the misfortune.

Sel. What! could my Emma wish me to stay, and be branded with dishonour?

Bloom. Not she, indeed, she'd sooner lose you for ever than think you a coward.

Em. Woman as I am, the thought is hateful; yet, my Selby, preserve yourself; let not impetuous zeal drive you into danger; do not seek wounds; for any drop of blood you lose flows from your Emma's heart.

Sel. Fear not, my love, I'll——

Bloom. Selby, take heed, my friendship cannot suffer you to incur censure; you should be gone—a greater power than love commands.

Sel. True; I feel the reproach——

Em. One moment stop, and hear my resolution in the presence of our mutual friend; I voluntarily and solemnly pledge myself to exclude all society till your return; nor do I blush to own my heart is, and shall continue yours.

Sel. Bewitching goodness!—Farewell—Should our arms prove successful, with what joy shall I return to Emma and my native place; or, should I fall, my last breath shall cry to Heaven for blessings on my Emma, and victory to my sovereign.   [*Exit.*

Em. Oh! heavens! my poor heart.

Bloom. What! is this your boasted resolution? These tears disgrace the noble love you bear him.

Em. They do, I own it—my Selby, I shall pray for your return with the same fervency as departing

sinners offer their supplications for felicity hereafter.   [*Exit.*

Bloom. Fortune ! Fortune ! Well may the world
pronounce thee unkind, when merit and virtue are
deserted, while ingratitude and villainy revel in your
smiles—Ha ! here comes the gay, the elegant, accomplish'd, inconstant, Sir Charles Leslie, who happily blends gallantry, mirth, and bravery, with every
amiable qualification, and, notwithstanding all his levity, has a soul susceptible of friendship, and a heart
capable of every noble act.

Enter SIR CHARLES LESLIE.

Sir Cha. Bloomfield ! who expected to have seen
you quit the matrimonial yoke thus early ? Prodigious ! Turtles will cease to coo, and the waking
nightingale forget to sing, when thus, by break of
day, you leave the downy bed of love.

Bloom. Sir Charles, 'twas in obedience to the call
of friendship I deserted my pillow.—Poor George
Selby and the regiment he belongs to were this morning under marching orders.

Sir Cha. Selby ! I don't know him.

Bloom. The loss is yours. He has so much worth
and honour, that if you knew him as well as I do,
you'd love him as well as I do ; were merit any title
to advancement, he should be a general; but fortune
often bestows preferment where 'tis least deserved.

Sir Cha. Why never introduce me to him ?

Bloom. Because his lieutenancy being his sole property, he lived within bounds, and devoted his time
chiefly to the woman of his heart, with whom he has
just now parted. His poverty and her father's avarice are the only bars to their union.

Sir Cha. He ought to thank his poverty for keeping at a distance a greater evil.

Bloom. Come, come, Sir Charles, matrimony is
like hazard, there are mains.

Sir Cha. Ay, and chances too—you have made a
very just simile.   Dice and marriage are two things
I could preach upon whole nights together—'tis hard
to distinguish which are worst, the pride, folly, and
extravagance of a wife, or the rattling of a box and
dice, whose noise proclaims that the infatuated idiot
is forcing into a prison himself, and providing alms-
houses for the rest of his family.—These ideas set liberty and interest at war within me to determine
which shall conquer—ruin or the widow.

Bloom. Wou'dn't you be content this instant to go
to church with her?

Sir Cha. Yes, upon condition I might follow her,
in a month, to the church-yard——Marry her!—horrid!—then I must not be commonly civil to a pretty
girl, or I shall be look'd on by her father and mother
worse than a tax-gatherer in a country village, and
all this for an ugly woman.—Nay what's worse, an
old woman!—No, no, matrimony and the country
are two things on which we shall never think alike.

Bloom. Why object to the country? Can mankind
have greater delight than in contemplating the works
of nature?

Sir Cha. I contemplate the chief works of nature,
fine women: in my opinion, half a score well-dress'd
ladies are infinitely superior to a wilderness of syca-
mores, oaks, or poplars: and I would forego all the
luxury of purling streams and chirping birds for
that ravishing music, the rustling of a silk petticoat.

Bloom. You may rail against retirement and matrimony, yet I am mistaken if you'll not shortly be
reconciled to the latter, and that with Lady Supple;
a widow possess'd of eighty thousand pounds, and
the redemption of your estate mortgaged to her deceased husband, you'd find much better than being
eternally teaz'd with officers lurking about your house,
and even your servants impudent for want of wages.

Sir Cha. To be sure duns are intolerable; and when some poor devil of a tradesman has told a lamentable tale of his distress, and that discharging my bill wou'd instantly relieve him and his indigent family, I have in desperation flown to her, said ten thousand fine things, and told her as many lies as invention on the rack could supply me with, but all would not do.

Bloom. I fear you have a rival that has possess'd himself of her good opinion, and when once she comes to fancy him seriously, she'll think no more of you than of her dead husband or his poor relations.

Sir Cha. You allude to that young fop, Sir Rakeish Spangle? They first met at the opera, where I should have been to attend her, but the bottle deluded me till twelve that night, the dice till six in the morning, and bed till five next evening : at which time I dress'd, went to visit her, and, to my great surprise, found him there. We rattled of indifferent things, but I soon perceived my six months address was all to no purpose.

Bloom. If you hope to gain her you must flatter ——Oh ! here comes your servant, seemingly in a great hurry—Something has happened.

Sir Cha. Don't be alarmed——He is very busy about nothing—He is a most extraordinary fellow. He formerly lived with an actor, and has pick'd up quotations which he eternally misapplies. I would part with him, but he is so attach'd to me ; and when the other servants are teazing for wages, he begs I'll take the trouble of keeping his till he wants them.

Enter KILLEAVY.

Kill. Sir, sir, sir—

Sir Cha. What ails the fellow ?

Kill. Beg pardon, sir,—but yonder is the tame

wild duck we have been catching these two months, without being once able to lay our hands on her.

Sir Cha. Where? ha! 'tis she, by heaven—the adorable she!

Bloom. She! What she?

Sir Cha. Oh! the she that—a—I can't tell, but I must follow her.

Bloom. Follow her—Where?

Sir Cha. I don't know.

Bloom. Where did you see her?

Sir Cha. In the street.

Bloom. What street?

Sir Cha. This—That—The—I don't remember —Farewell!

Bloom. Stay—What's her name?

Sir Cha. I never could find out—but now I hope I shall discover all. Adieu! [*Exit* SIR CHA.

Bloom. Killeavy, do you know the lady?

Kill. Yes, sir, that I do; yet I can't say exactly what she is, only she's flesh and blood— Sometimes I think she's a fairy, for I no sooner catch a hold of her, but she flies away, and 'tis impossible to know where she's going, or how to find her when she is gone.

Bloom. Oh! some jilt or other.

Kill. Jilt! she's a very handsome jilt then, sir. —But I shall lose sight of 'em, and then woe betide me for not being ready at her heels to follow her from mercer's shop to mercer's shop: the Park, the play, and all public places, let them be ever so private; then, sir, after five or six hours jaunt, she whips away like Will-o'-the-Wisp in a fog; leaves me in broad day-light, like a fool in the dark, to return to my master, and be heartily bless'd with curses for my pains.

Bloom. Tell him, should he enquire for me, I shall be at home.

Kill. Yes, sir, he'll not be long disengaged with

the lady, I'll answer, sir. She'll soon give us both
the slip, and then I shall pay for it. A disappointed
lover in his rage will strike stone walls, and other
animated creatures, much more a poor live footman
—but, as Gibbet says, " My master is the goddess
I adore. He placed me near his person, and thinks
me much dishonour'd by his service."

Bloom. Ha! ha! ha! Why you're a child of the
muses—quite a son of Thespis, ha!

Kill. No, sir, you have been misinform'd—I am
the only son and heir of Paddy Killeavy, and so is
my five brothers and sisters.

Bloom. I mean, I think you are a person of understanding; a man of wit.

Kill. Lord, sir, no, sir; I've no pretensions that
way—if I had any wit, I shou'd have left my place
before I got into it.

Bloom. Why so, pray?

Kill. Because, sir, my master has turned away his
estate, and 'tis not the fashion now for wise men to
hold places, when there is no hope of reward for their
services.   [*Exit.*

Bloom. Poor Sir Charles! What a crime have I
been guilty of in advising my friend to enter into that
state which to me is only productive of misery; fondly and tenderly doting on my wife, I feel accessary
to the ruin her extravagance must bring on us both.
Balls, routs, operas, masquerades, and other excesses,
now engage all those moments which ought to be devoted to our mutual happiness. In the country she
appeared like the genius of virtue, and guardian
of innocence, dispensing comfort and blessings.
The widow smiled under her protection; the orphan
forgot its sorrows, and the weakness of age and infancy was sustained by her bounty. O for some gentle means to reclaim her, and make her virtuous mind
returns to its former pursuits!   [*Exit.*

SCENE II.

Changes to a different part of the Park, with various Walks.

Enter LADY SUPPLE, *followed by* MISS RUSSEL.

L. Sup. For shame! I am amazed you have not more delicacy than to attack me in this public manner; canst thou think I trouble myself about right and wrong, child?—My lawyer tells me, all I at present possess is my own; and I have so entire a confidence in him, I can never alter or deviate from that opinion. Therefore, I beseech you, don't incommode the serenity of my mind.

Miss Rus. Keep down, my swelling heart, and let tame patience speak my wrongs; for wrongs like mine need not the force or fire of passion. My deceased father, madam, left me, an only child, and twenty thousand pounds, to the care of your rapacious husband, who cruelly betrayed that generous confidence, by saying one thousand was more than the bequest, and with it banish'd me his dwelling; he dying, you became possess'd of all his ill-got wealth.

L. Sup. Prodigious!

Miss Rus. That sum being now almost exhausted, I see the monster Penury approach with such terror, that to you I once more appeal, and sure my injuries must find redress, if misery can touch your heart, and any spark of honour, honesty, or tenderness remain there.

L. Sup. Tenderness for such insolence!

Miss Rus. Do you think the injured will not speak, that the oppressed can sleep on the hard ground, and

never groan? Or that sufferings like mine can go un-
told? No—violence, oppression, and injustice will
make silent meekness find a tongue to accuse the unfeeling heart that wrongs an helpless orphan!

L. Sup. Bless me! What will become of me? I
sha'n't recover my complexion, temper, health, and
quiet these six months.

Miss Rus. Six months! Not while you live shall
you know ease, or peace of mind, unless your wounded conscience forces you to yield me up my right.

L. Sup. Your right! Why your right is your poverty, and that I yield you.—Keep it—People that's
wise never think now-a-days of right or wrong, so they
get money;—but I can stay no longer to be entertained with your right and conscience.—Baubles for children—Will conscience keep a coach? Will conscience
buy a title? Will conscience maintain an equipage?
Will conscience provide an elegant estate? No, no,
conscience!—It's like a negligee or long ruffles—
quite out of fashion.　　　　　　　　　　*[Exit.*

Enter SIR CHARLES LESLIE, *in haste.*

Sir Cha. Ay, here she is—I thought she had escaped me again. Well encounter'd, madam.

Miss Rus. Sir! how unlucky this, and my mind in
such a state; but, dear, kind, good spirits, on you must
I rely.　　　　　　　　　　　　　　*(Aside.*

Sir Cha. You see, madam, I am a true sportsman,
and never change my game.

Miss Rus. But pray, sir, don't you hunt more for
the love of sport than for the sake of the prey?

Sir Cha. No, by heaven! I loved you from the first
moment I saw you, and have not since so much as
dream'd, thought, or look'd at any creature in petticoats but your dear self.

Miss Rus. Ah! poor gentleman! to fall under such
unhappy circumstances, as to love, admire, nay adore
the woman whose face you have hardly seen; her fortune and character unknown to you; but if you'd per-

suade me to credit the assertion, you must wear your
arms across, sigh, look dismal, turn up your eyes now
and then, hum a languishing air, appear confused,
careless in your dress, pale-faced, speak but little, and
that abrupt sentences; turn poet, and write soft son-
nets; but you are quite the opposite of all these, and
appear like a sturdy beggar, who asks only for form's
sake, and wou'd, if you durst, boldly rob to gratify
your inclination.

Sir Cha. What then have you resolved? Am I to
hang or drown myself?

Miss Rus. Use your own discretion, sir; just which
you please.

Sir Cha. Come, come; as your beauty bred my affection, let your kindness nourish it—Do, pr'ythee,
acquaint me with your name, that a mutual agreement
may take place between Sir Charles Leslie, Baronet,
of one part, and miss—or lady—pray, ma'am, what
do you call your name?—on the other.

Miss Rus Really, Sir Charles, you are tolerably
agreeable, and I design, one time or other, to let you
know who thinks you so; but it shall not be until I
am convinced you have not the least penchant for any
one but myself; then, I fancy, I cou'd like you longer than a new suit, a fine chariot, a diamond necklace, or any other pretty little nick-nack.

Sir Cha. My future moments shall be devoted to
you, and only you——

Miss Rus. Stop! stop, Sir Charles—your equipage,
I'm told, is frequently seen waiting at a certain elderly lady's door, in——

Sir Cha. Oh! the widow, Lady Supple, you mean,
surely—she's the last thing of all her sex I would be
thought to address. Why, she's as disgusting as the
frizeur's block her head is dress'd upon—ay, and as
much painted too.

Miss Rus. Oh, shame—and you'd have me believe
you really admire me?

Sir Cha. By heavens, I do. Your charms, like

fate, compel my trembling steps and my fixed eyes
to gaze and follow where you fly.

Miss Rus. Undone ! As I live the man is in love.
He begins to talk nonsense ! then must I take my
leave, and bid adieu for the present to Sir Charles
the Inconstant.

Sir Cha. Surely, you won't be so cruel as to carry
away my heart, and not even tell me where I may hear
of it.

Miss Rus. I'll keep it safe for you : if you had it
you'd bestow it much worse. Adieu, Sir Charles.

[*Exit up the walk.*

Sir Charles *solus.*

Adieu ! nay, now I have you in view, I shall not
quit you till I have some satisfaction, I am determined. [*Exit after her.*

Enter Killeavy.

Kill. So, so, there they go. Indeed, miss, we have
you snug ; the devil's in't if she escapes us now ! Hey-
day, here they come again—I must keep at a snug
distance, and be quite close to observe them.

[*Retires.*

Miss Russel, *followed by* Sir Charles *from the top
of the stage.*

Sir Cha. Confide in me so far—I'll prove constant
as the sun, and daily pay my devoirs to you.

Miss Rus. What shall I do ? (*Screams.*) Undone
and ruined for ever !

Sir Cha. What's the matter, madam ?

Miss Rus. Mercy on me ! I have lost——

Sir Cha. What, madam ?

Miss Rus. My father's picture, which I value above
all things in the world.

Sir Cha. How, or where, did you lose it ?

Miss Rus. I can't tell. I had it at the upper end
of that walk !—Oh heavens !

Sir Cha. Nay, be not uneasy: it cannot be lost.
Here, Killeavy.

Kill. Sir.

Sir Cha. This lady has lost a picture somewhere
here.

Miss Rus. Oh! the only relic of a deceased parent!

Sir Cha. I am distressed to see you so afflicted. It
can't be lost, madam: Killeavy, go search carefully
up that walk, whilst I seek in this.

[*Exit* SIR CHARLES.

Kill. Don't fret, madam; Oh, don't fret a vurneen.
—May be you did not lose it here; but, whether you
did or did not, I'll be bound I'll find it for you.

[*Exit.*

Miss Rus. Oh! I shall never have a moment's ease,
unless——Ha! ha! your most obedient, Sir Charles.

[*Makes her escape.*

KILLEAVY *returns.*

Kill. The devil a lady or gentleman's picture I can
find, except——

Enter SIR CHARLES.

Sir Cha. Well, Killeavy, have you found it?—
Where's the lady, sirrah?

Kill. Where, sir!—O ho! As usual, sir, because
we had her fast, she's gone.

Sir Cha. Damnation, villain!—fly and overtake her;
or——

Kill. Lord, sir, it's impossible; if you were to
murder me, and then to divide me into as many
pieces as there are points in the globe, I could not
catch her.

Sir Cha. Follow her, rascal, quick as lightning.

Kill. Yes, sir, yes,—which—a—now I'm sure I'll
follow her the way she didn't go.   [*Exit.*

Sir Cha. Where can she have escaped to? Why
does she fly me thus? What can she be?—She's a

riddle made up of so many contradictions, that the
whole sex is but an epitome of her : She's serious, gay,
and seemingly virtuous—Sometimes jiltish, young,
and an appearance of discretion, now confidently pert,
by-and-by very modest; she has wit, good-humour,
and ill-nature.—She has—yes, I feel—I am satisfied
—she has possession of my heart.

Enter KILLEAVY.

Sir Cha. Well, sir, have you overtaken her?

Kill. Overtaken her, sir! I thought I did—but
when I spoke to her, I found it was another person.
Why, sir, you might as soon overtake a Lapland witch
posting through the clouds on a broomstick.

Sir Cha. By heavens, villain, you must have seen
this lady! you are in league with her to impose upon
me. I suppose she bribes you to——

Kill. Bribes me! No, no, sir, I'm above that, I assure you, though I might take it very innocently without knowing what it was; for 'tis so long since I saw
a guinea, the devil burn me if I recollect whether it
is round or square.

Sir Cha. Who can—Why does she—but rat her
—I'll think no more of her—I'll take Bloomfield's
advice, and marry the widow. Attend me at Lady
Supple's in an hour—Yes—I'll—I don't know what
to do.—Let your wise men say what they will of our
being lords of the creation, I am convinced they are
wrong, for a woman is more than a match for any
man in Christendom.   [*Exit.*

Kill. A woman more than a match! I can't think
that, and I am certain, I'd be a beautiful match for
Sally—She's a nice—Oh she's a charm—I believe
the gods have in futurity told and ordained that my
master should love old ugly always, only that I might
have an opportunity of being the chained-down ado-
rer of her maid; now I know she'll be at the old story,
and vow to marry me the moment I destroy myself

for love of her—What an odd caper—She's so full of
whims too—then the worst of her is, to be quite genteel, she despises the produce of her own country,
and is fond of every thing foreign—I'll break her of
that, or I'll break her delicate heart.—Yes, yes, yes,
we have enemies enough abroad, without encouraging any within ourselves.   [*Exit.*

ACT THE SECOND.

SCENE I.

Lady SUPPLE'S *Dressing Room —*SALLY *discovered
reading Don Quixote.*

Sal. Oh! the dear fellow—What a pity he wasn't killed—I wou'dn't care a farthing for a sweetheart that
wou'd refuse to die for me.——There is my dear Mr
Killeavy, I do think he'll be persuaded,—then another thing makes me love him,—he's not English—
That's so elegant—How charmingly my lady's lover
Sir Rakeish Spangle looks ; but I should like him still
better, if he did not speak our common language.—

Enter Servant.

Serv. A letter for Mrs Flounce.
Sal. Let's see.—(*Exit Servant.*)—Oh ! what a

seal!—a heart stuck with darts, like pins in a pincu-
shion. (*Reads.*) "Thou fairest of the fair,—I send
you this by the penny-post,—and if the letter carrier
does not give it to you directly, run to the post-office
to inquire for it, and then we'll be sure to meet, for
I am going to your house immediately, where I hope
you'll receive with ecstacy your ever agreeable and
transported,   WILLIAM KILLEAVY."
Pshaw!—what signifies transported!—it would be
something indeed if he had been hang'd,—or shot,—
or——

Enter KILLEAVY.

Kill. I wish he was with all my heart.—If the rascal is troublesome to you—Who is he, my pet?

Sal. Who!—why a person that pretends to love
me.

Kill. Oh, then I join you with all my heart,—and
wish he was hang'd, shot, cut in smithereens, or——

Sal. Ha, ha, ha! that's a very good joke,—why
it was yourself I meant.

Kill. A good joke to see me hang'd, or cut up!—
Well, what an ignorant rascal I am.—So a thing that
makes one wretched, is—a—By the powers, I thought
a good joke was an action that caused mirth and delight to all parties.

Sal. O you fool! among some people nothing's a
joke, but what's malicious, and hurts the feelings of
intimate friends, or brings a burning blush into the
cheeks of innocence and virtue.

Kill. Ay! this is all new,—but every thing is so
changed, that curse me if I know what to make of the
place or the people. Such fashions! nothing looks
like what it is,—the men are all women, and the women are all men;—formerly they used to marry in
order to love, and keep close to one another,—but
now they are always walking together in separate

places, and their beds are so large, that it seems as
if they only went together to keep asunder.

Sal. You know nothing of taste—you——

L. Sup. (*Without.*) Where is Flounce?

Sal. Heavens!—here is my lady.

Kill. Well, suppose she is,—I'm waiting for my
master.

Sal. What, in her dressing room? Here—step in,
or I'm ruined—she'll not remain long.—Don't stir
till I come to release you.—Oh make haste, or—Oh,
dear!

Kill. Well,—weep not, my fair.

Sal. I'm not weeping—I say, go in.

Kill. I came to tell you—" Your lady approaches
like the rugged Prussian bear."

Sal. I tell you, go in,—or I shall be discharged.

(*Pushes him into a closet.*

Enter LADY SUPPLE.

L. Sup. What impertinence am I fatigued with!—
That Sophia Russel has so deranged me.——Where's
the sal volatile?

Sal. Here, ma'am.

L. Sup. Oh, dear! I wou'dn't for all my jointure,
that any of my admirers were to see me so disconcerted.

Sal. Lord, ma'am, I shou'd not mind any of them
seeing me, except Sir Rakeish Spangle. He is worth
being uneasy about—If I was your ladyship, I'd prefer him to all the rest, for surely he's handsomer than
Sir Charles Leslie, and I am certain he's much rich-
er; then as for old Mr Hale, there can be no——

L. Sup. An idiot, to think of me!—Does he imagine
I should sacrifice my fortune, life, and (if this glass
don't flatter) I may still say beauty, to such a crabbed old mortal—What return could I possibly hope
from him?

Sal. Why, the return an old man generally

makes; he'll prefer ye to the office of being his nurse, my lady.

Enter Servant.

Serv. Here's your ladyship's nephew, Master Neddy Dash.

L. Sup. Shew him up.

Serv. He's here, madam.

Dash. (*Without.*) Come, Tim, and I'll inquire where you'll place the gig.   (*They enter.*

(Tim *brings on a portmanteau, sword, and cane.* My dear aunt, I rejoice to see you, and am your truly devoted and obedient slave.

L. Sup. My dear nephew, I am very glad to see you; I hope you have brought manners and good breeding from the academy?

Dash. Yes, aunt, I flatter myself—I—a—I've had singing, fencing, and dancing masters.   At the assembly last week I was all the choice, so damn'd graceful in my allemandes and cotillions——I did spring from the floor—not a soul cou'd rise like me.

Tim. That's true,—his honour was always up by break o' day.

Dash. Hold your tongue—stifle the fellow,—I mean rising high in my dancing.

Tim. Yes, his honour jumps like our jack-daw, that has one wing cut.

L. Sup. Could not you have selected another sort of servant, nephew?

Dash. Excuse him, aunt; he's ignorant, but very honest.—He shall refine.—He must, stifle me.   I'll have him taught to read, and so forth; then he'll be wise as well as honest.

L. Sup. You are very kind to him, poor creature.

Tim. So he is, your ladyship, and when I learn to be wise,—if I don't forget to be honest—'twill be very well.   Where shall I put your honour's gig?

Dash. Aunt, can you accommodate ?—'Tis the nice thing—must not be exposed to the weather.

L. Sup. I dare say there's room in my coach-house. —Flounce, take him to the groom, and he'll dispose of 'em.

Sal. Yes, ma'am. Come along you,—a—where did you grow, I wonder! Come quickly, for if any of our visitors shou'd see such a mongrel, they'd be— Come along, I say.

Tim. Yes, ma'am, I'm coming,—I'm coming, ma'am ; if you'd see me dressed, you wou'dn't look so cross,—no nor think me such a gumril : then you'd say I was as handsome a lad as ever peep'd out of a suit of clothes.   [*Exit with* SALLY.

Dash. Be sure to take care of Prancer.—Well, my dear aunt, I superabundantly rejoice to see you,— stifle me but you look most delightfully.—Damme, if she is not uglier than ever ; but I must hum the old tabby !   (*Aside.*

L. Sup. Why, considering all I have fretted, 'tis wonderful that I have preserved my looks.   And indeed you seem greatly altered, I shou'd scarcely have known you,—quite a new being.

Dash. New ! I protest, ma'am, I don't know myself.—Bless me—I vow to gad—I have forgot where the bank stands,—may I be stifled, if the Exchange is not a mere bear-garden, all noise and confusion. —Stew me, madam, if I don't think you have saved me from ruin.

L. Sup. Indeed, I think the education of youth shou'd never be neglected.

Dash. Absolutely, had I remained in the city, behind a counter, I should never have been fit for any thing but an alderman, or a justice of peace.—Oh, horrid, filthy, quite a bore, stifle me !

L. Sup. Yet, my dear nephew, I know nothing better than trade and business for a young man.

Dash. Certainly 'tis very well in some cases, for

heavy, plodding, inanimate, stupid souls, stiver-cramp-
ed geniuses without estates ; then trade is very proper ; but fellows with exalted notions, great spirits,
little understandings, and large fortunes, all of which
I possess so amply, or I shall possess, being your
heir——

L . Sup. I once had some such thought, but I am
half prevailed on to listen to the persuasions and solicitations of one of my suitors, and enter into the
happy enjoyment of connubial love.

Dash. What ?—con——nu——love,—here's a rig—
why, stifle me—What's this ?—I thought you never
meant to love any thing but me.

L. Sup. Those were my sentiments, 'tis true, nephew ; but Sir Charles Leslie, Mr Hale, and Sir
Rakeish Spangle, are tormenting me eternally, saying
how wrong I should be to deprive mankind of my
society.

Dash. Your money they mean,—but sure you're
not such a young one, not such a green-horn, to be
had ?

L. Sup. I don't well understand you,——but
know, that this day I mean to determine on an alli-
ance either with Sir Charles Leslie or Sir Rakeish
Spangle.

Dash. What ! the fop I saw with you at the opera ?—Why, he's no bigger than a wax-doll.—If he's
your purchase, you're out, I tell you.—Stifle me, but
you have bought at the top of the market, and when
stocks fall, you'll be damn'd mad at your bargain.

L. Sup. Insolence ! since you provoke me, know
that I will marry.

Dash. So will I, if that be all, dowager.

L. Sup. I hope you'll ask my consent !

Dash. Not I——you don't ask mine ; and as to
your grasshopper, Sir Rakeish——

L. Sup. I say, sir——

Dash. Damme, if I care three per cent. what you

say—perhaps I'll convince you the house is mine,
—my father left it in trust for me, with your late
husband ; your own lawyer says he knows every
foot of the terra firma and the terra inscripta—
He's a devilish honest fellow.   He offer'd to insure
it all to me if I'd give him half.

L. Sup. Villain, have you been tampering with
my lawyer ? What a world ! at the very moment
that I was thinking of your welfare—I intended you
should marry that charming, amiable girl, Sophia
Russel, and would have given five hundred pounds
between you, with which you might have taken a
shop, and—

Dash. Shop ! Wife !—Five hundred pounds !—
that's good—No, no, I have had a taste of what
it is to be a gentleman,—yes, and I've got some hints
about my estate—I know what it is, where it is, and
how much it is—Mr Demur is my friend.   He'll
pilot me into this house, and all the rest of my property—I'll go to law ; stifle me, but I'll go to law.

L. Sup. Is this your gratitude for my care of
your education and morals ? out of pure humanity
to—

Dash. Yes, your humanity would leave me as it
has Miss Russel ;——but law, O glorious law, and
glorious lawyers ; yes, yes, they'll shew me the
straight road into my property through Chancery-
lane.

L. Sup. They'll be apter to shew you the
straight road into the Fleet through Chancery-lane.

Dash. We'll see that : indeed, old one, we've
twigg'd you.

L. Sup. Old one !—monstrous impudence !——
you take these liberties because I'm an unprotected
woman ; but, perhaps before to-morrow, you may
hear of a person being master of this house, that shall
secure me from ever being troubled with your impertinence.   [*Exit.*

Dash. Master of this—O damme, but I'll keep possession,—I'll go to law.

Enter MISS RUSSEL.

Ah! my lass of spirit—how do you do? how do you do? I haven't seen you this age; my aunt wants me to marry you, but I won't, not I; no, "I'll rove and I'll range, I'll love and I'll change;" that's my way; besides, I'm to have a great fortune, and you know you are stiver-cramp'd,—you haven't a shilling.

Miss Rus. Wretch! upbraid me with my poverty, that poverty which the credulity of a noble-minded, unsuspecting parent has brought on me! I now come for the last time to require justice from the hands of your cruel aunt—should she refuse——

Dash. Apply to me.

Miss Rus. Never ;—my soul must spurn an obligation where I scorn even an acquaintance ; no,—my next appeal shall be very different ;—thank heaven, I enjoy the blessing of residing in a country where the law provides a guardian for the fatherless ; who, with a parent's care, redresses the complaints of oppressed, helpless orphans.

Dash. What, you'll go to law? That's right; it's the only way to manage this old quiz. Life must be supported. I'll tell you how I live : I gallant all day, drink all night, walk the streets, break lamps, kick up rows, (I'm first at a row ;) how they do ogle me in the theatres—the women, ay, and the men too, they're all afraid of me. The moment I go into a box, off the party set to another, all owing to my way, the careless twirl of my stick. Two watches! glass, look bold, courageous, and negligent, just as if I could cane a man without being out of humour.

Miss Rus. I dare say you are very courageous, that is, if courage consists in boasting to women of exploits that never happen'd ; insulting them, and shrinking from any man that has honour to defend or protect 'em.

Dash. What's that you say ?—Shrink——stay till Mr Demur gets my fortune, then I'll—damme, I wish I was a captain——I believe I'll go into the army. I'll be a great officer. How I'll command and strut, and—don't you think so, my love ?

Miss Rus. Don't mistake, sir ; a good soldier is polite, brave, humane, and generous. He holds his life dear only to offer it in the service of his king and country. Pray where is Lady Supple ? I must see her.

Dash. She's in the next room ; but you sha'n't stir ; don't mind her ; I'll take a snug house, that's my way ; I'm a man of honour ; I told you I should not marry—but——

Miss Rus. Stop, thou reptile ; let me pass this instant, or I'll call for assistance.

KILLEAVY *comes from the door.*

Kill. And assistance you shall have, whether you call for it or not. Ha?—Well, to be sure—Oh! may be it's not our tame wild duck.

Dash. Eh ! what !—who's this ?

Kill. Who ? why me, to be sure ; who the devil else cou'd it be ? What ails you, ma'am ?

Miss Rus. Dare to talk to me in a style——

Kill. Oh, the——damme, if I know what to call him !—a beast, sure, that's a human creature, must love and regard a pretty woman. Come, madam, with your leave, I'll be after handing you from this agreeable villain to the care of Sir Charles Leslie.

Miss Rus. As I live, 'tis Sir Charles's man—Now I am discover'd.

Dash. You hand her ! I command you to quit the house, and leave the lady as you found her.

Kill. To be sure, sir ; yes, you shall see me go directly, *exit signum,*—but if this lady chuses, or wishes, to be of my party, she most assuredly shall go out of this room with me all alone by herself.

Dash. Shall she? (*Drawing the sword which* TIM *brought in with the portmanteau.*) Now resign the lady, or else—damme, but the sun shall shine thro' you this instant.

Miss Rus. Oh, heavens! leave me, sir, pray do!

Kill. Pray, ma'am, discompose yourself;—— though you stand arm'd there, before me, *non est inventus,* if you were my own mother, and to behave so, I'd tell you plainly you're no gentleman. Oh! I wish there was an act of parliament against any man's wearing a sword that could draw it in a bad cause!

Dash. Come, no rudeness—acknowledge what brought you here. Give up the lady, and beg pardon this moment.

Miss Rus. Pray do, sir.

Kill. Madam, if you gave a thousand worlds, I could not say, " Sir, I beg your pardon,"—but I'll settle it this way. We'll talk a little jocosely.

Dash. By heavens, I'll run you through—take care—there's no jesting with edge·tools.

Kill. Well, I think it's better jesting than being in earnest with 'em. So, sir, if you please, I'll tell you how—a—this lady is in love. No, my master, ——no, not that: 'tis my friend Horatio loves—the —he's running away every-where, and I'm running after him. He's like Cleopatra, walking up silver in cinders to meet Mr Marc Antony. There she stands ——only look. (*During this speech he approaches* DASH, *and seizes his sword.*) Now I believe the sun will shine through you.

Miss Rus. O, sir, don't kill him,—'twill be cruel.

Dash. Cruel! damme, 'twill be murder. Sure you wou'dn't be so mean, so ungenteel—was there ever such a thing—Draw on an unarm'd, defenceless man! Throw away the sword, and then——

Kill. There, and what then?

Dash. Why then—I'll give you my address.——— Where is yours?

Kill. Mine is and ever shall be to him that could insult an innocent female—This! (*Canes him.*)—— How he canters! Do you think I'm to leather you by the mile? This fellow has run heats at the Curragh, or Newmarket—but I'll——

Miss Rus. Hold, sir, hold, for heaven's sake.

Kill. I ask your pardon, madam, for the liberty I have taken of dusting his jacket in your presence: but I have done—though a little more of it would be of great service to him.

Dash. Stifle me, if you're a gentleman, there's my card—that's my way.

Miss Rus. He is out of danger. I'll make my escape. Fortune, I once more thank thee.   [*Exit.*

Kill. Card. (*Reads.*) " Set pin—silver buckles —four guineas!" Why, this address is a pawn-broker's ticket.

Dash. A pawn-bro—Death and hell—some rascal has put it in my pocket!

Kill. Rascal! that you may swear, for it was your own sweet-scented self. Don't you think so, madam? Ha! Where is the lady?

Dash. Lady! he's a terrible passionate fellow!

Kill. Villain! Where's the lady?

Dash. I don't know.

Kill. Who is she?

Dash. I don't know.

Kill. What's her name?

Dash. I don't know.

Kill. What brought her here?

Dash. I don't know.

Kill. Was there ever such an intelligent rascal! I I believe you've pawn'd her. How——What—— Where are you?   [*Exit* DASH.

Dash. (*Without.*) I don't know.

Enter SIR CHARLES LESLIE.

Sir Cha. What's the matter?

Kill. O, sir, I've catch'd the lady!

Sir Cha. What lady?

Kill. Oh, you know the tame wild duck.

Sir Cha. Ha! Where is she?

Kill. She's here——that is——she's just gone this moment.

Sir Cha. Which way?

Kill. The devil a know I know, sir,—but there she was, and there I was, and there he was, behaving clandecently; and when I had her to a certainty in my hands, I found she was off again, gone—and so here I am *solus omnes*.

Sir Cha. 'Sdeath, sir! why didn't you come and tell me?

Kill. Lord, sir, when I was with her, how cou'd I be with you! Sure I cou'dn't be in two places at one time, unless I was a bird.

Sir Cha. Can you give no account of her? I must pursue her: she cannot be out of the neighbourhood. Follow me.

Kill. Sir, sir, didn't you come to see the old Lady Supple, with her beautiful cash?

Sir Cha. Damn the old——   [*Exit.*

Kill. Och, honey, with all my heart. The devil fire the old—Stop, master Billy—She's a woman, and don't abuse her. Oh, the darling babbies, with their coaxings, and their wheedlings, and their little noses turn'd up, and their scolding so sweetly, who'd abuse or be angry with them? Sure, we know all the time what they're about,—poor things, myself dotes upon 'em; by—a—the honestest man in the world, that behaves like a rogue to a woman, must be a downright villain.   [*Exit.*

SCENE II.

A Street.

Enter MISS RUSSEL.

Miss Rus. I can hardly think myself safe; that poor
honest fellow—I'm inclined to think his master, Sir
Charles, loves me,—and could I recover from that
avaricious Lady Supple even a part of what I am
justly entitled to, he should not long remain ignorant
of my name, my fortune, or the state of my heart.
For his sake, I believe, I must try to obtain by stratagem, what I never can expect from her justice.
As I live, yonder comes Sir Charles. He has not
seen me. I'll make this effort, though a desperate
one, to avoid him (*Knocks at a door. Servant enters.*)
I desire instantly to speak with your lady.
                              [*Goes in with Servant.*

Enter SIR CHARLES.

Sir Cha. Ah! madam! have I caught you?—
Here she went in. I'll follow—Hold, hold! this may
not be her house—I'll watch her coming out—no,
that might be too long to wait; I'll boldly ask to
see her.   [*Knocks.*

Enter Servant.

Serv. Servant, sir.
Sir Cha. Sir, your servant—pray, sir,—a—

Serv. What's your business, sir? Did you want my master?

Sir Cha. No, good sir, I wanted your mistress.

Serv. Oh! my young lady, is it, sir, you want?

Sir Cha. Upon my soul I can't tell. Yes, yes, I believe it is.

Serv. I don't imagine——indeed, sir, I'm sure she'll not see you, sir, (SIR CHARLES *gives money.*) but if you please to walk into the parlour, I'll go and try.

Sir Cha. Much obliged to you. Say I must speak with her.

Serv. I shall, sir.

Sir Cha. Yes, I have her now—providentially— happy discovery!   [*Exit, following the Servant.*

SCENE III.

The Inside of MR HALE's *House.*

Enter EMMA *and* MISS RUSSEL.

Miss Rus. Your excusing this intrusion, and so kindly accepting my apology, lays me under the most sensible obligations—it imports me extremely not to be seen.

Enter Maid.

Maid. Madam, the gentleman says he cannot be mistaken—he insists that you are here. He saw you come in. I had much ado to keep him from coming up—Lor, I think I hear him on the stairs.   [*Exit.*

Miss Rus. 'Tis in your power to assist me most essentially—suffer me to retire into this room.   Fortunately our dresses correspond, and——

Miss Em. With regret I'm forced to decline what you propose.   A resolution I have made to converse with no man, (my father excepted,) until the return of a dearly esteem'd friend, whose absence——

Enter Maid.

Maid. Ma'am, I never met such a boisterous gentleman in my life.   In spite of every thing I can say or do, he insists on coming up stairs.

Miss Rus. By that dear friend, and by the hopes you have of his return, let me conjure you to keep me from the sight of this gentleman.

   [*Leaves her cloak with* EMMA, *and exit.*
Maid. As I live, ma'am, here he is.

Enter SIR CHARLES.

Sir Cha. My dear ma'am, I have found so much difficulty in approaching you, that nothing but your beauty can atone, or apologize, for the apparent rudeness, that—Hey-day!—she is gone again !

Em. Inform me, sir, what could encourage you to this strange pursuit.

Sir Cha. Yes, I am mistaken——what shall I say ?
        [*Aside.*

Em. Why should you follow me, sir ?

Sir Cha. Faith, madam, because you run away from me.

Em. Do you know me then, sir ?

Sir Cha. Not I—Devil take me, but I must on now. (*Aside.*) When I saw you to-day, madam, I own I took you for another lady.   Your statures and habits are much the same,——yet, shou'd any chance give you an opportunity of seeing her, you wou'd be satisfied how much she is honour'd in a supposed resemblance to you—and faith she is tolerably handsome—to a man that had not seen you.

Em. You are now convinced of your mistake, sir, which I excuse ; my father I expect every moment, to whom I shou'd find a difficulty in accounting for your being here.

Sir Cha. I understand you, madam. But suffer this heart to take a distant gleam of hope along with it, only to——·

Em. Pray, sir, be assured no pretence—no delay —not all your rhapsody or eloquence, can give me other impressions of you than those I've already form'd.

Sir Cha. Ten thousand blessings on you for these last words,—they're mysterious, yet they are kind. To a soul like mine, that wakes and starts at the least dawn of joy, they set its every faculty on fire. I go, that I may hope to return. This charming girl is almost as handsome as little fly-away. (*Aside.*) Adieu, thou lovely creature. O the overflowing springs of cool refreshing beauty !   [*Exit.*

Em. Madam, permit me to release you,——(*Bringing on* Miss Russel.) I congratulate your escape from the levity and wildness of your pursuer.

Miss Rus. Ó my heart ! When the service you have done, ma'am, proves an obligation or an injury, be satisfy'd I shall not be insensible to either.

Em. Bless me ! I fear, madam, you are as liable to mistakes as the gentleman.

Miss Rus. I fear I am more subject to 'em, madam, particularly when I make a friend of one who wou'd destroy all my hopes of happiness, by encouraging the addresses of him who is dearer to me than life.

Em. Is it thus you thank me ?—To serve a stranger, I have violated a most solemn vow ! But, as our interview commenced abruptly, so let it end. The servant shall attend you to the door.

                              [*Rings, and exit.*

Miss Rus. False Sir Charles ! Duped by a man I thought sincere ; robb'd by her who shou'd protect

me. Wretched, wretched Sophia! Yet why shou'd
I despair? those spirits which have supported me
hitherto, I trust, will not forsake me.—I'll inquire
of the servant this lady's name—Write a letter to
Sir Charles as from her, desiring an interview, by
which means I shall discover his real sentiments.

Mr H. (*Without.*) If any body brings me money,
call me immediately—(*Enters.*)—and, do you hear, if
any one want money, I'm not at home, nor sha'n't
be to-day. (*Seeing* MISS R., *bows.*) Egad, the very
identical pretty girl I have so often followed in the
street. Madam.   (*Bows.*

Miss Rus. Sir,—as I live, old Mr Hale, one of the
widow's lovers!—How unfortunate!—but I am certain
he don't know me, though I do him.   (*Aside.*

Mr H. Who is—ah! I suppose 'tis the young woman that wanted a place, and was recommended to
Emma. She's very beautiful. (*Aside.*) I hope you
and my daughter have not disagreed?

Miss Rus. Pardon me, sir, we have; but I fear the
fault was mine.

Mr H. No, no, it could not be your fault, you are
faultless—you—Egad I don't know what to say to
her:——she looks so fine, and so—yet why should I
be afraid?——she's only a lady's waiting woman.
                                                (*Aside.*

Miss Rus. Sir, your most obedient.
                                         (*Offering to go.*

Mr H. O thou charming girl! Ten thousand fe-
vers are not equal to the tortures I endure!

Miss Rus. Sir, what's the matter? what sudden fit
has seiz'd you?

Mr H. Love! my angel! love! One smile, my
goddess!

Miss Rus. Ridiculous! I desire, sir—

Mr H. The sweets of lilies, jessamin, and roses
dwell on those lips; to touch would be transporting.

Miss Rus. Was ever any thing so absurd! Yet I am

tempted to humour this wretch, and punish his folly.
(*Aside.*) It shall be so——Lord, sir, how can you
flatter me ? I——

Mr H. Flatter ! Not I—No, no, 'tis your fops
that are in love with themselves who flatter, and don't
regard what they say : Why, child, one of these cold-
cream coxcombs will spend half a-day doting on his
glass, prating to himself, and practising grimaces
against he goes abroad, in hopes every female he
meets will be as much in love with the animal as he
is himself.

Miss Rus. Indeed, sir, I don't think any thing more
disgusting than the impertinent vanity and conceit of
these creatures, who have robb'd our sex of trifles,
which were agreeable enough in women, but are in-
tolerably nauseous in those who wou'd be thought
men.

Mr H. And faith, my love, your sex is pretty even
with 'em ; for 'tis no novelty now to see a Venus in
every street with a helmet and plume, like an Alexander, mounted as if in a triumphal car, managing
six in hand, with the ease and appearance of a Her-
cules—but this is going from the subject we were talking of—O thou enchanting---were I possess'd of
Ovid's softness, I should want art to tell the vastness
of my passion !

Miss Rus. What an old rogue ! (*Aside.*) Don't be
angry, sir, if I am rather an infidel. I cannot help
distrusting you.

Mr H. I'll put it beyond the power of doubt ;
and, to confirm your wavering faith, here's a convincing proof. Till now my chief and only bliss was
wealth, but you have made a convert of me—This
purse is yours.

Miss Rus. Mine, sir ?

Mr H. Yours ! This ring is yours, and this bank
bill : I'll load you with riches enough to satisfy the

craving appetite of avarice itself.   Can I offer greater
proofs of my sincerity—my love—my——

Miss Rus. Prudence, a moment by your leave.—
(*Aside.*) Lord, sir, who knows but perhaps you may
be as false and cruel as those insignificant fops you
were just describing.—They, I am told, protest and
make love exactly as you do.

Mr H. Not they: damn 'em, they ha'n't it in their
power to make love as I do, poor devils! not worth a
groat.

Miss Rus. Ah, sir! but you'll allow I'm right in
not believing too hastily.

Mr H. Yes, I do, I do, thou charmer! Always be
sure the bill is good before you discount it.   I admire
your caution; but surely you cannot doubt me when
I give such security.—Your beauty caught me, but
your sense has enslaved me : where did'st thou get
it ? How came you so accomplished ?

Miss Rus. I have studied, sir, only in the school
of nature, which does not always bestow birth and
fortune, yet sometimes gives sense enough not to be
unhappy without them.   Excuse me, sir; indeed I
cannot remain any longer here.

Mr H. Well, well—give me a smile to live upon,
—bless me with one kind word: only say when and
where we may meet again.

Miss Rus. You shall see me, when, perhaps, you'll
blush to own you ever spoke to me.

Mr H. Impossible !

Miss Rus. Well, you shall see me very shortly.—
Adieu, adieu, thou agreeable deceiver !

Mr H. Agree——Oh ravishing !—I'm distracted !
Farewell ! Ten thousand transports on this sweet hand.
You'll let me hear from you, or see you soon—when ?
—say when ?

Miss Rus. I can't exactly say at present.

Mr H. Well, well, you'll think of me.

Miss Rus. Rest assured I shall think of tormenting

you, you old sinner, as far as the scope of my invention will allow. (*Aside.*) Farewell, sir. Oh! now for my letter. (*Aside.*) (*Going out, turns back, looks at him, then sighs, and exit.*

Mr H. O I'm overcome! I'm—I have her! I have her!—What shall I do with myself? where shall I go? How shall I—Eh!—Stop! It's time I shou'd visit Lady Supple. If I can marry her, get possession of her estates, and of this young creature's affection, I shall have enough to make me happy while I live. Oh wealth! how wilt thou bless me. Oh beauty! how wilt thou delight me. Joy! Joy! Oh, how I shall hug myself thus wrapt in pleasure!   (*Exit.*

ACT THE THIRD.

SCENE I.

A Chamber in Mr BLOOMFIELD'S *House.*

BLOOMFIELD *sen. and Child discovered.*

Child. Ah! but when I grow a big man, then my papa says I shall have a real gun, and be a captain.

Bloom. sen. Ah! but I hope he'll change his mind, when I recollect the many anxious heart-rending hours his absence caused me to endure.—But, thank heaven, he returned laden with wealth, accompanied

7

by honour, and rescued from penury these grey hairs
—Oh, how painful to see his virtuous wife squander
such a noble property—I cannot live to see the fatal
end of it, and pray heaven their lovely boy here may
never feel it.

Child. Sure you'll live till I'm a captain, and have
an army ?

Bloom. sen. An army, child ! you should say a
company : to raise an army of men requires more
wealth and power than you can ever hope to have.

Child. Ah! but I'll have an army for all that—I'll
tell you what I'll do—I'll coax all the pretty women,
and take them with me, then, you know, the men will
all be sure to come after them.

Bloom. sen. My lovely boy—

Enter Mrs BLOOMFIELD *and* CAREFUL *the Steward.*

Mrs Bloom. Tell not me of patience.   Shall I deprive myself of every joy the world affords ?—Was I
not born and bred in elegance ? taught only to wish,
and then possess that wish ? Are the new liveries
brought home, the pharaoh, hazard, and card tables
set ? The perfumed wax-lights ready, and etherial
spirits for the lamps—I'll create admiration abroad,
and excite wonder at home.

Bloom. sen. Consider how vast the expence must
be, my dear child—not even the first nobility make
such an appearance.

Mrs Bloom. Then I shall be the more regarded—
Go instantly—pay for my box at the opera, and secure tickets for the first concert.

Stew. To-day I cannot, madam—the money I had
is entirely exhausted.

Mrs Bloom. What!

Bloom. sen. Softly—perhaps to-morrow——

Mrs Bloom. To-morrow ! I say go instantly—am
I to be——

Enter Mr BLOOMFIELD.

Bloom. What! angry, my dear?

Mrs Bloom. I am angry to be so miserably re-strained, impeded in my pleasures, even by your do-mestics; your very steward presumes to follow your's and your father's example, and preach frugality.

Bloom. Obey your lady without hesitation. (*Exit Steward.*) My example! in what do you accuse me?

Bloom. sen. Let not passion possess your minds—my children, reason with mildness, and the goodness of your own hearts will bring you to a sense of what is right. (*Takes the child's hand.*) Live in affection, my children—happy in thy father's blessing, and still happier in your own virtues.   (*Exit with the child.*

Bloom. My dear, how can you complain? Have I not complied with all your desires even to a fault? against my own reason? quitted the country, changed a calm and retired life for this luxuriant town, com-posed of noise, dissipation, and profligacy?

Mrs Bloom. The country! I would not endure the country conversation again to be a lady of six manors —What a bustle they make about housewifery, and breeding their daughters as if they were designed for service—then the men are such wretches! To hear a creature make himself and his horse merry with whistling—Oh! what delight there is in cock-fighting —then the harmonious music of the hounds, and the charming melody of their masters' snoring after a hard day's hunting.

Bloom. When content and those pleasures surround-ed you, you lived secure and innocent—beloved of all, praised for your hospitality; you might be envied, but malice knew not where you dwelt.

Enter Steward.

Stew. Here, madam, is the perfumer's bill—the particulars are enormous.

VON. IX.   D

Mrs Bloom. No matter, let him have his money—
I detest an argument with such creatures.

Stew. The jeweller, madam, is——

Mrs Bloom. Oh pay him, pay him directly—he
must not be disobliged.

Stew. Then the mercer's bill is out of all reason,
madam—'tis but three months, and the amount is
four hundred pounds.

Mrs Bloom. He earns what's extravagant by his
attendance; 'tis diverting to have half-a dozen of
them here in a morning, to tumble their goods, buy
nothing, and send them off, by saying, Lord, what an
odious assortment you have got!

Stew. Here are several small bills of 30 or 40 pounds,
madam, and I have not ten guineas in the——

Mrs Bloom. How can you, Mr Bloomfield, suffer
me to be thus tortured by a——

Bloom. Have you really no money?

Stew. You'll see by that account, sir, that I have
not ——

Bloom. Amazing! shall I have my doors beset with
honest men, made poor and wretched through the
indiscretion of my family—go directly, take the writings of my Dorsetshire estate, raise what money you
can upon them, and pay every creature.—(*Exit Steward.*) Let me not suffer the disgrace of being forced
to that which common honesty shou'd dictate to every
feeling mind.—What misery and desolation must this
extravagance occasion!

Mrs Bloom. Extravagance! Is it more than is requisite for a woman of my birth, education, and fortune?

Bloom. I'm not ignorant of your quality, madam,
but surely some of these expences might be re-
trenched with credit to that birth and education which
you boast.

Mrs Bloom. Upon my word, this is a most delightful sermon—any thing more?

5

Bloom. Yes—your midnight revels, your masquerades, which affect as much your character as my
estate. Take heed—the virtuous know 'tis not
enough to clear themselves, but to give no cause even
for suspicion; and how despicable a state must matrimony be, when a husband, who is the sanctuary
and guardian of a woman's honour, must be obliged
to the discretion of his wife for the security of his
own!

Mrs Bloom. Mr Bloomfield, you may live as you
please; but society, pleasure, and elegance I am entitled to, and those I will have.

Bloom. Yes, I fear you will, to our ruin.—Is there
no means to prevent it?—I'll try (*Aside.*)—Well, my
love, perhaps you're in the right, and my conduct
has been erroneous. We live but to edify, therefore
be witness of the resolution I have taken, which is
from this moment to pursue what you call the joys
of life, spare no expence, but revel, enjoy society,
laugh at penury, and—

Mrs Bloom. Penury! 'tis the miser's curse, who
dares not use the wealth he is possessed of—the very
chest wherein it lies concealed enjoys as much of it,
as he—that cannot taste, the owner dares not.

Bloom. True, my love.—O pleasure! why hast thou
fled from me so long! But now I bid thee welcome
to this habitation.—Let my steward attend, and all
my servants; my hospitable doors shall open wide,
and the world shall find a welcome here.

Mrs Bloom. You surprise and delight me—now
you are obliging indeed——this is the way to be truly
happy.

Bloom. (*Aside.*) Truly wretched, I fear.

Mrs Bloom. Do you dine at home to-day, my love?

Bloom. Yes, and shall have an elegant assemblage
of our most intimate friends.

Mrs Boom. Dear me—I'm sorry my engagements
are so particular—they force me from you—but I

shall return early, to meet a party I have invited to
cards.—Will you excuse me ?

Bloom. Certainly. But I had much rather your
engagement would——

Mrs Bloom. That is so gallant, and at the same
time so affectionate—It causes,—good heaven!—I
declare it brings tears—What can—but we must not
be melancholy —Adieu !   [*Exit.*

Bloom. A strange humour this that I have taken ;
I am determined to dance, play, entertain, appear
as gay, and squander money as fast as she can. If
she has any judgment, 'twill awake her into reason.
It must—it shall—my flattering hopes assure me of
success.—Again, I shall enjoy her friendly confidence,
her cheerful smiles, and all the hoarded joys of her
indulgent heart.—Wou'd husbands, in general, tenderly endeavour to reclaim, by gentle means, wives
who innocently stray, divorces wou'd become rare,
Doctors Commons useless, and many virtuous minds
escape from public odium.

Enter LIEUTENANT SELBY.

Is it possible ! I am astonished and rejoiced, my
dear friend, at this unlooked-for, but welcome return
—but what—I hope love, all powerful love, has
not——

Sel. Oh no !—I had scarce got to the place of
embarkation, when I received my noble patron's letter, with an account of his having obtained an exchange for me to a regiment of cavalry. I lost no
time, you may easily imagine, in coming to town to
acknowledge my gratitude to him, friendship to you,
and ardent love for my dearest Emma.

Bloom. Well, she keeps pace with you, love as
much as you please—your absence has made her a
second Penelope.

Enter Servant.

Serv. Sir Charles Leslie, sir.

Sel. Allow me to retire, and send a note to acquaint my Emma I am here, and shall wait on her
the moment her father's absence grants me an opportunity.

Bloom. In my study you'll find pen and ink.   I
don't expect Sir Charles to delay ; or, if he should, I
know he would be proud of your acquaintance.

(Exit SELBY.

Enter SIR CHARLES.

Sir Cha. Oh, Bloomfield! my dear fellow—such
an adventure—such a circumstance.

Bloom. What adventure? What circumstance?
Does it pertain to love or war?

Sir Cha. Love! love! my good friend! Oh, Bloomfield, such a woman!

Bloom. Yes, all yours are such women; but who
is she?

Sir Cha. I don't know, therefore am come to you
to inquire.   She lives just five doors off on the right
hand.

Bloom. Five doors! let me consider : ah ! 'tis impossible : it can't be.

Sir Cha. True, upon my soul—I observed the
house exactly.   Do you know who lives there?

Bloom. Yes, so well, that I am certain you're
mistaken.

Sir Cha. Mistaken! Is there a young lady in that
house of extraordinary beauty?

Bloom. There is Emma, the daughter of my friend
Mr Hale.

Sir Cha. Then I have been in conversation with
her—I tell you I followed her home.

Bloom. Psha! 'twas the maid you saw.   Where's

the lady you went in pursuit of this morning ?—What
was she ?

Sir Cha. Why she—I can't tell any thing about
her—I own she lives more in my heart than any woman I have ever seen ; and I am obliged to be in love
elsewhere, to divert the melancholy thoughts which
intrude on her account.

Enter Servant.

Serv. Your man, sir, brought this letter—he says,
'twas left with directions to deliver it immediately
into your own hands.

Sir Cha. From some creditor, I suppose. Here,
Bloomfield, is a damper. Can any thing be more
distressing than having the most anxious desire to be
just, and, through the villainy of others, be deprived
of the power (*Opens the letter.*) Hey-day !—(*Reads.*)
" Approach—a—love—um—um—unhappy
                              EMMA HALE."
Pray, did not you say the lady's name was Emma
Hale ?

Bloom. Yes, I did.

Sir Cha. Oh ! the heavenly, bewitching !—D—m—
me, but I thought she looked as if her name was
Emma Hale. Here, here, thou infidel, here's conviction that I have seen her—nay, more—that I am
to see her again—the sweet, delicious—O, I must
send to her directly !   (*Going.*

Bloom. I blush for you, Sir Charles,—a man of
your sense and honour attempt to insinuate any thing
so prejudicial to a lady's virtue.

Sir Cha. I insinuate any thing prejudicial to a lady's virtue—no ! May he that could slander any part
of that sex, whom we are bound in nature and honour
to protect and defend,—may he—the greatest ill I
can wish him in this world is to be excluded their
dear society—may he never even have a quarrel with
'em, that he may never enjoy the superlative felicity

of a reconciliation ;—no, by heavens !—nothing—
not even our friendship could induce me to mention
the circumstance to you, but that I required your assistance in discovering who she is.

Bloom. Believe me, you are in an error.

Sir Cha. Will her hand-writing convince you?

Bloom. The letter must be a forgery.

Sir Cha. I have it—suffer me to appoint her here,
and——

Bloom. Here! surely you have more respect for
Mrs Bloomfield than to propose meeting——

Sir Cha. 'Tis for the sake of the lady's honour I
propose it. She desires me to—nay, you shall have
the entire letter. (*Reads.*) " The surprise of your
unexpected approach, and the apprehension of my
father's return, I fear betrayed me into rudeness.
Your declarations of love seemed to be uttered with
a degree of sincerity. If really so, your honour I
shall trust to as a security for mine : I wish to explain
the motives for my behaviour. Send your servant to
Storey's Gate directly, and he shall conduct you to
the unhappy   EMMA HALE."
Now, my dear Bloomfield, 'twill be acting the part
of a mutual friend to let me appoint her here.

Enter SELBY, *hastily.*

Sel. Pardon me, sir ; being in the next room, 'twas
impossible to avoid hearing your conversation, and
having some influence over my friend Bloomfield,
ventured out to join my solicitations in entreating
him to comply with your request.

Sir Cha. Sir, you're extremely kind. I am infinitely obliged to you—what say you, Bloomfield?

Bloom. Say—that you are mad.

Sel Oh ! you must grant permission ; being a lady of honour, there can be no impropriety in admitting her to your house. I request it as a most particular favour.

Sir Cha. Sir, your friendship binds me to you—
Ah! I see you are a man of gallantry. You know
how to feel for a man in my situation——but this
Bloomfield, is coldness itself—an anchorite.

Bloom. Well, as you (*To* SELBY) so particularly
wish it, Sir Charles may give her the meeting here,
but I'll wager my life you are wrong—when do you
expect her?

Sir Cha. In a few minutes. I'll go and dispatch
my servant instantly—for your kind interference, I
must take another opportunity, sir, to offer my acknowledgments, and hope to be honour'd with your
acquaintance.   (*Exit.*

Sel. Is this your Penelope? This the woman
that——

Bloom. Why, can you believe 'tis she?

Sel. 'Tis impossible to doubt it.

Bloom. Have you written to her?

Sel. No.

Bloom. Mind not her father in this case, but go
see her, and, take my word, you'll find her innocent.
(*Seeing* EMMA.) Amazing! whom have we here?

Sel. 'Tis she, by Heavens! O deceitful, cruel woman! (*He retires. Throws himself on a sofa.*)

Enter EMMA.

Em. Mr Bloomfield, your servant.

Bloom. Madam!

Em. You seem astonished, sir.

Bloom. I must confess I am, madam.

Em. The confidence your friend reposes in you,
sir, is the cause of mine. Where is he?—He'll scarce
believe that I am here.

Bloom. Indeed, madam, I scarcely can myself believe that you are here.

Em. Sir, if my visit be troublesome, or unseasonable, 'tis your friend's fault. Where is he? Let me
see him.

Sel. (*Coming forward.*) This is beyond all bearing! Wretched, imprudent woman!

Em. Mr Selby, are you displeased to see me?

Sel. Displeased! that guilt can so assume the face of innocence! (*Going.*

Em. Why! why! wherefore would you go?

Sel. To make room for the gentleman you came to meet.

Em. What gentleman? I came to you, and only you.

Sel. Deceitful woman! You knew not I was here. No, no—you thought me too far off to disturb your assignation—and I assure you, madam, 'twas my ill fortune, not my design. However, I leave the field open for my happier rival, as no doubt your lover will be shortly here.

Em. That is a title none can claim but you.

Sel. Madam, I'm not fool enough to be your sport —Farewell! (*Going.*

Bloom. Nay, stay! I'm certain she's innocent.— Her tongue, her eyes, and that flood that swells 'em, vindicate her heart.

Sel. They do but shew her practice in dissimulation—I go, perhaps, never to return. Adieu! my dearest friend! (*Exit.*

Em. Oh! Mr Bloomfield, follow him—his manner of leaving me is still more severe than even his censures against me.

Enter Sir Charles Leslie.

Sir Cha. Ha! here! my happiness is greater than I cou'd have hoped: I didn't expect you quite so soon; I trust I have not made you wait.

Em. Wait, sir! What can he mean? as I live 'tis the strange gentleman who followed the lady into our house. (*Aside.*

Sir Cha. You are offended I was not here to receive you, but——

Em. Indeed, sir, I am not.

Sir Cha. Confirm it by a smile then ; beg pardon, Bloomfield,—'tis your presence displeases the lady.

Bloom. I shou'd be sorry to intrude——

Em. Mr Bloomfield, pray don't leave me with an entire stranger.

Sir Cha. Oh, I perceive your caution, though you might rely on his secrecy—I shall withdraw, as if I did not know you.   (*Aside to her.*

Em. No whispering, pray, sir. I have not the vanity to be thought of your acquaintance, and I resolve you shall never have the mortification of being mine.

Bloom. Not acquainted with you, madam! I thought you came hither to meet him. Of this I'm confident, he came to meet you

Em. Pray, sir, did you come here to meet me ?

Sir Cha. To be sure I did—and, as Mr Bloomfield is apprized of the whole affair, there can be no impropriety in shewing the commission which authorised me to expect you.

Em. What is this, sir ?

Sir Cha. What is this, madam! Why 'tis your letter—surely you won't deny it.

Em. I must, upon my honour.

Sir Cha. Oh! I see she is determined to deny every thing. Well, ma'am, and you'll deny perhaps ever seeing me before, and you'll deny that I follow'd you home to your house, and you'll deny that I was admitted, and you'll deny——

Em. Allow me to undeceive you, sir, in one particular ; upon my veracity it was not me you follow'd in the street.

Sir Cha. Not you !

Em. No, indeed, sir, the lady was an entire stranger to me ; she seemed so anxious to avoid you, that, with the most earnest solicitation, she prevailed on me (being nearly the same stature) to acknowledge myself the person you pursued, and Heaven knows how fatal it has been to me.

Sir Cha. I thought 'twas—I cou'dn't have been deceived. Yes, 'twas Miss Fly-away again. It must be some fiend—but, madam, this letter—

Em. I am entirely ignorant of every thing relating to—

Bloom. I perceive 'tis a plot upon you, Sir Charles. Did you know of Selby's return ?   (*To* EMMA.)

Em. I did.   My maid told me she had seen him enter your house : I knew he would not venture to my father's, and, without hesitation, flew to meet him here.

Sir Cha. Yes, she has hummed me again—this must be her letter.

Em. Mr Bloomfield, let me entreat you to go in search of him.   Explain this mystery, and bring him to his faithful wretched Emma.

Bloom. I will about it directly.   In the mean time, permit me to solicit the honour of your company this evening ; Sir Charles, we rely on you.   Adieu. You'll excuse me—we wou'd not leave you ; but I see your servant—he may have some business.

Sir Cha. You know, Mr Bloomfield, I hate ceremony ; madam, your most obedient ; for what is past I have not power to offer even an apology.   Farewell, and may you be happy as your goodness merits.

(*Exit* MR BLOOM. *and* EMMA.

Enter KILLEAVY.

Well, sir, where have you been ?

Kill. Where, sir ? Didn't you send me to the lady ?

Sir Cha. And have you seen her ?

Kill. Faith an I have, sir ; she was waiting for me an hour after I got to the place ; and, to my great joy, the very identical tame wild duck, that has so often

given us the slip.   O she is the sort—she is the prettiest—

Sir Cha. Where is she?

Kill. Sir, the moment I saw her I cou'dn't help
looking at her—by the—She is the prettiest—she is
all the style—she—

Sir Cha. But where is she?

Kill. She—a—I was completely blind, cou'd see
nothing while I was looking at her, for she quite
fill'd my eyes.

Sir Cha. Well, sir, and where—

Kill. Well, sir, she bid me call a coach, which I did
in a minute without saying a word, handed her in,
stept up behind, told the man to drive her here, which
he did, sir, and while I rapped at the door, she spoke
to him, and off he drove as if the devil was in him.

Sir Cha. And why didn't you pursue, rascal?

Kill. I did pursue the rascal, sir, and roar'd, Stop
thief! I was amazed at her going away after behaving so civil to me, and done all in my power to
overtake her, but it was not to be done.

Sir Cha. To let her escape when you had her so
completely in your power, as the coach must—

Kill. I cou'dn't help it, sir; will you only consider, the horses had eight feet, and I had but two.

Sir Cha. 'Sdeath, villain, you have been drinking!

Kill. Oh, yes, the villain did drive as if he had
been drinking.

Sir Cha. When I depended on you, to think of
your getting in such a state; but I discharge you
from this hour.

Kill. Who me? Upon my soul, sir, I——

Sir Cha. Leave me this moment, sirrah.

Kill. I can't sir; it's impossible: Get your estate,
and then discharge me as soon as you please; we've
shared good fortune together, and bad shall never
part us.

Sir Cha. Insolent scoundrel, I command you to trouble me no more.

Kill. Scoundrel!——

Sir Cha. Yes, sirrah, deliver up your charge, and never let me see your face.

Kill. Scoundrel!—You have wounded me in the tenderest part, " the heart that loved you, and wou'd have followed you in beggary through the world;" —but I am off my charge—there is—no, I'll say nothing about wages, for I know there are two things we can't do—he can't pay, and I can't ask.—Here, sir, is—I wish to avoid giving you uneasiness; but since we are to part, I feel bound to return every thing that belongs to you. Here are a number of tradesmen's bills; you'll find a receipt to the shoemaker's, and some others, that I paid out of the board-wages I never received. Since I have been with him I have " lived like the camel, on the solid air." Here are a parcel of new tooth-picks; but these are furniture we neither of us have much use for. There's some protests from notaries, and a few copies of writs; I leathered the fellows that brought 'em, and wou'dn't take them in; but there they are. I didn't wish to distress your mind, so would not shew them. Now, sir, farewell—but consider, sir, pray was it any wonder, Miss Will-o'-th'-Wisp should distance me with such a weight as all that about my——   (*Laying his hand on his heart.*

Sir Cha. Begone, sir; I'll send you your wages, you shall no longer impose on my credulity.

Kill. Impose!—I can lay my hand on my heart, and say I never imposed on you, sir; I wish all men going out of place could say the same by their superiors.   (*Exit.*

Sir Cha. Damnation! Was ever mortal born to suffer as I am; but intrigues, honourable or dishonourable, fashionable or unfashionable, I from this

hour bid adieu to. My privilege shall no longer be
my protection—I'll mortify for the advantage of
my creditors, and redeem my estate by marrying the
widow—I'll go this minute, make her a formal, serious offer, and then adieu for ever to Mis Fly-away.
D—mn——No, bless her—bless her—ten thousand
blessings on her, and on the whole sex—They are
lovely—all divine—all charming. Miss Emma Hale
is lovely—little Fly-away's divine—Lady Supple—
Oh! she is the devil.   (*Exit.*

ACT THE FOURTH.

SCENE I.

A Chamber in LADY SUPPLE'S *House.*

Enter DASH, *meeting* TIM.

Tim. A letter for your honour.
Dash. (*Reads.*) " I have filed another bill, and
proceedings are going forward with the greatest success and rapidity"—Huzza! law for ever ! " I am
concerned in so many expensive cases, that I must
request you'll send me instantly 200 pounds, or we
are ruined, our cause is lost. Your's, faithfully,
                          " CAPIUS DEMUR."
Stifle me, what's this ?

Tim. A letter sure, sir. I just brought it to you; ecod, this place is turning young master's brain.

(Aside.

Dash. Why, he promised to do all without any trouble or expence to me, and asked only half of what he gained. I gave him every guinea I had this morning, and now he sends for more. What shall I do? I am completely stiver-cramp'd; not a face about me, but the one I look through.

Tim. Troth'en, maister, you'd best come and live in my country, where 'tis the fashion for people to look through their own faces.

Dash. Get away, sirrah! Do you think I'd go and live in your damned country—leave my lawyer and my Chancery suit?

Tim. You'd better leave him the Chancery suit, or may be he'll soon leave you without even my livery suit.

Dash. Pho! pho! you don't understand—he's to give me possession of all my estate. I must away to him. But hold! if I leave the house, my aunt's new husband may—I'll bar that—the servants are all my friends, I'll leave them in trust for me—possession is nine points of the law, and that I'll keep—Tim, desire Rummer the butler, and all the servants, to come here directly.

Tim. Yes, sir.   *(Exit.*

Dash. I'll leave these fellows in charge for me, whilst I go to Demur—(*Looking at the letter.*) 200*l.* Stifle me if I know where to get 200 pence, except from him—the law and the lawyers must do all for me.

Re-enter TIM, RUMMER, *Coachman, Footman, two others, &c.*

Serv. Ah! master Neddy, welcome! welcome!

Dash. Stop, my boys, I'll tell you, this is my house, the whole property was left in trust for me;

and now my lady aunt wants to cheat me out of it—
but I know it's mine, and, as you are honest fellows,
and my particular friends, I give it in charge to
you; we'll have open house directly—nothing shall
be here but plenty, pleasure, mirth, Burgundy, oceans
of stingo and claret, my boys.

Serv. Bravo! master Neddy.

Dash. That's my way—stifle me—the bells shall
ring—the fiddles play, trumpets sound—drums beat,
and the house shall be in an uproar; I'll have money
to keep a jubilee all my life—the cellar shall be left
open—Butler, you shall throw away your keys, and,
cook, you shall sleep with your knife in your hand.

Foot. You are a charming gentleman to talk this
way to your servants.

Rum. He, Lord love him! he has no more pride
than one of us out of place.

Dash. Pride! not I—Stifle me, I detest it—Now,
my boys, only take care of the house in my absence,
and I'll provide for you all. As for you, Rummer,
you shall be my steward directly. I'm only going to
my lawyer, and shall be back directly. What a capital fellow this law-suit will make me! (*Going.*

Tim. Master Neddy, master Neddy—you never
told me what you'd make of me. What shall I be?

Cook. No, sir, nor you hav'n't said what I shou'd
be?

Serv. No, nor I, sir?

Dash. You! Oh, stifle me, don't be particular;
you shall all have places when I'm a great man, if I
don't forget, as great men generally do.   [*Exit.*

[*Servants all following him huzzaing, except* TIM.

Enter SALLY.

Sal. For Heaven's sake, what is the meaning of all
this noise? my lady is almost distracted.

Tim. So is my master.

Sal. My lady vows he shall quit this house directly : she expects company that must not be disturbed, therefore prepare to be setting off.

Tim. Setting off! Where, Mrs Flounce?

Sal. Oh! no matter where, so the house is rid of such lumber.

Tim. I shall be very sorry when the lawyer men turn you all out, for sure you and I would be very agreeable.

Sal. What?

Tim. You and I would agree the best in the world.

Sal. Asunder it must be then.   No, no, Mr Killeavy is the lad that can be agreeable and attentive; and to be sure there is one way, and only one, that you can ever hope to gain my affections; if you will oblige me in that one particular, I think I should love you immensely ever after.

Tim. I'll do it, let it be what it will.

Sal. Why I want the glory of having somebody die for the love of me.   It's what I have heard a great deal of talk about, but never experienced it. I do think I should be most prodigiously fond of a man that loved me enough to hang or drown himself for my sake ?

Tim. Eh ?—What ?—You'd love a man that wou'd kill himself for your sake.

Sal. Yes, dearly—I'd adore him !

Tim. What, for shooting himself ?

Sal. Yes, thou dear fellow—shooting will be still more genteel.   I'll borrow you a pistol.   And, oh! Tim, Tim, how I shall cry and lament you, and say, Oh! the dear, delightful fellow ! Oh ! Oh ! Oh !

Tim. I'm very much obliged to you—I cou'dn't think of giving you so much trouble, for I should be sorry to make any one that loves me cry.   I'd rather make 'em laugh : so, do you see, I don't think nature ever intended me for a dear delightful fellow.

Sal. And you won't ?

Tim. I'd rather not.

Sal. What, shrink when you've such an opportunity of immortalizing yourself, to be sung about in ballads, to be quoted when you're in the grave.

Tim. I'd sooner be coated out of the grave, ay, and I'd rather people should say, Timothy Thickness was cowardly enough to refuse killing himself to oblige his sweetheart, than, Here lies the brave fellow who shot himself through the head for love of the beautiful Miss Sally Flounce.

Sal. Oh very well, sir.—Leave the room, nor never dare, or hope, to have a smile from me: I wonder how I could lose my time with such a ninny-hammer.

Tim. To be sure, I may be a ninny-hammer, or a yellow-hammer, but I'd rather live two days in this world, bad as it is, than be sung about in ballads for a hundred years: so your servant; I'll warrant I'll find a reasonable sweetheart, that won't ask me to undergo any punishment more than marrying her, but be happy and contented with what I can do with her in this life.   [*Exit.*

Sal. Astonishing! The creature, who this morning appeared to me a downright idiot, is metamorphosed into a sensible being.

Enter KILLEAVY.

Kill. See where she stands.——

" She never told her love, but let revealment, like a worm
        i' the mud,
Feed on her damsel's cheek."——

Sally, my darling, I just called to take leave of you, and tell you my good fortune—I've lost my place.

Sal. Indeed! how came you to lose it?

Kill. I won't own I was discharged. (*Aside.*) Why, like all great politicians, I resigned my appointment, and gave up my salary, when I found I could get nothing by keeping them.

Sal. Oh! then your wages are——

Kill. Why I can't exactly tell how much they'll be when I get 'em, but they are nothing at all now.

Sal. Then, as you have no money, nor place, and that you despair, may be you'd die for love of me.

Kill. Have a little patience, and if I live long enough this way, I'll die for hunger; and to shew how I love you, I'll commission you as a friend when I'm gone, to make your fortune by publishing all the bad things I've done, by way of an apology for my life. It's all the fashion now.

Sal. Will you marry me?

Kill. Why I love you so well, I'd marry you and twenty like you, if I had enough to make you comfortable in the misery that I must bring on you. Oh, you crator, " Can'st thou bear cold and hunger; can these limbs, framed for the tender offices of love, endure the pleasing pipe of smarting poverty? When"——

Enter SIR CHARLES.

Sir Cha. Ha! my little sprightly! What, Killeavy, are you there, my honest fellow?

Kill. No, sir, I am not, nor ever will be your honest fellow,

" While memory holds a seat within this horrid, headless trunk."

Sir Cha. I have been betrayed by passion—I am in your debt—I've given——

Kill. That you have, given me a receipt in full —Scoundrel—

" Words would but wrong the gratitude I owe you."

Sir Cha. I know your disposition too well to ask you to return to my——but pray oblige me, and go directly to Mr Bloomfield's; you'll hear of something there to your advantage.

Kill. I thank you, sir; I'll go this instant, and though I'll never serve you as long as I live, I'd lose my life with pleasure for you, if I could afterwards see you possessed of your fortune.   [*Exit.*

Sir Cha. Can I speak to your lady ? Is your goddess visible ?

Sal. No, sir, she is not—she won't be at home this day to any living creature, except Sir Rakeish Spangle.

Sir Cha. Confound this little body, I thought we had lost him. It's an age since I've seen him.

Sal. He has written to my lady, that he means this day to wait on her, and have her final determination.

Sir Cha. The devil! What can she discover in him, to be partial to a little——

Sal. Sir, I cannot bear to hear him disparaged in such a manner. He is a gentleman, sir, and knows how to gain a lady's favour, sir.

Sir Cha. Then pr'ythee tell me how he has completely gained your favour, and why you seem so much my enemy ?

Sal. Enemy, sir! lord, sir! really, sir, I am nobody's enemy ; but when gentlemen behave like gentlemen, and act with elegance, as a body may say, why 'tis impossible not to treat them like what they are, and throw in a favourable word with one's lady, which I do for Sir Rakeish, because he is a generous, accomplished, thoughtful, attentive, clever, encouraging, well-disposed, pretty youth ; and as to my lady, she is not at home, nor won't be at home, for she has a thousand engagements to-day, to-morrow, the next day, the day after ; so that 'tis impossible to say whether she'll ever be at home again or not.

Sir Cha. Bless me, child! I'm sorry to see you so ill.

Sal. I'm very well, sir, but my lady——

Sir Cha. Never saw more desperate symptoms ; but don't be alarmed : I've got a medicine about me—

Sal. A medicine for what ?

Sir Cha. To cure talkativeness : look here ; this is the first potion I'll administer.   (*Shewing a purse.*

Sal. Lord, sir, is that dose pretty strong ?

Sir Cha. Yes, and there is a possibility of its being repeated.   It contains ten pills made up of pure gold ; five pennyweights eight grains each.

Sal. Lord, how lucky to meet so learned a physician ! I never could bear doctor's stuff of any kind, but I'll venture to take this. (*Puts it in her pocket.*) It's down—a—the—Lord, sir, I beg pardon.   I believe I was indisposed, but your prescription has effectually cured me.

Sir Cha. What have you to say of——

Sal. Not a word, sir ; you've deprived me of the power of speech.   When I hear his name mentioned, I conceit I have got a locked jaw.

Sir Cha. Take care he does not find a key to open your lock jaw ; for here he comes, dressed like an emperor.

Sal. Then, sir, I must fly to tell my lady.   I heartily wish you success ;—like a modern elector, I have sold my interest to both parties, and now determine not to vote for either.   (*Aside, and exit.*

Enter Miss Russel, *dressed as* Sir Rakeish Spangle.

Ha ! Sir Charles Leslie ! in any other place I should have been rejoiced to see you.

Sir Cha. Sir Rakeish, your most obedient ; you still lay siege to her ladyship.   I hoped you had considered the superiority of my claim : you know I courted her long before you knew her.

Miss Rus. Why—a—that's very true ; but then, without vanity, I believe I may affirm, I stept further into her favour at first sight, than you have reached for many months ; you know I can't help it if the lady will love me, poor thing.

Sir Cha. You have for some time crossed my ad-

dresses : if you don't desist, I shall expect proper satisfaction.

Miss Rus. Sir Charles, I have crossed your addresses, and mean to give you proper satisfaction at a
proper time.

Enter MR HALE.

Oh! you are come most fortunately, Mr Hale; Sir
Charles seems resolved to have the widow, right or
wrong, contrary to her own inclinations and our pretensions.

Mr H. To be sure I can't dance, cock my hat,
sing an opera air, repeat soft lines, and swear a thousand false oaths; but what o' that? her ladyship is a
woman of understanding: it must be substance and
merit, both in purse and person, that will persuade
her. I'm strong and hearty, sound, wind and limb;
here is persuasion from head to foot. I am Lady
Supple's choice.

Enter LADY SUPPLE.

Miss Rus. So looked the Paphian Goddess, when
rising from the sea, and with such ecstacy the god of
war flew from the field to her embrace.

Sir Cha. That flight exceeds all the lies I ever
told her.   (*Aside.*

Mr H. I shou'd have thought him nearer the
mark to have said, "so Vulcan looked when coming
from his forge, and I am Venus in breeches flying to
his embrace."   (*Aside.*

Sir Cha. But this young gentleman shall not carry matters so. Your ladyship's humble servant.

L. Sup. Ah! Sir Charles Leslie! Mr Hale too, I
protest. I beg pardon, but the attraction of Sir
Rakeish is so powerful, I really did not see you, gentlemen.

Mr H. Your ladyship may please your eye with a
fair appearance, a kickshow, a mere puft paste, a

whipp'd trifle ; but, madam, consider, I have an hundred thousand pounds in my pocket : stock in abundance : no mortgage on my person or estate : both
free from incumbrances, as this indenture witnesseth.

Sir Cha. Tempting offers you have made—Stock !
the lady can't converse with your stock, drink tea
with your stock, go to the opera with your stock,
dance——

Miss Rus. No, sir, a young fellow's worth a million
of your stock. I am your rival. Look at me. I
hope I make a better figure than a bundle of tallies,
or a roll of orders.

Mr H. Not you, indeed : They are of value ; but
such a thing as thee—Here's English oak, an hundred years a growing, an hundred in perfection, and
an hundred decaying—You'll allow, younker, that I
am something more of a man than you are.

Miss Rus. Yes, I allow you are much older—Pray,
ma'am, do you like a man the better for being old ?
ha, ha !

Mr H. But, madam, I am no rake, no libertine—
your hours of rest shall never be broken by me.

Sir Cha. No, that I'll be sworn they won't.

Mr H. I don't employ my money in paying tailors
for fantastic habits ; my back shall never be a foundation for tradesmen to erect summer-houses.

Miss Rus. How can you listen to him, ma'am ? the
old wicked deceiver !

Mr H. I a wicked deceiver.—Ma'am, do I look
like a deceiver ? Sir, my reputation's too firmly established to be hurt by your raillery. I am a man of
integrity, and confine my addresses to this lady only ;
think of no other, admire no other, love no other,
and can be made happy by no other.

Miss Rus. Sly sinner ! Ah ! you wicked devil !—
What, and you this morning had not an interview
with an artless, foolish girl? you made her no offer, no
presents?—" The sweets of lilies, jessamin, and roses,

dwell on those lips.—Were I possessed of Ovid's softness, I shou'd want art to tell the vastness of my passion."—Has he ever uttered raptures like these to your ladyship?

L. Sup. Never that I recollect.

Mr H. No, nor any one else—it's all his own invention, my lady.

Miss Rus. Invention! Now, madam, hear a most solemn repetition of his own words: " Till now my chief and only bliss was wealth; but you have made me a convert—this purse is yours."

Mr H. Confusion! How the devil should he know all this?   (*Aside.*

Miss Rus. Mine, sir?—your's, is it not, Mr Hale? —" This ring is your's and this Bank bill, were they not all your's? Ha! ha!—give me a smile to live upon."—A lovely fellow to be smiled on.

Mr H. I am thunderstruck, tricked, bubbled, and disappointed; damned jilt, I have not courage to attempt an excuse,—confound it, sir——

Miss Rus. And, sir——

Mr H. I don't understand——

L. Sup. Then I understand you are a wicked old dissembler, and wou'd betray me to misery.

Miss Rus. Yes, and has basely attempted to ruin a woman of virtue.

Sir Cha. And yet, poor devil, he bid high,—'tis pity he shou'd be baulked. She was a cruel, hard-hearted baggage to betray you thus.

Mr H. Madam, I shall find a time to justify myself.

L. Sup. Then do it now, before your accuser, or never see me more.

Miss Rus. Ay, now, now or never, what can you say?

Mr H. I say, madam,—Sir,—a—that, as I hope for pardon,—I wish,—I wish,—may misery, plagues, and poverty, seize you altogether!   [*Exit.*

Miss Rus. Ha! ha! ha!—Now, my lady, having defeated the enemy, I shall possess myself of the treasure.

Sir Cha. Hold, hold, sir; you have only routed the advanced guard, the main body continues unshaken. Madam, the attentions I have shewn you, the sincerity with——

Miss Rus. What I am to attack you too? With all my heart—have at you. When you address a person of her ladyship's discerning judgment, you should disengage yourself from all other intrigues whatever, as well as our friend Hale.

L. Sup. Surely, Sir Charles, you cou'd not be so deceit——

Miss Rus. Only a small piece of gallantry to divert himself in your absence or so.

Sir Cha. Hark ye, young gentleman, I desire you'd keep within the bounds of truth and good manners. You hav'n't Mr Hale to deal with now.

Miss Rus. No, I have the free, the gay, the unconfined, inconstant, general lover—did you not this morning protest never to see this lady again—"Psha! hang Lady Supple, she's more disgusting than the frizeur's block her head is dressed upon; ay, and more painted."

L. Sup. I painted! compare me to a block!

Sir Cha. Sir, you are——

Miss Rus. You did not find the picture the lady dropt this morning?

L. Sup. A block! From this moment I detest——

Sir Cha. My dear lady, be assured—

Miss Rus. Did you overtake the lady that was insulted here?

L. Sup. Here—under my roof?

Sir Cha. That was a woman, that——

Miss Rus. That you followed in the street, pursued into a house, made love to another lady—an assignation was the result. Mr Bloomfield can witness how you were tricked there—Have you discovered who the abominable jilt is ?

Sir Cha. Very well, and pray are you not ashamed of all this ?

L. Sup. I think you shou'd, Sir Charles.   I wish you a good day, sir—A block indeed !

Sir Cha. I scorn to intrude, madam ; and, notwithstanding all this facetious little gentleman has advanced, I hope to convince you of the very—a—hem ! —sincere—affection—I bear you—and——

Miss Rus. A—hem—sincere—Ah! ha!—the block, madam.

Sir Cha. You'd better be quiet, sir.——Ma'am, I—

L. Sup. Compare me to a block !

Sir Cha. Ma'am, ha !—the—this damned block has been the ruin of me.   [*Exit.*

Miss Rus. Victory ! victory !—*Veni, vide, vici.* Now your ladyship can't in honour deny me your hand ; 'tis the only way you can effectually punish the deceit of such lovers, revenge the affronts they have offered you, and reward my boundless passion.

L. Sup. Laird, you are so young ; but then you are so engaging, you can persuade me to any thing. I—a —do consent—I will be yours.   There's no denying you.

Miss Rus. O my angel ! you've sealed the bond, and from this moment I date my happiness ! I have a special licence ready, and the ceremony shall be performed directly.

Welcome, bright joy, to Hymen lead away :
Thus bliss and rapture crown each future day. [*Exeunt.*

SCENE II.

A Hall in MR BLOOMFIELD'S *House.*

Porter. KILLEAVY *enters.*

Kill. Sir, your servant.

Por. Your servant. What do you want?

Kill. I want to hear something to my advantage, " for I am fortune's fool."

Por. I know nothing about you : who are you?

Kill. Why, sir, I'm a man of no estate worth mentioning ; for the sea covers half the land that belonged to it, and the tenants can't make the rent of the other half, because it is all covered with stones ; I am only like a great many private gentlemen here, that live on the public ; as a proof of it, I'll treat you to a bottle of wine, if there's a tavern near where you have credit, for the devil a teaster myself has in the world.

Enter Steward, seeing KILLEAVY.

Stew. Oh! I am glad you are come.   Sir Charles Leslie recommended you to my master ; he desired me to hire you immediately, and give you whatever wages you asked.   What had you in your last place ?

Kill. In my last place, I had—I won't take the same here.

Stew. What had you from your former master ?

Kill. Nothing at all.   He used me very ill ; he went to bed one night as well as any man in the world, and when he awoke in the morning he found himself stiff dead ; so I'd live with him no longer.

Stew. You've been very unfortunate : but you shall
have good wages here. There's a set of new liveries
come home—take one of 'em, and get to business directly; we are to have a great entertainment.

Kill. To be sure this is luck; I was just going to
seek my fortune; but I did not know where to find it.

Stew. You shou'd have gone abroad.

Kill. I was there before; in my travels I had a
taste for every thing. There's Ratsbone diet—and
there's Polish diet; but the devil a morsel I could
find equal to your good old English diet; and so, sir,
if you please to shew me where I am to begin my
work, I'll be at it directly, and the only way I wish
to go abroad again is to stay at home all the rest of
my life.   [*Exeunt.*

ACT THE FIFTH.

SCENE I.

Enter MR BLOOMFIELD *in full dress, a Gentleman,
and Servant.*

Bloom. Where is Mr Careful?

Serv. In his own room, sir.

Bloom. Desire him to bring the money instantly
that I ordered. (*Exit Servant.*) The new-married

Lady Supple and her bridegroom appear quite fashionable already—Their's is the shortest honeymoon I ever witnessed.

Enter MRS BLOOMFIELD.

Mrs Bloom. My dear, I wish I cou'd have been with you sooner, but 'twas not in my power.

Enter CAREFUL, *the Steward.*

Stew. Here is five more, which makes fifteen thousand since dinner, sir.

Bloom. Very well, get the remainder instantly—(*Exit* CAREFUL.) There, sir, is the five thousand, and if you are inclined to pursue madam Fortune, her frowns have not terrified me.

Gent. As you please, sir.

Bloom. With all my heart again, sir, I'll attend you. (*Exit Gent.*

Mrs Bloom. Fifteen, my dear—have you been playing?

Bloom. Playing! yes, and am delighted—'tis charming—but I must return.

Mrs Bloom. Don't your losses disturb you?

Bloom. Disturb! no! by heaven I'd rather lose ten times the sum than have one sad thought come near my heart.

Mrs Bloom. Say you so? I'll have another carriage to-morrow richly lined, and superbly painted—O that I cou'd get a coronet!—Do try for one. 'Twill be such an addition to you.

Bloom. I don't think so.

Mrs Bloom. What, not better to be a lord than a simple private gentleman?

Bloom. Not in my mind—Interest can make a lord, but it requires merit, manners, and inborn virtue to make a real gentleman. I have given orders, that the four elements shall furnish out the table with their choicest delicacies—I have summed up my estates, and find we have a twelve-month good yet.

Mrs Bloom. What do you mean?

Bloom. That I had rather be lord of pleasure a single year, than be whole ages consuming what we have in foolish temperance.

Mrs Bloom. You get beyond all bounds!— A year? and what then pray?

Bloom. Why, then retire into the Bench, till my debts are paid by an act of parliament; after that carry a musket, and fight for my king. If the fortune of war shou'd deprive me of a limb, 1 can end my days in that glorious establishment provided for the brave fellows who are maimed in defending their country.

Mrs Bloom. If you see all this so plainly, why not endeavour to prevent it?

Bloom. No, my dear, 'tis only you that can prevent it.

Mrs Bloom. Me! Do I know your income?—Do you men ever suffer your wives to concern themselves with your estates? You must retrench your own expences—I will not be controled, Mr Bloomfield, that's my resolution.   (*Exit.*

Bloom. But you shall be ruled, that's my resolution. —Since I have found persuasion, good-nature, and indulgence all in vain, this is my last effort, nor can I doubt of its success.   (*Exit.*

SCENE II.

A superb Drawing-room, with an elegant Assemblage, at different Amusements—several Servants attending.

Enter MR HALE *from amongst the Company.*

Mr H. I have received an invitation from Mr Bloomfield; I shou'd not have accepted it, but to

observe my daughter, for I hear Selby's in town, and
to a certainty he'll be of the party ; but I'll watch
'em. In the mean time I may as well take a share
of the good things here.

[*Goes to sideboard, looks at labels as choosing his
wine.* KILLEAVY *comes forward dressed in
MR BLOOMFIELD'S livery, a salver in his hand,
in waiting.*]

Kill. Well this is cruel! I am working hard here
upon earth like a collier, or a grave-digger under
ground, and I am doing nothing. (*Seeing MR HALE.*)
What's this you are at ?

Mr H. At ! Why if you must know, the room is
so warm I was going to take a taste of this by way
of a cooler.

Kill. A taste of this ! (*Drinks.*) Oh ! for shame,
you never can expect to stay here, if you go on this
way. (*Drinks.*) Sure this wou'd be the ruin of you
(*Drinks.*)—Here's more yet—(*Drinks.*) You look
damned bad ; this is the way you are killing yourself.
(*Drinks.*

Mr H. I think it's the way you are killing yourself—you're a strange fellow.

Kill. You're out—I never was more at home in
my life.

Mr H. It seems so : let me have a glass of wine.

Kill. That I will, a dozen, when your business is
done; but come, you shall have one glass to raise your
old heart. Here's every thing—what shall I introduce to you?

Mr H. No matter ; any French wines. They are
the coolest.

Kill. French ! No not the devil a sup ; I'll take
more care than that of you : Introducing any thing
French among us is enough to ruin our constitution.

Mr H. I'm choking, and this fellow keeps prating
and drinking. I desire you'll give me a glass of claret this moment.

Kill. To be sure I will—let me look for it—why didn't you say that at first ? You shall have plenty of claret, for that's Irish, my Grecian—Here it is. I'll help you, and you shall have a bumper. Here's the land we live in, and I wish I was there with all my heart ; O sweet Ireland !   (*Slapping his back.*

Mr H. What do you mean by all this freedom ? Pray do you know Mr Hale ?

Kill. No, nor I don't desire to know him: He's a spalpeen.——

Mr H. What ?

Kill. Why, he's a dirty congrawnaigh ! the servants here, " our partners in exile," tell me, Mr Hale comes whenever he's invited. Mr Hale gives more trouble and less money than any one in the house living or dead ; they always laugh in Mr Hale's face when they see his back out of the door, for the head of Mr Hale's thirteen was never impudent enough to look at any of us, so I'm sure you'll join with me, in pitching Mr Hale and all such customers to the devil.

Mr H. I'll be damn'd if I do ! Why you infamous scoundrel—

Kill. Infamous ! infamy on thy head, thou fool of power, thou grander in authority.

Serv. What are you doing to Mr Hale ?

Mr H. Doing !

Kill. Why sure that's not Mr Hale ?

Serv. I tell you it is.

Kill. Well, listeners never heard good of themselves. He had no business listening to me, when I did not know him.   (*Retires up.*

LADY SUPPLE, *dressed, comes forward with a Gentlewoman.*

L. Sup. Oh ! my dear ma'am, only a few hours married, and do but observe his inhuman negligence, his cruelty, after resigning to him all I was worth in the world—Oh !——

SIR CHARLES *comes from amongst the Company.*

Sir Cha. Ah, widow, no, bride I mean—Hey-day!
weeping! I see nature will keep its course; as man
and wife are one flesh, so repentance and matrimony are inseparable.—Why did you credit his assertions; and refuse with such indignation the offer I
made you?

L. Sup. I am most heartily sorry—Oh!—

Mr H. Ha! and I am most heartily glad; give
you joy, ma'am, give you joy,—you despised me—I
was a wicked old deceiver, and wou'd betray you to
misery; but what cou'd you expect from such a pa-
per-built thing.—Why a strong puff of wind wou'd
blow him into his original nothingness.—Here he
comes—I hope he has not heard me.

MISS RUSSEL *comes forward, dressed as before.*

Miss Rus. Ha! Sir Charles, your hand,—give me
joy.—Mr Hale, are you there?—We have been rivals,—no matter—we are now friends.——All is sunshine,—why don't you laugh, my lady? (*Aside to*
LADY SUP.) I shall expect to see you all at my
house, where gaiety, festivity, and joy, shall crown
the hours—Look good-humour'd, laugh, my adorable
dowager.　　　　　　　　　(*Aside to* LADY SUP.

L. Sup. I can't laugh, but I can cry.—Oh! Oh!

Miss Rus. There, true wife; always in opposition
with the husband. If I had bid her cry, I'll lay fifty
pounds she'd ha' laugh'd.

Sir Cha. Come, sir, you must behave in another
manner.

Miss Rus. Sir, she's mine—who dares interfere between a man and his wife?

Sir Cha. Her estate shall be taken care of.

Miss Rus. That I'm in possession of, and all her
bank notes, writings, bonds, and leases. (*To a Servant.*) Desire one of my footmen to step home, and

bid Flounce instantly bring the seal'd box of papers that's in her lady's chamber—(*Exit Servant.*) I am lord of her, and all she's worth.

Sir Cha. You are a fine pert little fellow—Pray, sir, after all, who the devil are you?

Miss Rus. A gentleman.

Sir Cha. Of what estate?

Miss Rus. None, but what this lady through her bounty has bestow'd on me.

L. Sup. Oh! Oh! Oh! what will become of me?

Miss Rus. I'll tell you—You shall retire into Wales, and live comfortably among the mountains on the fifty pounds a year, which my unbounded generosity shall settle on you for life.

L. Sup. If we must separate, let me know your conditions.

Miss Rus. I shall be moderate in the extreme, but for worlds I will not deviate from what I now propose.—I shall only demand out of the entire property, twenty thousand pounds, and the mortgage you have upon this gentleman's estate.

(*Pointing to* SIR CHARLES.

Sir Cha. The mortgage on me!—Sir, you and I must meet, and—

Miss Rus. With all my heart, sir; when I have settled this affair, I am your's, when and where you please.

Enter SALLY, *with a small box.*

Sal. A servant came for this box; but, as I know your ladyship always kept papers of the utmost consequence in it, I wou'dn't venture to trust it with him.

Miss Rus. You were right: stay a moment, and you may take it back. (*Unlock the box.*) Here, my lady, it shall be your own act and deed,—your own free gift.

Sir Cha. Surely your ladyship won't yield me up a sacrifice to one that has no regard to honour.

L. Sup. I wou'd preserve you, Sir Charles, but it is not in my power; I must prevent my own total ruin.—Here is the mortgage!

Sir Cha. Confusion.

L. Sup. And there's the twenty thousand pounds in bank bills. I hope you are satisfied?

Miss Rus. Perfectly, and exonerate you from every engagement.—You on your part agree never to molest me for what you have now frankly given?

L. Sup. I do.

Miss Rus. Then I take my leave.

Sir Cha. By Heavens, sir, you shall take my life, before you take that mortgage out of this house.—Draw, sir.

Miss Rus. What, before the ladies? Quarrel where you are sure to be parted. (*Aside.*) What shall I do? the discovery, whenever it occurs, shall be my own voluntary act, I'm determined.

Sir Cha. I'll perish before I suffer myself to be in the power of such a villain. Relinquish that mortgage, or one of us dies this moment.

Miss Rus. Well, since you are determined on an engagement with me, rely on it, you'll not find me the lad, the stripling you think—By all—but there is no need of passion—Let me tell you, you don't know who you have to deal with—I am a person of property—You don't imagine I am to risque my life in a moment, and leave my affairs at sixes and sevens—I must make my will in case of an accident: Flounce, do you come and witness it.—I'll be with you in a few minutes, sir, d—mn me if I don't.

                (*Exit* SALLY, *following.*

Sir Cha. There's a little rascal—he certainly meditates some act of villainy against me; but I'll watch him—he sha'n't escape, I'm resolved.—Was ever mortal so tormented! Distressed in circumstances—

wretched in my love—Oh! that obdurate little Fly-away! I fear I shall see her no more—No more be blessed with her agreeable prattle—Never have the pleasure of almost losing my breath in pursuit of her, the delight of looking like a fool, the felicity of being badgered by a coxcomb, and turned out by an ugly old woman. Oh! cruel, unkind, hard-hearted woman, to deprive me of all this comfort!

(*Goes up the stage.*

Enter MRS BLOOMFIELD.

Mrs Bloom. The more I think, the more dreadful it appears. Poverty, shame, and reproach will soon overtake us.——To live here in town is delightful— the place where all pleasures flow ; but how shall I enjoy those pleasures—oh no,—'tis paying slow years of repentance for hasty moments that fly so fast, they stay not to be welcomed.

MR BLOOMFIELD *comes from the Company.*

Bloom Well, my dear, is not this charming ?—now we are both pleased, and may our happiness never know a change.

Enter CAREFUL.

Care. All's done, as you commanded, sir; but with much difficulty, and a large premium, I raised the money.

Bloom. Oh! no matter so I have to pay my losses.

Enter Father and BLOOMFIELD *Jun.*

Fath. My dear children, it grieves my old heart to mention any thing that can damp your joy, but there are at this moment three executions in your house

Mrs Bloom. Heavens!

Bloom. Don't be alarmed, love. Sell that manor

which is your ladyship's jointure. (*Exit* CAREFUL.)
You have no objection, my dear?

Mrs Bloom. No—never shall I object to any thing
you think right.

Bloom. 'It's unavoidable.

Fath. Good heaven! is it come to so low an ebb
already?—Oh, 'tis not to be supported—To prevent
such acute misery to my latter days, there is but
one way, that is, at this instant to bid you eternally
adieu.

Bloom. My father, whither wou'd you go?

Fath. Attempt not to stop me—Farewell.—I take
my final leave. Adieu, my child.

(Embraces the boy.

Bloom. Thou shalt not go, unfriended and unfur-
nished.

Mrs Bloom. No, by no means: If you will leave
us, take something to guard you from necessity.

Fath. What! think you I'll give speed to your misfortunes, and by depriving you of some of that little
you have left, invite ruin to fall on you a day sooner
—no, no. (*Going.*)

Bloom. If not from us, take from your darling
boy—Here, sir, give these to your grandfather, and
say, when they are gone, you'll again supply him.

(Gives him two bank notes.

Boy. Here, dear papa, take this. (*Giving one.*)

Fath. From the child, it is——

Bloom. That—why not both, sir?—Is this your gratitude, your love?

Boy. Oh! though I love him very well, I love you
too, and so I'll keep this (the other note) until I'm
a man, and my wife's extravagance makes you go
away from me, then I'll give it to support you.

Fath. Oh! my dear child! (*Embraces him.*) Thy
innocent prattle has afforded a lesson that—reflect
on his words, my children: I know the purity of your
minds; should a reformation be the happy result, in

what tranquillity and content shall I close the scene
of life in the society of you and my dear boy.

> (*Retires up with the boy.*

Mrs Bloom. Reproach from my infant! my husband's aged father threaten to fly from us! sell my
jointure! then misery is inevitable.   (*Aside.*

Bloom. What! grave and thoughtful in the midst
of all you can desire?

Mrs Bloom. Really, my dear, I begin to be tired of
the formality of paying and receiving visits; with all
this bustle, there's little society, and, I fear, less sincerity—say, that to-morrow you'll accompany me to
our villa, and bid adieu to all this folly and dissipation
—you sha'n't deny me.

Bloom. My dear, I have a thousand engagements
that can't be dispensed with—then I must to Bath,
Brighton, and Newmarket, where I have horses to
run, and from the bets already made, I must win or
lose considerably.

Mrs Bloom. I can contain myself no longer, but on
my knees entreat you'd summon all your reason, and
with tender patience hear me.

Bloom. Rise, my dear; I cannot bear to see you
in this posture.   What wou'd you say?

Mrs Bloom. I'd warn you of the precipice before
you.   If you advance, we are both inevitably lost—
think when you have sold all, how dreadful it must
be to be driven out by rude hands, and the severer
law, to be forced to labour for our bread, be scorned
by strangers, slighted by friends, receive an alms
given with a severe rebuke for our past follies, which
will be yet more bitter than want itself, and we must
endure it, for the fallen wretch that will not cringe
for support, may linger in poverty without pity or relief.— Frugality may yet retrieve our sinking fortune
—let me beseech you retire into the country, for I
am now convinced, that where innocence inhabits,
there content is only to be found.

Bloom. Be it as you please; I can't refuse, when you thus tenderly entreat.

Mrs Bloom. Then I am blessed! kind Providence has saved me from the brink of ruin, and restored me once more to every earthly happiness.

SIR CHARLES *comes forward.*

Sir Cha. My gentleman within here takes a long time in settling his affairs.

MR HALE *comes forward with* EMMA, SELBY *following.*

Sel. Only suffer me to explain, sir—

Mr Hale. Explain, sir, what business you have with my daughter?

Sir Cha. Your daughter, and this the gentleman! —yes, I see it is—I'm sorry for the confusion I occasioned, and—come, come, do give your daughter to this man of worth and mettle.

Mr H. Is it the right sort of mettle? Is he a man of fortune?

Sir Cha. He's a man of honour, that's better; and, from my friend Bloomfield's account, possesses truth, justice, and integrity: those articles you don't always find about men of fortune.

Mr H. Well, as his patron, Lord Wealthy, has got him a company, and is so firmly his friend, why I'll be his friend too, and tell him his father in the hour of death entreated I would give him my daughter; made me his executor, and left ten thousand pounds to his boy George. The will and cash I secreted: now I'll produce 'em; give 'em to you with all my heart, and my dear girl's hand into the bargain—there—I am easier now than I have been since I took charge of your property.

Sel. Oh! give me joy, for—

Enter Dash, *very shabbily dressed.*

Dash. No, no, give me joy—give me joy, I have got it—give me joy, I have got it.

Sir Cha. Got it! Got what? And why is all this joy?

Dash. I have got my fortune—Well, aunt! What! have you heard the news? you seem down in the mouth; you may fret, but you can't blame me for getting what's my own.

Sir Cha. I rather think, from your present appearance, you've lost what was your own : when last I had the honour of seeing you, I observed a diamond ring, pin, large buckles, two watches—

Dash. Oh! they are all gone : they and my wardrobe went to raise money for the counsel, and to carry on the suit. These clothes were lying by, so I just put them on for convenience, having no others. I shall now blaze forth with more splendour than ever, stifle me, eh, old one? I told you I'd make you stare; how damned mad they are at my good fortune!

Enter Servant.

Serv. Two men, who followed Mr Dash into the hall, desired me to give him this. [*Exit.*

Dash. Oh! 'tis from my friend Mr Demur—let me see—(*Reads.*) "Sir, every thing being now finally adjusted"—Bravo! I suppose here follows a draft on his banker—Law for ever—" and your part of the property producing only two thousand pounds, you now remain indebted to me the sum of six hundred and seventy-three pounds sixteen shillings and eightpence. Your paying the bearer instantly will prevent his executing the writ he has against you, and the uneasiness which your going to prison must occasion in the breast of,—yours, Capius Demur, uneas·pris."
—What the devil is all this?

Sir Cha. 'Tis your good fortune, which we all envy so much.

Dash. Well, but stifle me, if ever I thought of this. A prison!—is that the great house he promised to give me possession of?

Mr H. Hold, young man; sometimes out of evil good will arise. My design on this lady's person and property made me attentive to all the proceedings of your lawyer, by which I shall be enabled to free you from the gripe of a scoundrel, and put you in possession of what is really yours.

Dash. Strike me crooked, but you are a good one! You'll get me my own! take my advice though, and don't go to law! stifle me, if ever I go to law while I breathe.

Sir Cha. What, not to recover your right, sir?

Dash. No, sir; for there's no such thing as right in law, I think.

Sir Cha. Don't mistake, sir, you have only to lament that you have fallen into bad hands : your agent was dishonest.—English laws, like English liberty, properly treated, are our greatest blessings they were established on the noblest basis, to protect us from oppression, and are the chief supporters of our glorious constitution.

Miss Rus. (*Within.*) Is Sir Charles Leslie there? I suppose by his patience he has thought better of the affair.

Sir Cha. My patience! You requested time, and I have granted it. Come forth thou——

Miss Rus. I will, and I hope you have spirit to meet me.

Sir Cha. You shall feel whether I have spirit or not.

Mr H. No, no, though he is a little impudent—

Enter SALLY, *dressed as* SIR RAKEISH.

Hey-day! why this is Sally.

Sir Cha. Sally!

Sal. Yes, I am Sally, sir, at your service——

(*Curtsies.*

Sir Cha. Where is this impostor, this coward? I'll make him an example. I'll sacrifice him to——

Sal. Oh! dear sir, don't hurt him, poor sweet gentleman, if you had seen him throw himself on his knees to me, and cry, O, my dear Mrs Sally, you and only you can save my life, says he. Sir, says I, I'd have you to know I am a very honest—O, nonsense, says he—Ho, sir, 'tis not nonsense, says I, and I vow I'll cry out. Will you have me, says he? No, I won't, says I. Only let me tell you what I want, says he. I know what you want well enough, says I. So then, with all the civility and all the modesty in the world, says he, here is a purse of guineas, if you'll save my life by exchanging clothes with me. Oh, sir, who could refuse a pretty young fellow and a purse of guineas.

Sir Cha. Ah, the coward!

Sal. So I did, sir. Go boldly out, says he—Sir Charles will follow, and then I can escape. Oh, sir, for all your passion, if you'd ha' seen him as I saw him, you'd have done more than that for him.

Sir Cha. His impositions shall now be checked. I am the instrument that must punish thee, thou wretch, nor think that any disguise shall shield thee from——

Enter Miss Russel, *in* Sally's *clothes.*

Miss Rus. Truth and honour shall shield me. To my disguise I bid adieu. It has answered every purpose I wished; first, through it I have obtained 20,000 l. my own just patrimony; then knowing your mortgage was gained by extortion, I made bold to get that, and justice points you out as the right owner of it.   (*Gives a bond to* Sir Cha.

Sir Cha. Generous, charming woman!—share it

with me.   License my honourable passion, and give
me leave to love.

Miss Rus. O, Sir Charles! he that will love, and
knows what it is to love, will ask no leave of any but
himself—there's my fortune—there's my hand, and
with those be satisfied—you have long possessed my
heart.

Sir Cha. Bloomfield, ma'am, Selby—rejoice—ay,
and Lady Supple shall be happy : whatever your late
husband's fair demands on my estate may have been
shall be discharged most faithfully.

L. Sup. I ask no more.   To your agency, Mr
Hale, I commit my property, and desire to retain
only what is truly mine.

Fath. (*Comes forward.*) I see you amidst your
friends; may I venture to say, I participate in your
return to happiness ?

Mrs Bloom. You may, sir.—To-morrow we shall
retire into the country, where to see this company
must be a gratification as often as our shattered fortune will allow.

Bloom. Our fortune is not shattered, not even hurt
—my excesses have been all pretended; they were
put on to awaken in your mind——

Mrs Bloom. And it has most effectually—Your
conduct was so clear a mirror of my own, that 'twas
impossible not to see and blush at my glaring impro-
prieties : but we will advert to the past only to make
permanent our present felicity.—I will discard the
sycophants that used to surround me ; I will associate
only with the virtuous, and never will I suffer cunning
villainy to sit at my feast, while innocent honesty pe-
rishes at my door.   [*Exeunt omnes.*

THE

CHAPTER OF ACCIDENTS.

A

COMEDY,

IN FIVE ACTS.

AS PERFORMED AT THE

THEATRE-ROYAL, HAY-MARKET.

BY

MISS LEE.

DRAMATIS PERSONÆ.

LORD GLENMORE,	Mr Bensley.
GOVERNOR HARCOURT,	Mr Wilson.
WOODVILLE, *only Son to my Lord,*	Mr Palmer.
CAPTAIN HARCOURT, *Nephew to both,*	Mr Bannister, Jun.
GREY, *an infirm Clergyman,*	Mr Aickin.
VANE, *Valet to Lord Glenmore,*	Mr La Mash.
JACOB, *Servant to Cecilia,*	Mr Edwin.
CECILIA, *Mistress to Woodville,*	Miss Farren.
MISS MORTIMER, *Ward to Lord Glenmore,*	Mrs Cuyler.
WARNER, *Housekeeper to Lord Glenmore,*	Mrs Love.
BRIDGET, *Maid to Cecilia,*	Mrs Wilson.

SCENE—*London.*

Time, Twenty-four hours.

CHAPTER OF ACCIDENTS.

ACT THE FIRST.

SCENE I.

A Hall.

Enter VANE *in a riding dress, and a Footman.*

Vane. Run, and tell Mrs Warner my lord is at hand ; and bid the butler send me a bottle of hock. — (*Throws himself along the hall chairs, wiping his forehead.*) Phew ! the months have jumbled out of their places, and we have July in September !

Enter MRS WARNER.

War. Servant, Mr Vane.

Vane. Ah ! my dear creature ! how have you done these fifty ages ?

War. Why, methinks you are grown mighty grand, or you would have come to the still room to ask. Will you choose any chocolate ?

Vane. Why, don't you see I am dead?—absolutely dead; and, if you was to touch me, I should
shake to mere dust, like an Egyptian mummy.—Because it was not provoking enough to lounge away
a whole summer in the country, here am I driven up
to town, as if the devil was at my heels, in the shape
of our hopeful heir; who has neither suffered my
lord nor me to rest one moment, through his confounded impatience to see his uncle.

War. Umph!—he'll have enough of the old gentleman presently.   He is the very moral of my poor
dear lady, his sister, who never was at peace herself,
nor suffered any one else to be so.   Such a house as
we have had ever since he came!—Why, he is more
full of importance and airs than a bailiff in possession:
and hectors over Miss Mortimer, till she almost keeps
her chamber to avoid him.

Vane. Hates Miss Mortimer!—Why, here'll be
the devil to pay about her, I suppose!

War. Hate her? ay, that he does.   He look'd as
if he could have kill'd her the moment she came
down to see him; and got into his chamber presently after, where he sends for me.—Who is this young
woman, Mrs What's your name? says he.   Why,
sir, says I, she is the orphan of a Colonel Mortimer,
whose intimacy with my lord, says I——Pho, pho,
says he, all that I know, woman—What does she do
in this house? says he, his face wrinkling all over,
like cream when it's skimming.   Why, sir, says I,
her father unluckily died just before the duke his
brother, and so could not leave her one shilling of
all that fine fortune; and so my lord intends to marry her to Mr Woodville, says I.——He does? cries
he; Heaven be praised, I'm come in time to mar
that dainty project, however.   You may go, woman,
and tell Miss I don't want any thing more to-night.
——So up goes I to Miss Mortimer, and tells her

7

all this. Lord! how glad she was, to find he intended to break the match, though she cann't guess what he means.

Vane. Upon my soul, I think it is full as hard to guess what she means. What the devil, will not my lord's title, fortune, and only son, be a great catch for a girl without a friend or a shilling?

War. Ay; but I could tell you a little story would explain all.——You must know——(*Sitting down; a loud knocking.*)

Vane. (*Starts up.*) Zounds, here's my lord!

[*Exeunt confusedly.*

SCENE II.

An Antichamber.

LORD GLENMORE *and the Governor meet; the latter hobbling.*

Ld Glen. You are welcome to England, brother! I am sorry your native air pays you so ill a compliment after sixteen years absence.

Gov. Faith, my lord, and so am I too, I promise you: I put up with these things tolerably well in the Indies; I did not go there to be happy; but, after all my labours, to find I have just got the money when it is out of my power to enjoy it, is a cursed stroke:—like a fine ship of war, I am only come home to be dismasted and converted into an hospital. However, I am glad you hold it better: I don't think you look'd as well when we parted. My sister, poor Susan! she is gone too:—well, we can

never live a day the longer for thinking on't. Where's
Frank ? Is he still the image of his mother?

Ld Glen. Just as you left him, but that the innocence of the boy is dignified by the knowledge of
the man.

Gov He will hardly remember his old uncle !——
I did love the rogue, that's the truth on't : and never
look'd at my money-bags but I thought of him. However, you have provided him a wife !

Ld Glen. I have ; you saw her on your arrival, I
suppose, for I left her in town to attend a sick aunt.
Poor Mortimer ! he died one month before the duke
his brother, and missed a fine title and estate. You
know how I loved the honest fellow, and cannot wonder I took home his orphan'd daughter, as a match
for Woodville.

Gov. Brother, brother, you are too generous! it is
your foible, and artful people know how to convert
it to their own advantage.

Ld Glen. It is, if a foible, the noblest incident to
humanity. Sophia has birth, merit, accomplishments,
and wants nothing but money to qualify her for any
rank.

Gov. Can she have a worse want on earth ? Birth,
merit, accomplishments, are the very things that
render money more essential; if she had been brought
up in a decent plain way indeed,—but she has the
airs of a peeress already ; and if any philosopher
doubts of the perpetual motion, I would advise him
to watch the knocker of your house. Then you
have, out of your precise decorums, removed your
son, to make way for this flirt of fashion ; and what
is the consequence of rendering him thus early his
own master ?

Ld Glen. If you run on thus, only to divert yourself, with all my heart ; but if you would throw a
real imputation on Miss Mortimer's conduct, she is

entitled to my serious defence. I never saw any good
arise from secluding young people ; and authorise
Woodville and Sophia to live with that innocent elegance, which renders every rank easy, and prevents
pleasure from seducing the heart, or ignorance the
senses

Gov. My lord, I am amazed at you! Was there
ever yet a woman who didn't mean to pass for a goddess? Do they not gain upon us continually, till
nothing of our prerogative remains but the name?
We are wise fellows truly, if we do not keep down this
humour of their's as long as possible, by breeding
them in retirement. Every tinsel fop will find address enough to convince a wife she is an angel; and
the husband must be lucky, as well as sensible, who
reconciles her to treatment so inferior to her deserts.
Woodville will agree with me, I dare say; for the
character suits with his intended ; and, faith, he will
make but a modish husband, or he could not endure
to see her flying about, like the queen-bee, with the
whole hive at her heels

Ld Glen. You are too captious, brother!

Gov. And you too placid, brother! If, like me,
you had been toiling a third of your days to compass
a favourite design, and found it disappointed at the
moment you thought it complete, what would even
your serene lordship say and do?—Here have I promised myself a son in your's,—an heir in your's ;—
instead of which——

Ld Glen. His marriage with Miss Mortimer will
not make him unworthy either title.

Gov. Never mention her name to me, I beg, my
lord !—I hate all mode-mongers of either sex : the
wife I would have given him has beauty without
knowing it, innocence without knowing it, because
she knows nothing else; and, to surprise you farther,
forty thousand pounds without knowing it ;—nay,

to bring all your surprises together, is my daughter without knowing it.

Ld Glen. Your daughter ! Why, have you married since my sister's death ? Your daughter by her you lost before you went abroad ?

Gov. Yes, but I shall find her again, I believe.— I know you will call this one of my old whims, as usual, but we have all some ; witness this dainty project of your's ; and so I will tell you the truth in spite of that project.—From the very birth of this girl, I saw her mother would spoil her, and, had she lived, proposed kidnapping Miss in her infancy.

Ld Glen. Kidnap your own daughter !—Why, brother, I need only prove this to obtain a commission of lunacy, and shut you up for life.

Gov. Why, though my wife was your lordship's sister, I will venture to tell you she was plaguy fantastical, and contrived to torment me as much with her virtues, as others by their vices—Such a fuss about her delicacy, her sensibility, and her refinement, that I could neither look, move, nor speak, without offending one or the other, and execrated the inventor of the jargon every hour in the four and twenty ;—a jargon I resolved my girl should never learn ; and Heaven no sooner took her mother, (Heaven be praised for all things !) than I dispatch'd her draggle-tail'd French governess, made a bonfire of every book on education, whip'd Miss into a postchaise, under a pretence of placing her in a nunnery; instead of which, I journeyed into Wales, and left her in the care of a poor curate's wife, whose name was up as the bes housewife in the whole country ; then return'd, with a solemn history of her death in the small-pox.

Ld Glen. Well, this is indeed astonishing ! an admirable tutoress truly for my niece !

Gov. Yes, but there's a better jest than that.

Ld Glen. Indeed!—is that possible ?

Gov. How do you think I contrived to make them obey my instructions ?—I saw they suspected I was some rich humourist, and was afraid they would, after all, make a little bit of a gentlewoman of her; for which reason, except the first year in advance, they never had a single shilling of my money.

Ld Glen. This is almost incredible ! And so you left your only child to the charity of strangers ?

Gov. No, no, not so bad as that neither.—You remember my honest servant Hardy ? After the poor fellow's leg was shot off in my tent, I promised him a maintenance ; so, entrusting him with the secret, I ordered him to live in the neighbourhood, have an eye on the girl, and claim her if ill used.—Fine accounts I had from him, faith ! The old parson and his wife, having no children, and not finding any one own her, gave out she was their's, and doted on her ; in short, she is the little wonder of the country : tall as the palm-tree; with cheeks that might shame the drawing-room ; and eyes will dim the diamonds I have brought over to adorn them.—This confounded gout has kept me in continual alarm, or else she should have spoke for herself.

Ld Glen. Why then does not Hardy bring her up to you ?

Gov. Why, for two very sufficient reasons :—In the first place, that identical parson paid him the last compliment, that is, buried him a twelvemonth ago ; and in the second, they would hardly entrust her to any man but him who delivered her to them.—Here was a girl, my lord, to support your title, of which I dare swear you are as fond as ever : she would have brought you a race of true Britons ; instead of which, from the painted dolls and unjointed macaronies of these days, we shall produce our own enemies, and have a race of Frenchmen born in England.

Ld Glen. I thank your intention, brother; but am

far from wishing the chief accomplishments of Woodville's lady should be the making cream cheeses,
goats' whey, and alder wine.

Gov. Let me tell your lordship, women were never better than when those were their chief accomplishments.—But I may be ridiculous my own way
without being singular.—Harcourt shall have my girl,
and my money too.—Cream cheeses, quotha? No,
no, making cream faces is an accomplishment which
the belles of these days oftener excel in.

Ld Glen. I would not advise you to publish this
opinion, governor.

Gov. But where is this son of your's ? Sure he has
not totally forgot his old uncle?

Ld Glen. He will be here immediately.

Gov. Nay, I must e'en take an old man's fate, and
follow his mistress without complaint.

Ld Glen. You have no reason for the reproach ;
this is not his hour for visiting Miss Mortimer.

Gov. Miss Mortimer!—Ha, ha, ha! why, do you
think I took her for his mistress ?—What, I warrant,
I can tell you news of your own family, though I have
hardly been three days in it !—Woodville keeps a girl,
and in great splendour !—nay, they tell me that the
unconscionable young rogue encroaches so far on the
privileges of threescore, as to intend marrying the
slut.

Ld Glen. You jest, surely ?

Gov. There's no jest like a true one—ha, ha, ha!
how foolish you look ! this is your innocent elegance,
this is the blessed effect of letting him live out of your
own house !——

Ld Glen. Pr'ythee reserve your raillery, sir, for
some less interesting occasion ;—to have my views
thus in a moment overturned !—Where does she live ?

Gov. Ha, ha, ha!—Oh, the difference of those little syllables me and thee !—Now you can guess what

made me so peevish, I suppose ?—As to where Miss lives, I have not heard ; but somewhere near his lodgings.—A devilish fine girl she is, by the bye.—Ah I told you, twenty years ago, you would spoil this boy —entirely spoil him.

Ld Glen. Zounds ! governor, you have a temper Socrates himself could not have supported.—Is this a time for old sayings of twenty years ago ?—Finish dressing ; by that time your nephew will be here, and I shall have reflected on this matter.

Gov. With all my heart.—'Tis but a boyish frolick, and so good morning to you.—Here ; where's my triumvirate ? Pompey, Antony, Cæsar !   (*Exit.*

Ld Glen. A boyish frolick truly !—many a foolish fellow's life has been marked by such a boyish frolick ! —But her residence is the first object of my inquiry. —Vane !

Enter VANE.

Is not my son come ?

Vane. This moment, my lord; and waits till the governor is ready.

Ld Glen. Vane !—I have deserved you should be attached to me, and I hope you are ?

Vane. My lord ! (what the devil is he at ?) [*Aside.*

Ld Glen. This strange old governor has alarmed me a good deal ;—you are more likely to know whether with reason than I can be.—Have you heard any thing important of my son lately ?

Vane. Never, my lord.

Ld Glen. Not that he keeps a mistress ?—What does the fool smile at !

Vane. I did not think that any thing important, my lord.

Ld Glen. I do, sir—and am told a more important thing ; that he even thinks of marrying her—Now, though I cannot credit this, I would chuse to know what kind of creature she is.   Could not you assume a clownish disguise, and, scraping an acquaintance with her people, learn something of her character and designs ?

Vane. Doubtless, to oblige your lordship, I could do such a thing.——But, if Mr Woodville's sharp eyes (and love will render them still sharper) should discover me, I might chance to get a good drubbing in the character of a spy.

Ld Glen. Oh, it is very improbable he should suspect you: at the worst, name your employer, and your bones are safe.——The office, perhaps, is not very agreeable, but I impose few such on you : execute it well, and you shall remember it with pleasure.—— I will detain Woodville till you are ready ; and, as I doubt not that his next visit will be to this creature, by following him you will find out where she lives. Prepare then as quick as possible, and send me word when you are ready ; for, till then, I will not suffer him to depart. (*Exit.*

Vane. A pretty errand this his formal lordship has honour'd me with !—Um ; if I betray him, shall I not get more by it ;—ay, but our heir is such a sentimental spark, that, when his turn was served, he might betray me. Were he one of our hare-um skare-um, good-natured, good-for-nothing fellows, it would go against my conscience to do him an ill turn.——I believe I stand well in my lord's will, if Counsellor Puzzle may be trusted, (and when he can get nothing by a lie, perhaps he may tell truth,) so, like all thriving men, I will be honest, because it best serves my interest. (*Exit.*

SCENE III.

A confined Garden.

WOODVILLE *walking about.*

Wood. How tedious is this uncle !—how tedious every body !—Was it not enough to spend two detestable months from my love, merely to preserve the secret, but I must be tantalized with seeing without arriving at her? Yet how, when I do see her, shall I appease that affecting pride of a noble heart, conscious too late of its own inestimable value?—Why was I not uniformly just?—I had then spared myself the bitterest of regrets.

Enter CAPTAIN HARCOURT.

Har. Woodville! how dost?—Don't you, in happy retirement, pity me my Ealing and Acton marches and countermarches, as Foote has it?—But, methinks thy face is thinner and longer than a forsaken nymph's, who is going through the whole ceremony of nine months' repentance.——What, thou'st fall'n in love? —rustically too?—nay, pr'ythee don't look so very lamentable!

Wood. Ridiculous!—keep this Park conversation for military puppies!—How can we have an eye or ear for pleasure, when our fate hangs over us undecided?

Har. I guess what you mean; but why make mountains of mole-hills? Is the rosy-fisted damsel so obstinately virtuous?

Wood. Imagine a fair favourite of Phœbus in all respects; since, while her face caught his beams, her heart felt his genius!—Imagine all the graces hid under a straw hat and russet gown ; imagine—

Har. You have imagined enough of conscience ! and now for a few plain facts, if you please.

Wood. To such a lovely country maid I lost my heart last summer ; and soon began to think romances the only true histories; all the toilsome glories recorded by Livy phantoms of pleasure, compared with the mild enjoyments described by Sir Philip Sidney ; and happiness not merely possible in a cottage, but only possible there.

Har. Well, all the philosophers, ancient and modern, would never be able to convince me a coach was not a mighty pretty vehicle, and the lasses as good-natured in town as country ; but pray let us know why you laid aside the pastoral project of eating fat bacon, and exercising a crook all day, that thou might'st conclude the evening with the superlative indulgence of a peat-fire and a bed stuff'd with straw ?

Wood. Why, faith, by persuading the dear girl to share mine.

Har. Oh, now you talk the language of the world : and does that occasion thee such a melancholy face ?

Wood. How ignorant are you both of me and her ! —Every moment since I prevailed has only served to convince me I can sooner live without every thing else than her ; and this fatal leisure (caused by my absence with my father) she has employ'd in adding every grace of art to those of nature ; till, thoroughly shocked at her situation, her letters are as full of grief as love, and I dread to hear every hour I have lost her.

Har. I dread much more to hear you have lost yourself.   Ah, my dear Woodville, the most dangerous charm of love is, every man conceits no other ever found out his method of loving : but, take my word for it, your Dolly may be brought back to a milk-maid. —Leave her to herself a while, and she'll drop the celestials, I dare swear.

Wood. She is too noble : and nothing but the duty I owe to so indulgent a father prevents me from offering her all the reparation in my power.

Har. A fine scheme truly ! Why, Woodville, art frantic ?—To predestinate yourself among the horned cattle of Doctors Commons, and take a wife for the very reason which makes so many spend thousands to get rid of one——

Wood. To withdraw an amiable creature from her duty, without being able to make her happy, is to me a very serious reflection ;—nay, I sinned, I may say, from virtue ; and, had I been a less grateful son, might have called myself a faultless lover.

Har. Well, well, man ! you are young enough to trust to time, and he does wonders.—Don't go now and ruin yourself with your uncle ;—I have found him out already, and advertise you, none of your formal obsequious bows and respectful assents will do with him ; having been cheated in former times of half his fortune by a parasite, he mistrusts every one, and always mistakes politeness for servility.   Maintain your own opinion, if you would win his ; for he generally grows undetermined the moment he knows those around him are otherwise : and, above all, shake off this mental lethargy.

Wood. I will endeavour to take your advice.—— Should she fly, I were undone for ever !—but you are no judge of my Cecilia's sincerity.   How should you know those qualities, which rise with every following hour ?—Can you think so meanly of me, as that I could be duped by a vulgar wretch, a selfish wanton ? Oh no !—she possesses every virtue but the one I have robbed her of.   [*Exit.*

HARCOURT *alone.*

Har. Poor Frank! thy sponsors surely, by intui-
tion, characterised thee when they gave thee that name.
——Did I love your welfare less, I could soon ease
your heart, by acquainting you of my marriage with
Miss Mortimer; but now the immediate consequence
would be this ridiculous match.—How, if I apprize
either my lord or the governor, both obstinate in
different ways? I might betray only to ruin him.—
A thought occurs;—my person is unknown to her.
—Chusing an hour when he is absent, I'll pay her a
visit, offer her an advantageous settlement, and learn
from her behaviour her real character and intentions.
[*Exit.*

ACT THE SECOND.

SCENE I.

*An elegant Dressing-Room, with a Toilet richly or-
namented. A Harpsichord, and a frame with Embroidery.*

BRIDGET *fetches various small jars with flowers, and
talks as she places them.*

Brid. Lord help us!—How fantastical some folks
not an hundred miles off are!—If I can imagine
what's come to my lady.—Here has she been sighing

and groaning these two months, because her lover
was in the country; and now, truly, she's sighing
and groaning because he is come to town.—Such
maggots indeed!—I might as well have staid in our
parish all the days of my life, as to live mewed up
with her in this dear sweet town. I could but have
done that with a virtuous lady—although I knew she
never was at Fox-hall in all her jaunts: and we two
should cut such a figure there!—Bless me! what's
come to the glass? (*Setting her dress.*) Why, sure,
it is dulled with her eternal sighing, and makes me
look as frightful as herself!—O! here she comes,
with a face as long and dismal as if he was going to
be married, and to somebody else too.

CECILIA *enters, and throws herself on the sofa,
leaning on her hand.*

Cec. What can detain Woodville such an age?—
It is an hour at least since he rode by.—Run, Bridget, and look if you can see him through the drawing-room window.

Brid. Yes, madam. (*Exit, eyeing her with contempt.*)

Cec. How wearisome is every hour to the wretched!—They catch at each future one, merely to while
away the present. For, were Woodville here, could
he relieve me from the torment of reflection, or the
strong, though silent, acknowledgment my own
heart perpetually gives of my error?

Brid. (*Without.*) Here he comes, ma'am, here he
comes!

Cec. Does he?—Run down then. (*Fluttered.*)

Brid. Dear me, no; 'tis not neither; (*Enters.*) 'tis
only the French ambassador's new cook, with his
huge bag and long ruffles.

Cec. Blind animal!—Sure nothing is so tormenting as expectation!

Brid. La', ma'am!—any thing will torment one,

when one has a mind to be tormented ; which must
be your case for sartin. What signifies sitting mope,
mope, mope, from morning to night ?—You'd find
yourself a deal better if you went out only two or
three times a day. For a walk, we are next door to
the Park, as I may say ; and for a ride, such a dear
sweet vis-a-vis and pretty horses might tempt any
one : then, as to company, you'll say, a fig for your
starched ladies, who owe their virtue to their ugli-
ness !—mine is very much at your service—(*Curtsies.*)

Cec. How could I endure this girl, did I not know
that her ignorance exceeds even her impertinence !
—I have no pleasure in going abroad.

Brid. Oh la, ma'am ! how should you know till
you try ? Sure every body must wish to see and be
seen.—Then there's such a delightful hurricane ; all
the world are busy, though most are doing nothing ;
to splash the mob, and drive against the people of
quality !—Oh, give me a coach and London for ever
and ever !—You could but lock yourself up, were you
as old and ugly as gay Lady Grizzle, at next door.

Cec. Had I been so, I had continued happy.

Brid. La, ma'am, don't ye talk so profanely !—
Happy to be old and ugly —Or, I'll tell you what,
as you don't much seem to fancy going out, suppose
you were to come down now and then, (you know
we have a pure large hall,) and take a game of
romps with us ? If you were once to see our Jacob
hunt the slipper, you would die with laughing !—
Madam Frisk, my last mistress, used, as soon as ever
master was gone, (and indeed he did not trouble her
much with his company,) to run down, draw up her
brocaded niggle-de-gee, and fall to play at some good
fun or other '—Dear heart, we were as merry then
as the day was long !—I am sure I have never been
half so happy since !

Cec. I cannot possibly imitate the model you propose ; but though I don't choose to go abroad, you may.

Brid. I don't love to go much among the mobility, neither. If indeed, madam, next winter, you'd give me some of your tickets, I would fain go to a masquerade, (it vexes me to see um stick in the thing-um-bobs for months together,) and Mrs Trim promises me the lent of a Wenus's dress, which, she says, 1 shall cut a figure in. Now, madam, if I had but some diamonds, (for beggars wear diamonds there, they say,) who knows but I might make my fortune, like you?

Cec. Mar it, much rather, like me.—That is no place for girls of your station, which exposes you to so much insult.

Brid. Ah, let me alone, madam, for taking care of number one. I ware never afeared but once in my whole life, and that ware of grand-far's ghost ; for he always hated I, and used to walk, poor soul! in our barken, for all the world like an ass with a tie-wig on.— (*Knocking hard.*)

Cec. Hark! that sure is Woodville's knock! Fly, and see !—(*Walks eagerly to the door, and returns as eagerly.*)—Alas! is this my repentance?—Dare I sin against my judgment?

Enter WOODVILLE.

Wood. My Cecilia!—My soul!—Have I at last the happiness of beholding you?—You know me too well to imagine I would punish myself by a moment's voluntary delay.

Cec. Oh no ; it is not that—(*Both sit down on the sofa.*)

Wood. Say, you are glad to see me ; afford me one kind word to atone for your cold looks!—Are you not well?

Cec. Rather say, I am not happy.—My dear Woodville, I am an altered being !—Why have you redu-

ced me to shrink thus in your presence ? Oh ! why
have you made me unworthy of yourself?—(*Leans
against his shoulder, weeping.*)

Wood. Cruel girl!—Is this my welcome ?—When
did I appear to think you so ?

Cec. Tell me when any one else would think me
otherwise ?

Wood. Will you never be above so narrow a prejudice ?—Are we not the whole world to each other ?
—Nay, dry your tears ! allow me to dry them : (*Kisses her cheek.*) What is there, in the reach of love or
wealth, I have not sought to make you happy ?

Cec. That which is the essence of all enjoyments
—innocence !—Oh, Woodville! you knew not the
value of the heart whose peace you have destroyed.
My sensibility first ruined my virtue, and then my
repose.—But, though for you I consented to abandon an humble happy home, to embitter the age of
my venerable father, and bear the contempt of the
world, I can never support my own !—My heart
revolts against my situation, and hourly bids me
renounce a splendour, which only renders guilt
more despicable.—(*Rises.*) I meant to explain
this hereafter ; but the agitation of my mind obliged me to lighten it immediately.

Wood. Is your affection then already extinct ?
for sure it must, when you can resolve to torture me
thus.

Cec. Were my love extinct, I might sink into a
mean content.—Oh no !—'Tis to that alone I owe
my resolution.

Wood. Can you then plunge me into despair ?—
So young, so lovely too !—Oh! where could you find
so safe an asylum as my heart ?—Whither could you
fly ?

Cec. I am obliged to you, sir, for the question ;
but who is it has made me thus destitute ?—I may
retain your protection, indeed, but at what price ?

Wood. Give me but a little time, my love !—I am equally perplexed between my father and my uncle, each of whom offers me a wife I can never love.—Suffer them to defeat each other's schemes !—Let me, if possible, be happy without a crime; for I must think it one to grieve a parent hitherto so indulgent. —I will not put any thing in competition with your peace ; and long for the hour when the errors of the lover will be absorbed in the merits of the husband.

Cec. No, Woodville !—That was, when innocent, as far above my hopes, as it is now beyond my wishes. —I love you too sincerely to reap any advantage from so generous an error : yet you at once flatter and wound my heart in allowing me worthy such a distinction ; but love cannot subsist without esteem; and how should I possess your's, when I have lost even my own ?

Wood. It is impossible you should ever lose either, while so deserving of both.—I shall not be so easily denied hereafter, but am bound by the caprices of others at present.—I am obliged to return directly, but will hasten to you the very first moment.—When we meet again, it must be with a smile, remember !

Cec. It will when we meet again.—Oh, how those words oppress me ! (*Aside.*)—But do not regulate your conduct by mine, nor make me an argument with yourself for disobeying my lord; for here I solemnly swear never to accept you without the joint consent of both our fathers ; and that I consider as an eternal abjuration !—But may the favoured woman you are to make happy have all my love without my weakness ! [*Exit in tears.*

Wood. Disinterested, exalted girl !—Why add such a needless bar ? For is it possible to gain my father's consent ?—And yet, without her, life would be insupportable !—The censures of the world !—What is that world to me ?—Were I weak enough to sacrifice her to the erroneous judgment of the malicious and unfeeling, what does it offer to reward me?—Commendations I can never deserve, and riches I can never enjoy.   [*Exit.*

SCENE II.

A Street before CECILIA'S *House.*

JACOB *opens the door, and lets out* WOODVILLE, *who passes over the stage* ; JACOB *remains with his hands in his pockets, whistling.*

Enter VANE, *disguised, with a basket of game in his hand.*

Vane. So, there he goes at last.   I may open the attack without fear of a discovery, since our hopeful heir will hardly return directly.—This intelligence of my landlord's at the Blue Posts has made the matter much easier.—Um, a good subject!—Sure I ought to know that bumpkin's face!—As I live, my playfellow at the parish school, Jacob Gawky!—Now for a touch of the old dialect.—D'ye hire, young mon!—Prey, do ye know where one Bett Dowson do live ?

Jac. Noa, not I.

Vane. Hey!—Why, zure as two-pence, thou beest Jacob Gawky !

Jac. Odsbodlikins ! zo I be indeed!—But, who beest thee ?

Vane. What doest not knaw thy ould zkhoolvellow, Wull, mun ?

Jac. Hey!—What—Wull!—Od rabbit it, if I ben't desperate glad to zee thee ; where doost live now, mun ?

Vane. Down at huome, in our parish.——I be coom'd up with Zur Isaac Promise, to be made excoiseman.

Jac. Thee'st good luck, faith! wish, no odds to thee, my fortin ware as good!—but theed'st always a muortal good notion of wroiting and cyphers, while I don't knaw my own neame when I do zee it.——What didst leave zea for?

Vane. Why, I ware afraid I should be killed before I com'd to be a great mon! But what brought thec into this foine house?

Jac. Fortin, Wull! Fortin.——Didst thee knaw Nan o' th' mill?

Vane. Noa, not I.

Jac. Od rabbit it! I thought every mortal zoul had knawd zhe —Well, Nan and I ware such near neighbors, there ware only a barn between us;—she ware a desperate zmart lass, that's the truth on't: and I had half a moind to teake to feyther's business, and marry zhe:—but ecod the zimpletony grow'd so fond, that, some how or other, I ware tired first! when, behold you, zquire takes a fancy to me, and made I cuome and live at the hall; and, as my head run all on tuown, when aw comed up to London, aw brought I wi' un: zo I thought to get rid that way of the bullocking of Nan.

Vane. But, Jacob, how didst get into thic foine house?

Jac. Dang it, doan't I zeay, I'll tell thee present —Zoa, as I ware zaying, one holiday I went to zee thic there church, wi' the top like a huge punch-bowl turned auver; and, dang it! who should arrive in the very nick, but madam Nan—Well, huome comes I as merry as a cricket;—zquire caals for I in a muortal hurry; when who should I zee, but madam Nan on her marrowbones, a-croying for dear loife!—dang it, I thought at first I should ha zwounded;—zo a made a long zarmant about 'ducing a poor girl, and

zaid I should zartainly go to the divil for it, and then
turned I off.   But the best fun is to come, mun ;—
rabbit me ! if aw did not teake Nan into keeping himself ; and zhe do flaunt it about as foine as a duchess.

Vane. A mighty religious moral gentleman, truly !
(*Aside.*) Well, how came you to this pleace ?

Jac. Why, Meay-day, walking in Common Garden
to smell the pozeys, who should I zee but our Bridget ?—I was muortal glad to zee her, you must needs
think, and zhe got I this here pleace.

Vane. Wounds ! dost live wi' a lord in this foine
house ?

Jac. Noa, a leady, you fool ! but such a leady,
zuch a dear, easy, good-natured creature !—zhe do
never say noa, let we do what we wull.

Vane. Now to the point. (*Aside.*)—Is your lady
married ?

Jac. Noa : but she's as good ; and what'st think,
mun !—to a lord's zon !—though if a ware a king, aw
would not be too good for zhe.—A mortal fine comely mon too, who do love her as aw do the eyes in his
head.   Couzin Bridget do tell I, zhe zeed'd a letter
wh re aw do zay aw wull ha her any day of the week,
whatever do come o' th' next.—Why I warrant they
have 'pointed wedding-day !

Vane. The devil they have ! my lord will go mad
at this news.   [*Aside.*

Jac. Lauk a deazy ! how merry we will be on that
day ! Wo't come and junket wi' us ?

Vane. Yes, yes, I shall certainly make one among
you, either then or before ; (*Aside.*) but now I must
goa and give this geame to zquire—zquire—what the
dickens be his neame ! I do always forget it—there
zhould be a ticket somewhere—zoa, rabbit me ! if
some of your London fauk ha' no' cut it off out o'
fun !

Jac. Ha, ha, ha ! ecod, nothing more likelier—
(*Both laugh foolishly.*) The rum people be zo zharp as

needles.—But there's no pleace like it for all that—
I be set upon living and dying in it.

Vane. Now to secure my return if necessary. (*Aside.*)
—I'll tell thee what, Jacob, seeing as how I ha' lost
thic there direction, do thee teake the basket : 'tis
only a present of geame from the parson o' our parish ;
and, if zo be I can't find the gentleman, why 'tis honestly mine.—Meay be I'll come, and teake a bit o'
supper wi' ye.

Jac. Wull ye indeed ?—dang it ! that's clever ; and
then you'll see our Bridget.   She's a mortal zmart
lass, I promise ye !—and, meay be, may'st get a peep
at my leady, who's desperate handsome !—Good bye
t'ye.—Bridget's zo comical !—Od rabbit it, we'll be
main merry !   [*Exit.*

VANE *alone.*

Vane. Thus far I have succeeded to admiration !
Our young heir has really a mind to play the fool, and
marry his mistress !—though, faith, marrying his own
does not seem very inexcusable, when so many of his
equals modestly content themselves with the cast-offs
of half their acquaintance.   [*Exit.*

SCENE III.

An Apartment in CECILIA'S *House.*

Enter BRIDGET.

Brid. So, just the old story again ! crying, crying
for ever !—Lord, if I was a man, I should hate such
a whimpering—What would she have, I wonder ? to
refuse such a handsome, genteel, good-natured man !

and I'll be sworn, he offer'd to marry her, for I listened with all my ears!—Oh, that he would have me now!—I should become my own coach purdigiously, that's a sure thing. Hey, who knocks?

Enter JACOB.

Jac. A young mon do want my leady.

Brid. A man!—what sort of a man?

Jac. Why a mon—like—just such another as I.

Brid. No, no, no;—that's not so easy to find.—What can any man want with her?—Shew him in here, Jacob.

Jac. *(Returning in a kind of glee.)* When shall we have the wedding, Bridget?

Brid. We shall have a burying first, I believe.

Jac. Od rabbit it! we won't be their seconds there, faith !   [*Exit.*

Brid. Now, if he mistakes me for my lady, I shall find out what he wants.

Enter CAPTAIN HARCOURT, *disguised, with* JACOB.

Har. (*Surveying her.*)——Is that your lady ?

Jac. He, he, he! lauk, zur, don't you know that's our Bridget?

Brid. So, deuce on him, there's my whole scheme spoilt!—My lady, sir, is engaged; but if you tell me your business, it will do just as well.

Har. For yourself it may, child! (*Chucks her under the chin.*)

Brid. What, you belong to Mr Gargle the apothecary? or come from the jeweller on Ludgate-hill? or have a letter from——

Har (*Interrupting her.*)—The very person; you have hit it.   And now, do me the favour to tell your lady a stranger wishes to speak to her on particular business.

Brid. Very well, sir:—Was ever handsome man so crabbed!

Har. Egad, if the mistress have half as much tongue as the maid, Woodville may catch me in the midst of my first speech.——Now for my credentials! and here she comes!—A lovely girl, indeed! I can scarce blame Frank, for she awes me.

Enter CECILIA, *followed officiously by* BRIDGET.

Cec. I was informed, sir, you had particular business with me?

Har. I took the liberty, madam,—I say, madam, I——

Cec. As I have neither friends or relations in London, (*Sighs*) I am at a loss to guess——

Har. What I would communicate, madam, requires secrecy.

Cec. Bridget, go where I ordered you just now.

Brid. Yes, madam, but if I an't even with you for this—   [*Exit.*

Cec. I complied with your request, sir, without inquiring the motive; because you, I think, can have only one—My father, if I may trust my heart, has made you his messenger to an unwilling offender.

Har. Pardon me, madam, but I refer you to this.

Cec. (*Reads.*)—" Madam,—being certainly informed Mr Woodville is on the point of marrying a lady chosen by his friends, when it is presumed you will be disengaged, a nobleman of rank, and estate above what he can ever possess, is thus early in laying his heart and fortune at your feet, lest some more lucky rival should anticipate him.——The bearer is authorised to disclose all particulars, and offer you a settlement worthy your acceptance ——Deign, madam, to listen to him on the subject, and you will find the unknown lover as generous and not less constant than Woodville." Good heavens! to what an insult have I exposed myself! (*She bursts into tears, and sinks into a chair, without minding* HARCOURT, *who watches her with irresolution.*)

Har. What can I think ?—there is an air of injured delicacy in her, which teaches me to reproach myself for a well-meant deceit.——If, madam,——

Cec. I had forgot this wretch. (*Rises.*) Return,
sir, to your vile employer; tell him, whoever he is, I
am too sensible of the insult, though not entitled to
resent it—tell him, I have a heart above my situation,
and that he has only had the barbarous satisfaction
of adding another misery to those which almost overwhelmed me before.

Har. Hear me, madam, I conjure you!

Cec. Never! a word would contaminate me——
(*Struggling to go off.*)

Har. Nay, you shall—You do not know half the
good consequences of this letter; I am the friend, the
relation of Woodville—my name Harcourt!

Cec. Is it possible he should be so cruel, so unjust——

Har. He is neither cruel nor unjust, but only unfortunate.—Hear—he designs to marry you; this I
learnt from himself only this morning. As a proof
of my sincerity, I will own I doubted your right to
that mark of his esteem, and made this trial in consequence. Pleased to find you worthy of his rank, I
feel shock'd at reminding you, you ought not to share
it. But, madam, if you truly love him, you cannot
wish that, to be just to you, he should be unjust to
those who have a prior right over him.—This shall
positively be my last effort. (*Aside.*)

Cec. A motive like your's, sir, will excuse any
thing. How little my happiness, honour, or interest,
ever weighed against his, need not be repeated. Far
be it from me now to disgrace him; he is apprized of
my invincible objections to a match which will never
take place. May he form a happier, while I, by a voluntary poverty, expiate my offence!

Har. Ma—Ma—what the devil choaks me so!—
I am struck with your sentiments, and must find you

a proper asylum. The moment I saw you, I had hopes such manners could not veil an immoral heart; I have proved your sincerity, and owe a reparation to your delicacy. The proposed bride of Woodville is every way worthy that distinction ; nor am I without hopes even she will be prevailed on to protect you.—But I must not leave a doubt of my sincerity :—Do you know Miss Mortimer ?

Cec. I have seen the lady, sir. But dare I credit my senses ?—Has heaven form'd two such hearts, and for me ?—

Har. With her, your story will be buried for ever: and, I think, the sooner you disappear, the more easily will you prevent Woodville's disobedience. I will open the affair to Miss Mortimer directly, and, if she acquiesces, desire her to call for you in person, to prevent the possibility of any artifice.

Cec. He who inspired such sentiments alone can reward them ! Oh, sir, you have raised a poor desponding heart !—but it shall be the business of my future life to deserve those favours I can never half repay.

Har. I find, by punishing me with acknowledgments, you are resolved to be obliged to me. The time is too precious to be wasted on such trifles. At seven, you shall have certain intelligence of my success; employ the interim to the best advantage, and hope every thing from daring to deserve well. (*Exit.*

CECILIA *alone.*

Astonishing interposition of heaven !—Hope !—What have I to hope ?—But let the consciousness of acting rightly support me in the sad moment of renouncing Woodville ; and, in him, all that rendered life desirable. [*Exit.*

SCENE IV.

LORD GLENMORE'S *House.*

LORD GLENMORE *and* VANE.

Ld Glen. And are you sure of all this?

Vane. Absolutely, my lord; I have known the bumpkin, her footman, from the height of his own club.

Ld Glen. What a cursed infatuation!—these are the comforts of children!—our fears beginning from the moment our power ends; the happiest of fathers is not to be envied:—I know not what to resolve on!

Vane. If I may be permitted to advise, my lord—

Ld Glen. And who asked your advice, sir?

Vane. You have, my lord, formerly.

Ld Glen. Take care you stay till I do! Leave me, sir.

Vane. If you don't like my advice, I shall give you my opinion very shortly.—A crusty crab!

[*Exit muttering.*

Ld Glen. This is the certain consequence of entrusting low people;—and yet there is no doing without them.—I can never master my feelings enough to speak properly to Woodville on the subject, therefore must fix on some other method—(*Pauses.*)—That's a sure one, and falls heavy on the artful, aspiring creature only!—Vane!

Re-enter VANE.

—Could not you procure me a travelling-chaise and four stout fellows immediately?

Vane. To be sure, my lord, I can order a chaise at any inn, if you choose it.

Ld Glen. Pho, pho!—don't put on that face;—you must go through with this thing like a man.—Here's something for the share you have already had in it.—Do what I have ordered, and wait near the Horse-guards in about an hour, when I shall seize this insolent baggage, and convey her out of my son's reach.—You gave me a high-flown account of her; —and, as you are a smart young fellow, and she must at least be pretty, if we can contrive to frighten her into taking you as a husband, it will end all my fears, and shall be the making of your fortune.

Vane. 'Gad, I like the project well!—A handsome wife is the best bait, when we fish for preferment;—and this gives me a double claim both on father and son. (*Aside.*)—Nothing but the profound respect I have for your lordship could induce me to think of this;—though born without rank and fortune, I have a soul, my lord——

Ld Glen. Come, come, my good lad! I guess what you would say; but we have no time for speeches.—I have set my heart on the success of this project, and you shall find your interest in indulging me.

[*Exeunt different ways.*

SCENE V.

Miss Mortimer's *Apartment.*

Enter CAPTAIN HARCOURT, *meeting* Miss MORTIMER.

Har. If I were to judge of your temper by your looks, my dear, I should say it was uncommonly sweet this morning.

Miss Mor. A truce with compliment ! I must, in reason, renounce dear flattery after marriage.

Har. To flattery you never paid court; but the language of the heart and the world will sometimes resemble.—I ought, however, to praise your temper, for I am come to try it, and give you a noble opportunity of exerting its benevolence.

Miss Mor. A benevolence you certainly doubt, by this studied eulogium.

Har. I might, did I not know it well.—In short, my love, I have taken the strangest step this morning——

Miss Mor. What step, for heaven's sake ?

Har. In regard to a lady——

Miss Mor. Not another wife, I hope ?

Har. No,—only a mistress.

Miss Mor. Oh, a trifle ! a trifle !

Har. You may laugh, madam, but I am serious ; and a fine girl she is;—nay, to shew you I have not read Chesterfield in vain, I have robbed my dearest friend of her: In plain English, Woodville has a mistress he dotes on so madly, as even to intend marrying her.—Imagining her, like most of her stamp, only an artful, interested creature, I paid her a visit as a stranger, with an offer which must have unveiled her heart, had it been base; but I found her, on the contrary, a truly noble-minded girl, and far above her present situation, which she earnestly wishes to quit.—In short, my dear, I thought it prudent to part them; and, in your name, offered her an asylum.

Miss Mor. In my name ! You amaze me, Mr Harcourt ! Would you associate your wife with a kept mistress ? Bring such an acquisition into the house of Lord Glenmore, and deprive Woodville of, perhaps, his only reason for not interfering with us ?—Do you think I credit this sudden acquaintance ?

Har. I deceived myself, I find ;—I thought you

above such low suspicion, that you could make distinctions.

Miss Mor. Yes, yes, I can make distinctions more clearly than you wished. You must excuse my interference in this affair, sir; and let me hint to you, that your own will do as little credit to your heart as to your understanding.

Har. Mighty well, madam; go on! Settle this with respect to yourself, but do not be concerned about me; for, in one word, if you cannot resolve on protecting this poor unfortunate, I will!

Miss Mor. (*Aside.*) That must not be; yet his warmth alarms me.—Nay, but, my dear, think deliberately!—Supposing her all you say, the world judges by actions, not thoughts, and will bury her merit in her situation.

Har. It is that cruel argument perpetuates error in so many of your frail sex; be the first to rise above it. That you are in Lord Glenmore's house, will be your justification, both to the world and himself; for what but a generous motive can actuate you? In my eyes, my dear Sophia, virtue never looks so lovely as when she stretches out her hand to the fallen!

Miss Mor. Oh, Harcourt! I am ashamed of my suspicion; I ought to have known all the candour and generosity of your heart, and received, in a moment, the unhappy woman it patronized;—yet, at this crisis in our own affairs, to run the chance of farther exasperating my benefactor——

Har. I am not to learn, that friendship and love have been mere masks to fraud and folly in the great world; no one would blame me, were I to suffer Woodville to ruin himself, as the shortest way of fixing my own fortune, and obtaining my lord's approbation of your choice; but I know not how it happened, that, when a mere boy, I took it into my head truth was as much to the purpose as lying; and, as I never got into more scrapes than others, why, I still pursue my system, and prefer honour to art. Then, if we fail, we have something better to console us than a pond or pistol; and, if we succeed, what is there wanting to our happiness?

Miss Mor. And how do you mean to manage her escape?

Har. That, my dearest, is the difficulty. I found she had seen you, and, therefore, was obliged to satisfy her of my honour, by assuring her you would call for her in person.

Miss Mor. Very well; we must carefully watch our opportunity. You dine here—the word of command you are accustomed to obey, but you must now become obedient to the look: for, you know, I have my difficulties, however strong my desire of obliging you.   [*Exeunt.*

ACT THE THIRD.

SCENE I.

A magnificent Drawing-Room.

MISS MORTIMER *pouring out coffee, sends it to the company ;* CAPTAIN HARCOURT *leans against a pannel near her, sipping it ; at a little distance, the Governor and* WOODVILLE *playing at Back-gammon, while* LORD GLENMORE *leans over his Chair, thoughtfully observing the behaviour of his son, who loses merely to make his uncle leave off.*

Har. It grows near the appointed hour, my love !— but how to make sure of Woodville—

Miss Mor. You should have thought of that before, my sagacious confidant ! However, as I do not need your company, fasten it upon him ;—pretend a duel, —pretend an intrigue ;—in short, if all else fails, pretend you are dying, and keep him to make your will, rather than suffer him to interrupt me.

Ld Glen. (*To himself.*) What way can I secure the absence of this son of mine ? For, I see plainly, another lucky hit would almost provoke him into throwing the dice in the governor's face ; yet Vane, I doubt, has hardly been able to procure me every convenience in so short a time. However, I will

make one of my own garrets his minx's prison, rather than suffer her to interfere with my serious
views.

Gov. (*Rising from play.*) Zounds, Frank! you are
like the French; so ready to be beat, that there is
hardly any triumph in conquering you. But you
shall take your revenge, I insist upon it.

Wood. Another time, sir;—my head aches;—my
—in short, I cannot play any longer; my cousin will
engage with you.

Har. (*Twitching his sleeve.*) Kind sir, your cousin
is infinitely indebted to you; but he, like yourself,
may have something else to do; and so indeed has
every body, for we all seem impatient to separate.

Miss Mor. (*To the servant, removing coffee.*) Bid
Warner send my cloak.

Ld Glen. Going abroad, my dear?

Miss Mor. Only a formal round, my lord.

Ld Glen. Woodville, you attend Miss Mortimer.

Miss Mor. Sweetly contrived, that, however; and
my lover seems posed. (*Aside to* HARCOURT.)—I
will not so severely tax Mr Woodville's politeness,
my lord.

Wood. You are very obliging, madam;—(*To* HAR-
COURT.) and the only thing she has said or done to
oblige me this day, *entre nous.*

Har. (*Aside.*) Um! not quite sure of that, if you
knew all—(*Turning to* MISS MORTIMER.) I will
march off quietly, and lie in wait for Woodville, so
that I think you may depend on his not meeting you.
[*Goes off unobserved.*

[WOODVILLE, *having taken his hat and sword,*
offers his hand to MISS MORTIMER.

Ld Glen. So, he is going to escape!—They all
take pleasure in perplexing me.—Frank, return to
me directly; I have bethought myself of something
very important, in which I need your assistance.

Wood. Would I had bethought myself of vanishing, like Harcourt!—How devilishly vexatious!

[*Leads* MISS MORTIMER *off.*

Gov. So there goes madam to coquette, curtesy, and talk nonsense with every well-dressed ape of either sex. Before I would allow a girl such freedom——

Ld Glen. Brother, do not judge till you know her, and give me leave to tell you, these prejudices of your temper will render you very ridiculous.

Gov. The prejudices of my temper! Oh, lord! oh, lord! this is an excellent jest. Zounds, because you have not the use of your eyes.

Ld Glen. I shall never have patience!—My head is just now full of something too important to examine which of us is most in the wrong.—I am fixed on removing this ambitious minx of my son's for ever out of his reach immediately. Will you oblige me with the company of your servants? Being slaves, they will not dare reveal the affair; and, were they so inclined, can hardly comprehend it.

Gov. Will I? Ay, that I will! and with my own company into the bargain!

Ld Glen. Hist! He returns; and if we may judge by his countenance, mortified enough to lose the evening away from her—

Re-enter WOODVILLE.

—Go, my dear Frank, first to Puzzle's chambers, for the mortgage of Hayfield-house, and don't fail to learn his whole opinion upon the subject;—(*Aside to the Governor.*) and that will take two long hours by a very moderate computation; then proceed to the London Tavern, and ask if Levi, the Jew, waits there by my appointment; otherwise, do you wait there till either he or I join you.

Wood. A pretty round-about employment my father has invented for me! (*Aside.*) and I dare not

give the least symptoms of disgust, lest that troublesome old uncle of mine should pry into the cause.
—I shall observe your orders, my lord,—though if
the devil has called upon the counsellor a little before his time, I shall consider it as an eternal obligation.   [*Exit.*

Ld Glen. Now I must inquire after Vane.   [*Exit.*

Gov. And I will give a little lecture to my myr-
midons, and wait, with them, your pleasure.—Od, it
will be precious sport, to catch madam so unawares,
and see her play off every virtuous grimace with
which she entangled young Scape-grace.

[*Exeunt severally.*

SCENE II.

The Hall.

Enter VANE *looking about.*

Hey-day! sure his old-fashion'd lordship has not
employed two of us on one errand!—An old man has
been hovering about madam's house, and has followed me here, without my knowing what to make of
him! However, ears befriend me!

[*Retires listening.*

Enter the Governor, and his black Servants soon after.

Here, Antony, Pompey, Cæsar! you dogs! be
ready to attend my lord and me on a little expedition.—No; no flambeaus, boobies!—the chaste Miss
Diana will surely take a spiteful pleasure in lighting
us to catch another kind of Miss.—And, do ye hear?
not one syllable of the when, where, or how, except

you intend to dangle on one string, like a bunch of
black grapes. [*Talks to them apart.*

Enter GREY.

Grey. It is here, I am at length informed, the father of this abandoned seducer resides.—Yet what
redress can poverty hope from pride ?—Surely, however, for his own sake, he will assist me in regaining
the poor girl, and afterwards prevent the wretch
from pursuing her !—There I suppose he is !—My
lord !

Gov. (*Turns short upon him.*) Well, old sturdy !
what do you want with my lord ?

Grey. Merciful Heaven ! the father of Cecilia.

Vane. (*Listening.*) Hey !—indeed !

Grey. Oh ! how my heart misgives me !—perhaps
this base Woodville—her very brother—

Gov. What, is the old man ill ?—Sure I know this
honest—it is not—yet it is—Grey ?

Grey. The same indeed, my lord.

Gov. No my lord to me, man ! my name is Harcourt.

Grey. Blessed be Heaven for that, however !

Gov. Be not righteous over-much ! for that my
name is Harcourt, I do not reckon among the first
favours of Heaven.—But, ha, ha ! perhaps you thought
I had no name at all by this time ?—Faith, I put a
pretty trick upon—well, well, well !——(*To the blacks.*)
you may retire till my lord is ready.   (*Exeunt.*
I am a riddle, honest Grey ! but now I am come to
expound myself, and make thy fortune into the bargain.—It is many a long day since I saw old England.
—But at last I am come home with a light heart and
a heavy purse, design to fetch up my Cicely, give
her and my money to the honestest fellow I can find,
and grow old amid a rosy race of Britons, springing
from a stem reared after my own fashion.—There's
news for you, my honest friend !

Grey. Alas! How little will he think I deserve his favour when he hears my account of her! And how can I shock a parent with what too severely shocks even myself!   [*Aside.*

Gov. What!—Silent, man?—ha, ha, ha!—I can't but laugh to think how foolish you looked at the second year's end, when no allowance came—but that was my own contrivance; all done on purpose, my good old soul! and now it will come in a lump; there's the whole difference.—Well, and so my dame made her a pattern of housewifery, hey?—Oh! I don't intend to touch another pickle or preserve that is not of my little Cicely's own doing; and I'll build her a dairy with every bowl and churn of silver!—Zounds, it shall be a finer sight than the Tower of London!—and we'll set up Dame Deborah's statue before it, like Queen Anne's in St Paul's Churchyard!—But, why dostn't enjoy this discovery, man? Art afraid I shall take her from thee? Oh, never think of that; for thou shalt bless everypie she makes; ay, and taste it afterwards, old pudding-sleeves.

Grey. Ah, sir! (*Sighing.*)

Gov. Hey? Zounds!—What dost mean? Sure my Cicely isn't dead!

Grey. No, not dead, sir!

Gov. She's very near it then, I suppose?

Grey. No, sir.

Gov. No, sir? Then what the devil do you mean, by alarming me thus, with your "No, sirs," after all?

Grey. Alas! Is there no greater evil?

Gov. None, that I know of;—but your whole fraternity are not more like ravens in colour than note. —Come, let us know what this mighty evil is?

Grey. For years did she increase in goodness as in beauty; the charm of every young heart, and the sole comfort of those old ones, to whom Heaven and man seemed to have consigned her for ever.

Gov. Well, well, I had a little bird told me all this—

Grey. About a twelve month ago, during a little absence of mine, a young man of fashion introduced himself into my house; and, my wife being void of suspicion, and the dear girl uninstructed in the ways of this bad world——

Gov. The dog betrayed her!—And is this your care, you old—and that ignoramus, your wife!—Zounds! I am in such a fury!—I want to know no more of her infamous conduct.—Od! I am strangely tempted to have you strangled this moment, as a just reward for your negligence, and so bury the secret with you.

Grey. It is as effectually buried already, sir—I love the dear unhappy girl too well ever to tell her heaven gave her to such a father.

Gov. Yes, yes; you are better suited to the—I hope she pays for this severely!—You make her stand in a white sheet, to be pointed at by the whole village every Sunday, to be sure?

Grey. Alas, sir! She put it out of my power even to forgive her——

Gov. Forgive her! forgive her, truly!

Grey. By flying immediately from her only friend. —Infirm and poor, I struggled with the joint evils till now; when, having collected enough to support me, I walked up in search of her;—it was only yesterday I discovered her in a splendid coach, which I traced to her house.

Gov. A house! I shall run mad entirely! A coach! —Why, dare the little brazen-face pretend to elegance, when I took such pains to quench every spark of gentility in her?

Grey. In the neighbourhood I discovered the name of her seducer; and, in seeking him, met with you.—Moderate your passion, sir—Reflect! When

age is frail, what can we expect in youth?—Shall
man desert humanity?

Gov. So, so, so!—Now I am to be tortured with
your preaching.—I renounce the unworthy little slut.
—I have no friend—no daughter—no any thing.—
Od! I would sooner build an hospital for idiots, like
Swift, and endow it with all my fortune, than bestow
it on one who thus perverts reason.—Hark ye, sir—
Forget the way to this house!—Forget you ever saw
my face!—Would I had never seen your's!—For, if
you dare to send her whining to me, I'll torment
you with every plague, power, wealth, law, or even
lawyers can set in motion—By heaven, I abjure the
audacious little wretch for ever! and will sooner return to India, and bury my gold with those from
whom it was taken, than bestow a single shilling on
her, when she loses her coach and her house!

Grey. (*Contemptuously.*) And I will sooner want
a shilling, than suffer her to waste her youth in a
state which will render her age an insupportable burthen!—Fear not, sir, ever seeing her or me again;
for the bosom which reared, will joyfully receive her,
nor farther embitter her remaining days with the
knowledge she was born the equal of her undoer;
and deprived herself of all those blessings Heaven
only hid, never denied her.   [*Exit.*

Governor alone.

Gov. Who would have a daughter?—Zounds! I
am as hot as if I was in the black hole at Calcutta.
—If Miss had only married a lout, from ignorance of
her birth, I could have forgiven it; but, her puppy
being of fashion, the papers will get hold of it, and I
shall be paragraphed into purgatory.—Fools can turn
wits on these occasions; and, " A certain governor
and his daughter," will set the grinners in motion
from Piccadilly to Aldgate.—This insolent old fellow,
too!—I need not wonder where she got her courage!

—Not but I like his spirit—Od! I like it much!—
It proves his innocence.—What the devil did I drive
him away for!—Here, dogs!—Run after that old
man in black, and order him to return to me this
moment.

Enter LORD GLENMORE.

Ld Glen. And now, brother, I am ready for you.

Gov. Yes; and now, brother, I have something
else to mind; and my servants, moreover— [*Exit.*

Ld Glen. What new whim can this troublesome
mortal have taken into his head? (*A rapping at the
door.*) I am not at home, remember.—Miss Mortimer!—Who's with her?

MISS MORTIMER *enters with* CECILIA, *in mourning.*

Miss Mor. Nay, as to that circumstance—Bless me,
here's my lord!

Cec. My lord!—Good heavens, I shall sink into
the earth!

Miss Mor. He can never guess at you—Recover,
my dear creature!

Ld Glen. Is the lady indisposed, Miss Mortimer?

Miss Mor. Yes, my lord;—that is, no—I don't
know what I am saying.—She has been ill lately, and
riding has a little overcome her; that's all.—(*Aside
to* CECILIA.) Struggle to keep up, for heaven's sake
and your own.

Cec. Impossible! (LORD GLENMORE *draws a hall-
chair, in which she faints.*)

Ld Glen. Warner! drops and water in a moment.
—How beautiful she is!—her features are exquisitely
fine!

Miss Mor. They are thought so, my lord.—Bless
me! where can I have crammed my *Eau de Luce!*—
Oh, I have it.

Ld Glen. Her pulse returns—she revives.

Cec. I beg your pardon, madam!—my lord, too!—I am shocked to have occasioned so much trouble.

Miss Mor. Absurd, to apologize for the infirmity of nature:—My lord, I do assure you, was quite anxious.

Ld Glen. The man must surely have lost every sense, who can see this lady, even when deprived of her's, without emotion;—but to me, the languor of illness had ever something peculiarly interesting.—(*Aside.*) I wonder who this elegant creature is.—Her hand seems to tremble strangely.

Cec. Oh, madam!—

Miss Mor. Silence and recollection alone can secure you from suspicion;—I confess, I relied on his absence.

Re-enter the Governor.

Gov. He won't return, hey?—Od! I like the old Cambrian the better for it:—I have fired his Welch blood finely.—Why, what a blockhead was I not to go after him myself!—Methinks, I should like to know miss when I meet her in her coach too.—Um—did he not tell me something of tracing the seducer into this house! (*Stands in amazement a moment, then whistles.*) Woodville's mistress, by every thing contrary! Od, I shall seize the gipsy with redoubled satisfaction! but I must keep my own counsel, or my old beau of a brother will roast me to death on my system of education.—Hey! who has he got there? (CECILIA *rises.*) A pretty lass, faith!—Ah, there is the very thing I admire!—there is gentility, without the fantastical flourishes of fashion!—just the very air I hoped my minx would have had.   (LORD GLEN-MORE, *having led off* CECILIA, *returns.*)

Ld Glen. I don't know how, but my inclination to this business is over.   I think I'll let the matter alone at present.

Gov. The devil you will!—Why, by to-morrow Woodville may have married her.

Ld Glen. D'ye think so ?—well, then let's go.

Gov. And what d'ye intend to do with her, pray ?

Ld Glen. (*Aside.*) I won't trust this weathercock till all is safe.—I care not what becomes of her, so she is out of my way ;—send her to Bridewell, perhaps—

Gov. To Bridewell, truly !—no, that you sha'n't, neither ; Bridewell, quotha !—why, who knows but the fault may be all that young rake-hell, your son's ?

Ld Glen. My son's, sir !—Let me tell you, I have not bred him in such a manner.

Gov. Oh, if breeding were any security—Zounds, I shall betray all by another word ! (*Aside.*

Ld Glen. What now can have changed you ?—but you are more inconstant than our climate.—Did you ever know one minute what you shou'd think the next ? However, to satisfy your scruples, I intend to dispatch her to a nunnery ; and, if that don't please you, e'en take charge of her yourself. (*Exeunt together.*

VANE *comes forward.*

Vane. Ha, ha, ha ; why, this would make a comedy !—and so, of all birds in the air, his dignified lordship has pitched on me for the husband of the Governor's daughter and his own niece !—Well, if I can but go through with this, it will be admirable !— Thank'd by one for making my fortune, and safe from the anger of all.

Enter a Servant.

Serv. Mr Woodville, sir, is just gone into the house you bad me watch. (*Exit.*

Vane. The devil he is !—Why, then I must consign my intended to him for one more night, and persuade my lord to delay our seizure till morning ;—for, to meet with him, would certainly produce an agreement of all parties, and a marriage which would never en-

roll my name in the family pedigree, or Governor's
will.   [*Exit.*

SCENE III.

CECILIA's *Dressing-room.—Candles burning, and her
clothes scattered.*

Enter WOODVILLE.

Thanks to that dear lawyer's lucky absence, I have
a few happy hours, my love, to spend with thee——
(*Looks at her clothes.*) Already retired? sure I have not
left my key in the garden gate.—No, here it is. (*Rings
the bell, and takes off his sword, then throws himself into
a chair.*) Nobody answer—I don't understand this
—Perhaps I shall disturb her—I'll steal into her
chamber—(*Goes off, and presently returns disordered.*)
Not there! her clothes too, the same she had on last:
—Oh, my heart misgives me!—But where are all the
servants? (*Rings very violently, calling at the same
time,* BRIDGET! ROBERT! JACOB!)

Enter BRIDGET, *with her hat on.*

—Bridget! what's become of your lady?
  Brid. Really, sir, I can't say;—don't you know?
  Wood. If I did, I shou'dn't have asked you.
  Brid. (*After a little pause.*) Why, sure, sir, my
lady has not run away? and yet something runs in my
head, as if she had.—I thought that spark came for no
good to-day.
  Wood. What spark, girl?
  Brid. Why, just after you went away, comes a
young man, a monstrous genteel one, and very hand-

some too, I must needs say ; with fine dark eyes, and
a fresh colour.

Wood. Damn his colour ! tell me his business.

Brid. So he axed for my lady, and would not tell
me what he wanted : I came with her, however, but
she no sooner set eyes on him than she sent me out,
which argufied no good, you'll say ; and, before I
could possibly come back, though I ran as fast as ever
my legs could carry me, he was gone, and she writing, and crying for dear life ;—but that was no news,
so I did not mind it : and when she gave me leave to
go to the play, thought no more harm than the child
unborn.

Wood. It must be a scheme beyond all doubt, and
I am the dupe of a dissembling, ungrateful—Oh, Cecilia ! (*Throws himself in a chair.*)

Brid. (*Softening her voice, and setting her dress.*)
If I was as you, sir, I would not fret about her : there
is not a lady in the land would slight a gentleman so
handsome and sweet-tempered—I scorns to flatter,
for my part.—Inferials mustn't direct their betters ;
but, had I been in my lady's place, a king upon his
throne would not have tempted me.—Handsome him
that handsome does, say I ; and I am sure you did
handsome by her ; for, if she could have eat gold, she
might have had it.—He might take some notice truly.

(*Aside.*

Wood. (*Starting up.*) Where was she writing ?

Brid. In the little drawing-room, sir.

[*Exit* WOODVILLE.

BRIDGET *alone.*

This ridiculous love turns people's brains, I think.
—I am sure I said enough to open his eyes :—but,
may be, I don't look so handsome, because I am not
so fine.—Hey,—a thought strikes me ! My lady is
gone, that's plain.—Back she will not come, is as
plain. (*Gathers together* CECILIA's *elegant clothes.*)

I'll put on these, and he'll think she gave 'em to me; —then he may find out I am as pretty as she : if not, he and I are of very different opinions.   [*Exit.*

Re-enter WOODVILLE *more disordered.*

Wood. Cruel, ungrateful, barbarous girl !—to forsake me in the very moment I was resolving to sacrifice every thing to her !—but 'tis just.—First dupes to the arts of man, the pupil soon knows how to foil him at his own weapons. Perhaps the discovery is fortunate. In a short time, I must have borne the whole disgrace of her ill conduct, and my father's resentment had the bitterest aggravation.—But is she indeed gone ? and will continual to-morrows come, without one hope to render them welcome ?

Enter JACOB.

Wood. Villain! where's your lady?
Jac. 'Las a deazy, how can I tell, zur?
Wood. Where are all your fellows ?
Jac. Abroad, making haliday.
Wood. When did you go out? who gave you leave ?
Jac. My leady, her own zelf; and I'll tell you how 'tware.—Arter dinner I geed her a noate ; and, when zhe had red un, she axed me if zo be as how I had ever zeed the lions ? Zoa I told her noa ; nor no mour I never did.—Zoa zhe geed me half-a-crown, and bid me goa and make myself happy. I thought it were desperate koind of her ; zoa I went and zeed the huge cretors : and arter, only stopped a bit to peap at the moniment, and hay my fortin tuold by conj'rer in the Old Bailey ; and aw zaid——
Wood. What the devil does it signify to me what he said ?—Hark'e, sir, I see in your face you know more of your mistress ?
Jac. Dang it then my feace do lie hugely !
Wood. Tell me the whole truth, villain, or I'll stab you to the heart this instant!   (*Draws his sword.*

Jac. (*Kneels.*) I wull, zur, indeed I wull; doan't ye terrify me zoa! I do forget every thing in the whole world.

Wood. Be sincere, and depend upon my rewarding you.

Jac. Why I wish I meay die this maument, if conj'rer did not zey I should lose my pleace! nay, aw do verily think aw zaid zomething o' my being put in fear o' my loife. Loard knaws, I little thought how zoon his words would come to pass.

Wood. Will you dally?

Jac. Zoa, as I zaid, zur, when I comed huome again, I found all the duors aupen, and not a zoul to be zeed.

Wood. (*Aside.*) This fellow can never mean to impose on me, and I must think it a planned affair.— While I was in the country, Jacob, did your mistress see much company?

Jac. Cuompany!—noa, not to speak an— not gentlewomen.

Wood. Gentlewomen, blockhead! Why, had she any male visitors?

Jac. Anan!

Wood. I must brain thee at last, booby! Did any men come to see her then?

Jac. Oh yes, zur, yes—two gentlemen com'd almost every deay.

Wood. How! two gentlemen? I shall run distracted! Young and handsome?

Jac. Not auver young, zur, nor auver handsome; but drest muortal foine.

Wood. So they came almost every day?—Very pretty, indeed, Miss Cecilia!—Was you never called up while they staid?—Did they come together or alone?

Jac. Alone.

Wood. I thought as much; yes, I thought as much. But was you never called up, Jacob?

Jac. Yes, zur, when one aw um ware here one deay, I ware caaled up for zomething or other.

Wood. Well! why don't you go on? I am on the rack!

Jac. Don't yé look so muortal angry, then.

Wood. Well, well, I won't, my good fellow!—— There's money for thy honesty.

Jac. Well;—there aw ware——

Wood. Speak out freely, you can tell me nothing worse than I imagine; you won't shock me in the least; not at all.

Jac. Well; theare aw ware playing on that theare music-thing like a coffin, and madam ware a zin ng to un like any blackbird——

Wood. A music-master!—Is that all, booby? (*Pushes him down.*)

Jac. Yes—but t' other, zur—

Wood. Ay, I had forgot;—what of him, good Jacob, what of him?

Jac. I ware never caalled up while aw steayed; zoa (I can't but zeay I had a curiosity to know what brought he here) one deay I peaped through the keay-hoole, and zeed un—(*Titters.*)—I shall ne'er forgeat—

Wood. Tell me this instant, or I shall burst with rage and suspense.

Jac. Screaping on a leetle viddle, no bigger than my hond; while madam ware a huolding out her quoats, and danzing all round the room, zoa—(*Mimicks the minuet awkwardly.*)

Wood. Why, I believe the impudent bumkin dares to jest with my misery! and yet I have no other avenue; for the rest I fear are knaves, and he seems only a fool—And are these all that came, Jacob?

Jac. Noa, thare ware one moare, zur; a leetle mon in a black quoat—but aw only cuomed now and tan.

Wood. A disguise, no doubt! Yes, yes, they were artful enough!

Jac. And zoa, arter he'd done wi' my leady, aw did zhut hiz zelf up wi' Bridget ; and zoa I axed her all about un, and zhe zaid az how aw coomed to teeach madam to turn themmin great round balls, all bleue, and red, and yaller, that do stond by the books, and larned zhe to wroite——

Wood. Yes, yes, Mrs Bridget was in all her secrets, I don't doubt.—If that fellow in black comes here again, keep him, if you value your life, and send for me.—I know not what to do or think, and must renew my search, though hopeless of success. [*Exit.*

JACOB *alone.*

Jac. Dang it ! but he's in a desperate teaking !—Rabbit me, but I ware muortally afcard aw un too, for aw flurished hiz zword az yeazy az I cou'd a cudgel.—I do think conjuror moight as well ha' tould me madam would ha' run away, while aw ware abeout it, and then I moight ha' run'd away first. (*Exit.*

Enter GREY.

Grey. At length I have gained entrance into this house of shame, which now, alas! contains my darling Cecilia—plunged in vice, and lost to every sentiment I spent so many anxious years in implanting. This does not seem to be the abode of pleasure, nor have I met a single being.

WOODVILLE *entering behind, sees* GREY, *and drawing his sword, flies at and seizes him.*

Wood. Ha !—a man !—and in black, as Jacob said. —Villain, this moment is your last !

Grey. (*Turning suddenly upon him.*) Yes, young seducer, add to the daughter's ruin, the father's murder !—Stab my heart, as you already have my happiness !

Wood. Alas ! Was this her visitor ? I dare not speak to him.

Grey. Embosomed by affluence, exalted by title, peace still shall be far from thy heart ; for thou, with the worst kind of avarice, hast, by specious pretences, wrested from poverty its last dear possession—virtue.

Wood. Pierced to the soul, as I am, by your reproaches, I dare appeal to Cecilia herself for a testimony of my contrition !—How shall I convince you ?

Grey. Hardly by a life of repentance.—But I debase myself to exchange a word with you. Give me back my Cecilia !—Ruined as she is, I yet would recover her !—Give her back then to a father you first taught her to fear, and an habitation too humble for any but the good to be happy in.

Wood. Alas, sir ! Can you trifle with my misery ? —Do you give her back to the wretch who cannot survive her loss ! Let me owe her hand to your bounty, though her heart to her own !—Did you know what this elopement of her's has cost me—

Grey. Oh ! most accomplished villain !—but think not to dupe me too !

Wood. Who but you can have robbed me of her since morning ?

Grey. Shallow artifice !

Wood. Hear me, sir ! and even believe me, when I solemnly swear I have deeply repented my crime, and offered her all the reparation in my power ;—but, since then—

Grey. What since then ?

Wood. Either by your means, or some other, she has fled !

Grey. Impossible !

Wood. 'Tis too true, by heaven !

Grey. Perhaps, while you are thus ingeniously deluding me, she indeed flies.—Study some other deception, while I examine the whole house, for nothing else can convince me. (*Exit.*

WOODVILLE *alone*.

Surely this injured venerable man was sent by heaven to complete my misfortunes!—My passions subside, but only into a vague horror and despondency, even more dreadful!—If with rash hand she has shortened her days, what remain of mine will be, indeed, all her father predicts—(*Walking by the toilet*.)—Ha, a letter!

Re-enter GREY.

Grey. A total loneliness in the house!

Wood. Now, sir, be convinced.—I have just found a letter from her.

Grey. This cannot be the invention of a moment; —let me read it—it is, indeed, her hand—(*Opens and reads it.*) " Receive this as my last farewell.—Providence has unexpectedly sent me a friend, whose protection I dare accept; and time may perhaps subdue a passion which seems interwoven with my being.— Forget me, I entreat : and seek that happiness with another, I can never hope to bestow or partake.— Consoled only by reflecting, that the grief my error occasions is inferior to that I should have felt, had I, by an ungenerous use of my power, made you, in turn, my victim.—Once more, adieu!—All search will certainly be fruitless.

P. S. In the cabinet you will find your valuable presents; and the key is in a dressing box."

[WOODVILLE *snatches the letter, and bursts into tears.*]

Grey. Cecilia ! I may say, with tears of joy, thou art, indeed, my daughter! more dear (if possible) than ever! A daughter monarchs might contend for, though thy weak father abjures thee!—May the friend you have found have a heart but like your own!— For you, young man—But I leave you to your anguish; the loss of such a woman is a sufficient punishment.

Wood. Stay, sir! (*Rises.*) by your holy profession, I conjure you stay!—Plunge me not into total despair!—Though without a clue to her asylum, I would fain believe my heart will lead me to it; and let me then hope you will bestow her on me?

Grey. There is a something in your manner, young gentleman, that affects me.—I have been young, wild, and extravagant, myself; and, what is more strange, have not forgot I was so: my own experience proves reformation possible; act up to her, and atone your error.

Wood. I will endeavour it, sir; and, oh! could those who yet but waver, know what has passed in my heart during the last hour, who would dare to deviate!   [*Exeunt.*

ACT THE FOURTH.

SCENE I.

CECILIA'S *House.*

BRIDGET *dressed in* CECILIA'S *clothes, mixed with every thing vulgar and tawdry.*

Brid. So—I am ready against our gentleman comes. —Deuce on him, to run away last night, the moment

I was drest—and with an inferial fellow too !—Lard,
how can people of quality demean themselves by keeping company with inferials !—However, one thing I
am sure of, he's too much on the fidgets to stay long
away from our house; and, in the mean while, I can
entertain myself extremely well.   (*Sits down to the
toilet.*)

Jac. (*Without.*) I tell ye, my leady's not at huome.

Gov. I tell you, I won't take your word for it ;—
so come, my lord, and see.

Brid. Hey-day, my lord !—What's the news now,
I wonder ?

Enter LORD GLENMORE *and the Governor ; both stop
short.*

Gov. Oh, I thought madam had learnt enough of
the ton to lie by proxy.

Brid. Dear heart ! —I am all of a twitteration !—
Who can these be ?—That's my lord, for certain !

Ld Glen. The vulgarity of the wench is astonishing !

Gov. Um—why, a little gawky, or so—there's no
denying it.—(*Aside.*) Here's a pretty discovery now,
after all my projects !—Thank fortune, the secret is
yet my own, though——

Ld Glen. (*Advancing to her.*) I ought to beg your
excuse, madam, for so abrupt an intrusion ; but the
opportunity, and so fair a temptation, will, I flatter
myself, be a sufficient apology.

Brid. (*Aside.*) He takes me for my lady, that's a
sure thing !—Oh, this is charming !—You need not
make no 'pologys, my lord ;—inferials never knows
how to suspect people of quality ; but I understands
good breeding better.

Ld Glen. (*Aside.*) Why, what a barn-door mawkin
it is !—Your politeness, madam, can only be equalled
by your beauty !

Brid. Dear heart, my lord, you flatter me !—

Won't you please to sit? (*Waits affectedly till they consent to seat themselves.*)

Ld Glen. (*To the Governor.*) Surely, by using my title, she knows me!

Gov. Zounds! I have a great mind to make her know me!—Od! I shall never be able to contain!

Ld Glen. I was afraid, madam, I should prove an unwelcome guest—but beauty like your's—

Brid. Does your lordship think I so very handsome then!—Lord, how lucky was my dressing myself!

Ld Glen. (*Aside.*) Affected idiot!—I was afraid, madam, too, of meeting Woodville here. (*Aside.*) I know not what to say to her.

Brid. He has not been here this morning; but, if he had, he knows better than to ax arter my company, I do assure you, my—lordship.

Ld Glen. I have been told he intends marrying you; what a pity to monopolize such merit!

Brid. If he has any such kind intention, 'tis more than I knows of, I assure you.

Ld Glen. His keeping that wise resolution from you, is some little comfort, however.

Brid. But, I promise ye, I shall make a rare person of quality; for I loves, cards, coaches, dancing, and dress, to my very heart—nothing in the world better—but blindman's-buff. I had some thoughts of taking a trip to Sadler's-Wells or Fox-Hall, but they don't begin till five o'clock.

Gov. (*Aside.*) Ha! ha!—though she can hardly spell out the ten commandments, she could break every one with as much ease and impudence, as if she had been bred in the circle of St James's.

Ld Glen. But, madam, you know, allowing Woodville willing to marry you, it is not in his power while his father lives, without forfeiting his fortune, the value of which you doubtless understand?

Brid. Oh yes, yes, for sartin, my lord.

Ld Glen. Who knows, too, how far an incensed parent may carry his resentment ?—He might find means to entrap and punish you.

Brid. Ha, ha, ha!—he entrap me!—that would be a good jest!—No, no, I have more of the lady of quality than to be so easily catch'd.

Gov. (*Mimicking her.*) He, he, he!—that is the only particular in which you have nothing at all of the lady of quality.

Ld Glen. With me you may share a higher rank and larger fortune without those fears—I am of an age—

Brid. Yes, one may see that without being a con-juror—Why, will you marry me, my lord?

Ld Glen. Convince me that you don't love this Woodville, and I know not how far my passion may carry me.

Brid. Love him!—Do you think I knows no more of high life than that comes to?—To be sure, he is a sweet pretty man, and all that—but as to love, I loves nobody half so well as myself!

Ld Glen. Upon my soul, I believe you; and wish he had the whole benefit of the declaration.—(*To the Governor.*) Her ingratitude is as shocking as her ignorance, and Bridewell too gentle a punishment.

Gov. Then build a Bridewell large enough to con-tain the whole sex; for the only difference between her and the rest is—this country mawkin tells what the town-bred misses conceal.

Ld Glen. Why, governor, you are as testy as if you had the care of her education.

Gov. I the care !—Zounds, what I say is merely from friendship to your lordship.—I hate to see you deceive yourself.—(*Aside.*) Surely he can never suspect! (BRIDGET *is employed in cramming trinkets from the dressing-table into her pockets.*)

Brid. Now I am ready to go, my lord.

Ld Glen. Reflect, madam; it would hurt me to

have you say I deceived you—if you should repent
—I am much afraid you will.

Brid. What, when I am a lady? Oh, I'll venture
that, and attend you.

Gov. (*Roughly snatching her other hand.*) To
where you little dream of, you vain, affected, presuming, ignorant baggage.

Brid. Hey-day!—my lord!

Ld Glen. Appeal not to me, base woman!—Know
I am the father of that poor dupe, Woodville.

Brid. Dear heart! be ye indeed?—What will become of me, then?

Ld Glen. And, as a moderate punishment for your
hypocrisy, ambition, and ingratitude, sentence you
to be shut up for life in a monastery.

Brid. O lord! among monsters?

Gov. No, ignoramus!—No, among nuns; though
they are but monsters in human nature either.

Brid. What! where they'll cut off my hair, and
make me wear sackcloth next my skin?

Gov. Yes, if they leave you any skin at all.

Brid. Oh dear, dear, dear! (*Sobs and groans.*)
Upon my bended knees, I do beg you won't send
me there!—Why, I shall go malancholy—I shall
make away with myself for sartin; and my ghost will
appear to you all in white.

Gov. All in black, I rather think; for the devil a
speck of white is there in your whole composition.

Ld Glen. Your conduct, wretch! justifies a severer
sentence.—To seduce him from his duty was crime
enough!

Brid. Who, I seduce him? I did not, my lord—
indeed I did not.

Ld Glen. Have you not owned—

Brid. No, indeed, no; that I wished to take my
lady's place, I believe I did own—

Gov. Ha, ha, ha! Very prettily devised, faith, for
a young beginner!—Come, come, (*Chucking her un-*

der the chin.) we must give you credit for this, Miss
—Your lady! Ha, ha, ha!

Ld Glen. Shallow subterfuge !——

Enter VANE *and the Slaves.*

Vane, is all ready ?—Seize this woman, and observe
my orders !

Brid. Ah, dear heart! I shall die away if the
blacks do but touch me—Indeed you do mistake !—
I be no lady——I be only Bridget !

Gov. I would give ten thousand pounds that you
were only Bridget, you artful puss !—Zounds ! though
I could one moment strangle the pug's face in her
own necklace, yet the next I can hardly prevail on
myself to punish her—What the devil had I now to
do in England ? or what the devil had I ever to do
in Wales ?—Phew ! I could dethrone fifty nabobs
without half the fatigue and anxiety of this moment.
—Take her away, however ! and let us try how Miss
likes riding out in her own coach.

[VANE *and the slaves seize her ; she screams out*,
and catches LORD GLENMORE'S *coat, falling on*
her knees.—JACOB *enters, her back to him.*

Jac. Why, what a dickens be ye all at here?—
Zoa, what's my lady theare?

Ld Glen. See there now—Oh, the artful Jezebel !

Brid. Oh, Jacob !—Why, don't ye see I am Bridget ? Pray satisfy my lord, here.

Jac. Why, be ye Bridget?——Never trust me
else !

Gov. Here's a fool of t'other sex now, can hardly
take a hint though so plainly given him !—Thanks to
the natural difference, for art is nature in woman.

(LD GLEN. *draws him aside.*

Jac. Auh, Bridget, Bridget ! Where didst thee
get theesum foin claws ?—Noa, noa, as theest brew'd,
thee meay'st beake.

Brid. Oh, do you take pity on me !—Why, they

be going to carry me to some outlandish place, and make a nunnery of me!

Jac. A nunnery!—What's that? any thing Cristin?—Well, if I do spake to um, will ye ha'e me?

Brid. Oh, yes, yes, yes!

Ld Glen. Brother, I shall leave you to the completion of this affair—I am sick to the soul of the gawky——

Gov. Yes, yes; I don't doubt it—I don't doubt it.

Ld Glen. (*To* VANE.) Convey her to my house, and lock her up in one of the lofts over the stables. ——Go the back way, and even the family need know nothing of the matter.—The chaplain will provide a licence, and be ready.—Courage, my lad, and depend upon my gratitude!.   [*Exit.*

Gov. Will you take her, or no?—I shall never be able to stifle my agitation; and burst with rage if I show it.—

Jac. Why, zure, zure, ye won't carr' away our Bridget?

Vane. Ha, ha, ha!

Gov. Oh, she has beat her meaning into thy thick scull at last!—Pr'ythee, keep thy blockhead out of my way, if thou mean'st to keep it on thy own shoulders.

Jac. Why, be ye in arnest then? Dear heart alive! Why, this is cousin Bridget!

Brid. Only send for Mr Woodville.

Gov. Prettily devised again!—Ha, ha, ha!—Dost think, my little dear, we have lived three times as long as your ladyship to learn a quarter as much!—Send for Mr Woodville, hey?—No, no; you won't find us quite so simple.

Jac. Oh doan't ye, doan't ye carr' off zhe, or if ye wull, do pray take I.

Vane. Yes, you would be a choice piece of lumber, truly.

Gov. Drag her away this moment.

Brid. Oh, dear, oh dear ! to be hanged at last for another's crime is all that vexes me !

[They carry her off, Governor follows.

SCENE II.

MISS MORTIMER'S *Apartment.*

CECILIA *enters, and sits down to embroidery.*

How fond, how weak, how ungrateful, are our hearts !—Mine still will presumptuously fancy this house its home, and ally itself to every one to whom Woodville is dear.

LORD GLENMORE *enters.*

Cec. Oh heavens, my lord !—How unlucky !—if I go, he may find the captain with Miss Mortimer !

Ld Glen. You see, madam, you have only to retire to engage us to pursue you even to rudeness.—But, tell me, can it be your own choice to punish us so far as to prefer solitude to our society ?

Cec. I know myself too well, my lord, to receive distinctions of which I am unworthy :—yet think not, therefore, I fail in respect.

Ld Glen. But is that charming bosom susceptible of nothing beyond respect ?—Why is it capable of inspiring a passion it cannot participate ?

Cec. Your goodness, my lord—my profound veneration, will always attend you—but the more generously you are inclined to forget what is due to yourself, the more strongly it is impressed on my memory.

Ld Glen. Were what you say true, the bounties of nature atone amply to you for the parsimony of fortune, nor would your want of every other advantage lessen your merit, or my sense of it.

Cec. (*Aside.*) Had he thought thus a few months since, how happy had I now been! Your approbation at once flatters and serves me, by justifying Miss Mortimer's protection of me.

Ld Glen. Her partiality for you does her more honour than it can ever do you advantage. But you must tell me how she gained first the happiness of knowing you?

Cec. My—my lord, by a misfortune so touching—

Ld Glen. Nay, I would not distress you neither ; yet I own, madam, I wish to make a proposal worth a serious answer ; but ought first to know, why you affect a mystery? Tell me then, my dear, every incident of your life, and I will raise you to a title, I may without vanity say, many have aspired to !

Cec. You oppress my very soul, my lord ! But, alas ! unconquerable obstacles deprive me for ever of that title. Neither would I obtain it by alienating such a son from such a father.

Ld Glen. Put him entirely out of the question ; the meanness of his conduct acquits me to myself. Do you know, madam, he has resolved to marry a creature of low birth, illiterate, vulgar, and impudent? And, to complete her perfections, she has been his mistress at least !

Cec. Surely he knows, and purposely shocks me thus. (*Aside.*)

Ld Glen. But your integrity doesn't render you less amiable in my eyes ; it greatly enhances every other merit. As to this wretch, I have her in my power, and shall make her dearly repent.

Cec. Then I am lost indeed ! (*Aside.*)—You have, my lord, though I know not how, discovered—(*Rises in confusion.*)

Ld Glen. (*Rises, taking snuff, without looking at her.*) Oh, nothing more easy, madam; I had him carefully traced to her house; and, during his absence, took servants, and forced her away.

Cec. (*Aside.*) That, however, cannot be me: every word seems to add to a mystery I dare not inquire into.

Ld Glen. But why waste one precious moment on such an animal? What are these unconquerable obstacles?

Cec. Spare me, my lord; your indulgence induces me to try again to soften your resolutions respecting your son: deprived of the weak, the guilty, the miserable wretch you justly condemn, a little time will no doubt incline him to his duty. I should have your pardon to solicit, my lord, but that your own openness authorizes mine.

Ld Glen. But can you, who so powerfully plead the cause of another, be deaf to the sighs of a man who adores you? who offers you a rank——

Cec. Be satisfied, my lord, with knowing I have all that esteem your merit claims, which influences me beyond every casual advantage.

Ld Glen. But, madam——

Cec. Alas! my lord!—(*Bursts into tears, aside.*) —Be silent, if possible, both pride and virtue. I have deserved, and will submit to it—yet surely the bitterness of this moment expiates all past offences.

(*Exit.*

Ld Glen. Amiable creature! what an amazing elegance of mind and person! Tears were her only answers to my questions, and blushes to my looks, yet these only heighten a curiosity they have softened into love.   (*Exit.*

SCENE III.

WOODVILLE'S *Apartment.*

WOODVILLE *alone.*

Wood. No intelligence of my Cecilia yet!—Were I only assured of her safety, it would be some consolation.

Enter JACOB.

Jac. Zur, zur!—I do meake so bowld as to ax to spake to you.

Wood. Jacob! my honest fellow, the very sight of thee revives my hopes, and sets my heart in motion! —Well, what's the news?

Jac. Zurprising news indeed, zur!—Loord, I thought I should never meat wi' ye;—I comed to your lodgings twice, and ye wan't up.

Wood. Up! 'Sdeath, you ignorant booby! why didn't you order them to rouse me that moment?

Jac. Loord, zur! why your gentleman (as they do caal un) ware so terrable foine, I ware afeard of affronting un!

Wood. Plague on the stupidity of both, say I!— But what's all this to the purpose? The news? the news?

Jac. Las-a-deasy! mortal bad news, indeed!—

Wood. You tedious blockhead! is your lady returned?

Jac. Noa, zur. (*Shaking his head very mournfully.*)

Wood. (*Aside.*) The horrid forebodings of my heart recur; yet surely she could not be so desperate!—Shocking as the suspense is, I more dread the certainty.—Speak, however, my good fellow! (JACOB *wipes his eyes.*)—I shall ever value your sensibility.—Tell me then the simple truth, whatever it may be?

Jac. I wull, zur, I wull.—There has com'd two foine gentlemen, wi' zwords by their zides, just for all the world like yourn—

Wood. Well, and what did these gentlemen say?

Jac. Why they went up stears, willy, nilly, and carr'd off——our Bridget.   (*Bursts out a crying.*

Wood. You impudent, ignorant clown! I'll give you cause for your tears.   (*Shakes him.*

Jac. Loord! Loord!—do ye ha a little christin commiseration—Well, if ever I do cuome nigh ye again, I do wish ye may break every buone in my skin.

Wood. (*Walking about in a rage.*) To insult me with your own paltry love affairs! These great and mighty gentlemen were only constables, I dare swear, and your fears converted their staves to swords.

Jac. Ay, but that an't the worst neither. I do verily think my turn wull come next; can't sleep in my bed for thinking on't, nor enjoy a meal's meat: —zo, except you do bring your zword, and cuome and live in our houze, I woll gou out on't, that's a zure thing; for I had rather sceare craws at a graat a deay all my loife long, than bide here to be so terrifoid.

Wood. Sceare craws truly? why the craws will sceare you, ye hen-hearted puppy!—There, teake that, (*Gives him money.*) and guo home, or to the devil, so you never fall in my way again.

Jac. Zome faulk that I do know wull zee the black gentleman first, 'tis my belief—zoa I had best keep out o' his woy too.

Enter HARCOURT.

Har. Woodville, what's the matter? Why you will raise the neighbourhood.

JACOB *returns.*

Jac. Here's a peaper housemaid do zend you, wi' her humble duty; but, if zo be it do put ye in another desperate teaking, I do huope ye wull zend for zhe to beat, and not I.—Loord! Loord! what wull becuome of me in this woide world of London!

(*Exit* JACOB.

Har. Ha! ha! ha! he is a choice fellow!

Wood. A heart oppressed with its own feelings fears every thing. I have hardly courage to open a letter without an address.

Har. Come, come, give it me then. Hey, what? confusion!—Was ever any thing so unlucky?

(*Attempts to tear it.*

Wood. (*Snatches it from him.*) Ha! it is important then?

Har. Why will you invent torments for yourself? (*Aside.*)—My own letter, by every thing careless!— Here's a stroke—

Wood. (*Reads in a broken voice and manner.*) " Woodville on the brink of marriage—You will be disengaged—A nobleman—(Damnation!)—Heart and fortune at her feet"—I'll let his soul out there! Hell and furies!—but I will find him, if money— Never will I close my eyes till—Oh Cecilia—(*Throws himself into a seat.*)

Har. This is the most unforeseen—I know not what to say to him—Pr'ythee, Woodville, do not sacrifice so many reasonable presumptions in her favour, to a paper that may be a forgery, for aught you know!

Wood. Oh Charles! that I cou'd think so!—but I

have seen the villain's execrable hand somewhere! Did you never see the hand?

Har. Um—I can't but own I have—What the devil shall I say to him. (*Aside.*

Enter the Governor.

Gov. Woodville, my dear boy! I am come to have a little talk with thee.—Charles! don't run away! —you are in all your cousin's secrets.

Wood. What should possess this tiresome mortal to come here?—I should have waited on you in half an hour, sir.

Gov. Ay, and that's what I wanted to avoid:—— The more I talk to your father, Frank, the more I find him fixed on the match with his Miss Mortimer! Nay, he tells me he will have you married this very day.

Wood. That's mighty probable, in the humour I am in.

Gov. Ah, Frank! the girl I offer thee—

Wood. Is no more agreeable to me than her you despise.

Gov. How do you know that, peppercorn?—How do you know that?—Od, I could tell you—

Wood. And to tell you my full mind, sir, I had rather make myself miserable to gratify my father, than any other man.

Gov. Od! thou art so obstinate, boy, I can't help loving thee.—(*Aside.*) I don't see why I am obliged to know his Miss is my daughter—I have a great mind to own what we have done with her; and, if he will marry, e'en take care nobody hinders him! then, trump up a farce about forgiving them:——and yet it goes against my conscience to punish the puppy for life, though he has punished me pretty sufficiently, by the Lord Harry.

Har. I don't like this affair at all, and tremble for my Sophia, when I see this odd soul so inveterate against her.

Gov. (*To* WOODVILLE.) Well, my lad! do you know I am as deep in all your secrets as your favourite valet de chambre?

Wood. I don't understand you, sir.

Gov. Pho, pho, pho! keep that face till I shew thee one as solemn as my lord's. Why should not you please yourself, and marry your Miss, instead of your father's?

Both. Astonishing!

Gov. Od, if you turn out the honest fellow I take you for, I know a pretty round sum, an onion, and a black coat may one day or other entitle you to; so never mind Lord Gravity's resentment.

Wood. I act from better motives, sir, and were unworthy your wealth could it tempt me to disobey the best of fathers.

Gov. (*Passionately.*) Why then marry Miss Mortimer, and oblige him : take a back seat in your own coach, get a family of pale-faced brats, born with ostrich feathers on their heads ; and hate away a long life with all due decorum !—Zounds, here's a fellow more whimsical than—even myself!—Yesterday you would have the puss, spite of every body ; but you no sooner find it in your power to oblige your best friend, by humouring your inclinations, than, lo! you are taken with a most violent fit of duty and submission !—Od, you don't know what you have lost by it !—But, since you are bent on crossing me, I'll cross you, and once for all too—My secret shall henceforth be as impenetrable as the philosopher's stone.—Ay, stare as you please, I'll give you more years than you have seen days to guess it in. (*Exit.*

Har. What this uncle of our's can mean, is quite beyond my guess!

Wood. What signifies seeking to expound by reason, actions in which it had no share?—His brain is indubitably touched! But Cecilia lies heavy on my heart, and excludes every other thought.

Har. Time may explain the secret of that letter, which, I will lay my life, she despises :—A woman who did not would have kept it from your hands.

Wood. That's true, indeed !—If I wrong her, and this was but an insult,—there is a noble sincerity in her own letter which sets suspicion at defiance.—If he stumbled on one word of truth during this visit, the crisis of my fate approaches. Oh, wherever thou art, if the exalted being I will still hope my Cecilia, thou shalt know I have at least deserved thee !

[*Exeunt.*

ACT THE FIFTH.

SCENE I.

A mean Room ; Boots, Bridles, &c. hanging all round.

BRIDGET *sitting very mournfully, her fine clothes in great disorder.——A table by her, with a small roll, a glass of water, an old dogs-eared book, and a bit of looking-glass.*

Brid. Dear heart ! dear heart ! what a miserable time have I passed ! and, where I be to pass my whole life, my lord here only knows !—I have not much stomach indeed ; neither have I much break-fast.   (*Eats a bit of bread, and bursts into tears.*

Enter the Governor.

Gov. Had I more sins to answer for, than a college of Jesuits, I surely expiate them all, by going through a purgatory in this life beyond what they have invented for the other. This vulgar minx of mine haunts my imagination in every shape but that I hoped to see her in; I dare hardly trust myself to speak to her!—Od, I would not have the extirpation of the whole female sex depend upon my casting vote, while I am in this humour!

Brid. Mercy on me! here's that cross old gentleman again! What will become of me?—Do, pray, strange sir! be so generous as to tell me what is next to be done with me?

Gov. Why, just whatever I please, you audacious baggage!—(*Aside.*) Od, now I think on't, I have a great mind to try a few soft words, and dive into all the secrets of the little ignoramus.—Come, suppose I had a mind to grant you your freedom, how would you requite me?

Brid. Dear heart! why I'd love you for ever and ever.

Gov. Zounds, that's a favour I could very readily dispense with!—and yet 'tis natural to the poor wench.—Ah! if thou had'st been a good girl, thou had'st been a happy one.—Hark ye, miss! confess all your sins; that's the only way to escape, I promise you! and, if you conceal the least, I'll do—I don't know what I'll do to you.

Brid. I will, I will, sir, indeed, as I hope to be married.

Gov. Married, you slut! bad as that is, it's too good for you.—Come, tell me all your adventures.—Describe the behaviour of the young villain who seduced you.—Where did you see him first?

Brid. Ugh, ugh!—At church, sir.

Gov. At church, quotha—a pretty place to commence an intrigue in!—and how long was it before you came to this admirable agreement?

Brid. Umh—Why—Sunday was Midsummer-eve, —and Sunday after was madam's wedding-day,—and Monday was our fair, and——

Gov. Oh curse your long histories!—and, what then said Woodville?

Brid. Oh, Lord, nothing at all—why, it warn't he.

Gov. No!—(*Ready to burst with passion.*) Who, who, who? tell me that, and quite distract me!

Brid. Timothy Hobbs, 'squire's gardener.

Gov. An absolute clown—(*Walks about half groaning with rage and disappointment.*) Who, oh! who would be a father?—I could laugh,—cry,—die,— with shame and anger!—Since the man, who corrupted, left her only one virtue, would he had deprived her of that too!—Oh, that she had but skill enough to lie well!

Brid. Whether I can or no, I'll never speak truth again, that's a sure thing!—What do I get by it, or any poor souls of the female kind?

Gov. I am incapable of thinking;—every plan, every resource, thus overturned.—I must be wiser than all the world!—This fool's head of mine must take to teaching, truly! as if I could eradicate the stamp of nature, or regulate the senses, by any thing but reason.—Don't pipe, baggage, to me!—you all can do that, when too late:—when I have considered whether I shall hang myself or not, I'll let you know whether I shall tuck you up along with me, you little wretch, you!   (*Exit.*

BRIDGET *alone.*

Well, sure I have at last guessed where I am shut up!—It must be Bedlam; for the old gentleman is out of his mind, that's a sure thing.

Enter VANE.

Vane. Ha, ha, ha! my future father-in-law seems to have got a quietus of my intended : and, faith, so wou'd any man who was not in love with a certain forty thousand ;—to be sure, in plain English, she is a glorious mawkin!—(*To her.*)—Well, madam, how are you pleased with your present mode of living?

Brid. Living, do you call it?—I think, 'tis only starving.—Why, I shall eat my way through the walls very shortly.

Vane. Faith, miss, they use you but so so, that's the truth on't : and I must repeat, even to your face, what I said to my lord, that your youth, beauty, and accomplishments, deserve a better fate.

Brid. Dear heart! Bedlam, did I say, I was in? why, I never knew a more sensibler, genteeler, prettier sort of a man in my life—(*Aside.*)—I am sure, sir, if I was to study seven years, I should never know what I have done to discommode them, not I.

Vane. Oh lard, my dear! only what is done every day by half your sex without punishment—however, you are to suffer for all, it seems.—You see your fare for life!—a dungeon, coarse rags, and the same handsome allowance of bread and water twice a-day.

Brid. Oh, dear me!—Why, I shall be an otomy in a week!

Vane. And an old black to guard you, more sulky and hideous than those in the Arabian Nights Entertainments.

Brid. Why, sure they will let you come and see me, sir? I shall certainly swound away every time I look at that nasty old black.

Vane. This is the last time your dungeon (which your presence renders a palace to me) will ever be open to one visitor—unless—unless—I cou'd contrive —but no, it would be my ruin : yet who wouldn't venture something for such a charming creature? you could endear even ruin.—Tell me, then, what reward you would bestow on a man who ventured all to give you freedom?

Brid. Nay I don't know; you're such a dear sweet soul, I sha'n't stand with you for a trifle.

Vane. Ahey! Miss will be as much too complying in a minute.—Well, then, my dear, I must marry you, or you will still be in the power of your enemies.

Brid. Hey?—what? do I hear rightly? marry me! —(*Aside.*)—Why, this will be the luckiest day's work I ever did!—Nay, sir, if you should be so generous, I hope I shall live to make you amends.

Vane. (*Aside.*) The only amends you can make me, is by dying—and now, my dear, I will own to you, I have the license in my pocket; and my lord as eager as myself.—Our chaplain will do us the favour with more expedition than he says grace before meat!—Well done, Vane! egad, thy lucky star predominates!—(*Aside—takes her arm.*)

Brid. Surely my locking up does end very comical.
[*Exeunt arm in arm.*

SCENE II.

The Drawing-room.

MISS MORTIMER *and* CAPTAIN HARCOURT.

Miss Mor. Woodville is now with his father, and both in the decisive mood.—Oh, Charles! as the moment approaches nearer, your influence becomes insensibly less powerful:—the frantic fits of the Governor; the solemn absurdity of my lord,—but, above all, the behaviour of Woodville, hurts and alarms me!

—still cautious not to offend his father, he had tried every way to extort the refusal from me ; but, by a pardonable equivocation, I left him hopeless, and assured him I should, to the utmost of my power, obey my benefactor—Why, why, did you marry one who could give you nothing but her heart !

Har. I shall not answer, till you can name me an equivalent—Trust to my management, my dear Sophia.—I still flatter myself one storm will settle the tenor of our lives—If not, while acquitted to heaven, the world, and ourselves, we may struggle with spirit against fortune ; and sometimes owe our dearest enjoyments to her fluctuations.

Miss Mor. By sentiments like these you won my very soul ; and to retain for ever a heart so invaluable, I have ventured the displeasure of my benefactor : but our hearts will not always follow the lead of our reason ; nor, when I consider the cause, can I repent the deviation of mine.

Har. Think, if you pity yourself, what you can give to Cecilia ; and fortify her mind against too strong a sense of her frailty. For my part, I must watch whatever is going on.

Miss Mor. So you leave me out of the plot ?— Well, if it ends happily, I shall be contented ; and, like the world, measuring your merit by your success, will declare you a most inimitable schemer.—Adieu !

Har. Nay, stay a moment.

Miss Mor. Not for the world ; for here comes your uncle, with a face more petrifying than Medusa's.   (*Exit.*

Enter the Governor, musing.

Gov. I have lived fifty-eight years, five months, and certain odd days, to find out I am a fool at last ; but I will live as many more, before I add the discovery that I am a knave too.

Har. What the devil can he be now hatching?—
mischief, I fear.

Gov. Dear Fortune! let me escape this once undiscovered, and I compound for all the rest.—Charles!
the news of the house? for the politics of this family
are employment for every individual in it.

Har. *Bella, horrida bella,* sir!—My lord is determined to bring his son's duty to an immediate test—
(*Aside.*) Thanks to his friend's schemes and his mistress's beauty.

Gov. What poor malicious wretches are we by nature!—Zounds, if I could not find in my heart to rejoice at thinking every one here will be as mortified
and disappointed as a certain person that shall be
nameless!—So, so, here they come, faith, to argue
the point in open court.

Enter LORD GLENMORE, *followed by* WOODVILLE.

Ld Glen. Without this proof of your obedience, all
you can urge, sir, is ineffectual.

Wood. While obedience was possible, I never
swerved, my lord; but, when you command me to
make myself wretched, a superior duty cancels that:
—already bound by a voluntary, an everlasting vow,
I cannot break it without offending heaven, nor keep
it without offending you.

Gov. (*Aside.*) What's this?—Chopped about again!

Wood. Did you once know the incomparable merits of my love, even your lordship's prejudices must
give way to your reason.

Ld Glen. Mere dotage.—Doesn't her conduct equally evince her folly and depravity?

Wood. Covered, as I ought to be, with confusion
and remorse, I will own she was seduced and deceived.

Gov. (*Aside.*) Ah, poor boy!—one of the two was
woefully deceived, sure enough.

Ld Glen. Oh, your conscience may be very easy

on that account; it could not require much art to deceive such an idiot.

Gov. No, no, my lord! Why paint the devil blacker than he is? Not an idiot neither.

Wood. Sir, my father's freedom of speech I must endure;—but your's——

Gov. You must endure too, young sir, or I shall bite my tongue off.

Wood. But, my lord! that dear unhappy girl is no longer a subject of debate.—She evidently proves her merit by her flight.

Ld Glen. Would you make a virtue from not doing ill, when it is no longer in your power?—Woodville! I was once weak enough to believe indulgence the surest way of obtaining your duty and esteem.—My eyes are at last opened.—Miss Mortimer is worthy a better husband; but you are her's, or no son of mine.—I solemnly promised this to her dying father, and will acquit myself at all events.

Wood. Can you resolve to sacrifice me to a promise made before we could judge of each other?— You never felt, sir, the compulsion you practise.— Will you dissolve the first band of morality, and see your highly-estimated title end in me? for never will I on these terms continue it.

Ld Glen. I almost wish I never had continued it.— (*Walks in anger.*) I am determined, Woodville! and nothing but Miss Mortimer's refusal can break the match.

Wood. I shall not put that in her power, my lord. Permit me to tell you, no son was ever more sensible of a father's kindness: but, if I can purchase its continuance only with my honour and my happiness, it would be too dearly bought.

Ld Glen. 'Tis well, sir.—I have listened to you sufficiently. Now hear me. Know, this worthless wretch you prefer to your duty, is in my power; nay, in this house.

2

Har. (*Aside.*) The devil she is! How in the name of ill-luck should he find that out?—My fine scheme entirely blown up, by Jupiter!

Wood. Why play thus upon me, my lord?—Her letter——

Ld Glen. What, has she wrote to you?—That I was not aware of, nor indeed suspected she could write.

Gov. No, not so ignorant as that neither. I ordered she should write too.

Ld Glen. You ordered she should write!—let me tell you, sir, it was wronging my confidence!

Gov. No, I did not order she should write;—I mean,—I mean,—Zounds! I don't know what I mean!

Wood. So it seems, indeed, since hardly half an hour ago my uncle himself persuaded me to marry my love.

Gov. Here's a cursed affair now!

Ld Glen. Can this be possible? Let me tell you, Governor, if, presuming upon your wealth, you play a double part in my family——

Gov. Zounds! nobody knows his own part in your family that I see! and this fellow, too, to teaze me, whom I loved above all in it. Why, I spoke entirely from regard to him. If since then I have discovered a bumpkin was before-hand with him in the possession of his miss——

Wood. If any one, besides yourself, sir, durst tell such a falsehood, it would cost a life.

Gov. Yes; and if any one beside myself durst tell me such a truth, it would cost a soul perhaps. (*Exit.*

Har. This is more unintelligible than all the rest.

Ld Glen. To end these altercations;—upon yourself, Woodville, shall depend the fortune of this wretch to whom you have been so gross a dupe as to justify the imputation of folly. Why, even without knowing

me, she ridiculed your passion, and offered to leave
you.

Wood. Impossible!

Ld Glen. Dare you disbelieve me, sir?—nay, she
shall be produced, and obliged to confess her arts;—
then blush and obey! Here, Vane! Governor! the
keys!   (*Exit.*

(WOODVILLE *walks behind in great agitation.*

Har. Now could I find in my heart to make this
story into a ballad, as a warning to all meddling puppies; and then hang myself, that it may conclude with
a grace.   Zounds, he must be endued with superna-
tural intelligence! Just when I was saying a thousand civil things to myself on my success, to have my
mine sprung before my eyes by the enemy; and instead of serving my friend and myself, become a mere
tool to old Gravity's revenge! 'Pshaw! however, we
must make the best of a bad matter.—Woodville,
what dost mean to do, man?

Wood. Let them produce my Cecilia!—I will then
seize and protect her to the last moment of my life.

Har. And I will assist you to the last moment of
mine.

Wood. My generous cousin! this is indeed friendship.

Har. Not so very generous, if you knew all.

Re-enter LORD GLENMORE *and the Governor with*
BRIDGET, *holding a handkerchief to her eyes,* VANE
following; WOODVILLE *flies and clasps her in his
arms;* HARCOURT *takes her hand.*

Wood. My love! my life!—do I once again behold
thee?—fear nothing!—you here are safe from all the
world!—will you not bless me with one look?

Brid. (*Looking at him and* HARCOURT *with ridiculous distress.*) Oh, dear me!

Ld Glen. I have put it out of your power to marry,
sir, otherwise you may take her.

Wood. Take her!—What poor farce is this?

Har. Hey-day! more incomprehensibilities?

Vane. (*Aside.*) Now for the eclaircissement—since, if the Governor doesn't acknowledge her in his first rage and confusion, I may never be able to make him!—I humbly hope Mr Woodville will pardon me, if, with her own consent and my lord's, I this morning married this young lady.

Gov. Zounds, you dog, what's that?—you married her?—Why, how did you dare?—And you too, my lord!—what the devil, did you consent to this?

Vane. Believe me, sir, I didn't then know she was your daughter.

Ld Glen. Daughter!

Gov. So, it's out, after all:—It's a lie, you dog! you did know she was my daughter;—you all knew it;—you all conspired to torment me!

All. Ha, ha, ha!

Gov. Ha, ha, ha! confound your mirth!—as if I had not plagues enough already.—And you have great reason to grin too, my lord, when you have thrown my gawky on your impudent valet.

Ld Glen. Who could ever have dreamt of—ha, ha, ha!—of finding this your little wonder of the country, brother?

Har. Nay, my lord, she's the little wonder of the town too.

All. Ha, ha, ha!

Gov. Mighty well,—mighty well,—mighty well; pray, take your whole laugh out, good folks; since this is, positively, the last time of my entertaining you in this manner.—A cottage shall henceforth be her portion, and a rope mine.

Brid. If you are my papa, I think you might give some better proof of your kindness;—but I sha'n't stir;—why, I married on purpose that I might not care for you.

Gov. Why, thou eternal torment! my original sin!

—whose first fault was the greatest frailty of woman ; and whose second, her greatest folly ! dost thou, or the designing knave who has entrapped thee merely for that purpose, imagine my wealth shall ever reward incontinence and ingratitude ?—no ; go knit stockings to some regiment, where he is preferred to be drummer !—warm yourself when the sun shines !—soak every hard-earn'd crust in your own tears, and repent at leisure.   (*Exit in a rage.*

All. Ha, ha, ha !

Ld Glen. He to ridicule my mode of education !— But what is the meaning of all this ?

Wood. Truly, my lord, I believe it would be very hard to find any for either my uncle's words or actions. —I am equally at a loss to guess as to Bridget here.

Vane. Hey, what ? Bridget, did you say, sir ? Why, you little ugly witch, are you really Bridget ?

Brid. Why, I told you so all along ; but you wou'dn't believe me.

All. Ha, ha, ha !

Brid. Oh dear heart !—I am now as much afeard of my new husband as father !

Ld Glen. For thee, wench—

Brid. (*Pops upon her knees.*) Oh, no more locking up, for goodness sake, my lord !—I be sick enough of passing for a lady : but, if old Scratch ever puts such a trick again in my head, I hope—your lordship will catch me ! that's all.   (*Exit.*

Vane. I shall run distracted ! have I married an— and all ! for nothing, too ?

Ld Glen. A punishment peculiarly just, as it results from abusing my confidence—Hence, wretch ! nor ever, while you live, appear again in my presence.

    (*Exit* VANE, *looking furiously after* BRIDGET.

Ld Glen. 'Tis time to return to ourselves. We shall soon come to an eclaircissement, Woodville !—Since you won't marry, I will.

Wood. My lord !

Ld Glen. And you shall judge of my choice. (*Exit.*

Har. Now for it ;—whatever devil diverts himself among us to-day, I see he owes my sagacious lord here a grudge, as well as the rest ; and I foresee that his wife and the Governor's daughter will prove equally entertaining.

Enter LORD GLENMORE *leading* CECILIA, *followed by* MISS MORTIMER.

Ld Glen. This lady, sir, I have selected ;—a worthy choice.

Wood. I dream, surely !—that lady your choice ! —your's !

Ld Glen. Ungrateful son ! had such been your's—

Wood. Why, this very angel is mine, my Cecilia, my first, my only love.

Ld Glen. How !—

Cec. Yes, my lord !—you now know the unhappy object at once of your resentment, contempt, and admiration !—my own misfortunes I had learnt to bear, but those of Woodville overpower me !—I deliver myself up to your justice; content to be every way his victim, so I am not his ruin.

Ld Glen. But to find you in this house——

Cec. Your generous nephew and the amiable Miss Mortimer distinguished me with the only asylum could shelter me from your son !

Ld Glen. They distinguished themselves !——Oh, Woodville ! did I think an hour ago I could be more angry with you ?—How durst thou warp a mind so noble ?

Wood. It is a crime my life cannot expiate,—yet, if the sincerest anguish—

Ld Glen. I have one act of justice still in my power ; —my prejudice in favour of birth, and even a stronger prejudice, is corrected by this lovely girl :—of her goodness of heart and greatness of mind I have had incontestible proofs ; and if I thought you, Frank—

Cec. Yet, stay, my lord! nor kill me with too much kindness. Once your generosity might have made me happy, now only miserable. My reason, my pride, nay even my love, induces me to refuse, as the only way to prove I deserve him!—he has taught me to know the world too late, nor will I retort on him the contempt I have incurred. Mr Woodville will tell you whether I have not solemnly vowed—

Wood. Not to accept me without the consent of both fathers; and if mine consents, what doubt—

Governor without.

Stop that old man! stop that mad parson! stop him!

GREY *without.*

Nothing shall stop me in pursuit of my——(*Enters.*) Ha! she is—she is here indeed! Providence has at length directed me to her. (*Runs to* CECILIA.

Cec. My father! covered with shame let me sink before you.

Ld Glen. and Har. Her father!

Enter Governor.

Grey. Rise, my glorious girl! rise purified and forgiven! rise to pity with me the weak minds that know not all thy value, and venerate the noble ones that do.

Gov. Hey! is it possible! Grey, is this my——

Grey. Yes, sir; this is your Cecilia, my Cecilia, the object of your avowed rejection and contempt!

Gov. Rejection and contempt! stand out of the way—let me embrace my daughter—let me take her once more to my heart— (*Runs and embraces her.*

Ld Glen. His daughter!

Gov. Yes, my friend, this is really my daughter—my own Cecilia; as sure as I am an old fool after being a young one, this good girl has a right to call

me by the name of father.—Hasn't she, Grey?—
Why, my lord, this is the very parson I told you of.
—(*Taking* CECILIA's *arm under his.*) And now,
young sir, what do you say to your uncle's freaks?

Wood. Say, sir? that, had you ten thousand such,
I would go through a patriarchal servitude, in hopes
of Cecilia's hand for my reward.

Gov. And, had I ten millions of money, and this
only girl, thou should'st have her, and that, too, for
thy noble freedom!—And what says my Cecilia to
her father's first gift?

Cec. Astonishment and pleasure leave me hardly
power to say, that a disobedience to you, sir, would
only double my fault; nor to worship that heaven,
which has led me through such a trial to such a reward!—Take all I have left myself to give you,
Woodville, in my hand.

(WOODVILLE *kisses first her hand, and then herself.*

Grey. Now, let me die, my darling child! since I
have seen thee, once more, innocent and happy.

Gov. And now, kiss me, my Cecilia!—Kiss me!
—Od! Miss Mortimer shall kiss me too, for loving
my poor girl here!—Kiss me all of you, old and
young! men, women, and children!—Od. I am so overjoyed, I dread the consequences.——D'ye hear
there?——Fetch me a surgeon and a bottle of wine!
——I must both empty and fill my veins on this occasion!—Zooks, I could find in my heart to frisk it
merrily in defiance of the gout, and take that cursed
vixen below, whoever she is, for my partner!

Ld Glen. Methinks all seem rewarded, but my poor
Sophia here! and her protection of Cecilia deserves
the highest recompence!—But whenever, my dear,
you can present me the husband of your choice, I
will present him with a fortune fit for my daughter.

Gov. Protect Cecilia!—Od! she is a good girl,
and a charming girl, and I honour the very tip of her
feathers now!—If she could but fancy our Charles,

I'd throw in something pretty on his side, I promise you.

Miss Mor. Frankness is the fashion. What would you say, sir, and you, my lord, if I had fancied your Charles so much as to make him mine already ?

Gov. Hey-day! more discoveries!—How's this, boy ?

Har. Even so, sir, indeed.

Ld Glen. It completes my satisfaction.

Gov. Od, brother ! Who'd have thought you in the right all the while ?—We'll never separate again, by the Lord Harry ! but knock down our Welch friend's old house, and raise him one on the ruins, large enough to contain the whole family of us, where he shall reign sole sovereign over all our future little Woodvilles and Cecilias.

Cec. Oppressed with wonder, pleasure, gratitude, I must endeavour to forgive myself, when heaven thus graciously proves its forgiveness, in allying me to every human being my heart distinguishes.

Grey. Yes, my Cecilia, you may believe him, who never gave you a bad lesson, that you are now most truly entitled to esteem ; since it requires a far greater exertion to stop your course down the hill of vice, than to toil slowly up toward virtue.

[*Exeunt.*

THE

ENGLISH MERCHANT,

A

COMEDY,

IN FIVE ACTS.

AS PERFORMED AT THE

THEATRE-ROYAL, DURY-LANE.

BY

GEORGE COLMAN.

DRAMATIS PERSONÆ.

LORD FALBRIDGE,	Mr Powell.
SIR WILLIAM DOUGLAS,	Mr Havard.
FREEPORT,	Mr Yates.
SPATTER,	Mr King.
OWEN,	Mr Burton.
LA FRANCE,	Mr Baddeley.
Officer,	Mr Strange.
Servants, &c.	
LADY ALTON,	Mrs Abington.
AMELIA,	Mrs Palmer.
MRS GOODMAN,	Mrs Hopkins.
MOLLY,	Miss Pope.

SCENE—London.

ENGLISH MERCHANT.

ACT THE FIRST.

SCENE I.

A Room in MRS GOODMAN'S *House.*

Enter MOLLY, *struggling with* SPATTER.

Mol. Be quiet, Mr Spatter! let me alone, pray
now, sir! It is a strange thing a body can't go about
the house without being pestered with your impertinence—Why sure—

Spat. Introduce me to your mistress then; come,
there's a good girl!—and I will tease you no longer.

Mol. Indeed I sha'n't—Introduce you to my lady!
for what, pray?

Spat. Oh! for a thousand things.   To laugh, to
chat, to take a dish of tea, to—

Mol. You drink tea with my lady! I should not
have thought of that—On what acquaintance?

Spat. The most agreeable in the world, child; a
new acquaintance.

Mol. Indeed you mistake yourself mightily; you
are not a proper acquaintance for a person of her
quality, I assure you, sir!

Spat. Why, what quality is she, then?

Mol. Much too high quality for your acquaintance,
I promise you.   What, a poet man! that sits write,
write, write, all day long, scribbling a pack of nonsense for the newspapers.   You're fit for nothing
above a chambermaid.

Spat. That's as much to say, that you think me
just fit for you, eh, child?

Mol. No, indeed, not I, sir.   Neither my lady nor
I will have any thing to say to you.

Spat. Your mistress and you both give yourselves
a great many airs, my dear.   Your poverty, I think,
might pull down your pride.

Mol. What does the fellow mean by poverty?

Spat. I mean that you are starving.

Mol. Oh the slanderous monster! We starving!
Who told you so? I'd have you to know, sir, my lady has a very great fortune.

Spat. So 'tis a sign, by her way of life and appearance.

Mol. Well, she lives privately indeed, because she
loves retirement; she goes plain, because she hates
dress; she keeps no table, because she is an enemy
to luxury: In short, my lady is as rich as a Jew,
and you are an impertinent coxcomb.

Spat. Come, come! I know more of your mistress
than you imagine.

Mol. And what do you know of her?

Spat. Oh, I know what I know.

Mol. Well!   (*Alarmed.*

Spat. I know who she is, and where she came from; I am very well acquainted with her family, and know her whole history.

Mol. How can that be?

Spat. Very easily—I have correspondence every where. As private as she may think herself, it is not the first time that I have seen or heard of Amelia

Mol. Oh gracious! as sure as I am alive this man will discover us! (*Apart.*) Mr Spatter, my dear Mr Spatter, if you know any thing, sure you would not be so cruel as to betray us!

Spat. My dear Mr Spatter! O ho! I have guessed right—there is something then.

Mol. No, sir, there is nothing at all; nothing that signifies to you or any body else.

Spat. Well, well, I'll say nothing; but then you must—

Mol. What?

Spat. Come, kiss me, hussy!

Mol. I say kiss you, indeed!

Spat. And you'll introduce me to your mistress.

Mol. Not I, I promise you.

Spat. Nay, no mysteries between you and me, child! Come, here's the key to all locks, the clue to every maze, and the discloser of all secrets; money, child! Here, take this purse; you see I know something; tell me the rest, and I have the fellow to it in my pocket.

Mol. Ha, ha, ha! poor Mr Spatter! Where could you get all this money, I wonder? Not by your poetries, I believe. But what signifies telling you any thing, when you are acquainted with our whole history already. You have correspondence every where, you know. There, sir! take up your filthy purse again, and remember that I scorn to be obliged to any body but my mistress.

Spat. There's impudence for you! when, to my certain knowledge, your mistress has not a guinea in the world; you live in continual fear of being discovered; and you will both be utterly undone in a fortnight, unless Lord Falbridge should prevent it, by taking Amelia under his protection. You understand me, child?

Mol. You scandalous wretch! Did you ever hear such a monster? I won't stay a moment longer with him; but you are quite mistaken about me and my mistress, I assure you, sir.   We are in the best circumstances in the world; we have nothing to fear; and we don't care a farthing for you.   So your servant, Mr Poet.   (*Exit.*

SPATTER *alone.*

Your servant, Mrs Pert! "We are in the best circumstances in the world." Ay, that is as much as to say, they are in the utmost distress. "We have nothing to fear;" that is, they are frightened out of their wits.——"And we don't care a farthing for you," meaning that they will take all the care in their power that I shall not find them out.   But I may be too hard for you yet, young gentlewoman! I have earned but a poor livelihood by mere scandal and abuse; but if I could once arrive at doing a little substantial mischief, I should make my fortune.

Enter MRS GOODMAN.

Oh! your servant, Mrs Goodman! Your's is the most unsocial lodging-house in town.   So many ladies, and only one gentleman! and you won't take the least notice of him.

Mrs Good. How so, Mr Spatter?

Spat. Why, did not you promise to introduce me to Amelia?

Mrs Good. To tell you the plain truth, Mr Spatter, she don't like you.   And, indeed, I don't know how it is, but you make yourself a great many enemies.

Spat. Yes; I believe I do raise a little envy.

Mrs Good. Indeed you are mistaken, sir. As you are a lodger of mine, it makes me quite uneasy to hear what the world says of you. How do you contrive to make so many enemies, Mr Spatter?

Spat. Because I have merit, Mrs Goodman.

Mrs Good. May be so; but nobody will allow it but yourself. They say that you set up for a wit, indeed; but that you deal in nothing but scandal, and think of nothing but mischief.

Spat. I do speak ill of the men sometimes, to be sure; but then I have a great regard for women—provided they are handsome: and that I may give you a proof of it, introduce me to Amelia.

Mrs Good. You must excuse me; she and you would be the worst company in the world: for she never speaks too well of herself, nor the least ill of any body else. And then her virtue—

Spat. Pooh, pooh, she speaks ill of nobody, because she knows nobody; and as for her virtue, ha, ha, ha!

Mrs Good. You don't believe much in that, I suppose?

Spat. I have not over much faith, Mrs Goodman. Lord Falbridge, perhaps, may give a better account of it.

Mrs Good. Lord Falbridge can say nothing but what would be extremely to her honour, I assure you, sir. (SPATTER *laughs.*) Well, well, you may laugh, but it is very true.

Spat. Oh, I don't doubt it; but you don't tell the whole truth, Mrs Goodman. When any of your friends or acquaintance sit for their pictures, you draw a very flattering likeness. All characters have their dark side, and if they have but one eye, you give them in profile. Your great friend, Mr Freeport, for instance, whom you are always praising for his benevolent actions—

Mrs Good. He is benevolence itself, sir.

Spat. Yes, and grossness itself too. I remember him these many years. He always cancels an obligation by the manner of conferring it; and does you a favour, as if he were going to knock you down.

Mrs Good. A truce with your satire, good Mr Spatter! Mr Freeport is my best friend; I owe him every thing; and I can't endure the slightest reflection on his character. Besides, he can have given no offence to Lady Alton, whatever may be the case with Amelia.

Spat Lady Alton! she is a particular friend of mine, to be sure; but, between you and me, Mrs Goodman, a more ridiculous character than any you have mentioned. *A belle esprit* forsooth! and as vain of her beauty as learning, without any great portion of either. A fourth grace, and a tenth muse! who fancies herself enamoured of Lord Falbridge, because she would be proud of such a conquest; and has lately bestowed some marks of distinction on me, because she thinks it will give her credit among persons of letters.

Mrs Good. Nay, if you can't spare your own friends, I don't wonder at your attacking mine—and so, sir, your humble servant.—But stay, here's a post-chaise stopped at our door; and here comes a servant with a portmanteau; 'tis the gentleman for whom my first floor was taken, I suppose.

Spat. Very likely: well, you will introduce me to him at least, Mrs Goodman.

Enter a Servant with a portmanteau—SIR WILLIAM DOUGLAS *following.*

Sir Wil. You are Mrs Goodman, I suppose, madam?

Mrs Good. At your service, sir.

Sir Wil. Mr Owen, I believe, has secured apartments here?

Mrs Good. He has, sir.

Sir Wil. They are for me, madam—Have you any other lodgers ?

Mrs Good. Only that gentleman, sir, and a young lady—

Spat. Of great beauty and virtue, eh, Mrs Goodman ?

Mrs Good. She has both, sir ; but you will see very little of her, for she lives in the most retired manner in the world.

Sir Wil. Her youth and beauty are matter of great indifference to me, for I shall be as much a recluse as herself.—Are there any news at present stirring in London ?

Mrs Good. Mr Spatter can inform you, sir, for he deals in news. In the mean while, I'll prepare your apartments.   (*Exit, followed by the servant.*

Manent Sir William Douglas *and* Spatter; Sir William *walks up and down without taking notice of* Spatter.

Spat. This must be a man of quality by his ill manners. I'll speak to him. (*Aside.*) (*To* Sir William.) Will your lordship give me leave—

Sir Wil. Lordship ! I am no lord, sir, and must beg not to be honoured with the name.

Spat. It is a kind of mistake, that cannot displease at least.

Sir Wil. I don't know that. None but a fool would be vain of a title, if he had one ; and none but an impostor would assume a title to which he has no right.

Spat. Oh, you're of the house of commons then, a member of parliament, and are come up to town to attend the sessions, I suppose, sir ?

Sir Wil. No matter what I am, sir.

Spat. Nay, no offence I hope, sir. All I meant was to do you honour. Being concerned in two Evening-Posts, and one morning paper, I was willing to know the proper manner of announcing your arrival.

Sir Wil. You have connections with the press then, it seems, sir?

Spat. Yes, sir; I am an humble retainer to the muses, an author. I compose pamphlets on all subjects, compile magazines, and do newspapers.

Sir Wil. Do newspapers! What do you mean by that, sir?

Spat. That is, sir, I collect the articles of news from the other papers, and make new ones for the postscript, translate the mails, write occasional letters from Cato and Theatricus, and give fictitious answers to supposed correspondents.

Sir Wil. A very ingenious as well as honourable employment, I must confess, sir!

Spat. Some little genius is requisite, to be sure. Now, sir, if I can be of any use to you—if you have any friend to be praised, or any enemy to be abused, any author to cry up, or minister to run down, my pen and talents are entirely at your service.

Sir Wil. I am much obliged to you, sir, but at present I have not the least occasion for either. In return for your genteel offers, give me leave to trouble you with one piece of advice. When you deal in private scandal, have a care of the cudgel; and when you meddle with public matters, beware of the pillory.

Spat. How, sir! are you no friend to literature? Are you an enemy to the liberty of the press?

Sir Wil. I have the greatest respect for both; but railing is the disgrace of letters, and personal abuse the scandal of freedom: foul-mouthed critics are in general disappointed authors; and they who are the loudest against ministers only mean to be paid for their silence.

Spat. That may be sometimes, sir; but give me leave to ask you——

Sir Wil. Do not ask me at present, sir! I see a particular friend of mine coming this way, and I must beg you to withdraw.

Spat. Withdraw, sir! first of all allow me to——

Sir Wil. Nay, no reply : we must be in private.

[*Thrusting out* SPATTER.

SIR WILLIAM DOUGLAS *alone.*

What a wretch! as contemptible as mischievous. Our generous mastiffs fly at men from an instinct of courage; but this fellow's attacks proceed from an instinct of baseness—But here comes the faithful Owen, with as many good qualities as that execrable fellow seems to have bad ones.

Enter OWEN.

Well, Owen, I am safe arived you see.

Owen. Ah, sir! would to heaven you were as safe returned again! Have a care of betraying yourself to be Sir William Douglas!—During your stay here, your name is Ford, remember.

Sir Wil. I shall take care—But tell me your news —What have you done since your arrival ? Have you heard any thing of my daughter? Have you seen Lord Brumpton? Has he any hope of obtaining my pardon ?

Owen. He had, sir.

Sir Wil. And what can have destroyed it then ?

Owen. My Lord Brumpton is dead, sir.

Sir Wil. Dead!

Owen. I saw him within this week in apparent good health; he promised to exert his whole interest in your favour : by his own appointment I went to wait on him yesterday noon, when I was stunned with the news of his having died suddenly the evening before.

Sir Wil. My Lord Brumpton dead! the only friend I had remaining in England ; the only person, on whose intercession I relied for my pardon ! Cruel

fortune ! I have now no hope but to find my daughter. Tell me, Owen ; have you been able to hear
any tidings of her ?

Owen. Alas, sir ! none that are satisfactory. On
the death of Mr Andrews, in whose care you left her,
being cruelly abandoned by the relation who succeeded to the estate, she left the country some months
ago, and has not since been heard of.

Sir Wil. Unhappy there too! When will the measure of my misfortunes be full ? When will the malice of my fate be satisfied ? Proscribed, condemned,
attainted, (alas, but too justly !) I have lost my rank,
my estate, my wife, my son, and all my family. One
only daughter remains. Perhaps a wretched wanderer like myself, perhaps in the extremest indigence,
perhaps dishonoured—Ha ! that thought distracts me.

Owen. My dear master, have patience ! Do not be
ingenious to torment yourself, but consult your safety,
and prepare for your departure.

Sir Wil. No, Owen. Hearing, providentially, of
the death of my friend Andrews, paternal care and
tenderness drew me hither ; and I will not quit the
kingdom till I learn something of my child, my dear
Amelia, whom I left a tender innocent in the arms of
the best of women twenty years ago. Her sex demands protection ; and she is now of an age, in which
she is more exposed to misfortunes than even in helpless infancy.

Owen. Be advised ; depart, and leave that care to
me. Consider your life is now at stake.

Sir Wil. My life has been too miserable to render
me very solicitous for its preservation—But the complexion of the times is changed ; the very name of
the party, in which I was unhappily engaged, is ex-
tinguished, and the whole nation is unanimously devoted to the throne. Disloyalty and insurrection are
now no more, and the sword of justice is suffered to
sleep. If I can find my child, and find her worthy

of me, I will fly with her to take refuge in some foreign country; if I am discovered in the search, I
have still some hopes of mercy.

Owen. Heaven grant your hopes may be well
founded!

Sir Wil. Come, Owen! let us behave at least with
fortitude in our adversity! Follow me to my apartment, and let us consult what measures we shall take
in searching for Amelia.   [*Exeunt.*

SCENE II.

AMELIA'S *Apartment.*

Enter AMELIA *and* MOLLY.

Amel. Poor Molly! to be teazed with that odious
fellow, Spatter!

Mol. But, madam, Mr Spatter says he is acquainted with your whole history.

Amel. Mere pretence, in order to render himself
formidable. Be on your guard against him, my dear
Molly; and remember to conceal my misery from
him and all the world. I can bear poverty, but am
not proof against insult and contempt.

Mol. Ah, my dear mistress, it is to no purpose
to endeavour to hide it from the world. They will
see poverty in my looks. As for you, you can live
upon the air; the greatness of your soul seems to support you; but, lack-a-day! I shall grow thinner and
thinner every day of my life.

Amel. I can support my own distress, but yours
touches me to the soul. Poor Polly! the labour of
my hands shall feed and clothe you—Here, dispose

of this embroidery to the best advantage ; what was formerly my amusement must now become the means of our subsistence.   Let us be obliged to nobody, but owe our support to industry and virtue.

Mol. You're an angel : let me kiss those dear hands that have worked this precious embroidery ; let me bathe them with my tears! You're an angel upon earth.   I had rather starve in your service, than live with a princess.   What can I do to comfort you ?

Amel. Thou faithful creature—only continue to be secret : you know my real character ; you know I am in the utmost distress : I have opened my heart to you, but you will plant a dagger there if you betray me to the world.

Mol. Ah, my dear mistress, how should I betray you ! I go no where, I converse with nobody but yourself and Mrs Goodman : besides, the world is very indifferent about other people's misfortunes.

Amel. The world is indifferent, it is true ; but it is curious, and takes a cruel pleasure in tearing open the wounds of the unfortunate.

Enter Mrs Goodman.

Mrs Goodman !

Mrs Good. Excuse me, madam : I took the liberty of waiting on you to receive your commands.   'Tis now near three o'clock.   You have provided nothing for dinner, and have scarce taken any refreshment these three days.

Amel. I have been indisposed.

Mrs Good. I am afraid you are more than indisposed—You are unhappy—Pardon me ! but I cannot help thinking that your fortune is unequal to your appearance.

Amel. Why should you think so ? You never heard me complain of my fortune.

Mrs Good. No, but I have too much reason to believe it is inferior to your merit.

Amel. Indeed you flatter me.

Mrs Good. Come, come; you must not indulge this melancholy. I have a now lodger, an elderly gentleman, just arrived, who does me the honour to partake of my dinner; and I must have your company too. He seems to be in trouble as well as you. You must meet; two persons in affliction may perhaps become a consolation to each other. Come, let us take some care of you.

Amel. Be assured, Mrs Goodman, I am much obliged to you for your attention to me; but I want nothing.

Mrs Good. Dear madam! you say you want nothing, and you are in want of every thing.

Enter Servant.

Serv. (*To* Mrs Good.) Lady Alton, madam, sends her compliments, and will wait upon you after dinner.

Mrs Good. Very well; my best respects to her ladyship, and I shall be ready to attend her. (*Exit Servant.*) There, there is one cause of your uneasiness! Lady Alton's visit is on your account. She thinks you have robbed her of Lord Falbridge's affections, and that is the occasion of her honouring me with her company.

Amel. Lord Falbridge's affections!

Mrs Good. Ah! my dear Amelia, you don't know your power over his heart. You have reconciled it to virtue—but come! let me prevail on you to come with me to dinner.

Amel. You must excuse me.

Mrs Good. Well, well, then I'll send you something to your own apartment. If you have any other commands, pray honour me with them, for I would fain oblige you if I knew how it were in my power.

(*Exit.*

Manent AMELIA *and* MOLLY.

Amel. What an amiable woman ! If it had not been for her apparent benevolence and goodness of heart, I should have left the house on Mr Spatter's coming to lodge in it.

Mol. Lady Alton, it seems, recommended him as a lodger here ; so he can be no friend of yours on that account ; for to be sure she owes you no good will on account of my Lord Falbridge.

Amel. No more of Lord Falbridge, I beseech you, Molly. How can you persist in mentioning him, when you know that, presuming on my situation, he has dared to affront me with dishonourable proposals ?

Mol. Ah, madam, but he sorely repents it, I promise you, and would give his whole estate for an opportunity of seeing you once more, and getting into your good graces again.

Amel. No ; his ungenerous conduct has thrown him as much below me, as my condition had placed me beneath him. He imagined he had a right to insult my distress ; but I will teach him to think it respectable.   [*Exeunt.*

ACT THE SECOND.

SCENE I.

An Apartment at MRS GOODMAN'S.

Enter LADY ALTON *and* SPATTER.

Spat. But you won't hear me, madam!

Lady Al. I have heard too much, sir! This wandering *incognita* a woman of virtue! I have no patience!

Spat. Mrs Goodman pretends to be convinced of her being a person of honour.

Lady Al. A person of honour, and openly receive visits from men! seduce Lord Falbridge! No, no: reserve this character for your next novel, Mr Spatter—it is an affront to my understanding. I begin to suspect you have betrayed me; you have gone over to the adverse party, and are in the conspiracy to abuse me.

Spat. I, madam! Neither her beauty nor her virtue—

Lady Al. Her beauty! her virtue! Why, thou wretch, thou grub of literature, whom I as a patroness of learning and encourager of men of letters, willing to blow the dead coal of genius, fondly took under my protection, do you remember what I have done for you?

Spat. With the utmost gratitude, madam.

Lady Al. Did not I draw you out of the garret, where you daily spun out your flimsy brain to catch the town flies in your cobweb dissertations? Did not I introduce you to Lord Dapperwit, the Apollo of the age? And did not you dedicate your silly volume of Poems on Several Occasions to him? Did not I put you into the list of my visitors, and order my porter to admit you at dinner-time? Did not I write the only scene in your execrable farce, which the audience vouchsafed an hearing? And did not my female friend, Mrs Melpomene, furnish you with Greek and Latin mottoes for your two-penny essays?

Spat. I acknowledge all your ladyship's goodness to me. I have done every thing in my power to shew my gratitude and fulfil your ladyship's commands.

Lady Al. Words, words, Mr Spatter! You have been witness of Lord Falbridge's inconstancy. A perfidious man! False as Phaon to Sappho, or Jason to Medea! You have seen him desert me for a wretched vagabond; you have seen me abandoned like Calypso, without making a single effort to recall my faithless Ulysses from the Siren that has lured him from me.

Spat. Be calm but one moment, madam, and I'll——

Lady Al. Bid the sea be calm, when the winds are let loose upon it. I have reason to be enraged. I placed you in genteel apartments in this house, merely to plant you as a spy; and what have you done for me? Have you employed your correspondence to any purpose? or discovered the real character of this infamous woman, this insolent Amelia?

Spat. I have taken every possible method to detect her. I have watched Amelia herself like a bailiff, or a duenna; I have overheard private conversations, have sounded the landlady, tampered with the servants, opened letters, and intercepted messages.

Lady Al. Good creature! my best Spatter! And what, what have you discovered?

Spat. That Amelia is a native of Scotland; that her surname Walton is probably not real, but assumed; and that she earnestly wishes to conceal both the place of her birth and her family.

Lady Al. And is that all?

Spat. All that I have been able to learn as yet, madam.

Lady Al. Wretch! of what service have you been then? Are these your boasted talents? When we want to unravel an ambiguous character, you have made out that she wishes to lie concealed; and when we wish to know who she is, you have just discovered that she is a native of Scotland!

Spat. And yet, if you will give me leave, madam, I think I could convince you that these discoveries, blind and unsatisfactory as they may appear to you at first, are of no small consequence

Lady Al. Of what consequence can they possibly be to me, man?

Spat. I'll tell you, madam. It is a rule in politics, when we discover something, to add something more. Something added to something makes a good deal; upon this basis I have formed a syllogism.

Lady Al. What does the pedant mean? A syllogism!

Spat. Yes, a syllogism: as for example; any person who is a native of Scotland, and wishes to be concealed, must be an enemy to the government. Amelia is a native of Scotland, and wishes to be concealed; ergo, Amelia is an enemy to the government.

Lady Al. Excellent! admirable logic! but I wish we could prove it to be truth.

Spat. I would not lay a wager of the truth of it, but I would swear it.

Lady Al. What, on a proper occasion, and in a proper place, my good Spatter?

Spat. Willingly; we must make use of what we know, and even of what we don't know. Truth is of a dry and simple nature, and stands in need of some little ornament. A lie, indeed, is infamous; but fiction, your ladyship, who deals in poetry, knows is beautiful.

Lady Al. But the substance of your fiction, Spatter?

Spat. I will lodge an information that the father of Amelia is a disaffected person, and has sent her to London for treasonable purposes: nay, I can upon occasion even suppose the father himself to be in London: in consequence of which you will probably recover Lord Falbridge, and Amelia will be committed to prison.

Lady Al. You have given me new life. I took you for a mere stainer of paper; but I have found you a Machiavel.—I hear somebody coming.—Mrs Goodman has undertaken to send Amelia hither. Ha! she's here—Away, Spatter, and wait for me at my house: you must dine with me; and after dinner, like true politicians, we will settle our plan of operations over our coffee. Away, away, this instant!

[*Exit* SPATTER.

LADY ALTON *alone.*

A convenient engine this Mr Spatter: the most impudent, thorough-paced knave in the three kingdoms! with the heart of Zoilus, the pen of Mævius, and the tongue of Thersites. I was sure he would stick at nothing. The writings of authors are public advertisements of their qualifications; and when they profess to live upon scandal, it is as much as to say, that they are ready for every other dirty work in which we chuse to employ them.—But now for Amelia; if she proves tractable, I may forego the use of this villain, who almost makes me hate my triumph, and be ashamed of my revenge.

Enter AMELIA.

Amel. Mrs Goodman has informed me that your ladyship has desired to see me: I wait your commands, madam.

Lady Al. Look you, young woman, I am sensible how much it is beneath a person of my rank to parley with one of your condition; for once, however, I am content to wave all ceremony; and, if you behave as you ought to do, you have nothing to fear, child.

Amel. I hope I have never behaved otherwise than as I ought to do, madam.

Lady Al. Yes; you have received the visits of Lord Falbridge; you have endeavoured to estrange his affections from me: but, if you encourage him in his infidelity to me, tremble for the consequence: be advised or you are ruined.

Amel. I am conscious of no guilt, and know no fear, madam.

Lady Al. Come, come, Mrs Amelia; this high strain is out of character with me. Act over your Clelia, and Cleopatra, and Cassandra, at a proper time; and let me talk in the style of nature and common sense to you. You have no Lord Falbridge, no weak young nobleman to impose upon at present.

Amel. To impose upon! I scorn the imputation, and am sorry to find that your ladyship came hither merely to indulge yourself in the cruel pleasure of insulting one of the unhappiest of her sex. (*Weeping.*

Lady Al. You are mistaken: I came hither to concert measures for your happiness, to assist your poverty, and relieve your distress. Leave this house; leave London; I will provide you a retirement in the country, and supply all your wants; only renounce all thoughts of Lord Falbridge, and never let him know the place of your retreat.

Amel. Lord Falbridge! What is Lord Falbridge to me, madam?

Lady Al. To convince me you have no commerce with him, accept of my proposals.

Amel. No, madam; the favours which you intend me I could not receive without blushing. I have no wants but what I can supply myself; no distresses which your ladyship can relieve; and I will seek no refuge but in my own virtue.

Lady Al. Your virtue! Ridiculous! If you are a woman of virtue, what is the meaning of all this mystery? Who are you? What are you? Who will vouch for your character?

Amel. It wants no vouchers; nor will I suffer myself to be arraigned like a criminal, till I know by what authority you take upon you to act as my judge.

Lady Al. Matchless confidence! Yes, yes, it is too plain; I see you are the very creature I took you for; a mere adventurer; some strolling princess, that are perhaps more frugal of your favours than the rest of your sisterhood, merely to enhance the price of them.

Amel. Hold, madam! This opprobrious language is more injurious to your own honour than to mine. I see the violence of your temper, and will leave you. But you may one day know that my birth is equal to your own; my heart is perhaps more generous; and whatever may be my situation, I scorn to be dependent on any body; much less on one who has so mean an opinion of me, and who considers me as her rival.   (*Exit.*

LADY ALTON *alone.*

Her rival! Unparalleled insolence! An open avowal of her competition with me! Yes; I see Spatter must be employed. Her rival! I shall burst with indignation!

Enter MRS GOODMAN.

Lady Al. Mrs Goodman! where is Mr Spatter?

Mrs Good. He went out the moment he left your
ladyship. But you seem disordered : shall I get you
some hartshorn, madam ?

Lady Al. Some poison!—Rival!—I shall choak with
rage.—You shall hear from me. You, and your
Amelia. You have abused me ; you have conspired
against my peace ; and be assured you shall suffer for
it.   (*Exit.*

MRS GOODMAN *alone.*

What a violent woman ! Her passion makes her
forget what is due to her sex and quality. Ha! Mr
Freeport !

Enter FREEPORT.

My best friend! Welcome to London! When did
you arrive from Lisbon ?

Free. But last night.

Mrs Good. I hope you have had a pleasant voyage ?

Free. A good trading voyage—I have got money,
but I have got the spleen too.—Have you any news
in town ?

Mrs Good. None at all, sir.

Free. So much the better : the less news, the less
nonsense.—But what strange lady have you had here ?
I met her as I was coming up : she rushed by like a
fury, and almost swept me down stairs again with
the wind of her hoop-petticoat.

Mrs Good. Ah! jealousy ! jealousy is a terrible
passion, especially in a woman's breast, Mr Freeport.

Free. Jealousy ! Why, she is not jealous of you,
Mrs Goodman ?

Mrs Good. No, but of a lodger of mine.

Free. Have you any new lodgers since I left you ?

Mrs Good. Two or three, sir ; the last arrived but

to-day; an elderly gentleman, who will see no company.

Free. He's in the right. Three parts in four of mankind are knaves or fools; and the fourth part live by themselves.—But who are your other lodgers?

Mrs Good. An author and a lady.

Free. I hate authors. Who is the lady?

Mrs Good. She calls herself Amelia Walton; but I believe that name is not her real one.

Free. Not her real one! Why, sure she is a woman of character?

Mrs Good. A woman of character! She is an angel. She is most miserably poor; and yet haughty to an excess.

Free. Pride and poverty! A sad composition, Mrs Goodman.

Mrs Good. No, sir; her pride is one of her greatest virtues: it consists in depriving herself of almost all necessaries, and concealing it from the world. Though every action speaks her to be a woman of birth and education, she lives upon the work of her own hands without murmur or complaint. I make use of a thousand stratagems to assist her against her will; I prevail on her to keep the money due for rent for her support, and furnish her with every thing she wants at half its prime cost; but if she perceives or suspects these little artifices, she takes it almost as ill as if I had attempted to defraud her. In short, sir, her unshaken virtue and greatness of soul under misfortunes, make me consider her as a prodigy, and often draw tears of pity and admiration from me.

Free. Ah! women's tears lie very near their eyes. I never cried in my life, and yet I can feel too; I can admire, I can esteem, but what signifies whimpering? Hark ye, Mrs Goodman! this is a very extraordinary account you give of this young woman; you have raised my curiosity, and I'll go and see this lodger of yours; I am rather out of spirits, and it will serve to amuse me.

Mrs Good. Oh, sir, you can't see her; she neither pays visits nor receives them, but lives in the most retired manner in the world.

Free. So much the better: I love retirement as well as she. Where are her apartments?

Mrs Good. On this very floor, on the other side of the staircase.

Free. I'll go and see her immediately.

Mrs Good. Indeed you can't, sir. It is impossible.

Free. Impossible! where is the impossibility of going into a room? Come along!

Mrs Good. For heaven's sake, Mr Freeport—

Free. Pshaw! I have no time to lose, I have business half an hour hence.

Mrs Good. But won't it be rather indelicate, sir? Let me prepare her first!

Free. Prepare her—With all my heart—But remember that I am a man of business, Mrs Goodman, and have no time to waste in ceremony and compliment.   [*Exeunt.*

SCENE II.

AMELIA'S *Apartment.*

AMELIA *at work, and* MOLLY.

Amel. No, Polly! If Lord Falbridge comes again, I am resolved not to see him.

Mol. Indeed, madam, he loves you above all the world; I am sure of it, and I verily believe he will run mad, if you don't hear what he has to say for himself.

Amel. Speak no more of him.

Enter MRS GOODMAN.

Mrs Goodman!

Mrs Good. Pardon me, madam! Here is a gentleman of my acquaintance begs you would give him leave to speak with you.

Amel. A gentleman! who is he?

Mrs Good. His name is Freeport, madam. He has a few particularities; but he is the best hearted man in the world. Pray let him come in, madam!

Amel. By no means; you know I receive visits from nobody.

Enter FREEPORT.

Bless me, he's here! This is very extraordinary indeed, Mrs Goodman.

Free. Don't disturb yourself, young woman; don't disturb yourself.

Mol. Mighty free and easy, methinks!

Amel. Excuse me, sir; I am not used to receive visits from persons entirely unknown.

Free. Unknown! There is not a man in all London better known than I am. I am a merchant, my name is Freeport, Freeport of Crutched-Friars; inquire upon 'Change.

Amel. Mrs Goodman, I never saw the gentleman before. I am surprised at his coming here.

Free. Pooh! Pr'ythee—Mrs Goodman knows me well enough. (MRS GOODMAN *talks apart with* AMELIA.) Ay! that's right, Mrs Goodman. Let her know who I am, and tell her to make herself easy.

Mrs Good. But the lady does not chuse we should trouble her, sir.

Free. Trouble her! I'll give her no trouble; I came to drink a dish of tea with you; let your maid get it ready, and we will have it here instead of your parlour.—In the mean time I will talk with this lady ; I have something to say to her.

Amel. If you had any business, sir—

Free. Business ! I tell you I have very particular business, so sit down, and let's have the tea.

Mrs Good. You shou'd not have followed me so soon, sir.

Free. Pooh, pr'ythee ! (*Exit* MRS GOODMAN.

Mol. This is the oddest man I ever saw in my life.

Amel. Well, sir, as I see you are a particular acquaintance of Mrs Goodman—But pray what are your commands for me, sir ? (*They sit.*

Free. I tell you what, young woman, I am a plain man, and will tell you my mind in an instant. I am told that you are one of the best women in the world, very virtuous, and very poor ; I like you for that : but they say you are excessively proud too ; now I don't like you for that, madam.

Mol. Free and easy still, I see.

Amel. And pray, sir, who told you so ?

Free. Mrs Goodman.

Amel. She has deceived you, sir ; not in regard to my pride, perhaps, for there is a certain right pride which every body, especially women, ought to possess ; and as to virtue, it is no more than my duty ; but as to poverty, I disclaim it ; they who want nothing, cannot be said to be poor.

Free. It is no such thing : you don't speak the truth, and that is worse than being proud. I know very well that you are as poor as Job, that you are in want of common necessaries, and don't make a good meal above once in a fortnight.

Mol. My mistress fasts for her health, sir.

Free. Hold your tongue, hussy ! what, are you proud too ?

Mol. Lord, what a strange man !

Free. But however, madam, proud or not proud,

does not signify two-pence.—Hark ye, young woman! it is a rule with me (as it ought to be with
every good Christian) to give a tenth part of my fortune in charity. In the account of my profits there
stands at present the sum of two thousand pounds on
the credit side of my books, so that I am two hundred pounds in arrear. This I look upon as a debt
due from my fortune to your poverty; yes, your poverty, I say; so never deny it. There's a bank note
for two hundred pounds; and now I am out of your
debt.—Where the deuce is this tea, I wonder?

Mol. I never saw such a man in my life.

Amel. I don't know that I ever was so thoroughly
confounded (*Apart.*)—Sir!   (*To* FREEPORT.

Free. Well?

Amel. This noble action has surprised me still
more than your conversation; but you must excuse
my refusal of your kindness; for I must confess, that
if I were to accept what you offer, I don't know
when I should be able to restore it.

Free. Restore it! why, who wants you to restore
it? I never dreamt of restitution.

Amel. I feel, I feel your goodness to the bottom
of my soul; but you must excuse me. I have no
occasion for your bounty; take your note, sir, and
bestow it where it is wanted.

Mol. Lord, madam! you are ten times stranger
than the gentleman.—I tell you what, sir: (*To* FREE-
PORT.) it does not signify talking; we are in the
greatest distress in the world, and if it had not been
for the kindness and good-nature of Mrs Goodman,
we might have died by this time. My lady has concealed her distress from every body that was willing
and able to relieve her; you have come to the
knowledge of it in spite of her teeth; and I hope
that you will oblige her, in spite of her teeth, to accept of your generous offer.

7

Amel. No more, my dear Polly; if you would not have me die with shame, say no more! Return the gentleman his note with my best thanks for his kindness; tell him, I durst not accept of it; for when a woman receives presents from a man, the world will always suspect that she pays for them at the expence of her virtue.

Free. What's that! what does she say, child?

Mol. Lord, sir, I hardly know what she says. She says, that when a gentleman makes a young lady presents, he is always supposed to have a design upon her virtue.

Free. Nonsense! why should she suspect me of an ungenerous design, because I do a generous action?

Mol. Do you hear, madam?

Amel. Yes, I hear, I admire; but I must persist in my refusal: if that scandalous fellow Spatter were to hear of this, he would stick at saying nothing.

Free. Eh! what's that?

Mol. She is afraid you should be taken for her lover, sir.

Free. I for your lover! not I. I never saw you before. I don't love you, so make no scruples upon that account; I like you well enough, but I don't love you at all, not at all, I tell you.—If you have a mind never to see my face any more, good bye t'ye! —You shall never see me any more. If you like I should come back again, I'll come back again; but I lose time, I have business—your servant.   (*Going.*

Amel. Stay, sir! do not leave me without receiving the sincerest acknowledgments of my gratitude and esteem: but, above all, receive your note again, and do not put me any longer to the blush!

Free. The woman is a fool.

Enter Mrs Goodman.

Amel. Come hither, I beseech you, Mrs Goodman.

Mrs Good. Your pleasure, madam?

Amel. Here! take this note which that gentleman
has given me by mistake, return it to him, I charge
you; assure him of my esteem and admiration, but
let him know I need no assistance, and cannot accept it.   [*Exit.*

Manent Freeport, &c.

Mrs Good. Ah! Mr Freeport! you have been
at your old trade.   You are always endeavouring
to do good actions in secret, but the world always
finds you out, you see.

Mol. Well, I don't believe there are two stranger
people in England than my mistress and that gentleman, one so ready to part with money, and the
other so unwilling to receive it;—but don't believe
her, sir, for, between friends, she is in very great
need of assistance, I assure you.

Mrs Good. Indeed I believe so.

Free. Oh, I have no doubt on't, so I'll tell you
what, Mrs Goodman, keep the note, and supply her
wants out of it without her knowledge; and, now I
think of it, that way is better than t'other.

Mol. I never saw such a strange man in my life.
                                                (*Exit.*

Mrs Good. I shall obey your kind commands, sir.
Poor soul! my heart bleeds for her, her virtue and
misfortunes touch me to the soul.

Free. I have some little feeling for her too, but
she is too proud.   A fine face, fine figure, well behaved, well bred, and I dare say an excellent heart!
—But she is too proud, tell her so, d'ye hear? tell
her she is too proud. I shall be too late for my busi-

ness—I'll see her again soon—It is a pity she is so
proud.   [*Exeunt.*

ACT THE THIRD.

SCENE I.

A Hall.

SIR WILLIAM DOUGLAS *alone.*

A young woman! a native of Scotland! her name
Amelia! supposed to be in the greatest distress, and
living in total retirement! If fortune should for once
smile upon me, and have thrown me into the very
same house! I don't know what to think of it, and
yet so many uncommon circumstances together recall the memory of my misfortunes, and awaken all
the father in my bosom.   I must be satisfied.

Enter MOLLY *crossing the stage.*

Sir Wil. Madam! will you permit me to speak one
word to you ?

Mol. (*Coming forward.*) If you please—what is
your pleasure, sir ?

Sir Wil. I presume, madam, you are the charming young woman I heard of ?

Mol. I have a few charms in the eyes of some folks,
sir, sure enough.

Sir Wil. And you are a native of Scotland, they tell me?

Mol. I am, at your service, sir.

Sir Wil. Will you give me leave to ask the name of your family? Who is your father?

Mol. I really don't remember my father.

Sir Wil. Ha! not remember him, do you say?
(*Earnestly.*

Mol. No, sir, but I have been told that he was—

Sir Wil. Who, madam?

Mol. One of the most eminent bakers in Aberdeen, sir.

Sir Wil. Oh, I conceive! You live, I suppose, with the young lady I meant to speak to. I mistook you for the lady herself.

Mol. You did me a great deal of honour, I assure you, sir.

Sir Wil. But you are acquainted with your mistress's family?

Mol. Family, sir!

Sir Wil. Ay, who are her parents?

Mol. She comes of very creditable parents, I promise you, sir.

Sir Wil. I don't doubt it; but who are they? I have particular reasons for inquiring.

Mol. Very likely so, but I must beg to be excused, sir.

Sir Wil. Of what age is your mistress? you will tell me that at least.

Mol. Oh, as to her age, she don't care who knows that, she is too young to deny her age yet a while. She is about one-and-twenty, sir.

Sir Wil. Precisely the age of my Amelia. (*Apart.*) One-and-twenty, you say? (*To* MOLLY.

Mol. Yes, sir, and I am about two-and-twenty; there is no great difference between us.

Sir Wil. (*Apart.*) It must be so; her age, her country, her manner of living, all concur to prove her mine, my dear child, whom I left to taste of misfortune from the cradle.

Mol. (*Apart.*) What is he muttering, I wonder, I wish this one-and-twenty has not turned the old gentleman's head.

Sir Wil. Let me beg the favour of you to conduct me to your mistress; I want to speak with her.

Mol. She will see no company, sir; she is indisposed, she is in great affliction, and receives no visits at all.

Sir Wil. Mine is not a visit of form or ceremony, or even impertinent curiosity; but on the most urgent business. Tell her I am her fellow countryman.

Mol. What! are you of Scotland too, sir?

Sir Wil. I am. Tell her I take part in her afflictions, and may, perhaps, bring her some consolation.

Mol. There is something mighty particular about this old gentleman! He has not brought another two hundred pounds, sure! (*Apart.*) Well, sir, since you are so very pressing, since you say you are our fellow-countryman, if you will walk this way, I'll speak to my mistress, and see what I can do for you.

Sir Wil. I am obliged to you. (*Exit* MOLLY.) And now, if I may trust the forebodings of an old fond heart, I am going to throw my arms about my daughter.   (*Exit.*

As SIR WILLIAM *follows* MOLLY *out on one side,* SPATTER *appears on the other.*

SPATTER *alone.*

There they go! what the deuce can that old fellow and Amelia's maid do together? The slut is certainly conducting him to her mistress! In less than half an hour I expect that Amelia will be apprehended. In the mean time I must be upon the watch; for, since I have laid the information, it is high time that I should collect some materials to support it.—Who comes here? Lord Falbridge's valet de chambre : his errand is to Amelia, without doubt ; something may be learnt there, perhaps.

Enter LA FRANCE.

Ha! Monsieur La France! your servant.

La Fr. Serviteur! ver glad to see you, Monsieur Spatter.

Spat. Well; what brings you here, eh, Monsieur La France?

La Fr. Von lettre, monsieur.

Spat. A letter to whom?

La Fr. From my lor to Mademoiselle Amelie.

Spat. Oh, you're mistaken, monsieur; that letter is for Lady Alton.

La Fr. Lady Alton! no, *ma foi!* it be for mademoiselle. I am no mistake. *Je ne me trompe pas la dessus.*

Spat. Why, have not you carried several letters from Lord Falbridge to Lady Alton?

La Fr. *Oh, que oui!* but dis be for de young laty dat lif here ; for mademoiselle : mi lor lov her! *ma foi*, he lov her *à la folie.*

Spat. And he loved Lady Alton *a la folie*, did not he?

La Fr. *Oh, que non!* he lov her so *gentely! si tranquiliment ; ma foi*, he lov her *a la Françoise.*— But now he lov mademoiselle, he no eat, no sleep, no speak, but mademoiselle ; no tink but of mademoiselle ; quite an oder ting, Monsieur Spatter, quite an oder ting!

Spat. Well, well; no matter for that; the letter is for Lady Alton, I promise you.

La Fr. *Ah, pardonnez moi!*

Spat. It is, I assure you ; and to convince you of it, see here, monsieur! Lady Alton has sent you five guineas to pay the postage.

La Fr. Five guineas! *ma foi*, I believe I was mistake, indeed.

Spat. Ay, ay; I told you you were mistaken : and,
after all, if it should not be for her ladyship, she will
inclose it in another case, and send it to Amelia, and
nobody will be the wiser.

La Fr. *Fort bien ;* ver well; *la voila. (Gives the
letter.)* I have got five guinées ; I don't care.

Spat. Why should you? Where's the harm, if one
woman should receive a letter written to another ?
There will be nothing lost by it ; for if Amelia don't
receive this, she will receive others ; and letters of
this sort are all alike, you know.

La Fr. Begar dat is ver true.   Adieu, sir.—I have
execute my commission : adieu. *Oh ! je fais bien mes
commissions, moi !*   [*Exit.*

SPATTER *alone.*

See the effects of secret-service-money! Intelligence must be paid for ; and the bribing couriers is
a fair stratagem, by all the laws of war.   Shall I break
open this letter ; or carry it to Lady Alton as it is ?
No, I'll read it myself, that I may have the credit of
communicating the contents.   Let me see ! (*Opens
the letter and reads.*) " Thou dearest, most respectable, and most virtuous of women !" So! this is *a la
folie,* indeed, as Monsieur La France calls it.—" If
any consideration could add to my remorse for the
injury I have offered you, it would be the discovery
of your real character."   Ah, ah! " I know who you
are.   I know you are the daughter of the unhappy
Sir William Douglas."—So, so !—"Judge then of the
tumult of my soul, which is only preserved from the
horrors of despair, by the hopes of rendering some
service to the father, which may, perhaps, in some
measure atone for my behaviour to his too justly offended daughter.   Give me leave, this evening, to
sue for my pardon at your feet, and to inform you of

the measures I have taken.   In the mean time believe
me unalterably yours.   FALBRIDGE."
This is a precious pacquet, indeed.—Now if I could
discover the father too!—His lordship's visit will be
too late in the evening, I fancy ; the lady will not
be at home; but before she goes, once more to my
old trade of eaves-dropping about her apartments!
The old gentleman and she are certainly together,
and their conversation perhaps may be curious.   At
all events, Lady Alton must be gratified.   Men of
letters never get any thing of their patrons, but by
sacrificing to their foibles.   [*Exit.*

SCENE II,

AMELIA'S *Apartment.*

SIR WILLIAM DOUGLAS *and* AMELIA *discovered*
sitting.

Sir Wil. Every word you utter touches me to the
soul.   Nothing but such noble sentiments could have
supported your spirit under so many misfortunes.

Amel. Perhaps it is to my misfortunes that I owe
those sentiments ; had I been brought up in ease and
luxury, my mind, which has learnt fortitude from
distress, might have been enfeebled by prosperity.

Sir Wil. Thou most amiable of thy sex, I conjure
thee to hide nothing from me.   You say you were
born at Aberdeen ; you confess that you are derived
from one of those unhappy families who suffered
themselves to be so fatally deluded, and drawn from
their allegiance to the best of kings.   Why, why then,

will you not tell me all ? Why do you endeavour to conceal your name and family ?

Amel. My duty to my family obliges me to silence. My father's life is forfeited by the sentence of the law; and he owes his existence at this hour to flight or secrecy. He may be in England; he may, for aught I know, be in London ; and the divulging my name and family might create a fresh search after him, and expose him to new perils. Your conversation, it is true, has inspired me with respect and tenderness ; but yet you are a stranger to me ; I have reason to fear every thing, and one word may undo me.

Sir Wil. Alas ! one word may make us both happy. Tell me ; of what age were you when your cruel fortune separated you from your father?

Amel. An infant; so young, that I have not the least traces of him in my memory.

Sir Wil. And your mother; what became of her ?

Amel. She, as I have often heard, was carried off by a fever, while she was preparing to embark with me, to follow the fortunes of my father. He, driven almost to despair by this last stroke of ill fortune, continually shifted his place of residence abroad ; but for some years past, whether by his death, the miscarriage of letters, the infidelity of friends, or other accidents, I have not received the least intelligence of him : and now I almost begin to despair of hearing of him again, though I still persist in my inquiries.

Sir Wil. (*Rising.*) It must be so ; it is as I imagined. All these touching circumstances are melancholy witnesses of the truth of it. Yes, my child ! I am that unhappy father whom you lost so early : I am that unfortunate husband, whom death and my unhappy fate, almost at the very same period, divorced from the best of wives ; I am—I am Sir William Douglas.

Amel. Sir William Douglas ! have I lived to see

my father! then heaven has heard my prayers; this
is the first moment of my unfortunate life. (*Embracing.*)—And yet your presence here fills me with apprehensions; I tremble for your safety, for your life;
how durst you venture your person in this kingdom?
how can you expose yourself to the danger of discovery in this town? My whole soul is in a tumult of
fear and joy.

Sir Wil. Do not be alarmed, my Amelia; fear nothing; heaven begins to smile upon my fortune. To
find thee so unexpectedly, to find thee with a mind
so superior to distress, softens the anguish of my past
life, and gives me happy omens of the future.

Amel. Oh, sir! by the joy I receive from the embraces of a father, let me conjure you to provide for
your safety! do not expose me to the horror of losing
you for ever! Quit this town immediately; every
moment that you remain in it, is at the hazard of your
life; I am ready to accompany you to any part of
the world.

Sir Wil. My dear child! how I grieve that your
youth and virtue should be involved in my misfortunes! Yes, we will quit this kingdom; prepare for
your departure, and we may leave London this even·
ing.

Enter OWEN *hastily.*

Ha! Owen! thou art come at a happy moment; I
have found my daughter. This is your young mistress, the paragon of her sex, my dear, my amiable
Amelia.

Owen. Oh, sir, this is no time for congratulation.
You are in the most imminent danger.

Sir Wil. What is the matter?

Owen. The officers of government are at this instant in the house. I saw them enter; I heard them
say they had authority to apprehend some suspected

person, and I ran immediately to inform you of your danger.

Amel. Oh, heaven! My father, what will you do?

Owen. Do not be alarmed, sir; we are two; we are armed; and we may perhaps be able to make our way through them; I will stand by you to the last drop of my blood.

Sir Wil. Thou faithful creature! Stay, Owen; our fears may betray us; till we are sure we are attacked, let us shew no signs of opposition.

Enter MOLLY, *hastily.*

Mol. My dear mistress! we are ruined; we are undone for ever.

Amel. There are officers of justice in the house; I have heard it; tell me, tell me this instant, whom do they seek for?

Mol. For you, madam; for you; they have a warrant to apprehend you, they say.

Amel. But they have no warrant to apprehend any body else?

Mol. No, madam; nobody else; but I will follow you to the end of the world.

Amel. My dear Polly, I did not mean you. Retire, sir! (*To* SIR WILLIAM.) For heaven's sake leave me to their mercy; they can have no facts against me; my life has been as innocent as unfortunate, and I must soon be released.

Sir Wil. No, my child; I will not leave thee.

Mol. My child! This is Sir William Douglas then, as sure as I am alive!

Sir Wil. Besides, retiring at such a time might create suspicion, and incur the danger we would wish to avoid.

Mol. They will be in the room in a moment; I think I hear them upon the stairs; they would have been here before me, if Mr Freeport had not come in and stopt them.

Sir Wil. Courage, my dear Amelia!

Amel. Alas, sir! I have no terrors but for you!

Owen. They are here, sir.

Mol. Oh, lord! here they are indeed; I am frighted out of my wits.

Enter MRS GOODMAN, FREEPORT, *and Officer.*

Free. A warrant to seize her? A harmless young woman? it is impossible.

Offi. Pardon me, sir; if the young lady goes by the name of Amelia Walton, I have a warrant to apprehend her.

Free. On what account?

Offi. As a dangerous person.

Free. Dangerous!

Offi. Yes, sir; suspected of disaffection and treasonable practices.

Amel. I am the unhappy object of your search, sir; give me leave to know the substance of the accusation.

Offi. I cannot tell you particulars, madam: but information upon oath has been made against you, and I am ordered to apprehend you.

Mrs Good. But you will accept of bail, sir? I will be bound for all I am worth in the world.

Offi. In these cases, madam, bail is not usual; and if ever accepted at all, it is excessively high, and given by persons of very large property and known character.

Free. Well; my property is large enough, and my character very well known. My name is Freeport.

Offi. I know you very well, sir.

Free. I'll answer for her appearance; I'll be bound in a penalty of five hundred pounds, a thousand, two thousand, or what sum you please.

Offi. And will you enter into the recognizance immediately?

Free. With all my heart, come along.   (*Going.*

Offi. And are you in earnest, sir ?

Free. Ay, to be sure. Why not?

Offi. Because, sir, I'll venture to say there are but few people that place their money on such securities.

Free. So much the worse ; he who can employ it in doing good, places it on the best security, and puts it out at the highest interest in the world.

(*Exit with the Officer.*

Manent SIR WILLIAM DOUGLAS, &c.

Sir Wil. I can hardly trust my eyes and ears ; who is this benevolent gentleman ?

Mrs Good. I don't wonder you are surprised at Mr Freeport's manner of proceeding, sir ; but it is his way. He is not a man of compliment ; but he does the most essential service in less time than others take in making protestations.

Mol. Here he is again ; heaven reward him !

Re-enter FREEPORT.

Free. So ! that matter is dispatched ; now to our other affairs ! this is a busy day with me.—Look ye, Sir William ; we must be brief ; there is no time to be lost.

Sir Wil. How ! am I betrayed then ?

Free. Betrayed ! no ; but you are discovered.

Owen. What ! my master discovered !

(*Offers to draw.*

Free. (*To* OWEN.) Nay, never clap thy hand to thy sword, old Trusty ! your master is in danger, it is true ; but it is not from me, I promise you. Go, and get him a post-chaise ; and let him pack off this instant ; that is the best way of shewing your attachment to him at present.—Twenty years, Sir William, have not made so great an alteration in you, but I knew you the moment I saw you.

Mrs Good. Harbour no distrust of Mr Freeport, sir ; he is one of the worthiest men living.

Amel. I know his worthiness. His behaviour to the officer but this moment, uncommonly generous as it appeared, is not the first testimony he has given me to-day of his noble disposition.

Free. Noble! pshaw! nonsense!

Sir Wil. (*To* FREEPORT.) Sir, the kind manner in which you have been pleased to interest yourself in my affairs, has almost as much overpowered me, as if you had surprised me with hostile proceedings. Which way shall I thank you for your goodness to me and my Amelia?

Free. Don't thank me at all; when you are out of danger, perhaps, I may make a proposal to you, that will not be disagreeable; at present think of nothing but your escape; for I should not be surprised, if they were very shortly to make you the same compliment they have paid to Amelia; and in your case, which is really a serious one, they might not be in the humour to accept of my recognizance.

Mrs Good. Mr Freeport is in the right, sir; every moment of delay is hazardous; let us prevail upon you to depart immediately! Amelia being wholly innocent, cannot be long detained in custody, and as soon as she is released, I will bring her to you, wherever you shall appoint.

Free. Ay, ay, you must be gone directly, sir! and as you may want ready money upon the road, take my purse.   (*Offering his purse.*

Sir Wil. No, thou truest friend, I have no need of it. With what wonderful goodness have you acted towards me and my unhappy family!

Free. Wonderful! why wonderful? Would not you have done the same, if you had been in my place?

Sir Wil. I hope I should.

Free. Well then, where is the wonder of it? Come, come, let us see you make ready for your departure.

Sir Wil. Thou best of men!

Free. Best of men ! Heaven forbid ! I have done no more than my duty by you. I am a man myself; and am bound to be a friend to all mankind, you know.   [*Exeunt.*

ACT THE FOURTH.

SCENE I.

SPATTER'S *Apartment.*

LADY ALTON, *with a letter in her hand, and* SPATTER.

Lady Al. Thanks, my good Spatter, many thanks for this precious epistle ! more precious at present than one of Ovid, Pliny, or Cicero. It is at once a billet-doux and a state paper ; and serves at the same time to convict her of conspiring against me and the public.

Spat. It is a valuable manuscript, to be sure, madam ; and yet that is but the least half of my discoveries since I left your ladyship.

Lady Al. But is not this half, according to the Grecian axiom, more than the whole, Mr Spatter ?

Spat. When you know the whole, I believe you will think not, madam.

Lady Al. Out with it then! I am impatient to be mistress of it.

Spat. By intercepting this letter of Lord Falbridge's,

your ladyship sees that we have discovered Amelia
to be the daughter of Sir William Douglas.

Lady Al. True.

Spat. But what would you say, madam, if I had
found out the father himself too ?

Lady Al. Sir William Douglas !

Spat. Is now in this house, madam.

Lady Al. Impossible !

Spat. Nothing more certain. He arrived this
morning under a feigned name. I saw him conduct-
ed to Amelia's apartment. This raised my suspicion,
and I planted myself at her door, with all the circumspection of a spy, and address of a chambermaid.
There I overheard their mutual acknowledgments of
each other ; and a curious interview it was. First
they wept for grief; and then they wept for joy ; and
then they wept for grief again. Their tears, however,
were soon interrupted by the arrival of the officer,
whose purpose was partly defeated, as you have already heard, by the intervention of Freeport.

Lady Al. Yes, the brute ! But that delay was not
half so unfortunate as your discoveries have been
happy, Spatter ; for my revenge shall now return on
them with redoubled fury.—Issue out upon them
once more ; see what they are about ; and be sure
to give me immediate notice if Lord Falbridge should
come.   (*Going.*

Spat. Stay, madam. After intercepting the letter,
I sent for your ladyship, that, at so critical a juncture,
you might be present on the spot : and if you go
home again, we shall lose time, which perhaps may
be precious, in running to and fro. Suppose you step
into the study till I return. You will find my own
answer to my last pamphlet, and the two first sheets
of the next month's magazine, to amuse you.

Lady Al. Planned like a wise general ! Do you
then go, and reconnoitre the enemy, while I lie here
in ambush to reinforce you as soon as there shall be

occasion. Do but give the word, we'll make a vigorous sally, put their whole body to rout, and take
Amelia and her father prisoners. [*Exeunt severally.*

SCENE II.

The Hall.

FREEPORT *alone.*

I don't know how it is, but this Amelia here runs
in my head strangely.   Ever since I saw her, I think
of nothing else.   I am not in love with her.—In love
with her! that's nonsense.   But I feel a kind of uneasiness, a sort of pain that—I don't know what to
make of it—I'll speak to her father about her.

Enter OWEN.

Well, old true-penny! Have you prepared every
thing for Sir William's departure?

Owen. We had need be going, indeed, sir; we are
in continual danger while we stay here. Who d'ye
think lodged the information against madam Amelia?

Free. Who?

Owen. A person who lodges in this very house, it
seems : one Mr Spatter, sir.

Free. Spatter! how d'ye know?

Owen. I had it from one of the officers who came
to apprehend her.

Free. A dog! I could find it in my heart to cut
off his ears with my own hands, and save him the
disgrace of the pillory.

Owen. My poor master is always unfortunate. If
Lord Brumpton had lived a week longer, Sir William

might perhaps have been out of the reach of their malice.

Free. Lord Brumpton?

Owen. Yes, sir. He was soliciting my master's pardon; but died before he had accomplished his benevolent intentions.

Free. Ha! A thought strikes me. (*Apart.*) Hark ye, friend, (*To* OWEN.) does Sir William know the present Lord Brumpton?

Owen. No, sir. The late lord had no children, or near relations, living; and, indeed, he was the only surviving friend of my poor master in the kingdom.

Free. Is the chaise at the door?

Owen. Not yet, sir; but I expect it every moment.

Free. Run to your master, and desire him not to go till I see him. Tell him I am going out upon his business, and will be back within this hour.

Owen. I will let him know immediately.—Ah, you're a true friend indeed, sir!

(*Shaking him earnestly by the hand.*

Free. Pooh! pr'ythee!

Owen. Ah! Heaven preserve you!   (*Exit.*

FREEPORT *alone.*

Fare thee well, old Honesty!—By the death of Lord Brumpton, without children or near relations living, as Owen says, the title and estate came to my old friend Jack Brumpton, of Liverpool; who is of a distant branch; a fortieth cousin, for aught I know; who has past his whole life in a compting-house; and who, a few years ago, no more dreamt of being a lord than Grand Signior, or Great Mogul. He has so good a heart, that I believe it is impossible even for a title to corrupt it. I know he is in town; so I'll go to him immediately; acquaint him with the obligation entailed on him to be of service to Sir William, and make him heir to the benevolence of his predecessor as well as his wealth and dignity. (*Going, stops.*) Who's here? Mrs Goodman and Spatter, as I live! Oh the dog! my blood rises at the villain. If I don't take care, I shall incur an action of battery for caning the rascal.

Enter MRS GOODMAN *and* SPATTER.

Mrs Good. In short, Mr Spatter, I must beg leave to give you warning, and desire that you would provide yourself with another lodging as soon as possible.

Spat. What now? What the deuce is the matter with you, Mrs Goodman?

Mrs Good. I see now the meaning of Lady Alton's recommendation of such a lodger to my house, as well as of her visits to Amelia, and her frequent conferences with you, sir.

Spat. The woman is certainly out of her senses.

Free. What has been laid to your charge is no joke, sir.

Spat. What! are you there to keep up her back-hand, Mr Freeport? What is all this?

Free. You are found out to be a spy, sir.

Mrs Good. A person who pries in the secrets of families merely to betray them.

Free. An informer.

Mrs Good. An eaves-dropper.

Free. A liar.

Spat. Right-hand and left! this is too much: what the plague is the matter with you both?

Mrs Good. Did not you go and tell that Amelia was a native of Scotland?

Spat. Well; and where's the harm of being born in Scotland?

Free. None; except by your malicious interpretation, rascal; by means of which you made it the ground of an information against her, and were the cause of her being apprehended.

Spat. And you were the cause of her being released: every man in his way, Mr Freeport!

Free. Look you, sirrah! you are one of those wretches, who miscall themselves authors; a fellow, whose heart, and tongue, and pen, are equally scandalous; who try to insinuate yourself every where, to make mischief if there is none, and to increase it if you find any.—But if you fetch and carry like a spaniel, you must be treated like one. I have observed that you are always loitering in the passages; but if I catch you within the wind of a door again, I'll beat you till you are as black as your own ink, sirrah. Now you know my mind.   [*Exit.*

Spat. Very civil and very polite, indeed, Mr Freeport. Ha! here comes my friend Lord Falbridge.

Mrs Good. Lord Falbridge your friend! For shame, Mr Spatter!

Enter Lord Falbridge *hastily.*

Ld Fal. Mrs Goodman, I rejoice to see you. Tell me, how does my Amelia? I have heard of her distress, and flew to her relief. Was she alarmed? Was she terrified?

Mrs Good. Not much, my lord: she sustained the shock with the same constancy that she endures every other affliction.

Ld Fal. I know her merit; I am too well acquainted with her greatness of soul; and hope it is not yet too late for me to do justice to her virtue.—Go to her, my dear Mrs Goodman, and tell her I beg to see her: I have something that concerns her very nearly to impart to her.

Mrs Good. I will, my lord.   [*Exit.*

Ld Fal. Oh, Mr Spatter! I did not see you. What have you got there, sir?

(*Seeing a paper in his hand.*

Spat. Proposals for a new work, my lord! May I beg the honour of your lordship's name among my list of subscribers?

Ld Fal. With all my heart, sir. I am already in your debt on another account.

(*Pulling out his purse.*

Spat. To me, my lord? You do me a great deal of honour; I should be very proud to be of the least service to your lordship.

Ld Fal. You have been of great service to me already, sir. It was you, I find, lodged the information against this young lady.

Spat. I did no more than my duty, my lord.

Ld Fal. Yes, you did me a favour, sir. I consider only the deed, and put the intention quite out of the question. You meant to do Amelia a prejudice, and you have done me a service: for, by endeavouring to bring her into distress, you gave me an opportunity of shewing my eagerness to relieve her.—There, sir! there is for the good you have done, while you meant to make mischief. (*Giving him a few guineas.*) But take this along with it; if you ever presume to mention the name of Amelia any more, or give yourself the least concern about her, or her affairs, I'll—

Spat. I am obliged to your lordship.   (*Bowing.*

Ld Fal. Be gone, sir, leave me.

Spat. Your most humble servant, my lord!—So! I am abused by every body, and yet I get money by every body;—egad, I believe I am a much cleverer fellow than I thought I was.   [*Exit.*

LORD FALBRIDGE *alone.*

Alas! I am afraid that Amelia will not see me! What would I not suffer to repair the affront that I have offered her!

Enter MOLLY.

Ha! Polly! how much am I obliged to you for sending me notice of Amelia's distress!

Mol. Hush, my lord! Speak lower, for heaven's sake! My mistress has so often forbad me to tell any thing about her, that I tremble still at the thoughts of the confidence I have put in you. I was bewitched, I think, to let you know who she was.

Ld Fal. You were inspired, Polly, heaven inspired you to acquaint me with all her distresses, that I might recommend myself to her favour again, by my zeal to serve her, though against her will.

Mol. That was the reason I told you, for else I am sure I should die with grief to give her the least uneasiness.

Ld Fal. But may I hope to see Amelia? Will she let me speak with her?

Mol. No indeed, my lord, she is so offended at your late behaviour, that she will not even suffer us to mention your name to her.

Ld Fal. Death and confusion! What a wretch have I made myself! Go, Polly, go and let her know that I must speak with her; inform her that I have been active for her welfare, and have authority to release her from the information lodged against her.

Mol. I will let her know your anxiety, my lord, but indeed I am afraid she will not see you.

Ld Fal. She must, Polly, she must. The agonies of my mind are intolerable: tell her, she must come, if it be but for a moment, or else, in the bitterness of despair, I fear I shall break into her apartment, and throw myself at her feet.

Mol. Lud! you frighten me out of my wits! Have a little patience, and I'll tell my mistress what a taking you are in.

Ld Fal. Fly, then! I can taste no comfort, till I hear her resolution.   (*Exit* MOLLY.

LORD FALBRIDGE *alone*.

How culpably have I acted towards the most amiable of her sex! But I will make her every reparation in my power. The warmth and sincerity of my

repentance shall extort forgiveness from her. By
heaven, she comes !—Death ! how sensibly does an
ungenerous action abase us ! I am conscious of the
superiority of her virtue, and almost dread the encounter.

Enter AMELIA.

Amel. I understand, my lord, that by your application I am held free of the charge laid against me ;
and that I am once more entirely at liberty. I am
truly sensible of your good offices, and thank you for
the trouble you have taken.   (*Going.*

Ld Fal. Stay, madam ! do not leave me in still
greater distraction than you found me. If my zeal
to serve you has had any weight with you, it must
have inspired you with more favourable dispositions
towards me.

Amel. You must pardon me, my lord, if I cannot
so soon forget a very late transaction. After that
all your proceedings alarm me : nay, even your present zeal to serve me creates new suspicions, while I
cannot but be doubtful of the motives from which it
proceeds.

Ld Fal. Cruel Amelia ! for, guilty as I am,   I
must complain, since it was your own diffidence that
was in part the occasion of my crime.—Why did you
conceal your rank and condition from me ? Why did
not you tell me, that you were the daughter of the
unhappy Sir William Douglas?

Amel. Who told you that I was so, my lord ?

Ld Fal. Nay, do not deny it now : it is in vain to
attempt to conceal it any longer ; it was the main
purport of my letter to apprise you of my knowledge
of it.

Amel. Your letter, my lord !

Ld Fal. Yes, wild as it was, it was the offspring
of compunction and remorse ; and if it conveyed the

dictates of my soul, it spoke me the truest of peni-
tents. You did not disdain to read it, sure ?

Amel. Indeed, my lord, I never received any letter from you.

Ld Fal. Not received any! I sent it this very morning. My own servant was the messenger. What
can this mean ? Has he betrayed me ? At present,
suffer me to compensate, as far as possible, for the
wrongs I have done you : receive my hand and heart,
and let an honourable marriage obliterate the very
idea of my past conduct.

Amel. No, my lord, you have discovered me, it is
true : I am the daughter of Sir William Douglas.
Judge for yourself then, and think how I ought to
look upon a man who has insulted my distress, and
endeavoured to tempt me to dishonour my family.

Ld Fal. Your justice must acquit me of the intention of that offence, since at that time I was ignorant of your illustrious extraction.

Amel. It may be so, yet your excuse is but an
aggravation of the crime. You imagined me, perhaps, to be of as low and mean an origin as you
thought me poor and unhappy. You supposed that
I had no title to any dowry but my honour, no dependence but on my virtue, and yet you attempted
to rob me of that virtue, which was the only jewel
that could raise the meanness of my birth, or support me under my misfortunes; which, instead of
relieving, you chose to make the pander to your vile
inclinations.

Ld Fal. Thou most amiable of thy sex, how I
adore thee! Even thy resentment renders thee more
lovely in my eyes, and makes thee, if possible, dearer to me than ever. Nothing but our union can
ever make me happy.

Amel. Such an union must not, cannot be.

Ld Fal. Why ? What should forbid it ?

Amel. My father.

Ld Fal. Your father! where is he? In whatever part of the world he now resides, I will convey you to him, and he shall ratify our happiness.

Enter MOLLY *hastily.*

Mol. Oh Lord, madam! here's the angry lady coming again—she that made such a racket this morning!

Amel. Lady Alton?

Mol. Yes, madam.

Ld Fal. Lady Alton! Confusion! Stay, madam.

(*To* AMELIA, *who is going.*

Amel. No, my lord, I have endured one affront from her already to-day; why should I expose myself to a second? Her ladyship, you know, has a prior claim to your attention.   (*Exit.*

Ld Fal. Distraction! I had a thousand things to say to her.—Go, my dear Polly, follow my Amelia! Plead earnestly in my behalf, urge all the tenderest things that fancy can suggest, and return to me as soon as Lady Alton is departed.

Mol. I will, my lord. Oh lud! here she is, as I am alive!   [*Exit.*

Ld Fal. Abandoned by Amelia! and hunted by this fury! I shall run wild.

Enter LADY ALTON.

Lady Al. You may well turn away from me; at length I have full conviction of your baseness. I am now assured of my own shame, and your false-hood.   Perfidious monster!

Ld Fal. It is unjust to tax me with perfidy, ma-dam.   I have rather acted with too much sincerity. I long ago frankly declared to you the utter impos-sibility of our reconciliation.

Lady Al. What! after having made your addresses to me? after having sworn the most inviolable af-fection for me? Oh, thou arch-deceiver!

VOL. IX.   T

Ld Fal. I never deceived you : when I professed a passion, I really entertained one ; when I made my addresses to you, I wished to call you my wife.

Lady Al. And what can you alledge in excuse of your falsehood ? Have you not been guilty of the blackest perjury ?

Ld Fal. The change of my sentiments needs no excuse from me, madam ; you were yourself the occasion of it.——In spite of the torrent of fashion, and the practice of too many others of, my rank in life, I have a relish for domestic happiness, and have always wished for a wife who might render my home a delightful refuge from the cares and bustle of the world abroad. These were my views with you ; but, thank heaven, your outrageous temper happily betrayed itself in good time, and convinced me that my sole aim in marriage would be frustrated : for I could neither have been happy myself, nor have made you so.

Lady Al. Paltry evasion ! You have abandoned me for your Amelia ; you have meanly quitted a person of letters, a woman of rank and condition, for an illiterate vagabond, a needy adventurer.

Ld Fal. The person you mention, madam, is indeed the opposite of yourself ; she is all meekness, grace, and virtue.

Lady Al. Provoking traitor ! You urge me past all sufferance. I meant to expostulate, but you oblige me to invective.——But, have a care ! You are not so secure as you suppose yourself ; and I may revenge myself sooner than you imagine.

Ld Fal. I am aware of your vindictive disposition, madam ; for I know that you are more envious than jealous, and rather violent than tender ; but the present object of my affections shall be placed above your resentment, and challenge your respect.

Lady Al. Away, fond man ! I know that object of your affections better than yourself ; I know who she is ; I know who the stranger is that arrived for

her this morning, I know all : men more powerful
than yourself shall be apprised of the whole immediately, and within these two hours, nay, within this
hour, you shall see the unworthy object, for which
you have slighted me, with all that is dear to her and
you, torn away from you perforce. (*Going.*

Ld Fal. Ha! how's this? Stay, madam! Explain
yourself! But one word, do but hear me.

Lady Al. No, I disdain to hear you : I scorn an explanation. I have discovered the contemptible cause
of your inconstancy, and know you to be mean, base,
false, treacherous, and perfidious. You have forfeited my tenderness, and be assured you shall feel the
effects of my revenge. (*Exit.*

Ld Fal. What does she mean? The stranger that
arrived to day!—That arrived for my Amelia! Sure
it cannot be. (*Pausing.*) Is it possible that——
(*Re-enter* MOLLY.) Ha, Polly! explain these riddles to me. Lady Alton threatens me, she threatens
my Amelia : does she know any thing? Her fury
will transport her to every extravagance : how dreadful is jealousy in a woman!

Mol. Ay, it is a dreadful thing, indeed, my lord.
Well, heaven send me always to be in love, and
never to be jealous!

Ld Fal. But she talked of tearing Amelia from
me perforce—and then some stranger—she threatens him too ; what is it she means?

Mol. What, a gentleman that came to madam
Amelia! (*Alarmed.*

Ld Fal. Yes, to Amelia ; and arrived this very
day, she says.

Mol. We are ruin'd for ever : she means Sir William Douglas!

Ld Fal. The father of my Amelia! Is he here?

Mol. Yes, my lord, I was bound to secrecy ; but
I can't help telling you the whole truth, because I

am sure you will do all in your power to be of service to us.

Ld Fal. You know my whole soul, Polly: this
outrageous woman's malice shall be defeated.

Mol. Heaven send it may.

Ld Fal. Be assured it shall: do not alarm your
mistress, I fly to serve her, and will return as soon
as possible.

Mol. I shall be miserable till we see you again, my
lord.   [*Exit.*

Ld Fal. And now, good heaven! that art the protection of innocence, second my endeavours! enable
me to repair the affront I have offered to injured virtue, and let me relieve the unhappy from their distresses!   [*Exit.*

———

ACT THE FIFTH.

SCENE I.

Continues.

LORD FALBRIDGE *and* MOLLY *meeting.*

Mol. Oh, my lord! I am glad to see you returned.

Ld Fal. Where is your mistress?   (*Eagerly.*

Mol. In her own chamber.

Ld Fal. And where is Sir William Douglas?

Mol. With my mistress.

Ld Fal. And have there been no officers here to apprehend them?

Mol. Officers! No, my lord. Officers! you frighten me. I was in hopes, by seeing your lordship so soon again, that there were some good news for us.

Ld Fal. Never was any thing so unfortunate. The noble persons, to whom I meant to make application, were out of town; nor could by any means be seen or spoken with till to-morrow morning: and, to add to my distraction, I learnt that a new information had been made, and a new warrant issued to apprehend Sir William Douglas and Amelia.

Mol. O dear! What can we do then?

Ld Fal. Do! I shall run mad. Go, my dear Polly, go to your mistress and Sir William, and inform them of their danger. Every moment is precious, but perhaps they may yet have time to escape.

Mol. I will, my lord!   (*Going.*

Ld Fal. Stay! (Molly *returns.*) My chariot is at the door; tell them not to wait for any other carriage, but to get into that, and drive away immediately.

Mol. I will, my lord. Oh dear! I never was so terrified in all my life.   (*Exit.*

Lord Falbridge *alone.*

If I can but save them now, we may gain time for mediation. Ha! what noise? Are the officers coming? Who's here?

Enter La France.

La Fr. Milor, Mons. le Duc de——

Ld Fal. Sirrah! Villain! You have been the occasion of all this mischief. By your carelessness, or treachery, Lady Alton has intercepted my letter to Amelia.

La Fr. Ledy Alton?

Ld Fal. Yes, dog; did not I send you here this morning with a letter?

La Fr. Oui, Milor.

Ld Fal. And did you bring it here, rascal?

La Fr. Oui, Milor.

Ld Fal. No, sirrah, you did not bring it; the lady never received any letter from me, she told me so herself—whom did you give it to? (LA FRANCE *hesitates.*) Speak, sirrah, or I'll shake your soul out of your body. (*Shaking him.*

La Fr. I give it to——

Ld Fal. Who, rascal?

La Fr. Monsieur Spatter.

Ld Fal. Mr Spatter?

La Fr. Oui, Milor, he promis to give it to Mademoiselle Amelie, vid his own hand.

Ld Fal. I shall soon know the truth of that, sir, for yonder is Mr Spatter himself: run, and tell him I desire to speak with him!

La Fr. Oui, Milor;—*ma foi,* I was very near kesh; I never was in more *vilain embarras* in all my life.
(*Exit.*

LORD FALBRIDGE *alone.*

My letter's falling into the hands of that fellow accounts for every thing. The contents instructed him concerning Amelia. What a wretch I am! Destined every way to be of prejudice to that virtue which I am bound to adore.

Re-enter LA FRANCE *with* SPATTER.

Spat. Monsieur la France tells me that your lordship desires to speak with me; what are your commands, my lord? (*Pertly.*

Ld Fal. The easy impudence of the rascal puts me out of all patience. (*To himself.*

Spat. My lord!

Ld Fal. The last time I saw you, sir, you were rewarded for the good you had done ; you must expect now to be chastised for your mischief.

Spat. Mischief, my lord ?

Ld Fal. Yes, sir ; where is that letter of mine, which La France tells me he gave you to deliver to a young lady of this house ?

Spat. Oh the devil ! (*Apart.*) Letter, my lord ?
(*Hesitates.*

Ld Fal. Yes, letter, sir ; did not you give it him, La France ?

La Fr. Oui, Milor !

Spat. Y—e—e—s, yes, my lord, I had the letter of Monsieur la France, to be sure, my lord, but——but—

Ld Fal. But what, sirrah ? give me the letter immediately, and if I find that the seal has been broken, I will break every bone in your skin.

Spat. For heaven's sake, my lord !—(*Feeling in his pockets.*) I—I—I have not got the letter about me at present, my lord ; but if you will give me leave to step to my apartment, I'll bring it you immediately.
(*Offering to go.*

Ld Fal. (*Stopping him.*) No, no, that will not do, sir ; you shall not stir, I promise you.—Look ye, rascal ! tell me, what is become of my letter, or I will be the death of you this instant.   (*Drawing.*

Spat. (*Kneeling.*) Put up your sword, my lord ; put up your sword ; and I will tell you every thing in the world.   Indeed I will.

Ld Fal. Well, sir, be quick then !
(*Putting up his sword.*

Spat. Lady Alton——

Ld Fal. Lady Alton ! I thought so—Go on, sir.

Spat. Lady Alton, my lord, desired me to procure her all the intelligence in my power concerning every thing that past between your lordship and Amelia.

Ld Fal. Well, sir, what then?

Spat. A little patience, I entreat your lordship. Accordingly, to oblige her ladyship——one must oblige the ladies, you know, my lord—I did keep a pretty sharp look-out, I must confess; and this morning, meeting Monsieur la France, with a letter from your lordship in his charge, I very readily gave him five guineas of her ladyship's bounty-money, to put it into my hands.

La Fr. *Oh Diable! me voila perdu!*   (*Aside.*

Ld Fal. How! A bribe, rascal?

(*To* LA FRANCE.

La Fr. *Ah, Milor!*   (*On his knees.*

Spat. At the same price for every letter, he would have sold a whole mail, my lord.

La Fr. *Ayez pitie de moi.* (*Holding up his hands.*

Ld Fal. Betray the confidence I reposed in you!

Spat. He offered me the letter of his own accord, my lord.

La Fr. No such ting, *en verité, Milor!*

Spat. Very true, I can assure your lordship.

Ld Fal. Well, well; I shall chastise him at my leisure. At present, sir, do you return me my letter.

Spat. I—I have it not about me, my lord.

Ld Fal. Where is it, rascal? tell me this instant, or—

La Fr. Ledy Alton—

Ld Fal. (*To* SPATTER.) What! has she got it? speak, sirrah!

Spat. She has indeed, my lord.

Ld Fal. Are not you a couple of villains?

La Fr. Oui, Milor.
Spat. Yes, my lord!   } (*Both speak at once.*

Ld Fal. (*To* SPAT.) But hold, sir! a word more with you! As you seem to be Lady Alton's chief agent, I must desire some further information from you.

Spat. Any thing in my power, my lord.

Ld Fal. I can account for her knowledge of Amelia by means of my letter: but how did she discover Sir William Douglas?

Spat. I told her, my lord.

Ld Fal. But how did you discover him yourself?

Spat. By listening, my lord.

Ld Fal. By listening!

Spat. Yes, by listening, my lord! Let me but once be about a house, and I'll engage to clear it, like a ventilator, my lord. There is not a door to a single apartment in this house but I have planted my ear at the key-hole.

Ld Fal. And were these the means by which you procured your intelligence?

Spat. Yes, my lord.

Ld Fal. Impossible.

Spat. Oh dear! nothing so easy; this is nothing at all, my lord! I have given an account of the plays in our Journal, for three months together, without being nearer the stage than the pit-passage; and I have collected the debates of a whole session, for the magazine, only by attending in the lobby.

Ld Fal. Precious rascal!—Ha! who comes here? Lady Alton herself again, as I live!

Spat. (*Apart.*) The devil she is! I wish I was out of the house.

Enter LADY ALTON.

Lady Al. What! still here, my lord? still witnessing to your own shame and the justice of my resentment?

Ld Fal. Yes, I am still here, madam, and sorry to be made a witness of your cruelty and meanness, of your descending to arts so much beneath your rank, and practices so unworthy of your sex.

Lady Al. You talk in riddles, my lord.

Ld Fal. This gentleman shall explain them. Here, madam! here is the engine of your malice, the instrument of your vengeance, your prime minister, Mr Spatter.

Lady Al. What have I to do with Mr Spatter?

Ld Fal. To do mischief, to intercept letters, and break them open, to overhear private conversations, and betray them to—

Lady Al. Have you laid any thing of this kind to my charge, sir? (*To* SPATTER.

Spat. I have been obliged to speak the truth, though much against my will, indeed, madam.

Lady Al. The truth! thou father of lies, did ever any truth proceed from thee? What! is his lordship your new patron! A fit Mæcenas for thee, thou scandal to the belles lettres!

Ld Fal. Your rage at this detection is but a fresh conviction of your guilt.

Lady Al. Do not triumph, monster! you shall still feel the superiority I have over you. The object of your wishes is no longer under your protection, the officers of the government entered the house at the same time with myself, with a warrant to seize both Amelia and her father.

Ld Fal. Confusion! Are not they gone then? La France! villain! run, and bring me word!

La Fr. I go, Milor. (*Exit.*

Lady Al. Do not flatter yourself with any hopes; they have not escaped; here they are, secured in proper hands.

Ld Fal. Death and distraction! now I am completely miserable.

Enter SIR WILLIAM DOUGLAS, AMELIA, OWEN, *and Officers.*

Lady Al. Yes, your misery is complete indeed; and so shall be my revenge. Oh! your servant, madam! (*Turning to* AMELIA.) You now see to what a condition your pride and obstinacy have reduced you. Did not I bid you tremble at the consequences?

Amel. It was here alone that I was vulnerable. (*Holding her father's hand.*) Oh, madam, (*Turning to* LADY ALTON.) by the virtues that should adorn your rank, by the tenderness of your sex, I conjure you pity my distress! do but release my father, and there are no concessions, however humiliating, which you may not exact from me.

Lady Al. Those concessions now come too late, madam. If I were even inclined to relieve you, at present it is not in my power. (*Haughtily.*) Lord Falbridge perhaps may have more interest.

(With a sneer.

Ld Fal. Cruel, insulting woman! (*To* LADY ALTON.) Do not alarm yourself, my Amelia!—Do not be concerned, sir! (*To* SIR WILLIAM.) Your enemies shall still be disappointed. Although ignorant of your arrival, I have for some time past exerted all my interest in your favour, and by the mediation of those still more powerful, I do not despair of success. Your case is truly a compassionate one, and in that breast, from which alone mercy can proceed, thank heaven, there is the greatest reason to expect it.

Sir Wil. I am obliged to you for your concern, sir.

Ld Fal. Oh, I owe you all this, and much more —But this is no time to speak of my offences, or repentance.

Lady Al. This is mere trifling. I thought you knew on what occasion you came hither, sir.

(To the Officer.

Offi. Your reproof is too just, madam. I attend you, sir. (*To* SIR WILLIAM.

Ld Fal. Hold! Let me prevail on you, sir, (*To the Officer.*) to suffer them to remain here till to-morrow morning. I will answer for the consequences.

Offi. Pardon me, my lord! we should be happy to oblige you, but we must discharge the duty of our office.

Ld Fal. Distraction!

Sir Wil. Come then! we follow you, sir! Be comforted, my Amelia! for my sake be comforted! Wretched as I am, your anxiety shocks me more than my own misfortunes.

(*As they are going out, enter* FREEPORT.

Free. Hey-day! what now? the officers here again! I thought we had satisfied you this morning. What is the meaning of all this?

Offi. This will inform you, sir.

(*Giving the warrant.*

Free. How's this? Let me see! (*Reading.*) " This is to require you"—um um—" the bodies of William Ford and Amelia Walton"—um—um—" suspected persons"—um—um—Well! well! I see what this is: but you will accept of bail, sir?

Offi. No, sir; this case is not bailable, and we have already been reprimanded for taking your recognizance this morning.

Sir Wil. Thou good man! I shall ever retain the most lively sense of your behaviour: but your kind endeavours to preserve the poor remainder of my proscribed life are in vain. We must submit to our destiny.   (*All going.*

Free. Hold, hold! one word, I beseech you, sir! (*To the Officer.*) a minute or two will make no difference—Bail then, it seems, will not do, sir?

Offi. No, sir.

Free. Well, well; then I have something here that will perhaps.   (*Feeling in his pocket.*

Ld Fal. How!

Lady Al. What does he mean?

Free. No, it is not there.—It is in t'other pocket, I believe. Here, Sir William! (*Producing a parchment.*) Ask the gentleman if that will not do.—But,

7

first of all, read it yourself, and let us hear how you
like the contents.

Sir Wil. What do I see! (*Opening and perusing
it.*) My pardon! the full and free pardon of my offences! Oh heaven! and is it to you then, to you,
sir, that I owe all this? Thus, thus let me shew my
gratitude to my benefactor! (*Falling at his feet.*

Free. Get up, get up, Sir William! Thank heaven
and the most gracious of monarchs. You have very
little obligation to me, I promise you.

Amel. My father restored! then I am the happiest
of women.

Ld Fal. A pardon! I am transported!

Lady Al. How's this? a pardon!

Free. Under the great seal, madam.

Lady Al. Confusion! what, am I baffled at last
then? am I disappointed even of my revenge?—
Thou officious fool, (*To* FREEPORT.) may these
wretches prove as great a torment to you as they
have been to me! As for thee, (*To* LORD FALBRIDGE.)
thou perfidious monster, may thy guilt prove thy
punishment! May you obtain the unworthy union
you desire! May your wife prove as false to you as
you have been to me! May you be followed, like
Orestes, with the furies of a guilty conscience; find
your error when it is too late; and die in all the horrors of despair! [*Exit.*

Free. There goes a woman of quality for you!
what little actions, and what a great soul!—Ha!
Master Spatter! where are you going?

(*To* SPATTER, *who is sneaking off.*

Spat. Following the muse, sir! (*Pointing after*
LADY ALTON.) But if you have any further commands, or his lordship should have occasion for me
to write his epithalamium—

Ld Fal. Peace, wretch! sleep in a whole skin, and
be thankful! I would solicit mercy myself, and have
not leisure to punish you. Be gone, sir!

Spat. I am obliged to your lordship—This affair will make a good article for the Evening Post to-night, however.   (*Aside, and exit.*

Sir Wil. How happy has this reverse of fortune made me !—But my surprise is almost equal to my joy. May we beg you, sir, (*To* FREEPORT.) to inform us how your benevolence has effected what seems almost a miracle in my favour ?

Free. In two words then, Sir William ; this happy event is chiefly owing to your old friend, the late Lord Brumpton.

Sir Wil. Lord Brumpton!

Free. Yes ; honest Owen there told me that his lordship had been employed in soliciting your pardon. Did not you, Owen?

Owen. I did, sir.

Free. Upon hearing that, and perceiving the danger you were in, I went immediately to the present Lord Brumpton, who is a very honest fellow, and one of the oldest acquaintance I have in the world. He, at my instance, immediately made the necessary application ; and guess how agreeably we were surprised to hear that the late lord had already been successful, and that the pardon had been made out on the very morning of the day his lordship died. Away went I, as fast as a pair of horses could carry me, to fetch it ; and should certainly have prevented this last arrest, if the warrant to apprehend you, as dangerous persons, had not issued under your assumed names of William Ford and Amelia Walton, against whom the information had been laid. But, however, it has only served to prevent your running away, when the danger was over ; for at present, Sir William, thank heaven and his majesty, you are a whole man again ; and you have nothing to do but to make a legal appearance, and to plead the pardon I have brought you, to absolve you from all informations.

Ld Fal. Thou honest excellent man! How happily have you supplied what I failed to accomplish!

Free. Ay, I heard that your lordship had been busy.—You had more friends at court than one, Sir William, I promise you.

Sir Wil. I am overwhelmed with my sudden good fortune, and am poor even in thanks. Teach me, Mr Freeport, teach me how to make some acknowledgment for your extraordinary generosity!

Free. I'll tell you what, Sir William; notwithstanding your daughter's pride, I took a liking to her the moment I saw her.

Ld Fal. Ha! What's this?

Free. What's the matter, my lord?

Ld Fal. Nothing. Go on, sir!

Free. Why then, to confess the truth, I am afraid that my benevolence, which you have all been pleased to praise so highly, had some little leaven of self-interest in it; and I was desirous to promote Amelia's happiness more ways than one.

Ld Fal. Then I am the veriest wretch that ever existed.—But take her, sir! for I must confess that you have deserved her by your proceedings; and that I, fool and villain that I was, have forfeited her by mine. (*Going.*

Free. Hold, hold! one word before you go, if you please, my lord! You may kill yourself for aught I know, but you sha'n't lay your death at my door, I promise you. I had a kindness for Amelia, I must confess; but in the course of my late negotiation for Sir William, hearing of your lordship's pretensions, I dropt all thoughts of her. It is a maxim with me, to do good wherever I can, but always to abstain from doing mischief.—Now, as I can't make the lady happy myself, I would fain put her into the hands of those that can.—So, if you would oblige me, Sir William, let me join these two young folks together, (*Joining their hands.*) and do you say amen to it.

Sir Wil. With all my heart !—You can have no objection, Amelia ?   (AMELIA *bursts into tears.*

Ld Fal. How bitterly do those tears reproach me ! It shall be the whole business of my future life to atone for them.

Amel. Your actions this day, and your solicitude for my father, have redeemed you in my good opinion ; and the consent of Sir William, seconded by so powerful an advocate as Mr Freeport, cannot be contended with.   Take my hand, my lord ! a virtuous passion may inhabit the purest breast; and I am not ashamed to confess, that I had conceived a partiality for you, till your own conduct turned my heart against you ; and if my resentment has given you any pain, when I consider the occasion, I must own that I cannot repent it.

Ld Fal. Mention it no more, my love, I beseech you! You may justly blame your lover, I confess ; but I will never give you cause to complain of your husband.

Free. I don't believe you will.   I give you joy, my lord! I give you all joy.   As 'for you, madam, (*To* AMELIA.) do but shew the world that you can bear prosperity, as well as you have sustained the shocks of adversity, and there are few women who may not wish to be an Amelia.   [*Exeunt.*

DRAMATIS PERSONÆ.

GENERAL SAVAGE,	*Mr King.*
BELVILLE,	*Mr Reddish.*
TORRINGTON,	*Mr Weston.*
LEESON,	*Mr Palmer.*
CAPTAIN SAVAGE,	*Mr Brereton.*
CONNOLLY,	*Mr Moody.*
SPRUCE,	*Mr Baddely.*
GHASTLY,	*Mr W. Palmer.*
LEECH,	*Mr Bransby.*
CROW,	*Mr Wright.*
WOLF,	*Mr Ackman.*
MISS WALSINGHAM,	*Mrs Abington.*
MRS BELVILLE,	*Miss Younge.*
LADY RACHEL MILDEW,	*Mrs Hopkins.*
MRS TEMPEST,	*Mrs Greville.*
MISS LEESON,	*Miss Jarratt.*
Maid,	*Mrs Millidge.*

THE

SCHOOL FOR WIVES.

ACT THE FIRST.

SCENE I.

An Apartment at BELVILLE'S.

Enter CAPTAIN SAVAGE *and* MISS WALSINGHAM.

Capt. Ha! ha! ha! Well, Miss Walsingham, this fury is going; what a noble peal she has rung in Belville's ears!

Miss Wal. Did she see you, Captain Savage?

Capt. No, I took care of that : for though she isn't married to my father, she has ten times the influence of a wife, and might injure me not a little with him, if I didn't support her side of the question.

Miss Wal. It was a pleasant conceit of Mr Bel-

ville, to insinuate the poor woman was disordered in
her senses!

Capt. And did you observe how the termagant's
violence of temper supported the probability of the
charge?

Miss Wal. Yes, she became almost frantic in reality, when she found herself treated like a mad woman.

Capt. Belville's affected surprise too was admirable!

Miss Wal. Yes, the hypocrital composure of his
countenance, and his counterfeit pity for the poor
woman, were intolerable!

Capt. While that amiable creature, his wife, im-
plicitly believed every syllable he said—

Miss Wal. And felt nothing but pity for the accuser, instead of paying the least regard to the accusation. But pray, is it really under a pretence of
getting the girl upon the stage, that Belville has
taken away Mrs Tempest's niece from the people she
boarded with?

Capt. It is: Belville, ever on the look-out for fresh
objects, met her in those primitive regions of purity,
the green-boxes; where, discovering that she was
passionately desirous of becoming an actress, he improved his acquaintance with her, in the fictitious
character of an Irish manager, and she eloped last
night, to be, as she imagines, the heroine of a Dublin
theatre.

Miss Wal. So, then, as he has kept his real name
artfully concealed, Mrs Tempest can at most but
suspect him of Miss Leeson's seduction.

Capt. Of no more, and this only from the description of the people who saw him in company with
her at the play: but I wish the affair may not have
a serious conclusion; for she has a brother, a very
spirited young fellow, who is a counsel in the Tem-

ple, and who will certainly call Belville to an account
tho moment he hears of it.

Miss Wal. And what will become of the poor creature after he has deserted her?

Capt. You know that Belville is generous to profusion, and has a thousand good qualities to counter-
balance this single fault of gallantry, which contami-
nates his character.

Miss Wal. You men! you men!—You are such
wretches that there's no having a moment's satisfaction with you! and what's still more provoking,
there's no having a moment's satisfaction without
you!

Capt. Nay, don't think us all alike.

Miss Wal. I'll endeavour to deceive myself; for it
is but a poor argument of your sincerity, to be the
confidant of another's falsehood.

Capt. Nay, no more of this, my love; no people
live happier than Belville and his wife; nor is there
a man in England, notwithstanding all his levity, who
considers his wife with a warmer degree of affection:
if you have a friendship, therefore, for her, let her
continue in an error so necessary to her repose, and
give no hint whatever of his gallantries to any body.

Miss Wal. If I had no pleasure in obliging you,
I have too much regard for Mrs Belville not to follow your advice; but you need not enjoin me so
strongly on the subject, when you know I can keep
a secret.

Capt. You are all goodness, and the prudence with
which you have concealed our private engagements
has eternally obliged me; had you trusted the secret
even to Mrs Belville, it wou'dn't have been safe; she
would have told her husband, and he is such a rattle-
skull, that, notwithstanding all his regard for me, he
wou'd have mentioned it in some moment of levity,
and sent it in a course of circulation to my father.

Miss Wal. The peculiarity of your father's temper, joined to my want of fortune, made it necessary

for me to keep our engagements inviolably secret;
there is no merit, therefore, either in my prudence,
or in my labouring assiduously to cultivate the good
opinion of the general, since both were so necessary
to my own happiness : don't despise me for this acknowledgment.

Capt. Bewitching softness!—But your goodness, I
flatter myself, will be speedily rewarded ; you are now
such a favourite with him, that he is eternally talking
of you ; and I really fancy he means to propose you
to me himself; for last night, in a few minutes after
he had declared you would make the best wife in the
world, he seriously asked me if I had any aversion to
matrimony ?

Miss Wal. Why, that was a very great concession
indeed, as he seldom stoops to consult any body's inclinations.

Capt. So it was, I assure you; for, in the army,
being used to nothing but command and obedience,
he removes the discipline of the parade into his family, and no more expects his orders shou'd be dispu-
ted, in matters of a domestic nature, than if they
were delivered at the head of his regiment.

Miss Wal. And yet Mrs Tempest, who you say is
as much a storm in her nature as her name, is dis-
puting them eternally.

Enter MR *and* MRS BELVILLE.

Bel. Well, Miss Walsingham, hav'n't we had a
pretty morning's visitor ?

Miss Wal. Really, I think so ; and I have been
asking Captain Savage how long the lady has been
disordered in her senses ?

Bel. Why will they let the poor woman abroad
without some body to take care of her ?

Capt. O, she has her lucid intervals.

Miss Wal. I declare I shall be as angry with you
as I am with Belville.   (*Aside to the Captain.*

Mrs Bel. You can't think how sensibly she spoke at first.

Bel. I should have had no conception of her madness, if she hadn't brought so preposterous a charge against me.

Enter a Servant.

Serv. Lady Rachel Mildew, madam, sends her compliments, and if you are not particularly engaged, will do herself the pleasure of waiting upon you.

Mrs Bel. Our compliments, and we shall be glad to see her ladyship.   (*Exit Servant.*

Bel. I wonder if Lady Rachel knows that Torrington came to town last night from Bath.

Mrs Bel. I hope he has found benefit by the waters, for he is one of the best creatures existing; he's a downright parson Adams in good nature and simplicity.

Miss Wal. Lady Rachel will be quite happy at his return, and it would be a laughable affair, if a match could be brought about between the old maid and the old bachelor.

Capt. Mr Torrington is too much taken up at Westminster-Hall, to think of paying his devoirs to the ladies, and too plain a speaker, I fancy, to be agreeable to Lady Rachel.

Bel. You mistake the matter widely ; she is deeply smitten with him ; but honest Torrington is utterly unconscious of his conquest, and modestly thinks that he has not a single attraction for any woman in the universe.

Mrs Bel. Yet my poor aunt speaks sufficiently plain, in all conscience, to give him a different opinion of himself.

Miss Wal. Yes, and puts her charms into such repair, whenever she expects to meet him, that her cheeks look for all the world like a rasberry ice upon a ground of custard.

Capt. I thought Apollo was the only god of Lady

Rachel's idolatry, and that, in her passion for poetry, she had taken leave of all the less elevated affections.

Bel. O, you mistake again ; the poets are eternally in love, and can by no means be calculated to describe the imaginary passions, without being very susceptible of the real ones.

Enter Servant.

Ser. The man, madam, from Tavistock-street has brought home the dresses for the masquerade, and desires to know if there are any commands for him.

Mrs Bel. O, bid him stay till we see the dresses.
                                        (*Exit Servant.*

Miss Wal. They are only dominos.

Bel. I am glad of that; for characters are as difficult to be supported at the masquerade, as they are in real life.   The last time I was at the Pantheon, a vestal virgin invited me to sup with her, and swore that her pocket had been pick'd by a justice of peace.

Miss Wal. Nay, that was not so bad, as the Hamlet's ghost that box'd with Henry the Eighth, and afterwards danced a hornpipe to the tune of Nancy Dawson.   Ha! ha! ha!—We follow you, Mrs Belville.   [*Exeunt.*

SCENE II.

Changes to LEESON'S *Chambers in the Temple.*

Enter LEESON.

Lees. Where is this clerk of mine ? Connolly !

Con. (*Behind.*) Here, sir !

Lees. Have you copied the marriage-settlement as I corrected it?

Con. (*Enters with pistols.*) Ay, honey, an hour ago.

Lees. What, you have been trying those pistols?

Con. By my soul I have been firing them this half hour, without once being able to make them go off.

Lees. They are plaguy dirty.

Con. In troth, so they are; I strove to brighten them up a little, but some misfortune attends every thing I do, for the more I clane them, the dirtier they are, honey.

Lees. You have had some of your usual daily visitors for money, I suppose.

Con. You may say that! and three or four of them are now hanging about the door, that I wish handsomely hanged any where else for bodering us.

Lees. No joking, Connolly! my present situation is a very disagreeable one.

Con. Faith, and so it is; but who makes it disagreeable? your aunt Tempest would let you have as much money as you please, but you won't condescend to be acquainted with her, though people in this country can be very intimate friends, without seeing one another's faces for seven years.

Lees. Do you think me base enough to receive a favour from a woman, who has disgraced her family, and stoops to be a kept mistress? You see, my sister is already ruined by a connection with her.

Con. Ah, sir, a good guinea isn't the worse for coming through a bad hand; if it was, what would become of us lawyers? and by my soul, many a high head in London would at this minute be very low, if they hadn't received favours even from much worse people than kept mistresses.

Lees. Others, Connolly, may prostitute their honour, as they please; mine is my chief possession, and I must take particular care of it.

Con. Honour, to be sure, it is a very fine thing, sir; but I don't see how it is to be taken care of without a little money; your honour, to my knowledge, hasn't been in your own possession these two years, and the devil a crum can you honestly swear by, till you get it out of the hands of your creditors.

Lees. I have given you a licence to talk, Connolly, because I know you faithful; but I ha'n't given you a liberty to sport with my misfortunes.

Con. You know I'd die to serve you, sir; but of what use is your giving me leave to spake, if you oblige me to hould my tongue? 'tis out of pure love and affection that I put you in mind of your misfortunes.

Lees. Well, Connolly, a few days will, in all probability, enable me to redeem my honour, and to reward your fidelity; the lovely Emily, you know, has half-consented to embrace the first opportunity of flying with me to Scotland, and the paltry trifles I owe will not be missed in her fortune.

Con. But, dear sir, consider you are going to fight a duel this very evening, and if you should be kilt, I fancy you will find it a little difficult to run away afterwards with the lovely Emily.

Lees. If I fall, there will be an end to my misfortunes.

Con. But surely it will not be quite genteel to go out of the world without paying your debts.

Lees. But how shall I stay in the world, Connolly, without punishing Belville for ruining my sister?

Con. O, the devil fly away with this honour! an ounce of common sense is worth a whole ship-load of it, if we must prefer a bullet or a halter to a fine young lady and a great fortune.

Lees. We'll talk no more on the subject at present. Take this letter to Mr Belville; deliver it into his own hand, be sure; and bring me an answer; make haste, for I shall not stir out till you come back.

Con. By my soul, I wish you may be able to stir out then—O, but that's true—

Lees. What's the matter?

Con. Why, sir, the gentleman I last lived clerk with died lately, and left me a legacy of twenty guineas—

Lees. What! is Mr Stanley dead?

Con. Faith, his friends have behaved very unkindly if he is not, for they have buried him these six weeks.

Lees. And what then?

Con. Why, sir, I received my little legacy this morning, and if you'd be so good as to keep it for me, I'd be much obliged to you.

Lees. Connolly, I understand you, but I am already shamefully in your debt: you've had no money from me this age.

Con. O sir, that does not signify; if you are not kilt in this damned duel, you'll be able enough to pay me: if you are, I sha'n't want it.

Lees. Why so, my poor fellow?

Con. Because, though I am but your clerk, and though I think fighting the most foolish thing upon earth, I'm as much a gentleman as yourself, and have as much right to commit a murder in the way of duelling.

Lees. And what then? You have no quarrel with Mr Belville?

Con. I shall have a damned quarrel with him though if you are kilt: your death shall be revenged, depend upon it, so let that content you.

Lees. My dear Connolly, I hope I sha'n't want such a proof of your affection.—How he distresses me!

Con. You will want a second, I suppose, in this affair: I stood second to my own brother in the Fifteen Acres, and though that has made me detest the very thought of duelling ever since, yet if you want a friend, I'll attend you to the field of death with a great deal of satisfaction.

Lees. I thank you, Connolly, but I think it extremely wrong in any man who has a quarrel, to expose his friend to difficulties; we shou'dn't seek for redress, if we are not equal to the task of fighting our own battles; and I choose you particularly to carry my letter, because you may be supposed ignorant of the contents, and thought to be acting only in the ordinary course of your business.

Con. Say no more about it, honey; I will be back with you presently. (*Going, returns.*) I put the twenty guineas in your pocket, before you were up, sir; and I don't believe you'd look for such a thing there, if I wasn't to tell you of it. (*Exit.*

Lees. This faithful, noble-hearted creature!—but let me fly from thought; the business I have to execute will not bear the test of reflection. (*Exit.*

Re-enter CONNOLLY.

Con. As this is a challenge, I shou'dn't go without a sword; come down, little tickle-pitcher. (*Takes a sword.*) Some people may think me very conceited now; but as the dirtiest black-legs in town can wear one without being stared at, I don't think it can suffer any disgrace by the side of an honest man. (*Exit.*

SCENE III.

An Apartment at BELVILLE'S.

Enter MRS BELVILLE.

Mrs Bel. How strangely this affair of Mrs Tempest hangs upon my spirits, though I have every reason, from the tenderness, the politeness, and the generosity of Mr Belville, as well as from the woman's behaviour, to believe the whole charge the result of a disturbed imagination, yet suppose it shou'd be actually true—heigho !—well, suppose it should ;—I wou'd endeavour—I think I wou'd endeavour—to keep my temper :—a frowning face never recovered a heart that was not to be fixed with a smiling one :— but women in general forget this grand article of the matrimonial creed entirely; the dignity of insulted virtue obliges them to play the fool, whenever their Corydons play the libertine ; and, poh ! they must pull down the house about the traitor's ears, though they are themselves to be crushed in pieces by the ruins.

Enter a Servant.

Serv. Lady Rachel Mildew, madam.
                                                    [*Exit Servant.*

Enter LADY RACHEL MILDEW.

Lady Rach. My dear, how have you done since the little eternity of my last seeing you ? Mr Torrington is come to town, I hear.

Mrs Bel. He is, and must be greatly flattered to find that your ladyship has made him the hero of your new comedy.

Lady Rach. Yes, I have drawn him as he is, an honest practitioner of the law ; which is, I fancy, no very common character.

Mrs Bel. And it must be a vast acquisition to the theatre.

Lady Rach. Yet the managers of both houses have refused my play ; have refused it peremptorily, though I offered to make them a present of it.

Mrs Bel. That's very surprising, when you offered to make them a present of it.

Lady Rach. They alledge that the audiences are tired of crying at comedies; and insist that my de-

spairing shepherdess is absolutely too dismal for re-
presentation.

Mrs Bel. What, though you have introduced a
lawyer in a new light?

Lady Rich. Yes, and have a boarding-school romp,
that slaps her mother's face, and throws a bason of
scalding water at her governess.

Mrs Bel. Why surely these are capital jokes!

Lady Rach. But the managers can't find them
out.—However, I am determined to bring it out
somewhere; and I have discovered such a treasure
for my boarding-school romp, as exceeds the most
sanguine expectation of criticism.

Mrs Bel. How fortunate!

Lady Rach. Going to Mrs Le Blond, my milliner's,
this morning, to see some contraband silks, (for you
know there's a foreign minister just arrived,) I heard
a loud voice rehearsing Juliet from the dining-room;
and upon inquiry, found that it was a country girl
just eloped from her friends in town, to go upon the
stage with an Irish manager.

Mrs Bel. Ten to one, the strange woman's niece,
who has been here this morning.   (*Aside.*

Lady Rach. Mrs Le Blond has some doubts about
the manager, it seems, though she hasn't seen him
yet, because the apartments are very expensive, and
were taken by a fine gentleman out of livery.

Mrs Bel. What am I to think of this?—Pray,
Lady Rachel, as you have conversed with this young
actress, I suppose you could procure me a sight of
her?

Lady Rach. This moment if you will; I am very
intimate with her already; but pray keep the matter
a secret from your husband, for he is so witty, you
know, upon my passion for the drama, that I shall be
teazed to death by him.

Mrs Bel. O, you may be very sure that your secret is safe, for I have a most particular reason to

keep it from Mr Belville; but he is coming this way
with Captain Savage; let us at present avoid him.

[*Exeunt.*

Enter BELVILLE *and* CAPTAIN SAVAGE.

Capt. You are a very strange man, Belville; you
are for ever tremblingly solicitous about the happiness
of your wife, yet for ever endangering it by your passion for variety.

Bel. Why, there is certainly a contradiction between
my principles and my practice; but if ever you marry, you'll be able to reconcile it perfectly. Possession,
Savage! O, possession, is a miserable whetter of the
appetite in love! and I own myself so sad a fellow,
that though I wou'dn't exchange Mrs Belville's mind
for any woman's upon earth, there is scarcely a woman's person upon earth, which is not to me a stronger object of attraction.

Capt. Then, perhaps, in a little time you'll be
weary of Miss Leeson.

Bel. To be sure I shall; though, to own the truth,
I have not yet carried my point conclusively with
the little monkey.

Capt. Why, how the plague has she escaped a moment in your hands?

Bel. By a mere accident.—She came to the lodgings, which my man Spruce prepared for her, rather
unexpectedly last night, so that I happened to be engaged particularly in another quarter—you understand me?—and the damned aunt found me so much
employment all the morning, that I could only send
a message by Spruce, promising to call upon her the
first moment I had to spare in the course of the day.

Capt. And so you are previously satisfied that you
shall be tired of her?

Bel. Tired of her!—Why I am at this moment in
pursuit of fresh game against the hour of satiety :—
game that you know to be exquisite; and I fancy I

shall bring it down, though it is closely guarded by
a deal of that pride, which passes for virtue with the
generality of your mighty good people.

Capt. Indeed! and may a body know this wonder?

Bel. You are to be trusted with any thing, for you
are the closest fellow I ever knew, and the rack itself
would hardly make you discover one of your own secrets to any body—what do you think of Miss Walsingham?

Capt. Miss Walsingham!—Death and the devil!
                                                    (*Aside.*

Bel. Miss Walsingham.

Capt. Why surely she has not received your addresses with any degree of approbation?

Bel. With every degree of approbation I cou'd
expect.

Capt. She has?

Bel. Ay: why this news surprises you?

Capt. It does indeed!

Bel. Ha, ha, ha: I can't help laughing to think
what a happy dog Miss Walsingham's husband is likely to be!

Capt. A very happy dog, truly!

Bel. She's a delicious girl, isn't she, Savage?—
but she'll require a little more trouble;—for a fine
woman, like a fortified town, to speak in your father's
language, demands a regular siege; and we must
even allow her the honours of war, to magnify the
greatness of our own victory.

Capt. Well, it amazes me how you gay fellows
ever have the presumption to attack a woman of
principle; Miss Walsingham has no apparent levity
of any kind about her.

Bel. No; but she continued in my house after I
had whispered my passion in her ear, and gave me a
second opportunity of addressing her improperly;
what greater encouragement cou'd I desire?

Enter SPRUCE.

Well, Spruce, what are your commands?

Spruce. My lady is just gone out with Lady Rachel, sir.

Bel. I understand you.

Spruce. I believe you do. (*Aside.*)   (*Exit.*

Capt. What is the English of these significant looks between Spruce and you?

Bel. Only that Miss Walsingham is left alone, and that I have now an opportunity of entertaining her. You must excuse me, Savage; you must upon my soul; but not a word of this affair to any body; because, when I shake her off my hands, there may be fools enough to think of her upon terms of honourable matrimony.   (*Exit.*

Capt. So, here's a discovery! a precious discovery! and while I have been racking my imagination, and sacrificing my interest, to promote the happiness of this woman, she has been listening to the addresses of another; to the addresses of a married man! the husband of her friend, and the intimate friend of her intended husband!—By Belville's own account, however, she has not yet proceeded to any criminal lengths—But why did she keep the affair a secret from me? or why did she continue in his house after a repeated declaration of his unwarrantable attachment?—What's to be done?—If I open my engagement with her to Belville, I am sure he will instantly desist;—but then her honour is left in a state extremely questionable—It shall be still concealed—While it remains unknown, Belville will himself tell me every thing;—and doubt, upon an occasion of this nature, is infinitely more insupportable than the downright falsehood of the woman whom we love.   (*Exit.*

ACT THE SECOND.

SCENE I.

An Apartment in GENERAL SAVAGE'S *House.*

Enter GENERAL SAVAGE *and* TORRINGTON.

Gen. Zounds! Torrington, give me quarter, when I surrender up my sword: I own that for these twenty years I have been suffering all the inconveniences of marriage, without tasting any one of its comforts, and rejoicing in an imaginary freedom, while I was really grovelling in chains.

Tor. In the dirtiest chains upon earth;—yet you wou'dn't be convinced, but laughed at all your married acquaintance as slaves, when not one of them put up with half so much from the worst wife, as you were obliged to crouch under from a kept mistress.

Gen. 'Tis too true. But, you know, she sacrificed much for me ;—you know that she was the widow of a colonel, and refused two very advantageous matches on my account.

Tor. If she was the widow of a judge, and had refused a high chancellor, she was still a devil incarnate, and you were in course a madman to live with her.

Gen. You don't remember her care of me when I have been sick.

Tor. I recollect, however, her usage of you in health, and you may easily find a tenderer nurse, when you are bound over by the gout or the rheumatism.

Gen. Well, well, I agree with you that she is a devil incarnate ; but I am this day determined to part with her for ever.

Tor. Not you indeed.

Gen. What, don't I know my own mind ?

Tor. Not you indeed, when she is in the question : with every body else, your resolution is as unalterable as a determination in the house of peers : but Mrs Tempest is your fate, and she reverses your decrees with as little difficulty as a fraudulent debtor now-a-days procures his certificate under a commission of bankruptcy.

Gen. Well, if, like the Roman Fabius, I conquer by delay, in the end there will be no great reason to find fault with my generalship.   The proposal of parting now comes from herself.

Tor. O, you daren't make it for the life of you !

Gen. You must know that this morning we had a smart cannonading on Belville's account, and she threatens, as I told you before, to quit my house if I don't challenge him for taking away her niece.

Tor. That fellow is the very devil among the women, and yet there isn't a man in England fonder of his wife.

Gen. Poh ! if the young minx hadn't surrendered to him, she would have capitulated to somebody else, and I shall at this time be doubly obliged to him, if he is any ways instrumental in getting the aunt off my hands.

Tor. Why at this time ?

Gen. Because, to shew you how fixed my resolution is to be a keeper no longer, I mean to marry immediately.

Tor. And can't you avoid being pressed to death, like a felon who refuses to plead, without incurring a sentence of perpetual imprisonment?

Gen. I fancy you would yourself have no objection to a perpetual imprisonment in the arms of Miss Walsingham.

Tor. But have you any reason to think that, upon examination in a case of love, she would give a favourable reply to your interrogatories?

Gen. The greatest—do you think I'd hazard such an engagement without being perfectly sure of my ground? Notwithstanding my present connection won't suffer me to see a modest woman at my own house, she always treats me with particular attention whenever I visit at Belville's, or meet her any where else—If fifty young fellows are present, she directs all her assiduities to the old soldier, and my son has a thousand times told me that she professes the highest opinion of my understanding.

Tor. And truly you give a notable proof of your understanding, in thinking of a woman almost young enough to be your grand-daughter.

Gen. Nothing like an experienced chief to command in any garrison.

Tor. Recollect the state of your present citadel.

Gen. Well, if I am blown up by my own mine, I shall be the only sufferer—There's another thing I want to talk of—I am going to marry my son to Miss Moreland.

Tor. Miss Moreland!—

Gen. Belville's sister.

Tor. O, ay, I remember that Moreland had got a good estate to assume the name of Belville.

Gen. I haven't yet mentioned the matter to my son, but I settled the affair with the girl's mother yesterday, and she only waits to communicate it to Belville, who is her oracle, you know.

Tor. And are you sure the captain will like her?

Gen. I am not so unreasonable as to insist upon his liking her, I shall only insist upon his marrying her.

Tor. What, whether he likes her or not?

Gen. When I issue my orders, I expect them to be obeyed; and don't look for an examination into their propriety.

Tor. What a delightful thing it must be to live under a military government, where a man is not to be troubled with the exercise of his understanding!

Gen. Miss Moreland has thirty thousand pounds— That's a large sum of ammunition money.

Tor. Ay, but a marriage merely on the score of fortune, is only gilding the death-warrant sent down for the execution of a prisoner. However, as I know your obstinate attachment to what you once resolve, I sha'n't pretend to argue with you: where are the papers which you want me to consider?

Gen. They are in my library—File off with me to the next room, and they shall be laid before you— But first I'll order the chariot; for the moment I have your opinion, I purpose to sit down regularly before Miss Walsingham—Who waits there?

Enter a Servant.

Gen. Is Mrs Tempest at home?

Serv. Yes, sir, just come in, and just going out again.

Gen. Very well: order the chariot to be got ready.

Serv. Sir, one of the pannels was broke last night at the Opera-house.

Gen. Sir, I didn't call to have the pleasure of your conversation, but to have obedience paid to my orders.

Tor. Go order the chariot, you blockhead.

Serv. With the broken pannel, sir ? ·

Gen. Yes, you rascal, if both pannels were broke, and the back shattered to pieces.

Serv. The coachman thinks that one of the wheels is damaged, sir.

Gen. Don't attempt to reason, you dog, but execute your orders.—Bring the chariot without the wheels—if you can't bring it with them.

Tor. Ay, bring it, if you reduce it to a sledge, and let your master look like a malefactor for high treason, on his journey to Tyburn.

Enter Mrs Tempest.

Mrs Tem. General Savage, is the house to be for ever a scene of noise with your domineering ?—The chariot sha'n't be brought—it won't be fit for use till it is repaired—and John shall drive it this very minute to the coach-maker's.

Gen. Nay, my dear, if it isn't fit for use, that's another thing.

Tor. Here's the experienced chief that's fit to command in any garrison !   (*Aside.*

Gen. Go, order me the coach then. (*To the Serv.*

Mrs Tem. You can't have the coach.

Gen. And why so, my love ?

Mrs Tem. Because I want it for myself.—Robert, get a hack for your master—though indeed I don't see what business he has out of the house.

(*Exeunt* Mrs Tempest *and* Robert.

Tor. When you issue your orders, you expect them to be obeyed, and don't look for an examination into their propriety.

Gen. The fury !—this has steeled me against her for ever, and nothing on earth can now prevent me from drumming her out immediately.

Mrs Tem. (*Behind.*) An unreasonable old fool—But I'll make him know who governs this house !

Gen. Zounds ! here she comes again ; she has been

lying in ambuscade, I suppose, and has overheard us.

Tor. What if she has? you are steeled against her for ever.

Gen. No, she's not coming—she's going down stairs;—and now, dear Torrington, .you must be as silent as a sentinel on an out-post about this affair. If that virago was to hear a syllable of it, she might perhaps attack Miss Walsingham in her very camp, and defeat my whole plan of operations.

Tor. I thought you were determined to drum her out immediately.   (*Exeunt.*

SCENE II.

BELVILLE'S *Apartment.*

Enter MISS WALSINGHAM, *followed by* BELVILLE.

Miss Wal. I beg, sir, that you will insult me no longer with solicitations of this nature—give me proofs of your sincerity indeed! What proofs of sincerity can your situation admit of, if I could be even weak enough to think of you with partiality at all?

Bel. If our affections, madam, were under the government of our reason, circumstanced as I am, this unhappy bosom wouldn't be torn by passion for Miss Walsingham.—Had I been blessed with your acquaintance before I saw Mrs Belville, my hand as well as my heart wou'd have been humbly offered to your acceptance—fate, however, has ordered it otherwise, and it is cruel to reproach me with that situation as a crime, which ought to be pitied as my greatest misfortune.

Miss Wal. He's actually forcing tears into his eyes.—However, I'll mortify him severely. (*Aside.*

Bel. But such proofs of sincerity as my situation can admit of, you shall yourself command, as my only business in existence is to adore you

Miss Wal. His only business in existence to adore me ! (*Aside.*

Bel. Prostrate at your feet, my dearest Miss Walsingham, (*Kneeling.*) behold a heart eternally devoted to your service.—You have too much good sense, madam, to be the slave of custom, and too much humanity not to pity the wretchedness you have caused. Only, therefore, say that you commiserate my sufferings—I'll ask no more—and surely that may be said, without any injury to your purity, to snatch even an enemy from distraction—Where's my handkerchief ? (*Aside.*

Miss Wal. Now to answer in his own way, and to make him ridiculous to himself—(*Aside.*) If I thought, if I could think, (*Affecting to weep.*) that these protestations were real—

Bel. How can you, madam, be so unjust to your own merit ? how can you be so cruelly doubtful of my solemn asseverations ?—Here I again kneel, and swear eternal love !

Miss Wal. I don't know what to say—but there is one proof—(*Affecting to weep.*)

Bel. Name it, my angel, this moment, and make me the happiest of mankind !

Miss Wal. Swear to be mine for ever.

Bel. I have sworn it a thousand times, my charmer ; and I will swear it to the last moment of my life.

Miss Wal. Why then—but don't look at me I beseech you—I don't know how to speak it.

Bel. The delicious emotion !—do not check the generous tide of tenderness that fills me with such extasy.

Miss Wal. You'll despise me for this weakness ?

Bel. This weakness !—this generosity, which will demand my everlasting gratitude.

Miss Wal. I am a fool—but there is a kind of fatality in this affair—and I do consent to go off with you.

Bel. Eternal blessings on your condescension !

Miss Wal. You are irresistible, and I am ready to fly with you to any part of the world.

Bel. Fly to any part of the world indeed !—you shall fly by yourself then ! (*Aside.*) You are the most lovely, the most tender creature in the world, and thus again let me thank you : O, Miss Walsingham, I cannot express how happy you've made me !—But where's the necessity of our leaving England ?

Miss Wal. I thought he wou'dn't like to go abroad —(*Aside.*) That I may possess the pleasure of your company unrivalled.

Bel. I must cure her of this taste for travelling.
                                                    (*Aside.*

Miss Wal. You don't answer, Mr Belville ?

Bel. Why I was turning the consequence of your proposal in my thoughts, as going off—going off— you know—

Miss Wal. Why going off, you know, is going off— And what objections can you have to going off ?

Bel. Why going off will subject you, at a certainty, to the slander of the world ; whereas, by staying at home, we may not only have numberless opportunities of meeting, but at the same time prevent suspicion itself from ever breathing on your reputation.

Miss Wal. I didn't dream of your starting any difficulties, sir.—Just now I was dearer to you than all the world.

Bel. And so you are, by heaven !

Miss Wal. Why won't you sacrifice the world then at once to obtain me ?

Bel. Surely, my dearest life, you must know the

necessity, which every man of honour is under, of keeping up his character ?

Miss Wal. So, here's this fellow swearing to ten thousand lies, and yet talking very gravely about his honour and his character. (*Aside.*) Why, to be sure, in these days, Mr Belville, the instances of conjugal infidelity are so very scarce, and men of fashion are so remarkable for a tender attachment to their wives, that I don't wonder at your circumspection—But do you think I can stoop to accept you by halves, or admit of any partnership in your heart?

Bel. O you must do more than that, if you have any thing to say to me. (*Aside.*) Surely, madam, when you know my whole soul unalterably your own, you will permit me to preserve those appearances with the world, which are indispensably requisite—Mrs Belville is a most excellent woman, however it may be my fortune to be devoted to another—Her happiness, besides, constitutes a principal part of my felicity, and if I was publicly to forsake her, I should be hunted as a monster from society.

Miss Wal. Then, I suppose it is by way of promoting Mrs Belville's repose, sir, that you make love to other women ; and by way of shewing the nicety of your honour, that you attempt the purity of such as your own roof peculiarly entitles to protection ? For the honour intended to me, thus low to the ground I thank you, Mr Belville.

Bel. Laughed at, by all the stings of mortification !

Miss Wal. Good bye.—Don't let this accident mortify your vanity too much ;--but take care, the next time you vow everlasting love, that the object is neither tender enough to sob—sob—at your distress, nor provoking enough to make a proposal of leaving England.—How greatly a little common sense can lower these fellows of extraordinary impudence !

(*Exit.*

Bel. (*Alone.*) So then, I am fairly taken in, and she has been only diverting herself with me all this time :—however, lady fair, I may chance to have the laugh in a little time on my side ; for if you can sport in this manner about the flame, I think it must in the run lay hold of your wings.—What shall I do in this affair ?—she sees the matter in its true light, and there's no good to be expected from thumping of bosoms, or squeezing white handkerchiefs ;—no, these won't do with women of sense, and in a short time they'll be ridiculous to the very babies of a boarding-school.

Enter CAPTAIN SAVAGE.

Capt. Well, Belville, what news ? You have had a fresh opportunity with Miss Walsingham.

Bel. Why, faith, Savage, I've had a most extraordinary scene with her, and yet have but little reason to brag of my good fortune, though she offered in express terms to run away with me.

Capt. Pr'ythee explain yourself, man ; she cou'dn't surely be so shameless !

Bel. O, her offering to run away with me was by no means the worst part of the affair.

Capt. No? then it must be damn'd bad indeed : but, pr'ythee, hurry to an explanation.

Bel. Why then, the worst part of the affair is, that she was laughing at me the whole time ; and made this proposal of an elopement with no other view, than to shew me in strong colours to myself, as a very dirty fellow to the best wife in England.

Capt. I am easy. (*Aside.*

Enter SPRUCE.

Spruce. Sir, there is an Irish gentleman below with a letter for you, who will deliver it to nobody but yourself.

Bel. Shew him up then.

Spruce. Yes, sir.

Capt. It may be on business, Belville; I'll take my leave of you.

Bel. O, by no means; I can have no business which I desire to keep from you, though you are the arrantest miser of your confidence upon earth, and wou'd rather trust your life in any body's hands, than even a paltry amour with the apprentice of a milliner.

Enter CONNOLLY.

Con. Gintlemin, your most obedient; pray, which of you is Mr Belville?

Bel. My name is Belville, at your service, sir.

Con. I have a little bit of a letter for you, sir.

Bel. (*Reads.*)

" SIR—The people where Miss Leeson lately lodged asserting positively that you have taken her away in a fictitious character, the brother of that unhappy girl thinks himself obliged to demand satisfaction for the injury you have done his family; though a stranger to your person, he is sufficiently acquainted with your reputation for spirit, and shall, therefore, make no doubt of seeing you with a case of pistols, near the ring in Hyde Park, at eight o'clock this evening, to answer the claims of   GEORGE LEESON.

" To CRAGGS BELVILLE, Esq."

Capt. Eight o'clock in the evening! 'tis a strange time!

Con. Why so, honey? A fine evening is as good a time for a bad action as a fine morning; and if a man of sense can be such a fool to fight a duel, he shou'd never sleep upon the matter, for the more he thinks of it, the more he must feel himself ashamed of his resolution.

Bel. A pretty letter!

Con. O yes, an invitation to a brace of bullets is a very pretty thing.

Bel. For a challenge, however, 'tis very civilly written!

Con. Faith, if it was written to me, I shou'dn't be very fond of such civility : I wonder he doesn't sign himself, your most obedient servant.

Capt. I told you Leeson's character, and what wou'd become of this damned business ; but your affairs—are they settled, Belville ?

Bel. O, they are always settled ; for, as this is a country where people occasionally die, I take constant care to be prepared for contingencies.

Con. Occasionally die !—I'll be very much obliged to you, sir, if you tell me the country where people do not die; for I'll immediately go and end my days there.

Bel. Ha ! ha ! ha !

Con. Faith, you may laugh, gintlemin, but though I am a foolish Irishman, and come about a foolish piece of business, I'd prefer a snug birth in this world, bad as it is, to the finest coffin in all Christendom.

Bel. I am surprised, sir, that, thinking in this manner, you would be the bearer of a challenge.

Con. And well you may, sir ; but we must often take a pleasure in serving our friends, by doing things that are very disagreeable to us.

Capt. Then you think Mr Leeson much to blame, perhaps, for hazarding his life where he can by no means repair the honour of his sister.

Con. Indeed and I do—But I shall think this gintlemin, begging his pardon, much more to blame for meeting him.

Bel. And why so, sir?—You wou'dn't have me disappoint your friend ?

Con. Faith, and that I wou'd—He, poor lad, may have some reason at present to be tired of the world,

but you have a fine estate, a fine wife, a fine parcel
of children—in short, honey, you have every thing
to make you fond of living, and, the devil burn me,
was I in your case, if I'd stake my own happiness
against the misery of any man.

Bel. I am very much obliged to your advice, sir,
though on the present occasion I cannot adopt it;
be so good as to present my compliments to your
friend, and tell him I shall certainly do myself the
honour of attending his appointment.

Con. Why then upon my soul I am very sorry
for it.

Capt. 'Tis not very customary, sir, with gentlemen
of Ireland to oppose an affair of honour.

Con. They are like the gintlemin of England, sir,
they are brave to a fault; yet I hope to see the day
that it will be infamous to draw the swords of either
against any body but the enemies of the country.

(*Exit.*

Bel. I am quite charmed with this honest Hibernian, and would almost fight a duel for the pleasure
of his acquaintance.

Capt. Come, step with me a little, and let us consider, whether there may not be some method of ac-
commodating this cursed business.

Bel. Poh! don't be uneasy upon my account; my
character, with regard to affairs of this nature is unhappily too well established, and you may be sure
that I sha'n't fight with Leeson.

Capt. No—you have injured him greatly?

Bel. The very reason of all others why I should
not cut his throat. (*Exeunt.*

Enter SPRUCE.

Spruce. What the devil, this master of mine has
got a duel upon his hands! Zounds! I am sorry for
that; he is a prince of a fellow, and a good subject

must always love his prince, though he may now and then be a little out of humour with his actions.

Enter GENERAL SAVAGE.

Gen. Your hall-door standing open, Spruce, and none of your sentinels being on guard, I have surprised your camp thus far without resistance : Where is your master ?

Spruce. Just gone out with Captain Savage, sir.

Gen. Is your lady at home ?

Spruce. No, sir, but Miss Walsingham is at home ; shall I inform her of your visit ?

Gen. There is no occasion to inform her of it, for here she is, Spruce.   (*Exit* SPRUCE.

Enter MISS WALSINGHAM.

Miss Wal. General Savage, your most humble servant.

Gen. My dear Miss Walsingham, it is rather cruel that you should be left at home by yourself, and yet I am greatly rejoiced to find you at present without company.

Miss Wal. I can't but think myself in the best company, when I have the honour of your conversation, general.

Gen. You flatter me too much, madam, yet I am come to talk to you on a serious affair, Miss Walsingham ; an affair of importance to me and to yourself: Have you leisure to favour me with a short audience, if I beat a parley ?

Miss Wal. Any thing of importance to you, sir, is always sufficient to command my leisure.—'Tis as the captain suspected.   (*Aside.*

Gen. You tremble, my lovely girl, but don't be alarmed ; for though my business is of an important nature, I hope it won't be of a disagreeable one.

Miss Wal. And yet I am greatly agitated.

                                        (*Aside.*

Gen. Soldiers, Miss Walsingham, are said to be generally favoured by the kind partiality of the ladies.

Miss Wal. The ladies are not without gratitude, sir, to those who devote their lives peculiarly to the service of their country.

Gen. Generously said, madam. Then give me leave, without any masked battery, to ask, if the heart of an honest soldier is a prize at all worth your acceptance?

Miss Wal. Upon my word, sir, there's no masked battery in this question.

Gen. I am as fond of a coup de main, madam, in love as in war, and hate the tedious method of sapping a town, when there is a possibility of entering sword in hand.

Miss Wal. Why, really, sir, a woman may as well know her own mind, when she is summoned by the trumpet of a lover, as when she undergoes all the tiresome formality of a siege. You see I have caught your own mode of conversing, general.

Gen. And a very great compliment I consider it, madam: But now that you have candidly confessed an acquaintance with your own mind, answer me with that frankness for which every body admires you so much—Have you any objection to change the name of Walsingham?

Miss Wal. Why then, frankly, General Savage, I say no.

Gen. Ten thousand thanks to you for this kind declaration!

Miss Wal. I hope you won't think it a forward one.

Gen. I'd sooner see my son run away in the day of battle:—I'd soon think Lord Russel was bribed by Lewis the XIVth, and sooner vilify the memory of Algernon Sidney.

Miss Wal How unjust it was ever to suppose the general a tyrannical father! (*Aside.*

Gen. You have told me condescendingly, Miss

2

Walsingham, that you have no objection to change your name—I have but one question more to ask.

Miss Wal. Pray propose it.

Gen. Would the name of Savage be disagreeable to you?—Speak frankly again, my dear girl!

Miss Wal. Why then again I frankly say, no.

Gen. You make me too happy; and though I shall readily own, that a proposal of this nature would come with more propriety from my son——

Miss Wal. I am much better pleased that you make the proposal yourself, sir.

Gen. You are too good to me.—Torrington thought that I should meet with a repulse!   (*Aside.*

Miss Wal. Have you communicated ·this business to the captain, sir?

Gen. No, my dear madam, I did not think that at all necessary. I have always been attentive to the captain's happiness, and I propose that he shall be married in a few days.

Miss Wal. What, whether I will or no?

Gen. O, you can have no objection.

Miss Wal. I must be consulted, however, about the day, general: but nothing in my power shall be wanting to make him happy.

Gen. Obliging loveliness!

Miss Wal. You may imagine, that if I was not previously imprest in favour of your proposal, it wou'd not have met my concurrence so readily.

Gen. Then you own that I had a previous friend in the garrison?

Miss Wal. I don't blush to acknowledge it, when I consider the accomplishments of the object, sir.

Gen. O this is too much, madam; the principal merit of the object is his passion for Miss Walsingham.

Miss Wal. Don't say that, general, I beg of you, for I don't think there are many women in the kingdom who could behold him with indifference.

Gen. Ah, you flattering, flattering angel!—and

yet, by the memory of Marlborough, my lovely girl, it was the idea of a prepossession on your part which encouraged me to hope for a favourable reception.

Miss Wal. Then I must have been very indiscreet, for I laboured to conceal that prepossession as much as possible.

Gen. You cou'dn't conceal it from me ! you cou'dn't conceal it from me !—The female heart is a field which I am thoroughly acquainted with, and which has more than once been a witness to my victories, madam.

Miss Wal. I don't at all doubt your success with the ladies, general; but as we now understand one another so perfectly, you will give me leave to retire.

Gen. One word, my dear creature, and no more : I shall wait upon you some time to-day, with Mr Torrington, about the necessary settlements.

Miss Wal. You must do as you please, general ; you are invincible in every thing.

Gen. And, if you please, we'll keep every thing a profound secret till the articles are all settled, and the definitive treaty ready for execution.

Miss Wal. You may be sure that delicacy will not suffer me to be communicative on the subject, sir.

Gen. Then you leave every thing to my management ?

Miss Wal. I can't trust a more noble negociator.
(*Exit.*

Gen. The day's my own.   (*Sings.*

Britons, strike home ! strike home ! Revenge, &c.
(*Exit singing.*

ACT THE THIRD.

SCENE I.

MISS LEESON'S *Lodgings.*

Enter LADY RACHEL MILDEW, MRS BELVILLE, *and*
MISS LEESON.

Lady Rach. Well, Mrs Belville, I am extremely
glad you agree with me, in opinion of this young lady's qualifications for the stage. Don't you think
she'd play Miss Headstrong admirably in my comedy?

Miss Eel. Yes, indeed, I think she possesses a
natural fund of spirit very much adapted to the character.—'Tis impossible, surely, that this hoyden can
have a moment's attraction for Mr Belville! (*Aside.*

Miss Lees. You are very obliging, ladies; but I
have no turn for comedy; my forte is tragedy entirely.

Alphonso!—O Alphonso! to thee I call, &c.

Lady Rach. But, my dear, is there none of our comedies to your taste?

Miss Lees. O, yes; some of the sentimental ones

are very pretty, there's such little difference between them and tragedies.

Lady Rach. And pray, my dear, how long have you been engaged to Mr Frankly?

Miss Lees. I only came away last night, and hav'n't seen Mr Frankly since, though I expect him every moment.

Mrs Bel. Last night! just as Mrs Tempest mentioned.   (*Aside.*

Lady Rach. You had the concurrence of your friends?

Miss Lees. Not I, madam; Mr Frankly said I had too much genius to mind my friends, and as I should want nothing from them, there was no occasion to consult them in the affair.

Lady Rach. Then Osbaldiston is not your real name perhaps?

Miss Lees. O no, nor do I tell my real name; I chose Osbaldiston, because it was a long one, and wou'd make a striking appearance in the bills.

Mrs Bel. I wish we cou'd see Mr Frankly.

Miss Lees. Perhaps you may, madam, for he designs to give me a lesson every day, till we are ready to set off for Ireland.

Lady Rach. Suppose then, my dear, you wou'd oblige us with a scene in Juliet, by way of shewing your proficiency to Mrs Belville.

Miss Lees. Will you stand up for Romeo?

Lady Rach. With all my heart, and I'll give you some instructions.

Miss Lees. I beg pardon, ma'am; I'll learn to act under nobody but Mr Frankly. This room is without a carpet; if you will step into the next, ladies, I'll endeavour to oblige you.

Shall I not be environ'd, distraught——
This way, ladies.

Lady Rach. Pray, madam, shew us the way.

(*Exeunt* MISS LEES. *and* LADY RACH.

Mrs Bel. I'll prolong this mummery as much as possible, in hopes the manager may come.   Lie still, poor fluttering heart! it cannot be the lord of all your wishes! it cannot surely be your adored Belville?   (*Exit.*

Re-enter MISS LEESON.

Miss Lees. Hav'n't I left my Romeo and Juliet here? O yes, there it is.

Enter BELVILLE.

Bel. ————O, were those eyes in heav'n,
They'd through the starry region shine so bright,
That birds would sing, and think it was the morn!

Miss Lees. Ah, my dear Mr Frankly! I'm so glad you are come! I was dying to see you.
Bel. Kiss me, my dear;—why didn't you send me word of your intention to come away last night?
Miss Lees. I hadn't time: but as I knew where the lodgings were, I thought I should be able to find you by a note to the coffee-house I always directed to.
Bel. Kiss me again, my little sparkler!
Miss Lees. Nay, I won't be kissed in this manner; for though I am going on the stage, I intend to have some regard for my character.   But, ha! ha! ha! I am glad you are come now: I have company above stairs.
Bel. Company! that's unlucky at this time, for I wanted to make you entirely easy about your character. (*Aside.*) And pray, my dear, who is your company? You know we must be very cautious, for fear of your relations.
Miss Lees. O, they are only ladies.—But one of them is the most beautiful creature in the world!
Bel. The devil she is!
Miss Lees. " An earth-treading star, and makes dim heaven's light."

Bel. Zounds! I'll take a peep at the star—who knows but I may have an opportunity of making another actress.   (*Aside.*

Miss Lees. Come, charmer! charmer!

Bel. ————Wer't thou as far,
As that vast shore, washed by the farthest sea,
I wou'd adventure for such merchandise.

Now let's see what fortune has sent us above stairs.
                                    [*Exeunt.*

SCENE II.

A Dining Room at MISS LEESON'S.

MRS BELVILLE *and* LADY RACHEL *discovered.*

Mrs Bel. This is a most ignorant young creature, Lady Rachel.

Lady Rach. Why I think she is—Did you observe how she slighted my offer of instructing her?

Enter MISS LEESON.

Miss Lees. Ladies!—ladies!—here he is! here is Mr Frankly!

Enter BELVILLE, *bowing very low, and not seeing the ladies.*

Bel. Ladies, your most obedient.

Mrs Bel. Let me, if possible, recollect myself— Sir, your most obedient humble servant.

Bel. Zounds! let me out of the house.

Lady Rach. What do I see?

Miss Lees. You seem, ladies, to know this gentleman?

Mrs Bel. (*Taking hold of him.*) You sha'n't go, renegade—You laughed at my credulity this morning, and I must now laugh at your embarrassment.

Bel. What a kind thing it would be in any body to blow out my stupid brains!

Lady Rach. I'll mark this down for an incident in my comedy.

Miss Lees. What do you hang your head for, Mr Frankly?

Bel. Be so good as to ask that lady, my dear.— The devil has been long in my debt, and now he pays me home with a witness.

Mrs Bel. What a cruel thing it is to let Mrs Tempest out, my love, without somebody to take care of her!

Miss Lees. What, do you know Mrs Tempest, madam?

Mrs Bel. Yes, my dear;—and I am pretty well acquainted with this gentleman.

Miss Lees. What, isn't this gentleman the manager of a play-house in Ireland?

Bel. The curtain is already dropt, my dear; the farce is nearly over, and you'll be speedily acquainted with the catastrophe.

Enter MRS TEMPEST.

Mrs Tem. Yes, sir, the curtain is almost dropt: I have had spies to watch your haunts, and the catastrophe ends in your detection—Come, you abandoned slut——

Miss Lees. And have I eloped after all, without being brought upon the stage?

Mrs Tem. I don't know that you would be brought upon the stage; but I am sure you were near being

brought upon the town.   I hope, madam, for the future, you'll not set me down a mad-woman.

(To Mrs Bel.

Mrs Bel. Mr Belville, you'll make my apologies
to this lady, and acknowledge that I think her perfectly in her senses.

Bel. I wish that I had entirely lost mine.

Lady Rach. (*Writing.*) " I wish that I had entirely
lost mine,"—a very natural wish in such a situation.

Mrs Tem. Come, you audacious minx, come away.
You shall be sent into Yorkshire this very evening;
and see what your poor mother will say to you,
hussey.

Miss Lees. I will go on the stage, if I die for't ; and
'tis some comfort there's a play-house at York.

[Exeunt Mrs Tempest and Miss Lefson.

Bel. Nancy, I am so ashamed, so humbled, and so
penitent, that if you knew what passes here, I am
sure you wou'd forgive me.

Mrs Bel. My love, though I cannot say I rejoice
in your infidelity, yet, believe me, I pity your distress : let us therefore think no more of this.

Lady Rach. (*Writing.*) "And think no more of this."
—This conduct is new in a wife, and very dramatic.

Bel. Where, my angel, have you acquired so many
requisites to charm with ?

Mrs Bel. In your society, my dear ; and believe
me, that a wife may be as true a friend as any bot-
tle-companion upon earth, though she can neither get
merry with you over night, nor blow out your brains
about some foolish quarrel in the morning.

Bel. If wives knew the omnipotence of virtue,
where she wears a smile upon her face, they'd all
follow your bewitching example, and make a faithless
husband quite an incredible character.

Lady Rach. " Quite an incredible character !"—Let
me set down that.   (*Writing.*)   [*Exeunt.*

SCENE III.

GENERAL SAVAGE'S.

Enter General and Captain.

Gen. Yes, Horace, I have been just visiting at Belville's.

Capt. You found nobody at home but Miss Walsingham?

Gen. No, but I'd a long conversation with her, and upon a very interesting subject.

Capt. 'Tis as I guessed.   (*Aside.*

Gen. She is a most amiable creature, Horace.

Capt. So she is, sir, and will make any man happy that marries her.

Gen. I am glad you think so.

Capt. He's glad I think so!—'tis plain,—but I must leave every thing to himself, and seem wholly passive in the affair.   (*Aside.*

Gen. A married life after all, Horace, I am now convinced, is the most happy as well as the most reputable.

Capt. It is indeed, sir.

Gen. Then, perhaps, you wou'd have no objection to be married, if I offered you as agreeable a young woman as Miss Walsingham?

Capt. 'Twould be my first pride on every occasion, sir, to pay an implicit obedience to your commands.

Gen. That's sensibly said, Horace, and obligingly said; prepare yourself therefore for an introduction to the lady in the morning.

Capt. Is the lady prepared to receive me, sir?

Gen. O yes: and you can't think how highly delighted Miss Walsingham appeared, when I acquainted her with my resolution on the subject.

Capt. She's all goodness!

Gen. The more I know her, the more I am charm'd
with her. I must not be explicit with him yet, for
fear my secret should get wind, and reach the ears
of the enemy. (*Aside.*) I propose, Horace, that
you should be married immediately.

Capt. The sooner the better, sir, I have no will
but your's.

Gen. (*Shaking hands with him.*) By the memory
of Marlbro', you are a most excellent boy!—But what
do you think? Miss Walsingham insists upon naming
the day.

Capt. And welcome, sir; I am sure she won't
make it a distant one.

Gen. O, she said, that nothing in her power shou'd
be wanting to make you happy.

Capt. I am sure of that, sir.

Gen. (*A loud knocking.*) Zounds, Horace! here's
the disgrace and punishment of my life! let's avoid
her as we would a fever in the camp.

Capt. Come to the library, and I'll tell you how
whimsically she was treated this morning at Belville's.

Gen. Death and the devil! make haste. O, I must
laugh at marriage, and be curst to me! But I am providing, Horace, against your falling into my error.

Capt. I am eternally indebted to you, sir.

[*Exeunt.*

SCENE IV.

BELVILLE'S *House.*

Enter MRS BELVILLE *and* LADY RACHEL.

Lady Rach. Nay, Mrs Belville, I have no patience, you act quite unnaturally.

Mrs Bel. What! because I am unwilling to be miserable?

Lady Rach. This new instance of Mr Belville's infidelity—this attempt to seduce Miss Walsingham, which your woman overheard, is unpardonable!

Mrs Bel. I don't say but that I am strongly wounded by his irregularities; yet, if Mr Belville is unhappily a rover, I would much rather that he should have twenty mistresses than one.

Lady Rach. You astonish me!

Mrs Bel. Why, don't you know, my dear madam, that while he is divided amidst a variety of objects, 'tis impossible for him to have a serious attachment?

Lady Rach. Lord, Mrs Belville, how can you speak with so much composure! a virtuous woman should be always outrageous upon such an occasion as this.

Mrs Bel. What, and weary the innocent sun and moon from the firmament, like a despairing princess in a tragedy—No—no—Lady Rachel, 'tis bad enough to be indifferent to the man I love, without studying to excite his aversion.

Lady Rach. How glad I am that Miss Walsingham made him so heartily ashamed of himself! Lord, these young men are so full of levity! Give me a husband of Mr Torrington's age, say I.

Mrs Bel. And give me a husband of Mr Belville's, say I, with all his follies: However, Lady Rachel, I am pretty well satisfied that my conduct at Miss Leeson's will have a proper effect upon Mr Belville's generosity, and put an entire end to his gallantries for the future.

Lady Rach. Don't deceive yourself, my dear.— The gods in the shilling gallery would sooner give up roast beef, or go without an epilogue on the first night of a new piece.

Mrs Bel. Why should you think so of such a man as Mr Belville?

Lady Rach. Because Mr Belville is a man: However, if you dare run the risque, we will try the sincerity of his reformation.

Mrs Bel. If I dare run the risque! I would stake my soul upon his honour.

Lady Rach. Then your poor soul would be in a very terrible situation.

Mrs Bel. By what test can we prove his sincerity?

Lady Rach. By a very simple one. You know I write so like Miss Walsingham, that our hands are scarcely known asunder.

Mrs Bel. Well——

Lady Rach. Why then let me write to him as from her.

Mrs Bel. If I did not think it would look like a doubt of his honour—

Lady Rach. Poh! dare you proceed upon my plan?

Mrs Bel. Most confidently: Come to my dressing-room, where you'll find every thing ready for writing, and then you may explain your scheme more particularly.

Lady Rach. I'll attend you, but I am really sorry, my dear, for the love of propriety, to see you so calm under the perfidy of your husband; you should be quite wretched—indeed you should.   [*Exeunt.*

SCENE V.

The Temple.

Enter LEESON.

The hell-hounds are after me, and if I am arrested at this time, my honour will not only be blown upon by Belville, but I shall perhaps lose Emily into the bargain.   (*Exit.*

Enter LEECH, CROW, *and* WOLF, *dressed in fur habits.*

Leech. Yonder, my lads, he darts through the cloisters; who the devil cou'd think that he wou'd smoke us in this disguise? Crow, do you take the Fleet-Street side of the Temple as fast as you can, to prevent his doubling us that way—and, Wolf, do you run round the Garden Court, that he mayn't escape us by the Thames—I'll follow the strait line myself, and the devil's in the dice if he is not snapped by one of us.   [*Exeunt.*

SCENE VI.

Another part of the Temple.

Enter LEESON *on one side,* CONNOLLY *on the other.*

Lees. Fly, open the chambers this moment—the bailiffs are after me!

Con. Faith and that I will—but it will be of no use to fly a step neither, if I hav'n't the key.

Lees. Zounds! didn't you lock the door?

Con. Yes, but I believe I left the key on the inside—however your own key will do the business as well.

Lees. True, and I forgot it in my confusion; do you stay here, and throw every impediment in the way of these rascals.

Con. Faith and that I will.   [*Exit* LEES.

Enter CROW *and* WOLF.

Crow. Pray, sir, did you see a gentleman run this way drest in green and gold?

Con. In troth I did.

Wolf. And which way did he run?

Con. That I can tell you too.

Wolf. We shall be much obliged to you.

Con. Indeed and you will not, Mr Catchpole, for the devil an information shall you get from Connolly; I see plainly enough what you are, you blackguards, though there's no guessing at you in these fur coats.

Crow. Keep your information to yourself and be damn'd; here the cull comes, a prisoner in the custody of Master Leech.

7

Enter LEESON *and* LEECH.

Lees. Well, but treat me like a gentleman—Don't expose me unnecessarily.

Leech. Expose you, master! we never expose any body; 'tis gentlemen that expose themselves, venever they compels their creditors to arrest them.

Con. And where's your authority for arresting the gentleman? let us see it this minute, for may be you hav'n't it about you.

Leech. O here's our authority; ve knew as we had to do vid a lawyer, and so we came properly prepared, my master.

Lees. What shall I do?

Con. Why hark'e, sir—Don't you think that you and I could beat these three theeves to their hearts content?—I have nothing but my carcase to venter for you, honey, but that you are as welcome to as the flowers in May.

Lees. O, by no means, Connolly, we must not fly in the face of the laws.

Con. That's the reason that you are going to fight a duel.

Lees. Hark'e, officer—I have some very material business to execute in the course of this evening: here are five guineas for a little indulgence, and I assure you, upon the honour of a gentleman, that if I have life, I'll attend your own appointment to-morrow morning.

Leech. I can't do it, master—Five guineas to be sure is a genteel thing, but I have ten for the taking of you, do you see, and so, if you please to step to my house in Southampton Buildings, you may send for some friend to bail you, or settle the affair as well as you can with the plaintiff.

Con. I'll go bail for him this minute, if you don't want somebody to be bail for myself.

Lees. Let me reflect a moment.

Crow. (*To* Con.) Can you swear yourself worth one hundred and seventy pounds when your debts are paid?

Con. In troth I cannot, nor one hundred and seventy pence—unless I have a mind to perjure myself.—But one man's body is as good as another's, and since he has no bail to give you but his flesh, the fattest of us two is the best security.

Wolf. No, if we can't get better bail than you, we shall lock up his body in prison according to law.

Con. Faith, and a very wise law it must be, which cuts off every method of getting money, by way of making us pay our debts.

Leech. Well, Master Leeson, what do you determine upon?

Lees. A moment's patience—Yonder I see Mr Torrington—a thought occurs—yet it carries the appearance of fraud——however as it will be really innocent, nay laughable in the end, and as my ruin or salvation depends upon my present decision, it must be hazarded.

Crow. Come, master, fix upon something, and don't keep us waiting for you.

Con. By my soul, honey, he don't want you to wait for him; he'll be very much obliged to you if you go away, and leave him to follow his own business.

Lees. Well, gentlemen—here comes Mr Torrington: you know him, I suppose, and will be satisfied with his security.

Leech. O, we'll take his bail for ten thousand pounds, my master—Every body knows him to be a man of fortune.

Lees. Give me leave to speak to him then, and I shall not be ungrateful for the civility.

Leech. Well, we will—But, hark'e, lads, look to the passes, that no tricks may be played upon travellers.

Enter TORRINGTON.

Lees. Mr Torrington, your most obedient.

Tor. Your humble servant.

Lees. I have many apologies to make, Mr Torrington, for presuming to stop a gentleman to whom I have not the honour of being known; yet when I explain the nature of my business, sir, I shall by no means despair of an excuse.

Tor. To the business, I beg, sir.

Lees. You must know, sir, that the three gentlemen behind me are three traders from Dantzic, men of considerable property, who, in the present distracted state of Poland, wish to settle with their families in this country.

Tor. Dantzic traders !—Ay, I see, they are foreigners by their dress.

Leech. Ay, now he is opening the affair.

Lees. They want therefore to be naturalized, and have been recommended to me for legal advice.

Tor. You are at the bar, sir ?

Lees. I have eat my way to professional honour some time, sir.

Tor. Ay, the cooks of the four societies take care that the students shall perform every thing which depends upon teeth, young gentleman.—The eating exercises are the only ones never dispensed with.

Lees. I am, however, a very young barrister, Mr Torrington ; and as the affair is of great importance to them, I am desirous that some gentleman of eminence in the law shou'd revise my poor opinion, before they make it a ground of any serious determination.

Tor. You are too modest, young gentleman, to entertain any doubts upon this occasion, as nothing is clearer than the laws with respect to the naturalization of foreigners.

Con. Faith the old gentleman smiles very good-naturedly.

Leech. I fancy he'll stand it, Crow, and advance the crop for the younker.

Lees. To be sure the laws are very clear to gentlemen of your superior abilities ; but I have candidly acknowledged the weakness of my own judgment to my clients, and advised them so warmly to solicit your opinion, that they will not be satisfied unless you kindly consent to oblige them.

Tor. O, if nothing but my opinion will satisfy them, let them follow me to my chambers, and I'll satisfy them directly.

Lees. You are extremely kind, sir, and they shall attend you.—Gentlemen, will you be so good as to follow Mr Torrington to his chambers, and he'll satisfy you entirely.

Wolf. Mind that !

Con. Musha ! the blessing of St Patrick upon that ould head of yours.

Tor. What, they speak English, do they ?

Lees. Very tolerably, sir !—Bred up general traders, they have a knowledge of several languages ; and it would be highly for the good of the kingdom, if we cou'd get more of them to settle among us.

Tor. Right, young gentleman ! the number of the people forms the true riches of a state; however, now-a-days, London itself is not only gone out of town, but England itself, by an unaccountable fatality, seems inclined to take up her residence in America.

Lees. True, sir ; and, to cultivate the barbarous borders of the Ohio, we are hourly deserting the beautiful banks of the Thames.

Tor. (*Shaking him by the hand.*) You must come and see me at chambers, young gentleman ! we must be better known to one another.

Con. Do you mind that, you thieves ?

Lees. 'Twill be equally my pride and my happiness to merit that honour, sir.

Tor. Let your friends follow me, sir;—and pray do you call upon me soon ; you shall see a little plan which I have drawn up to keep this poor country, if possible, from undergoing a general sentence of transportation.—Be pleased to come along with me, gentlemen—I'll satisfy you.   (*Exit.*

Leech. Well, master ! I wish you joy.—You can't say but we behaved to you like gemmen !

                              [*Exeunt Bailiffs.*

Lees. And if you were all three in the cart, I don't know which of you I wou'd wish to have respited from execution. I have played Mr Torrington a little trick, Connolly, but the moment I come back I shall recover my reputation, if I even put myself voluntarily into the hands of these worthy gentlemen.

                              (*Exit.*

Con. Musha ! long life to you, old Shillaley ; I don't wonder at your being afraid of a prison, for 'tis to be sure a blessed place to live in !—And now let my thick skull consider if there's any way of preventing this infernal duel.—Suppose I have him bound over to the peace !—No, that will never do : it would be a shameful thing for a gentleman to keep the peace ! besides, I must appear in the business, and people may then think, from my connection with him, that he hasn't honour enough to throw away his life !—Suppose I go another way to work, and send an anonymous letter about the affair to Mrs Belville ; they say, though she is a woman of quality, that no creature upon earth can be fonder of her husband !—Surely the good genius of Ireland put this scheme in my head.—I'll about it this minute, and if there's but one of them kept from the field, I don't think that the other can be much hurt, when there will be nobody to fight with him.   (*Exit.*

SCENE VII.

CAPTAIN SAVAGE'S *Lodgings.*

Enter CAPTAIN SAVAGE *and* BELVILLE.

Capt. Why, faith, Belville, your detection, and so speedily too, after all the pretended sanctity of the morning, must have thrown you into a most humiliating situation.

Bel. Into the most distressing you can imagine: had my wife raved at my falsehood, in the customary manner, I could have brazened it out pretty tolerably; but the angel-like sweetness, with which she bore the mortifying discovery, planted daggers in my bosom, and made me at that time wish her the veriest vixen in the whole creation.

Capt. Yet the suffering forbearance of a wife is a quality for which she is seldom allowed her merit: we think it her duty to put up with our falsehood, and imagine ourselves exceedingly generous in the main, if we practise no other method of breaking her heart.

Bel. Monstrous! monstrous! from this moment I bid an everlasting adieu to my vices: the generosity of my dear girl—

Enter a Servant to BELVILLE.

Serv. Here's a letter, sir, which Mr Spruce has brought you.

Bel. Give me leave, Savage—Zounds! what an industrious devil the father of darkness is, when, the

moment a man determines upon a good action, he
sends such a thing as this, to stagger his resolution.

Capt. What have you got there?

Bel. You shall know presently. Will you let
Spruce come in?

Capt. Where have you acquired all this ceremony?

Bel. Bid Spruce come in.

Serv. Yes, sir.

Capt. Is that another challenge?

Bel. 'Tis, upon my soul, but it came from a beautiful enemy, and dares me to give a meeting to Miss
Walsingham.

Capt. How!

Enter SPRUCE.

Bel. Pray, Spruce, who gave you this letter?

Spruce. Miss Walsingham's woman, sir: she said
it was about very particular business, and therefore I
wou'dn't trust it by any of the footmen.

Capt. O, damn your diligence!   (*Aside.*

Bel. You may go home, Spruce.

Spruce. (*Looking significantly at his master.*) Is
there no answer necessary, sir?

Bel. I shall call at home myself, and give the necessary answer.

Spruce. (*Aside.*) What can be the matter with
him all on a sudden, that he is so cold upon the
scent of wickedness?   (*Exit.*

Capt. And what answer do you propose making
to it, Belville?

Bel. Read the letter, and then tell me what I
should do—You know Miss Walsingham's hand?

Capt. O perfectly!—This is not—yes, it is her hand!
—I have too many curst occasions to know it.

          (*Aside.*

Bel. What are you muttering about?—Read the
letter.

Capt. If you are not entirely discouraged by our

last conversation, from renewing the subject which then
gave offence——

Bel. *Which* then *gave offence !*—You see, Savage,
that it is not offensive any longer.

Capt. 'Sdeath ! you put me out !—*You may at the
masquerade, this evening*—

Bel. You remember how earnest she was for the
masquerade party.

Capt. Yes, yes, I remember it well :—and I remember, also, how hurt she was this morning about
the affair of Miss Leeson. (*Aside.*)—*Have an opportunity of entertaining me*——O the strumpet !
(*Aside.*

Bel. But mind the cunning with which she signs
the note, for fear it shou'd by any accident fall into
improper hands.

Capt. Ay, and you put it into very proper hands.
(*Aside.*) *I shall be in the blue domino*—The signature
is—   You know who.

Bel. Yes, *you know who.*

Capt. May be, however, she has only written this
to try you.

Bel. To try me ! for what purpose ? But if you
read a certain postscript there, I fancy you'll be of a
different opinion.

Capt. *If Mr Belville has any house of character to
retire to, it wou'd be most agreeable, as there cou'd be
no fear of interruption.*

Bel. What do you say now ?—Can you recommend me to any house of character, where we shall
be free from interruption ?

Capt. O, curse her house of character ! (*Aside.*)
But surely, Belville, after your late determined resolution to reform——

Bel. Zounds ! I forgot that.

Capt. After the unexampled sweetness of your
wife's behaviour——

Bel. Don't go on, Savage : there is something here

(*Putting his hand upon his bosom.*) which feels already not a little awkwardly.

Capt. And can you still persist ?

Bel. I am afraid to answer your question.

Capt. Where the plague are you flying ?

Bel. From the justice of your censure, Horace, my own is sufficiently severe ; yet I see that I shall be a rascal again, in spite of my teeth ; and good advice is only thrown away upon so incorrigible a libertine. (*Exit.*

Capt. (*Alone.*) So then, this diamond of mine proves a counterfeit after all, and I am really the veriest wretch existing at the moment in which I conceived myself the peculiar favourite of fortune. O the cursed, cursed sex ! I'll see her once more to upbraid her with her falsehood, then acquaint my father with her perfidy, to justify my breaking off the marriage, and tear her from my thoughts for ever.

Enter a Servant.

Serv. Sir ! sir ! sir !—

Capt. Sir, sir, sir.—What the devil's the matter with the booby !

Serv. Miss Walsingham, sir !

Capt. Ah ! what of her ?

Serv. Was this moment overturned at Mr Belville's door ; and John tells me carried in a fit into the house.

Capt. Ha ! let me fly to her assistance. (*Exit.*

Serv. Ha, *let me fly to her assistance*—O, are you thereabouts ! (*Exit.*

SCENE VIII.

MR BELVILLE'S.

Enter MRS BELVILLE, MISS WALSINGHAM, *and*
LADY RACHEL MILDEW.

Mrs Bel. But are you indeed recovered, my dear ?

Miss Wal. Perfectly, my dear—I wasn't in the
least hurt though greatly terrified, when the two
fools of coachmen contended for the honour of being
first, and drove the carriages together with a violence
incredible.

Lady Rach. I sincerely rejoice at your escape;
and now, Mrs Belville, as you promised to choose a
dress for me if I went in your party to the masquerade this evening, can you spare a quarter of an hour
to Tavistock-Street ?

Mrs Bel. I am loth to leave Miss Walsingham
alone, Lady Rachel, so soon after her fright.

Miss Wal. Nay, I insist that you don't stay at
home upon my account; and Lady Rachel's company to the masquerade is a pleasure I have such an
interest in, that I beg you won't delay a moment to
oblige her.

Mrs Bel. Well, then I attend your ladyship.

Lady Rach. You are very good, and so is Miss
Walsingham.   (*Exit.*

Miss Wal. I wonder Captain Savage stays away
so long! where can he be all this time?—I die with
impatience to tell him of my happy interview with
the general.

Enter a Servant.

Serv. Captain Savage, madam.

Miss Wal. Shew him in. (*Exit Serv.*) How he must rejoice to find his conjectures so fortunately realized.

Enter CAPTAIN SAVAGE.

Capt. So, madam, you have just escaped a sad accident.

Miss Wal. And by that agreeable tone and coun-tenance, one would almost imagine you were very sorry for my escape.

Capt. People, madam, who doubt the kindness of others, are generally conscious of some defect in themselves.

Miss Wal. Don't madam me, with this accent of indifference. What has put you out of humour?

Capt. Nothing.

Miss Wal. Are you indisposed?

Capt. The crocodile! the crocodile! (*Aside.*

Miss Wal. Do you go to the masquerade to-night?

Capt. No, but you do.

Miss Wal. Why not? Come, don't be ill-natured, I'm not your wife yet.

Capt. Nor ever will be, I promise you.

Miss Wal. What is the meaning of this very whimsical behaviour?

Capt. The settled composure of her impudence is intolerable. (*Aside.*) Madam, madam, how have I deserved this usage?

Miss Wal. Nay, sir, sir, how have I deserved it, if you go to that?

Capt. The letter, madam!—the letter!

Miss Wal. What letter?

Capt. Your letter, inviting a gallant from the mas-querade to a house of character, madam!—What, you appear surprised?

Miss Wal. Well I may, at so shameless an asper-
sion.

Capt. Madam, madam, I have seen your letter !
Your new lover cou'dn't keep your secret a moment.
But I have nothing to do with you, and only come
to declare my reasons for renouncing you everlast-
ingly !

Enter Servant.

Serv. General Savage, madam.

Miss Wal. Shew him up. (*Exit Serv.*) I am glad
he is come, sir; inform him of your resolution to
break off the match, and let there be an end of every
thing between us.

Enter GENERAL SAVAGE.

Gen. The news of your accident reached me but
this moment, madam, or I should have posted much
sooner to reconnoitre your situation. My aid-de-
camp, however, has not been inattentive I see, and
I dare say his diligence will not be the least lessened,
when he knows his obligations to you.

Capt. O, sir, I am perfectly sensible of my obligations ; and the consciousness of them was one motive
of my coming here.

Gen. Then you have made your acknowledgments
to Miss Walsingham, I hope.

Miss Wal. He has indeed, General, said a great
deal more than was necessary.

Gen. That opinion proceeds from the liberality of
your temper ; for 'tis impossible he can ever say
enough of your goodness.

Capt. So it is ; if you knew but all, sir.

Gen. Why, who can think more of the matter than
myself ?

Miss Wal. This gentleman, it seems, has something, General Savage, very necessary for your information.

Gen. How's this?

Capt. Nay, sir, I only say, that for some particular reasons which I shall communicate to you at a more proper time, I must beg leave to decline the lady whose hand you kindly intended for me this morning.

Gen. O you must!—Why then I hope you decline at the same time all pretension to every shilling of my fortune? It is not in my power to make you fight, you poltroon, but I can punish you for cowardice.

Miss Wal. Nay, but, General, let me interpose here. If he can maintain any charge against the lady's reputation, 'twould be very hard that he should be disinherited for a necessary attention to his honour.

Capt. And if I don't make the charge good, I submit to be disinherited without murmuring.

Gen. 'Tis false as hell! the lady is infinitely too good for you in every respect; and I undervalued her worth when I thought of her for your wife.

Miss Wal. I am sure the lady is much obliged to your favourable opinion, sir.

Gen. Not in the least, madam; I only do her common justice.

Capt. I cannot bear that you should be displeased a moment, sir; suffer me therefore to render the conversation less equivocal, and a few words will explain every thing.

Gen. Sirrah, I'll hear no explanation; ar'n't my orders that you shou'd marry?

Miss Wal. For my sake hear him, General Savage.

Capt. Madam, I disdain every favour that is to be procured by your interposition.   (*Exit.*

Miss Wal. This matter must not be suffered to proceed farther though, provokingly, cruelly as the captain has behaved.   (*Aside.*

Gen. What's that you say, my bewitching girl?

Miss Wal. I say that you must make it up with the Captain, and the best way will be to hear his charge patiently.

Gen. I am shocked at the brutality of the dog ; he has no more principle than a suttler, and no more steadiness than a young recruit upon drill. But you shall have ample satisfaction :—this very day I'll cut him off from a possibility of succeeding to a shilling of my fortune. He shall be as miserable as——

Miss Wal. Dear General, do you think that this wou'd give me any satisfaction ?

Gen. How he became acquainted with my design I know not, but I see plainly that his mutiny proceeds from his aversion to my marrying again.

Miss Wal. To your marrying again, sir ! why shou'd he object to that ?

Gen. Why, for fear I should have other children, to be sure.

Miss Wal. Indeed, sir, it was not from that motive ; and, if I can overlook his folly, you may be prevailed upon to forgive it.

Gen. After what you have seen, justice shou'd make you a little more attentive to your own interest, my lovely girl.

Miss Wal. What, at the expence of his ?

Gen. In the approaching change of your situation, there may be a family of your own.

Miss Wal. Suppose there shou'd, sir, won't there be a family of his too ?

Gen. I care not what becomes of his family

Miss Wal. But, pray let me think a little about it, General.

Gen. 'Tis hard, indeed, when I was so desirous of promoting his happiness, that he shou'd throw any thing in the way of mine.

Miss Wal. Recollect, sir, his offence was wholly confined to me.

Gen. Well, my love, and isn't it throwing an obstacle in the way of my happiness, when he abuses you so grossly for your readiness to marry me?

Miss Wal. Sir!—

Gen. I see, with all your good nature, that this is a question you cannot rally against.

Miss Wal. It is indeed, sir.—What will become of me?   [*Aside.*

Gen. You seem suddenly disordered, my love?

Miss Wal. Why really, sir, this affair affects me strongly.

Gen. Well, it is possible, that for your sake I may not punish him with as much severity as I intended: in about an hour I shall beg leave to beat up your quarters again with Mr Torrington, for 'tis necessary I should shew you some proof of my gratitude, since you have been so kindly pleased to honour me with a proof of your affection.

Miss Wal. (*Aside.*) So, now indeed we're in a hopeful situation.   [*Exeunt.*

SCENE IX.

TORRINGTON's *Chambers in the Temple.*

Enter TORRINGTON, LEECH, CROW, *and* WOLF.

Tor. Walk in, gentlemen—A good pretty young man that we parted with just now—Pray, gentlemen, be seated.

Leech. He is indeed a very pretty young man.

Crow. And knows how to do a genteel thing.

Wolf. As handsome as any body.

Tor. There is a rectitude besides in his polemical principles.

Leech. In what, sir ?

Tor. His polemical principles.

Crow. What are they, sir ?

Tor. I beg pardon, gentlemen, you are not sufficiently intimate with the English language to carry on a conversation in it.

Wolf. Yes, we are, sir.

Tor. Because, if it is more agreeable to you, we'll talk in Latin.

Leech. We don't understand Latin, sir.

Tor. I thought you generally conversed in that language abroad.

Crow. No, nor at home neither, sir ; there is a language we sometimes talk in, called slang.

Tor. A species of the ancient Sclavonic, I suppose ?

Leech. No, it's a little rum tongue, that we understand among von another.

Tor. I never heard of it before—But to business, gentlemen—The constitution of your country is at present very deplorable, I hear.

Wolf. Why indeed, sir, there never was a greater cry against people in our way.

Tor. But you have laws, I suppose, for the regulation of your trade ?

Leech. To be sure we have, sir, nevertheless ve find it very difficult to carry it on.

Crow. Ve are harrassed with so many oppressions—

Tor. What, by the Prussian troops ?

Crow. The Prussian troops, sir—Lord bless you, no, by the courts of law ; if ve make never so small a mistake in our duties—

Tor. Then your duties are very high, or very numerous ?

Leech. I am afraid we don't understand one another, sir.

Tor. I am afraid so too—Pray where are your papers, gentlemen ?

Leech. Here's all the papers we have, sir—You'll find every thing right.

Tor. I dare say I shall. (*Reads.*) " Middlesex to wit"—Why this is a warrant from the sheriff's office to arrest some body.

Crow. To be sure it is, sir.

Tor. And what do you give it to me for ?

Wolf. To shew that we have done nothing contrary to law, sir.

Tor. Who supposes that you have ?

Leech. Only because you asked for our papers, sir.

Tor. Why what has this to do with them ?

Crow. Why, that's the warrant for arresting the young gentleman.

Tor. What young gentleman ?

Wolf. Lord bless your heart, sir, that stopped you in the street, and that you bail'd for the hundred and seventy pounds.

Tor. I bail'd for an hundred and seventy pounds !

Leech. Sure, sir, you told me to follow you to chambers, and you would satisfy us.

Tor. Pray hear me, sir ; aren't you a trader of Dantzic ?

Leech. I a trader ! I am no trader, nor did I ever before hear of any such place.

Tor. Perhaps this gentleman is.

Crow. Lord help your head, I was born in Claremarket, and never was farther out of town in my life than Brentford, to attend the sheriff at the Middlesex election.

Tor. And it may be that you don't want to be naturalized ?   [*To* WOLF.

Wolf. For what, my master ? I am a liveryman of London already, and have a vote besides for the four counties.

Tor. Well, gentlemen, having been so good as to tell me what you are not, add a little to the obligation, and tell me what you are ?

Leech. Why, sir, the warrant we have shewed you, tells that ve are sheriff's officers.

Tor. Sheriff's officers are you?—O ho—sheriff's officers—then I suppose you must be three very honest gentlemen.

Crow. Sir !—we are as honest—

Tor. As sheriff's officers usually are.—Yet cou'd you think of nobody but a man of the law for the object of your conspiracy ?

Leech. Sir, we don't understand what you mean.

Tor. But I understand what you mean, and therefore I'll deal with you properly.

Wolf. I hope, sir, you'll pay us the money, for we can't go till the affair is certainly settled in some manner.

Tor. Oh, you can't—why then I will pay you; but it shall be in a coin you won't like, depend upon it.—Here, Mr Molesworth—

Enter MOLESWORTH.

Tor. Make out mittimusses for the commitment of these three fellows; they are disguised to defraud people; but I am in the commission for Middlesex, and I'll have you all brought to justice.—I will teach you to go masquerading about the streets.—So take them along, Mr Molesworth.

Leech. Ve don't fear your mittimus.

Crow. We'll put in bail directly, and try it with you, though you are a great lawyer.

Wolf. He'll make a flat of himself in this Nantzick affair.

Tor. Mighty well—And, if I find the young barrister, he may, perhaps, take a trip to the barbarous borders of the Ohio from the beautiful banks of the Thames.   [*Exeunt.*

ACT THE FOURTH.

SCENE I.

An Apartment at BELVILLE'S.

Enter Mrs BELVILLE *and Captain* SAVAGE.

Mrs Bel. Don't argue with me, Captain Savage; but consider that I am a wife, and pity my distraction.

Capt. Dear madam, there is no occasion to be so much alarmed; Mr Belville has very properly determined not to fight; he told me so himself, and should have been effectually prevented, if I hadn't known his resolution.

Mrs Bel. There is no knowing to what extremities he may be provoked, if he meets Mr Leeson; I have sent for you, therefore, to beg that you will save him from the possibility, either of exposing himself to any danger, or of doing an injury to his adversary.

Capt. What wou'd you have me do, madam?

Mrs Bel. Fly to Hyde-Park, and prevent, if yet possible, his meeting with Mr Leeson: do it, I conjure you, if you'd save me from desperation.

Capt. Though you have no reason whatever to be apprehensive for his safety, madam, yet, since you are so very much affected, I'll immediately execute your commands.   [*Exit.*

Mrs Bel. Merciful Heaven! where is the generosity, where is the sense, where is the shame of men, to find a pleasure in pursuits which they cannot remember without the deepest horror; which they cannot follow without the meanest fraud; and which they cannot effect without consequences the most dreadful? The single word pleasure, in a masculine sense, comprehends every thing that is cruel, every thing that is base, and every thing that is desperate: yet men, in other respects the noblest of their species, make it the principal business of their lives, and do not hesitate to break in upon the peace of the happiest families, though their own must be necessarily exposed to destruction!—O Belville! Belville!—my love!—The greatest crime which a libertine can ever experience, is too despicable to be envied; 'tis at best nothing but a victory over his own humanity; and if he is a husband, he must be dead indeed, if he is not doubly tortured upon the wheel of recollection!

Enter MISS WALSINGHAM *and* LADY RACHEL MILDEW.

Miss Wal. My dear Mrs Belville, I am extremely unhappy to see you so distressed.

Lady Rach. Now I am extremely glad to see her so, for if she wasn't greatly distressed it wou'd be monstrously unnatural.

Mrs Bel. O, Matilda!—my husband! my husband! my children! my children!

Miss Wal. Don't weep, my dear, don't weep; pray be comforted, all may end happily. Lady Rachel, beg of her not to cry so.

Lady Rach. Why, you are crying yourself, Miss

Walsingham; and though I think it out of character to encourage her tears, I can't help keeping you company.

Mrs Bel. O, why is not some effectual method contrived to prevent this horrible practice of duelling!

Lady Rach. I'll expose it on the stage, since the law now-a-days kindly leaves the whole cognizance of it to the theatre.

Miss Wal. And yet if the laws against it were as well enforced as the laws against destroying the game, perhaps it would be equally for the benefit of the kingdom.

Mrs Bel. No law will ever be effectual till the custom is rendered infamous.—Wives must shriek— mothers must agonize—orphans must multiply, unless some blessed hand strips the fascinating glare from honourable murder, and bravely exposes the idol who is worshipped thus in blood. While it is disreputable to obey the laws, we cannot look for reformation :—But if the duellist is once banished from the presence of his sovereign;—if he is for life excluded the confidence of his country ;—if a mark of indelible disgrace is stamped upon him, the sword of public justice will be the sole chastiser of wrongs; trifles will not be punished with death, and offences really meriting such a punishment will be reserved for the only proper avenger, the common executioner.

Lady Rach. I cou'dn't have expressed myself better on the subject, my dear : but, till such a hand as you talk of is found, the best will fall into the error of the times.

Miss Wal. Yes, and butcher each other like madmen, for fear their courage should be suspected by fools.

Mrs Bel. No news yet from Captain Savage ?

Lady Rach. He can't have reached Hyde-park yet, my dear.

Miss Wal. Let us lead you to your chamber, my dear; you'll be better there.

Mrs Bel. Matilda, I must be wretched any where; but I'll attend you.

Lady Rach. Thank heaven I have no husband to plunge into such a situation.

Miss Wal. And, if I thought I cou'd keep my resolution, I'd determine this moment on living single all the days of my life. Pray don't spare my arm, my dear.   [*Exeunt.*

SCENE II.

Hyde-Park.

Enter BELVILLE.

Bel. I fancy I am rather before the time of appointment; engagements of this kind are the only ones in which, now-a-days, people pretend to any punctuality:—a man is allowed half an hour's law to dinner, but a thrust through the body must be given within a second of the clock.

Enter LEESON.

Lees. Your servant, sir.—Your name I suppose is Belville?

Bel. Your supposition is very right, sir; and I fancy I am not much in the wrong when I suppose your name to be Leeson?

Lees. It is, sir; I am sorry I shou'd keep you here a moment.

Bel. I am very sorry, sir, you shou'd bring me here at all.

Lees. I regret the occasion, be assured, sir, but 'tis not now a time for talking—we must proceed to action.

Bel. And yet talking is all the action I shall proceed to, depend upon it.

Lees. What do you mean, sir? where are your pistols?

Bel. Where I intend they shall remain till my next journey into the country—very quietly over the chimney in my dressing-room.

Lees. You treat this matter with too much levity, Mr Belville; take your choice of mine, sir.

Bel. I'd rather take them both, if you please, for then no mischief shall be done with either of them.

Lees. Sir, this trifling is adding insult to injury, and shall be resented accordingly. Didn't you come here to give me satisfaction?

Bel. Yes, every satisfaction in my power.

Lees. Take one of these pistols then.

Bel. Come, Mr Leeson, your bravery will not at all be lessened by the exercise of a little understanding: if nothing less than my life can atone for the injury I have unconsciously done you, fire at me instantly, but don't be offended because I decline to do you an additional wrong.

Lees. 'Sdeath, sir! do you think I come here with an intention to murder?

Bel. You come to arm the guilty against the innocent, sir; and that, in my opinion, is the most atrocious intention of murder.

Lees. How's this?

Bel. Look'e, Mr Leeson, there's your pistol— (*Throws it on the ground.*) I have already acted very wrongly with respect to your sister; but, sir, I have some character (though perhaps little enough) to maintain, and I will not do still a worse action, in raising my hand against your life.

Lees. This hypocritical cant of cowardice, sir, is too palpable to disarm my resentment ; though I held you to be a man of profligate principles, I neverthe-less considered you as a man of courage ; but, if you hesitate a moment longer, by heaven I'll chastise you on the spot. (*Draws.*)

Bel. I must defend my life ; though, if it did not look like timidity, I would inform you—(*They fight,* LEESON *is disarmed.*) Mr Leeson, there is your sword again.

Lees. Strike it through my bosom, sir ;—I don't desire to out-live this instant.

Bel. I hope, my dear sir, that you will long live happy, as your sister, though to my shame I can claim no merit on that account, is recovered unpol-luted by her family ; but let me beg that you will now see the folly of decisions by the sword, when success is not fortunately chained to the side of jus-tice : before I leave you, receive my sincerest apolo-gies for the injuries I have done you ; and be assured no occurrence will give me greater pleasure, than an opportunity of serving you, if, after what is past, you shall at any time condescend to use me as a friend.

[*Exit.*

Lees. Very well—very well—very well.

Enter CONNOLLY.

Lees. What, you have been within hearing I sup-pose ?

Con. You may say that.

Lees. And isn't this very fine ?

Con. Why I can't say much as to the finery of it, sir, but it is very foolish.

Lees. And so this is my satisfaction after all.

Con. Yes, and pretty satisfaction it is. When Mr Belville did you but one injury, he was the greatest villain in the world ; but now that he has done you two, in drawing his sword upon you, I suppose he is a very worthy gentleman.

Lees. To be foil'd, baffled, disappointed in my revenge !—What, though my sister is by accident un-stained, his intentions are as criminal as if her ruin was actually perpetrated ; there is no possibility of enduring this reflection !—I wish not for the blood of my enemy, but I would at least have the credit of giving him his life.

Con. Arrah, my dear, if you had any regard for the life of your enemy, you shou'dn't put him in the way of death.

Lees. No more of these reflections, my dear Con-nolly ; my own feelings are painful enough. Will you be so good as to take these damned pistols, and come with me to the coach ?

Con. Troth and that I will ; but don't make your-self uneasy : consider that you have done every thing which honour required at your hands.

Lees. I hope so.

Con. Why you know so ; you have broke the laws of heaven and earth, as nobly as the first lord in the land, and you have convinced the world, that where any body has done your family one injury, you have courage enough to do it another yourself, by hazard-ing your life.

Lees. Those, Connolly, who would live reputably in any country, must regulate their conduct in many cases by its very prejudices.—Custom, with respect to duelling, is a tyrant, whose despotism no body ven-tures to attack, though every body detests its cruelty.

Con. I didn't imagine that a tyrant of any kind would be tolerated in England. But where do you think of going now ? For chambers, you know, will be most delightfully dangerous, till you have come to an explanation with Mr Torrington.

Lees. I shall go to Mrs Crayons's.

Con. What, the gentlewoman that paints all manner of colours in red chalk ?

Lees. Yes, where I first became acquainted with Emily.

Con. And where the sweet creature has met you two to three times, under pretence of sitting for her picture.

Lees. Mrs Crayons will, I dare say, oblige me in this exigency with an apartment for a few days. I shall write, from her house, a full explanation of my conduct to Mr Torrington, and let him know where I am : for the honest old man must not be the smallest sufferer, though a thousand prisons were to stare me in the face.—But come, Connolly, we have no time to lose.—Yet if you had any prudence, you would abandon me in my present situation.

Con. Ah, sir, is this your opinion of my friendship ? Do you think that any thing can ever give me half so much pleasure in serving you, as seeing you surrounded by misfortunes ?   (*Exeunt.*

SCENE III.

An Apartment at BELVILLE'S.

Enter GENERAL SAVAGE, TORRINGTON, *and* SPRUCE.

Spruce. Miss Walsingham will wait on you immediately, gentlemen.

Gen. Very well.

Spruce. (*Aside.*) What can old Holifernes want so continually with Miss Walsingham?   (*Exit.*

Gen. When I bring this sweet mild creature home, I shall be able to break her spirit to my own wishes

—I'll inure her to proper discipline from the first moment, and make her tremble at the very thought of mutiny.

Tor. Ah, General, you are wonderfully brave, when you know the meekness of your adversary.

Gen. Envy, Torrington—stark, staring envy : few fellows on the borders of fifty have so much reason as myself to boast of a blooming young woman's partiality.

Tor. On the borders of fifty, man !—beyond the confines of threescore.

Gen. The more reason I have to boast of my victory then; but don't grumble at my triumph : you shall have a kiss of the bride, let that content you, Torrington.

Enter MISS WALSINGHAM.

Miss Wal. Gentlemen, your most obedient ; General, I intended writing to you about a trifling mistake ; but poor Mrs Belville has been so very ill, that I cou'dn't find an opportunity.

Gen. 1 am very sorry for Mrs Belville's illness, but I am happy, madam, to be personally in the way of receiving your commands, and I wait upon you with Mr Torrington, to talk about a marriage settlement.

Miss Wal. Heavens ! how shall I undeceive him !
                                                (Aside.

Tor. 'Tis rather an awkward business, Miss Walsingham, to trouble you upon ; but as the General wishes that the affair may be as private as possible, he thought it better to speak to yourself than to treat with any other person.

Gen. Yes, my lovely girl ; and to convince you that I intended to carry on an honourable war, not to pillage like a free-booter, Mr Torrington will be a trustee.

Miss Wal. I am infinitely obliged to your intention, but there's no necessity to talk about my settlement —for——

Gen. Pardon me, madam,—pardon me, there is—besides, I have determined that there shall be one, and what I once determine is absolute.—A tolerable hint for her own behaviour, when I have married her, Torrington.   (*Aside to* Tor.

Miss Wal. I must not shock him before Mr Torrington. (*Aside.*) General Savage, will you give me leave to speak a few words in private to you?

Gen. There is no occasion for sounding a retreat, madam; Mr Torrington is acquainted with the whole business, and I am determined, for your sake, that nothing shall be done without him.

Tor. I can have no objection to your hearing the lady *ex parte*, General.

Miss Wal. What I have to say, sir, is of a very particular nature.

Tor. (*Rising.*) I'll leave the room then.

Gen. (*Opposing him.*) You sha'n't leave the room, Torrington. Miss Walsingham shall have a specimen of my command, even before marriage, and you shall see that every woman is not to bully me out of my determination.   (*Aside to* Tor.

Miss Wal. Well, General, you must have your own way.

Gen. (*To* Tor.) Don't you see that 'tis only fighting the battle stoutly at first with one of these gentle creatures?

Tor. (*Significantly.*) Ah, General!

Gen. I own, madam, your situation is a distressing one; let us sit down—let us sit down——

Miss Wal. It is unspeakably distressing indeed, sir.

Tor. Distressing however as it may be, we must proceed to issue, madam; the General proposes your jointure to be 1000l. a year.

Miss Wal. General Savage!

Gen. You think this is too little, perhaps?

Miss Wal. I can't think of any jointure, sir.

Tor. Why to be sure, a jointure is at best but a

melancholy possession, for it must be purchased by the loss of the husband you love.

Miss Wal. Pray don't name it, Mr Torrington.

Gen. (*Kissing her hand.*) A thousand thanks to you, my lovely girl.

Miss Wal. For heaven's sake let go my hand.

Gen. I shall be mad till it gives me legal possession of the town.

Miss Wal. Gentlemen—General—Mr Torrington, I—beg you'll hear me.

Gen. By all means, my adorable creature; I can never have too many proofs of your disinterested affection.

Miss Wal. There is a capital mistake in this whole affair—I am sinking under a load of distress.

Gen. Your confusion makes you look charmingly, though——

Miss Wal. There is no occasion to talk of jointures or marriages to me; I am not going to be married.

Tor. What's this?

Miss Wal. Nor have I an idea in nature, however enviable I think the honour, of being your wife, sir.

Gen. Madam!

Tor. Why here's a demur!

Miss Wal. I am afraid, sir, that in our conversation this morning, my confusion, arising from the particularity of the subject, has led you into a material misconception.

Gen. I am thunder-struck, madam! I cou'dn't mistake my ground.

Tor. As clear a *nol. pros.* as ever was issued by an attorney-general.

Gen. Surely you can't forget, that at the first word you hung out a flag of truce, told me even that I had a previous friend in the fort, and didn't so much as hint a single article of capitulation?

Tor. Now for the rejoinder to this replication.

Miss Wal. All this is unquestionably true, General,

and perhaps a good deal more ; but in reality my
confusion before you on this subject to-day was such,
that I scarcely knew what I said ; I was dying with
distress, and at this moment am very little better ;—
permit me to retire, General Savage, and only suffer
me to add, that, though I think myself highly flattered by your addresses, it is impossible for me ever to
receive them.   Lord ! Lord ! I am glad 'tis over in
any manner !   [*Exit*.

Tor. Why, we are a little out in this matter, General ; the judge has decided against us, when we
imagined ourselves sure of the cause.

Gen. The gates shut in my teeth, just as I expected the keys from the governor !

Tor. I am disappointed myself, man ; I sha'n't have
a kiss of the bride.

Gen. At my time of life too !

Tor. I said from the first you were too old for her.

Gen. Zounds, to fancy myself sure of her, and to
triumph upon a certainty of victory !

Tor. Ay, and to kiss her hand in a rapturous return for her tenderness to you : let me advise you
never to kiss before folks as long as you live again.

Gen. Don't distract me, Torrington ! a joke, where
a friend has the misfortune to lose the battle, is a
downright inhumanity.

Tor. You told me that your son had accused her
of something that you would not hear ; suppose we
call at his lodgings, he perhaps, as an *amicus curiæ*,
may be able to give us a little information.

Gen. Thank you for the thought ;—but keep your
finger more than ever upon your lips, dear Torrington.   You know how I dread the danger of ridicule,
and it wou'd be too much, not only to be thrashed
out of the field, but to be laughed at into the bargain.

Tor. I thought when you made a presentment of
your sweet person to Miss Walsingham, that the bill
wou'd be returned ignoramus.   [*Exeunt.*

SCENE III.

BELVILLE'S.

MRS BELVILLE *and* LADY RACHEL MILDEW, *discovered on a Sopha.*

Lady Rach. You heard what Captain Savage said?

Mrs Bel. I would flatter myself, but my heart will not suffer it ; the Park might be too full for the horrid purpose, and, perhaps they are gone to decide the quarrel in some other place.

Lady Rach. The Captain inquired of numbers in the Park without hearing a syllable of them, and is therefore positive that they are parted without doing any mischief.

Mrs Bel. I am, nevertheless, torn by a thousand apprehensions, and my fancy, with a gloomy kind of fondness, fastens on the most deadly. This very morning I exultingly numbered myself in the catalogue of the happiest wives—Perhaps I am a wife no longer ;—perhaps, my little innocents, your unhappy father is at this moment breathing his last sigh, and wishing, O, how vainly ! that he had not preferred a guilty pleasure to his own life, to my eternal peace of mind, and your felicity !

Enter SPRUCE.

Spruce. Madam ! madam ! my master ! my master !

Mrs Bel. Is he safe ?

Enter BELVILLE.

Bel. My love !

Mrs Bel. O, Mr Belville !   (*Faints.*

Bel. Assistance, quick !

Lady Rach. There she revives.

Bel. The angel-softness ! how this rends my heart!

Mrs Bel. O, Mr Belville, if you cou'd conceive the agonies I have endured, you would avoid the possibility of another quarrel as long as you lived, out of common humanity.

Bel. My dearest creature, spare these tender reproaches ; you know not how sufficiently I am punished to see you thus miserable.

Lady Rach. That's pleasant indeed, when you have yourself deliberately loaded her with affliction.

Bel. Pray, pray, Lady Rachel, have a little mercy : Your poor humble servant has been a very naughty boy,—but if you only forgive him this single time, he will never more deserve the rod of correction.

Mrs Bel. Since you are returned safe, I am happy. Excuse these foolish tears, they gush in spite of me.

Bel. How contemptible do they render me, my love !

Lady Rach. Come, my dear, you must turn your mind from this gloomy subject.—Suppose we step up stairs, and communicate our pleasure to Miss Walsingham ?

Mrs Bel. With all my heart.   Adieu, recreant!

    [*Exeunt* Mrs Bel. *and* Lady Rach.

Bel. I don't deserve such a woman, I don't deserve her.—Yet, I believe I am the first husband that ever found fault with a wife for having too much goodness.

Enter Spruce.

What's the matter ?

Spruce. Your sister——

Bel. What of my sister ?

Spruce. Sir, is eloped.

Bel. My sister !

Spruce. There is a letter left, sir, in which she says, that her motive was a dislike to match with Captain Savage, as she has placed her affections unalterably on another gentleman.

Bel. Death and damnation!

Spruce. Mrs Moreland, your mother, is in the greatest distress, sir, and begs you will immediately go with the servant that brought the message; for he, observing the young lady's maid carrying some bundles out, a little suspiciously, thought there must be some scheme going on, and dogged a hackney coach, in which Miss Moreland went off, to the very house where it set her down.

Bel. Bring me to the servant, instantly;—but don't let a syllable of this matter reach my wife's ears, her spirits are already too much agitated. (*Exit.*

Spruce. Zounds! we shall be paid home for the tricks we have played in other families! (*Exit.*

SCENE IV.

CAPTAIN SAVAGE'S *Lodgings.*

Enter CAPTAIN SAVAGE.

Capt. The vehemence of my resentment agains this abandoned woman has certainly led me too far. I shou'dn't have acquainted her with my discovery of her baseness;—no, if I had acted properly, I should have concealed all knowledge of the transaction till the very moment of her guilt, and then burst upon her when she was solacing with her paramour in all the fulness of security. Now, if she should either alter her mind with respect to going to the masque-

rade, or go in a different habit to elude my observation, I not only lose the opportunity of exposing her,
but give her time to plan some plausible excuse for
her infamous letter to Belville.

Enter a Servant.

Serv. General Savage and Mr Torrington, sir.
Capt. You blockhead, why did you let them wait
a moment? What can be the meaning of this visit?
                                          [*Exit Servant.*

Enter GENERAL SAVAGE *and* TORRINGTON.

Gen. I come, Horace, to talk to you about Miss
Walsingham.
Capt. She's the most worthless woman existing,
sir: I can convince you of it.
Gen. I have already changed my own opinion of
her.
Capt. What, you have found her out yourself, sir?
Tor. Yes, he has made a trifling discovery.
Gen. 'Sdeath, don't make me contemptible to my
son!   (*Aside to* TOR.
Capt. But, sir, what instance of her precious behaviour has come to your knowledge? For an hour
has scarcely elapsed since you thought her a miracle
of goodness.
Tor. Ay, he has thought her a miracle of goodness
within this quarter of an hour.
Gen. Why she has a manner that wou'd impose
upon all the world.
Capt. Yes, but she has a manner also to undeceive
the world thoroughly.
Tor. That we have found pretty recently; however, in this land of liberty, none are to be pronounced guilty till they are positively convicted; I can't
therefore find against Miss Walsingham upon the
bare strength of presumptive evidence.

Capt. Presumptive evidence ! hav'n't I promised you ocular demonstration ?

Tor. Ay, but till we receive this demonstration, my good friend, we cannot give judgment.

Capt. Then I'll tell you at once who is the object of her honourable affections.

Gen. Who—who——

Capt. What would you think if they were placed on Belville ?

Gen. Upon Belville ! has she deserted to him from the corps of virtue ?

Capt. Yes, she wrote to him, desiring to be taken from the masquerade to some convenient scene of privacy, and though I have seen the letter, she has the impudence to deny her own hand.

Gen. What a fiend is there then disguised under the uniform of an angel !

Tor. The delicate creature that was dying with confusion !

Capt. Only come with me to the masquerade, and you shall see Belville carry her off: 'Twas about the scandalous appointment with him I was speaking when you conceived I treated her so rudely.

Gen. And you were only anxious to shew her in her real character to me, when I was so exceedingly offended with you ?

Capt. Nothing else in the world, sir; I knew you would despise and detest her the moment you were acquainted with her baseness.

Gen. How she brazened it out before my face, and what a regard she affected for your interest ! I was a madman not to listen to your explanation.

Tor. Though you both talk this point well, I still see nothing but strong presumption against Miss Walsingham : Mistakes have already happened, mistakes may happen again ; and I will not give up a lady's honour upon an evidence that wou'd not cast a common pickpocket at the Old Bailey.

Capt. Come to the masquerade then, and be convinced.

Gen. Let us detach a party for dresses immediately. Yet remember, Torrington, that the punctuality of evidence which is necessary in a court of law is by no means requisite in a court of honour.

Tor. Perhaps it would be more to the honour of your honourable courts if it was.   (*Exeunt.*

SCENE V.

An Apartment at Mrs CRAYONS'S.

Bel. (*Behind.*) My dear, you must excuse me.

Maid. Indeed, sir, you must not go up stairs.

Bel. Indeed but I will ; the man is positive to the house, and I'll search every room in it, from the cellar to the garret, if I don't find the lady. James, don't stir from the street door.

Enter BELVILLE, *followed by a Maid.*

Maid. Sir, you are the strangest gentleman I ever met with in all my born days :—I wish my mistress was at home.

Bel. I am a strange fellow, my dear ; but if your mistress was at home, I shou'd take the liberty of peeping into the apartments.

Maid. Sir, there's company in that room, you can't go in there.

Bel. Now that's the very reason I will go in.

Maid. This must be some great man, or he wou'dn't behave so obstropolous.

Bel. Good manners, by your leave a little. (*Forcing the door.*) Whoever my gentleman is, I'll call him to

a severe reckoning :—I have just been called to one
myself, for making free with another man's sister.

Enter LEESON, *followed by* CONNOLLY.

Lees. Who is it that dares commit an outrage
upon this apartment ?

Con. An Englishman's very lodging, ay, and an
Irishman's too, I hope, is his castle ;—an Irishman
is an Englishman all the world over.

Bel. Mr Leeson !

Maid. O we shall have murder !   (*Running off.*

Con. Run into that room, my dear, and stay with
the young lady.   (*Exit Maid.*

Lees. And, Connolly, let nobody else into that room.

Con. Let me alone for that, honey, if this gentleman has fifty people.

Lees. Whence is it Mr, Belville, that you persecute
me thus with injuries ?

Bel. I am filled with astonishment !

Con. Faith, to speak the truth, you do look a little
surprised.

Lees. Answer me, sir ; what is the foundation of
this new violence ?

Bel. I am come, Mr Leeson, upon an affair, sir—

Con. The devil burn me if he was half so much
confounded a while ago, when there was a naked
sword at his breast.

Bel. I am come, Mr Leeson, upon an affair, sir,
that—How the devil shall I open it to him, since the
tables are so fairly turned upon me ?

Lees. Dispatch, sir, for I have company in the
next room.

Bel. A lady, I suppose ?

Lees. Suppose it is, sir ?

Bel. And the lady's name is Moreland, isn't it, sir ?

Lees. I can't see what business you have with her
name, sir. You took away my sister, and I hope you
have no designs upon the lady in the next room ?

Bel. Indeed but I have.

Lees. The devil you have!

Con. Well, this is the most unaccountable man I ever heard of; he'll have all the women in the town, I believe.

Lees. And pray, sir, what pretensions have you to the lady in the next room, even supposing her to be Miss Moreland?

Bel. No other pretensions than what a brother should have to the defence of his sister's honour: You thought yourself authorised to cut my throat a while ago in a similar business.

Lees. And is Miss Moreland your sister?

Bel. Sir, there is insolence in the question; you know she is.

Lees. By heaven, I did not know it till this moment; but I rejoice at the discovery: This is blow for blow!

Con. Devil burn me but they have fairly made a swop of it.

Bel. And you really didn't know that Miss Moreland was my sister?

Lees. I don't conceive myself under much necessity of apologizing to you, sir; but I am incapable of a dishonourable design upon any woman; and though Miss Moreland, in our short acquaintance, repeatedly mentioned her brother, she never once told me that his name was Belville.

Con. And he has had such few opportunities of being in her company, unless by letters, honey, that he knew nothing more of her connections, than her being a sweet pretty creature, and having thirty thousand pounds.

Bel. The fortune, I dare say, no way lessened the force of her attractions.

Lees. I am above dissimulation—it really did not.

Bel. Well, Mr Leeson, our families have shewn

such a very strong inclination to come together, that it would really be a pity to disappoint them.

Con. Upon my soul and so it would; though the dread of being forced to have a husband, the young lady tells us, quickened her resolution to marry this gentleman.

Bel. O she had no violence of that kind to apprehend from her family : therefore, Mr Leeson, since you seem as necessary for the girl's happiness as she seems for your's, you shall marry her here in town, with the consent of all her friends, and save yourself the trouble of an expedition to Scotland.

Lees. Can I believe you serious ?

Bel. Zounds, Leeson, that air of surprise is a sad reproach ! I didn't surprise you when I did a bad action, but I raise your astonishment when I do a good one.

Con. And by my soul, Mr Belville, if you knew how a good action becomes a man, you'd never do a bad one as long as you lived.

Lees. You have given me life and happiness in one day, Mr Belville ! however, it is now time you shou'd see your sister ; I know you'll be gentle with her, though you have so much reason to condemn her choice, and generously remember, that her elopement proceeded from the great improbability there was of a beggar's ever meeting with the approbation of her family.

Bel. Don't apologize for your circumstances, Leeson : a princess could do no more than make you happy, and if you make her so, you meet her upon terms of the most perfect equality.

Lees. This is a new way of thinking, Mr Belville.

Bel. 'Tis only an honest way of thinking ; and I consider my sister a gainer upon the occasion ; for a man of your merit is more difficult to be found than a woman of her fortune.

(*Exeunt* LEESON *and* BELVILLE.

Con. What's the reason now that I can't skip and laugh and rejoice at this affair? Upon my soul my heart's as full as if I had met with some great misfortune. Well, pleasure in the extreme is certainly a very painful thing: 1 am really ashamed of these woman's drops, and yet I don't know but that I ought to blush for being ashamed of them, for I am sure nobody's eye ever looks half so well as when it is disfigured by a tear of humanity.   (*Exit.*

ACT THE FIFTH.

SCENE I.

A Drawing-Room.

Enter BELVILLE.

Bel. Well, happiness is once more mine, and the women are all going in tip-top spirits to the masquerade. Now, Mr Belville, let me have a few words with you: Miss Walsingham, the ripe, the luxurious Miss Walsingham, expects to find you there burning with impatience:—But, my dear friend, after the occurrences of the day, can you be weak enough to plunge into fresh crimes? Can you be base enough to abuse the goodness of that angel your wife; and wicked enough, not only to destroy the innocence which is sheltered beneath your own roof, but to ex-

pose your family perhaps again, to the danger of losing a son, a brother, a father, and a husband ? The
possession of the three graces is surely too poor a recompence for the folly you must commit, for the
shame you must feel, and the consequence you must
hazard   Upon my soul, if I struggle a little longer,
I shall rise in my own opinion, and be less a rascal
than I think myself:—Ay, but the object is bewitching ;—the matter will be an eternal secret—and if it
is known that I sneak in this pitiful manner from a
fine woman, when the whole elysium of her person
solicits me :—Well, and am I afraid the world should
know that I have shrunk from an infamous action ?—
A thousand blessings on you, dear conscience, for
that one argument;—I shall be an honest man after
all—Suppose, however, that I gave her the meeting?
That's dangerous,—that's dangerous;—and I am so
little accustomed to do what is right, that I shall certainly do what is wrong, the moment I am in the way
of temptation.   Come, Belville, your resolution is not
so very slender a dependence, and you owe Miss
Walsingham reparation for the injury which you have
done her principles.   I'll give her the meeting—I'll
take her to the house I intended—I'll—Zounds !
what a fool I have been all this time, to look for pre-
carious satisfaction in vice, when there is such exquisite
pleasure to be found at a certainty in virtue. (*Exit.*

Enter Lady Rachel *and* Mrs Belville.

Lady Rach. For mirth sake don't let him see us :
There has been a warm debate between his passion
and his conscience.

Mrs Bel. And the latter is the conqueror, my life
for it.

Lady Rach. Dear Mrs Belville, you are the best
of women, and ought to have the best of husbands.

Mrs Bel. I have the best of husbands.

Lady Rach. I have not time to dispute the matter

with you now ; but I shall put you into my comedy
to teach wives, that the best receipt for matrimonial
happiness is to be deaf, dumb, and blind.

Mrs Bel. Poh ! poh ! you are a satirist, Lady
Rachel—But we are losing time : shou'dn't we put
on our dresses, and prepare for the grand scene ?

Lady Rach. Don't you tremble at the trial ?

Mrs Bel. Not in the least, I am sure my heart has
no occasion.

Lady Rach. Have you let Miss Walsingham into
our little plot ?

Mrs Bel. You know she could not be insensible of
Mr Belville's design upon herself, and it is no farther
than that design we have any thing to carry into
execution.

Lady Rach. Well, she may serve to facilitate the
matter, and therefore I am not sorry that you have
trusted her.

Mrs Bel. We shall be too late, and then what
signifies all your fine plotting.

Lady Rach. Is it not a little pang of jealousy that
wou'd fain now quicken our motions ?

Mrs Bel. No, Lady Rachel, it is a certainty of my
husband's love and generosity that makes me wish
to come to the trial.   I would not exchange my confidence in his affections for all the mines of Peru ; so
nothing you can say will make me miserable.

Lady Rach. You are a most unaccountable woman ;
so away with you.   [*Exeunt.*

SCENE II.

Continued.

Enter SPRUCE *and* GHASTLY.

Spruce. Why, Ghastly, the old General your master is a greater fool than I ever thought he was: He wants to marry Miss Walsingham!

Ghast. Mrs Tempest suspected that there was something going forward, by all his hugger-mugger consulting with Mr Torrington; and so set me on to listen.

Spruce. She's a good friend of your's, and that thing she made the General give you the other day in the hospital, is, I suppose, a snug hundred a year?

Ghast. Better than two: I wash for near four thousand people: there was a major of horse who put in for it, and pleaded a large family.

Spruce. With long services, I suppose.

Ghast. Yes, but Mrs Tempest insisted upon my long services; so the major was set aside—However, to keep the thing from the damned newspapers, I fancy he will succeed the barber, who died last night, poor woman, of a lying-in fever, after being brought to bed of three children.—Places in public institutions—

Spruce. Are often sweetly disposed: I think of asking Belville for something one of these days.

Ghast. He has great interest.

Spruce. I might be a justice of peace, if I pleased, and in a shabby neighbourhood, where the mere swearing would bring in something tolerable; but

there are so many strange people let into the commission now-a-days, that I shou'dn't like to have my
name in the list.

Ghast. You are right.

Spruce. No, no, I leave that to paltry tradesmen,
and shall think of some little sinecure, or a small pension on the Irish establishment.

Ghast. Well, success attend you. I must hobble
home as fast as I can, to know if Mrs Tempest has
any orders. O, there's a rare storm brewing for our
old goat of a General.

Spruce. When shall we crack a bottle together?

Ghast. O, I sha'n't touch a glass of claret these
three weeks; for last night I gave nature a little fillip
with a drunken bout, according to the doctor's directions; I have entirely left off bread, and I am in
great hopes that I shall get rid of my gout by these
means, especially if I can learn to eat my meat quite
raw like a cannibal.

Spruce. Ha, ha, ha!

Ghast. Look at me, Spruce, I was once as likely
a young fellow as any under ground in the whole parish of St James's;—but waiting on the General so
many years—

Spruce. Ay, and following his example, Ghastly.

Ghast. 'Tis too true: has reduced me to what you
see. These miserable spindles wou'd do very well
for a lord or a duke, Spruce; but they are a sad disgrace to a poor valet de chambre.   (*Exit.*

Spruce. Well, I don't believe there's a gentleman's
gentleman, within the weekly bills, who joins a prudent solicitude for the main chance to a strict care
of his constitution better than myself. I have a little
girl who stands me in about three guineas a week; I
never bet more than a pound upon a rubber of whist;
I always sleep with my head very warm; and swallow
a new-laid egg every morning with my chocolate.

(*Exit.*

SCENE III.

The Street.

Two Chairs cross the Stage, knock at a door, and set down BELVILLE *and a Lady.*

Bel. This way, my dear creature !   (*Exeunt.*

Enter GENERAL SAVAGE, CAPTAIN SAVAGE, *and* TORRINGTON.

Capt. There ! there they go in : You see the place is quite convenient, not twenty yards from the masquerade.

Gen. How closely the fellow sticks to her !

Tor. Like the great seal to the peerage patent of a chancellor. But, gentlemen, we have still no more than proof presumptive :—Where is the ocular demonstration which we were to have ?

Capt. I'll swear to the blue domino ; 'tis a very remarkable one, and so is Belville's.

Tor. You wou'd have rare custom among the Newgate solicitors, if you'd venture an oath upon the identity of the party under it.

Gen. 'Tis the very size and shape of Miss Walsingham.

Tor. And yet I have a strange notion that there is a trifling *alibi* in this case.

Gen. It would be a damned affair if we shou'd be countermined.

Capt. O, follow me, here's the door, left luckily open, and I'll soon clear up the matter beyond a question.   (*Enters the house.*

Tor. Why your son is mad, General. This must produce a deadly breach with Belville. For heaven's sake, let's go in, and prevent any excesses of his rashness.

Gen. By all means, or the poor fellow's generous anxiety on my account may be productive of very fatal consequences. (*Exeunt.*

SCENE IV.

An Apartment.

BELVILLE *unmasked, and a Lady in a blue domino masked.*

Bel, My dear Miss Walsingham, we are now perfectly safe; yet I will by no means entrust you to unmask, because I am convinced, from the propriety with which you repulsed my addresses this morning, that you intend the present interview should make me still more deeply sensible of my presumption.—I never lied so awkwardly in all my life; if it was to make her comply, I should be at no loss for language. (*Aside.*) The situation in which I must appear before you, madam, is certainly a very humiliating one ; but I am persuaded that your generosity will be gratified to hear, that I have bid an everlasting adieu to my profligacy, and am now only alive to the virtues of Mrs Belville.—She won't speak—I don't wonder at it; for, brazen as I am myself, if I met so mortifying a rejection, I should be cursedly out of countenance.
(*Aside.*

Capt. (*Behind.*) I will go in.
Gen. (*Behind.*) I command you to desist.

5

Tor. (*Behind.*) This will be an affair for the Old Bailey. (*The noise grows more violent, and continues.*

Bel. Why, what the devil is all this?—Don't be alarmed, Miss Walsingham, be assured I'll protect you at the hazard of my life;—step into this closet, —you sha'n't be discovered, depend upon it; (*She goes in.*) and now to find out the cause of this confusion.   (*Unlocks the door.*

Enter GENERAL SAVAGE, CAPTAIN SAVAGE, *and* TORRINGTON.

Bel. Savage! what is the meaning of this strange behaviour?

Capt. Where is Miss Walsingham?

Bel. So, then, sir, this is a premeditated scheme, for which I am obliged to your friendship.

Capt. Where's Miss Walsingham, sir?

Gen. Dear Belville, he is out of his senses; this storm was entirely against my orders.

Tor. If he proceeds much longer in these vagaries, we must amuse him with a commission of lunacy.

Bel. This is neither a time nor place for argument, Mr Torrington; but as you and the General seem to be in the possession of your senses, I shall be glad if you'll take this very friendly gentleman away; and depend upon it I sha'n't die in his debt for the present obligation.

Capt. And depend upon it, sir, pay the obligation when you will, I sha'n't stir till I see Miss Walsingham.—Look'e, Belville, there are secret reasons for my behaving in this manner; reasons which you yourself will approve, when you know them;—my father here—

Gen. Disavows your conduct in every particular, and would rejoice to see you at the halberds.

Tor. And for my part, I told him previously 'twas a downright burglary.

Bel. Well, gentlemen, let your different motives

VOL. IX.   2 E

for breaking in upon me in this agreeable manner, be what they may, I don't see that I am less annoyed by my friends than my enemy; I must therefore again request that you will all walk down stairs.

Capt. I'll first walk into this room.

Bel. Really, I think you will not.

Gen. What phrenzy possesses the fellow to urge this matter farther?

Capt. While there's a single doubt she triumphs over justice; (*Drawing.*) I will go into that room.

Bel. Then you must make your way through me.

Enter MRS BELVILLE.

Mrs Bel. Ah!

Capt. There, I knew she was in the room :—there's the blue domino.

Gen. Put up your sword, if you don't desire to be cashiered from my favour for ever.

Bel. Why wou'd you come out, madam? But you have nothing to apprehend.

Capt. Pray, madam, will you have the goodness to unmask?

Bel. She sha'n't unmask.

Capt. I say she shall.

Bel. I say she shall not.

Mrs Bel. Pray let me oblige the gentlemen!

(*Unmasks.*

Capt. Death and destruction, here's a discovery!

Gen and Tor. Mrs Belville!

Mrs Bel. Yes, Mrs Belville, gentlemen : Is conjugal fidelity so very terrible a thing now-a-days that a man is to suffer death for being found in company with his own wife?

Bel. My love, this is a surprise, indeed; but it is a most agreeable one, since you find me really ashamed of my former follies, and cannot now doubt the sincerity of my reformation.

Mrs Bel. I am too happy! this single moment wou'd overpay a whole life of anxiety.

Bel. Where shall I attend you? Will you return to the masquerade?

Mrs Bel. O no! Lady Rachel and Miss Walsingham are by this time at our house, with Mr Leeson, and the Irish gentleman whom you pressed into our party, impatiently expecting the result of this adventure.

Bel. Give me leave to conduct you home then from this scene of confusion. To-morrow, Captain Savage, I shall beg the favour of your explanation; (*Aside to him as he goes out.*) Kind gentlemen, your most humble servant.

Mrs Bel. And when you next disturb a *tête à tête,* for pity to a poor wife, don't let it be so very uncustomary a party as the matrimonial one.

(*Exeunt* BEL. *and* MRS BEL.

Gen. (*To the Capt.*) So, sir, you have led us upon a blessed expedition here.

Tor. Now don't you think that if your courts of honour, like our courts of law, searched a little minutely into evidence, it wou'd be equally to the credit of their understandings?

Capt. Though I am covered with confusion at my mistake (for you see Belville was mistaken as well as myself,) I am overjoyed at this discovery of Miss Walsingham's innocence.

Gen. I should exult in it too, with a *feu de joy,* if it didn't now shew the impossibility of her ever being Mrs Savage.

Capt. Dear sir, why should you think that an impossibility? Though some mistakes have occurred in consequence, I suppose, of Mrs Belville's little plot upon her husband, I dare say Miss Walsingham may yet be prevailed upon to come into our family.

Tor. Take care of a new error in your proceedings, young gentleman.

Gen. Ay, another defeat would make us completely despicable.

Capt. Sir, I'll forfeit my life, if she does not consent to the marriage this very night.

Gen. Only bring this matter to bear, and I'll forgive you every thing.

Tor. The captain should be informed, I think, general, that she declined it peremptorily this evening.

Gen. Ay, do you hear that, Horace?

Capt. I am not at all surprised at it, considering the general misconception we laboured under. But I'll immediately to Belville's, explain the whole mystery, and conclude every thing to your satisfaction.

[*Exit.*

Gen. So, Torrington, we shall be able to take the field again, you see.

Tor. But how, in the name of wonder, has your son found out your intention of marrying Miss Walsingham? I looked upon myself as the only person acquainted with the secret.

Gen. That thought has marched itself two or three times to my own reflection. For though I gave him some distant hints of the affair, I took particular care to keep behind the works of a proper circumspection.

Tor. O, if you gave him any hints at all, I am not surprised at his discovering every thing.

Gen. I shall be all impatience till I hear of his interview with Miss Walsingham: suppose, my dear friend, we went to Belville's, 'tis but in the next street, and we shall be there in the lighting of a match.

Tor. Really this is a pretty business for a man of my age and profession, trot here, trot there. But, as I have been weak enough to make myself a kind of party in the cause, I own that I have curiosity enough to be anxious about the determination.

Gen. Come along, my old boy, and remember the old song, " Servile spirits," &c.   [*Exeunt.*

SCENE V.

BELVILLE'S.

Enter CAPTAIN SAVAGE *and* MISS WALINGHAM.

Capt. Nay, but, my dearest Miss Walsingham, the extenuation of my own conduct to Belville made it absolutely necessary for me to discover my engagements with you; and, as happiness is now so fortunately in our reach, I flatter myself you will be prevailed upon to forgive an error, which proceeded only from an extravagance of love.

Miss Wal. To think me capable of such an action, Captain Savage! I am terrified at the idea of a union with you; and it is better for a woman, at any time, to sacrifice an insolent lover, than to accept of a suspicious husband.

Capt. In the happiest unions, my dearest creature, there must be always something to overlook on both sides.

Miss Wal. Very civil, truly.

Capt. Pardon me, my life, for this frankness; and recollect, that if the lover has through misconception been unhappily guilty, he brings a husband altogether reformed to your hands.

Miss Wal. Well, I see I must forgive you at last, so I may as well make a merit of necessity, you provoking creature.

Capt. And may I hope, indeed, for the blessing of this hand ?

Miss Wal. Why, you wretch, would you have me

force it upon you? I think, after what I have said, a soldier might have ventured to take it without farther ceremony.

Capt. Angelic creature! thus I seize it as my lawful prize.

Miss Wal. Well, but now you have obtained this inestimable prize, Captain, give me again leave to ask if you have had a certain explanation with the General?

Capt. How can you doubt it?

Miss Wal. And he is really impatient for our marriage?

Capt. 'Tis incredible how earnest he is.

Miss Wal. What, did he tell you of his interview with me this evening when he brought Mr Torrington?

Capt. He did.

Miss Wal. O, then, I can have no doubt.

Capt. If a shadow of doubt remains, here he comes to remove it.——Joy, my dear sir! joy a thousand times.

Enter GENERAL SAVAGE *and* TORRINGTON.

Gen. What, my dear boy, have you carried the day?

Miss Wal. I have been weak enough to indulge him with a victory, indeed, General.

Gen. None but the brave, none but the brave, &c.
                                              [*Singing.*

Tor. I congratulate you heartily on this decree, General.

Gen. This had nearly proved a day of disappointment, but the stars have fortunately turned it in my favour, and now I reap the rich reward of my victory. (*Salutes her.*)

Capt. And here I take her from you, as the greatest good which heaven can send me.

Miss Wal. O, Captain !

Gen. You take her as the greatest good which heaven can send you, sirrah *? I* take her as the greatest good which heaven can send *me :* and now what have you to say to her ?

Miss Wal. General Savage !

Tor. Here will be a fresh injunction to stop proceedings.

Miss Wal. Are you never to have done with mistakes ?

Gen. What mistakes can have happened now, my sweetest ? you delivered up your dear hand to me this moment.

Miss Wal. True, sir; but I thought you were going to bestow my dear hand upon this dear gentleman.

Gen. How ! that dear gentleman !

Capt. I am thunder-struck !

Tor. General—*None but the brave, &c.*   [Sings.

Gen. So the covertway is cleared at last ; and you have imagined that I was all along negociating for this fellow, when I was gravely soliciting for myself?

Miss Wal. No other idea, sir, ever once entered my imagination.

Tor. General—*Noble minds should ne'er despair, &c.*
[Sings.

Gen. Zounds ! here's all the company pouring upon us in full gallop, and I shall be the laughing-stock of the whole town.

Enter BELVILLE, MRS BELVILLE, LADY RACHEL, LEESON, *and* CONOLLY.

Bel. Well, General, we have left you a long time together.   Shall I give you joy ?

Gen. No ; wish me demolished in the fortifications of Dunkirk.

Mrs Bel. What's the matter ?

Lady Rach. The General appears disconcerted.

Lees. The gentleman looks as if he had fought a hard battle.

Con. Ay, and gained nothing but a defeat, my dear.

Tor. I'll shew cause for his behaviour.

Gen. Death and damnation ! not for the world ! I am taken by surprise here ; let me consider a moment how to cut my way through the enemy.

Miss Wal. How cou'd you be deceived in this manner !   [*To the Captain.*

Lady Rach. O, Mr Torrington, we are much obliged to you ; you have been in town ever since last night, and only see us now by accident.

Tor. I have been very busy, madam ; but you look sadly, very sadly indeed ! your old disorder the jaundice, I suppose, has been very troublesome to you ?

Lady Rach. Sir, you have a very extraordinary mode of complimenting your acquaintance.

Con. I don't believe for all that, that there's a word of a lie in the truth he speaks.   [*Aside.*

Lees. Mr Torrington, your most obedient—You received my letter, I hope ?

Tor. What, my young barrister !—Have you any more traders from Dantzick to be naturalized ?

Con. Let us only speak to you in private, and we'll there clear up the affair before the whole company.

Tor. [*Speaking apart to* LEES. *and* CON.] This gentleman's letter has already cleared it up to my entire satisfaction ; and I don't know whether I am most pleased with his wit, or charmed with his probity.—However, Mr Leeson, I used the bailiffs sadly. —Bailiffs are generally sad fellows, to be sure ; but we must love justice for our own sakes.

Lees. Unquestionably, sir, and they shall be amply recompensed for the merit of their sufferings.

Con. And the merit of suffering, I fancy, is the only merit that is ever likely to fall to the share of a sheriff's officer.

Tor. One word—one word more, Mr Leeson—I have inquired your character, and like it—like it much.—Forgive the forwardness of an old man.— You must not want money—you must not indeed—

Lees. Sir—

Tor. Pray, don't be offended—I mean to give my friends but little trouble about my affairs when I am gone.—I love to see the people happy that my fortune is to make so; and shall think it a treason against humanity, to leave a shilling more than the bare expences of my funeral.—Breakfast with me in the morning.

Lees. You overwhelm me with this generosity; but a happy revolution in my fortunes, which you will soon know, renders it wholly unnecessary for me to trouble you.

Con. [*Wiping his eyes.*] Upon my soul, this is a most worthy old crater—to be his own executor. If I was to live any long time among such people, they'd soon be the death of me with their very goodness.

Mrs Bel. Miss Walsingham, Captain Savage has been telling Mr Belville and me of a very extraordinary mistake.

Miss Wal. 'Tis very strange indeed, mistake on mistake.

Bel. 'Tis no way strange to find every body properly struck with the merit of Miss Walsingham.

Miss Wal. A compliment from you now, Mr Belville, is really worth accepting.

Gen. If I thought the affair cou'd be kept a secret, by making the town over to my son, since I am utterly shut out myself—

Capt. He seems exceedingly embarrassed.

Gen. If I thought that,—why, mortified as I must be in giving it up, I think I could resolve upon the manœuvre, to save myself from universal ridicule:

but it can't be,—it can't be; and I only double my
own disappointment in rewarding the disobedience
of the rascal who has supplanted me.   There!—
there! they are all talking of it, all laughing at me,
and I shall run mad.

Mrs Temp. [*Behind.*] I say, you feather-headed
puppy, he is in this house; my own servant saw
him come in, and I will not stir till I find him.

Gen. She here!—then deliberation is over, and I
am entirely blown up.

Lady Rach. I'll take notes of this affair.

Enter MRS TEMPEST.

Mrs Temp. Mighty well, sir.   So you are in love
it seems;—and you want to be married it seems?

Lees. My blessed aunt!—O how proud I am of
the relation!

Gen. Dear Bab, give me quarter before all this
company.

Mrs Temp. You are in love, you old fool, are you?
and you want to marry Miss Walsingham, indeed!

Con. I never heard a pleasanter-spoken gentlewoman—O hone, if I had the taming of her, she
shou'd never be abusive, without keeping a civil
tongue in her head.

Mrs Temp. Well, sir, and when is the happy day
to be fixed?

Bel. What the devil, is this true, General?

Gen. True—Can you believe such an absurdity?

Mrs Temp. Why, will you deny, you miserable
old mummy, that you made proposals of marriage to
her?

Gen. Yes I do—no I don't—proposals of marriage!

Miss Wal. In favour of your son—I'll help him
out a little.   [*Aside.*

Gen. Yes, in favour of my son—What the devil
shall I do?

Mrs Bel. Shall I take a lesson from this lady, Mr
Belville? Perhaps, if the women of virtue were to

pluck up a little spirit, they might be soon as well
treated as kept mistresses.

Mrs Temp. Hark'e, General Savage, I believe
you assert a falsehood; but if you speak the truth,
give your son this moment to Miss Walsingham, and
let me be fairly rid of my rival.

Gen. My son! Miss Walsingham!—Miss Walsingham, my son!

Bel. It will do, Horace; it will do.

Mrs Temp. No prevarications, General Savage;
do what I bid you instantly, or by all the wrongs of
an enraged woman, I'll so expose you—

Con. What a fine fellow this is to have the command of an army!

Gen. If Miss Walsingham can be prevailed upon.

Tor. O, she'll oblige you readily—but you must
settle a good fortune upon your son.

Mrs Temp. That he shall do.

Mrs Bel. Miss Walsingham, my dear—

Miss Wal. I can refuse nothing either to your request, or to the request of the General.

Gen. Oblige me with your hand then, madam:
Come here you—come here, Captain. There, there
is Miss Walsingham's hand for you.

Con. And as pretty a little fist it is as any in the
three kingdoms.

Gen. Torrington shall settle the fortune.

Lees. I give you joy most heartily, madam.

Bel. We all give her joy.

Capt. Mine is beyond the power of expression.

Miss Wal. [*Aside to the company.*] And so is the
General's, I believe.

Con. O faith, that may be easily seen by the sweetness of his countenance.

Tor. Well, the cause being now at last determined,
I think we may all retire from the court.

Gen. And without any great credit, I fear, to the
General.

Con. By my soul, you may say that.

Mrs Temp. Do you murmur, sir?—Come this moment home with me.

Gen. I'll go any where to hide this miserable head of mine : What a damned campaign have I made of it !   [*Exeunt Gen. and* MRS TEMP.

Con. Upon my soul, if I was in the General's place, I'd divide the house with this devil ; I'd keep within doors myself, and make her take the outside.

Lady Rach. Here's more food for a comedy.

Lees. So there is, madam ; and Mr Torrington, to whose goodness I am infinitely obliged, could tell you some diverting anecdotes, that would enrich a comedy considerably.

Con. Ay, faith, and a tragedy too.

Tor. I can tell nothing but what will redound to the credit of your character, young man.

Bel. The day has been a busy one, thanks to the communicative disposition of the Captain.

Mrs Bel. And the evening should be cheerful.

Bel. I sha'n't therefore part with one of you, till we have had a hearty laugh at our general adventures.

Miss Wal. They have been very whimsical indeed ; yet if represented on the stage, I hope they wou'd be found not only entertaining, but instructive.

Lady Rach. Instructive ! why the modern critics say that the only business of comedy is to make people laugh.

Bel. That is degrading the dignity of letters exceedingly, as well as lessening the utility of the stage. —A good comedy is a capital effort of genius, and should therefore be directed to the noblest purposes.

Miss Wal. Very true ; and unless we learn something while we chuckle, the carpenter who nails a pantomime together will be entitled to more applause than the best comic poet in the kingdom.

                                [*Exeunt omnes.*

HENRY THE SECOND,

OR

THE FALL OF ROSAMOND.

A

TRAGEDY.

BY

THOMAS HULL.

DRAMATIS PERSONÆ.

HENRY II. *King of England,*	*Mr Smith.*
PRINCE HENRY,	*Mr Wroughton.*
CLIFFORD, *Father to Rosamond,*	*Mr Hull.*
ABBOT,	*Mr Clarke.*
SALISBURY,	*Mr Gardner.*
VERULAM,	*Mr R. Smith.*
LEICESTER,	*Mr Thompson.*
QUEEN ELEANOR,	*Miss Miller.*
ROSAMOND,	*Mrs Hartley.*
ETHELINDA,	*Miss Pearce.*

SCENE,—Oxford and Places adjacent.

HENRY THE SECOND.

ACT THE FIRST.

SCENE I.

An Apartment in SALISBURY'S *House.*

Enter CLIFFORD *and* SALISBURY.

Clif. Salisbury, no more; seek not with empty
    words
To talk down grief like mine; hadst thou a child,
Whom thy fond heart had dwell'd and doted on,
As mine on Rosamond, and felt'st the pang
Of seeing her devote her matchless beauty
To lawless love, her dignity and virtue
To infamy and shame, thou wou'dst not brook
Vain consolation.

Salis. Judge not I esteem
Thy sufferings light, or think thy pains will yield
To cold philosophy.

   Clif. No—Wou'd'st thou ease
The tortured wretch, thou must sit down beside him,
Shed tear for tear, in sympathizing silence ;
List to the tale which sorrow loves to tell,
And, by partaking the distressful cause,
Sooth the strong woe that will not be controul'd.

   Salis. Give thy full bosom vent, thy friend shall
         wait
With patient and participating heart.

   Clif. I ask but that ; for shou'd'st thou weary lan-
         guage,
Ransack the stores of subtle sophistry,
For deepest arguments, my simple answer
Confutes and baffles all—I've lost my child.

   Salis. I grant it, lord, and meant alone to stand
A friendly mediator 'twixt thyself
And the o'er-ruling tumults of thy mind.
I dread their violence.   Did'st thou not talk
Of vengeance and redress ? Whence should they
         spring ?
Where wou'd'st thou point them ? Say, is this a time
To add to Henry's troubles ? now, when dark
Intestine feuds and foreign foes combine
To shake his throne and peace ?

   Clif. Cousin, thou callest
A blush to these old cheeks at the bare thought
Of what thy words imply.   Think'st thou I mean,
Had this weak arm the highest power of vengeance,
To stain my native land with civil slaughter ?
No, Heaven forefend ! nor should a danger reach
My sovereign's sacred life.   Were there a wretch
Accursed enough to raise his traitorous arm
'Gainst Henry's breast, Clifford would rush between,
Oppose himself to the assassin's point,
And glory in the death that saved his king.

Salis. My mind's at peace.

Clif. So rest it, noble Salisbury!
Shall I be plain, and tell thee all my weakness?
'Spite of ungrateful Henry's perfidy,
I love him still, I love this royal robber.
In early youth I led him to the field,
Train'd his advent'rous spirit, shared his dangers,
And by his side maintain'd my country's honour,
In many a gallant feat; Oh, hard return!
How hath he paid this love!

Salis. When headlong passions
Mislead him not from his instinctive greatness,
How noble shews he! wisdom, learning, policy,
Inform his mind, and generous honour sways it.

Clif. Where was it fled, that guardian of man's
          heart,
When, with insidious arts, in evil hour,
He lured my chaste, my duteous Rosamond
From virtue and obedience? Was she not
All that a parent's fondest wish could form?
In vain her modest grace and diffidence
Bore the dear semblance of her mother's sweetness,
And promised an unsullied length of days.
She's lost, and the bright glories of our line
Are stain'd in her disgrace.

Salis. The love of goodness
Not wholly leaves the breast that error stains,
But oft abides, a wholesome monitor,
To call the miserable culprit back
To its forsaken laws. So may it fare
With her.   'Tis true the king, when in her sight,
Engrosses all her thoughts; but, in her secret
And solitary hours, sad she regrets
Her ruin'd innocence, and mourns that love
Which led her to destroy a father's peace,
And stain the honours of a spotless line.

Clif. To save her from a deeper plunge in guilt
Is all my present purpose; against the king

No other weapons do I wish to use,
But those which best become the manly heart,
Reason and conscience; let him give her back
Stain'd and dishonour'd as the mourner is,
Let him restore her to these aged arms,
I ask no more.

    Salis. Unfold thy utmost wish,
And if a friend's assistance may avail,
Command thy kinsman's warmest services.

    Clif. Conceal my being here; let not the king
Know Clifford treads these bounds; he must be won
To my discourse, unconscious who I am.
I have devised a means—inquire not now,
But patient aid me, and await the issue.
I have good hopes that all the generous fires,
Which warmed his noble heart, are not extinct;
If so, I may once more embrace my child,
My still dear Rosamond.—Blame not my weakness,
I come not to inflict but banish pain;
To awaken in her breast a just remorse
For her past failings; and entice her steps
To some serene abode, where penitence
And contemplation dwell, and jointly sooth
The contrite sinner's mind with glowing hope
Of Heaven's indulgence, and returning peace.

                               [*Exeunt.*

SCENE II.

A retired Grove belonging to the Palace.

Enter PRINCE HENRY *and* LEICESTER.

Prince. My spirit will not brook it ! what avails

The empty name and title of a king,
Without imperial power ? Why with his son
Divide his throne, unless he meant to grant
A share of that supreme authority,
Which only lends stability to greatness
And gives its highest lustre ?—To be caught
With the gay tinsell'd garb of royalty
Befits an idiot only ; let him know
That Henry's son inherits Henry's pride,
And may in time, with daring hand, assume
What now he is debarr'd.

 Leices. Your wrongs are great ;
But be not too precipitate and rash,
Lest you therein defeat the means by which
You wish to gain.   Beware, the watchful eye
Of curiosity besets our paths ;
Speak not so loud.

 Prince. What danger ? Shou'd the king
Himself o'erhear, confront me face to face,
I would not shrink ; mine eye should not abate
Its angry fire, nor my sunk heart recall
The smallest drop of that indignant blood
That paints my glowing cheek ; but I would speak,
Avow, proclaim, and boast my settled purpose.
I have a double cause to urge me on,
A royal mother's wrongs joined to my own.
Do I not see her injured, scorn'd, abandon'd,
For the loose pleasures of a wanton's bed,
His beauteous minion, whom embower'd he keeps
In Woodstock's mazy walks ? Shall he do this
Unnoticed, unreproach'd, yet dare to check
My honest ardour ? He hath yet to learn,
That parent who expects his son to walk
Within the decent pale of rigid duty,
Should keep a heedful watch o'er his own steps,
And by his practice well enforce the doctrine
He means to have him learn.

 Leices. Yet check this passion,

And hear the dictates of my cooler mind.
Is not the council here convened this morn,
By Henry's order, to debate the courtesy
Of the French monarch, who even now invites
Thy royal presence to his gallant court,
On friendly visit ?

   Prince. Yes—and here the partner
In England's throne waits, till their mighty wisdoms
Shall have determined what his course must be,
And deign to call him in ; waits like a servile
And needy pensioner, that asks a boon.

   Leices. Again you lapse into this wild extreme.
Forget a while ambition and revenge,
And court cool wisdom ; act the politician ;
Play to their humours, yield to their decrees;
Use this French journey, as the happy step
To mount to your desires.—Though here deprived
Of power, in Normandy your half-king title
Enables you to scatter favours round,
Such as shall gain you popular applause,
And win your subjects' hearts—This point obtain'd,
All you can ask is yours ; you may command
Where now you sue, and Henry's self may fear
Your potency, and grant your highest wish.

   Prince. By Heaven thou hast inflamed my eager
       soul
With bright imaginations of renown,
Of conquest and ambition ; I awhile
Will try to sooth this proudly-swelling heart
Into mild heavings and submissive calms,
For this great purpose.

   Leices. To your aims devoted,
I'll privily away, and meet you there ;
Will worm myself into each Norman breast ;
Pour in their greedy ears your early virtues,
Your love of them, their interest and honour ;
Then join in any hardy enterprize

That fore-thought can suggest, and win the palm,
Or die beside thee.

    Prince. Generous, gallant friend!
I have not words to thank thee—to my breast
Let me receive the guardian of my glory,
In full assurance that his noble friendship
Shall never be forgot.

    Leices. Behold the queen;
She moves this way.

    Prince. I will retire a while;
I would not meet her, till this hoped departure
Be fix'd irrevocably, lest her fond
Maternal love and softness might prevail
O'er that instinctive yielding in the breast,
Which nature wakens when a mother sues,
And win some promise from my pliant heart,
That I should scorn to break.   [*Exit.*

    Leices. What if I try
To win her to our cause? The frequent wrongs,
Which fire her haughty mind, join'd to affection
For her young Henry, may engage her help
In any scheme that promises revenge.
But soft—the present is no time for that;
For with her comes that busy meddling Abbot,
That dealer in dark wiles, who rules and guides
The consciences of all who weakly crouch
To his mock sanctity.   I will avoid him—
Even now some mischief broods within his mind!
Perhaps toward me; for he, of late, hath shewn me
Marks of respect and courtesy, wherein
He was not wont to deal.   Time only will
Explain the object of his present aims,
For in his Proteus-face, or even his words,
No smallest trace of what employs his thoughts
Can ever be descry'd.   [*Exit.*

    Enter QUEEN *and* ABBOT.

    Queen. Tell me no more
Of long protracted schemes and tedious wiles;

My soul is all impatience : Talk to me
Of vengeance, speedy vengeance.

 Abbot. What can be
Devised to punish, pain, and mortify,
Beyond what is enjoin'd on Henry's head?
Though distant from the venerable shrine
Where martyr'd Becket's sacred blood was spill'd,
Is he exempt from penance? Doth not here
Our careful mother-church pursue her foe?
Is he not nightly doom'd to tread the lone
And solemn isles of Ida's holy house,
In deep atonement for the barbarous fall
Of that dear murder'd saint?

 Queen. And what atones
For Eleanor's loud wrongs, her murder'd peace?
Will all the penances e'er yet devised
By dronish priests relieve my tortured heart?
Will they recall my Henry's truant love,
Or blast the charms of that deluding witch,
Who lures him from me? This is the redress
Which Eleanor demands—this the revenge
Alone which she can condescend to take.

 Abbot. Nor is this past my hope to purchase for you:
My thoughts, devote to you and your repose,
Continually labour for your good.
Alas! you know not, mighty queen, the sighs
My heart has heaved, the tears mine eyes have shed,
For your injurious treatment; and, even now,
Would you but bid your just resentment cool,
I think the wish'd occasion is at hand,
That gratifies your most enlarged desire.

 Queen. Thy words are balsam to my wounded
    peace.
Go on, go on; dwell on this pleasing strain,
And I will worship thee.

 Abbot. Is not the council
Convened by Henry? Do they not decree
Your darling son shall strait for France?

Queen. Ay, there
Again is England's queen insulted, mock'd—
Have I no right of choice ? Shall the dear boy,
Whose noble spirit feels his mother's wrongs,
Shall he be banish'd from me, torn away,
My only comforter ?

Abbot. He must not go.
You must prevent it—practise every art ;
Nay, bid your pride and fierce resentment bend
To soft request and humblest supplication,
Ere suffer his departure.

Queen. Tell me, father,
How this is to be done ? Canst thou speak peace
To the tumultuous bosom of the deep,
When the loud tempest tears it ? Can I meet
With patient meekness my oppressor's sight ?
Wear an apparent calmness in my face,
While heaving anguish struggles in my mind ?
It will not be.

Abbot. There are no other means.
What though the council urge state policy,
And public good, for their consent herein,
Their inward aim is to oblige the king,
Who labours this great point. And what's his drift ?
No courteous scheme, to please his brother France,
But merely to remove the gallant prince.

Queen. Say'st thou ?

Abbot. He fears a rival in the hearts
Of discontented subjects ; the brave youth,
With speech undaunted, that disdains disguise,
Hath freely spoke your wrongs : Hence jealousy
Broods in the king, lest your aspiring son
May prove, in time, a bane to his pursuits,
In wanton dalliance and illicit love.

Queen. Is this the end of all his boasted care
For my son's weal, his happiness and honour ?
This the great cause his brother France must see
The all-praised heir of England's mighty throne ?

O, Henry! whither is thy greatness fled?
Is thy bold pride, thy majesty of heart,
Sunk in low stratagems and mean deceits?
So will it ever be, when perfidy
Pollutes the soul: the sense of honour flies,
And fraud and meanness fill the vacant seat.

 Abbot. Lose not the precious hours in useless
    reasonings;
Speed to the presence; seize the first fair moment:
Hang on his garment, clasp his stubborn knees;
Foil art with art, and practise every means
To win the king from this abhorr'd design.

 Queen. I go; howe'er ill-suited to the task,
I will essay it.—Stoop, exalted heart,
A moment stoop; and, tongue, learn thou a new,
An unbeseeming lesson; let the cause,
The noble motive, consecrate the means.
Remember, Eleanor, thou fall'st a while,
To rise more glorious; to record thy name
Amid the fairest legends of renown,
A brave avenger of thy sex's wrongs.   [*Exit.*

 Abbot. Go, shallow woman! thy impatient soul,
That mounts to frenzy at each slight surmise
Of injury, makes thee a precious tool
For deep-laid policy to work withal.
The prince must here abide—his tow'ring pride,
And Leicester's hot and enterprizing genius,
Assisted by my subtle aid, may raise
A storm, that shall destroy this haughty king,
This poison to our cause and holy order.
Henry, thou knowest not what a foe thou hast
In this unmitigable breast—my soul
Abhors thee, and will never know repose,
Till thou hast fallen a victim to my rage.
The greatest noblest cause inspires my deeds!
Look down, oh, sainted Becket! with delight,
On thy true servant! let thy blessed spirit
Assist my purpose, while I seek revenge

On him who dared insult our holy faith,
By instigating sacrilegious hands
With thy dear blood to stain our hallow'd shrine !

         [*Exit.*

ACT THE SECOND.

SCENE I.

An Apartment in the Palace.

Enter the KING *and* VERULAM.

 King. True, Verulam, and it must be thy care
To check this growing pride, which mounts so fast,
And, like the forward sapling, boldly strives
To emulate the lofty cedar's height,
Which long hath tower'd, in unrivall'd strength,
The glory of the wood.
 Ver. That zeal and love,
Which hitherto hath won my master's confidence,
Long as the life-blood warms this aged heart,
Shall be employ'd to serve him : but this asks
The nicest caution ; soft advice must sooth
His headstrong spirit, that, on the least surmise
Of an usurp'd authority, would start
Aside, indignant of controul.

VOL. IX.   2 G

King. To thee,
Thy love and prudence, we confide the whole :
Thy polish'd sense, thy knowledge of mankind,
And long experience, render thee most fit
For this great task.
　　Ver. The time of his departure,
Is it yet fixed ?
　　King. On our decree alone
That point depends ; he shall with speed away ;
These rude commotions, that assail us round,
May call us from our realm ; should it prove so,
He must not here remain ; his stay were fatal.
　　Ver. Not so, I hope, my liege.
　　King. Prudence enjoins
Our strictest caution. What his own ambition
Might of itself attempt, we cannot say ;
But there's a farther danger to be feared.
　　Ver. His virtues will defend him from such deeds
As honour and obedience must alike
Condemn ; and he has virtues which, I trust,
Will cast a lustre o'er his rising years,
When the slight indiscretions of his youth
Are buried in oblivion.
　　King. I trust so too ;
Yet, Verulam, where splendid virtues grow
Great errors also shoot ; his time of life
Is now in that capricious, wavering state,
When the soft bosom is susceptible
Of every new impression ; his colleague,
(From whom we wish him sunder'd) subtle Leicester,
Is ever at his ear, watchful to seize
The unguarded moment of the youthful heart,
When dark insinuations may prevail
Upon his ductile mind. Be thou in readiness,
On our first notice.
　　Ver. This important point,
Which waited only, what this morn hath given,

The council's sanction, hath been long debated.
I am prepared, my liege.
   King. Behold our son !

Enter the PRINCE.

Henry, the council, zealous for thy welfare,
The ripe improvement of thy growing virtues,
And the successive glories of our line,
Have by their voices sanctified our will,
In thy departure hence. Go, reap that profit
Which the discerning and ingenious mind
Gains from new climes; that knowledge of the world,
Of laws, of customs, policy, and states,
Which observation yields alone, and books
And learned guides imperfectly convey.
   Prince. I thank my father's love; the council
         wisely
Bend to thy will; they but allot what else
Had been demanded by the future heir
And present partner in the imperial seat.
My glowing youth and kindling spirit scorn
To live coop'd up within one scanty bound :
Would life permit, it were delight to trace
Each scepter'd region of the peopled world ;
To mark, compare, define their various modes,
And glean the wisdom that results from all.
   King. Blest in the inheritance of England's throne,
This ardour well befits thee. Go, my Henry,
Visit our brother France ; there shines a star
Of this rich diadem ; let the bright dawn
Of thy young virtues glitter in their eyes;
Those virtues which shall grace this glorious isle,
When we are low in dust.
   Prince. And shew a heart
Prepared to vindicate each royal due
With the last drop that warms its swelling veins.
   King. Spoke with a free-born spirit—Yet beware,
Be not impetuous to grasp at power,

Nor use it, when obtain'd, beyond the limits
Of reason and uprightness ; in the monarch
Do not forget the man.   This honest lord,
An able counsellor and steady friend,
We make companion of thy expedition;
Receive him, Henry, from thy father's hand,
Worthy thy friendship, wear him near thy heart ;
And should some hasty warmth mislead thy youth,
Be his white hairs the reverend monitor,
To warn thee back to the neglected path,.
From which thy steps had stray'd.

   Prince. I love his virtues,
And thus receive the man my sire esteems.

                       [Embraces VERULAM.

Enter the QUEEN.

   Queen. Must I then lose him ? Is he not my son ?
Or has a mother's tongue no right to plead
In her own sufferings? Oh, my lord, my Henry,
Stand thou between thy wife, and the hard sentence
Of men, who feel not the soft ties of nature,
And give me back my boy.

   King. Madam, forbear !
Parental feelings in my bosom sway
Strong as in thine.   Is he not lost alike
To Henry as to Eleanor ? Subdue
This unbecoming weakness, that prefers
Self-satisfaction to the public weal.
He must away.

   Queen. Alas ! there was a time
When Henry's speech had falter'd o'er and o'er,
Ere he had utter'd, with determined breath,
So harsh a sentence.   Is that time forgot ?
—Nay, turn not from me, Henry ! doth thy heart
Shame to avow the guests it harbour'd once,
Fond love and gentle pity ?

   Prince. Cease, my mother,
Oh, cease to interrupt my course of glory :

I go but for a season, to return
More worthy thy endearments.

   Queen. Art thou, too,
A traitor to my peace? And dost thou wish
To fly a mother's arms? To leave her here,
Helpless and unprotected! Oh, my son!
Oppose not thou my wish, but rather join
To melt a father's heart.

   King. 'Twere useless, madam;
Think who thy husband is, and what his ties.
How light, how wavering must he appear
In public eyes, should he abjure the point
He hath just labour'd! Recollect thyself—
Thou canst not wish him so to slight the claims
Of wisdom and of honour.

   Queen. Nor the claims,
The softening duties of domestic life;
The claims of happiness, of inward peace,
Which long my heart hath sigh'd for.

   King. Eleanor,
Once more, remember who we are; a king,
That will not brook to be arraign'd and school'd
For petty indiscretions; Henry judges
His own misdoings, and the chastisement
Must be inflicted by his conscious mind,
Not the bold railings of another's tongue.

   Queen. I will be mild, be patient, be advised
I do recall my words, revoke each free,
Each hasty breath of my unguarded speech,
Which hath offended thee; henceforth I bend
My temper to thy will, thy nicest wish,
So I may keep my son.

   King. No more—thou askest
What cannot be.

   Queen. Thus lowly on my knee
Will I turn suppliant for him.

   King. Oh, forbear!

That posture ill becomes us both.   I grieve
Thou shou'd'st be so importunate, for what
We must not, cannot, will not grant.
   Queen. For this
Have I debased myself? Hath England's queen
Bent lowly to the earth, to be denied
A suit the mother had a right to claim?
My heart swells high, indignant of the meanness,
And scorns itself for such servility.
   King. Prefer a proper suit, thou canst not ask
What Henry shall refuse.
   Queen. Oh no! thy grants,
Thy kind consenting smiles, thy soothing accents,
Thy love, thy faith, are all withdrawn from Eleanor,
And given to another; conscious shame
O'erpowers me, while I own they once were dear;
But I will now forget them, rase them out
From my officious memory, which hath dared
To call them back to my insulted heart.
   King. Well doth this railing, which thy fury pro-
          mised,
Warn us to part; our kindness meant to give
Some days indulgence to the mother's feelings.
   Queen. I scorn both that and thee.
   Prince. [*Aside.*] My bosom swells,
Impatient of her wrongs—down, down, a while,
The time—the time will come—
   King. Lord Verulam,
Prepare thee, on the instant; he shall hence
Before yon sun decline.   If thou hast aught
Of love or duty for thy mother's ear,
Thou hast free license, Henry, to employ
The present moments in that pious office:
Yet take good heed—let not a woman's weakness
Melt thy resolves, and tempt thee to forget
The debt thou ow'st thy country and thy king.
           (*Exit with* VERULAM.

Prince. Restrain those precious drops, my dearest
          mother,
That trembling stand in thy swoll'n eyes, and shew
Like the full bubblings on the fountain's brim,
Pressing to pass their bounds ; abate this grief,
And bid thy bosom rest.
    Queen. If thou behold'st
One tear disgrace mine eye, fierce indignation,
Not grief, has call'd it forth—Away, away—
Seem not solicitous about a cause
That pains thee not ; thou art no more a son,
No more a comfort to thy mother's woe.
    Prince. Oh, by the hopes I have of future fame,
I do not merit these ungentle terms.
Revoke thy words—resume those gentle strains
Which wont to fall upon thy Henry's ear,
And nature's feelings will unsluice my heart
In blood to thy complainings.
    Queen. Art not thou
Join'd with the rest, a foe to my repose ?
See'st thou not how thy mother is neglected,
Abandon'd, scorn'd ? Yet thou canst yield obedience
To the decrees of him who thus insults me,
And leave me to my wrongs.
    Prince. Can I oppose
A parent's absolute command ? Oh, madam !
Think on my state, how critically nice ;
'Twixt two such urgent claims, how hard to judge !
I must resist a king and father's power,
Or seem neglectful of a mother's woes.
Judge me not so : even while I own the strength
Of this imperial mandate, and prepare
To speed for France, I feel for your afflictions,
Lament your helpless state, and could with joy
Yield up my life to save you from disgrace.
    Queen. There spoke my son again ! Oh, my dear
          Henry !

If thy soul's truth confirms these precious words,
(And that it does, I trust that starting tear)
Reflect what further must betide my life,
What future hoards of misery and shame
Fate hath to pour upon my wretched head.
My share in the imperial seat, my life,
Even now perchance, is doubtful; all ills threaten;
And when the mighty measure is complete,
When every breast, but thine, is callous toward me,
Must I call out in vain for my defender?
Or must I yield my spirit to my wrongs,
And poorly die beneath them?
 Prince. Ere the hour
Arrive, that should behold that dire event,
I would myself redress thee, wou'd excite
My Norman subjects in thy just defence;
Wou'd head them, and oppose my vengeful sword
To each oppressive breast, (save one alone)
To vindicate thy rights.

     [Enter VERULAM.

 Ver. The king, my lord,
Expects you.
 Prince. I attend him strait. (*Exit* VERULAM.
 Queen. This haste
Hath malice in it.
 Prince. Heed it not, my mother;
This journey (if my guess deceive me not)
Shall be the source of good; and on thy head
May all that good descend! Be death my lot,
So I give peace to thee!
 Queen. I will not shame
Thy noble spirit with weak womanish tears,
Or one disgraceful sigh. Wilt thou remember
Thy mother's wrongs?
 Prince. I will.
 Queen. Adieu, begone;   (*Exit Prince.*

Glory and bliss be thine! This gallant boy
(So my prophetic mind forebodes) shall prove
My great avenger, and oppression's scourge.
Perfidious Henry! thou impell'st my soul
To these extremes; thou mak'st me what I am.
Hadst thou continued, what I knew thee once,
Endearing, tender, fond—but hence the thought!
Let me shun that, lest my great heart recoil,
And shrink inglorious from its mighty task.
Why comes he not, this abbot? Oh, 'tis well.

Enter the ABBOT.

Where are thy councils now? Thy subtle schemes?
All weak and unavailing—I am lost;
Sunk in my own esteem; have meanly bent
Beneath injurious Henry's lordly pride,
And heard my prayers rejected.
 Abbot. Hapless queen!
Thy wrongs, indeed, cry loud.
 Queen. My son's torn from me.
 Abbot. I've heard it all.
 Queen. And sat inactive down,
To wait the slow events of time and chance?
 Abbot. Misdeem me not, great queen; I have re-
  volved
Each circumstance with nicest scrutiny;
Ev'n from this journey, which we wished to thwart,
Much good may be derived; if the prince breathe
The spirit of his mother——
 Queen. Peace! my policy
Hath flown before thee there; I have explored
His active spirit; found him what I hoped;
For me he sallies forth; for me returns,
To vindicate my rights.
 Abbot. As we cou'd wish;
And a sharp spur, to forward his designs
In any daring enterprize, is Leicester.

By secret emissaries I have learn'd,
Within this hour, that warm, ambitious friend
Withdraws from court, and speeds to join the prince
In Normandy.

    Queen. But what avail these views
Of distant vengeance to my present pangs?
Here I endure the bitterness of woe,
While my curst rival, bane of all my joys,
Dwells in tranquillity and soft content;
In placid ease, within her fairy-bower,
Enjoys my Henry's smiles, his fond endearments,
And vows of love—Ah! due to me alone!

    Abbot. That dream shall vanish quickly.

    Queen. Say'st thou, father?

    Abbot. This very evening, my religious function
Demands me at the fair-one's bower.

    Queen. The fiends—

    Abbot. To thy sole use the time shall be employ'd.
I will awaken in her tim'rous mind
The dangers of her state; load her with scruples;
Then work her temper to some dang'rous scheme,
That shall undo her favour with the king.

    Queen. Its nature—speak——

    Abbot. Tax me not, gracious mistress,
To farther explanation—Let me have
The triumph and delight to pour at once
My subtle scheme and its desired success
In thy enraptured ear.

    Queen. Enough—go on,
And give me this great comfort; let me hear
The sorceress is sunder'd from his arms.
Work me this miracle—Renown, and wealth,
Unbounded power, and royal patronage
Shall be thy great reward.   *(Exit.*

    Abbot. For wealth and power
I on myself alone depend—vain dreamer!
Who weakly canst suppose I toil for thee.

No, I have further, higher views, beyond
Thy feeble stretch;—the supple Rosamond
Shall prove a greater bane to thy repose
Than thou divin'st; her will I instigate,
With her soft blandishments and witching phrase,
To practise on her lover, till she lure him
To cast thee from thy regal dignities,
Divorce thee from his bed and throne; that done,
The enchantress rises to the vacant seat;
Thus one great point of my desire is gain'd;
Power uncontroulable awaits my nod:
This gewgaw, dazzled with her pomp, shall rule
The king, and I rule all by ruling her.   (*Exit.*

SCENE II.

A Cloister.

Enter CLIFFORD, *dressed as an Abbot.*

Clif. Thou garb, for holy purposes design'd,
Assist my honest artifice; conceal
My aged form from recollection's trace,
And be my passport to my mourning child,
I'll hallow thee with gratitude and tears.
This is the awful hour, if right I learn,
When in these solemn isles the royal Henry
Treads, pilgrim-like, these flints, and pours his soul
In sighs for murder'd Becket—Where, alas!
Where are the deep laments, the bitter tears,
Which he should shed for Clifford's ruin'd peace!
He comes, the great disturber of my breast,
Ev'n noble in his guilt!—My heart avows
The fond affection that I bore his youth,

7

And melts within me.—Let me shun his sight
A moment, to retrieve my sinking spirit.   (*Retires.*

Enter the KING *as a pilgrim.*

  King. Must it be ever thus? Still doom'd to tread
This sullen course, and for a bitter foe?
Becket, though in his grave, torments me still.
And what avails it him, who sleeps unconscious
Of my forced penance? Heart, resume thy strength!
Rouse thee! resist the bigot imposition,
And be thyself again.
  Clif. Who thus vents forth   (*Advancing.*
His sore disquiets?
  King. What is he who asks?
If yon expiring lamp deceive me not,
Thy garb betokens a religious function.
  Clif. Thou judgest well.
  King. Inform me, holy guide,
What boot the punishments your laws enjoin;
Self-castigation, balmy sleep renounced,
And lonely wand'rings o'er the rugged flint,
Through the long cloister'd isle?
  Clif. Much, pious stranger,
Much they avail: within these silent walls
Chaste contemplation dwells; this hallow'd gloom
Inspires religious musings, ardent prayer,
Which, by their fervid impulse, waft the soul
Of erring man above this vale of weakness,
And teach him to regain, by heavenly aid,
What he had forfeited by human frailty.
  King. Divinely spoke! But well may'st thou de-
      claim
On their utility, who ne'er hast felt
Their harsh severities—Thou haply canst
Produce the legend of a life unstain'd.
  Clif. No—would to heaven I had that boast; but
      rank'd
'Mongst error's sons, I share the general weakness;

Too numerous are my faults; but one, alas!
Beyond the rest I mourn—Spare me a moment,
While I give respite to my swelling grief.

King. Methinks thou hast involved me in a share
Of thy distress.   For what art thou enjoin'd
This rigid duty, similar to mine?
Who hath inflicted it?

Clif. Myself—my conscience.

King. Thyself!

Clif. The mind that feels its own demerits,
Needs no infliction from another's tongue.

King. My ears, my soul, are open to thy words—
Give me to know thy crime.

Clif. How can I utter it,
And not sink down with shame?

King. Let shame betide
The coward heart that will not own its frailties;
If there's a grace in man superior far
To all beside, it must be that true pride,
That bids him speak his own misdeeds.   Proceed.

Clif. I had a friend—the darling of my soul——
He loved, he honoured me—the trade of war
He taught my youth; in many a hardy field
Have we together fought, asserted England's
And noble Henry's fame, Henry the greatest,
The best of kings!—

King. Oh, painful recollection!   (*Aside.*
Thou once hadst such a friend, ungrateful Henry!

Clif. A length of brotherhood we joy'd together,
Till all its blessedness was spoil'd by me.
He had a daughter, beauteous as the eye
Of fancy e'er imagined—

King. Spare me, spare me—
Oh, bitter tale! thou hadst a daughter, Clifford!
                                          (*Aside.*

Clif. I mark'd her for my own; pour'd the false
            tale
Of wily love into her credulous ear,

And won her artless heart.

    King. Tumultuous pangs   (*Aside.*
Rush like a torrent through my bursting breast ;
My crime, reflected by this stranger's tale,
Glares frightful on me ! Till this hour, I knew not
My trespass was so great—Oh, with what weak,
What partial eyes we view our own misdeeds !
The faults of others are a huge Olympus,
Our own an emmet's nest.

    Clif. Heart, heart, be strong !   (*Aside.*
He muses deeply on it—I have hurt (*To the King.*
Thy soft humanity, I fear.—Perchance
Thou hast a daughter, who, like this my victim,
Hath stray'd from virtue's path.

    King. Away, away—
I can endure no more—O conscience, conscience,
                             (*Aside.*
With what a wild variety of torments
Thou rushest through my soul !—'Tis all distraction,
And asks some more than human strength of reason,
To save me from despair.   (*Exit.*

    Clif. Kind Heaven, I thank thee ;
His noble nature is not quite extinguish'd,
He's wounded deep—Oh ! may he but retain
This sense of the sore pangs he brought on me,
Till I have rescued my repentant child,
And all my business in this life is done.   (*Exit.*

ACT THE THIRD.

SCENE I.

An Apartment in the Bower.

ROSAMOND *discovered writing.*—ETHELINDA *attending.*

Ros. It is in vain—my trembling hands deny
Their wonted office—my distracted mind
Revolves a thousand projects to regain
Its vanish'd peace; yet all by turns evade
My feeble efforts : like the lucid vapours,
Which rise successive in a summer's sky,
And court our observation, yet are lost
Ere fancy can assign them name or shape,
Lost in the wide expanse.　Ah me ! how weak,
How insufficient to its own desires,
Is the poor breast which honour hath deserted !
　Eth. Say, is it aught thy servant can discharge ?
She wishes to relieve thy woe, and shares
Thy every pang.
　Ros. Thy sympathizing heart
Hath oft consoled me, soften'd the rude hour
Of bitter recollection, and repell'd

Encroaching agony—My Henry gave thee
A servant to my use ; but thy mild nature,
So ill adapted to the lowly state
Wherein thy lot was cast, taught me to change
That servile title for the name of friend.

    Eth. Give me that office now, and let me speak
Thy meanings there.

    Ros. I know not what I mean.
In vain, alas ! she strives to please herself,
Who hath offended virtue.   On that paper
I wished to pour my duty to my father,
Implore his dear forgiveness, beg one blessing,
Ere yet he sleep in peace—Oh, Rosamond !
Well hast thou spoke ! for in the grave alone
Can Clifford rest.—Peace and repose on earth
Thine impious offences have denied him.
Ere this, perhaps, he is laid low in dust,
And his last hours were charged with grief and shame.

    Eth. Hope better, my fair mistress ; raise thy
                thoughts
From the dark musings of despondent woe,
To these bright scenes of happiness and joy.

    Ros. I have no title to them ; these bright scenes
May give delight to unpolluted breasts,
But not to mine ! the charmer Happiness,
Hath long deserted me ; with her loved mate,
Seraphic Innocence, she wing'd her flight,
I fear for ever.—This retired abode,
Graced with each ornament inventive Fancy
Can furnish, to allure the admiring eye,
Serves but to sting me deeper with remorse :
Upon my cheek imprint a stronger glow
Of conscious shame, reflecting on the cause,
The wretched cause, that brought me to their view.

    Eth. These are the dictates of deforming spleen,
That to the low dejected mind presents
False and disgustful objects.   Henry's absence
Is the sad source that casts this mournful gloom

On all around : three days have now elapsed
Unmark'd by him and love; when he arrives,
The bower, the groves, will wear a fairer aspect,
And all be dress'd in beauty and delight.

   Ros. 'Tis true, I try to wear the smile of joy
In my dear conqueror's sight : nay I do wear it,
My heart acknowledges the soft delight
His presence gives.   Had I not loved too well,
I had not been this wretch !—My soul dotes on him !
I live but in his looks.   Why was he not
By fate ordain'd some rustic villager,
And I the mistress of a neighbouring cot,
That we had met as happy equals do,
And lived in pleasures unallay'd by guilt !

   Eth. Yet to engage the dear, the tender hours,
Which royal Henry spares from public toils ;
To call that heart your own, which all agree
To love and honour; feast upon those smiles,
Which millions sigh for—

   Ros. Cease, my Ethelinda ;
Thou knowest not how thy words afflict my breast.
Think not, though fallen from innocence, my mind
Is callous to the feelings of humanity,
Of truth or justice.   I reflect full oft,
Even in my happiest moments, there lives one
Who has a right to Henry's every hour ;
Each tender vow, and each attractive smile :
I know it, and condemn my feeble heart,
For yielding to desires all moral laws
Forbid, and inborn reason disapproves.

   Eth. You school yourself too harshly.

   Ros. Oh, not so !
I have much more to bear.   I have not yet
Learn'd the great duty expiation claims :
To part, my Ethelinda.

   Eth. Part ! from whom ?

   Ros. From Henry—from the monarch of my heart,

My wishes' lord, my all of earthly bliss!
Thou marvel'st at my words—but it must be;
It is the sole atonement I can make
To a fond father's woes, his injured fame,
The tarnish'd glories of a noble line,
The royal Eleanor's insulted rights,
And my own conscious, self-arraigning heart.

Eth. Oh! do not flatter that fond heart with hope
Of such exertive power! beneath the trial,
Your strength would fail, your resolution droop;
You could not yield him up.

Ros. By my warm hopes
Of mild remission to my great offences,
I feel my bosom equal to the task,
Hard as it is; so Henry left me not
In anger or unkindness, but resign'd me,
With the dear care of a protecting friend,
To the soft paths of penitence and peace,
I would embrace the torment it entail'd,
And bless him for each pang.

Eth. Behold, he comes!   [*Exit.*

Enter the King.

King. My Rosamond! my ever-new delight!
Receive me to thy arms, enfold me there,
Where ever blooming sweets perpetual rise,
And lull my cares to rest.

Ros. It was not thus
My Henry used to visit this retreat;
Bright cheerfulness was wont to dance around him,
Complacent sweetness sat upon his brow,
And soft content beam'd lovely from his eye.

King. Well thou reprovest me; I will strive to
chace
The gloomy cloud, that overhangs my spirit,
The effect of public business, public cares.
My tell-tale looks, I fear, will speak the pain

My heart still suffers, from that stranger's converse.
                                            [*Aside.*
Oft do I mourn the duties of my station,
That call my thoughts to them, and claim the hours,
Which I would dedicate to love and thee.

   Ros. I meant not to reproach thee : 'twas my zeal,
For the dear quiet of thy mind, that spoke.
I cannot see the slightest shade of grief
Dim the bright lustre of thy cheering eye,
But apprehension pains me, lest for me
.Thy glory be diminish'd to the world.

   King. I seek not empty popular acclaims ;
Thy tender accents falling on mine ear,
Like rural warblings on the panting breeze,
Convey more rapture, more supreme delight,
Than io-pæans of a shouting world.

   Ros. To see bright satisfaction glow within
Thy manly cheek, behold the rising smile,
And hear thee speak the gladness of thy heart,
Is my best joy, my triumph, and my pride ;
And yet, my Henry, ought it to be so ?
Still should I listen to the syren Pleasure,
While awful Virtue lifts her sober voice,
And warns my heart of her neglected precepts ?

   King. Forbear, forbear these soft complaints, and
                    speak
Of rapture ; speak of my improving ardour,
And thy unceasing love.

   Ros. Oh ! thou divinest not
How many heavy hours and sleepless nights
Thy Rose endures ! how much my faulty state
(Bless'd as I am in thee) arraigns my mind ;
Oft in the bitter hours, when thou art absent,
My father's image rises to my view,
Array'd in gloomy grief and stern reproof.
Nay, do not eye me with that melting fondness ;
Hast thou not often bade me cast my cares
On thee, and told me thou wou'd'st bear them for me ?

Hear then, oh, hear me! for to whom but thee
Can I unload my heart?
   King. Oh, speak not thus.
Shou'd these sad accents stain the precious moments,
When Henry flies from a tumultuous world
To tranquil joys, to happiness and thee?
What busy fiend, invidious to our loves,
Torments thy gentle breast?
   Ros. Trust me, my Henry,
This is no sudden gust of wayward temper,
'Tis Reason's impulse; oft hath my heart endured
Afflictive pangs, when my unclouded face
Hath worn a forced and temporary smile,
Because I would not hurt thy noble mind.
Advancing time but multiplies my torments,
And gives them double strength; they will have vent.
Oh! my protector, make one glorious effort
Worthy thyself—remove me from thy arms;
Yield me to solitude's repentant shade.
   King. Renounce thee, did'st thou say, my Rosa-
      mond?
Were those the words of her and love?
   Ros. They were;
It is my love entreats; that love which owns
Thee for its first, its last, its only lord.
Allow me to indulge it, undisturb'd
By the sore miseries which now surround me,
Without the sense of guilt, that fiend who waits
On all my actions, on my every thought.
   King. By Heaven, I never knew distress till now!
Thy accents cleave my soul; thou dost not know
What complicated agonies and pangs
Thy cruelty prepares for Henry's heart!
He must endure a throe, like that which rends
The seated earth, ere he can summon strength
To banish thee for ever from his arms.
   Ros. Think,—conscience, honour, plead.
   King. Down, busy fiend;   [*Aside.*

That stranger's tale, and Clifford's crying wrongs,
Distract my tortured mind—in pity cease—

[*To* Ros.

I cannot part with thee.

Ros. A thousand motives
Urge thy compliance—Will not public claims
Soon call thee from thy realm ? When thou art gone,
Who shall protect me ? Who shall then provide
A safe asylum for thy Rosamond,
To guard her weakness from assailing fears
And threatning dangers ?

King. What can here alarm thee ?

Ros. Perpetual apprehensions rise ; perchance
The poignant sense, how much my crimes deserve,
Adds to the phantoms ; conscience-stung, I dread
I know not what of ill. Remove me hence,
My dearest lord ; thus on my knees I sue,
And my last breath shall bless thee. Give me misery,
But rescue me from guilt.

King. What, lead thee forth
From these once happy walls ! yield thee, abandon'd,
To an unpitying, unprotecting world !
Then turn, and roam uncomfortably round
The changed abode, explore in vain the bliss
It once afforded, like a restless sprite
That hourly haunts the desolated spot
Where all his treasure lay ! Bid me tear out
This seated heart, and rend each vital string,
I sooner could obey thee.

Ros. Turn, my Henry ;
Leave me not thus in sorrow ! Canst thou part
In anger from me ?

King. Anger !—Oh, thou sweet one !
Witness these pangs !—I cannot, will not lose thee—

[*Going.*

Ros. Confirm my pardon then ; pitying, reflect
'Tis the first hour I e'er beheld thy frown.
Forgive me—Oh, forgive me !

King. Spare me—spare
A moment's thought to my distracted soul,
To ease the throbs, and hush the swelling tumults,
Which my fond love would fain conceal from thee,
Thou exquisite tormentor !   (*Exit.*

Ros. Heaven sooth thy suffering mind, restore thy
     peace,
And win thy yielding spirit to my prayer !
For it must be—the blow must be endured,
Though Nature tremble at it—Heaven requires it :
I hear the secret voice, that claims aloud
Atonement for its violated laws.
When I am sunder'd from him, ne'er again
To feast my eyes on his loved form, or share
His converse more, it will be then no sin,
Nor Heaven nor man can be offended then,
If sometimes I devote a pensive hour
To dwell upon his virtues ; or, at night,
When sleep, like a false friend, denies his comfort,
I bathe my solitary couch with tears,
And weary Heaven for blessings on his head.

Enter the ABBOT.

Abbot. Health to the fair, whose radiant charms
     diffuse
Bright beams around, and shame meridian day
With rival lustre and superior beauty !

Ros. Alas, good father, my dejected heart,
Ill-suited now to Flattery's soothing breath,
Is wrapp'd in other thoughts.

Abbot. An old man's praise
Is of small worth; nor shou'd'st thou term it flattery,
The approbation which the ready tongue
Spontaneous utters, at thy beauties' sight :
But thy sad eyes are swoln with tears ; I trust
They flow from holy motives.

Ros. Thou hast oft
Preach'd, in persuasive accents, the great duty

Of combating temptation; teaching Virtue
To gain dominion o'er assailing passions,
And with her pious firmness guard the breast.
　　Abbot. I have, fair daughter.
　　Ros. These thy holy precepts,
My melancholy heart, I hope, hath learn'd;
The self-convicted mourner hath resolved
To turn from guilt's delusive dangerous way,
And seek the penitential paths of peace.
　　Abbot. Explain thyself, my pupil; lay thy meanings
Clear to my view.
　　Ros. I have resolved to leave
This culprit-state of unchaste, lawless love,
And, in some solitude's protecting shade,
Atone, by future purity of life,
My errors past.
　　Abbot. 'Tis nobly purposed, daughter;
Worthy the precepts I have given thy youth,
And the great efforts of exalted virtue:
But why retire to moping solitude?
The heart is weak that finds itself unable,
In any situation, to repent
Its past misdeeds; it is the principle,
And not the place, atones; we may be good,
And yet abide in active, cheerful life;
There are a thousand pleasures and delights
Not inconsistent with the strictest truth
And sanctity of mind.
　　Ros. It may be so,
And such may be indulged, by those whose lives
Have ne'er been branded with a flagrant crime;
But wretches like myself, whom conscience taxes
With violated chastity and justice,
Have forfeited those rights.
　　Abbot. I like not this—
She dares debate—she judges for herself—
I must restrain this freedom—'tis presumption.
　　　　　　　　　　　　　　　　　(*Aside.*

Ros. Yes, all shall be renounced, all that conspired
To make my guilty situation wear
The face of bliss ; splendour and affluence,
All shall be given up, and well exchanged,
If they obtain remission for my crimes.

    Abbot. Some farther meaning lurks beneath these
           words,
Which my foreboding fears dislike.   (*Aside.*

    Ros. My Henry
I have solicited to this great purpose,
Of my new-open'd, new enkindled mind.

    Abbot. As I divined—destruction to my views !
                         (*Aside.*

    Ros. Why turn'st thou from me ? Breathe thy pious
           comforts
To nourish my resolves.

    Abbot. Think'st thou, fond pupil,
Thy paramour will yield to thy request ?
Oh no ! his passion is too much his master.
Think'st thou, can he, who dotes upon thy beauties,
Dotes even to folly—

    Ros. Spare me, holy father—
Wound not my ear with one contemptuous word
Against his dignity : I cannot bear it.

    Abbot. My recollection, zealous for thy ease,
Recalls the casual word.   I grieve to see thee
Misled by phantoms : but there is a way,
A clear and certain way to happiness,
Which thou hast not descry'd.

    Ros. Inform me, father,
How I may compass the religious ends
My state demands, and my whole soul aspires to,
Without disquieting my Henry's peace,
And I will bless thee for it.

    Abbot. Love alone
Confers true honour on the marriage-state.
Without this sanction of united hearts,
The sacred bond of wedlock is defiled,

And all its holy purposes o'erthrown.
  Ros. Be plain, good father.
    Abbot. Happiness should crown
The altar's rites—and Henry sure deserves
To be supremely happy—thou alone
Canst make him so.   Need I say more?
  Ros. Speak on.
Clear, unambiguous phrases best befit
My simple sense.
    Abbot. His union with the queen
Cannot be term'd a marriage; Heaven disdains
The prostituted bond, where hourly jars
Pervert the bless'd intent; thy vain retirement—
What boots it Eleanor? who now retains
The name alone of queen; or what avails
The title of a wife? Thou art the espoused
Of his affections; let the church then shed
Her holy sanction on your plighted loves;
A pious duty calls, assert thy claim,
Let thy fond lord divorce her from her state,
And Rosamond shall mount the vacant throne.
  Ros. Thy specious arguments delude me not;
My soul revolts against them.   Hence! I scorn
Thy further speech—Have I not crimes enough?
Have I not amply injured Henry's wife,
But I must further swell the guilty sum?
Fly with thy wicked, thy pernicious schemes,
To breasts whence every trace of good is banish'd.]
I am not yet so vile; 'twas Henry's self
I loved, not England's king; not for the wealth
Of worlds, for all that grandeur can afford,
The pride of dignity, the pomp of power,
Nor even to fix my Henry mine alone,
Will I advance one added step in sin,
Or plant another torment in her breast,
Whom too severely I have wrong'd already.   (*Exit.*
  Abbot. Bane to this coward heart, that shrunk
      beneath

The peevish outrage of a frantic girl!
The vain presumer sorely shall repent
Her bold licentious pride, that dared oppose
Her upstart insolence 'gainst my controul,
Whose bidding shou'd direct her every thought.
Had she obey'd, the doting king perchance
Had raised the painted moppet to his throne,
And by that deed, had lost his people's love:
A ready victim to the daring bands
That threaten him around.   That hope is lost—
New schemes must be devised—all arts employ'd:
For nothing shall appease my fierce resentment,
Till the foul wounds given to our mitred saint
Be deep avenged in Henry's impious heart.   (*Exit.*

ACT THE FOURTH.

SCENE I.

The Palace.

The ABBOT *alone.*

It shall be so—the queen herself shall be
My instrument of vengeance, both on Henry,
And that audacious minion, who presumed
To disobey my dictates.   This new project

Cannot deceive my hopes : The haughty Eleanor,
Fired by those demons, Jealousy and Anger,
Will set no bounds to her outrageous will,
And she hath suffer'd wrongs that might inflame
A colder breast.   But why recoils my heart
At thought of harm to this presumptuous wanton ?
Why feel reluctant strugglings, as if Virtue
Check'd and condemned my purpose ? 'Tis not harm,
'Tis piety, 'tis mercy.—Will she not
Be taken from a life of sin and shame,
And placed where she at leisure may repent
Her great offences ? This is giving her
Her soul's desire.—But Eleanor, not I,
Shall be the means.   Night gathers round apace :
Ascend, thick gloom, and with thy sable wings
Veil Henry's peace for ever from his eyes!

Enter the QUEEN.

Hail, honoured queen !
    Queen. Art thou a comforter ?
Thine order calls thee such ; but thou approachest
Unlike the messenger of gladsome tidings ;
Delay is in thy step, and disappointment
Sits on thy brow.
    Abbot. Oh, skilful in the lines,
Which the mind pictures on th' obedient visage,
To speak her inward workings !
    Queen. Thy designs
Have failed ?
    Abbot. To thee I yield the palm of wisdom,
Effective policy, and deep contrivance ;
To thee resign it all.
    Queen. Lose not the moments
In vain lamentings o'er mischances past :
One project foil'd, another should be try'd,
And former disappointments brace the mind
For future efforts and sublimer darings.
    Abbot. Thy noble spirit may perchance succeed

Where all my arts have fail'd.   I boast no power
O'er this perverse, this self-directed wanton;
She seems new-framed—her gentle disposition,
Which erst was passive to Instruction's breath,
As vernal buds to zephyr's soothing gale,
Is banished from her breast; imperious tones
Exalt her voice, and passion warms her cheek.

    Queen. Whence can it spring, this new presump-
           tuous change?

Can she assume the port of arrogance?
She whose soft looks and hypocritic meekness
Have won admiring eyes and pitying tongues,
While I am tax'd with warm and wayward temper,
For that I have not meanness to conceal
A just resentment for atrocious wrongs,
But bid them glow within my crimson cheek,
And flash indignant from my threatening eye.

    Abbot. The lures of greatness, and ambition's baits,
Are eagerly pursued by soaring minds:
When first their splendour is display'd before them,
Anticipating hope exalts their brightness,
And fires the wretched gazer, ev'n to frenzy.

    Queen. What hope—what greatness—what ambi-
           tion? Speak,
Explain thy meaning, ease the gathering tumult
That struggles here, and choaks me with its fulness.

    Abbot. I fear to speak.

    Queen. Why fear? Look on me well;
I am a woman with a hero's heart.
Be quick—be plain—thou hast no tale t' unfold,
Can make me shudder, though it make me feel.

    Abbot. Her wild imagination hurries her
Beyond belief, or ev'n conception's limit;
Safely protected by the royal favour
Of her great master (may I say his love?)—

    Queen. On with thy speech—dispatch!

    Abbot. She threats defiance
To every other power, and all controul;

Bids me, with haughty phrase, no more assume
The right to check her deeds; exalts herself
Above the peers and worthies of the realm :
Nay, frantic in her fancied excellence,
Becomes the rival in imperial rule,
And plumes herself on future majesty.

    Queen. The trait'ress ! but thou err'st, it cannot be:
Thou hast mista'en her words ; her coward heart
Cou'd not conceive such insolence of speech,
Such arrogant presuming.

    Abbot. In effect
All was express'd, though not in open terms :
Hearts so determined rarely speak their meaning,
Lest just prevention intercept their purpose :
But thus much, in the fulness of her passion,
Fell from her lips : Let her a while enjoy
(These were her words) her transitory greatness !
Anon the beam may take a different poise ;
The mistress may become the exalted wife,
The haughty wife become the abandon'd mistress.

    Queen. Breathed she those daring, those audacious
        accents,
And doth the wretch survive it ? Be it so !
She only lives to gratify my vengeance.
Ere the vain dreamer mount her airy throne,
She shall be taught the power of royalty
O'er her own littleness, her pigmy pride.

    Abbot. You do not mean to see her ?

    Queen. Yes—I do—
She thirsts for honour ; I will shew it her ;
Will deign to set before her shrinking view
Majestic Eleanor, the exalted wife,
And with a glance destroy her.

    Abbot. All you seek
May be obtain'd by this great condescension ;
Within your power, beneath your eye abashed,
Whelm'd with her crimes, and shrinking in her fears,
She'll crouch to any terms ; bind her by oath

No more to see your lord; or, if you doubt
The efficacy of that tie, remove her
From the gay bower her infamy hath stain'd.
Perform a holy work; force her to quit
The wanton course of her abandon'd life,
And in some dim, secure retreat, where you
Alone command, conceal the sorceress
For ever from the godlike Henry's eyes.

    Queen. Oh, precious doctrine! learned comforter!
Continue thus to counsel; leave my heart,
My dauntless heart, to execute thy schemes.

    Abbot. When mean you—

    Queen. Now; this night—my eager fury
Brooks no delay—thou must advise the hour.

    Abbot. About the season when imperial Henry
Speeds to his midnight penance at the convent;
I will with nicest caution watch the moments—

    Queen. And be my guide?

    Abbot. Devoted to your bidding.

    Queen. But soft—the means of our access—did not
This grand apostate to his nuptial bond
Contrive some childish toy, some subtle clue,
Without whose aid Inquiry's foot in vain
Attempts to find the wanton's close retreat?

    Abbot. He did; but that device is only practised,
When public duties call him from his realm;
Then is the minion deep immured within
The very heart of the obscure recess;
But now that he with frequent eye o'erlooks
And watches his caged turtle, she enjoys
Free range of the whole bower, by few attended,
And none but who submissive yield obedience
To our grave habit and religious order.

    Queen. Enough; use wary watch—and hie with
        speed
To my impatient soul.   (*Exit Abbot.*
Conceal her! yes,
In that deep cavern, that eternal gloom,

Where all her shames may be conceal'd—in death;
Atonement less than this were insufficient
To gratify my boundless thirst of vengeance.
Long have they revell'd in the mighty pangs
That rent my heart—'tis now my turn to triumph.
When I behold the traitor sunk in grief,
Plaining to her whose bosom will be cold
To his distress, superior will I rise,
Proudly exult in his severest pangs,
Point at her lifeless corse, for whom he scorn'd me,
And loud exclaim in his afflicted ear,
Behold the victim of despair and love !   (*Exit.*

SCENE II.

An Apartment in the Bower.

Enter ROSAMOND *with a letter, and* ETHELINDA.

Ros. No, Ethelinda—Never from that hour,
That fatal hour, when first I saw my hero,
Saw him returning from the field of war,
In manly beauty, flush'd with glorious conquest,
Till our last grievous interview, did Henry
Shew word or look ungentle—Nay, even now,
Here in the full distraction of his soul,
O'er his strong woes soft tenderness prevails,
And all the fondness of unbounded love.
   Eth. But what does he resolve ?
   Ros. There, Ethelinda,
He gives me fresh disquiet; frenzy seems
To guide his wayward pen ; he talks of life
As of a load he wishes to lay down,

If I persist in my unnatural purpose,
For such he terms it.   Canst thou think, my Henry,
I suffer not affliction great as thine ?
Yes, let the present tumults in my breast
Be witness how I struggle with affection,
Stand up, and war with nature's strongest power,
In duty and religion's righteous cause.

   Eth. And must your gentleness abide such trials,
Such hard extremity of wretchedness ?
Is here no middle course to steer ?

   Ros. Forbear !
Seek not to tempt me from that proper sense
Of my deep faults, which only can sustain me
In this sore trial : to remit my fervour
Were to be lost again.

   Eth. He'll ne'er consent
To yield you up, resign you to your woe,
Unfriended, unsustain'd, to heave alone
The bitter sigh and pour the unpitied tear.

   Ros. He says he will return to me, and soon ;
Then paints the anguish of his bleeding heart
In unconnected phrase and broken periods ;
Adjures me, by our loves, no more to urge
The hard request on which his life depends.
Oh, did I ever think I could refuse
What Henry ask'd—But this—It must not be—
Lend me thy arm, my friend ; a sudden faintness
Comes o'er me, and instinctive bodings whisper
I shall not long survive my Henry's loss.

   Eth Oh, chide them from you ! at the sad idea
My sorrows stream afresh.

   Ros. Weep not for that,
'Tis my best comfort.   In the grave alone
Can I find true repose, that quiet haven,
Whereto the wretched voyager in life,
Whose little helpless bark long time hath strove
'Gainst the rude beatings of tumultuous guilt,

Oft casts an ardent look, an eager wish,
To gain a shelter there from future storms.
    Eth. Let me conduct thee to the cheering breeze,
Thy looks are pale.
    Ros. Oh thou, that art all mercy,   (*Kneels.*
Look down, indulgent, on the child of frailty;
With pity view her errors, and instruct her
How to obtain returning peace and pardon. (*Going.*

    Enter CLIFFORD *in his disguise.*

    Clif. Stay thee, fair mourner; wherefore dost thou
        shun
The messenger of comfort?
    Ros. Ethelinda!
What voice was that? My startled fancy wakes
New terrors! Yet it cannot be—
    Clif. My daughter!
    Ros. All-gracious heaven! 'tis he——   (*Faints.*
    Clif. Oh, let me clasp her
To a fond father's aged breast, and call
Her sinking spirit from the shades of death.
    Eth. Oh, reverend stranger, if thou be'st her
        father,
With gentle voice allure her; do not cast
The frown of anger on her meek distress;
Her softness cannot bear it.
    Clif. Fear not, virgin!
Assist to raise her—the returning blood
Faintly renews its course! her timid eye
Speaks painful apprehension.
    Ros. Where is fled
That reverend form? Even now it hover'd o'er me,
Sent by kind Heaven, the sacred delegate
Of comfort and protection.
    Clif. Rosamond!—
Nay! turn not from me—do not shun my sight,
In pity shrink not from a father's eye,

Who comes to chace thy sorrows; comes to shed
Some pious drops o'er thy afflicted heart,
Ere he is mingled with the dust.

   Ros. Thus lowly
Bent to the earth, with abject eye, that dares not
Look up to that much-injured reverend face,
Let me implore thy pardon.

   Clif. Rise, my child,
Oh rise, and let me gaze on that loved form,
Which once was all my comfort.

   Ros. But which now
You look upon with anger and disgust.
My crimes deserve it all.

   Clif. Nay, meet my eye—
Survey me well: dost thou behold therein
A rigid judge? Oh no, the father melts
In these fast-streaming tears.

   Ros. Has pitying Heaven
Heard the sad prayer of such a guilty wretch,
And granted, in the moment of affliction,
A parent's presence, and returning blessing,
To his repentant child!

   Clif. Dost thou repent?—
And didst thou wish once more to see thy father?
Dry up thy tears, and answer me with firmness,
Dost thou repent?—Hast thou the fortitude
To break the fatal tie, that link'd thy soul
To lawless love, and all its false allurements?
Canst thou look up, with steady resolution,
To that great Power who loves repentant hearts,
And say thou wilt no more transgress?

   Ros. I can,
I can, my father; that all-seeing Power,
To whom thou hast appeal'd, can witness for me,
I have renounced the paths of sin and shame,
And mean to spend my sad remains of life
In deep contrition for my past offences.

Clif. To find thee thus is rapture to my soul!
Enter my breast, and take again possession
Of all the fondness that I ever bore thee.——
By my best hopes, when in thy smiling youth
Mine eye hath hung enamour'd on thy charms,
Thou shew'd'st not then so lovely as now,
Dress'd in these graceful penitential tears.

Ros. Oh, my father!
And may I still look up to thee with hope
That the dear love and tenderness thy breast
Once cherish'd for thy darling Rosamond
Is not extinguish'd quite?

Clif. Alas, my child!
I am not lost to nature and her ties.
We all are frail; preach stoicks how they will,
'Tis not a parent's duty to cast off,
But to reclaim, the wand'rer of his blood.——
One question more, on that depends my peace——
Shall I behold my child redeem'd from shame,
Or must I sink with sorrow to the grave,
Ere this great business of my soul's accomplish'd?

Ros. Command my heart; can I, thus lost to good-
      ness,
Assuage thy cares, and soften the decline
Of weary nature? say, my dearest father,
And by the zeal of my obedience, prove
The truth of my contrition.

Clif. Hear me then,
Thou darling of my bosom!——Westward hence,
On the slow rising of a fertile hill,
A virtuous dame of honourable race
Hath founded and endow'd a hallow'd mansion,
To pure devotion's purposes assign'd.
No sound disturbs the quiet of the place,
Save of the bleating flocks and lowing herds,
And the meek murmurs of the trilling stream,
That flows sweet-winding through the vale beneath;

No objects intercept the gazer's eye,
But the neat cots of neighb'ring villagers,
Whose lowly roofs afford a pleasing scene
Of modest resignation and content.
There Piety, enamour'd of the spot,
Resides; there she inspires her holy fervour,
Mild, not austere; such piety, as looks
With soft compassion upon human frailty,
And sooths the pilgrim-sinner to embrace
Repentant Peace beneath her holy roof.—
Say, wilt thou quit, for such serene delights,
This gay abode of shame?

 Ros. I will, my father;
My wish invites to such a soft retreat.
Oh, lead me forth!

 Clif. Thy words give added strength
To my weak frame, and warm my languid blood.
Some two hours hence, when midnight veils the
   globe,
Disguised, as now, in this religious garb,
Again expect me, to redeem thee hence,
And guide thy steps to that abode of bliss—
Here break we off—

 Ros. Once more thy blessing on me,
While I pour forth the silent gratitude
Of my full soul for thy returning love. [*Kneeling.*

 Clif. Warm as thy soul can wish, my child, re-
   ceive it.   [*Embracing her.*
Oh, the supreme delight 'twill be to see thee
Restored to holy peace and soft content,
And sometimes share thy converse; then devote
My lonely intervals to ceaseless prayer,
That Heaven will pour on thy repentant heart
Its healing mercy and its promised grace! [*Exit.*

 Ros. Propitious Power, who cheer'st thy mourn-
   er's spirit,
Accept my boundless thanks—thy pitying goodness
Inspired my father's heart, and sent him hither

To succour and sustain me.   Oh, continue
Thy strength'ning fervour, that I may not shrink
From the great task I have begun, but rise
An object worthy thy returning grace !
   Eth. My gentle mistress, I partake your transport,
Yet apprehension checks the rising joy.
What agonies will pierce your Henry's heart—
   Ros Peace, on thy life ! seek not to wake again
Those thoughts which I must hush within my breast ;
The lover is forgot ; what Clifford's daughter
Leaves unperform'd Clifford himself will perfect.
That tongue, whose wholesome counsels Henry wont,
In early life, to listen and obey ;
That heart, which loved his virtues, will again
Exert its power, and win him to applaud
The minister of peace, who leads me hence
To that asylum my offences claim.   (*Exeunt.*

ACT THE FIFTH.

SCENE I.

The Bower.   Table with Tapers, &c.

Enter ROSAMOND *and* ETHELINDA.

Ros. Is it the vain suggestion of my fears,

Or do unwonted sounds and buzzing murmurs
Ride in each breeze ?

   Eth. 'Tis fancy's coinage all :
Your mind, alarm'd lest any thwart event
Should interrupt this night's important business,
Creates false terrors.

   Ros. Twice within this hour
Hath it presented to my tortured sight
My father in the agonies of death,
Gasping and pale, and stretching forth his hands
To me for aid and pity.

   Eth. When suspense
And expectation hold dominion o'er
The agitated bosom, these illusions
Are busy to torment us.

   Ros. Angels speed him
In safety to me ! and console my Henry,
When he shall seek his Rosamond in vain
Around this once-loved bower ! When thou be-
       hold'st him,
(O ! can it be a crime to leave a sigh,
One soft adieu, for him who was so dear ?)
Say, Ethelinda, that I left these walls
Not with a harden'd, but a tutor'd mind,
Not desperate, but resolved ; arm'd with that due,
That holy resolution, which becomes
My state and purpose ; and when busy memory
Recalls the sad idea of our loves,
(Too oft, alas ! I fear 'twill press my mind,)
I'll pour my fervent prayers, that bliss and honour
May crown the hero's days !

   Eth. I will do all
My mistress bids ; but must I stay behind ?
Must I renounce the sweet companionship,
Her gentleness and soft humanity
Have taught me to esteem my highest bliss ?

   Ros. This once obey—this night's great business
      done,

I claim no duty more ; but when the storm
Shall be o'erblown, and all be calm again,
If aught of good befall my after-hours,
Thou, Ethelinda, shalt partake it with me.
Go now, collect together those dear pledges,
(The only treasure I shall carry hence,)
My Henry's letters ; my o'er-harrass'd spirits
Would sink beneath the task.   [*Exit* ETHEL.
Ill-boding fears
Possess me still ; such as I oft have heard
Haunt the sick couch, Death's sable harbingers.

Enter QUEEN *with a bowl and dagger.*

  Queen. Ay, there the trait'ress sits. Who could
          surmise
Guilt kept abode in such an angel-form ?
Approach, thou beauteous fiend ! Well may'st thou
          start,
'Tis Eleanor that calls ; she comes to wake thee
From the vain dream, which thou hast long enjoy'd,
To justice and atonement.
  Ros. Shield me, powers,
From that wrong'd form ! My fears are all explain'd.
  Queen. No power can shield thee now—Thy
          prayers are fruitless ;
Now cry in vain to him who hath undone thee,
Who robb'd thee of thy innocence of heart,
And taught thee to be rival to a queen.
  Ros. Most injured majesty, thus to the earth
I bow myself before thee ; I confess
My heinous crimes ; I sink beneath their weight :
Yet oh ! take pity on a hapless creature
Misled by fatal love, immersed in guilt,
And blinded to the evils that ensued !
  Queen. And plead'st thou that in thy defence,
          fond wretch,
Which loudest cries against thee ? Knew'st thou not
Who Henry was, what were his noble ties ?

How did thy passion dare aspire so high?
Thou should'st have sought within thine own degree
Mates for thy wanton hours; then had'st thou not
Debased a monarch in his people's eyes,
Nor waked the vengeance of an injured queen.

    Ros. Alas, thou look'st on me as on a wretch
Familiar with pollution, reconciled
To harden'd guilt, and all its shameless arts;
I am not such.   Night's holy lamps can witness
What painful sighs my sad afflicted heart
Hath heaved, what streaming tears my eyes have
          pour'd,
To be released from the pernicious snare
Wherein I was involved!

    Queen. Those sighs and tears,
Had true contrition been their holy source,
Should have inspired thy heart to break the snare,
And set itself at freedom.

    Ros. O! 'tis true
They should; but in my rebel breast they found
Too strong resistance; love hath been my fault,
My bane, my ruin;—
O let this very weakness plead my cause,
Within your royal breast; revolve, great queen,
How you have loved, and let those tender feelings
Win you to pity me!

    Queen. [*Aside.*] What witchery
Of language hangs upon this Circe's tongue?
Why droops my resolution? Rouse thee, Eleanor,
Remember the great cause that brought thee hither,
Nor let a harlot's sigh, or treach'rous tear,
Subdue thy fortitude.

    Ros. What shall I do
To humble me yet lower in thy sight?
What form of language shall my lips adopt
To move thy mercy? I confess my crimes,
Confess their heinousness, and sue for pardon:
Can I do more? Even Heaven is won by tears,
By contrite heart, and fervent supplication:

Shall thou be harder to appease ?—O hear!
A woman's weakness claims a woman's pity.
Exert that dignity of soul that rises
Above resentment to a pleaded wrong,
And teach me how to make atonement.
   Queen. Hence!   (*Aside.*
Encroaching weakness! coward heart, abjure it—
Think on thy mighty wrongs—arm thee to meet
My words with noble firmness! Death alone
Appeases Eleanor's insulted love.
   Ros. Death, said'st thou ?—Death!—O yet—
   Queen. Behold, deluder!
I will not stain me in thy blood; this cup
Contains thy doom.
   Ros. Oh! do not bid me die,
Steep'd as I am in guilt; closed in a convent,
Where Heaven's clear air and animating light
Ne'er found an entrance; let me be condemn'd
To all the hardships ever yet devised;
Or banish me to roam far-distant realms,
Unfriendly climates, and unsocial wastes,
So thou afford me some remaining hours
To reconcile my soul to that great summons,
When Heaven shall deign to call.
   Queen. Prophane no more
The name of Heaven with thy polluted breath,
Thou who hast spurn'd its laws! Justice demands
Thy forfeit life. Thou shalt no more mislead
A monarch's noble mind; no more devise
Insidious art, to work a queen's disgrace:
Thou shalt not live to rob her of her rights,
Her lord's affection, and imperial pride,
That thou may'st seize the abdicated seat,
And triumph in her fall.
   Ros. By Heaven's pure grace,
My mind ne'er harbour'd such an impious thought!
   Queen. Heap not fresh crimes, thou hast enough
       already.

Ros. Have I no evidence on this side heaven ?
And must I fall alone, unjustified ?
Where is the holy abbot ? Where my Henry ?
    Queen. Thy Henry ! thine !—That word hath fired
        anew
My failing spirit.   Drink !
    Ros. Yet, yet relent——
    Queen. Drink ! or this poniard searches every vein.
    Ros. Is there no pity ? None—This awful silence
Hath answer'd me, and I entreat no more.
Some greater power than thine demands my life ;
Fate summons me ; I hear, and I obey—
O, Heaven ! if crimes like mine may hope forgiveness,
Accept a contrite heart !   (*Drinks.*
    Queen. O, beauteous witch !
Hadst thou been less alluring, or had I
Forgot to love, thou hadst not met this fate ! (*Aside.*
    Ros. Thou art obey'd—Once more I bend before
        thee—
Nay, harden not thy heart to the last accents
Of a poor wretch, that hurries to her grave.
Look, look upon me ; I behold thee not
With unforgiving and resentful eyes ;
I deem thee but the destined instrument
Of righteous Heaven, to punish my misdeeds.
    Queen. A flood of agony o'erwhelms my soul,
And all my pride and rage is wash'd away.   (*Aside.*
    Ros. Now cast an eye of pity on my tears,
Now, in these awful, these tremendous moments,
Thou canst not doubt my truth.   By my warm hopes
Of mercy at that throne where all must bow,
My only crime was love.   No power on earth
Could have impell'd me to a further wrong
Against thy state or peace.
    Queen. I must believe thee—
What then remains for me ? O rise, and wreak
Thy vengeance on my now-relenting rage.
Behold these tears—My wrongs are all forgot—

Excess of passion, love that knew no bounds,
Drove me, with execrable haste, to act—
What now I would resign all earthly bliss
To have undone again.

 King. (*Within.*) Seize all that haunt
These winding avenues—let none escape.

 Ros. Ah me! that voice!

 Queen. 'Tis Henry's: let him come,
And take his share of misery.

 Enter the KING, ETHELINDA, *and Attendants.*

 King. Where, where is she?—
O fell, vindictive fiend, what horrid act
Hath thy dark rage been dealing?

 Queen. Mad revenge!

 Eth. Lo! the dread means! all this my mind
   foretold,
When the queen's train first met my startled eye.

 Ros. Ev'n now my flitting spirit is on the wing;
The deadly draught runs through my scorching blood,
I feel it at my heart—O, Henry! Henry!

 King. Malicious rage, thou rid'st the lightning's
   flash
To execute thy vengeance! Ethelinda,
Thy zeal was cool, thy expedition slow,
Compared to that fell tyrant's rapid heat.
Lift up thine eyes—O! do not leave me yet—
Why melts compassion in thy languid looks?
The flames of fury should be kindled there,
'Gainst him, who left thee to invading fate,
Who saw not thy distress, heard not thy cries,
When black revenge was pouring torments on thee!
 cruel woman, unrelenting fiend!

 Ros. Calm, calm thy mind; vent not thy fury there,
Her wrongs cried loud, and her great heart is wrapt
In sorrow for the deed.

 King. What now avails it?
Compunction should have sprung when she beheld

The streaming tears course one another down
Thy beauteous cheek, and read the speechless grief
Of thy imploring eyes.   O! was it thus
I thought to see my Rosamond again!—
Hath fury, like an eastern blast, destroy'd
The sweetest, loveliest flower that ever bloom'd?
But I will die beside thee; never more
Revisit cheerful day, nor dream of comfort,
When thou art parted from me.
   Ros. Cease, O! cease
These useless plainings; consecrate to peace
The few remaining moments—nor let rage
Impel thy soul to meditate revenge
For a poor wretch, who justly thus atones
Her numerous crimes.   O, royal Eleanor!
Hear these last accents—Howsoe'er I loved,
However guilty I have seem'd to you,
This very night I had resolved to leave
These fatal walls, and, by my father's guidance,
Devote my future days to penitence.
   King. Doth not thy blood, like mine, halt in thy
      veins,
And chill the seat of life?
   Ros. Extend thy pity,
(I cannot wrong thee further,) grant me now
One moment to indulge the tender feelings
Of hapless love, and breathe a fond adieu,
Ere this poor harass'd spirit quit my breast.
   King. Why this compassion to the wretched cause
Of all thy miseries! I am the source
Of every pang that feeds on thy loved heart—
Of this thy fatal end.—Reproach, revile me—
Do any thing but look thus kindly on me,
And I will struggle with my mighty woes,
Taught by the great example.
   Ros. O, my Henry!
Let not the sad remembrance of my fate
Sit on thy heart, nor call my present state

A misery: I wish'd some sure retreat
From grief and shame, and Heaven hath heard my
                    prayer.
 Queen. Unhappy victim of my blinded fury,
I almost envy thee thy present state ;
Thou soon wilt be at ease ; while I must liv
To all the torments which a guilty mind
Inflicts upon itself.
 King. Canst thou feel thus,
Yet couldst remain obdurate to her tears
And deaf to her entreaties ?
 Queen. A deed like this
Was foreign to my heart, had not the fraud
Been pour'd into my ears, that I was meant
To be divorced for ever from thine arms,
Be made an outcast from thy bed and throne,
That she might rise my substitute in all.
 King. What black-soul'd dæmon could possess thy
                    mind
With such a hellish falsehood?
 Queen. He—that fiend !

CLIFFORD brought on, in his disguise.

 King. Wretch, take thy death.
 Ros. Forbear !   [*Faints.*
 Clif. Strike, Henry, strike !   [*Discovers himself.*
Why start'st thou back ? I shrink not from the blow ;
New woes assail me at that sinking object,
And all thy sword can do is mercy now.
 King. Thou, night, in tenfold darkness close me
                    round,
From that much-injured form !
 Clif. My child, my child,
Oh ! wake, and let me once more hear thy voice !
Speak, speak, my Rosamond ; tell my sad heart
What further woe awaits it.   Hath affliction
Robb'd me of sense ? or do I see the pangs
Of ruthless death within thy struggling eye ?

Ros. Thou dost, my father; let me bless thy good-
ness
Ere speech forsake me ; thou art come to execute
Thy pious promise—Fate prevents thy care,
And I submit.   My penitential tears,
My hopes of heavenly mercy, and thy pardon,
Alleviate death's sharp terrors.

    Clif. O ! what hand
Hath robbed me of the latest ray of hope,
That trembling glitter'd on my eve of life ?

    Queen. In me behold the murderer of thy peace !
Vent thy reproaches, load me with thy curses,
I bear them all ; high as I am in rank,
And proud in heart, I bend to make atonement.
My rage unsex'd me ; and the dire remembrance
Will ever haunt my mind.

    King. It will have vent.
Lo, injured Clifford, Henry kneels before thee !
Henry, who spurn'd the holy ties of friendship,
The kindly brotherhood of human nature,
And robb'd thee of thy child ; yet let me mingle
My penitential with thy pious tears
O'er this loved form, for whom my heart weeps
    blood.

    Ros. Peace, peace, a moment! let my parting
    spirit
Glide gently hence ; death hurries on apace.
O ! welcome ! hide me in thy peaceful breast
From the dread horrors that surround me here.—
Confusion, shame, oppress my languid thoughts
In this dread moment.—Ye, much-injured, pour
Compassion on me now ! Thou, royal Eleanor—
Thou best of fathers—O forgive !—And thou,
Beloved Henry !—Oh !—   [*Dies.*

    King. Art thou then gone ?—
And did thy dying looks and words speak pardon
To thy destroyer ? In that parting sigh
The meekest, kindest spirit took its flight,

That ever held abode in human breast.
O, sorrowing Clifford! how shall I atone
Thy bleeding injuries?

   Clif. It needs not, Henry;
My child lies dead before me—'Tis enough—
One grave will hold us both—My failing heart
Hath but few drops of life's warm stream remaining,
Grief soon will drink them all—

   King. What now can fate do more?
Rain, eyes, rain everlasting floods of tears
O'er this sad monument of lawless love.

   Queen. If thy torn heart can spare from its own
        anguish
A moment's respite, hear! Thou knewest me, Henry;
Was cruelty an inmate of this breast,
When thou wert kind and constant? Think what pang
I must have felt, ere wrought to this black deed;
Let that reflection win one pitying tear
For all my sufferings, and I ask no more.

   King. It shall be so; and we will reign together
In solemn, sad, uncomfortable woe.

   Queen. Henry, farewell! the hand that's foul with
        murder,
(Bear witness, Heaven!) shall ne'er be closed in
        thine.
To the sad cloister and repentant prayer
I give my future life.   Hail, gloomy shades!
Ye best befit the execrable wretch,
Who, daring to assume the bolts of vengeance,
Dealt desolation with unbounded fury,
And shew'd the faults, she meant to punish, slight,
Compared to her, and her atrocious crimes.

                     [*Exit Queen.*

   King. In this great deed thou hast out-gone thy
        Henry.
Peace, to thy troubled soul! Ye hapless pair,

Accept these tears,—for ever will they flow,
While memory recalls this dreadful scene.

Here let the gay seducer turn his eyes,
And see the dread effects of lawless love:
Learn, 'tis no single crime,—the mischief spreads
To all the dearest ties of social life.
Not only the deluded virgin's heart
Falls the sad victim of his trait'rous art,
But oft, a prey to one licentious deed,
The friend, the lover, and the parent bleed.

[Exeunt.

END OF VOLUME NINTH.

THE

MODERN THEATRE;

A COLLECTION OF

SUCCESSFUL MODERN PLAYS.

THE MODERN THEATRE

A collection of plays

selected by

MRS. ELIZABETH INCHBALD

First published London, 1811

in ten volumes

Reissued in 1968
in five volumes
by Benjamin Blom, Inc.

Benjamin Blom, Inc.

New York

THE

MODERN THEATRE;

A COLLECTION OF

SUCCESSFUL MODERN PLAYS,

AS ACTED AT

THE THEATRES ROYAL, LONDON.

PRINTED FROM THE PROMPT BOOKS UNDER THE
AUTHORITY OF THE MANAGERS.

SELECTED BY

MRS INCHBALD.

———

IN TEN VOLUMES.

VOL. X.

LONDON:

PRINTED FOR LONGMAN, HURST, REES, ORME, AND BROWN,
PATERNOSTER-ROW.

1811.

First published London, 1811
Reissued 1968,
by Benjamin Blom, Inc. Bx 10452

Library of Congress Catalog Card No. 67-13004

Manufactured in the United States of America

FASHIONABLE LEVITIES;

A COMEDY,

IN FIVE ACTS.

BY LEONARD MACNALLY, ESQ

CHARACTERS.

Welford,	Mr Lewis.
Sir Buzzard Savage,	Mr Quick.
Captain Douglas,	Mr Wroughton.
Cheaterly,	Mr Farren.
Colonel Staff,	Mr Wewitzer.
Nicholas,	Mr Edwin.
Mr Ordeal,	Mr Henderson.
Widow Volatile,	Mrs Bates.
Clara,	Mrs Martyr.
Constance,	Mrs T. Kennedy.
Mrs Muslin,	Miss Platt.
Grace,	Mrs Wilson.
Honour,	Mrs Webb.
Lady Flippant Savage,	Miss Younge.

SCENE—*Bath.*   Time—*One day.*

FASHIONABLE LEVITIES.

ACT I.

SCENE—*Lady* FLIPPANT SAVAGE'S *Dressing-room.*

Enter GRACE *and Mrs.* MUSLIN.

Mrs. Mus. AND do you really prefer London Bath, Mrs. Grace?

Grace. Why, I do; in London there's such a noise—such rattling of carts, waggons, coaches, chariots and vis-a-vis; then at night its so charming to see the flambeaux flying about from house to house, like blazing stars!—But what have you got there for my lady, Mrs. Muslin?

Mrs. Mus. A few cards of laces.

Grace. Foreign, I hope—we hate every thing English, and wear nothing but foreign manufactures. (*Bell rings.*) My lady's bell.—— Any new company come down?

Mrs. Mus. Have heard of none, except the wife and daughter of big Mr. Minikin, the great pin-maker from Threadneedle street. (*Bell rings.*)

Grace. Coming, my lady (*goes to a door in the back scene.*) It is only Mrs. Muslin, my lady.

Lady Flip. (*within.*) I'll be with her immediately.

Grace. Let me have a few words with you before you go—Sir Buzzard and my lady had such tifting yesterday, you never heard the like——They hate each other most affectionately, that is the truth of it——

Enter Lady FLIPPANT SAVAGE *through a door in the back scene.*

Lady Flip. So, Muslin, (*sits.*) Heigh ho! I'm all languor and lassitude!—Never knew Bath so dull— Scarce any person of fashion—Nobody one knows —This patch has a pretty effect—And you may go, Grace: and do you hear, Grace, let Miss Constance know I shall be ready to go out in half an hour.

Grace. Yes, my lady.   [*Exit.*

Lady Flip. Muslin, take a chair;—this is certainly English rouge, a vulgar natural red.—Did you see my brute as you came in, Muslin?

Mrs. Mus. Saw two of them, dear pretty animals, in the hall, my lady; the little French dog was playing with the Spanish monkey.

Lady Flip. Muslin, are you mad!—my dog and monkey brutes! sweet creatures! I was enquiring after the brute my husband.

Mrs. Mus. I ask your ladyship's pardon; I saw Sir Buzzard with Colonel Staff, and Mr. Cheaterly in the great parlour.—But I have something to mention to your ladyship—here are the laces—(*opening the box*) but it is not about the laces I want to speak —but——

Lady Flip. But what?—Heigh ho! hand me the Olympian dew—Muslin, I saw a charming fellow at the play last night, and he saw me—Lady Holden certainly pencils her eyebrows—But the charming fellow, he took up my whole attention from the per-

formance——I flatter myself I engaged his—his
eyes were never off me—was dressed in a new Pa-
risian frock.   Hand me the volatile salts, Muslin.

Mrs. Mus. My lodger, I protest!—pick'd the pinion of a chicken at my humble table, last night,
and never ceased talking of your ladyship.

Lady Flip. Hand me the rose water—he spoke of
me, you say?—

Mrs. Mus. Heavens, said he, what an air!—what
grace! then run on in praise of your ladyship's person and beauty; but when he heard your ladyship
was married, poor youth, how piteously he sigh'd.

Lady Flip. Good natured charitable soul!—but
his name—who is he?—what is he? whence came
he?—and who are his relations, Muslin?

Mrs. Mus. Cannot answer one of your ladyship's
questions, except that his name is Welford; he
came to my house yesterday, and talks of leaving
Bath to-morrow morning.

Enter GRACE.

Grace. Mr. Cheaterly requests permission to wait
upon your ladyship.

Lady Flip. Shew him up.   [*Exit* GRACE.
Come to demand his winnings;—lost two hundred
last night, could think of no card but the knave of
hearts I saw at the theatre.

Mrs. Mus. The knave—the king of hearts your
ladyship means; and let me tell you a trump—never
saw finer eyes; then he has the leg of a soldier, and
the hand of a lady——but is he to have the honour
of——

Lady Flip. Of what?

Mrs. Mus. He says he has something of a serious
nature to communicate to your ladyship.

Lady Flip. Perhaps letters from some of my friends
in Paris.

Mrs. Mus. Saw a large bundle of letters on his table.

Lady Flip. Then, Muslin, I leave his introduction to you—shall be at home all the morning.

Mrs. Mus. Your ladyship's most obedient—I leave the laces. (*going.*) Never saw a handsomer gentleman.   [*Exit.*

Lady Flip. What a giddy creature am I?   But a body must kill time—then the fellow is so elegant, (*rises*) and Sir Buzzard so peevish!——the fatigue and apprehension which body and mind suffer after an unlucky run are insupportable; my nerves are quite out of tune, but Muslin has in some degree elevated my spirits.

Enter CHEATERLY.

Cheat. I condole with your ladyship on your hard run last night; the aces conspired against you:—Renounce brag, the cunning of the game lies, not in —judgment of mind, but in command of muscles.

Lady Flip. To which I impute your uninterrupted series of good luck.

Cheat. I am unfit for brag;—the warmth of my heart, particularly in your ladyship's presence, (*bows low*) keeps my features in continual rebellion,—but no person with a flexible countenance should touch brag, the impenetrable looks of lady Frigid Midnight have established her an adept at the game.

Lady Flip. And her nimble fingers give her command of the cards; but she lost temper when I got the black knaves; it was when you stood on my right, and lord Lackacre on my left hand.—" I have got the black knaves," said I, " Lady Frigid"—" I see you have," said she, pointing to you and my lord,—then, as she puckered up her mouth in an affected smile, down fell a few flakes of paint, and her skin appeared under the fractures, like *old* brickwork peeping through the *new* invented composition.

Cheat. Her countenance was once tolerable, but a long run of ill luck has stamped that irrisible discordancy, of hill and dale, which marks her visage, and prevents the smiles of fortune, joy, or good humour, from unbending her to a laugh, or the smallest semblage of the amiable. (*Hums a tune.*) There is a small matter between us, for which I have a very pressing occasion.

Lady Flip. (*Aside.*) I expected this! Ha! ha! ha! I cannot but laugh at your description of Lady Frigid.

Cheat. For heaven's sake say no more of her;— but, let me have the money. (*Bows.*)

Lady Flip. The money! Psha! You must have patience.

Cheat. Patience for a debt of honour!

Lady Flip. I have bills to pay—my mercer, milliner, and mantua-maker, are to be with me to-morrow, and people of that class, you know, are rude and importunate.

Cheat. But suppose I point out a mode of discharging this debt of honour without diminishing your ladyship's purse—what say you?

Lady Flip. If you have any thing to propose I can honourably receive, speak out.

Cheat. Your ladyship is not usually slow of apprehension;—it is true, I have not made an open declaration of my passion.

Lady Flip. Sir!

Cheat. But my eyes, my looks, have spoke the workings of my soul.

Lady Flip. (*Goes from him confused.*) This I never suspected. (*Aside.*)

Cheat. May I hope for your assistance towards my happiness? I have long loved, doated, and despaired.

Lady Flip. Long loved and doated! I'm not surprised at that. *(Aside.)*

Cheat. Sir Buzzard knows of, and approves my
passion.

Lady Flip. Sir Buzzard approves it!

Cheat. He does,—and I cannot live——

Lady Flip. Hold, sir! *(Aside.)* I'm astonish'd.

Cheat. I cannot live without her.

Lady Flip. Without her! without whom?

Cheat. Who but Constance!—divine Constance!

Lady Flip. (Aside.) Though I despise the fellow!
—I—I—but why should I be ruffled?

Cheat. She thought I was making love to herself. *(Aside.)*

Lady Flip. And would you have me accessary to
the ruin of a young creature?

Cheat. There is no ruin intended;—I have open'd
my mind to the lady,—Sir Buzzard is my friend,
and I only solicit your interest; I would marry
Constance.

Lady Flip. No ruin intended! could a greater
curse befal a young creature than to marry you!—
who are you, sir?

Cheat. Who am I, madam! a gentleman.

Lady Flip. I don't mean to asperse your birth,
sir; but is not your ruling passion play; your principal dependance cards and dice; your most intimate connections jockeys, grooms, game-cocks, and
race-horses? I am surprised you could look up to
her.

Cheat. My fortune and family entitle me to look
up to any woman.

Lady Flip. Then it must be merely to look up;
you are, no doubt, one of fortune's favourites, and
her favours follow you;—you have large estates in
expectancy, and considerable rents in Bath, Wells,
Scarborough, Southampton and Margate; nay, more,

you have as many agents as the first landed gentleman in the country.

Cheat. I don't understand this treatment.

Lady Flip. Your connections, manners and conversation would be perfectly agreeable to Constance's turn of mind;—her respect for religion, her morality, philosophy, and knowledge of the belles lettres, would exactly coincide with your studies in the arts and sciences of play.

Cheat. Arts and sciences of play—

Lady Flip. I insinuate nothing injurious to your profession; the respect which professors of play receive in preference to all other professors proves it a profession the most liberal, as well as most profitable. *(ironically.)*

Cheat. She will never forgive the insult of preferring another woman to herself; *(Aside.)* Your tradesmen's bills, madam, are unpaid, your ladyship's mercer and milliner—and people of that class are so importunate and rude;—I do not solicit you to take an active part in my favour; only promise not to be an enemy, and the debt of honour is cancelled.

Lady Flip. You say the debt of honour shall be cancelled. Are you aware that Constance has bestowed her favours on young De Courcy, of York?

Cheat. Yes; and that his passion for play was cooled at the last York races, which obliged him to take a trip to France for the recovery of his finances.

Lady Flip. And his losses she imputes to a conspiracy between you and those friends of yours, who were the ostensible winners, and to whom you introduced him;—I fear you have no chance.

Cheat. Chance!—leave me to that;—I have often won with the odds against me: then she is a beggar, but my passion is disinterested.

Lady Flip. And pray now, how much of the uncle's

debt of honour is to be paid by this parental kindness to the niece?—I see into the scheme,—and
here comes the unfortunate sacrifice.

Enter CONSTANCE.

Con. I understand your ladyship desired to speak
with me.

Lady Flip. To inform you, my dear, of some engagements; but particular business calls me away
for a few minutes, so I leave you to entertain Mr.
Cheaterly.   [*Exit Lady* FLIPPANT.

Cheat. (*Aside.*) Her modest blush puts even my
impudence out of countenance!—your solicitude,
madam, to avoid me, so strongly indicates apathy to
my addresses, I almost dread the possibility of convincing you I am sincere;—do not turn from me in
scorn; I may have some claim upon your gratitude,
though no interest in your heart.

Con. Gratitude! Oh! Your absence, sir, I must
insist on; I will not, in future, be persecuted by your
presumption!

Cheat. I acknowledge my weakness in pursuing
the impulse of my passion; reason checks me, but
such is the imperious violence of my affection, that
even your scorn increases my desires, by making
you lovely in the midst of anger, and the blessing I
sigh for appears still more valuable, more worthy
pursuit, from the distant prospect you give me of
the possession.

Con. Prospect, sir!

Cheat. Yes, madam, prospect.

Con. You will be pleased, sir, to withdraw—you
are insolent.   [*Walks disconcerted.*

Cheat. Insolent! a hard word, madam, to a man
who prefers you to every other woman,—I may be
bold, madam, but—

Con. I repeat it, you are insolent. [*Walks from him.*

Cheat. I am calm, madam; I know the impedi-

ment to my happiness, young lady, and have spirit
to remove it.—Insolent! ha; you prefer a clandes-
tine correspondence with a bankrupt in fame and
fortune to the generous addresses of a man, honoured with your uncle's approbation, and independent of the world.

Con. The engagements of my heart—but I will
not weep—(*wiping her eyes*)—Sir——you have,
with a base and mean cowardice, dared to traduce
a generous, unsuspecting youth, whose fortune you
have assisted to ruin, but whose honour you can
never taint;—a youth who, if present, you would not
dare to look on without trembling. (*Going.*)

Enter Sir BUZZARD SAVAGE.

Sir Buz. What's the matter now?

Con. Enquire of that gentleman, sir.

Sir Buz. What a life I lead! my mind kept in a
continual fever, you and your aunt are a perpetual
ague to me;—her hot fits of levity, and your cool
fits of prudery, operate alternately, and I am tortured by you from morning till night.

Con. I must tell you, sir, that since your house
cannot afford me protection, I shall leave it; and,
though destitute of fortune, I know where to apply
for an asylum.   [*Exit* CONSTANCE.

Sir Buz. " I know where to apply for an asylum!"
—She cannot have a knowledge of our secret, or I
would suppose she meant the Chancery; a man must
now pay as much attention to his ward, as if she was
his child.

Cheat. True, and what adds to the grievance, if a
young fellow marries an heiress, he is obliged to
settle her fortune on herself, though, perhaps, her
person was a secondary object,—I shall never succeed here, Sir Buzzard.

Sir Buz. Pish, why not succeed? a hundred to one
but all she has said is pretence,—you know nothing

of women's subtilty; they smile, they frown, they laugh, they weep, they move but to deceive us, and lay a snare in every article of their dress.

Cheat. De Courcy is the object of her choice.

Sir Buz. Why afraid of De Courcy? his friends at York races plucked the poor devil of a pigeon so bare, they scarcely left him feathers to fly into France.

Cheat. I was present;—may I depend on your assistance?

Sir Buz. Is not our bargain concluded?—on the day of your marriage with my niece, you return me my mortgages, the bill of sale upon my horses, and an acquittance of all demands.

Cheat. Depend upon it—I have pledg'd my honour;—assist me, and I will pursue my game, though she keeps me at bay every step.

Sir Buz. Cheaterly, I must look about me; I came down here for the recovery of my health, and am suffering under a precipitate consumption of my purse. Do you think the young clergyman plays fair?

Cheat. You mean Parson Spruce; could you suspect a divine?

Sir Buz. Why, yes; I do suspect your divines in their own hair, and boots: many of them I believe have thrown off morality with their wigs, and kicked away religion with their shoes.

Cheat. But Dr. Spruce has three hundred a year in the church——he won a cool fifty from me.

Sir Buz. A fifty! I lost more to him than would purchase four years of his income.

Cheat. Do you want cash? I can lend you a hundred; here (*gives him a note*) with friends money should be a common commodity.

Sir Buz. Why I lost this note to Parson Spruce last night—he gave me a fifty, and took it.

Cheat. Aye, Oh, I had it from him, he gave it to me for a bill on London.

Sir Buz. Here comes Colonel Staff and old Ordeal yoked together, very naturally, as two asses should be;—I despise them both: the colonel never served abroad, yet he prates as bold as if he had experienced half a dozen foreign campaigns.

Cheat. And is poor and proud.

Sir Buz. Yes, but hopes to mend his fortune by marrying my sister; I wish him success, that they may mutually torment each other.

Cheat. Mark Ordeal, he is not a less extraordinary character than the colonel: the fellow was a foundling, and never knew his parents; but having acquired a fortune by trade, impudently insults his betters, by preaching what he calls generosity.

Sir Buz. O, confound his generosity; he is always setting a bad example with his charities, relieving widows, providing for orphans, and portioning off young maidens: though ignorant as a Hottentot, he has got himself rank'd among the literati, and sets up for a philosopher—the fellow has come into life through as many shapes as an Orkney barnacle; he was first a block, then a worm, and is now a goose.

Enter Colonel STAFF, *and Mr.* ORDEAL.

Col. Ha! ha! ha! I have been accusing Ordeal of avarice, and he denies the charge.

Ord. I do: avarice, though too often an attendant on age, is a vice foreign to my nature; no man can accuse me of accumulating money by unjust means, or of hoarding it when in my possession; whereas avarice is a dropsy of the mind—a disease that irritates and increases by the means used to assuage its thirst.

Col. Have you not refused to lend me a mere trifle, and being rich, is not that a proof of avarice?

Ord. Hear me;—I consider myself an agent,

B

bound to answer for the distribution of that wealth with which heaven has bless'd my industry—the charge of avarice is more applicable to the spend-thrift than the prudent; the spendthrift grasps at every man's property; yet no man is accounted avaricious who conforms to the custom of dissipation; though the spendthrift raises his rents, and starves his tenantry—borrows money and ruins his friend, or runs in debt, and makes bankrupts of his tradesmen, if he drives a carriage, keeps a train of servants, plays, drinks, and plunges into vice, the world will call him a damn'd generous fellow——I speak my mind—that's my way.

Sir Buz. Well, colonel, how goes on your affair with my fantastical sister? She is a jilt, colonel.—I hate a jilt.

Col. She will soon surrender: I have got possession of the counterscarp, and shall shortly set up the standard of matrimony upon the crown of the—

Sir Buz. Horn work—Eh?

Cheat. The widow has a considerable share of the *toujours gai* in her composition.

Sir Buz. Too much to promise constancy; but then you old bachelors have such winning ways—but, colonel, keep a centinel on my sister—time and possession are two dangerous pioneers, the first moulders the cement by degrees, and the other saps the foundation.

Cheat. Then the widow is so frank, dégagé and good natured, she may grant favours from charity and sensibility, which other women would refuse from principle, or the prejudice of education.

Ord. What Mr. Cheaterly has advanced contains profound gravity of judgment: but my Clary shall have no modern education; I have engaged a master to teach her the classics, to manure the soil by cultivating the seeds of virtue;—yes, I will have Clary cultivat d, for she is innocence itself: free from the bias of example, she is guided only by the impulse of pure nature.

Cheat. A young lady could not have a more dangerous preceptor; the impulse of pure nature will produce every evil that can arise from the politest education.

Ord. I am convinc'd she is delicate as the ermine, which would die to preserve the snowy whiteness of its fur.

Col. Well said, my old friend, amorous as May, though grey as December.

Ord. Grey! Nay, let me tell you, colonel, though snow has fallen upon the mountain, there is sunshine in the valley—Clara is an Aurora Borealis, a blaze in the regions of frigidity.

Sir Buz. Ordeal, seriously, now, are you going to marry this ward of yours for love?

Ord. Seriously, I love the girl as I love my life; but if I did not, having no relations nor friends to whom I owe any obligation, I am determined to make her my heir.

Sir Buz. And no doubt she will bring you an heir in return, and then bury you.

Ord. Bury me!—Granted: when I sleep peaceable under the green turf, let her marry some honest young fellow, and their children shall bear my name.

Cheat. A good way this to raise a family without trouble.

Ord. Family, I understand your sneer: I was a foundling it is true, and cannot boast ancestry; yet I have a heart susceptible of the tender feelings and sweet solicitudes of humanity. Though I cannot claim relations of particular descriptions, I know Adam and Eve were our primitive parents, therefore consider the world one common family, and hold myself bound to all mankind by ties of fraternal love.

Sir Buz. And your family kindness is ot con-

fined to your brothers, but extends to your sisters
too.

Ord. Clara's father was my friend; we serv'd our
apprenticeship together, set up in the same branch
of trade, he failed, and died poor, but I prospered—
he was a worthy soul, and I never speak of him
without tears. (*Weeps.*)

Cheat. Ah! very good, Sir Buzzard; because the
father was his juvenile friend, he would marry the
daughter in his old age.

Sir Buz. A pretty excuse for a vicious appetite.

Col. Hear, hear!

Ord. Clara's father, when on his death-bed, bequeathed her to me as a legacy; it was a bequest of
confidence, and I esteem it more than if it had been
a million: he bequeathed her to me an infant, without a mother, without relations, without friends,
without fortune.—Now, though rich in the liberal
gifts of nature, who hath endowed her with an exu-
berant hand, yet being poor in worldly substance,
she hath but few attractions for a husband; the
knight errants of these days are Argonauts—this is
the golden age, and every thing is bought and sold.

Sir Buz. Spoke in the true spirit of commerce,
my old merchant.

Ord. Let me tell you, Sir Knight, the spirit of
commerce is the best spirit in the nation; we mer-
chants live by barter and sale it is true, but take
this with you, sir, probity is our principle, and our
character nice as a lady's.

Sir Buz. Here comes my moiety of mortality—
here comes the origin of two thirds of my complaints,
with my widow'd sister, the colonel's tormentor that
is to be—see, they smile at some mischief in embryo
—Ah, candied ginger, sugar on the outside, fire
within, sweet on the palate, biting on the tongue.
Ordeal, keep a strict eye upon pure nature; the aloe
is most bitter when green. (*Going.*)

Cheat. Nay, stay, Sir Buzzard.

Sir Buz. Stay, and my wife coming! Excuse me, I avoid her as I would an epidemic complaint. [*Exit.*

Enter Lady FLIPPANT SAVAGE *and Widow* VO-
LATILE.

Wid. Are you here, colonel? I follow you as the little bird does the cuckoo—Mr. Ordeal, your most obedient: how is pretty Clara, and when are we to call her Mrs. Ordeal?—You rear her quite a domestic animal, she is never seen abroad.

Lady Flip. Nor at home, sister, not even at the windows.

Cheat. He fears the sun would spoil her complexion.

Ord. She hath indeed a lovely complexion, glowing and bright as the Tyrian dye, not a modern local blush, that hides shame instead of discovering it; but ruddy health moving in varied tints—the lily and the rose vying for pre-eminence on her cheek!—O she is pure nature!

Wid. But when introduced to life those roses will blow, those lilies will fade.

Ord. She shall never get into any life, but where they may blow and fade naturally—her real face shall never be concealed under a counterfeit; some ladies coin complexions, and should be punished for high treason in defacing beauty.

Cheat. Bravo, old Ordeal! bravo!

Ord. I reprobate imposition of charms! a reverend bishop declared to me he was married two years before he saw his wife's face, and that was by accident.

Lady Flip. I am astonished a gentleman of your age can be so scandalous, so malicious; but it is the nature of wasps to retain their buz after they have lost their sting.

Wid. Our gaiety provokes their spleen; these

ancient gentlemen rail at women for speaking scandal, yet resort in groupes to every place of public entertainment, ogling with their telescope eyes to discover blemishes on beautiful objects—now here's a piece of antiquity! (*turning Ordeal round.*)

Ord. I have not pretended to juvenility since the crow's feet appeared near my eyes: nay, don't bite your lips, widow; lines will appear in the skin after thirty, and are the harbingers to wrinkles.

Enter a Servant.

Serv. The chocolate is ready, my lady.

[*Exit Servant.*

Lady Flip. Sister, let us in—Mr. Cheaterly—

Cheat. I attend your ladyship.

Ord. Can I pay my respects to Constance, my old friend's daughter?

Lady Flip. You will probably find her in the study —poor Constance takes the humbleness of her situation too much to heart.

[*Exit Lady* FLIP. CHEAT. *and Widow.*

Ord. Colonel, I knew the father of Constance intimately, a stout fellow, and served his country long and well—he served abroad—

Col. Hem!

Ord. Strict honour was his principle—but alas, he experienced that was not the medium to promotion—so finding carpet soldiers like you promoted over his head, he went to India.

Col. This widow of mine, Ordeal, hath a prolific flow of wit and spirits.

Ord. Yes, and egad I thought she struck you dumb—she has a prolific tongue too, sharp as the arrow of a Bornean Indian, and tipp'd with poison; your union with her will be happy—perfectly happy —though I recollect she compared you to a cuckoo, a bird of omen; yes, a cuckoo is a very ominous bird—pray, colonel, is the widow skilled in augury?

Col. Damn your cuckoo! but your speaking of augury reminds me of a circumstance at the siege of Prague—a flock of rooks——

Ord. I must go pay my compliments to Constance.

Col. At the siege of Prague—when the Prussian grenadiers advanced. (*Holds Ordeal.*)

Ord. Were you at the siege, colonel?

Col. My regiment was there—I have served my country.

Ord. Oh, yes, you have done great service to your country—at home—by censuring those who have fought for her abroad.   [*Exit.*

ACT II.

SCENE I.—*A Chamber.*

Lady FLIPPANT *and* WELFORD, *seated.*

Lady Flip. Sir, I must say you presume too far.

Wel. I saw your ladyship and admired, and if that be presumption, who is free from it? Admiration naturally produced a more tender emotion—I communicated my feelings to Mrs. Muslin;—Mrs. Muslin reported them to your ladyship, and your ladyship, with a mind liberal as your person is elegant, permits me to throw myself at your feet.

Lady Flip. You have misconstrued the liberty I allowed—my house is always open to persons of fashion, and as a visitor only I expected you.

                                          [*Rises.*

Wel. Nay, madam, your privy counsellor informed me I should be admitted into the interior cabinet, and your principal lady in waiting introduced me in form accordingly.

Lady Flip. And shall I call her now, sir, to shew you the way back? [*Aside.*] Pleasant impudent fellow!

Wel. You are not so cruel—I see pardon beaming from your eye, and frolic smiling on your cheek.

Lady Flip. And should I pardon from that instant, the servile suppliant, now at my feet, would lose all sense of obligation, and from the mistress's slave aspire to be her tyrant.

Wel. I neither desire to be slave or tyrant, but to love upon equal terms—you consent—I read it in your eyes—and I am secret as the grave.

Lady Flip. Secret you may be, but it is not the mere colour of reputation can protect a woman's honour.—I might, perhaps, carry on an intrigue with secrecy, but my mind—

Wel. Upon my soul I have no design upon your ladyship's mind: my heart is captivated; and if I did not totally misunderstand my good friend, and your ladyship's very good friend, Mrs. Muslin, a certain person (whom modesty will not permit me to name) is not totally indifferent in your opinion. (*Bowing*).

Sir Buz. [*within.*] Grace, where is your lady?

Lady Flip. Sir Buzzard's voice!

Grace. [*within.*] My lady, sir!

Sir Buz. Yes, your lady, ma'am.

Grace. [*Speaking very loud.*] She is in her own room, sir, but I believe not yet dress'd—I'll let her know you want her, sir.

Enter GRACE.

Grace. As I hope to be saved, here is my master, and in one of his gruff humours, quite in a tantarum—the gentleman cannot go out that way—follow me.

Lady Flip. Into the next room—make haste—
[*Pushing* WELFORD.
Wel. I go, perhaps, into the interior cabinet—
This alarm, I trust, will convince your ladyship,
that in love, as in war, delays are dangerous—Go
on, Mrs. Grace.   [*Exeunt* WELFORD *and* GRACE.

Enter Sir BUZZARD. [*He sits.*]

Sir Buz. What an infernal life I lead!

Lady Flip. What has rais'd the storm now?

Sir Buz. Why ask!—you know I am married—and
married to you—I am my own master, and hate impertinent questions—I have lost my money—I am
glad of it.—Oh! I wish I had never married.

Lady Flip. [*sighs.*] And I, with all my heart.

Sir Buz. Yet you leaped at my offer—you were
glad to snatch at me—

Lady Flip. Who I? I was seduced into the
match!—Have I not brought reputation to your
house, sir?

Sir Buz. Reputation to my house!—you have
turned my house topsy turvy, inside out; you have
irritated me into a complication of complaints, and
reduced my fortune to galloping decay—have fretted me down to a mere skeleton.

Lady Flip. Sir, some respect is due to my birth;
—I am daughter to a nobleman, and till honoured
with my hand, your family could not boast a drop
of blood in their veins.

Sir Buz. No blood in their veins! I, indeed, have
lost both flesh and blood; no blood in my veins!—
Have I not lent your brother money—your uncle
money—your cousins money!—which of your honourable or right honourable relations are out of
my debt?——If I had no blood in my veins, how the
devil have you and yours bled me so plentifully?

Lady Flip. I despise your meanness—

Sir Buz. Your family are leeches—I could never shake them off.

Lady Flip. Sir, your connexion with me was an honour, which, with all your land and wealth, you had no right to expect. What was your family before your union with me?

Sir Buz. Men and women.

Lady Flip. Could they boast antiquity?

Sir Buz. Yes, my grandfather lived to ninety—my father to eighty-six.

Lady Flip. You married me———

Sir Buz. To perpetuate my family—are you satisfied?

Lady Flip. No, I am not satisfied.

Sir Buz. I know it, I know it.—I know it.

Lady Flip. My ancestors can be traced to the Normans—the Danes—the Saxons.

Sir Buz. Which only proves you have sprung from pirates and invaders; but what is it to me if you were related to the Picts, the Scots, or the Romans? —I am a Savage!

Lady Flip. Yes, you are a savage indeed—

Sir Buz. And the Savages, let me tell you, are the oldest and purest blood in the country.

Lady Flip. (*Aside.*) How shall I get rid of him ?— Sir Buzzard, you don't intend to stay here, I hope?

Sir Buz. You hope so, do you?—I am glad of that, then here I shall have a comfortable nap. (*Sits down and composes himself.*)

Lady Flip. (*aside.*) I'll raise the spirit of contradiction to send him off (*draws a chair and sits by him*). Now that is kind, thanks for your company, and I'll read, or sing a lullaby to compose you; shall I kiss you?—come now, smile, my dear. (*Takes off his hat.*)

Sir Buz. I hate smiling, smiling is the cunning covering of deceit ; (*rising*) and kissing———am I in a habit of constitution for kissing ?

Lady Flip. Am not I your wife?

Sir Buz. I feel you are—do not roll your basilisks
—they have lost their fascinating powers.

Lady Flip. But you shall not go—

Sir Buz. Not go!—I am master of my own house!

Lady Flip. Then I will be mistress of my time;—I
may find a companion.

Sir Buz. With all my heart—a woman who would
keep her husband at home is worse than a corn on
his foot, there is no stirring at ease for her!—O that
mine were cut off!

Lady Flip. You will go before me though; I shall
wear weeds for my love—your face looks this instant
pale as marble, and I can see " Here lieth Sir Buzzard Savage," written on your forehead.

Sir Buz. I am ill, it is true.

Lady Flip. Ill! you have a mortal blackness under
your eyes.

Sir Buz. Eh! What!

Lady Flip. Do not stare so—it alarms me!

Sir Buz. My head swims!——I feel a palpitation
here, just upon my temple.

Lady Flip. A dangerous symptom.

Sir Buz. I know it, and you are glad of it. Oh,
Lord! I shall presently be enrolled on death's list of
Bath patients, who die where they come to live for
the recovery of their health.   [*Exit.*

Lady Flip. Now to deliver my poor distressed
swain from confinement.   [*Exit.*

SCENE II.—*Another Apartment.*

WELFORD *and* GRACE *discovered.*

Wel. Nay, my nonpareil—my sweetest, dearest of
all girls, you may believe every word I say.

[*Lady* FLIPPANT *appears listening at a door in the scene.*

I have lov'd you——

Grace. Love me!—dear sir!—Well, whether you speak truth or no, I like to hear you say so—yet, I fear you are false-hearted; it was my lady you came to visit.

Wel. Your lady! no, no, child, you were the object, and I got myself introduced to the lady, that I might with more ease become intimate with the maid.

Grace. Cannot believe that—my lady is much handsomer than I—What a fine complexion!

Wel. Mere rouge!

Grace. White teeth!

Wel. For which she's obliged to the dentist—

Grace. Charming hair!

Wel. All false.

Grace. Then, what polite conversation!

Wel. Psha, child, she has not the native bloom of your cheeks, the nectarine of your lip, the pearl of your teeth, the natural curl of your tresses, nor the wit of your imagination.

Grace. (*Aside.*) How I likes to hear him praise me and abuse my lady!—And you really love me?

Wel. Most devoutly—could we not retire to a more private chamber? (*Shews a purse.*)

Grace. Swear you'll not be false-hearted.

Wel. By Jupiter, Venus, Cupid, and all the gods and goddesses, never. (*Shakes the purse.*)

Grace. Then hear me swear (*lays her hand upon the purse*) by this purse (*takes it*) I like you.

Wel. Take it, my girl—take it.

Grace. And by this ring, I'll—(*lays her hand on his ring.*)

Wel. My dear, don't swear so often—but kiss me, hussy—I have a secret to tell you.

Grace. A secret! but may not that secret speak for itself hereafter and discover all?

[*Lady* FLIPPANT *comes forward.*

Dear ma'am, you can't think how the gentleman has been praising your ladyship's complexion, teeth, hair, and I don't know what.

Wel. Yes, I was praising your ladyship's—I—I—I—don't know what.

Lady Flip. There's no impediment now, sir, to your retiring, and I request you will instantly withdraw.

Wel. For the present I submit to your rigid and peremptory sentence;—it is my way never to deny or palliate my faults. When I travel in pursuit of pleasure, I always take a view of such beautiful seats as lie before me, and for the life of me, I could not help casting an eye on this little snug box, which lay so convenient to your ladyship's mansion-house.

[*Exit* WELFORD.

Grace. I hope your ladyship will excuse me;—I thought I was doing no harm,—I thought your ladyship dismissed the gentleman, and your ladyship knows we chambermaids have the same claim to our ladies cast lovers, as to their cast clothes.

[*Exit* GRACE.

Lady Flip. Order chairs, and tell my sister I'll attend her to——Devil take the fellow, yet I admire him for his impudence.   [*Exit.*

SCENE III.—ORDEAL's *Study.*

Enter NICHOLAS *and* DOUGLAS, *disguised in a shabby Highland Dress.*

Nich. And so you were recommended by old Corderius, the schoolmaster, to teach our young lady the Latin lingo?

C

Doug. Yes; to instruct her in the reediments of the dead languages.

Nich. Dead languages! do you mean the languages spoken in the other world? for ecod she can chatter glibby enough in the living tongue.

Doug. I am to instruct her, man, in Greek and Latin.

Nich. Greek and Latin! will not that teach her strology and conjuration?

Enter ORDEAL.

Here, sir, is Mr.a—a—What's your name, Scotchey?

Doug. Alexander M'Classic.

Nich. He's Mr. M'Classic, come from Mr. Corderius to learn Miss Clary the dead languages, which he has got alive at his tongue's end.

Doug. Here, sir, are my credentials.

         [Gives a letter.

Ord. My friend Corderius gives you an excellent character, young man, for honesty, and literary abilities, and you may begin with your pupil when you please.

Nich. He has began with her already.

Ord. You are perfect master of the classics, I presume.

Doug. My father keept an academy, where I first acquired the roodiments, and after I matriculated at Aberdeen; there I made an intimate acquantance with the philosophers, Christian, and Heathen,— the logicians, mathematicians, astronomers, navigators, botanists, chemists, and aw the tribe of nateral philosophers.

Nich. What a number of scholars are in Aberdeen!

Ord. Be silent, fool.

Doug. As to the classics, I am maister of Homer, Xenophon, Sophocles, Seneca, Virgil, Ovid, Terence, Sallust, Livy and Horace.

Nich. Have you learned all those gentlemen?

Ord. Silence, you inquisitive puppy.

Doug. I teach them aw, and will make the young lady mistress of them aw.

Nich. Mistress of them all! Ecod she'll never remember half of her servants' names! but o' tag, rag, and bobtail; how comes it that with all those scholars you've taught, you go so poorly? Ecod your clothes are all in jeopardy. He! he! he!

Ord. Silence. Go you, sirrah, and call miss Clara.

Nich. I go—I go—I go—I go—I go—let me see —he teaches musicians, magicians, and physicians —and he'll teach her conjuration and star-gazing— and—mum.   [*Exit* NICHOLAS.

Doug. You are, I presume, sir, a scholar.

Ord. I never deny my ignorance—it is my misfortune, and a man should only be ashamed of his faults,—I do not understand a word of any language but my native tongue, except a few phrases I have picked up,—but I have read most English authors; born in poverty, I was debarred the benefit of a liberal education.—I am candid—that's my way.

Doug. This is a common case.

Ord. No doubt one half of the literati are unlettered, and, like light or Birmingham guineas, pass for more than they are worth.

Doug. You intend to mary the lady yourself?

Ord. Yes.

Doug. And you have secluded her frae company, aw that was judicious—be cautious what men you introduce to her.

Ord. Yes; and women too.

Doug. That's right,—recreations which prudence prohibits at home, and decency denies the exercise of in public, may easily be enjoyed at the preevate house of a confidential friend.

Ord. You are right; there are many obliging, convenient, liberal-hearted, female beauty brokers, who support elegance and expence by trading in a contraband commerce of the sexes.

Enter CLARA *and* NICHOLAS.

Well, my girl,—your tutor has given you a lesson, I understand.

Cla. Yes, sir. (*Loud knocking.*)

Ord. Who the devil is at the door? –I believe they have got a battering-ram, and are going to storm us after the manner of the Greeks and Romans.

[*Exit* NICHOLAS.

Enter NICHOLAS.

Nich. Such silks, and rustlings!

Ord. What's the matter?

Nich. There are cork rumps—hoops and high heels in the house.

Ord. Who knocks at the door?

Nich. They are covered with paint, patches and pomatum.

Ord. Who knock'd at the door?

Nich. False hair, curls and perfumes!—don't blame me, they came upon me unawares; I push'd, and they push'd,—but they push'd harder, and overturned me.

Ord. Who overturned you?

Nich. They are full of flirtation, and giggling, and bedizened with gauze and ribbands; Lady Savage and her sister, with their long tails sweeping behind.

Ord. Lady Savage and her sister! Lady Devil and her imp!—Where are they?

Nich. Running all over the house—up stairs and down stairs, to and fro,—in and out—backwards and forwards—round about—here and there, and every where.

Ord. I am not at home;—there is no body at home —we are all out—I'll retire to my closet; you will step with me, Mr. M'Classic, and do you, my lamb, lock yourself up to avoid 'em.

[*Exit* ORDEAL *and* DOUGLAS.

Nich. He, he, he,—here is a bluster.—Ecod we shall have rare sport.

Enter Lady FLIPPANT *and the Widow.*

Lady Flip. Where, my dear, in such haste?

Cla. Indeed I cannot stay—must I not go, Nicholas?

Nich. Yes, you must go,—go—go—go.

[*Pushing her out.*

Wid. Be not alarmed, miss, we are Mr. Ordeal's intimate friends.

Nich. Yes, miss, they are our intimate friends.

Lady Flip. Come to visit you, my dear.

Nich. Yes; they are come to visit us,—my dear.

Wid. Where is Sir Ordeal?

Nich. Out—out—out (*Points to the closet.*) we shall have swinging fun. (*Aside.*)

Cla. Ladies, farewell. (*Going.*)

Wid. Fie, my dear,—it would be impolite to leave company.

Nich. Miss Clary,—Manners makes the man— we are teaching her the Latin lingo.

Wid. Are you very happy, my dear, on being on the verge of matrimony?

Nich. Speak, my dear. (*Lady* FLIPPANT, *and the Widow, stand on each side of* CLARA.)

Cla. I cannot say I'm very happy; nor I cannot say I am displeased: I do not wish to be married, nor have I any objection to a husband——Heigho!

Lady Flip. But to confess the truth, you have no desire to marry Mr. Ordeal, he is such an old fellow; though if addressed by a handsome, wealthy, good natured youth, you'd—Heigho!

Cla. Do not speak disrespectfully of my guardian —he is very kind to me.

c 3

Lady Flip. I approve your prudence in preferring an old lover to a young one; after marriage you will no longer be confined like an infant;—then you will enjoy such pleasure in making his money fly, and in seeing him approach the grave.

Wid. But for fear he should live too long, be sure you get him a physician.

Nich. A physician! O, death!

Cla. My guardian has taught me how a married lady ought to conduct herself.

Wid. Let us hear, my dear pretty creature.

Cla. I have it by heart: he has taught me, that all young men are cunning and deceitful, and that I must never listen to or believe their flattering tongues; that a man and his wife are one person, and should act as if inspired by one soul!—that a wife should not complain of her husband to her most intimate friends, nor form any connections without his approbation.

Nich. There's instruction for you; you see we take care of her soul.

Cla. Moreover, he has taught me, that in private a wife should receive no company without her husband's knowledge, and in public should not think herself protected but by his presence ; that she should obey him in all things, and place her highest delight in making him happy.

Lady Flip. These were the duties of a wife in the last century,—but we will instruct you in the duties of a wife, who would cut a figure in the polite circles of the present day.—Sister, begin.

Wid. Must consider matrimony a means to increase liberty, and defy scandal.

Lady Flip. Must retain your favourite cicisbeo, confidante, maid servant and footman.

Nich. That will be, I.

Wid. See whom you please, where you please, and when you please.

Cla. That must be very pleasant!—Go on.

Lady Flip. Must be mistress of your own hours, —turn day into night, and night into day.——

Wid. Keep a separate purse, a separate carriage, and a separate bed.

Lady Flip. Never attend to œconomy, but sink, play, and squander your money, to the last shilling, and stretch your husband's credit to the utmost.

Nich. Here is work cut out for mantua-makers and milliners.

Wid. You must always dissimulate in conversation with your husband, and when you cannot deceive you must insist—if he opposes your will, rant, and laugh at him.

Nich. Ha, ha, ha!

Lady Flip. And if these fail, accuse him of cruelty, sigh, sob, weep, scream out, and fall into fits.

Enter ORDEAL *and* DOUGLAS.

Ord. I can contain no longer!—out of my house!—

Lady Flip. Shame! Shame! What, listening to the private conversation of ladies?

Ord. Private conversation! open, abominable instruction,—how can you answer to your conscience, for attempting to poison a young creature's morals! —retire, retire, my lamb.——

Cla. Farewell, ladies.

Wid. Adieu, pretty Clara.

Lady Flip. And remember our instructions.

[*Exit* CLARA.

Ord. Instructions!——downright libertine principles!—you may laugh, ladies,—you may laugh. Ha, ha, ha!

Lady Flip.
Wid. } Ha, ha, ha!

Doug. Perhaps the ladies think their beauty sufficient excuse for their levity,—but ah, they are wrong—naething can atone for want of delicacy,

without which there can be nae charms in the face,
nae elegance in the person.

Enter Colonel STAFF.

Col. Ordeal, your most obedient—call'd at your
ladyship's house, and Miss Constance inform'd me
you were on a visit here.

Wid. We came to see Mr. Ordeal's pure nature,
and he has affronted us!

Col. Affronted!—impossible!

Doug. Haud your tongue, lady, haud your tongue!
—levity degrades a woman, however her name may
be elevated by birth, teetle, or fortin.

Col. Who are you?

Doug. A man.

Nich. Yes, and a scholar ecod!

Ord. (*To the women.*) Out of my house!

Lady Flip. I'll prophecy for your comfort, if you
marry Clara she'll soon draw a comparison between
your winter frown and the summer smiles of a
pretty fellow.

Ord. I despise your prophecy—Oracles have long
since ceased; when they existed the devil spoke
through them, which may be your ladyship's case.

Col. Ordeal, take care; I wear a sword.

Doug. I weer a sword.

Col. Do you daar echo my words?

Doug. Do you daar echo my words?

Nich. Knock out his teeth with one of your hard
ones.

Col. Rascal! (*raises his hand.*)

Doug. Rascal! hear first, and strike after:—you
appear an officer, but I am convinced you are nae
soldier; touch but a hair o' my heed wi' your hand,
and the dee'l gang away wi' my soul, gin I dinna split
you through the crown.

Nich. Sir, sir, shall I bring him the old broad sword?

Col. There was just such a fellow as this at the Havannah——

Ord. There were several such fellows at the Havannah, and such fellows only could have beaten the brave fellows who defended it,—were you there?

Col. My regiment did service there—and if it had not been for a damn'd ague,—but no matter,—I overlook this fellow's insolence,—but Mr. Ordeal, you have been too severe on the ladies.

Doug. Too severe on the ladies—I am your echo again—zounds, do you take the man for a Shrove-tide cock, set up to receive blows without returning them?

Wid. Let's go: we are not likely to receive protection from the colonel.

Doug. I ken, madam, what you are.

Wid. Stand off, fellow——

Col. These are ladies of honour.——

Doug. Their honour, like your courage, is in their own possession; but remember the character of both is in the opinion of others.

Wid. Do you hear the fellow?

Col. He's mad, and not worth notice.

Lady Flip. Were I Clara, I should prefer a young Indian, though sure of being his widow, and burning with him in a month, to living with you for an age.

Col. Ordeal, you shall answer this—but——

Doug. But what dare you say?

Col. Say—I say—my immediate duty is to attend the ladies.

[*Exit Colonel, Lady* FLIPPANT *and Widow.*

Ord. My brave Caledonian! (*shakes hands.*) But here, here, step out and get yourself new rigged.— (*Gives* DOUGLAS *money.*)

Nich. Yes, he is out of feather, and wants pluming.

Ord. But you, you sirrah, if ever you let those women enter my doors again, cut you go—Oh, what a fierce beast, and a perilous enemy to the commonwealth, is a wicked woman!   [*Exeunt.*

ACT III.

SCENE I.

Enter Lady FLIPPANT SAVAGE *and* GRACE.

Grace. Shall I introduce the gentleman, my lady?

Lady Flip. Yes,—no,—yes, Grace.

Grace. I like the gentleman, because he likes your ladyship,—and that shews him a man of taste—I go.—(*Going.*)

Lady Flip. Stay, Grace,—let me consider, this interview may be attended with all the ill consequences of an illicit correspondence.—What are you musing on, Grace?

Grace. I am thinking how very ugly Sir Buzzard is in comparison with your ladyship's lover.——

Lady Flip. Sir Buzzard's plainness, Grace, is not his worst fault,—it is his peevish asperity of disposition renders him odious to me.—Grace, I will not see this gentleman, it will endanger my reputation.——

Grace. Nay, my lady, but consider, *my* reputation, my *honour* is pledged,—he is a delightful creature.—Then consider what an airy, nice dressed gentleman he is—and consider, Sir Buzzard wears flannel under-waistcoats, and swan-skin stockings.

Lady Flip. Can I ever again face Sir Buzzard?

Grace. If I was your ladyship, I would not face my lover too suddenly,—no, I would recline upon the sopha,—(*sits*) lost in thinking,—so,—with my

fan shading my face thus, and every thing about
me dégagée.——

Lady Flip. You say he waits.——

Grace. Or when the dear man approached, turn
short—strike him with a full flash of my charms, and
scream out. Ah!—(*Screams and starts up.*)

Lady Flip. Are you mad, girl?

Grace. A thousand pardons, my lady, but protest
I am beside myself.   [*Exit* GRACE.

Lady Flip. There is no retracting, and I think I
will take him by surprise.—I'll keep up the appearance of resentment, and have the satisfaction of
hearing him humbly plead for pardon.—(*Sits, with
her back to the door.*)

Enter GRACE, *and* WELFORD *full dressed.*

Grace. Now you must acknowledge I am your
friend.

Wel. My sweet girl, I do acknowledge it.—
                                  [*Exit* GRACE.
A fine figure! (*taps Lady* FLIPPANT *on the shoulder,
—she starts.*) Madam——

Lady Flip. Heaven defend me!

Wel. Not from an ardent lover!——

Lady Flip. (*Aside.*) I cannot scold the fellow, he
looks so pleasant!—Pray, sir, by what warrant do
you come here?

Wel. I understand from Mrs. Muslin, by warrant
from your own lips,—but the warrant is incomplete
till your ladyship has affix'd the privy seal to it. (*Offers to kiss her.*)

Lady Flip. A married woman can grant nothing
without the consent of her husband.

Wel. Well thought on; but I do not come un-
prepared: man and wife are one person, and when a
married lady gives me reason to think a tête-à-tête
would not be disagreeable, I always take care to
bring my authority along with me.

Lady Flip. But suppose a lady should acknowledge your authority;—your inclinations, I imagine, sir, could not easily be attached to a single object.

Wel. Yes, they could,—though I candidly acknowledge I entertain an affection for the whole sex.

Lady Flip. Then there is an individual you prefer to the whole sex?

Wel. There is.

Lady Flip. Handsome?

Wel. Yes.

Lady Flip. Sensible?

Wel. Yes.

Lady Flip. And you really prefer her——

Wel. If I denied it I should be insincere, and unworthy your attention.

Lady Flip. And pray, sir, may I inquire, who is the favourite fair?

Wel. Nay, the less we say, or think of her, the better: she is absent——

Lady Flip. Yes, sir,—I perceive she is absent— (*walks about*) and you too are absent.

Wel. Yes, she is absent,—and—Sir Buzzard is absent, and we are together,—and you are a fine woman,—and I am——.

Lady Flip. What, sir?

Wel. A man,—a young man, not a very ill made man, and a very well dress'd man, with a brisk flow of spirits, a warm heart, and a soul which at this instant vibrates with sensibility.

Sir Buzzard. (*Within.*) I say it is false, I left all the papers in London——

Lady Flip. I protest Sir Buzzard is at the door— you must be concealed again——

Wel. Unfortunate!—(*She pushes him in.*)

Lady Flip. You cannot get out of that room till I please.—(*Sits.*)

Enter Sir BUZZARD SAVAGE, *and* GRACE *walking lame.*

Grace. Oh, mercy, sir, you have ruin'd me; oh, my lady, my lady, oh, oh, I shall faint with pain: just when I got to the door, there was my master, and not knowing it, I run plump against him, and he trod upon my foot,—oh,—but it is much better.

Sir Buz. [*Sits.*] A messenger is come down from London for the title deeds of Prospect Farm,—do you know where they are?

Lady Flip. What should I know about your musty parchments?

Sir Buz. Why not?—you spend the rents fast enough—but I remember now, they are in a box that lies in the wardrobe in that room, and——

Grace. La, sir,—I will get it.

Sir Buz. You are not tall enough to reach it.

Grace. But I can stand on a chair, sir, though I need not do that,—our new footman is in the closet settling your clothes, sir.—Yes, sir,—our new footman, sir, is in the closet settling your honour's wardrobe, and he'll help me.   [*Exit* GRACE.

Lady Flip. [*Aside.*] What can she mean? shall I desire Grace to bring the box out to you?

Sir Buz. No, let the footman bring it out, I have not seen him yet.—Grace, bid the fellow bring in the box.

Grace. [*Within.*] He's taking it down, sir.

Sir Buz. Leave it in the closet; I must get some other papers out of the scrutoire. [*Rises.*]

Enter GRACE *and* WELFORD *in a Livery, with a Box.*

Grace. Come, young man, I'll get you my lady's cards for Wednesday's rout, and they mus tbe delivered immediately.

Lady Flip. [*Aside.*] What a metamorphosis!—you'll be expeditious.

Sir Buz. A good looking fellow;—but stand off;
—he is enough to suffocate a man with perfume!
What's your name, Civet Cat?

Wel. [*In a strong brogue.*] What's my name?   I
was christen'd Patrick, your honour.

Sir Buz. An Irishman!—eh!—heaven knows we
had blunders enough in the family before.—[*Looking on the box*]—this is the wrong box.

[*Exit Sir* BUZZARD *into the closet.*

Grace. Yes, we have all got into the wrong
box. [*Aside.*]

Wel. When next we meet—   [*Exit.*

Grace. Nothing could be more lucky, my lady,—
the new livery that came home for your last footman,
George, lay in the bottom of my master's wardrobe.
I must see him safe out—

Lady Flip. This is too mortifying, it hurts my
pride—had I met a man of a generous disposition—
but here comes my torment, and reflection flies.

Enter Sir BUZZARD *with* WELFORD'S *Clothes.*

Sir Buz. I have found more than I sought for,
Lady Flippant;—who am I to thank for this addition
to my wardrobe?

Lady Flip. These clothes!—you mean these clothes!
—he, he, he,—they are really very pretty clothes—
you like them, my dear?

Sir Buz. No, I don't like them, my dear; and who
the devil did they come from, my dear? and to
whom do they belong, my dear?

Lady Flip. Elegant manufacture!—nothing like
it made in England.

Sir Buz. Where did they come from?

Lady Flip. Paris.

Sir Buz. Who owns them?

Lady Flip. They are your clothes, my love!——

Sir Buz. Mine! Did you ever see me wear such
frippery?

Lady Flip. Yes, yours positively; but I did not intend you should have seen them—they were smuggled.

Sir Buz. Smuggled!

Lady Flip. Yes, smuggled from Paris, by my milliner, and sent here for the purpose of ornamenting you, my sweet love!—

Sir Buz. Sweet love!—now that's fulsome—yet thou art my sweet love!

Lady Flip. Am I?—[*Smiling.*]

Sir Buz. Yes, like an apothecary's dose,—my bitter sweet.—

Lady Flip. How ill-natur'd!—but no matter, you shall wear these clothes at the ball this evening.

Sir Buz. I will not.

Lady Flip. You shall.

Sir Buz. Damn me if I do.

Lady Flip. Very well, sir, then I'll send 'em back.

Sir Buz. They shall not be sent back, I begin to like them,—a good colour, and not too gaudy.—I'll keep them.

Lady Flip. Keep them!

Sir Buz. Yes, and wear them.

Lady Flip. Wear them,—where?

Sir Buz. At the ball this evening.—

Lady Flip. I fear you will take cold.

Sir Buz. You wish I should take cold, but I will not take cold,—and I will wear the clothes; you lay out a revenue on your back, and I will, at least for this once, follow your example.—I'll keep the clothes, and go to the ball in them this evening.

Lady Flip. [*Aside.*] The smuggled clothes are fairly forfeited.

Enter GRACE.

Grace. Dinner, my lady!—[*Seeing the clothes.*] Bless me!

Lady Flip. [*Apart.*] Silence, all is well.—Sir

Buzzard you see found the clothes I ordered Mrs.
Muslin to procure him from Paris.

Grace. Well, I am sure, sir, my lady has fitted you
nicely, and I admire her taste, that I do; but will
you wear them, sir?

Sir Buz. Yes, wear them, sir!

Grace. Not till after dinner, sir.

Sir Buz. Directly, Mrs. Prate,—I will surprise
the company in them:—let dinner be kept back.

[*Exit Sir* BUZZARD *with the clothes.*

Grace. It was good luck he did not find the gentleman's sword—yet little matter if he had, for in-
triguing with an incumbrance about him; but how
shall I get him away?

Lady Flip. Poor soul! he must have patience—
contrive to convey him through the garden, to a
chair; he may pretend he is a servant taken ill, which
will blind suspicion.   [*Exit Lady* FLIPPANT.

Grace. Well thought on,—my lady's no fool, but
she must be a great fool indeed who could not make
a fool of a husband.   [*Exit* GRACE.

SCENE II.—ORDEAL's *House.*

Enter NICHOLAS *and* CLARA.

Nich. He, he, he, lack a daisy, Miss Clara—the
Scotchman looks gaily in his new clothes,—he is a
brave youth,—what a leg [*looks at his leg*]—but I
have got more of the calf.

Cla. Yes, a good deal more calf, Nicholas;—but
what can be the reason that while he's teaching me,
he sighs as piteously as if in pain,—it goes to my
heart to hear him without being able to give him
ease.

Nich. Why—why—ecod now, Miss Clary, when
you speak to me, it makes me sigh, and gives me
the heart-burn.

Cla. What would you have me do, good Nicholas?

Nich. What would I have you do? I'll tell you—ecod I cannot—but I'll tell you what the Scotchman ought to do—he,—he ought—

Cla. What!

Nich. Ecod, he ought to,—to—sugar and honey!—what red lips you have!

Cla. What ought he to do?—

Nich. What ought he to do!—why he ought to—how old are you?

Cla. Do not tantalize me, Nicholas.

Nich. Well, I will tell you, he ought to—bless my eyes, what a fine face she has!—he ought to—he ought to—what pretty buckles yours are!—he ought to,—well, shake hands, I will tell you [*takes her hand*] soft as satin,—he ought to—ecod, I should like to do it.

Cla. Do what?

Nich. I mean no offence—but he ought to—[*kisses his hand*] that's what he ought—

Cla. Oh, shame, Nicholas,—shame.

Nich. What shame!—listen to me,—and I won't go behind the bush with you—my master is a fool, and thinks nobody knows any thing but himself—Now, when I see a young man and a young lady together,—and hear them sigh, and see them ogle—why, I sigh myself, and I—I—ecod, I know what's what.

Cla. And what is it you know, Nicholas?

Nich. That the Scotch scholard loves you, and that you like the Scotch scholard—I'ze been in love, and I'ze never think of it, but—Oh, but I can not tell you how it disturbs me—[*Whistles.*]

Cla. And I am disturbed too—heigh ho!

SONG.

What wakes this new pain in my breast?
  This sense that lay dormant before?
Lie still, busy flutt'rer, and rest,
  The peace of my bosom restore.

                    What wakes, &c

Why trickles in silence the tear,
  This sighing—ah! what does it mean?
This mixture of hope and of fear,
  Where once all was mild and serene.—

                    What wakes, &c.

Some pleasingly anxious alarm
  Now warms and then freezes my heart;
Some soft irresistible charm
  Alternate gives pleasure and smart.

                    What wakes, &c.

Enter ORDEAL *and* DOUGLAS, *in a neat Scotch
Dress.*

Ord. Clara, your tutor tells me, you make an
astonishing progress in your grammar, and I am
to hear you speak a lesson:—bring chairs, Nicholas. [*They sit.*]

Doug. Ha you got your grammar, lady?

Cla. Yes, sir, I have been studying my last lesson [*Takes a grammar from her pocket.*]

Doug. Be seated, lady. [*They sit.*]

Ord. Modest creature!—how the blush mantles
on her cheek!—don't be ashamed, Clary—Mac
Classic [*takes* DOUGLAS *aside*] what a subject for
speculation—she is an orange tree, possessing at
once the sprightly verdure of the spring, the sweet
blossom of the summer, and the ripe fruit of autumn.
It revives me to look on her.

Nich. It revives us to look on you.—

Ord. What think you of her eyes?—they shoot arrows of desire into the heart, but on her lips lies an honied salve to heal the wound,

Doug. [*Agitated.*] Will you hear her repeat a lesson?

Ord. See her mouth, a door of coral, opening to a colonnade of pearl.

Nich. Then her bosom, your honour.

Ord. Where the devil is the fellow going? [*Shakes him.*]

Doug. [*Aside.*] My spirits are so agitated, I shall betray myself.

Ord. Come, my lamb—begin.—There is a mild creature, wax of my own fashioning, and I have moulded her into the very temper of my affections.—

Nich. She can give you Latin for every thing about you.

Ord. Restrain your tongue, sirrah.   Go on with your lesson, sweetest, and never mind this fellow.

Cla. [*Tenderly.*] Amo, I love, [*looks at* DOUGLAS] amas, thou lovest, [*looks at* ORDEAL] amat, he loves!

Doug. [*Sighs.*] Oh!

Cla. Amamus, we love. Oh! [*Sighs.*]

Nich He, he, he, amo—I love!

Ord. Silence, rascal!—but, Mac Classic, are the first lessons in Lilly's grammar upon love?

Doug. Aw grammars begin wi' it, sir—because love is the primœval principle of nature.

Nich. He, he, he!

Ord. Out of the room, you scoundrel!

Nich. I go, zir. Amo, I love, amo, you love, amo, he loves, amo, we love,—he, he, he!

[*Exit* NICHOLAS.

Doug. Shall we proceed, sir?

Ord. If you please.

Re-enter NICHOLAS.

Nich. There are three poor people below you desired to call.

Ord. I shall return directly.—[NICHOLAS *following*] Where are you going? Stay here,—Clara
may want something—you'll give her a new lesson
now, Mr. M'Classic—I think she has got enough
of amo and amas.   [*Exit* ORDEAL.

Nich. Zooks! he's jealous, zure as a gun, and
left me here to watch you—but ecod, I'll be no
spoil-sport—so teach away—I love, you love—he
loves.   [*Exit* NICHOLAS.

Cla. What are you musing on?—I like to hear
your instructions when we are alone.

Doug. [*Aside.*] To seduce such innocence would
be damnable: when you are married to Mr. Ordeal,
my instructions will no longer please,—you love
him?

Cla. I do indeed, as much as if he was my father,
—but I never think of him when you are present.

Doug. Then you love him from gratitude?

Cla. Just so!—could I have any other motive?—
If there be any other kind of love, I wish you'd let
me know it.

Doug. There is another kind,—give me your
hand—there is a love known by its effects; it beats
on the pulse, trembles on the breath, gives eyes to
the thoughts, and thoughts to the eyes.

Cla. O la! then I'm sure you are in love, for your
eyes speak and laugh:—why did you touch my
hand?—indeed—indeed, I'm afraid I have taken it
from you—I hope there's no danger in it.

Doug. Love is the child of desire, nursed by delight—weaned by inconstancy, consumed by neglect,
killed by dissembling, and buried by ingratitude.

Cla. How cruel to kill it.

Doug. But then 'tis the parent of jealousy, the

disuniter of friendship, and cause of disobedience; an arbitrary tyrant of the mind, that triumphs over wisdom, tramples upon prudence, and vanquishes even virtue.

Cla. O, you fright me with that description.

Doug. But where virtue is the basis of this passion, it produces the utmost happiness enjoyed on earth, and gives mortals a taste of heaven.

Cla. Now that is delightful! and to tell you the truth, I have heard my guardian speak of it, but I could never feel it in his hand as I did in yours: he says " love is fire full of cold—honey full of gall—and pleasure full of pain ;"—but I see he knows nothing of the matter :—are you really in love?

Doug. Yes, my dear, deeply—deeply ; but why do you ask?

Cla. Because——

Doug. Here comes Mr. Ordeal.

Cla. [*Aside.*] I wish he was in Jericho.

Enter ORDEAL.

Ord. Very well—very well—here, Nicholas !—where's the rascal? Clara, my dear, seek him, and give orders for dinner, there's a good girl. [*Kisses her hand.*]

Cla. Heigho! [*looks at* DOUGLAS]—[*To* ORDEAL] I obey, sir.   [*Exit* CLARA.

Ord. An amiable, modest creature, Mr. M'Classic—nothing ardent in her disposition, has no more idea of love than an infant, yet a charming fertilizing constitution, but chaste as ice,—her heart like the salamander—cold, cold, in the midst of flame.

Doug. Virtue beams in her een, and animates her countenance; like the finishing touches of the painter, it enlivens the portrait, and increases the beauty of the object.

Ord. Poetically conceiv'd, and prettily pronounc'd ;—yes, she shrinks from the touch, like the sensitive plant—you have a prolific imagination, Mr. M'Classic, considering you come from a northern climate [*viewing* DOUGLAS]—yet, Mr. M'Classic, there is no judging of a woman's chastity, who has never been in the way of temptation.

Doug. Very true, sir.

Ord. And women are virtuous in proportion to the temptations they withstand.

Doug. A just conclusion, sir.

Ord. Then you think it would be difficult to find a young inexperienced girl proof against promises, sighs, and tears—and who could withstand the cunning insinuations of a lover.

Doug. Certainly, sir.

Ord. Well, I think differently; I think I could trust Clara—but she's a nonpareil—yes, cool as a cucumber in a hot-bed—yet not prone to vegetation—but M'Classic, I have an experiment to make, and you must assist me.

Doug. Command me, sir.

Ord. Clara, I think, is a pure lamb.

Doug. Sir, there can be no doubt ; but you were speaking of an experiment, sir.

Ord. I have fortified her mind with morals, which will prove a shield to her by day, and a breast-plate by night.—But the experiment—you must be my instrument.

Doug. In what respect, sir?

Ord. To sound the depth of her inclinations—to feel how the pulse of her affection beats towards me.

Doug. Sir !

Ord. If she should not like me—but that is a point for future consideration—if she should like me, I will marry her in the morning.

Doug. Marry her, sir!

Ord. Yes, marry her, sir.

Doug. And in the morning. O my heart! and must I lose her after all?

Ord. In the morning—I have had a special licence some time—yes, she loves me—I know she loves me —and soon as we have dined, I will go to Sir Buzzard's, to engage him and his friends to attend the ceremony. In the mean time you must try the experiment—come in to dinner, and I'll give you further instructions. [*Exeunt* ORDEAL *and* DOUGLAS.

ACT IV.

SCENE I.—*Sir* BUZZARD'S.

Enter Sir BUZZARD *and* CHEATERLY.   *Sir* BUZZARD *in* WELFORD'S *Clothes.*

Cheat. Consider, Sir Buzzard, we are in danger of a discovery every instant.

Sir Buz. What can I do?—Would you have me court the girl for you? Besides, this business raises a qualm in my conscience.

Cheat. Conscience!

Sir Buz. Yes, conscience!—my conscience cannot boast such extensive latitude and longitude as yours,—you have a convenient conscience, it stretches or contracts like India rubber: your conscience is a servant of all work—which you discharge at a moment's warning.

Enter Colonel STAFF.

Col. May the fire of a platoon never again raise my spirits, but it would be better for a man to attack a breach daily and on a forlorn hope, than to sit down before a coquet.

Cheat. Have you ever attacked a breach, colonel?

Sir Buz. You hear he has attacked a widow, and upon a forlorn hope.

Col. I say, sir, your sister is a coquet.

Sir Buz. I say she is a downright jilt. He who confides in the sex will be deceived—I despise them.

Cheat. Yet keep a girl in a corner.

Sir Buz. But not from affection to the girl. I keep her because it pleases my humour and vexes my wife. You know the sex but superficially: there is my rib; when we married, she was all delicacy and good humour, and from her smooth behaviour and oily tongue, I considered her a miracle of goodness. But the wind soon veer'd about, and before the end of the honey-moon blew a rank storm.

Col. Talking of storms!

Sir Buz. Hear me out—Upon refusing to indulge her in some fashionable subscriptions, there was a total eclipse of the amiable; her passion swell'd like a roaring sea, producing nothing but fury, outrage, and noise.

Enter ORDEAL *and Widow.*

Ord. I forgive you, madam,—I forgive you—being determined to marry Clara in the morning.

Sir Buz. Ordeal, I understand they have been abusing you—but their best friends can't 'scape their malignity—they have tongues of charcoal, with which they are for ever blackening or burning characters.

Ord. I shall immediately set off with my bride for London, from whence we will proceed on the grand tour.

Cheat. Have not I heard you exclaim against the grand tour?

Ord. You have heard me exclaim against sending our youth abroad without a proper controul. You have heard me say, that on such expeditions they too often contaminate their native virtue and constitutions, by bartering the honest habits acquired in old England, for the gew-gaw ornaments and despicable effeminacies of the continent.

Wid. Pray, Mr. Ordeal, what retinue do you travel with?

Cheat. The young Scotchman, Pure Nature's tutor, no doubt will make one.

Sir Buz. I wish he may not make two; I speak my mind, Ordeal.

Wid. What, the colonel's friend! split you through the crown?

Col. She is at it again—madam, you should recollect.

Wid. Then I suppose you will no longer restrain her taste in dress—but allow her to throw off her present thin attire, and appear like a fashionable christian—in feathers and a hoop.

Ord. A hoop! no—it makes a woman appear like a walking sphere, encircled from the nadir to the meridian—and if the effeminacy of the men was not so well known, one would be apt to imagine that the women were all in a state of—But I will not speak my mind now, though it is my way.

Enter a Servant.

Serv. Coffee is served in the saloon, madam.

Cheat. Have you seen Miss Constance? [*Aside to the servant.*]

Serv. I believe, sir, she is reading in the garden.
                                        [*Exit Servant.*

Ord. Sir Buzzard, I admire your dress,—you look as fine—as—as the King of Prussia in wax-work.
                                        [*Exit* ORDEAL.

Col. [*To the Widow.*] Shall I have the honour of your hand, madam?

E

Wid. No, sir, I shall never give my hand to a man who has lost my good opinion.   [*Exit Widow.*

Col. [*To Sir* BUZZARD.]—Do you hear that?

Cheat. After her.

Sir Buz. After her purse, you mean.

Col. Capricious woman! [*running, turns round.*] —I once knew a major—

Sir Buz. Know the widow, man—

Col. A major in the forty-second.

Cheat. Away with you! [*They push him out.*]
                                                          [*Exit Colonel.*

Cheat. You will excuse me to the ladies—Constance, you hear, is in the garden: I will seek her, and for the last time plead my passion; but if she perseveres in rejecting my addresses, I have your consent to carry her by stratagem.   [*Exit* CHEATERLY.

Sir Buz. Carry her off any way, and I will be satisfied.   [*Exit Sir* BUZZARD.

SCENE II.—*A Grotto.*

CONSTANCE *discovered sitting, sleeping, with a Handkerchief over her Face—a Book near her.*

Enter CHEATERLY.

Cheat. Asleep!—to disturb her would offend delicacy—and I must sooth her,—I will sit here till she wakes: here comes one of the servants. [*Retires.*]

Enter WELFORD. [*His sword under his arm.*]

Wel. How my landlady will laugh to see me thus caparison'd!—A woman sleeping, by the god of love! —what a fortunate fellow am I!—no sooner does one adventure vanish than another presents itself to my view—how gently she breathes,—the gale is reviving,—[*she sighs*] a sigh of sensibility,—poor soul!

—it were pity she should sigh in vain.   Yes, I will
see her face. [*Takes off the handkerchief.*] O, Heavens!—it is Constance—my life!—my heaven!—
[*Embraces her.*

Con. Help!—oh, help!—

Enter CHEATERLY.

Cheat. Unhand the lady, villain!
Con. O, heavens, it is De Courcy!—
Wel. Ha! is it you? I have met my blessing and
my curse.
Cheat. De Courcy!—
Wel. I have been your dupe, sir, and I know it.
—Am well inform'd of those combinations by which
you defrauded me,—and am determin'd, sir, to give
the law its course.
Cheat. I scorn to retort your assertions,—you
have been a dupe to your own folly. Pride and
high sounding language but ill suit with the meanness of your appearance, assumed for the purpose
of some low intrigue;—metamorphose into a gentleman, and I'll enforce satisfaction for this insolence.
[*Exit* CHEATERLY.

Con. O, I shall faint.
Wel. My dear love,—pardon the momentary
neglect into which passion led me.—I have been
but one day in England—to-morrow I should have
gone for York,—my soul was all impatience to see
you.—
Con. What, in a livery!
Wel. A livery—yes,—it is a disguise, I own, worn
for a purpose I'll not attempt to palliate or justify—
but your appearance like a heavenly vision inspires
me with virtuous thoughts.
Con. I do not urge an explanation which must increase your confusion.
Wel. I will explain all another time.—Here comes
some of the family.

Enter Sir BUZZARD *and* ORDEAL.

Sir Buz. These alarms will ruin my constitution,
—it was fortunate I took bark this morning, or my
whole nervous system would be shaken to pieces.—
Where is this gentleman?—Cheaterly tells me a
stranger has been rude to you. Have you turn'd
him out, Patrick?

Con. [*To* ORDEAL.] Sir, I shall send a letter to
your house immediately, to which I implore your
attention—I am wretched, you were my father's
friend.

Ord. Madam, if I was not, I am a man, and every
thing that affects my fellow-creatures concerns me.
[*Exit* CONSTANCE.

Sir Buz. Patrick,—do you hear?—no answer,—I
shall never recover my health,—don't irritate me,
rascal.—

Wel. Rascal!—to whom do you address yourself?

Sir Buz. To you, scoundrel.—

Wel. Why, you despicable,—that epithet again,
and this sword. —

Sir Buz. This is no Irishman!—what the devil is
become of your brogue?—Who are you?

Wel. A gentleman!—

Ord. A gentleman! ha, ha, ha, this is good!—a
gentleman in a livery!—but which are you? a gentleman in waiting, or a gentleman of the road?

Sir Buz. Ah, ah! I now see how I came by the
new suit, smuggled from Paris.

Ord. The servant is mad, and Sir Buzzard has
caught the contagion.

Sir Buz. I have it here. [*Striking his head.*]

Ord. What have you there?

Wel. Nothing that I know of, upon my honour.

Ord. Nothing in your master's head! How dare
you joke with your betters, young man?

Sir Buz. I shall be the laughing-stock of fools and jest of the malignant.

Enter GRACE.

Grace. Oh, dear, dear, sure there is no harm done! It is all my fault,—Miss Constance is ready to break her heart;—you must know, sir, I was the only person in the house who knew this gentleman ; he is her lover, and he wheedled me, and wheedled me, till I consented to bring him into the house, and so I shut him into my lady's closet.

Wel. The girl tells the truth.

Ord. He is a gentleman, and you shut him up in your lady's closet. [*To Sir* BUZZARD.] Now, I see what you conceive in your head.

Grace. And so, sir, my lady coming in, the gentleman was oblig'd to lie close.

Sir Buz. And he wheedled you, and wheedled you,—and he lay close,—eh—and he never saw your lady?

Grace. Never saw her, as I hope to be saved!

Wel. You hear the girl swear.

Ord. O, it's plain there was nothing between them.

Grace. Nothing between them indeed, sir, that is the naked truth. [*Exit* GRACE.

Sir Buz. Then give me leave, sir, to inquire who you are? and what are your pretensions to visit my niece?

Wel. As to my pretensions, sir, nothing can be better founded :—I love the lady,—but what is still more material, the lady has long since confessed that she loves me.

Ord. Candid and open.

Sir Buz. And your name is De Courcy?

Wel. To that name I was born, but an old good-natured uncle taking it into his head to visit elysium —in obedience to his will, and in gratitude for six-

teen hundred pounds a-year, I now bear the name
and arms of Welford.

Ord. You seem an honest fellow, worthy the love
of Constance.

Sir Buz. What is his honesty to me? I am to inform you, sir, the father of Constance is dead; I am
her natural guardian, and you shall never have my
consent to marry her.

Wel. May I never obtain her consent, if ever I
ask yours.

Sir Buz. She has not a shilling fortune.

Wel. I am glad of it, I have sufficient fortune for
both,—I will settle a fortune on her.

Ord. A fellow of noble generosity!—

Sir Buz. There is a gentleman I am determined
she shall marry.

Wel. Mark me,—let that gentleman be whom he
may, if he presumes to speak to her, write to her,
or even thinks of her as a wife, I shall make him
such an example—but this is losing time,—farewell,
I must wait on Constance. [*Going.*]

Sir Buz. [*Opposing him.*] You shall not go an inch
into my house,—that is your way out.

Wel. I will go into any man's house, sir, where
she is,—debar me access to my love!—Were you
the grand signor, and detain'd her, I would force
into the inmost recesses of your seraglio, put you to
death in the midst of your janissaries, and carry her
off in triumph.

Ord. I do not often swear, it is not my way, but
damn me if I would not assist you.

Sir Buz. Nay, then we must try your courage.
[*Lays his hand upon his sword.*]—O, for an astringent
to brace my nerves.

Wel. Excuse me from running you through the
body while you wear my clothes; that coat is in excellent taste, and I cannot think of running it
through the body.—

Ord. A soldier, and a wit!—

Sir Buz. Take it, take it; [*throws off* WELFORD'S *coat*]—now let me see if you get into my house.

[*Draws.*

Ord. What, going to fight a duel!—Oh, for shame! —duelling is a mode of satisfaction unworthy gentlemen, practised now by every vulgar fellow;—people of fashion should explode it.

Sir Buz. [*Trembling.*] You know I pay great respect to your opinion,—and if,—but he shall not go into my house.

Ord. Consider what an improper place for quarrelling.

Wel. You are right, sir, this is too cold a situation for stripping;—[*takes up the clothes and hands them to* ORDEAL] now for Constance, love, and happiness. [*Exit* WELFORD, *running.*

Ord. Bravo, my boy!—bravo!

Sir Buz. Sure some malign devil has determined to make me ridiculous!—let me after him.

[ORDEAL *holds him.*

Enter Lady FLIPPANT, MUSLIN, *and* GRACE.

Lady Flip. Are you mad, Sir Buzzard?

Sir Buz. Stark mad!

Ord. Nearly stark naked mad.

Sir Buz. The clothes,—the smuggled clothes you provided for me.

Lady Flip.
Ord.   } Ha, ha, ha!

Sir Buz. Away! you old——get home;—perhaps your Scotch tutor may prepare Pure Nature for the grand tour, and provide you more company than you expect.—Why did I marry?—why plunge into a mortal disease, for which there is no remedy but poison,—no relief but death? [*Exit Sir* BUZZARD.

Ord. Can I see Constance?

Lady Flip. She is lock'd up in her own apartment to avoid her lover.

Ord. To avoid him!—He is a noble fellow, and she must have him;—I will in to Sir Buzzard, and argue this case:—he presumes to controul this young lady, his niece, by parental authority; but I will convince him, the principle of that authority is to make our children or wards happy,—not miserable.

[*Exit* ORDEAL.

Mus. Sir Buzzard is in a horrid rage.

Lady Flip. I must contrive to appease him. Constance I suppose has her suspicions;—an amiable girl—I really love her, pity her situation, and am determined never to see Welford again, but for the purpose of facilitating a marriage between them.—I must also effectuate a breach between my sister and this pusillanimous colonel.

Mus. That may be easily accomplished—the widow has no small share of vanity.

Lady Flip. True!—

Mus. We must persuade her she was the object of Mr. Welford's admiration.

Grace. I will swear he brib'd me to introduce him to her.

Mus. And I will contrive to get her and the gentleman together at my house, and your ladyship shall send the colonel to surprise them, which will produce an irreconcileable quarrel.

Lady Flip. Here comes the widow—do you lay the train.

Enter the Widow VOLATILE.

Wid. De Courcy is gone, after a very loud altercation with Cheaterly, which terminated in mutual vows of vengeance: he charges Cheaterly with having imposed on him at play.

Lady Flip. There is nothing scandalous in that

—play has become a science, fashionable in practice, and like other *faux pas*, 'tis only blameable in
discovery.   Pray how has Constance behaved?

Wid. Remains locked up in her own room, and
perseveres in denying an interview to her lover:—
this De Courcy is in my opinion a charming fellow.

Lady Flip. But I must know for what purpose he
was brought into my closet.—I am certain Constance was not the object; so speak, Grace.

Grace. Well, my lady, the truth is, the gentleman
came after the widow.

Lady Flip. I thought so,—this duplicity, sister,
hurts me.

Grace. Dear, my lady, it is all my fault,—the
gentleman saw Mrs. Volatile at the play with your
ladyship, and sent for me in the morning—and,—
but am I sure of pardon if I tell?

Lady Flip. Yes, if you tell nothing but the truth.

Grace. Well, my lady, the poor young gentleman
to be sure swore bitterly he was smitten;—By all the
gods, says he, she is one of the most beautifulest,—
most youngest, and most elegantest creatures my
eyes ever beheld!—but I, telling him as how she
was positively engaged to Colonel Staff,—then he
began to curse.—

Wid. Why presume to tell him so?—Who gave
you knowledge of my engagements?

Lady Flip. Hear the girl, sister; [*Aside.*] she's caught.

Grace. Don't be angry, madam,—I told him, madam—thinking no harm, and so he curs'd, and call'd
on heaven, and poor gentleman sigh'd so, that I
took pity on him, and by his persuasions and promises brought him into the closet, where he was to
have been concealed,—Yes, ma'am—'till I could
have contriv'd to have brought you into the room,
which I should have done, but that my lady first
came, and then Sir Buzzard, who made up the
noise that disturb'd the house.

Lady Flip. You are an impudent girl: go wait in my dressing-room 'till my coming.

Grace. Yes, my lady,—but oh, sure, you don't intend to discharge me,—what could I do when so pretty a gentleman knelt to me, and cried to me for assistance—and squeez'd my hand, and forc'd a purse into my bosom—Oh! oh! [*crying, apart to the widow*]—you will speak to my lady.

Wid. I will, Grace! [*apart*] there [*gives money*] —let me see you presently. [*Exit* GRACE, *laughing.* A pretty scheme this!—your maid, Lady Flippant, has used me well—did I ever ,make any positive engagements with the colonel?

Lady Flip. I hope not, but really you take such pains to torment each other, I was apprehensive you were privately married.

Wid. Heaven forbid!—I have been prudently considering the colonel's situation some time past—his estate I understand has been long languishing in a decline, and his creditors no doubt are in expectation of mine.

Lady Flip. Then to bestow it on Welford—think of the pleasure of sweet five and twenty smiling upon you from morning 'till night.

Mus. And from night to morning—think of that, madam.

Lady Flip. Then our triumph over a girl of such beauty as Constance—the buz of the polite world, and their impertinent ill-nature.

Wid. Certainly there are inducements.

Lady Flip. Inducements! you will have the exquisite satisfaction of being lampoon'd, epigramm'd, and paragraph'd—or perhaps be etch'd in aqua fortis, and stuck up in the print shops. Then to have the tribe of antiquated maidens, disgusted wives, and disappointed widows railing at your prudence, yet envying your situation—" Lord bless us!"—ejaculates Lady Toothless, " I wonder at her

indiscretion, to marry a man so young. The colonel
would have been much more suitable."—Then she
takes five years from your lover's age, and adds to
yours—" That's he!—that's he!"—exclaims Miss
Squintum, as she ogles from a side-box, with one eye
worn out in searching for defects in beauty, and the
other on the decline—" That's he,—but I cannot
perceive what she saw in the fellow; he is as plain as
herself—and I wonder how women can follow fellows."—The blooming youth hands you to your seat
—the whole circle stare at you—a general whisper's
breath'd round—you gaze in return with perfect
composure—salute your acquaintance—adjust your
tucker, giggle behind your fan, assume a perfect indifference, whisper your handsome husband to mortify them, and laugh out to shew your inward satisfaction and ineffable contempt.

Wid. But how is all this to be brought about?

Mus. Call at my house within an hour, and if I
do not settle it, discard me from your confidence.—

Lady Flip. She shall be punctual—come, sister, I
see you were unacquainted with your lover's passion,—but you must acknowledge I had sufficient
cause for suspicion.

Wid. Yet you must allow there was no deceit on
my part.   [*Exit Widow.*

Mus. You have play'd your part admirably.

Lady Flip. Yes, Muslin, all good actresses are not
upon the stage.

                   [*Exeunt Lady* FLIPPANT *and* MUSLIN.

SCENE III.—ORDEAL'S *House.*

Enter DOUGLAS, CLARA, *and* NICHOLAS.

Nich. You are no longer a Scotchman, I zee—

Doug. Yes, Nicholas, I have only laid aside the

tone and accent, but am still a Scotchman; I have
no reason to be ashamed of my country, and I trust
my country will never have reason to be ashamed
of me.

Nich. Why zee master, I could never zee any
difference between your English and Scotch; though
to be zure I could hear it in their speaking, and
that is the only difference I think should ever be
between them: but take a fool's advice now,—
make the best use of your time.   [*Exit* NICHOLAS.

Doug. What employs your thoughts, my love?

Cla. In truth, love itself: if the pleasing description you have given me be true, and I have no reason to doubt your veracity, to live with those we
love must be the extent of human happiness;—but
then, Mr. Ordeal has told me that your sex often
requite the most sincere passion with cold indifference.

Doug. The charge is too true; but my affection
can only cease with life.

Cla. I owe every thing to Mr. Ordeal's goodness,
and the very arguments you urged to gain my love
persuade me against being ungrateful!—obedience
is the only return I can make his kindness, and how
can I disobey him, when my heart informs me that
ingratitude is one of those heinous sins at which
Heaven is most offended?

Doug. It is true, no quality of the soul is more
lovely than gratitude;—but Mr. Ordeal is not actu-
ated by passion,—he offers you his hand from motives of generosity, not love,—all you owe him is
friendship, which an union with me could not diminish.

Cla. You can persuade me to any thing;—you
swear you love me,—I believe you,—and if the pleasure I take in seeing you, and hearing you, and the
pain I feel when you leave me, be love, I love you
above all things.

Re-enter NICHOLAS.

Nich. Have you settled every thing?
Doug. Good Nicholas, do not interrupt her.
Nich. Who, I, a spoil-sport! mum!——
                                        [*Exit* NICHOLAS.
Cla. Would not my consenting to marry you be
injustice to my benefactor?
Doug. The value I set upon your love is such, I
would not accept it, but as the voluntary gift of
your soul!—I will obtain Mr. Ordeal's consent.
Cla. Then I am for ever yours. [*He kisses her
hand.*]

Enter ORDEAL *and* NICHOLAS.

Ord. [*Aside.*]—What do I see!
Cla. But when will you obtain his consent?
Ord. Never.
Cla. O, we are undone.
Ord. [*to* DOUGLAS.] Is this the way you repay my
confidence? And you, [*to* CLARA] innocent miss,
is this a grateful return for years of kindness?—But
[*to* NICHOLAS.] what shall I say to you, rascal!—you,
whom I thought watchful as a lynx, have slumbered
like another Argus—were your eyes piped into a
nap by this Mercury, or was your mouth stopped
by a sop, Mr. Cerberus?
Nich. Yes, I loves a sop ;—but I will be called no
names—zee master,—our bargain is this, a month's
warning, or a month's wages; zo, pay me, and I'll
go, but remember it was not I brought maister
M'Classic into the house.   [*Exit* NICHOLAS.
Doug. Your resentment, sir, must fall solely upon
me—I only have deceiv'd you,—a word in private,
—[*takes* ORDEAL *aside*] could human nature repel
the influence of such beauty?—[*points to* CLARA]
had I been less honourable, or Clara less virtuous, I
might now perhaps be imposing upon your credu-
                        F

lity a seduced maid, with a vitiated mind: I am young,—Clara is pure nature,—the experiment I have made was dangerous.——

Ord. But you were only to have made the experiment to try how far her inclinations coincided with mine.

Doug. Consider, she was an orange tree.

Ord. You were to have been the instrument for promoting my happiness.

Doug. She possess'd the verdure of the spring—

Ord. Hear me!

Doug. The blossom of the summer——

Ord. Hear me!

Doug. The ripe fruit of autumn.

Ord. And you would consider me the falling leaf in winter—hear me, sir!—[*loud*] Have you not been urging the temptations of pleasure to seduce her into your own designs?—have you not alienated her affections from me?

Doug. Sir, I came into your house for the very purpose of gaining her love.

Ord. Who are you, sir?

Doug. A soldier—my name Douglas,—my fortune a competency,—my country Scotland—the same person who assisted you when attack'd by ruffians on Marlborough Downs.

Cla. The kind gentleman in whose arms I fainted!

Doug. From the first instant I saw her, my soul caught the inspiration of virtuous love.

Ord. You are unfashionable, sir,—from the dissipated conversation of the young fellows of the times, one would imagine there was neither honesty in man, nor chastity in woman;—but your conduct contradicts their aspersions.

Doug. It is too true, the arts of seduction are so sedulously studied, that honest love appears in danger of being extirpated.

Ord. There are many, many melancholy examples;—but be assured, young man, though sensual pleasures arise from seducing innocence, it is plucking blossoms from a sweet-briar, which will rankle in the flesh.

Doug. Your observation, sir, is just,—though it does not apply to me.——

Ord. My censure does not fall solely on youth,—no, the gardens of beauty and innocence are also despoil'd by old debilitated wretches, who cannot cultivate the soil, but lay waste its beauties.

Cla. Do you forgive me, sir?

Ord. I blame you not, I am your debtor for many instances of duty and affection;—look on her, Douglas;——yet her beauty is the least of her excellence,——but as it is a principal part of benevolence to assist another most when there is most need of assistance,—and that you need not owe too much to the generosity of your husband,—as you cannot be my wife, I adopt you for my child—love inspires its votaries with sentiment, and I acknowledge the benign influence. [*Joins their hands.*]

Doug. You weep, my lovely Clara!

Ord. And so do you,—and so do I,——I see you are all joy,——but, my children, the transports of a virtuous passion are the least parts of its happiness,—we will this instant to Sir Buzzard Savage's,—a young lady, his niece, calls for my protection.

Doug. You mean Constance Heartfree; young De Courcy of York, my particular friend, is, I believe, betrothed to her.——

Ord. You are right;—take your bride by the hand;—the women will laugh at me for losing her, but I am above the laugh of the world, and I will laugh at the world in my turn,—that is my way.—

[*Exeunt.*

ACT V.

SCENE I.—*Lady* FLIPPANT'S *Dressing-Room.*

Enter Lady FLIPPANT.

Lady Flip. The storm bends this way, and here will I meet it.   [*Sits down, and takes a book.*

Enter Sir BUZZARD *and* GRACE.

Sir Buz. [*Pushing* GRACE *before him.*] You shall instantly march out of my house.   [*Pushes her.*
Grace. My lady scorns your suspicions.
Sir Buz. Stop your gabble, you diminutive pandar in petticoats!—It is clear that Constance was ignorant of Welford's arrival in England!—It is apparent he did not come to my house after her.—What, is your noble blood at a loss for an excuse?
Lady Flip. Who has instilled jealousy into that head of yours, barren of every thing but what is monstrous!   [*Reads.*
Sir Buz. It is your ladyship has made my head monstrous.

Enter Colonel STAFF.

Col. Sure the devil instigates some women!—the widow——
Sir Buz. Do not throw the blame on the poor *devil*—it is nature instigates them, and she is to the full as subtle and certain in her operations.
Col. I just now spoke to her as she stept out of a chair into Mrs. Muslin's, and in return was shot through the heart with a look of ill-nature and contempt——if I was not the coolest fellow in the service, I'd run mad,—aye,—mad, mad—

Lady Flip. You would have cause to run mad, if you knew she is now at Mrs. Muslin's, enjoying a tête-à-tête with Welford.

Col. Impossible!

Grace. I am ready to take my oath of it! [*To Sir* BUZZARD.] The truth is, I told a great lie to your honour.

Sir Buz. O, confound me, but I believe you now.
                                        [*Exit* GRACE.

Col. The widow gone to Welford, on an assignation—ha! ha! ha! I will after her this instant, and cut his throat!—No, I will not stir—I am pleas'd—perfectly pleas'd!—I will discharge such a volley about his ears:—gone to visit Welford!—but why should I be vex'd?—I will follow her, spring a mine, and blow them up together—Burst on her like a hand-grenade.

Lady Flip. Ridiculous—you are all gunpowder.

Col. Ungrateful woman!

Sir Buz. Deceitful sex!

Lady Flip. Surprise her and her lover!

Col. I will break with her——I mean I will pursue her.   [*Exit.*

Lady Flip. Well, you see it was your sister, not your wife, Welford came to visit: are you ready to make an apology for your vulgar suspicions?

Sir Buz. An apology to you! O, impudence! have you not been the rust of my health, have you not fretted me down to a mere skeleton? Make you an apology!—give me my wasted flesh.

Lady Flip. I shall for London in the morning.

Sir Buz. If you dare!

Lady Flip. Will shew out at every place of public entertainment.

Sir Buz. At your peril.

Lady Flip. At your cost.

Sir Buz. The law gives me authority to confine you, and I will exercise it—I am your husband.

Lady Flip. I am heartily sorry for it!—will have public breakfasts, public dinners, and public nights.

Sir Buz. You shall have bread and water, in a narrow room.

Lady Flip. A box at the Opera, and subscribe to all the concerts.

Sir Buz. You devil!

Lady Flip. Will purchase a new vis-a-vis—a town chariot and phaeton.

Sir Buz. You—you have a design upon my life.

Lady Flip. Heav'ns! how ardently I pant to be elevated in the phaeton, to take the circuit of Hyde Park, rolling in a cloud of dust, four horses, two outriders, whip in hand, flowing manes, hunters' tails, sweep down Piccadilly, turn into St. James's street,—up fly the club-house windows, out pop the powdered heads of the bucks and beaux of fashion—some nod, some smile, some kiss hands,—all praise —She is a goddess, exclaims one,—a Venus, ejaculates another,—an angel, sighs a third. I cut on, flash down Pall Mall swift as lightning, rattle furiously through Charing-Cross, overturn Lady Dapper's whim and cats at Northumberland House, lose a wheel in the Strand, leap from my seat as the carriage falls, and am received in the arms of some handsome fellow whom love has directed to my assistance.

Sir Buz. She is mad! she is mad! outrageous mad!

Lady Flip. He carries me into a house, fainting—

Sir Buz. Stop there; I will be divorc'd.

Lady Flip. Then I will have a separate maintenance.

Sir Buz. Not a shilling.

Lady Flip. You cannot deprive me of my settlement.

Sir Buz. Ay, there is the grievance! O, confound

all jointures and settlements, those encourage your
levities, and stimulate you all to transgress.

[*Exit Sir* BUZZARD.

Lady Flip. [*Sits.*] My poor spirits are exhausted!
Heigh ho! I am tired of this dissipated life.

Enter CONSTANCE.

Con. I wait upon your ladyship, to return grateful
thanks for the many favours you have conferred upon
me, and to take my leave, as I am determined to
quit this house.

Lady Flip. What! without your uncle's consent?

Con. I cannot think his consent necessary, while
he and your ladyship assent to the persecution I experienced from a man I despise.

Lady Flip. [*Rising.*] And pray where do you intend to go?

Con. I have found a protector—Mr. Ordeal, the
friend of my unfortunate father. Lady Flippant, it
hurts my heart to part you upon those terms.

[*Weeps and walks as going.*

Lady Flip. In tears, Constance! [CONSTANCE *returns.*] Why so distress'd?

Con. My heart is too full.

Lady Flip. Be seated; [*they sit*] you love this
Mr. Welford sincerely—but he is! [*Aside.*] what
is it to me what he is!   [*Rises.*

Con. To me he is every thing—and it is my
hope!—[*Rises.*]—but why should I hope?—

Lady Flip. Constance—I really love you—our
manners have divided us; but be assured, my dear
girl, though I run the circle of fashionable life, my
mind is not devoid of sensibility—our education has
been different.

Con. It was my happiness to receive instruction
from a pious and tender mother, who early taught
me the precepts of virtue, and impressed upon my
heart, that a pure reputation with humble poverty

was preferable to a suspicious character, though blazoned with all the pomp and ornaments of elevated life—but she is no more.

Lady Flip. [*Rises.*] Alas, Constance! it was my misfortune to be educated in all the giddy foibles and levities of the times.

Con. [*Rises.*] But I have observed a disposition in your ladyship susceptible of the tenderest offices of friendship,——and where there is feeling——

Lady Flip. There is hope of reformation—you would have said so—indeed, Constance, there are sentiments here, which often upbraid me; but sure nothing has transpir'd, injurious to my honour.

Con. The world is censorious, madam, and those whose conversation is the most entertaining are often the most dangerous; to simplicity they impute cunning, and give a criminal construction to the most innocent actions.

Enter ORDEAL *and* CLARA.

Ord. I am all joy, Lady Flippant! Constance, this is Clara; hereafter I trust you will be inseparable friends.

Cla. I shall endeavour to merit the lady's friendship.

Ord. They may boast of Queen Emma walking over burning ploughshares, but here is a girl has done more, she has lived in a fashionable family without censure.   [*Takes* CONSTANCE *by the hand.*

Lady Flip. But, Mr. Ordeal, what is the cause of your joy?

Ord. It must be disclos'd—Pure Nature has bestowed her hand and heart on the Scotch lad, who turns out to be Captain Douglas, Welford's intimate friend.

Con. Sir, I know the gentleman, and he bears a high character.

Lady Flip. Constance, take this young lady to the

drawing-room, send Grace to me, and order your maid over to Welford's, to let him know you will be there presently.   I have a serious reason for my request, and will not be denied.

Con. I obey.   [*Exeunt* CONSTANCE *and* CLARA.

Lady Flip. The poor girl's situation is truly pitiable—it was our subject when you came in—the tears are not yet out of my eyes.

Ord. Never blush for weeping; tears are the certain symptoms of a noble soul.

Lady Flip. Do you know that I have serious thoughts of throwing aside all fashionable levities?

Ord. I know it is almost time; I believe your inclinations are virtuous, and your irregularities I do not impute to nature;—no, my lady, nature has endowed you with amiable qualities, among which I think generosity is prevalent—like most of your sex, you have taken up levity through whim, and maintain it through habit, though perhaps your soul struggles to be delivered from the trammels.—break them, then, and you will do more than Cæsar;—he conquered countries,—but the greatest glory human nature can acquire is to conquer ourselves;—I have good news for Constance,—her father is living.

Lady Flip. Heavens!—are you serious?

Ord. I have had letters from London, and he returns by the next ships from India;——nay more,—he has remitted thirty thousand pounds to her sole use, with directions to prepare a house for his reception.

Lady Flip. O, I am overjoy'd—why has she never heard from him before?

Ord. He was sent upon an embassy to the interior parts of the country, and his letters were intercepted and destroyed.—But seriously, has your ladyship known nothing of this before?

Lady Flip. Never.

Ord. There is roguery on foot,—an express was

sent to your seat at York, which not meeting the lady there was forwarded to this city, and delivered at this house.

Lady Flip. I see into it; this accounts for the warm impetuous passion of Cheaterly; the girl and her fortune were no doubt to be sacrificed, between him and my worthy spouse. Then you must assist me in persuading Constance to go to Welford; it will produce an incident which will punish the young gentleman's passion for intrigue, and give Constance an authority over him; [*going, returns*] but do you believe my repentance sincere?

Ord. I hope so!—but I believe nothing without proof—that is my way—where there is levity the world will suspect, and when the world has once cause to suspect a woman, her character becomes as much the sport of its malice, as if there was a certainty of her having abandoned it.

Lady Flip. I am penitent! but do you really forgive my lecture to Pure Nature?

Ord. Yes, and am convinced you are no false prophet; for, as you foretold, Clara preferred the summer dimples of youth to the winter wrinkles of age,——I speak my mind, that is my way.

[*Exeunt* ORDEAL *and Lady* FLIPPANT.

SCENE II.—*Mrs.* MUSLIN'S.

The Widow, Mrs. MUSLIN, *and* WELFORD, *discovered at Tea.*

Wel. Your opinion, madam, is just! Vivacity is an attribute to woman,—gravity natural to man:—and probably the sexes were thus contrasted, that the saturnine disposition of the male might be relieved by the sprightliness of the female;—your smiles alleviate our pains, your approbation rewards our dangers.

Wid. And our conversation illustrates my opinion;
—you are grave,—I, perhaps, too volatile.

Mus. The poor gentleman seems as if something
preyed upon his mind; let me recommend matrimony,—it is the only cure for melancholy.

Wel. And often a specific for all complaints.

Mus. Well,—business must be minded.   [*Going.*

Wel. [*Rises.*] Must see you to the door.

Mus. [*Aside.*] A great fortune,—may I trust her
with you?

Wel. May *I* trust myself with *her?*   [*Aside.*
                                    [*Exit Mrs.* MUSLIN.
A good, merry, convenient, civil old woman;—she
recommends matrimony.—[*Sits.*] Pray, madam,
what kind of lover would you prefer?

Wid. I must tell you the lover I would not prefer.
I would not prefer a coxcomb,—a fluttering summer insect,—a talkative creature, full of insipid
gesture, laughter, and noise, who pays more attention to his hair than to his intellects,—who possesses
neither sentiment for friendship, nor sensibility for
love—but is curst with a soul devoid of manliness,
and bent on the gratification of its own puny affections.

Wel. An excellent picture; yet the species of
animal you describe are favourites.——The ladies
are grown so enamoured of delicate limbs, and effe-
minate faces, one would imagine they wished to have
their lovers women in every thing.

Enter Mrs. MUSLIN.

Mus. Dear sir, there is a woman below enquiring for you—she insists upon coming up, and
has such a tongue!

Wid. I would not be seen for the world.

Mus. She would surely blast the reputation of
my house.—Sir, you must go down to her.—O my
poor character!   [*Exit Mrs.* MUSLIN.

Wel. Any thing to save the reputation of your house.   [*Going.*

Enter Mrs. MUSLIN.

Mus. Madam, madam, the slut is upon the stairs.—Step into this closet till the impudent creature is gone.—[*Puts the widow in the closet.*] You do not know, sir, that you have been sitting with Mrs. Volatile, sister to Sir Buzzard Savage.

Hon. [*Within.*] Mr. Welford.

Wel. I know that voice.

Mus. It is the clack of Mrs. Honor, waiting-maid to Miss Constance.

Wel. Then keep her out, for Heaven's sake.

Hon. [*Within.*] I will have admittance.

Mus. Coming, Mrs. Honor.——O the audacious wretch!—I see, sir, you are a man of gallantry; but pray dispatch the creature as fast as possible.   [*Exit Mrs.* MUSLIN.

Hon. [*Within.*] Madam, I insist upon going in first.

Grace. [*Within.*] No, me'm—you will pardon me.

Enter GRACE *and* HONOR *pushing in together.*

Wel. What, two!——Ladies, your most obedient.——[*Bows—they curtsey.*]

Hon. You have no business here, me'm——

Grace. My business, me'm, is no business of yours ——or if it was your business, me'm, yet it is not the business of the likes of you to look down upon the likes of me, me'm.

Hon. The likes of you I look down upon with scorn.——It is not for the likes of you, to look up to the likes of me, me'm.——I serves a lady of vartue.

Grace. Vartue! Your insinuation is low, me'm, high as you carry your head.

Wel. Grace, stand on my right hand—Honor,

take your place on my left—How happy would it be for England, were all her great men in my situation—Grace supporting one side, Honor supporting the other.—Now, ladies, to the cause of your visit.

Grace. My lady understanding that her sister was here—— }
Hon. My lady sent me to let you know—— } *Together.*

Wel. One at a time.

Grace. Sir, you must know—— }
Hon. My lady sent—— } *Together.*

Wel. Here is a guinea for her who speaks *second* ——What, dumb!——But money seals as well as unseals the mouths of great speakers.

Hon. Me'm, I shall certainly speak first—Sir, you must know——.

Grace. Speak first, me'm! I serve a lady of quality.

Wel. Order in the house—let me settle this point of precedence—I believe it is regular that Grace should take the lead of Honor, so Mrs. Grace begin.

Hon. Thank you for preferring she. [*Walks about.*

Wel. Now Grace, what is your business with me?

Grace. La, sir, I have no business with *you*—I want to speak with Mrs. Volatile.

Wel. Child, she is not here.

Grace. Not *here*—but I believe she is *there*.
                        [*Points to closet.*

Wel. By this guinea she is not.   [*Gives money.*

Grace. By this guinea I will swear it—mum—but my lady wants to see her directly—Mrs. Honor, your very obedient—an audacious hussy !—[*Aside.*
                        [*Exit* GRACE.

Hon. Me'm, your most humble—— [*Aside.*] Lord, sir, I found it as difficult to get at you, as if you had been a great Turk.

Wel. Mrs. Muslin did not know you perhaps.

Hon. Not know me! she knew me to be vartuous; though as the saying is, " tell me your company and I will tell you what you are"———and I and my mistress live in a family where there is not much vartue practised—but I am silent—servants should neither have eyes, nor ears, nor tongues, therefore I am always blind, deaf, and dumb, let me hear or see what I may.

Wel. Lower your voice, you may be over-heard.

Hon. Then there is Sir Buzzard's sister, the widow, though her husband is not dead six months, is frisky and brisk—gadding about, and running mad for another——

Wel. Speak low, a gentleman lies ill in the next room.

Hon. As to Sir Buzzard, they have put their fingers into his eyes so often, he is blind as a beetle. I must make you laugh about the widow—

Wel. I cannot permit you to stay any longer from your lady. Here's for your good report.

[*Gives money.*

Hon. Dear sir, you distress me—

Wel. Farewell--[*Pushing her out.*] [*Exit* HONOR. Heaven be praised! I have got rid of you!—Now to relieve my widow; who I suppose is mortified into humility, or bursting with rage.

Enter Widow from the Closet.

Madam, I feel for your situation, and did every thing in my power to stop the impetuous flow of the woman's tongue—but be not affected at what she said—Censure and calumny are taxes paid by the most elevated characters; nor is it possible to make defence against the impost, but by obscurity.

Wid. It is beneath me, sir, to defend my character against the aspersions of so mean a wretch—I feel, however, for the impressions her falsehoods may have made on you.

Enter MUSLIN.

Mus. You seem frightened, madam; quite fluster'd, I protest—sure the gentleman attempted no rudeness—

Wid. That woman has slandered me grossly!

Wel. Sooth your passion, madam; nothing so prejudicial to beauty as intemperate warmth—consider the vulgar set up a prescription for exercising latitude of tongue, that shews no respect to persons.

Wid. Your hand, Mrs. Muslin—some drops—some water—I faint—I am overcome—I die! Oh!

[*Faints in* WELFORD'*s arms.*

Mus. Support her, dear sir, 'till I return—let me run for restoratives—[*going, returns*]—open her hands, chafe her temples,—a-lack a day—This is a master stroke of the widow's! [*Aside*]

[*Exit* MUSLIN.

Wel. This is worse than the state of Tantalus—human nature cannot hold out—she is really handsome. I will venture to kiss her, however—

Re-enter MUSLIN.

Mus. Madam, sir,—there is Miss Constance and Colonel Staff with her—

Wid. What will become of me? [*Springing from the couch.*]

Wel. What will become of me?

Enter Colonel STAFF.

Col. In his private chamber, and just sprung from his arms:—Oh, hell and furies! but I will be cool,—we, sir, will meet hereafter; this intrusion, madam, is, I see, as unseasonable as unexpected; I am sorry to have interrupted you.

Wid. I am unconcerned at your suspicions, colonel,——you will not be censorious, Miss Constance

—my business here was to prevent that imprudent
step which you are about to take.

Con. You have succeeded, madam.   [*Going,*

Wel. Will you hear me?

Con. I am sorry, sir, for the confusion I have
caused—having gained my esteem without difficulty
—you have resigned it with the same ease—

Col. [*To the Widow.*] This undeniable proof of
your duplicity has reinstated my senses, and I will
run the gauntlet no longer—you see I am calm—
quite calm,—but I will have revenge;—you, sir?—

Wel. Well, sir!—it is my duty to clear this lady
from suspicion, to which her situation lays her open,
and in which I am innocently involved.

Wid. You may have an interest in justifying yourself, sir, but I request not to be included in your
defence; I am going.

Col. I give up the pursuit——Madam, if my acts
and deeds——

Wid. Your acts and deeds! Yes, I have heard of
your acts and deeds from yourself, colonel——but,
be assured, a man without spirit shall never controul the acts and deeds of my fortune.

[*Exit Widow.*

Col. A true Parthian,—she shot as she flew.

[*Exit Colonel.*

Wel. Constance, will you attend to me?

Con. No, sir;—you need not take the trouble of
speaking to me now, or of enquiring for me hereafter.   [*Exit* CONSTANCE.

Wel. Was ever man so unfortunate!—to have all
my wishes blasted in the moment of ripening!—to
lose the object of my love in the instant of recovering her—who waits there? To have an intrigue
with a wife, a widow, and a maid, in the course of
one day, and be disappointed in all—will nobody
answer?   [*Calling loud,*

Enter MUSLIN.

Mus. What is the matter, sir?

Wel. Where is the lady?

Mus. She went out with the colonel.

Wel. I speak of the young lady.

Mus. She left the house in a chair,—but I cannot tell where she went.

Wel. I will this instant to Sir Buzzard's!—I will follow her over the world;—what an unfortunate fellow!—   [*Exit* WELFORD.

SCENE *changes to the Parade.   Enter* CHEATERLY, *followed by a Servant.*

Cheat. What answer has Doctor Spruce sent?

Serv. He said, sir, he would not write,—but remember your ungenerous treatment, and have revenge!—Pardon me, sir, but these were his words.

Cheat. Would have revenge?

Serv. Yes, sir, and I saw a letter on his table directed to Sir Buzzard Savage;—there was an attorney with him, and I heard him say the penalty is treble the money lost.

Cheat. How much is he arrested for?

Serv. Upwards of seventy pounds.

Cheat. Here is a note for a hundred—[*Gives a note.*] fly and get him discharged.   [*Exit Servant.*

A letter to Sir Buzzard!—an attorney with him! —treble the penalty!—this Spruce, I fear, will turn traitor.

Enter DOUGLAS.

Captain Douglas, your most obedient,——how long have you been in Bath?   I have not seen you for an age.

Doug. I believe, sir, not since the York meeting, when my friend De Courcy lost his money.

Cheat. He is too ardent to attempt play,—always off his guard.

Doug. And had the misfortune to play with those who kept a constant centinel upon his weakness;—he confided in you, and was deceived:—care, and a plain understanding, may preserve a man's property from the plunder of a common robber,—but honesty has no protection from the frauds of superior cunning.

Cheat. I won nothing from him;—I lost—the truth is, the knowing ones took us in.—

Doug. But you shared the winnings—

Cheat. Will you dare—

Doug. I will dare any thing that is honest.

Cheat. Your friend, sir, has dared to traduce my character by the imputation you insinuate. But he and you should know me better than to suppose any man could affront me with impunity.

[*Lays his hand on his sword.*

Doug. I know you have a mind capable of vindicating your conduct, even at the risque of your own life, and the life of him you have injured—men like you, habituated in deceit, become callous to humanity;—destitute of principle,—they are not deterred by the compunctions of conscience,—but will insure the profits of their cunning, even at the price of blood.

Cheat. My family, sir—

Doug. Is honourable!—speak not of your family —their virtues render your vices the more conspicuous.

Enter Sir BUZZARD.

Sir Buz. Oh you traitor!—the reverend Mr. Spruce has made a full confession.—So I have been your pigeon, but the law shall do me justice.

Cheat. This is your scheme, pusillanimous, mean wretch—[*To Sir* BUZZARD.] For you, sir, [*To* DOUGLAS.] we shall meet again. [*Exit* CHEATERLY.

Sir Buz. Yes,—at the next assizes;—the fellow's

mind is sowed with hempseed, and will yet produce a halter,—or if he escapes hanging, I shall see him perishing in a gaol, under as many wants as are in the Daily Advertiser;—have you been pigeon'd, sir?

Doug. No, sir.

Sir Buz. I have,—he has pluck'd some quill feathers from me,—he has pinion'd me!—Oh the rascal!—but I shall recover my mortgages, and bonds, with treble penalties!

Enter WELFORD *and Lady* FLIPPANT.

Wel. Distraction!—she is lost!—I have been at your house, my lady,—at Mr. Ordeal's—at every inn in the town,—but can get no tidings of her.

Lady Flip. It is surprising, you, who possess a heart open and liberal, panting with affection for the whole sex, should run distracted for the loss of an individual!

Doug. You overlook me, Welford—

Wel. Douglas!—my friend!—O, Douglas, I have lost my Constance!—I—

Lady Flip. No truant; I have been your advocate, and regained her for you—on condition of repentance—

Enter CONSTANCE *and* CLARA, *followed by* ORDEAL.

Wel. My life!—　　　　　　　　　　[*They embrace.*

Sir Buz. Repentance!—let him marry, and he will live and die in a state of repentance.

Con. What!—marry me, an orphan without a shilling?

Wel. Talk not of wealth,—were the riches of the world in your possession, by Heaven they would not add a grain to the estimation of your worth.

Ord. Generous and noble!

Con. [*To* ORDEAL.] How, sir, can I repay your generosity?

Ord. The satisfaction which results from aiding virtue in distress, is the only interest a generous mind can wish to receive for its services;--because it is the only interest such a mind can enjoy.

Lady Flip. Return to my house,--there you shall be acquainted with a matter which nearly concerns your happiness.

Sir Buz. Which I never expect to taste!

Ord. Your happiness is in your own power; commence the practice of virtue, and you will be enamoured of its sweets:--try the experiment, and never fear success.

Lady Flip. What say you to that, Sir Buzzard?

Sir Buz. I say a man can never be too old to mend—I say I have been positive all my life, and I say if you follow the advice of your ancient and sapient friend, my endeavours to procure domestic happiness shall not be wanting.—Ordeal, the laugh will be against us both.

Ord. Laugh at me as long as you please; but had I married Clara, the laugh would have been still stronger against me:—the Scot has done right, and the girl has done right;—the mutual inclination of two virtuous souls cannot but render them more virtuous;—the inhabitants of countries united by nature and policy should take every opportunity of strengthening the connexion;—I see you all think as I do!—and here I hope we shall also meet approbation.   [*Bowing to the audience.*

TIME'S A TELL-TALE:

A COMEDY,

IN FIVE ACTS,

AS PERFORMED AT THE

THEATRE ROYAL, DRURY-LANE.

———— Σὺ δὲ μεγαλήτορα θυμὸν,
Ἴσχειν ἐν ϛήθεσσι· φιλοφροσύνη γὰρ ἀμείνων·   HOM. Il.

BY HENRY SIDDONS,

TO THE READER.

DURING a short residence in France, thirteen or fourteen years ago, I amused myself with forming a little serious drama from a story by M. Marmontel, Blandford and Coraly appearing to me two very interesting characters. These scenes lay long neglected in my port-folio.

When I made the stage my profession, I was prompted to review them, but found my hero by far too grave for a comedy. The part of Benedick was one that I had ever contemplated with delight, and it struck me that a naval character of the description might combine eccentricity with the most exalted generosity.

The play of the Stranger had then rendered the writings of Kotzebue extremely popular; and on perusing his works I found that he had also made both Shakespear and Marmontel his models:—it occurred to me, that by paraphrasing a few of his speeches I might give a degree of sprightliness to my principal character, and I felt assured that what I was doing would be new to an English audience; the nautical phrases, however, which form the allusions and constitute the aggregate, were of my own suggestion.

The father of Coraly in Marmontel is destroyed at the commencement of his story. To heighten the dramatic effect, I embodied him in the character of the elder Hardacre. The genuine applause of tears at the end of the fourth act have convinced me that I was not mistaken. No man of education or liberality has blamed me for making an elegant novel the foundation on which I have erected the Delmar family, well knowing that the most excellent writers in the English language availed themselves of these resources. The busy Morris, the proud Delville, and the dissipated Harrel are calculated for an excellent moral: indeed I have long wondered that the attempt has never been made by abler pens than mine. I am willing to allow that I have availed myself of every advantage which my reading, my reflection, or experience in my profession may have placed within my reach. I may at least hope that the annexed Comedy is written in the spirit of a man anxious to serve the cause of truth. I believe this, because it has been criticised with candour (a solitary exception cannot change my opinions) and with impartiality. Even those who have censured it have expressed themselves in the language of gentlemen, and I was never foolish enough to imagine that my production was a perfect one.

Public approbation must ever be the dearest wish of my heart, but I trust that I shall never forget the respectful deference by which alone it is to be both obtained and preserved.

To Mr. Graham, who accepted my play in the most gentlemanly manner, I return my sincere thanks; also to Mr. Wroughton, who superintended it with a consummate skill, joined to an unremitted attention. All my brother performers exerted the most brilliant talents, with all the zeal of the most unaffected friendship :—this last consideration would have sweetened even the defeat of all my hopes. The song (the four concluding lines excepted) is a translation from Anacreon, Ode XL. Theocritus, Idyll XIX. has treated the same subject, but in a measure entirely different.

H. SIDDONS.

CHARACTERS.

Sir ARTHUR TESSEL,	*Mr Russel.*
Sir DAVID DELMAR,	*Mr Raymond.*
BLANDFORD,	*Mr Elliston.*
QUERY,	*Mr Matthews.*
RECORD,	*Mr Palmer.*
HARDACRE,	*Mr Dowton.*
Young HARDACRE,	*Mr Decamp.*
MC GREGOR,	*Mr Maddox.*
TOBY,	*Mr Tokely.*
Lady DELMAR,	*Miss Mellon.*
ZELIDY,	*Mrs H. Siddons.*
Miss LAUREL,	*Mrs Sparks.*
OLIVIA WYNDHAM,	*Miss Duncan.*

SCENE—*Surrey.*——TIME—*A Day.*

TIME'S A TELL-TALE.

ACT I.

SCENE I.—*An Inn.*

Enter Mc Gregor, *and* Toby *his Waiter.*

Mc Gregor. Hoot Toby lad—ye maun bustle boot bairn, Sir David's house over the way is quite crammed, some o the company to the—the—ave! the *Fête Champêtre*, ye ken will want beds wi us.

Toby. I'll take care, measter.

Mc Gregor. Gin we should stand in need o ony thing, only step to neighbour Hardacre, it is but twa miles off ye ken, and I am sure he will obleege us.

Toby. They say in these parts, that Farmer Hardacre be but a cross-grained sort of a mon, neither, measter.

Mc Gregor. Ah he kens the difference o personages, he kens the world! He and I ha baith been weel eeducated—baith come o guede families, but " *tempora mutantur,*" times are changed wi me Toby! Mr. Hardacre has been a traveller.

H

Toby. So they do say. Neighbour Thatch do tell I that he has bought his son measter Philip a army commission.

Mc Gregor. And why for no?

Toby. Nothing: only the young officers that do come recruiting here do look so grand and so fine, and it was but the last year I saw measter Philip, helping his feyther, to dig their own field.

Mc. Gregor. Why for no bairn? ye ha næ ony leeterature, or you would ken that mony an unco muckle general, has digged potatoes on his ain ground. [*A knock at the door.*] Gang Toby; gang and speer wha's at the door.   [*Exit* TOBY.

He returns conducting Captain BLANDFORD *and Mr.* QUERY.

Welcome your honours! welcome to the Grey Hound!

Query. A good smart house! Landlord! what county?

Mc Gregor. Surrey, an like your honour.

Query. Surrey! so it is. Had any rain lately? How far to Sir David Delmar's? got a newspaper in the house? Landlord, what's o'clock? Are you married?

Mc Gregor. Deel tak me gin I ken which o'these questions I ought to answer first.   [*Aside.*

Query. Why so gloomy, Blandford?—got the tooth-ache, head-ache? Can I be useful?

Blandford. Now comes my turn, prithee be quiet! Landlord!

Mc Gregor. Here an like your honour!

Blandford. Send this letter to Sir David Delmar's directly.

Mc Gregor. You shall be obey'd, sair.   [*Going.*

Query. Stop a moment, Mr. Landlord: I want to ask you a question.—Pray have you ever—that is—

I mean—couldn't you? never mind—it does not signify—you may go.   [*Exit* Mc GREGOR.

Blandford. What a fellow is this! will you never, Ned, get rid of this cursed habit of asking questions?

Query. Nay! upon my soul you are too severe; what's the harm of a little curiosity? Without questions, how would you get at information? Would not society stagnate without it? our assemblies be mute, our newspapers insipid? What gives slander the true piquant inuendo? Question, for instance— who is the fair lady D., that has lately eloped from the Earl of F., with the gallant Major E.?—question, question, question. A skilful Query can save a character, sink a character, recover a character, and after all the questions that are made about questionable circumstances, the only question is, whether there was ever an atom of foundation for the circumstance in question.

Blandford. Thou art an odd animal, Ned! but having brought thee down with me upon an affair in which my honour and my peace are both concerned, I entreat thee to check these wild sallies of that inquisitive disposition.

Query. Peace? Honour concerned? Pray, my dear George, give me leave to ask are you going to marry that little wild girl, you have brought up so slily in a Welch cottage, and left under the care of Sir David before your last voyage?

Blandford. Have you any reason to think so?

Query. No—not exactly——you have resolved against matrimony, you know—but every body has been wondering who she is—what she is, and where she came from. A man now that was fond of prying into other people's concerns would have teazed you to death about all this—you see how indifferent I am about it. Is she pretty? What's her name?

Blandford. Oh yes—that is quite evident.

Query. To be sure, when a man is about to——

when he keeps a pretty girl snug in the country, and
at last places her under the care of his own relative
—Now come, my dear dear fellow, who is she?—
What is she?—Any fortune?—Good family?   Only
answer me this time, and I'll never, never teaze you
again.

Blandford. On that condition, Ned, I will own that
I have something to tell you.

Query. Out with it: nay, hang ceremony, friends
like us should have none—your secret?

Blandford. Is this, where the name of a lady is
concerned—

Query. Well.

Blandford. Never to allow it to be endangered by
ridiculous vanity, or impertinent curiosity: hang ceremony, Ned: friends like us should have none, you
know.

Query. I see: I see you are laughing at me, and
look ye, George! If ever again I meddle with your
concerns—may I——I'll never ask another question
as long as I live.

> [*Sulkily, his back turned to* BLANDFORD.

Enter Mc GREGOR.

Mc Gregor. Ain Mr. Record, Sir David's steward,
desires to ken, whether he may speak wi Captain
Blandford.

Blandford. My old friend Record! admit him instantly.

Query. Up, and pray who is this Mr. —— mum.

Enter RECORD.

Record. My ever valued sir!

Blandford. In tears, old honesty! Is this the welcome you give to the man you have so often dan-
dled a boy in your arms?

Record. Ah those were happy days, they'll never
return!   [*Sighs.*

Blandford. Life's a voyage—Keep hope in the perspective—Well what news with the family—I hear my uncle has married during my last voyage. Well, well, it's too late to repent now—What sort of a woman is my lady, pray?

Query. Aye, honest Mr. Record, pray what sort of a woman is my lady? is she young? rich? good-looking? how long has she been married?

Blandford. At it again.

Query. Oh no—no, it's no concern of mine——thought you might like to hear—that's all.

Record. Ah, sir, my lady is a thorough bred woman of fashion, and the encumbered estate of Sir David was never equal to his ideas of the family dignity, I have told him so a hundred times, and mark the end on't.

Blandford. That's a tender subject, Record.

Record. I can't help speaking, sir, when I see all going to wrack and ruin. A gala one night in London, a *fête champêtre* the other, here, in Surrey; and my lady's sister too, Miss Laurel, giving large dinner parties every day to all who call themselves the wits and geniuses of the age; a set of hungry gentlemen who eat us out of house and home, and devour more good things in a quarter of an hour than they write in a quarter of a year.

Query. But why don't you ask after the young ladies, eh Blandford?

Blandford. Right! my lovely play-fellow Olivia Wyndham, is she with her guardian Hardacre?

Record. No, sir, it is Sir David's year. He and old Hardacre are greater enemies than ever. They have never seen or spoken to each other in their lives. Sir David thinks Hardacre wants to secure Miss Wyndham's fortune by a marriage with his son Philip, but so far from it, he has sent him to his regiment, that his honour might not be brought into a moment's question.

H 3

Blandford. Well, well! but there is another of whom you say nothing; I am sure, my uncle and his lady have both been kind to the poor girl I brought from Wales.

Record. Every body must be kind to her. She is so mild, so modest, and so grateful for what you have done.

Blandford. Nonsense! trifles not worth remembering.

Query. I dare say not: pray what were they?

Record. I know, sir, that your uncle would fain unite you to Miss Wyndham—yet when I look at the other poor girl————

Blandford. Why hark ye friend Record, you need not distress yourself on that subject. My ship is my wife, and while I live I am resolved to have no other. Marriage! in such times as these a sailor must not think on't.

Record. Yet she thinks some return for your goodness—

Blandford. Well, let her return it, by saying nothing about the matter. Sheer compassion was my only motive, I merely did my duty, and if I save a little pinnace from foundering in the ocean of adversity, I am not bound to tow it after me for life, am I, honest messmate?

Record. I have done, sir. Your uncle is anxiously expecting you at Delmar Hall.

Blandford. I attend. As my friend, you, Ned, will be sure of a hearty welcome [*to* QUERY.]. Lead the way, old acquaintance. Marriage! psha, put it out of your head, man, and when you hear of my being married—but why waste time in talking of impossibilities, come—[*he is going,* QUERY *stops* RECORD.

Query. Pray, Mr. Record, who is this Miss Zelidy that——

Blandford. [*Returns quick.*] What makes you loiter?

Query. Nothing; Mr. Record was asking a question, that was all. I follow you.

Blandford. Come then, I know [you, Ned—nay, you don't quit me. Come, come.

Query. I follow; pray, Mr. Record, allow me to ask—no answer! waiter! waiter! what a house, not a waiter to speak to one.—I will have an answer, I am determined. [*Looks at his watch.*] What's o'clock? past eight! thank ye.   [*Exit.*

SCENE II.—*Sir* DAVID DELMAR'S *private Study. He is reading a Packet of Letters, in evident Perturbation.*

Sir David. Will these torments never end? [*reads*] " Sir, the money which has been due since"—psha! " Honoured sir, you were pleased to say I should be paid," " large family," " rent due." [*Throws down the letters.*] The life of a galley-slave would be a state of ease to mine; would I could retreat; retrench! retrench! humiliating thought!—I see the upstarts of the day erect their crests, point the finger at the diminished equipage, the lessening retinue—I see my wife reduced to——

ZELIDY *enters.*

Ha! who's there? I'll have no spies upon my conduct. [*Angry.*]

Zelidy. Oh dear Sir David! you frightened me so! it's only Zelidy.

Sir David. Be not alarmed, my pretty charge; come hither: what would you say now, had I something to tell you which would make you happy?

Zelidy. Words are too poor for the expressions of my grateful feelings to you, your lady, and the sweet Miss Wyndham.

Sir David. Nay, Zelidy, it is the duty of high rank to give protection wheresoever 'tis needed. [*Proud-*

ly.] Blandford will be here this morning.—[*Gives her a note, which she eagerly kisses.*]

Zelidy. My preserver! my guardian angel!—and shall I then at last behold him?

Sir David. [*Alarmed at her emotion.*] You express yourself with warmth.

Zelidy. Ah! how can I refrain? what other human being has so strong a claim on my affection?

Sir David. Affection! affection, Zelidy, is a term that——

Zelidy. Forgive, forgive me, dear Sir David; I am a wild girl, by nature and by birth. 'Tis now eight years since last I saw the captain; I was then a prattling girl; yet has his image still been stamped upon my heart. I repose on the little bench beneath his favourite tree; and as the waving boughs of the majestic oak shade me from the scorching sun-beam, I exclaim in grateful fervour, Generous! noble-minded Blandford! here is the emblem of thyself and Zelidy! oh! still defend her from the ills of life! still protect the humble flower, torn ere it blossomed from the parent branch; and but for thee had withered, drooped, and died upon its stem!

Sir David. Poor girl! but I must check this sympathy, or all my schemes are fruitless. [*Aside.*] Zelidy, it is my duty to warn you of your danger: a union between Blandford and yourself is made by many circumstances a thing impossible: your future peace demands that you should banish these romantic notions from your mind and heart.

Zelidy. I must, I ought, I will. To pray for my preserver, to implore of Providence eternal blessings on his head; that consolation surely may be mine! The sun turns not from the grateful flower that blooms and fades in gazing on his fostering brightness: nor will Blandford, placed by fortune, far, far above his lowly Zelidy, reject the simple homage of a thankful heart.—The subject affects

me, sir; some one approaches—permit me to re-
tire.   [*She goes out.*

Sir David. Poor artless girl!—But I must steel
my heart against these claims. The fortune of my
ward Olivia can alone preserve me from disgrace
and ruin: a marriage with my nephew might secure
it; but then the cottager—this Hardacre, whom
Olivia's father degraded me by making my joint
guardian. I see his aims; he means his son Philip!
aye, there's the stumbling-block; but I shall coun-
teract their plots. Now, Mr. Record.

Enter RECORD.

Record. According to your command, Sir David,
I have been to the inn, and your nephew is now arrived; he and his friend are changing their travelling
dresses, that they may have the honour of paying
their respects to you and to my lady.

Sir David. 'Tis well: should my present plans
succeed, Record, my difficulties will be at an end.
A marriage between Blandford and my ward, Miss
Wyndham, aided by my sister-in-law's union with
Sir Arthur Tessel, will set me above the malice of
my fate.—I hope Lady Delmar does not suspect my
involvements.

Record. All hitherto is safe; how long it may
continue so, Heaven only knows.

Sir David. Only save me till Sir Arthur and my
nephew are united to my sister-in-law and Miss
Wyndham—you shall see me reform completely.

Record. Such hopes are fruitless, sir. Captain
Blandford's aversion to matrimony is more rooted
than ever: were it otherwise, Hardacre would not
give his consent; and as for Sir Arthur Tessel's attachment to your sister-in-law—

Sir David. Can you doubt it? his attentions at
Bath—his eagerness to be invited here—

Record. Remember, sir, that Miss Venusia is neither young nor rich: your ward is both.—Sir Arthur is what is called a man of leisure. [*Sneering.*]

Sir David. What do you mean?

Record. I mean that your men of leisure do many things that would startle a plain, drudging, plodding fellow like myself. The town is full of 'em. It is men of leisure fill the card-table and the gaming-table.—Leisure sends the senator to the horse-race, and the peer to the boxing-ring: the daughters of industry are seduced by men of leisure; the sons of plain citizens are corrupted by men of leisure; and it is high time for you, my master, to exert yourself, and give a proof, that spite of the prevalence of idleness and fashion, the commercial genius of this country shall never be crushed by the vices, follies, and debaucheries of men of leisure.

Sir David. Record, you have ever been the friend of my family: your blunt sincerity convinces me you still are mine. The desperate state of my affairs——

Record. Call them not so. Do you and my lady make a noble effort; all may yet go well. If not, I fear that you will find too late, your substance has been wasted on flatterers and sycophants, whilst you have forfeited the real pride of independency, and put your meanest creditor upon a level with yourself. For how, Sir David, can you ever call that man an inferior, who can justly accuse you of withholding the hard-earned profit of his industry from his little family?

Sir David. You go too far—you presume on your past services; leave me, Mr. Record. For the future, when I need your counsel, I shall ask it.

[RECORD *bows and retires.*

Sir David. And am I then truly so lost? are the honours, the dignities of my family really so di-

minished in my person? I fear they are.—Hark!
Sir Arthur and my ward Olivia: Record wrongs the
baronet; I cannot, will not doubt his honour.

Enter Sir ARTHUR and OLIVIA.

Sir Arthur. Stop, stop, my dear Miss Wyndham,
or my Lady Delmar will set me down for the most
unpolite, unfashionable fellow in the whole world.

Olivia. My Lady Delmar! what, then, Sir Arthur,
is it modern good breeding to pay all your attentions to the married dames, and leave us poor unfortunate spinsters to pine in seclusion, or sit " like
patience on a monument," oh fie!

Sir David. Well urged, my dear ward.

Sir Arthur. Why, I can't exactly say whether it
be good breeding or no; but I assure you upon my
honour, it's the way we have in London. It would
there, for instance, be quite unfashionable to be
seen in a curricle with any woman under forty; if
she happens to be fifty, so much the better: and if
she chances to be married, why, so much the better
still.

Olivia. But pray do not the ladies' husbands
sometimes object to their wives driving in curricles
with such facetious gentlemen as yourself, Sir Arthur?

Sir Arthur. Oh no! not in London, I assure you.
Ask the husband after his lady, he stretches, yawns,
and cries, she was very well the day before yesterday.—Ask my lady after her husband, she takes
out her visiting pocket-book.—Monday, Tuesday,
Wednesday! oh yes, it was Wednesday that I saw
him last! and on Friday I shall perhaps see him
again.—*Bon jour*, colonel, we shall meet at the new
play:—and this, madam, is a sample of matrimonial
life in London, led by all fashionable couples from
the Park and St. James's, to the sound of Bow
bells.

Sir David. And pray where have you left my Lady Delmar, and her sister?

Olivia. Oh, we left her in the beach-grove reading Xenophon's expedition of Cyrus.

Sir Arthur. Oh, Sir David, you should rouse her energies. She is too much of a recluse; too fond of shady groves and purling streams; they are quite out of taste, quite exploded. We hurry to our rural retreats to taste the fogs of November; and crowd to the metropolis when the leaves bud, to enjoy the beauties of Pall-Mall, Bond-street, and the two Parks; and, to say the truth, I have seen more beauties in those few places than I ever beheld at Vienna, Paris, Petersburgh, Madrid, Naples, Venice, Spa, or Rome.

Sir David. Venusia would be quite vain if she heard you; I fancy you are not quite of Sir Arthur's opinion, Miss Wyndham?

Olivia. Why I cannot say I am. I detest crowds and squeezes of all sorts and kinds.

Sir Arthur. What! not love a rout, Miss Olivia?

Olivia. I can't endure it.

Sir David. Why! may one ask?

Olivia. Perhaps from passing so much of my time with my rural guardian, Mr. Hardacre: however that may be, I am perpetually at a loss in your crowded assemblies, Sir David, and find myself compelled either to say nothing, or else talk nonsense.

Sir Arthur. So much the better, so much the better, my dear Miss Wyndham; most of our fashionable conversationes in London are composed of those who talk nonsense, and nothing but nonsense. We take our degrees, and have our regular professors of the art. We have, for instance, the scandalous nonsense, the slip-slop nonsense, and the philosophical nonsense.

Sir David. How—the philosophical nonsense!

Sir Arthur. Yes, Sir David; nothing can be more simple; the philosophical nonsense merely consists in doubting every thing. Trying to comprehend a system we find we cannot account for—the growth of a flower—what we don't understand we never admit possible—and so begin again, philosophising and philosophising in an agreeable see-saw of continual doubt, and metaphysical uncertainty, till we are able at last to dispute the self evident proposition of our own existence, and this is the true " darkness visible" which modern illuminés would wish to spread over our fashionable horizon.

Enter Lady DELMAR.

Sir David. Emily! what has so long detained you?

Lady Delmar. Oh, my sister Venusia, with one of her classical illustrations as she calls them. I hope you don't feel offended at—

Sir David. Offended, Emily? what a thought!

Lady Delmar. Sir Arthur, my love, has been proposing a kind of naval *fête champêtre* in honour of your nephew Captain Blandford's arrival. I have spoken to La Jeunesse, he tells me a few hundreds will do it; all will be prepared, and La Jeunesse will come to you for the money to-morrow.

Sir David. Confusion! I dare not own my embarrassments, and—[*aside*] well, well, my dear!

Lady Delmar. Have we your consent?

Sir Arthur. Oh I'll answer for Sir David.

Sir David. I fear you must.   [*Aside.*

Sir Arthur. Shall I hope the honour of your ladyship's hand at the ball?

Lady Delmar. Fie, Sir Arthur, what would my sister say?

Sir Arthur. Oh, she will never dance, I am sure; Miss Wyndham will perhaps favour me?

Olivia. Oh, by all means, Sir Arthur; we have a

I

plentiful lack of young men in this part of the world,
and as they are equally inanimate automatons, mere
wire-moved puppets—one may do just as well as
another for a country dance; and for this reason—I
have no objection to go down one with you—allons,
Sir Arthur. [*Exit* OLIVIA *and Sir* ARTHUR, *with*
OLIVIA, *singing*,

> Follow me, and I will show
> Where the rocks of coral grow.

Lady Delmar. Shall we follow?

Sir David. Shall I avow my situation, explain my
difficulties—pride—pride and shame constrain my
tongue.   [*Aside.*

Lady Delmar. Oh, a-propos, my dear. La Jeunesse tells me, we must cut down the hawthorn, as
it will impede the preparation for the fête.

Sir David. I must not, will not have that tree mo-
lested; it was planted, when my father lived, by my
poor sister.

Lady Delmar. Sister!—have you a sister, then?

Sir David. I had—I had—but unhappy girl—

Lady Delmar. And never mentioned her to me?

Sir David. I wished to banish her my memory
for ever. She married a man every way beneath
her rank—we abandoned, gave her up—she fled
the country, and I fear—

Enter WILLIAMS.

Williams. Captain Blandford's respects, and he is
now ready to wait on you, sir.

Sir David. I come. [*Bows, exit.*] Oh, Lady Delmar! amidst all the gaiety with which you have long
beheld me surrounded, I have been a prey to feelings which—

Lady Delmar. Pray droop not thus, my love; few
in this world are free from such upbraidings.—If we

could judge ourselves with half the rigour we exert
towards others, the self-accusing blush would mantle
o'er the cheek of many a rugged moralist, and the
angel of pity, dropping a tear upon the catalogue of
human failings, would avow, none are themselves so
pure, as to deny indulgence to the errors of a fellow-
creature.   [*Exeunt.*

ACT II.

SCENE—*Sir* DAVID'S *Study.* [*as before.*]

Enter BLANDFORD *dressed in full uniform, with*
WILLIAMS.

Williams. My master will be here directly, sir.

Blandford. Nay, let him not hurry: I can anchor
here awhile: by the way, now my friend is adorning
his person, you may inform me how my little Zelidy
goes on—she must be much taller than when I left
her last.

Williams. Aye, sir; and she is good as she is
beautiful, and beautiful as good—the whole family
doat upon her.

Blandford. I rejoice to hear it: you have a great
deal of company, I see.

Williams. Our house is never empty, sir—my
master—but I hear him coming.

Sir DAVID *enters,* WILLIAMS *bows, retires.*

Sir David. Dear Blandford.

Blandford. After all my perils, kind sir, trust me,
I truly rejoice to find myself safe in your hospitable
port once more; but you seem a little weather-

beaten: no rough gales, I hope, since you ventured
on the dangerous voyage of matrimony?

Sir David. None, George, none; and do you, my
young son of Neptune, still hold your resolution
against the happy state?

Blandford. Fixed, Sir David. Constant, as the
needle to the pole. I've made many a false tack in
my life, it must be confessed; but matrimony!—of
that quicksand, thank Heaven, I have contrived to
steer clear.

Sir David. Nay, be serious. I have urgent reasons for wishing you to be so.

Blandford. Well then, I am—I am serious: and
ask me any questions you think proper, I will answer them with all the plain, blunt sincerity, that
belongs to my profession.

[*Sir* DAVID *here assumes an air of the most serious
earnestness.*]

Sir David. You promise me to be direct in your
answer.

Blandford. Try me.

Sir David. What then, George, can be a wiser
plan, for a fellow at your time of life, than to marry?

Blandford. To shoot himself.

Sir David. I fear all my hopes are vain. [*Aside.*

Blandford. Look ye, Sir David—Matrimony is
your harbour, and I give you joy of it; for my own
part I have told you often, and I tell you again and
again, it's a voyage I have no mind to—at four and
thirty years of age I have four and thirty little
whims—and customs—and custom is a second nature. For instance, I have a favourite walk, a favourite book, a favourite chair—in comes a wife—
and east, west, north, and south, cannot blow from
more different quarters than our inclinations. I
am inured to hardship, she pines for delicacies; I
love walking, she must have a carriage to loll in;
madam dies for the opera, I had rather see a dancing

bear than a dancing coxcomb; she loves foreign music, I am for a sailor's artless ballad; she has the head-ache—grows nervous—enter doctors, apothecaries, salts, phials, cordials and restoratives, fits, faintings, and hysterics;—and so you have the whole log-book of the cruize of matrimony.

Sir David. Were we born to please ourselves alone, such maxims might be encouraged; but in all families where the pride of ancestry is to be supported—sacrifices must be made. Since you saw her last, Miss Wyndham is improved in every virtue, and in every grace   [*Earnestly.*

Blandford. I truly rejoice to hear it; she has been good to my poor Zelidy, whom I left under her care and yours.   [*Sir* DAVID *is here abstracted.*

Sir David. It is natural that her thoughts should now be directed to a change of situation. Her fortune is immense. George! I have loved you from infancy. I!—I say, if you saw me surrounded by perils, encumbered by difficulties, would—would you not do somewhat to relieve me?

Blandford. The question hurts me. My element is a rough one, I own; but I never saw the sinking enemy to whom I would not stretch a helping hand; the friend who doubts me then affronts my feelings as a man, a sailor, and a christian.

Sir David. My noble boy! this day will I entrust you with a secret which must place my happiness, and what is dearer far than happiness—my honour, in your keeping—meantime regard Miss Wyndham as a lady dear to the interests of your family.

Blandford. If you desire it, she shall find a brother in me.

Sir David. A brother!—and why—why not a—husband?   [*With great vehemence.*

Blandford. A husband!   [*Recoiling.*

Sir David. Blandford, my only hope remains with you. No more at present; my Lady Delmar waits

impatient to congratulate your return; with her you
will find Miss Wyndham.

Blandford. I attend her ladyship.

Sir David. Williams!——[*Enter* WILLIAMS.]——
Conduct the captain to her ladyship.—[*Exit* WIL-
LIAMS.]—And when you see Olivia, think, George,
think what I have said; I have cause to imagine the
poor girl loves you, and you are bound in honour—

Blandford. Not to deceive her. No, uncle, no!
The scoundrel that, beneath false colours, captures a
weaker vessel than his own, is a robber and a pirate,
a villain and a coward. What should I be if, professing to love no woman, I cheated any with a hand
without a heart?

Sir David. Hear me, George——

Blandford. No, uncle, try me any way but this.
If I wrong a man he calls me to account, and none
but a dastard will wound that sex, who have our
own sensibilities to feel an injury, though they may
not have the same strength to resent it—you will
feel my argument, and I trust the decision to your
own bosom.   [*Exit* BLANDFORD.

Sir David. And that decision must condemn me.
Blandford refuses then, and on Sir Arthur all my
hope must rest. He has written to the colonel of
young Hardacre—and in such terms that if all my
projects are not formed to be defeated, he is no
longer with his regiment. Have I then added ty-
ranny—oppression—to my failings? But where
can that man hope to stop, who once has listened to
the dictates of an unfeeling prodigality?   [*Exit.*

The Cottage of HARDACRE, *neat and plain.* RECORD
     reading: HARDACRE *at a Table smoking his Pipe.*

Hardacre. Well, Record, have you finished the
letter from my boy Philip?

Record. He here informs you that, having quar-
relled with his colonel, he has left his regiment.

Hardacre. Right.   [*Smokes.*

Record. He is afraid that some concealed enemy
has done him this ill turn.

Hardacre. Yes.   [*Coolly.*

Record. And that, scanty as he knows your means
to be, he is now returning to share them, assured
that you would never again admit him to your presence if he stooped to an act of servility.

Hardacre. Right! right! quite right!

Record. And all these ill tidings you hear with the
most complete unconcern?

Hardacre. Why should it concern me?

Record. Philip has been bred like a gentleman.

Hardacre. Granted.

Record. How is he to support himself now?

Hardacre. Why, like a gentleman.

Record. But how?

Hardacre. By independence.

Record. What independence?

Hardacre. The best—his own exertions.

Record. We are friends!

Hardacre. True.

Record. I suspect foul play has been used.

Hardacre. Um!

Record. Sir David likes you not.

Hardacre. May be so! 'Tis strange to hate a man
one never saw.

Record. He is proud.

Hardacre. So am I.

Record. Miss Wyndham's father left you joint
guardian with him.

Hardacre. He did.

Record. This hurt his dignity. The will which
I have before me ordains that she should pass the
summer with you at your cottage, and the winter
with Sir David at his house in town.

Hardacre. He had his reasons. Wyndham was

an odd fellow like myself. I knew him from early life.

Record. Indeed!

Hardacre. Poor as I seem, I did; and rendered him a service he has not forgotten:—you ever thought me an oddity—I am so.

Record. Colonel Wyndham was rich—If you served him, how comes it that he left you none of his wealth?

Hardacre. I am an oddity, I tell you; he knew I was so; he knew likewise that the services the heart renders, the heart and not the hand must repay— money can buy many things—but the friend that money can buy is hardly worth the purchasing.

Record. I comprehend:—Colonel Wyndham wished his daughter to pass her time equally between the town and country—because—

Hardacre. Both have their vices—you have hit it; and by seeing them, she might avoid their extremes.

Record. Sir David suspects that you intend your son for Miss Wyndham's husband.

Hardacre. Does he?

Record. I know he does—if you could convince him of your innocence—he would be your friend.

Hardacre. My what? [*Laying down his pipe, and rising with a cool disdain.*]

Record. Your friend.

Hardacre. And what right can Sir David Delmar have to the name of old Philip Hardacre's friend? a name he never wastes on every new comer, who can scrape a tune on a fiddle, or make a leg like a dancing-master—not carelessly given, or wantonly withdrawn—but once pledged with the rough grasp of an honest hand, held firm and fast, till the last struggle of expiring mortality.

Record. How!

Hardacre. For you, Mr. Record, is my attachment firm and real—but your master must deserve my esteem before he can gain my friendship.

Record. Recollect Sir David's interest in the country.

Hardacre. I hope he does his best to serve it, and while life and strength is left me, so will I. In peace I will serve it by my example to my poorer neighbours round me; and in war I will unite my arms to theirs against invading violence. I am Sir David's equal here—I want not his favours. I am loved by those round me—smoke a pipe with the curate—club a joke with the apothecary—talk of pronouns and participles with the school-master—and condemn smuggling with the exciseman—every face in the village meets me with a smile—I want not his friendship.

Enter PHILIP.

Hardacre. My boy!

Philip. Dear, dear father! Mr. Record!

Record. Welcome home, young gentleman.

Philip. Home would indeed be welcome to me, sir—Did I not come to overcharge a father—You received my letter?

Record. Yes; and your father approves.

Philip. Then am I blest. I know not wherefore I have been thus treated: long was I honoured with my commander's confidence; and, proud to hold, endeavoured to preserve it.

Record. His temper perhaps was overbearing.

Philip. Let me do justice to his character: as a soldier, he is an honour to his country and profession; as a man, he is an ornament to the society of which he is a member. He has an eye to discern merit; and under him the meanest private in his ranks has only to deserve, to find protection, friendship, and promotion.

Hardacre. You have been slandered, boy.

Philip. Alas! I fear so, father.

Hardacre. You've not been treated with indignity?

Philip. I stand before my father; that is at once an answer to your question. Had I endured the slightest insult, I would have fled to the earth's extremest verge ere I ventured to a roof where poverty has dwelt, but where disgrace has never dared to enter.

Hardacre. Your hand—your hand—excuse the old man, Record—tears are not constant visitors with me, and when they come I welcome them as strangers and as guests.

Philip. No, father, no—my resignation sprung from chilling apathies, from cold neglects, felt easier than described. They pierced my heart, used to the glow of social friendship; and finding it withdrawn, I come again to my parental roof; my former occupation. Convinced, that though no laurel graces my brow, as I return with an unsullied heart, a father's arms will be, as now I see they are, open to welcome, cheer, and bless me.   [*Embrace.*

Record. Your hand—Hardacre, you called me friend. I'll prove so.—I suspect treachery—I'll find it.

Hardacre. Will you?

Record. To be sure I will. I had as soon give in a false account as not do justice to my neighbour's character—yours, young man!

       [*Shakes* PHILIP's *hand heartily, and exit.*

Hardacre. And now, my boy, you must turn the sword to the sickle. Stop! one word—it is suspected that Miss Wyndham—you turn pale—tomorrow she sets out to London, I shall resign my guardianship, and you must—aye, must promise me never to see her more.

Philip. If it is your pleasure.   [*Faltering.*

Hardacre. It's my command—Sir David thinks I
have encouraged you—Did the proud man know—
Well, no matter—Rouse yourself; if you indulge a
hope, remember that you wrong Olivia—Your father and—my boy, I know the task is hard—I feel
—I feel for you.   [*Tenderly.*

Philip. Yes, sir, I will exert myself, and strive to
find in labour and activity an antidote to a passion
weakly, vainly cherished.

Hardacre. Why, that's well said; we'll toil again
together, and affluence shall envy us our occupation;
my little lands have been neglected in thy absence;
they now again shall smile and flourish—we'll—
we'll help the poorer cottagers about us—divide our
crust with the needy—administer to the afflicted—
divide the burthen with the weary, and make the
grateful hamlet bless, and laugh around us.
                    [*Exeunt affectionately.*

SCENE III.—*Sir* DAVID DELMAR'S *House.*

The general Apartment.

ZELIDY, *drawing at a Table.*

Zelidy. He has forgotten me; I know, I feel he
has—He has been with Lady Delmar and Olivia;
yet he asks not for me.   I have finished my picture
—Will it please him?   Here is a little vessel agitated by a storm; that will serve as an emblem of
poor Zelidy—Here a majestic bark hastening to its
relief; that is an emblem of Blandford—And here
is Hope smiling upon her anchor; ah! for whom
will that serve?   Not for Zelidy!

Enter BLANDFORD.

Blandford. What a confounded noise in every part
of this mansion!   This it is to be married.—Marriage!—quiet? pretty quiet state, forsooth! the

must be great happiness to be sure, when all these noises of routs, and balls, and *fête champêtres* are necessary to keep the heavy machine in motion: thank Heaven and thy stars, Blandford, thou art teazed with no piping but the piping of the storm; subject to no caprices but the caprices of the elements—Matrimony!—Love!—Away with 'em!— I'll none on't!

Zelidy. [*Starting up.*] 'Tis he! that voice! my grateful heart cannot delude—deceive me! oh, my guardian! my preserver!

[*Bursts into tears, and kneels before him.*

Blandford. Zelidy! why yes—yes, it must: well, if it be so I'm heartily glad to see—[*Kisses her.*]—I feel an odd sensation that—marriage! why the plague should people marry?

Zelidy. My benefactor! my father!

Blandford. Nay, nay, you need not call me father. Sir David is much older than I am, and you may call him father if you please.

Zelidy. Your goodness.—

Blandford. Well, never mind my goodness now; you have not wanted any thing in my absence, I hope —come, don't call me father again—I don't like it.

Zelidy. Brother, then.

Blandford. Yes, that's a little better, and more like the fact. Well, you have been in London— like it, I suppose—dress, equipage, jewels—eh?

Zelidy. Ah, no! ill would it become an orphan, from childhood a dependent on the generous bounties of another, to vie in splendour with the affluent, the prosperous, and the happy.

Blandford. I understand—but take one truth from him who never flattered in his life. The simple pinnace floating down life's tide, with the white pendant of truth and innocence, need never strike its modest flag to any painted gaudy vessel that, decked in gewgaw colours, rides in affected arrogance before it.

Here, here is some worthless ballast, of which it will be kind to lighten me.   [*Offers money.*

Zelidy. Ah no! no! no! you hurt, you distress me. I have hitherto received your bounties in silence and without a blush—should they assume a pecuniary form, I could no longer accept them with other sensations than those of sorrow and uneasiness.

Blandford. Rather than so, may every guinea I possess be buried in the ocean where I earned it. I now find that to give is in the power of every stupid fellow—to give properly is a science—and we sailors generally understand the liberal arts much better than the fine ones.

Zelidy. Ah, sir! you have already done too much for Zelidy. My wishes should be humble as my fortunes: my parents are, perhaps, in poverty, in want.

Blandford. Be satisfied, my dear Zelidy, your parents can now need no assistance from you—your father was——

Zelidy. Was—who—speak—oh speak, and I will bless you!—oh yes! doubly bless you. When last we saw you here, I was a child too young to be entrusted with my own sad story—but, when reflection dawned, my busy fancy drew the mournful picture of my parents' sufferings. Memory retraced the image of my father; my mother's person too I never can forget—pale was her cheek, and she would sit and weep—Oh, hear me, bounteous Heaven! thou who didst spread thy sheltering arm in infancy! if yet my parents live—oh guide me, guide me to them! these hands shall toil to aid, these active limbs shall bound with more than youthful vigour to repay the pious debt of gratitude, of feeling, and of nature!

Blandford. Rise, Zelidy—your supplications are no longer to be resisted. Listen to me.

Zelidy. Oh, I am all attention.

Blandford. The ship, which, in the absence of our captain, I fourteen years since commanded, was ordered on an expedition to the place of your nativity. One night, when all was dark and silent except the sullen wave which dashed against the vessel's side, I heard——

Enter QUERY, *curiously coming towards him.*

Query. Aye, my dear fellow, what did you hear?
Blandford. Provoking!
Zelidy. Cruel interruption!
Query. Beg pardon; fear I come a little *mal-a-propos.*
Blandford. Where the deuce have you been loitering?
Query. Couldn't be introduced *en deshabille,* miss.
Zelidy. Sir!
Query. Madam!—is it Miss Zelidy?
                                   [*Aside to* BLANDFORD.
Blandford. No, no.
Query. Miss Venusia?
Blandford. O no!—no, I tell you.
Query. Miss Olivia?
Blandford. No.
Query. Lady Delmar, mayhap?   [BLANDFORD *makes a sign to* ZELIDY, *who retires unseen by* QUERY.
Blandford. Why you seem to know the names of the whole family before you have set eyes upon one of them.
Query. Let me alone for that—hate to lose time; while my coiffeur equipped me, got it all out of him. Don't let me neglect the young lady, though:— pray, miss, give me leave to ask—[*turns round.*]— Hey, gone! what could drive her away?
Blandford. Your questions would drive away the very devil himself.
Query. Come, come—now do; do be good-na-

tured, and I won't plague you any more: never ask a single question till supper-time. I say, who do you think is down on a visit here?

Blandford. I know not, I care not.

Query. My old London acquaintance, Sir Arthur Tessel—on a love affair to one of the ladies of this mansion; don't know which—ask him though the first time I see him, since you wish it.

Blandford. Why should I wish it? I've nothing to do with love or marriage.

Query. You remember Sir Arthur's uncle, the Colonel—I've heard you speak of him. Could you introduce me to him? he's a brave fellow, they say.

Blandford. They do him justice then; I know him to be so.

Query. Ask Sir Arthur to introduce me. The Colonel will thank him: know I shall be a favourite —flatter myself few people more so in London. Always do my best to please the good folks there. I've one certain way of being agreeable—have you found it out?

Blandford. Upon my soul, I have not.

Query. No? tell you my secret then: always make myself useful. Any thing lost, I inquire—any reports going abroad, I inquire—any news stirring, I inquire—thus by little and little I gather like a snow-ball ; every body is glad to employ me, every body is glad to see me, and useful Ned Query can make his way into a drawing room nine times out of ten, when a poor poet, a celebrated general, or a man of family is told, not at home, for four and twenty times together.

Blandford. Indeed, then, I'm hearily glad, Ned, that it has been my good fortune to spend so much of my time at sea.

Query. Why so?

Blandford. Because I should be sorry to see noise and impudence admitted to any house where genius,

worth and virtue were kept waiting at the door: but
follow me to the ladies, and mind you are upon your
good behaviour.

Query. But pray, did you ever——

Blandford. Psha—   [*Exit.*

Query. Here's treatment; I'll never ask another
question as long as I live—never, never, never!
[*Servant passes the stage.*] Ah, John, how's your
wife?—Dumb—plague take it, people now a days
would rather talk of any body's wives than their
own.   [*Exit.*

SCENE—*The Fête Champêtre.*

*A grand Naval Trophy erected in the Middle of the
Stage; various Arbours filled with elegant Company,
Sir DAVID and his Party; Sir ARTHUR and OLI-
VIA come forward.*

Sir Arthur. Positively, Miss Wyndham, you must
preside at this *fête champêtre;* I cannot prevail on
your aunt Venusia to do the honours, because she says
a *fête champêtre* was a thing unknown to the ancient
dames of Greece and Rome. Ha! ha! ha!

Olivia. Yet, Sir Arthur, you can flatter the woman you laugh at; and pray give me leave to ask
your motives for a constant attendance on her you
are perpetually endeavouring to render ridiculous.

Sir Arthur. Can my motives be unknown to Miss
Wyndham, for whom I have deserted dear, dear
London, and all its charming ways?—Ah, Miss
Wyndham, Miss Wyndham! will you never under-
stand me?

Olivia. Oh yes, Sir Arthur, I understand you too
well: I see that your pretended regards to my aunt
are so many affronts in disguise.

Sir Arthur. Oh, no! no affront; I do quiz her a
little, to be sure; it's a way we have in London.

Olivia. I know it, worthy baronet, I know it. Quiz

is an elegant term, which supplies, in your vain ideas, those superior qualifications you only ridicule because you cannot imitate.

Sir Arthur. Hold! hold! my dear Miss Wyndham; if you put on the armour of Minerva I shall never venture to attack you.

Olivia. Nay, be not afraid, Sir Arthur; a choice spirit like yourself should never be alarmed at any thing. I have observed your whole fraternity in London; have waited hours in patient expectation of their lively sallies, and found them languid when not noisy, saying any thing for the mere purpose of saying any thing, and eager to gain the applauses of coxcombs, empty as themselves, though on such terms as would cover an honest man with confusion, or a delicate woman with blushes.—Oh fie! fie! Sir Arthur!   *[Goes up the stage—music.*

Sir Arthur. 'Tis plain she suspects my designs: can I then give her up, with such grace, such vivacity, and such fortune? forbid it, love! Is there any harm in making this antiquated spinster the means of obtaining such a treasure?—none. She watches me closely though.—Let me see how to get rid of her. I have it—the obsequious Mr. Query will stand in good stead. I will introduce him as a scholar and a wit, the good old lady will swallow the bait, he will engross some of her attentions, and thus I hope to make him useful every way.

                       *[*QUERY *comes forward.*

Query. Who useful, my dear Sir Arthur?—only make me so, I shall be the happiest fellow in the world.

Sir Arthur. You might now be of the greatest service to me.

Query. As how? you rejoice my heart! as how?

Sir Arthur. Come to our table, I'll tell you my scheme.

Query. Scheme! what scheme?—heard Lady Delmar ask for you—darted off like an arrow from a bow—are you a toxopholite?—

Sir Arthur. Psha! we are staid for.   [*Retire.*

Enter RECORD.

Record. Here is the temple of dissipation.

Sir David. Now, Record, what news?

Record. The old news, sir, the old visitors.

Sir David. 'Sdeath, have they presumed to venture here?

Record. Yes, sir, and threaten to expose you before all your company, unless——

Sir David. Hush! how much will satisfy their clamours?

Record. Not less than five hundred pounds.

Sir David. Confusion! I borrowed that sum of Miss Wyndham yesterday for a debt of honour; I must again apply to her: for the present take this [*Gives a bank-note*]—silence the harpies. I would not have Lady Delmar know it for a thousand worlds.

Record. And how is Miss Wyndham to be——

Sir David. No matter; do your duty, sir: leave me to——I cannot think——leave me, leave me to ——to-morrow all shall be set to rights.

                    [*Retires and joins his party.*

Record. My duty! yes, painful as that duty is, it must, it shall be done. Miss Wyndham must not fall a sacrifice to her own goodness. On this note, which I have been requested by Philip to deliver to her, I may pencil a few lines to warn her of her danger. Ha! they rise.

> [*Sir* DAVID *and Lady come forward;* Sir AR-
> THUR *and* QUERY *converse;* BLANDFORD *and*
> ZELIDY *engaged likewise in conversation: while*
> *all are occupied,* RECORD *secretly slips a letter*
> *into the hand of* OLIVIA.

Lady Delmar. My dear, you are thoughtful?

Sir David. Oh no! I was absorbed in—no matter —are the dancers ready?

Query. Oh yes, all ready. I have seen to that, Sir David.

Sir David. Let them commence.

Lady Delmar. My dear!

Sir David. Pray see to our friends; I, I will fol- low.—I like not the attentions of my nephew to this orphan girl; pity, they say, is akin to love: this must be looked to, and——

> [*The music here strikes up. Village girls dance, and present* PLANDFORD *with flowers, then re- turn with naval flags, laurels, &c. which they likewise lay at his feet.*

ACT III.

SCENE I.—*Sir* DAVID'S *House.*

Enter Sir ARTHUR, *musing.*

Sir Arthur. Surely, surely, of all plagues with which a man can be tormented, none was ever greater than being trusted with the secrets of a family. Sir David tells me, that spite of the brilliant figure he has so long been making, he is worried to death by the demands of creditors.—Strange! psha! not at all so, the thing is common enough in every circle in London; and were none there to ride in their own carriages but those who have paid for them, we might lounge down Bond-street with as much ease and as little difficulty as we stroll through a church- yard in a country village.

Enter RECORD *with a bundle of bills.*

Record. Sir David informs me, sir, that you have

kindly undertaken to settle with a few gentlemen
who are to call here for money this morning.

Sir Arthur. Oh! yes, yes; Sir David tells me these
people have very been troublesome, and as I am so
soon to have the honour of being nearly related to
him, it's my duty to do all I can to set his mind at
rest: send them to me, I'll settle them.

Record. If you would encharge me with the money, sir, it would save you much trouble.

Sir Arthur. Money! oh, never mind the money,
my dear fellow; with us men of fashion money is
neither here nor there. When they call, only let me
know, and flattery's the word. You shall hear me
praise the colouring of the painter, till instead of
payment he begs me to sit for the exhibition; and
tickle the wine-merchant over a bottle of his own
champagne, till he forgets what he came for, and
begs a fresh order with a bow down to the ground.
This is the London style of living, my old boy, and
without it, we have a number of very dashing fellows who would not know how to live at all.

Record. I am astonished!

Sir Arthur. Are you? that's a sign you know very
little of high life, then: any stupid fellow can manage these matters with money, the real art of the
business is to settle them without it; only send them
to me, and you shall see me put my theory in practice.   [*Exit* RECORD.

Sir Arthur. So! when I have accommodated matters with these gentry, I have promised Sir David to
call this young Hardacre to an account.—My letter
to the Colonel has taken effect, it seems; I hope he
did not suspect the writer. Oh! [*taking out a me-
morandum-book*] here is my young spark's address;
I was to drive Miss Wyndham in my curricle to-day,
and with all this business on my hands, how shall I
contrive to——

Enter QUERY.

Query. My dear Sir Arthur, can I drive the curricle for you? I am a dead good whip.

Sir Arthur. Are you?

Query. Am I! d'ye know Bob Squarewell? he taught me the rules, snug, short, concise—

> The rule of the road is a paradox quite,
> While driving your carriage along ;
> If you keep to the *left* you are sure to go *right,*
> And if you go *right* you go *wrong.*

Sir Arthur. Well! that will answer, go and prepare.

Query. I am gone; but stay—Sir Arthur, where do you live in London? you keep a great deal of company?

Sir Arthur. Well, what then ?

Query. Ah! if you would but introduce me to some of your parties. I'm a useful fellow ; will you? its of no great consequence, only it gives a man an air to have a large acquaintance : will you introduce me some morning to all your fashionable friends?

Sir Arthur. Any thing. Zounds! you'll keep Miss Wyndham waiting.

Query. I am gone, only give me leave to ask one question, do you know the marquis of——

Sir Arthur. 'Sdeath and plagues! ask me any thing when you come back ; only go now. [*Retires up.*

Query. I'm gone, noble baronet, I'm gone.
[*Exit* QUERY.

Sir Arthur. Now then for my defiance ; my heart upbraids me when I think : think, beware of that Sir Arthur Tessel.—Reflection is the very worst friend a duellist can cherish.

> [*During his soliloquy* OLIVIA *appears advancing through the folding doors, so earnestly employed in reading a letter that she does not observe his exit.*

But see, my charming Olivia comes this way. I will instantly dispatch the business of Sir David, and return to her immediately.   [*Exit Sir* ARTHUR.

Olivia. Generous Philip! this noble effort for your father adds esteem to pity :—Pity! beware, Olivia. Pity is a dangerous word.—Heigho! [*Looks at the letter.*] What have we here? lines on the back in pencil writing. " Beware, Miss Wyndham! beware of the immense sums Sir David is daily borrowing."—This hint confirms my former suspicions. —Ha! Miss Venusia.

[*Seeing Miss* VENUSIA LAUREL *advancing slowly down the stage, with a book in her hand, her air pensive, solemn, and absorbed.*

Miss Venusia. These pleasures Melancholy give,
And I with thee will choose to live.

Miss Wyndham! jaded to death with that foolish feminine amusement, dancing, I suppose—Cornelia never danced—a mere loco-motive exercise! I marvel my sister, Lady Delmar, has not more taste than to encourage it.

Olivia. It is a harmless diversion at least, my dear madam, promotes society, and brings young people together.

Miss Venusia. Fie, fie, Miss Olivia! You have caught up these notions in the mansion of that visigoth, that Hardacre.

Olivia. Would you then have a young woman totally lay aside the graces that characterise her own sex?

Miss Venusia. The graces!—ridiculous. No, Miss Olivia, no. Even when a child I was admired for the gravity of my looks.

Olivia. Indeed, madam!

Miss Venusia. Aye, indeed. As I grew to riper years, I never consulted the idle variations of fashion; for the last twenty years I have dressed with the same pure simplicity in which you see me now—ever keeping in my mind the favourite line of my favourite poet—

" Where half the skill is decently to hide."

A cautious maxim, that has been out of date for these six years past.

Olivia. And yet, my dear madam, I have observed that there is nothing in this world of which the men have so great an horror as a learned lady.

Miss Venusia. Mere ignorance, child. Sheer envy and malevolence.

Olivia. A mistake, a mistake—I can assure you; no miser grudges his neighbour a supernumerary shilling with more grumbling reluctance, than a husband envies a wife one single atom of superior intellect.

Miss Venusia. However it may be in the country, amongst ignorant rustics like old Hardacre, it is quite a different case in London, I assure you, miss: for I think you yourself will agree with me in a firm opinion, that in London a woman of genius and talent never yet went unnoticed or unrewarded.

Olivia. You are as partial to London as your admirer Sir Arthur, who will not allow the least shadow of merit to any thing that does not bear the stamp of the metropolis.

Miss Venusia. Sir Arthur is a man of sense, a great admirer of the classics. He likes to hear me read Milton and the poets of old times. Hush! sure I hear his step—will you do me the favour to see my dear?

Olivia. With all my heart, madam; but you must excuse my returning, as I have to prepare myself for an airing in the curricle.

Miss Venusia. Oh, just as you please, Miss Olivia.

[*Exit* OLIVIA.

Miss Venusia. If, as I suspect, Sir Arthur should disclose his long smothered passion, how am I to

behave?   My acquirements seem to have made an
impression on his friend Mr. Query too, who, he tells
me, is one of the most inquiring geniuses of the age.
—He comes.

Enter Sir Arthur.

Sir Arthur.   'Sdeath!   Miss Wyndham gone!—
[*Aside.*]—To interrupt Miss Venusia Delmar is an
act of sacrilege to the interests of literature—how
then am I to sue for forgiveness?

Miss Venusia. The interruptions of some persons
are indeed intolerable, but a man like you, who has
such an esteem for—

Sir Arthur. What does she mean now?   I must
humour her this time, however. [*Aside.*] Madam!

Miss Venusia. You, I say, Sir Arthur, never pay a
female so ill a compliment, as to be attentive to so
ridiculous an exterior as beauty! your present ideas
are derived from a different source.

Sir Arthur. By my honour, madam, you do me
justice.   No, Miss Venusia, beauty is in my eyes a
mere chimera: give me the female whose mental
graces can charm the imagination and captivate the
understanding, as my friend Mr. Query says.

Miss Venusia. Mr. Query makes me proud.   The
approbation of such a scholar as you say your friend
is——

Sir Arthur. Oh! one of the first in the world; the
most inquiring genius I ever met with in the whole
course of my life.

Miss Venusia. He has promised me the honour of
an hour's conversation this morning.   Ah! Sir Arthur, how futile are all other entertainments compared with the interchange of intellect.

Sir Arthur. The union of minds.

Miss Venusia. There is no accounting for the vanity of some females, you know, Sir Arthur; however, I must leave you for the present.

Sir Arthur. Oh madam! why so?

Miss Venusia. I must finish my nine and thirtieth book of my poem with satirical notes.

Sir Arthur. I would not for worlds, madam, do literature such an injury as to detain you—besides I see Mr. Query coming this way, and he would interrupt us.

Miss Venusia. For the present—adieu, then, Sir Arthur.

[*Sir* ARTHUR *hands her to the door in centre, she curtseys and goes off.*

Enter QUERY *at the wing.*

Sir Arthur. How Query! not started yet?

Query. The carriage is this moment at the door, and I only come to ask—

Sir Arthur. Zounds!—I can't stay to be asked any thing now—only take care that no accident—

Query. Depend on me, Sir Arthur, never met with an accident in all my life; so careful, that when I took lady Highflyer's little son an airing, kept steady as possible, looked at nothing but the horses' heads for twelve miles together—brought the carriage quite safe home—to be sure Master Highflyer was missing; for being cautious not to frighten him, never once perceived that the little gentleman had popped out on the other side of me. My lady in a great rage when I came back—but no harm done—Master Highflyer returned safe and sound the next morning in the basket of the Windsor coach.

Sir Arthur. A mighty careful fellow, truly so— it's lucky, now I remember, that you have not set out—my dear Query!

Query. Well.

Sir Arthur. As you say you wish to be useful to me, here is a letter to young Hardacre; you

L

guess its contents, and shall be my friend in this affair.

Query. Yes, yes, baronet—I do guess its contents, and I will be your friend in the affair—but not by carrying the letter—plague take such officious friends—what are they like?—why—the—the comet full of fire superfluous, heat unnecessary—gazed at by the curious—safest at a distance.

Sir Arthur. Very well, sir—since you refuse me—I must send my letter by—

Query. Any body but Ned Query—I am a strange fellow—I have spent my life in making people laugh —it never hurts me—the more they laugh at me, the better I like it. I love to be useful—I'd sail to Russia—make a voyage to Abyssinia—any thing to be useful—but the medler who runs about to set two fellows cutting each others throats, is not only the most useless, but the most mischievous being on the face of the earth.   [*Exeunt.*

SCENE II.—HARDACRE'S *Cottage.*

Enter PHILIP *in his rustic Dress through the Cottage Door in Centre.*

Philip. The day grows late—yet my father returns not: the heavy rustling of the leaves too, seem to foretel a coming storm. Well, let it rage: it can not drown the tempest here. [*Strikes his heart.*] Olivia! beloved Olivia! Hush, presumptuous heart! lie still. Crush these aspiring hopes, be faithful to thy promise given, and sacrifice thy happiness to hers—[*A crash heard at the door of the cottage.*]—What noise is this?—[*A servant enters rapidly.*]—Ha! who are you?

Servant. Oh, sir, make all the haste you can; a gentleman has just overturned a curricle at the door, and we fear the lady who was in it is severely hurt.

Philip. Where is the gentleman? with his assistance I may——

Servant. He ran off for help directly, sir, bidding me say he hoped you would give the lady the shelter of this house from the storm which is coming on.

Philip. To any human being in distress the shelter of this house was never yet refused—no words, but follow me.

> [*They rush out; noise of falling rain, flashes of lightning seen through the cottage window.* PHILIP *and servant re-enter with* OLIVIA, *who is too much agitated to take notice of what is going forwards. They seat her in a chair. Servant retires—and* PHILIP *speaks.*

Madam, may I presume—[*catching her eye.*]—Olivia!

Olivia. Where am I? Sure I should know this house, this——Philip—dear Philip.

> [*Approaching him, he averts his face.*

Philip. Where will the malice of my fortune end? To see—to love—and yet be forced to shun her! Olivia! you received my letter?

Olivia. I did: and it has both alarmed and terrified me. You tell me there that we must meet no more. Could Philip be in earnest?

Philip. Honour, justice, humanity—all—all demand the painful sacrifice. Too long already has the baleful presence of an unhappy man clouded your prospects and destroyed your hopes—go—go enjoy the fortune heaven has blessed you with— leave me to my fate.

Olivia. Unkindly said! if you forget your generous acts, 'tis fit that I refresh your memory. When in our childish rambles, arm in arm we climbed yon precipice, my dizzy sight betrayed my faltering step, when Philip boldly plunged the steep, and saved Olivia at the hazard of his life.

Philip. Forbear! recal not thus the scenes of happy infancy—they make life's landscape darken round me—and memory adds fresh pangs to one so lost—so wretched—and so hopeless—my conscience is as yet unsullied, let me retain that consolation, and——

Olivia. I know your heart is pure, dear Philip— look up then—look proudly up while here Olivia owns her sentiments to thee and all the world—telling the sneering, idle herd of coxcombs, that flutter round her person, she prizes the friendship of one honest, honourable man, before a tribe of those unfeeling rakes, who falsely would be reckoned men of honour.

Enter HARDACRE, *his Pipe in his Mouth; on seeing them, starts—throws it to the Ground, and advances towards them.*

Hardacre. What do I see? Is this your promise, Philip?

Philip. Sir—Sir—I——

Hardacre. You have hurt me. The toil of the day had overpowered me—and you—you have completed it.   [*Wiping his brow.*

Philip. I am innocent, sir.

Hardacre. What brings Olivia here then?

Olivia. Hear me, sir.

Philip. Place yourself in my situation, father; tell me then how you would have acted.

Hardacre. In all situations I trust old Hardacre would have acted like an honest man; you know me, Miss Wyndham, you know me. Sir David has insulted me with a suspicion that—he looks down upon the rustic—I am rough, I am plain—but he shall one day know, though the bark of the tree is rugged, and the top somewhat withered, the root is still sound, and the core as vigorous and as untainted as his own; you—you have grieved me, boy.

Philip. Then am I the most unfortunate as well as the most wretched of men.

Olivia. Hear me, guardian—or if you persist in denying me that title, hear me, friend of my father.

Hardacre. Friend of Wyndham—well—go on—speak.

Olivia. Philip is not to blame—a gentleman broke down our carriage at this door—when he sheltered an unprotected female—indeed—indeed he did not know that female was Olivia.

Hardacre. Is it so?—Philip, forgive me. As your guardian, dear Olivia, I must now resign my right.

Olivia. Dear sir, have I offended?

Hardacre. No, bless thee, no; but I am forced to beg your absence from my house. I am thought to have designs upon your fortune—this I cannot submit to. The poor man's probity is all that he can call his own—and I cannot afford to part with it—it is the harvest of a sixty years of toil; and, thanks to Heaven and my country, there is no man on earth that can prevent my reaping it.

Olivia. The justice of your sentiments have pierced me to the soul. Oh Philip!

Philip. Olivia!

Re-enter Servant.

Servant. Sir Arthur, madam, attends you with my Lady Delmar's chariot.

Olivia. I come—farewell, my guardian—Philip, adieu!

[*To* PHILIP, *who throws himself in a chair, and covers his face with his hands*—OLIVIA *looks at him and rushes out. The servant stays.*

L 3

Servant. I had forgot—Sir Arthur desired me to give this letter to young Mr. Hardacre.

Philip. To me?

Servant. To you, sir—if you are the gentleman.

Philip. I am.   [*Servant gives him the letter and exit.* PHILIP *is agitated as he reads it.*

Hardacre. The contents affect him—my son! give me that paper.

Philip. Your pardon, sir.

Hardacre. I entreat.

Philip. Excuse me, I——

Hardacre. I command.

Philip. I dare not disobey—but remember the honour of a son is in a father's hands.

[*Gives the letter.*

Hardacre. And where shall it be safer?—where shall the ivy find more firm support than clasping the rough trunk where first it grew? How's this!—a challenge—oppression on oppression!—well, boy! —how do you mean to act?

Philip. I am a soldier, and your son—do you decide.

Hardacre. 'Tis hard—but yet—yes—you shall meet him, Philip.   [*He reads the note.*

" Since Sir David's commands have no effect—answer me—though the difference of our ranks makes it a condescension,"——what!—" to put you on a level"—indeed!

Philip. Does he insult our poverty?

Hardacre. No. He insults his country! Whoever breaks the peaceful order of society has no rank in it; he has forfeited his claim: come, come, my Philip—thou art the only prop of my declining day—when in distant climes my other blossom, thy poor sister, perished—when she was lost to me for ever —thou yet remaindst to comfort me—and now—now—[*Grasps his hand and bursts into tears; after a struggle Philip kneels to him.*

Philip. Father! If you would have me shun this fatal meeting, teach me but how I can with honour —a soldier's honour.

Hardacre. [*Firmly raises, then embraces him.*] No! no! That must not be: yet something shall be done. For fourteen years I've shunned Sir David Delmar —this day I'll see him, and all mystery shall end— my selfish feelings shall be sacrificed. Philip, thy hand—woe to the wretch who seeks these bloody trials—a professed duellist is a mildew and a blight upon the fairest works of Heaven—he is a savage bird of prey, and like kites and vultures should be hunted by general consent from that harvest which he was only born to ruin and deface—come, come, my son.   [*Exeunt with firm resolution.*

ACT IV.

SCENE I.—*Sir* David's *Study.*

Sir David *and* Record—Record *has his Book of Accounts.*

Sir David. Again tormented! and am I never to be free from these devouring cormorants?—Is this your vigilance?

Record. You know how often I have told you that it must come to this at last.

Sir David. Well, Mr. Record—it's very, very well, sir.

Record. I can no longer answer the many demands that every hour press in—I have done all I could— and must now beg you to examine my accounts, and take my resignation.

Sir David. 'Tis well, 'tis very well, Mr. Record—

you see me in the toils of misery, and take that opportunity to insult, and to desert me.

Record. Insult! Desert you!—Sir David Delmar,
when I do a kind act, I do not wish to talk about
it.   I have served your family these five and thirty
years—I have during that time saved up one thousand pounds—I have this very morning disbursed
the last remaining guinea of it among your creditors—if this is either to insult or to desert you, I
ask your pardon—Desert you in your need!

Sir David. Then quit me not.

Record. Yes—as your steward this very day.   In
poverty I would serve you, with all my heart, and
all my strength—but pardon me when I respectfully
repeat that I will never contribute to the flattering
luxury, that ruins while it smiles upon you.

[*Bows and retires.*

Sir David. My hopes are past—my friends desert—my heart upbraids me!   Blandford stedfastly
refuses the marriage with Olivia, and all my hopes
now rest upon Sir Arthur.   Still while Miss Wyndham remains in my house, my ruin may be prevented; her fortune may amuse my creditors a while
—s'death! what a state is mine! obligation on obligation!

Enter Miss WYNDHAM.

Olivia. I come, Sir David, before I set out, to return my grateful thanks for the many civilities I
have received, both from yourself and Lady Delmar.

Sir David. Set out!—Miss Wyndham!—are—are
you then going to leave us?

Olivia. I informed you, sir, last week, that I had a
visit to pay to—

Sir David. To Philip Hardacre, perhaps.

[*Bitterly.*

Olivia. Sir?

Sir David. Your father, madam, thought proper to make me an associate with this Mr.—Mr. Hardacre—a name I never thought to have seen conjoined with mine even in a writing.

Olivia. Mr. Hardacre, sir, was my late father's friend, and he has acted towards me with a noble integrity that must ever claim my gratitude.

Sir David. Her words upbraid me!—[*Aside.*]—Miss Wyndham, I have a request to make.

Olivia. Sir, if in my power—   [*Hesitating.*

Sir David. It is; a few days cannot possibly incommode your plans: grant me the favour of remaining one week more with Lady Delmar.

Olivia. I will deal candidly with you, sir; young and thoughtless as I may appear, I have long observed you struggling with pecuniary difficulties—nay, be not angry—hear me with patience. When at age, my fortune will be at my own disposal; and if that fortune can be the means of restoring the lost comforts of an amiable woman, or a misguided man, I shall think it has wandered to me as a providential gift from heaven, and hail it as the smiling herald of the purest earthly happiness.

Sir David. You have touched, affected me. Of this hereafter: you consent then to remain one week?

Olivia. If that will contribute to your peace, I do.

Sir David. It will most seriously; two things more; not a word of your suspicions to my lady—let me next hope that you will think no farther of this Philip—this—

Olivia. On that subject I must entreat you to excuse me.

Sir David. By your father's will, my consent is requisite to your marriage; and though this artful rustic, under the specious semblance of blunt honesty——

Olivia. Again—again you allow your reason to
be blinded by your prejudice; permit me to retire.
Reflect, dear sir, on that which I have said: and
think me not intrusive when I add, that in keeping your embarrassments a secret from Lady Delmar, you wrong yourself and her.   Believe me,
when I assure you, that she who has shared the
splendour of your fortunes will esteem it an ill
compliment to be held incapable of supporting
your trials of adversity, or of partaking the sorrows
of your bosom.   [*Exit* OLIVIA.

Sir David. Again, again perplexed, defeated, and
confounded. 'Tis plain she loves this Philip, then!
she owned it not, 'tis true, but she did not deny it
—my affairs draw to a crisis—all doubts must end
this night.   Ha, Zelidy!

ZELIDY *enters.*

Zelidy. Your pardon, if I intrude, but—

Sir David. Another bar to all my projects: but for
her Blandford might have entered into my schemes.
                                  [*Aside.*

Zelidy. I thought Captain Blandford had been
here, sir; he has something to communicate that—

Sir David. 'Tis plain—'tis plain, and every hope
is wrecked—yet do not think, rash girl—what am I
about to say? my feelings all grow callous, and I
have reached the last step of the ladder of oppression, by outraging the sensibilities of an orphan and
a woman.   [*Aside.*

Enter BLANDFORD.

Blandford. Sir—you look disturbed—you tremble—can I do any thing to aid, assist, or——

Sir David. You once might have done so, George,
but now it is too late.   [*Wildly.*

Zelidy. Oh, heavens!

Sir David. Excuse me, George! something has

happened, which has ruffled my disposition—let
me see you in the course of an hour, when I shall
have something to communicate of the greatest
consequence. Now then the die is cast—irrevocably. [*Aside and exit.*

Zelidy. What can he mean? he alarms—he ter-
rifies me.

Blandford. Fear not, dear Zelidy, you shall never want a protector.

Zelidy. Why did you bring me from the cottage
of poor Ellen? there infancy was past in placid,
gentle joys.

Blandford. That Ellen was my mother's trusted
friend. Exposed to a dangerous profession, my
uncle was the only living being to whom, before my
last voyage, I could entrust you. This night all
shall be explained.

Zelidy. But—

Blandford. Nay, Zelidy, I pledge my word—my
uncle's looks alarm me—watch him, I conjure you;
and should any thing occur, speak to my friend
Query, and he will immediately bring you to me at
the cottage of old Hardacre: the servants will direct
you—leave me now, dear Zelidy, as I expect Sir
Arthur every moment upon business of importance.

Zelidy. I will not then detain you—adieu, my benefactor—wherever you may go, may Heaven protect and bless you.

[*Affectionately kisses his hand, and exit.*

Blandford. Now then for the baronet. The letter
to the Colonel, then, was his. Record, I fear, is
right in his suspicions. At all events this brave
young soldier shall not meet him—no—though I
run the risk myself: an aged parent depends on
Philip's assistance: but I—what am I? nobody cares
for me—nobody? yes, poor Zelidy; she esteems and
loves me—and I love her, and—Love! what have
I to do with love? I have forsworn it—if Zelidy was

to marry another, would it concern me?—not a whit—I would go to sea again, and hope—that the first bullet might—Zounds! this looks plaguy like love too—Psha! I'll have nothing to do with it —it's a dangerous enemy, and there's honour in conquering it—so I'll see Sir Arthur—set poor old Hardacre's heart at rest—and then, and then haste back to Zelidy as fast as my heels will carry me— love!—nonsense!   [*Exit.*

SCENE II.—Hardacre's *Cottage.*

HARDACRE, RECORD—RECORD *with Writings and a Casket in his Hand.*

Hardacre. Thus, Mr. Record, have I fully told you all my purposes.

Record. I trust you never will repent your confidence.

Hardacre. For that, old honesty, I will be sworn. Sir David and I at last must meet. You have examined those papers and the casket I intrusted to your care.—You are a man of business, and can inform me whether they are correct.

Record. Nothing can be more so. I shall see the casket, and return your papers, wishing you a prosperous issue to your hopes.

Hardacre. That must be left to time: the husbandman may sow the grain, but 'tis not allotted to man to answer for its growth.

Record. At my request Captain Blandford wrote to Philip's colonel—he has received an answer with the slanderous note inclosed—I know the hand— I'll swear it is Sir Arthur's—it insinuates that Philip had spoken disrespectfully of his colonel.

Hardacre. And this Sir Arthur Tessel did at Sir David's suggestion—

Record. Even so—the young gentleman's attachment to the sister was all a feint—Olivia was his aim—to gain her he would have complied with any request her guardian could have made—but Blandford has thus put the black scrawl into my hands—I place it in yours—take it—and may it confound its author.

Hardacre. It shall—be sure of that—shame on such cowardly practices. The plunderer that robs my farm, pleads want as his excuse—but the midnight incendiary that wantonly fires my corn-field in the dark has all the guilt of the thief to create my contempt, without the pretence of temptation to justify my compassion. By Blandford's opinion we will stand or fall—he is a noble fellow, and will come, you say.

Record. I expect him every moment—oh, I had forgot to tell you—I have left Sir David.

Hardacre. Will you share my purse?

Record. Excuse me, I am an oddity as well as yourself.

Hardacre. I know you are.

Record. When you barely do an act of justice, would you choose to be paid for it?

Hardacre. No.

Record. No more do I; judge of your neighbour by yourself—a knock—it is the captain—Farewell, for a time.   [*Exit* RECORD.

Hardacre. Now let any one dare to say, that there is no friendship, no honesty in this world—I answer it is false, there is abundance to be found for those who choose to seek for them: a few tares will start up in the finest soil; but none but a fool would burn a whole field because a weed or two has grown among the crop.

Enter BLANDFORD.

Your servant, sir; will you be seated?

Blandford. Nay, nay, honest farmer—no cere-

M

mony, that is out of the line of either of us; at my
old friend Record's request, I have written to Colonel Tessel.   I have likewise seen Sir Arthur, and
shewn him his uncle's letter.   I told him all I
thought upon the subject, confounded, shamed, convinced; and am proud to be the bearer of his ample
apology to you, and to your son.

Hardacre. And how is Philip now to act?

Blandford. As I would do; accept the offered
hand of his enemy, and feel prouder of having convinced one man by the rational appeal of mercy,
than to have punished an hundred by the argument
of brutal violence.

Hardacre. Sir, your voice decides it: you interest
me much, one doubt alone—excuse me—but Miss
Wyndham informs me you have for many years had
a young lady under your protection.

Blandford. Hold, my good friend; this is a point
on which I have refused to answer the interrogatories of my dearest relatives—they have indulged
my humour, and a stranger will surely do me the
same favour.

Hardacre. I was wrong, and ask your pardon—we
all have secrets.—Captain Blandford, I shall soon
leave this country—should your fortunes not chance
to be equal to your merits—I am a plain man—but
write to Mr. Osborne, at St. Domingo, and you
shall never want a friend.

Blandford. [*Starting.*] At St. Domingo, did you
say?—Excuse me, sir—but you interest me deeply;
and the young person you have just named may
have cause to bless you.

Hardacre. Her blessing would console me.   I
have known happier days. I will hide nothing from
you.   In an insurrection of our colony I was summoned some miles off in order to defend our property—my son was young, but he marched chearily
by my side—my wife, the best that ever blessed the

hope of man—had died about that time—excuse—
excuse me —   [*Weeps.*

Blandford. Proceed, I conjure you.

Hardacre. On our return all was a scene of terror—the insurrection had raged in our absence—
my faithful servants had all fallen in the defence of
my lands—and my poor child—was—was heard no
more of—she—she—Oh heart!   [*In anguish.*

Blandford. Take comfort, sir—she lives.

Hardacre. Lives! lives! it cannot—Oh yes! yes!
yes! you are too good to mock me.

Blandford. Nay, be firm, and listen.

Hardacre. I will endeavour, sir, to—Lives! Oh
mercy!

Blandford. About fourteen years since—

Hardacre. [*Clasping his hands.*] The time, the
very time!

Blandford. The ship in which I served was sta-
tioned for a while at St. Domingo. One night we
saw the town in flames, and heard the shrieks of
violence and murder—we ordered out the boat—
our men were few—but they were Englishmen.

Hardacre. Still—still—my girl—my child.

Blandford. We gained the land, and found a large
plantation blazing—then a scene of carnage I shudder to remember—a desperate savage ran with an
infant shrieking in his arms—her cries struck on my
ear—I flew like lightning, with one hand snatched
the baby from his grasp, and with the other felled
him to the ground.

Hardacre. Oh!—oh!—

[*Grasping his hand, and choaked with his emotions.*

Blandford. I bore her to the ship, which was next
morning to set sail for England; the insurrection
raged—nor could I trust my little charge on shore—
I was a stranger there.

Hardacre. You brought her home?

Blandford. I did; and tried in vain all means to

find her friends—no one in St. Domingo answered my enquiry.

Hardacre. Alas! it must be so. Thinking her dead, I changed my name, and came, unknown to every one, to this my native land—Wyndham, my only living friend, was privy to the secret—he died and kept it—the infant you have reared with so much care is mine—I have so long been near her, then, yet my old heart never once whispered——

ZELIDY speaks without.

Zelidy. I must see Captain Blandford.—[*She enters.*]—Oh hasten to Sir David's—all there is a scene of terror; I flew to tell you, my dear—dear protector, that—[HARDACRE *here gazes on her.*]—why does this gentleman so earnestly regard me?

Blandford. Now—now, sir, summon all the fortitude—all the resolution of a man.

Hardacre. How mean you that—young lady!—Blandford! tell me—is it?—[BLANDFORD *affirms.*]—I cannot be deceived—fly to these weak old arms, my long lost—darling child.

Zelidy. Child did he say? Oh yes! I feel—I know him—I remember him—Father! Oh father!—
[Rushes to embrace him.

Hardacre. Mr. Blandford—Sir—Thanks, blessings——
> [*Tries to speak—sinks down embracing the knee of* BLANDFORD—ZELIDY *kneels on the other side of her protector—and the Act ends.*

ACT V.

SCENE I.—OLIVIA's *Chamber in Sir* DAVID's *House.*

A Lute and Music on the Table.

OLIVIA, *seated in a pensive Posture.*

Olivia. I cannot read, I cannot play; music has lost its magic influence: why was I born an heiress? what have I gained by fortune? the confession of Sir Arthur, ere he left this house, too clearly proves, that it is only destined to expose me to the mercenary designs of mercenary men: world, world, I'm weary of thee! How do I regret the simple cottage of my rural guardian! when it was thought no harm of me to think of Philip; to sing to him his favourite ballad—ha! [*takes up a song*] here it is— yes, I will try if yet I can remember it.

[*Sings an artless ballad.*—PHILIP *enters in his uniform, towards the conclusion.*

SONG.

Little Cupid, one day, o'er a myrtle bough stray'd,
Among the sweet blossoms he wantonly play'd,
Plucking many a thorn, 'mid the buds of the tree,
He felt that his finger was stung by a bee.
Little Cupid then whimpered; he sobb'd and he sigh'd,
Then ran to his mother, and pettishly cry'd,
" Ah Venus! dear mother! I'm wounded, you see,
And I ask for revenge on the mischievous bee."
His mother then laugh'd at the story he told,
O'er his forehead of snow strok'd his ringlets of gold,
" Now, when you wound another, my lad," answered
*   she,*
" Ere your arrows are pointed, you'll think on the bee;
M 3

A lesson of love let the story impart,
Ere the beam of the eye light the flame of the heart,
Ye fair ones, remember, while yet ye are free,
That the rose holds the thorn, but the myrtle the bee."

Philip. Olivia.

Olivia. Heavens, you here! how you have frightened me! and does your father——

Philip. Be not alarmed; I wait on you by his
command, to inform you, that in a few hours an execution will be in this house, and to remove you to
his own, should you think proper.

Olivia. And is my guardian still so kind, then?

Philip. Under these circumstances, he holds it an
imperious act of duty. You wonder at my present
appearance: know then, dear Olivia, Sir Arthur
Tessel, at the instigation of Sir David, sent me that
sort of appeal, no man of honour can refuse.

Olivia. At the instigation of Sir David? unhappy
man!

Philip. Even so; my opponent affected to doubt
whether he could meet me upon equal terms; I
therefore resumed this garb, to set his mind at rest
upon that subject; since whoever appears as a soldier, must appear as a gentleman.

Olivia. Oh, heavens! and have you met?

Philip. We have; when instead of a pistol he ten-
dered an apology; gave me a letter for Sir David,
another for his sister-in law, and then immediately
set out for London.

Olivia. And your father?

Philip. Of him I have much to tell you. I must
now fulfil my commissions, if you will then leave
this house——

Olivia. Not till I have first rendered every assistance to poor Lady Delmar. Whatever her husband's errors may have been, her misfortunes are
unmerited. She shall share my home—for of what

value can fortune be to me, except when it offers these golden opportunities of comforting the wretched.   [*Exeunt.*

Enter Miss VENUSIA, *opposite side to which they exit.*

Miss Venusia. It must be so. Sir Arthur will soon come to the critical question. Yes, Miss Olivia shall soon perceive that the spear of Minerva may sometimes inflict as deep a wound as the arrows of Cupid.

Enter Maid.

Maid. Mr. Query, madam.

Miss Venusia. Bless me, the great scholar—I must put on my best appearance—a man of his critical sagacity will give a piercing glance, even at first sight—Dorothea; reach me down the Pursuits of Literature—So, now you may go.
                     [*She shews in* QUERY.

Query. Sir Arthur was right—she does regard me with an eye of favour [*aside.*] Happy at this opportunity of being introduced to a lady of whom the world talks so highly.

Miss Venusia. Such elegant praises from a man of your celebrity must be ever flattering—the little I have done to oblige the world, the opinion of such a judge must amply overpay.

Query. Oblige the world? judge? what does that mean? [*aside.*] Pray, ma'am, is there any thing new? any thing stirring?

Miss Venusia. No, sir, a mere dearth in the literary hemisphere; few people, now a days, are of your inquisitive turn of mind.

Query. Inquisitive! oh, she's found me out, Blandford has betrayed me; and I shall never be able to make myself useful here.—I see that.   [*Aside.*

Miss Venusia. You are silent, sir; most of our modern wise men are so: they say but little, but

they think more.   Happy would it be for the world
if all like us spoke in their works alone.

Query. Works? yes, madam, yes.   I am a great
admirer of works: pray what may yours be?

Miss Venusia. Oh, mere private ones, I assure
you; but my motives are the best, and the end is
for posterity.

Query. Indeed, madam! and if I may be so bold,
what may be your favourite work?

Miss Venusia. The Pleasures of Imagination.

Query. Really! an odd amusement for a lady at
her time of her life.   [*Aside.*

Miss Venusia. Though, I dare say, you prefer the
Pleasures of Hope?

Query. A broad hint, that; I see I am a favourite.
                                               [*Aside.*

Miss Venusia. You must indulge me by consulting your taste; pray, then, do you give the preference to the Rise and Progress, or to the Decline
and Fall?

Query. [*Bowing.*] To the Decline and Fall, by
all means, madam, out of compliment to you.

Miss Venusia. I am happy to find that we amal-
gamate so well; your inquiries must have been unceasing.

Query. Some of my friends tell me a little too
much so, madam.

Miss Venusia. Ignorant souls! no man can inquire
too much.

Query. A sensible woman!

Miss Venusia. You have the Pursuits, no doubt?

Query. Never without them.   She and I have
changed characters, I think; she's plaguy inquisitive.   [*Aside.*

Miss Venusia. Any thing you admire must be
excellent; and when you come to London, I hope
you will make one of my celebrated society.   I
assure you I have people of the highest eminence

at my club; we have the most delightful entertainment, the very first characters in the land—lords, doctors, generals, and reviewers.

Query. The reviewing generals, you mean, perhaps, madam?

Miss Venusia. Exactly so: opinions are discussed, merits adjudged, and many who little suspect it find their bad works most curiously carved, I promise you.

Query. Carved!

Miss Venusia. Cut up, root and branch.

Query. And if they cut up bad works, I suppose they are equally ready to encourage good ones; and if any bad works spread abroad, likely to do injury to man, woman, or child, your reviewing generals have my free consent to cut and lop away while they can hold a weapon in their hands; such works are as gangrenes on the bodies of good taste and good sense, and none but fools or knaves can complain of the operation.

Enter PHILIP.

Philip. I beg pardon, madam, but Sir Arthur Tessel requested me to deliver this letter into your hands alone.   [*Gives a letter.*

Miss Venusia. Alone, sir!

Philip. Alone, madam; I have executed my commission, and now respectfully take leave.   [*Exit.*

Miss Venusia. A very extraordinary youth, well-looking and retiring, and possesses the ancient quality of modesty—a rare gem, which has been lost among many other valuable antiquities for several centuries past. But now for my letter—it must be the declaration—a truly classical hand—the characters bear a strong similitude to the Grecian.

Query. Oh yes, madam, it's quite the thing; the writing of most ladies and gentlemen in modern days is very like the Greek.—Perhaps you mayn't have your spectacles about you, madam—pray allow me to decypher—always proud to be useful.

[*Reads.*

" Madam,

" Ere this letter arrives, I shall have quitted this house, and shall most probably never see you more.

Miss Venusia. What!   [QUERY *reading.*

" From motives of the worst nature, I have long been both trifling with and imposing on you. The only reparation I can make is, to fly a spot where every thing reproaches—the guilty but penitent Arthur Tessel."

Miss Venusia. The base man! but I will rise superior to my fall! I will expose him—I will publish my life—and you, learned sir—you shall be my biographer.

Query. Why, look ye, madam, to serve and please has ever been the business of my life, and if my exertions sometimes happen to fall short of my intentions, I argue thus—what was my motive? good-nature—my fear? censure—who wishes success? every body—who can command it? nobody—what was my plea? necessity—my excuse? friendship—I promise to do my best—no man on earth can promise more, so, madam, have with you. [*Hands her in.*

SCENE II.—*The general Room, which must have a folding Door in its Centre.*

Lady DELMAR *and* WILLIAMS.

Lady Delmar. What do you tell me? a chaise ordered? hurry and confusion in his looks?

Williams. Too true, indeed, madam—my master desired me to order the horses to be put to immediately.

Lady Delmar. Fly to him instantly, I intreat you: tell him, I intreat, I supplicate a moment's audience.

[*Exit* WILLIAMS.]   No, generous Olivia!—I am grateful for your noble offer, but a commanding duty now requires my presence here.

Enter SIR DAVID.

Sir David. Emily!

Lady Delmar. My love!

Sir David. I have not deserved that name—Oh, Emily! victim of false pride, I have ruined thee and all thy flattering train of smiling hopes. The sister I deserted is avenged! Her husband now may triumph, but that's my least of pangs; for thee, for thee I feel!

Lady Delmar. For me! my husband, rouse, exert your energies—speak comfort to your heart.

Sir David. Where shall I hope to find it? Driven from my native land, a prey to folly, shame, remorse, and guilt—where shall I fly for refuge?

Lady Delmar. To these arms.

Sir David. Such blessings I deserve not. No, no, my wife—the generous Olivia has consented to receive, to cherish you—with her forget my follies and my sorrows.

Lady Delmar. Hear me, my husband; when we wedded first, joy strewed our path with flowers. My happiness, my pleasures were your cares—you could not see your wife outshone by others of her sex—for her you struggled, and for her you fell—you knew me not—now put me to the proof—go where you will—I'll never, never quit you—I will divide your sorrows, chase your cares, wipe off the upbraiding tear of anguish from your cheek, and be, what every faithful wife has sworn to prove—your servant, guide, your counsellor, and friend.

[*Embracing him.*

Sir David. Friend of my bosom—hide thee ever there! Prepare thee, then; an hour will bring the carriage that bears me off from England, and a prison—

What will become of thee?—remain, my Emily!—
I cannot bear the thought—in foreign lands a fugi-
tive—a wanderer.

Lady Delmar. No earthly power can change my
resolution—doubt not my fortitude or faith. En-
riched by a husband's affection, what woman can be
poor? possessed of a husband's heart, what wife can
want a home?   [*Exit Lady* DELMAR.

Sir David. How have I trifled with each blessing
life afforded! Still, still, the carriage comes not—
it must be near the hour—Hark! I hear it.

Enter WILLIAMS.

Williams. The chariot, sir.

Sir David. 'Tis well; acquaint your lady, and
say I earnestly intreat her utmost speed. [*Exit* WIL-
LIAMS.] Ha! who comes here? Some creditor—
unlucky! now.

Enter HARDACRE.

Friend, your pleasure?

Hardacre. Excuse me, sir, I have taken the liberty of arresting the horses at the door, while I say a
few words to you.

Sir David. Arrest my horses! The measure was
a strong one, but I presume you knew your power,
and have thought proper to exert it.

Hardacre. My power!

Sir David. There are doubtless some accounts
between us, you wish immediately to be settled—I
confess—I confess my inability—so use your pleasure.

Hardacre. Yes, Sir David Delmar, there are some
accounts between us, which must immediately be
settled.

Sir David. I have told you, sir, it is out of my
power.

Hardacre. Excuse me, give me a patient hearing,
and you will find that it is in your power, if it is in

your inclination, to strike the balance of every difference between us.

Sir David. Speed, sir, is necessary; pray be seated.
                                        [*They sit.*

Hardacre. As I am but a bad orator, I shall merely
state a plain story.

Sir David. Well, sir.

Hardacre. Many years ago, a man of consequence
in this part of the world left his eldest son with a
title, an encumbered estate, and an only sister to
protect.

Sir David. Proceed.

Hardacre. The young man being then absent on
his travels, the sister formed an attachment to a
neighbouring yeoman's son. He had saved her from
the fury of an intoxicated ruffian. Gratitude struck
root in her heart, blossomed, and the fruit was love:
the brother's pride on his return was wounded, he
abandoned the newly married couple, and never
would admit them to his presence.

Sir David. He acted rightly—though you may
despise rank.

Hardacre. You wrong me—I respect it—I consider the nobility of my country as the lordly trees of
the forest, engrafted there to shelter all the hum-
bler shrubs around them. But to my tale—abandoned by their brother they sought a foreign land,
where two young cherubs crowned their happiness
—the climate carried off the wife, who dying in
her husband's arms, implored upon her brother's
head—

Sir David. What? her maledictions? [*Shuddering.*

Hardacre. Oh no, no, her blessing and forgiveness.

Sir David. Oh memory—Oh poor Cecilia! [*Aside.*

Hardacre. The husband mourned her virtues o'er
her grave.—His daughter's loss ensued—with wealth
immense, converted into jewels, he returned to England, to sow the seeds of virtue in the mind of his

remaining child—he bred him in adversity's rude
school, a school that learns him to feel for others, a
lesson of more value than all that pampered luxury
can teach the dissipated sons of idleness and folly.

Sir David. Your words upbraid me, sir.

Hardacre. Nay, mark the end. Much has my
boy endured the treasure of an honest name tra-
duced, his father scorned and hated (though unknown) by him he wished to serve and love; oppression on oppression, slander upon slander, roused
his resentment for a while; but when he saw the ag-
gressor beat to the ground like a fallen tree, he
sought his dwelling—resolved to make his story
known, and gratify the only vengeance an honest
mind can harbour, the severe revenge of—doing
good for evil.

Sir David. Osborne!

Osborne. Osborne! the farmer Osborne, in Record's hands placed sums which have retrieved your
debts—discharged your creditors—restored you to
your rights, and now, Sir David, the balance is
struck, and our accounts are settled.

[*While this speech is going on, Lady* DELMAR
and OLIVIA *advance through the centre door.*

Sir David. My benefactor! Oh, my wife—thank,
thank your preserver.   [PHILIP *enters.*

Hardacre. Madam, his friend—I wish no other
title. Philip, my boy, we need but little; what
remains of my wealth shall be the grateful but inade-
quate reward of him who saved my darling dear
Cecilia.

Sir David. For Philip's virtue one recompence remains, Olivia—you understand me, and are above
all narrow vanity.

Philip. If, dear Olivia—

Lady Delmar. Nay, no denial. [*Joins their hands.*

Osborne. Bless ye both.

Enter BLANDFORD.

Philip. Behold the man to whom we owe our happiness.

Osborne. How—how shall we reward him?

Blandford. The reward is easy, sir.—It may seem a little odd, uncle, but I have lately found reason for altering some of my opinions.

Sir David. I guess'd as much.

Blandford. I once held the marriage state incompatible with the duties of my profession.   I am now convinced to the contrary : the dearer the objects for whom we contend, the more ardent our exertions— nothing can be so dear to a man as the wife of his heart; and the armies and navies which are filled with husbands and with parents form the surest and most effective bulwarks of a country.   Zelidy ! you once called me father—I must now resign that title, but there still remains another which——

Osborne. Which her heart confirms; I have it from her own lips—there—[*Gives her to* BLAND- FORD.]   Thus prosperous in the happiness of those dearest to my heart, the occupations of my farm again require my presence.

Zelidy. Nay, dear father !

Olivia. You shall not leave us.

Osborne. Oh bless you, bless you, girls—you shall see enough of me, I warrant you [*Taking one in each hand.*]   The old man shall pay his annual visit, and as he waters the little shrubbery growing up around him with the tears of fond affection, pray that they may grow with all the virtues of their mothers, and all the vigorous bravery of their fathers.   The harvest of my toil at last is ripe, but I can never hope to gather it, unless our friends will lend their hands and help to bring it in.

WHICH IS THE MAN?

A COMEDY,

IN FIVE ACTS,

AS PERFORMED AT THE

THEATRE ROYAL, COVENT-GARDEN.

———

BY MRS. COWLEY.

CHARACTERS.

Lord Sparkle,	*Mr Lee Lewis.*
Fitzherbert,	*Mr Henderson.*
Beauchamp,	*Mr Lewis.*
Belville,	*Mr Wroughton.*
Pendragon,	*Mr Quick.*
Lady Bell Bloomer,	*Miss Younge.*
Julia,	*Miss Satchell.*
Sophy Pendragon,	*Mrs Mattocks.*
Clarinda,	*Mrs Morton.*
Kitty,	*Mrs Wilson.*
Tiffany,	*Mrs Davenett.*
Mrs Johnson,	*Miss Platt.*
Ladies,	*Miss Stewart, Mrs Poussin, &c.*
Gentlemen,	*Mr Booth, Mr. Robson, &c.*

Servants to Lord Sparkle, Belville, *Lady* Bell, *&c.*

WHICH IS THE MAN?

ACT I.

SCENE I.—*A Drawing-room.*

Mrs. JOHNSON crosses the Stage, a Boy following.

Mrs. Johns. HERE, Betty, Dick! Where are ye? Don't you see my Lord Sparkle's carriage?—I shall have my lodgers disturbed with their thundering.— What, in the name of wonder, can bring him here at this time in the morning?——Here he comes, looking like a rake as he is!

Enter Lord SPARKLE, yawning.

Spark. Bid 'em turn; I sha'n't stay a moment.— So, Mrs. Johnson, I pull'd the string just to see how your Sylvans go on.

Mrs. Johns. As usual, my lord; but, bless me! how early your lordship is!

Spark. How late, you mean.—I have not been in bed since yesterday at one!—I am going home now to rest for an hour or two, and then to the drawing-room.—But what are the two rustics about? I have not been plagued with them these three or four days.

Mrs. Johns. They are now out.

Spark. I suppos'd that, or I should not have call'd.——But, prithee, do they talk of returning to their native woods again?

Mrs. Johns. Oh no, sir!—The young gentleman seems to have very different ideas: Miss, too, has great spirits, though she seems now and then at a loss what to do with herself.

Spark. Do with herself! Why don't you persuade her to go back to Cornwall? You should tell 'em what a vile place London is, full of snares, and debaucheries, and witchcrafts.—You don't preach to 'em, Johnson.

Mrs. Johns. Indeed I do, my lord; and their constant answer is, " Oh, Lord Sparkle is our friend: Lord Sparkle would take it amiss if we should go; 'twould look like distrusting his lordship."

Spark. Was ever man so hamper'd!—Two fools! to mistake common forms and civilities for attachments.

Mrs. Johns. I fear, my lord, towards the young lady something more than forms——

Spark. [*Interrupting.*] Never, upon my honour!— I kissed her; so I did all the women in the parish —the septennial ceremony. The brother I us'd to drink vile port with, listen to his village-stories, call his vulgarity wit, and his impudence spirit; was not that fatigue and mortification enough, but I must be bored with 'em here in town?

Mrs. Johns. But Miss, Sir, talks of pressing invitations, and letters, and——

Spark. Things of course; they had influence, and got me the borough. I, in return, said she was the most charming girl in the world; that I adored her; and some few things that every body says on such occasions, and nobody thinks of.

Mrs. Johns. But it appears that Miss did think—

Spark. Yes, 'faith: and on my writing a civil note that I should be happy to see them in town, &c.— which I meant to have suspended our acquaintance till the general election—they took me at my word; and before I thought the letter had reach'd 'em, they were in my house, all joy and congratulation. I didn't chuse to be encumber'd with 'em, so placed 'em with you. The boy was at first amusing, but our circles have had him, and I must be rid of him.

Mrs. Johns. I must say, I wish I was quit of them at present; for my constant lodger, Mr. Belville, came to town last night, and he wants this drawing-room to himself: he's obliged to share it now with Mr. Pendragon and his sister.

Spark. Hey! Belville!—'Gad, that's lucky! There is not a fellow in town better receiv'd by the women.—Throw the girl in his way, and get quit of her at once.

Mrs. Johns. If you mean dishonestly, my lord, you have mistaken your person: I did not live so many years with your mother to be capable of such a thing. —Ah, my lord, if my lady were living——

Spark. She would scold to little purpose,—and you may spare yourself the trouble.——I tell you, I care nothing about the girl: I merely want to get rid of her, and you must assist me.—[*Mrs.* JOHN-SON *turns from him with disgust.*]——Hey-day! the nicety of your ladyship's honour is piqued! Ha! ha! ha!—the mistress of a lodging-house!—*Bien drole*— Ha! ha! ha!   [*Exit Mrs.* JOHNSON. But who is this hobbling up stairs?—Ha! old Cato the censor, my honourable cousin?—What the devil shall I do?—No avoiding him, however.—

Enter Mr. FITZHERBERT.

I wish I had been out of the house, Fitzherbert, before you appeared! I know I shall not escape without some abuse.

Fitz. I never throw away reproof where there are no hopes of amendment—your lordship is safe.

Spark. Am I to take that for wit?

Fitz. No; for then, I fear, you would not understand it.

Spark. Positively, you must give me more of the felicity of your conversation: I want you to teach me some of that happy ease which you possess in your rudeness; 'twould be to me an acquisition. I am eternally getting into the most horrid scrapes, merely by politeness and good-breeding.—Here are two persons now in this house, for instance——

Fitz. [*Interrupting.*] Who do not know, that the language of what you call politeness differs from that of truth and honour.—You see I know those to whom you allude.—But we only lose time!—Good day, my lord!

Spark. Lose time! Ha! ha! ha!—Why, of what value can time be to you? the greatest enemy you have, adding every day to your wrinkles and ill-humour. I'll prove to you now, that I have employ'd the last twelve hours to better purpose than you have. Nine of them you slept away—the last three you have been running about town, snarling and making people uneasy with themselves;—whilst I have been sitting peaceably at Weltjie's, where I have won—guess what?

Fitz. Half as much as you lost yesterday—a thousand or two guineas, perhaps.

Spark. Guineas! Poh! you are jesting! Guineas are as scarce with us, as in the coffers of the Congress. Like them we stake with counters, and play for solid earth.

Fitz. [*Impatiently.*] Well!

Spark. Bullion is a mercantile kind of wealth,

passing through the hands of dry-salters, vinegar-merchants, and Lord-Mayors.—Our goddess holds a cornucopia instead of a purse, from which she pours corn-fields, fruitful vallies, and rich herds. This morning she popp'd into my dice-box a snug villa, five hundred acres, arable and pasture, with the next presentation to the living of Guzzleton.

Fitz. A church-living in a dice-box! Well, well; I suppose it will be bestowed as worthily as it was gained!—Good day, my lord, good day!

[*Turning from him.*

Spark. Good night, Crabtree—good night!

[*Going off.*

Enter a Servant.

Tell Belville I call'd to congratulate his escape from the stupid country.   [*Going.*

Fitz. My lord!

Spark. [*returning.*] Sir!

Fitz. I am going this morning to visit Lady Bell Bloomer.—I give you this intimation, that we may not risk another rencontre.

Spark. Civilly design'd; and for the same polite reason I inform you, that I shall be there in the evening.   [*Exit Lord* SPARKLE.

Fitz. Your master in bed yet! What time was he in town yesterday?

Serv. Late, sir.—We should have been earlier, but we met with Sir Harry Hairbrain on the road, with his new fox-hounds.—Fell in with the hunt at Bagshot—broke cover, run the first burst across the heath towards Datchet;—she then took right an end for Egham, sunk the wind upon us as far as Staines, where Reynard took the road to Oxford, and we the route to town, sir.   [*Bowing.*

Fitz. Very geographical, indeed, sir.—Now, pray inform your master——Oh, here we come!

Enter BELVILLE *in a robe de chambre.*

Just risen from your pillows!——Are you not
ashamed of this? A fox-hunter, and in bed at
eleven!

Belv. My dear, morose, charming, quarrelsome
old friend, I am ever in character!—In the country,
I defy fatigue and hardship.—Up before the lazy
slut Aurora has put on her pink-coloured gown to
captivate the plough-boys—scamper over hedge and
ditch. Dead with hunger, alight at a cottage; drink
milk from the hands of a brown wench, and eat from
a wooden platter. In town, I am a fine gentleman;
have my hair exactly dressed; my clothes *au dernier
gout;* dine on made-dishes; drink burgundy; and,
in a word, am every-where the *ton.*

Fitz. So much the worse, so much the worse,
young man! To be the *ton* where Vice and Folly
are the ruling deities, proves that you must be sometimes a fool, at others a——

Belv. [*Interrupting.*] Psha! you satirists, like
moles, shut your eyes to the light, and grope about
for the dark side of the human character: there is
a great deal of good sense and good meaning in the
world. As for its follies, I think folly a mighty
pleasant thing; at least, to play the fool gracefully
requires more talents than would set up a dozen
cynics.

Fitz. Then half the people I know must have
wonderful talents, for they have been playing the
fool from sixteen to sixty.——Apropos: I found my
precious kinsman Lord Sparkle here.

Belv. Ay; there's an instance of the happy effects
of total indifference to the sage maxims you recommend.

Fitz. Happy effects do you call them?

Belv. Most triumphant. Who so much admired?

who so much the fashion?—the general favourite of the ladies, and the common object of imitation with the men. Is not Lord Sparkle the happy man, who's to carry the rich and charming widow Lady Bell Bloomer from so many rivals?—And will not you, after quarreling with him half your life, leave him a fine estate at the end of it?

Fitz. No, no!—I tell you, no!   [*With warmth.*

Belv. Nay, his success with the widow is certain.—He boasts his triumph every-where ; and as she is such a favourite of yours, every thing else will follow.

Fitz. No; for if she marries Sparkle, she will be no longer a favourite. Yet she receives him with a degree of distinction that sometimes makes me fear it; for we frequently see women of accomplishments and beauty, to which every heart yields homage, throw themselves into the arms of the debauched, the silly, and the vain.

Enter a Servant.

Serv. Mr. Beauchamp.   [*Exit.*

Fitz. Oh! I expected him to call on you this morning. You must obtain his confidence; it will assist me in my designs. When I found myself disappointed in my hopes of his lordship, I selected Beauchamp from the younger branches of my family: but of this he knows nothing, and thinks himself under high obligations to the patronage of the peer; an error in which I wish him to continue, as it will give me an opportunity of proving them both.——But here he comes!—This way I can avoid him.   [*Exit.*

Enter BEAUCHAMP.

Belv. Beauchamp!——and in regimentals!——Why, prithee, George, what spirit has seized thee now? When I saw thee last, thou wert devoted to

o

the grave profession of the law, or the church; and
I expected to have seen thee envelop'd in wig,
wrangling at the bar; or seated in a fat benefice, receiving tythe-pigs and poultry.

Beauch. Those, Belville, were my school-designs;
but the fire of youth gave me ardours of a different
sort. The heroes of the Areopagus and the forum
have yielded to those of Marathon; and I feel, that
whilst my country is struggling amidst surrounding
foes, I ought not to devote a life to learned indo-
lence, that might be gloriously hazarded in her defence.

Belv. [*Smiling.*] I shan't give you credit now for
that fine flourish.——This sudden ardour for " the
pride, pomp, and circumstance of glorious war."——
I dare swear this heroic spirit springs from the
whim of some fine lady, who fancied you would be
a smarter fellow in a cockade and gorget, than in a
stiff band and perriwig.

Beauch. If your insinuation means that my heart
has not been insensible of the charms of some fair
lady, you are right; but my transformation is owing
to no whim of hers: for, oh Charles! she never
yet condescended to make me the object of her
thoughts.

Belv. Modest too!—Ay, you were right to give
up the law.—But who, pray, may this exalted fair
one be who never condescended?

Beauch. I never suffer my lips to wanton with the
charming sounds that form her name. I have a kind
of miserly felicity in glutting on her dear idea, that
would be impaired, should it be known to exist in
my heart.

Belv. Ha! ha! ha! who can be the nymph who
has inspired so obsolete a passion?—In the days of
chivalry it would have been the *ton.*

Beauch. I will gratify you thus far: the lady has
beauty, wit, and spirit; but, above all, a mind.—Is

it possible, Charles, to love a woman without a mind?

Belv. Has she a mind for you? That is the most important question.

Beauch. I dare not feed my passion with so pre-sumptuous a hope; yet I would not extinguish it if I could: for it is not a love that tempts me into corners to wear out my days in complaints: it prompts me to use them for the most important purposes:—the ardours it gives me shall be felt in the land of our enemies; they shall know how well I love.

Belv. Poh! poh! this is the gallantry of One Thousand One Hundred and One; the kind of passion that animated our fathers in the fields of Cressy and Poictiers.——Why, no beauty of our age, man, will be won in this style!——Now, suppose yourself at the Opera [*looking through his hand.*] "Gad, that's a fine girl! Twenty thousand, you say? I think I'll have her. Yes, she'll do! I—I must have her! I'll call on her to-morrow and tell her so." Have you spirit and courage enough for that, my Achilles?

Beauch. No, truly.

Belv. Then give up all thoughts of being received.

Beauch. I have no thoughts of hazarding a reception. The pride of birth, and a few hundreds for my education, were the sole patrimony the imprudence of a father left me. My relation, Lord Sparkle, has procured for me a commission.—Generously to offer that and a knapsack to a lady of five thousand a-year, would be properly answered by a contemptuous dismission.

Belv. But suppose she should take a fancy to your knapsack?

Beauch. That would reduce me to the necessity of depriving myself of a happiness I would die to obtain; for never can I submit to be quartered on a

wife's fortune whilst I have a sword to carve subsistence for myself.

Belv. That may be in the great style; but 'tis
scarcely in the polite. Will you take chocolate in
my dressing-room?

Beauch. No; I am going to take orders at my colonel's: where shall we meet in the evening?

Belv. 'Faith, 'tis impossible to tell! I commit
myself to chance for the remainder of the day, and
shall finish it as she directs. [*Exeunt at opposite sides.*

Scene changes to an Apartment at CLARINDA'S.

Enter CLARINDA, *reading a Catalogue, followed by*
TIFFANY.

Cla. Poor Lady Squander! So Christie has her
jewels and furniture at last!——I must go to the
sale.——Mark that Dresden service, and the pearls.
[*Gives the catalogue to the maid.*] It must be a great
comfort to her to see her jewels worn by her friends.
—Who was here last night? [*Sitting down, and taking
some cards from the table.*] I came home so late, I
forgot to inquire!——Mrs. Jessamy—Lady Racket
—Miss Belvoir—Lord Sparkle [*starting up*]—Lord
Sparkle here! Oh heavens and earth! what possessed me to go to Lady Price's? I wish she and her
concert of three fiddles and a flute had been playing
to her kids on the Welsh mountains!—Why did you
persuade me to go out last night?

Tiff. Dear ma'am, you seem'd so low-spirited,
that I thought——

Cla. I missed him every-where!—At four places
he was just gone as I came in.—But what does it
signify?—'Twas Lady Bell Bloomer he was seeking,
I dare swear:—his attachment to the relict is every-
where the subject. Hang those widows! I really
believe there's something cabalistical in their names.

—No less than fourteen fine young fellows of fortune have been drawn into the matrimonial noose by them since last February.——'Tis well they were threatened with imprisonment, or we should not have had an unmarried infant above seventeen, between Charing-Cross and Portman-Square.

Tiff. Well, I am sure I wish Lady Bell was married; she's always putting you out of temper.

Cla. Have I not cause? Till she broke upon the town, I was at the top of fashion—you know I was. My dress, my equipage, my furniture, and myself, were the criterions of taste; but a new French chamber-maid enabled her ladyship at one stroke to turn the tide against me.

Tiff. Ay, I don't know what good these Mademoiselles——

Cla. [*Interrupting.*] But, Tiffany, she is to be at court to-day, out of mourning for the first time: I am resolved to be there.——No, I won't go neither, now I think on't.—If she should really outshine me, her triumph will be increased by my being witness to it.——I won't go to St. James's; but I'll go to her route this evening, and, if 'tis possible, prevent Lord Sparkle's being particular to her.—Perhaps that will put her in an ill-humour, and then the advantage will be on my side.   [*Exit* CLARINDA.

Tiff. Mercy on us! To be a chamber-maid to a Miss on the brink of thirty requires as good politics, as being prime minister! Now, if she should not rise from her toilette quite in looks to-day, or if the desertion of a lover, or the victory of a rival, should happen, ten to one but I shall be forced to resign, without even a pension to retire on.

[*Exit* TIFFANY.

ACT II.

SCENE I.—*An elegant Apartment at Lady* BELL BLOOMER'S.

Enter JULIA, *with Papers in her Hand.*

Julia. What an invaluable treasure! Those dear papers, that have lain within the frigid walls of a convent, insensible and uninteresting to every one around them, contain for me a world of happiness. He is in England! How little he suspects that I too am here!

Enter KITTY.

Kitty. Mr. Fitzherbert will be here immediately, ma'am.

Julia. Mr. Fitzherbert! Very well. Has Lady Bell finished dressing yet?

Kitty. [*Speaking exceedingly fast.*] No, ma'am.— Mr. Crape the hair-dresser has been with her these three hours, and her maid is running here and there, and Mr. John flying about to milliners and perfumers, and the new vis-a-vis at the door to carry her ladyship to court.—Every thing black banished, and the liveries come home shining with silver; and the moment she's gone out, every body will be in such a delightful hurry about the rout that her ladyship is to give this evening, that they say all the world——

Julia. Ha! ha! ha! Prithee stop! I can't wonder if Lady Bell should be transported at dropping her weeds, for it seems to have turned the heads of the whole family.

Kitty. Oh! dearee, ma'am, to be sure! for now we shall be so gay! Lady Bell has such fine spirits! ——And 'tis well she has; for the servants tell me

their old master would have broke her heart else.—
They all adore her.——I wish you were a little
gayer, ma'am!——Somehow we are so dull!—'Tis
a wonder so young and so pretty a lady—

Julia. Don't run into impertinence.—I have neither the taste nor talents for public life that Lady
Bell Bloomer has.

Kitty. Laws, ma'am, 'tis all use! You are always at home; but Lady Bell knows, that wit and a
fine person are not given for a fire-side at home
[*Drawling.*] She shines every evening in half the
houses of half a dozen parishes, and the next morning we have stanzas in the *Bevy of Beauties*, and son-
nets, and billets-doux, and all the fine things that
fine ladies are so fond of.

Julia. I can bear your freedoms no longer!—
Carry these flowers with my compliments, and tell
her ladyship I sent to Richmond for them, as I know
her fondness for natural bouquets; and bid Harry
deny me to every body this morning, except Mr.
Fitzherbert.   [*Exit* KITTY.

Enter Mr. FITZHERBERT.

Fitz. Happily excepted, my dear ward! But I suppose you heard my step, and threw in my name for a
douceur.   I can hardly believe, that when you shut
your doors on youth and flattery, you would open
them to a cross old man who seldom entertains you
with any thing but your faults.

Julia. How you mistake, sir! You are the greatest
flatterer I have: your whole conduct flatters me
with esteem and love : and as you do not squander
these things——   [*Smiling.*

Fitz. There I must correct you.——I do squander
them on few objects, indeed, and they are propor-
tionably warmer.   I feel attachments fifty times as
strong as your good-humoured smiling people, who
are every one's humble servant, and every body's
friend.   Where is Lady Bell?

Julia. Yet at her toilette, I believe. My dear sir, I am every hour more grateful to you for having given me so charming a friend.

Fitz. So I would have you. When you came from France, I prevailed on her ladyship to allow you her society, that you might add to the polish of elegant manners the graces of an elegant mind. Here she comes! her tongue and her heels keeping time.

Enter Lady BELL.

Ay, ay, if all the women in the world were prating young widows, love and gallantry would die away, and our men grow reasonable and discreet.

Lady Bell. Oh you monster! But I am in such divine spirits, that nothing you say can destroy them.——My sweet Julia, what a bouquet! Lady Myrtle will expire.——She was so enveloped in flowers and evergreens last night, that she looked like the picture of fair Rosamond in her bower.—My dear Fitz, do you know we dined yesterday in Hill-street, and had the fortitude to stay till eleven!

Julia. I was tired to death with the fatiguing visit.

Lady Bell. Now I, on the contrary, came away with fresh relish for society. The persevering civility of Sir Andrew, and the maukish insipidity of his tall daughter, act live olives—you can't endure them on your palate, but they heighten the gusto of your tokay.

Fitz. Then I advise your ladyship to serve up Sir Andrew and his daughter at your next entertainment.

Lady Bell. So I would; only one can't remove 'em with the dessert. But how do you like me? Did you ever see so delightful a head? Don't you think I shall make a thousand conquests to-day?

Fitz. Doubtless, if you meet with so many fools. —But pray, which of those you have already made will be the most flattered by all these gay insignia of your liberty?

Lady Bell. Probably, he whom it least concerns.

Julia. Pray tell us, which is that?

Lady Bell. Oh, Heavens! to answer that requires more reflection than I have ever given the subject.

Julia. Should you build a temple to your lovers, I fancy we should find Lord Sparkle's name on the altar.

Lady Bell. Oh! Lord Sparkle!——Who can resist the gay, the elegant, the all-conquering Lord Sparkle? the most distinguished feather in the plume of fashion—without that barbarous strength of mind which gives importance to virtues or to vices. Fashionable, because he's well-dressed—brilliant, because he's of the first clubs, and uses his borrowed wit like his borrowed gold, as though it was his own.

Fitz. Why now, this man, whom you understand so well, you receive as though his tinsel was pure gold.

Lady Bell. Aye, to be sure!——Tinsel is just as well for shew.—The world is charitable, and accepts tinsel for gold in most cases.

Fitz. But in the midst of all this sunshine for Lord Sparkle, will you not throw a ray on the spirited, modest Beauchamp?

Lady Bell. A ray of favour for Beauchamp!—Were I so inclined to make it welcome, I must change my fan for a spear, my feathers for a helmet, and stand forth a Thalestris. You know his mistress is war— [*sighing, and then recovering.*]—But why do I trifle thus?—The hour of triumph is at hand.

Fitz. Of what?

Lady Bell. The moment of triumph!—Anglice, the moment when, having shewn myself at half the houses in St. George's, I am set down at St. James's, my fellows standing on each hand as I descend—the whisper flying through the crowd, " Who is she? Who is that sweet creature?—One of the four heiresses?"—" No; she's a foreign ambassadress."

——I ascend the stairs—move slowly through the
rooms—drop my fan—incommode my bouquet—
stay to adjust it, that the little gentry may have
time to fix their admiration—again move on—enter
the drawing-room—throw a flying glance round the
circle, and see nothing but spite in the eyes of the
women, and a thousand nameless things in those of
the men.

Julia. The very soul of giddiness!

Lady Bell. The very soul of happiness!—Can I be
less?—Think of a widow just emerged from her
weeds for a husband to whom her father, not her
heart, united her—my jointure elegant, my figure
charming—deny it if you dare!—Pleasure, fortune,
youth, health, all opening their stores before me;
whilst innocence and conscious honour shall be my
handmaids, and guide me in safety through the
dangerous ordeal.

Fitz. To your innocence and conscious honour
add, if you have time [*archly*], a little prudence, or
your sentinels may be surprised asleep, and you reduced to a disgraceful capitulation.

Lady Bell. Oh, I am mistress of my whole situation, and cannot be surprised.——But, Heavens! I
am losing a conquest every moment I stay!—The
loves and pleasures have prepared their rosy gar-
lands—my triumphal car is waiting—and my proud
steeds neighing to be gone.——Away to victory!—
                    [*Exit with great spirit.*

Fitz. A charming woman, Julia!—she conceals a
fine understanding under apparent giddiness, and a
most sensible heart beneath an air of indifference.

Julia. Yes, I believe her ladyship's heart is more
sensible than she allows to herself. I rally her on
Lord Sparkle, but it is Mr. Beauchamp, whose
name is never mentioned but her cheeks tell such
blushing truths, as she would never forgive me for
observing.

Fitz. Upon my word, you seem well acquainted with your friend's heart!——Will you be equally frank as to your own?

Julia. [*In great confusion.*] Sir!——my heart!

Fitz. Yes; will you assist me in reading it?

Julia. To be sure, sir.

Fitz. Then tell me, if amongst the painted, powdered, gilded moths whom your beauty or fortune have allured, is there one whom you would honour with your hand?——Aye, take time; I would not have you precipitate.

Julia. [*Hesitatingly.*] No, sir—not one.

Fitz. I depend on your truth, and on that assurance inform you that a friend of mine is arrived in town, whom I mean this morning to present to you.

Julia. As a——

Fitz. As a lover, who has my warmest wishes that he may become your husband.

Julia. Do I know the person for whom you are thus interested, sir?

Fitz. You do not; but I have had long intimacy with him, and it is the dearest wish of my heart to see him and Julia Manners united.

Julia. I trust, sir, you will allow——

Fitz. Be under no apprehensions.——Much as I'm interested in this union, your inclinations shall be attended to.—I am now going to your lover, and shall introduce him to you this morning.——Come, don't look so distressed, child, at the approach of that period which will give you dignity and character in society. The marriage state is that in which your sex evinces its importance; and where, in the interesting circle of domestic duties, a woman has room to exercise every virtue that constitutes the great and the amiable.   [*Exit* FITZHERBERT.

Julia. The moment I so much dreaded is arrived! How shall I reveal to my guardian, and to Lady Bell, that I am married? that I have already dared to take on me those important duties? I must not reveal it—my solemn promise to my husband—But where is he?—Oh, I must write to him this moment, that I may not be left defenceless to brave the storm of offended authority and love.   [*Exit* JULIA.

SCENE II.—BELVILLE'S *Lodgings.*

Enter BELVILLE *new drest.*

Belv. Let my trunks be ready, and the chaise at the door to-morrow morning by six, for I shall dine in Dover.

Fitz. Ha! just in time, I see!—You are ready plumed for flight.

Belv. True; but my flight would have been to you.—Impatient to know the cause of your summoning me from the Dryades and Hamadryades of Berkshire, your letter reached me at the very instant I was setting out for Dover, in my way to Paris.

Fitz. Paris!

Belv. Yes.

Fitz. Poh! poh! stay where you are, stay where you are! The great turnpike between Dover and Calais is a road destructive to this kingdom; and I wish there were toll-gates erected on its confines, to restrain with a heavy tax the number of its travellers.

Belv. I fear the tax would be more generally felt than the benefit; for it would restrain not only the folly-mongers and the fashion-mongers, but the rational inquirer and the travelling connoisseur.

Fitz. So much the better! so much the better!— Our travelling philosophers have done more towards destroying the nerves of their country than all the politics of France. Their chief aim seems to be to establish infidelity, and to captivate us with delusive views of manners still more immoral and licentious than our own.——Hey-day! who's this?—Oh, the Cornish lad, I suppose, whom Lord Sparkle placed here.

Belv. [*Laughing.*] Yes; an odd being.—He was designed by nature for a clodpole, but the notice of a peer overset the little understanding he had, and so he commenced fine gentleman. He has a sister with him, who ran wild upon the commons till her father's death; but she fancies herself a wit, and satirizes Bruin.—Here he comes.

Enter PENDRAGON.

Pen. My dear fellow-lodger, I'm come to——Oh, your servant, sir! [*To* FITZHERBERT.]—Is this gentleman a friend of yours?

Belv. He is.

Pen. Your hand, sir. [*Passes* BELVILLE, *and stands between them.*] If you are Mr. Belville's friend you are my friend, and we are all friends; I soon make acquaintance.

Fitz. A great happiness.

Pen. Yes, so it is, and very polite too. I have been in the great world almost six weeks, and I can see no difference between the great world and the little world, only that they've no ceremony; and so as that's the mark of good breeding, I tries to hit it off.

Fitz. With success.

Pen. To convince you of that I'll tell you a devilish good thing.—You must know——

Fitz. [*Interrupting.*] Excuse me now, but I am convinced you will amuse me, and desire your company at dinner—they'll give you my address below. Mr. Belville, I have business of importance.

[*Exit* FITZHERBERT *and* BELVILLE.

Pen. Gad, I'm glad he asked me to visit him!— He must be a lord by his want of ceremony. [*Imitating.*] " Mr. Belville, I have business of importance"—and off they go.—Now in Cornwall we should have thought that damn'd rude—but 'tis easy.—" Mr. Belville, I have business of importance." [*Going.*] Easy—easy—easy!

P

Enter SOPHY PENDRAGON.

Sophy. Brother Bobby!—Brother Bobby!

Pen. [*Returning.*] I desire, Miss Pendragon, you won't brother me at this rate—making one look as if one didn't know life. How often shall I tell you, that it is the most ungenteel thing in the world for relations to brother, and father, and cousin one another, and all that sort of thing. I did not get the better of my shame for three days, when you bawled out to Mrs. Dobson at Launceston concert—" Aunt, aunt, here's room between brother and I, if cousin Dick will sit closer to father !"

Sophy. Lack-a-day !—and where's the harm ?— What d'ye think one has relations given one for ?— to be asham'd of 'em ?

Pen. I don't know what they were given us for ; but I know no young man of fashion cares for his relations.

Sophy. More shame for your young men of fashion ; but I assure you, Brother Bobby, I shall never give in to any such unnatural, new-fangled ways. As for you, since Lord Sparkle took notice of you, you are quite another thing. You used to creep into the parlour when father had company, hanging your head like a dead partridge ; steal all round the room behind their backs to get at a chair ; then sit down on one corner of it, tying knots in your handkerchief ; and if any body drank your health, rise up and scrape your foot so—" Thank you kindly, sir !"—

Pen. By Goles, if you—   [*Shaking his fist.*

Sophy. But now, when you enter a room, your hat is tossed carelessly on a table ; you pass the company with a half bend of your body ; fling yourself into one chair, and throw your legs on another :— " Pray, my dear sir, do me the favour to ring."— " John, bring lemonade."—" Mrs. Plume has been

driving me all morning in Hyde-Park against the
wind, and the dust has made my throat mere plaster
of Paris."—

Pen. Hang me, if I don't like myself at second-
hand better than I thought I should !—Why, if I do
it as well as you, Sophy, I shall soon be quite the
thing !—And now I'll give you a bit of advice:—As
'tis very certain Lord Sparkle means to introduce
you to high life, 'tis fitting you should know how to
behave ; and as I have been amongst 'em I can tell
you.

Sophy. Well!

Pen. Why, first of all, if you should come into a
drawing-room, and find twenty or thirty people in
the circle, you are not to take the least notice of any
one.

Sophy. No!

Pen. No! The servant will, perhaps, get you a
chair ;—if not, slide into the nearest. The conversation will not be interrupted by your entrance, for
they'll take as little notice of you as you of them.

Sophy. Psha !

Pen. Then, be sure to be equally indifferent to the
coming-in of others.—I saw poor Lady Carmine
one night dying with confusion, for the vulgarity and
ill-breeding of her friend, who actually rose from her
chair at the entrance of the Duchess of Dulcet and
Lady Betty Blowze.

Sophy. Be quiet, Bobby !

Pen. True, as I am a young man of fashion !—
Then you must never let your discourse go beyond
one word.—If any body should happen to take the
trouble to entertain the company, you may throw in
—" Charming !—Odious !—Capital !"——Never
mount to a phrase, unless to that dear delightful one,
of " all that sort of thing."—The use made of that
is wonderful ! —" All that sort of thing" is an apology for want of wit; it is a substitute for argument;

it will serve for the point of a story or the fate of a battle.

Sophy. Well then,—upon going away?

Pen. Oh, you go away as you came in!—If one has a mind to give the lady of the house a nod, [*nodding*] one may; but 'tis still higher breeding to leave her with as little ceremony as I do you.

[*Exit* PENDRAGON *without looking at her.*

Sophy. I wish I could be sure it was the fashion not to mind forms, I'd go directly and visit Lord Sparkle. I could tear my eyes out to think I was abroad to-day when he called on Mrs. Johnson!—In all the books I have read, I never met with a lover so careless as he is.—Sometimes I have a mind to treat him with disdain, and then I recollect all I have read about ladies' behaviour that break their lovers' hearts;—but he won't come near me.—Now I have been three days in a complying humour—but 'tis all one; still he keeps away. I'll be hang'd if I don't know what he's about soon!—He shan't think to bring me from the Land's End to make a fool of me:—Sophy Pendragon has more spirit than he thinks for. [*Exit* SOPHY.

Re-enter FITZHERBERT *and* BELVILLE.

Belv. A wife! Heaven's last best gift!—But—a —no—I shan't marry yet. I have a hundred little follies to act before I do so rash a thing.

Fitz. But I say you shall marry. I have studied you from eighteen, and know your character, your faults, and your virtues; and such as you are, I have picked you out from all the blockheads and fools about you, to take a fine girl off my hands with twenty thousand pounds.

Belv. 'Tis a bribe, doubtless!—But what is the lady; coquet, prude, or vixen?

Fitz. You may make her what you will. Treat her with confidence, tenderness, and respect, and she'll be an angel; be morose, suspicious, and neglectful, and she'll be—a woman.   The wife's character and conduct is a comment on that of the husband.

Belv. [*Gaily.*] Any thing more?—

Fitz. Yes, she is my ward, and the daughter of the friend of my youth.—I entertain parental affection for her, and give you the highest proof of my esteem in transferring to you the care of her happiness. Refuse it if you dare.

Belv. Dare! My dear friend, I must refuse the honour you offer me.

Fitz. How!

Belv. To be serious, it is not in my power to wed the lady.

Fitz. I understand you.—I am disappointed!—I should have mentioned this subject to you before I had suffered it to make so strong a feature in my picture of future happiness.

Belv. Would you had, that I might have informed you at once—that I am—married.

Fitz. Married!—Where, when, how, with whom?

Belv. Where?—In France.——When?—About eight months since.——How?—By an English clergyman.——With whom?——Ah! with such a one! Her beauty is of the Greek kind, which pleases the mind more than the eye.—Yet to the eye nothing can be more lovely. To this charming creature add the name of Julia Manners, and you know my wife.

Fitz. Julia Manners! Julia Manners, do you say?

Belv. Yes, Julia Manners. I first knew her at the house of a friend in Paris, whose daughters were in the same convent with herself. I often visited her at the grate; at length, by the assistance of Mademoiselle St. Val, prevailed on her to give me her hand, but was immediately torn from her by a summons from my uncle at Florence; whence I was dispatched to England on a ministerial affair.

Fitz. So, so, so, very fine! [*Aside.*]——I suppose you had the prudence to make yourself acquainted with the lady's family before you married her?

Belv. Yes: her family and fortune are elegant.— She has a guardian, whose address the sweet obstinate refused to give me, that she might herself reveal the marriage, which I had reasons, however, to request her not to do till we both arrived in England.

Fitz. Then you have not seen your bride in England?

Belv. Oh no!—My Julia is yet in her convent. I have been preparing for her reception in Berkshire, and have written to inform her that I would meet her at Calais; but I fear my letters have missed her, and shall therefore set out for Paris, to conduct to England the woman who must give the point to all my felicities.

Fitz. [*Aside.*] And has Julia been capable of this? —Ungrateful girl! is it thus she rewards my cares?

Belv. Your silence and your resentment, my dear friend, whilst they flatter distress me.

Fitz. I'm indeed offended at your marriage, but not with you:—on you I had no claims.

Belv. I do not apprehend you.

Fitz. Perhaps not; and at present I shall not explain myself. [*Going.*]

Belv. If you will leave me, adieu! I am going to run over the town. My mind, impatient for the moment which carries me to my sweet bride, feels all the intermediate time a void, which any adventure may fill up.   [*Exit.*

Fitz. Spite of my displeasure, I can hardly conceal from him his happiness!—Yet I will.—Julia must be punished. To vice and folly I am content to appear severe, but she ought not to have thought me so. I have not deserved this want of confidence, and must correct it. If I don't mistake, Pendragon is a fit instrument.—I'll take him home with me.—

Yes, yes, my young lady, you shall have a lover!—
Oh these headstrong girls!   [*Exit.*

ACT III.

SCENE I.—*Lord* SPARKLE's.

Lord SPARKLE *and* BEAUCHAMP *discovered at a
Table, on which are Pens, Paper, &c.* SPARKLE
superbly drest.

Spark. Poor George! and so thou wilt really be in
a few days in the bosom of the Atlantic!

   " Farewell to green fields and sweet groves,
   " Where Chloe engag'd my fond heart."——
                    [*Rises and comes forward.*
Hey for counterscarps, wounds, and victory!

Beauch. I accept your last words for my omen;
and now, in the true spirit of Homer's heroes, should
take my *congé*, and depart with its influence upon
me.

Spark. First take an office which I know must
charm you.—You admire Lady Bell Bloomer?

Beauch. Admire her!—Yes, by Heaven—
                         [*With great warmth.*

Spark. [*Interrupting.*] No heroics, dear George
—no heroics! They are totally out now—totally
out both in love and war.

Beauch. How, my lord!

Spark. Indifference!—that's the rule. We love,
hate, quarrel, and even fight, without suffering our
tranquillity to be incommoded:—nothing disturbs.—
The keenest discernment will discover nothing particular in the behaviour of lovers on the point of
marriage, nor in the married, whilst the articles of
separation are preparing.

Beauch. Disgustful apathy!——What becomes of

the energies of the heart in this wretched system?
Does it annihilate your feelings?

Spark. Oh no!—I feel, for instance, that I must
have Lady Bell Bloomer, and I feel curiosity to
know her sentiments of me, of which, however, I
have very little doubt: but all my art can't make her
serious ; she fences admirably, and keeps me at the
length of her foil.—To you she will be less on her
guard.

Beauch. Me! you surprise me, my lord! How
can I be of use in developing her ladyship's sentiments?

Spark. Why, by sifting them. When you talk of me,
see if she blushes. Mention some woman as one
whom I admire, and observe if she does not make
some spiteful remark on her shape, complexion, or
conduct ; provoke her to abuse me with violence, or
to speak of me with confusion—in either case I have
her.

Beauch. Your instructions are ample, my lord ;
but I do not feel myself equal to the embassy.

Spark. [*With pique.*] Your pardon, sir! You refuse then to oblige me?

Beauch. I cannot refuse you—my obligations to
your lordship make it impossible :—but of all mankind, I perhaps am the last you should have chosen
for the purpose.

Spark. Nay, prithee don't be ridiculous! It is
the last service you can do me; and you are the only
man whom I could entrust with so delicate a business.

Beauch. I accept it as a proof of your lordship's
confidence, and will discharge the commission faithfully.——[*Aside.*] It will at least give me an occasion to converse with Lady Bell, and to converse
with her on love.——Oh, my heart! how wilt thou
contain thy ardours in the trying moment?

[*Exit* BEAUCHAMP.

Spark. Ha! ha! ha! I am confirmed in my suspicions, that the fellow has had the vanity to indulge a passion for Lady Bell himself. Well, so much the better! the commission I have given him will sufficiently punish him for his presumption.

Enter a Servant.

Serv. Mrs. Kitty is below, my lord, Miss Manners's woman.

Spark. Ha!—Send her up, send her up. [*Exit Servant.*] I had began to give up that affair; but I think I won't neither. It will be rather a brilliant thing to have Lady Bell for a wife, and her friend for a mistress :—yes, it will be a point. I think I'll have the *eclat* of the thing. [*Enter* KITTY.]—Well, Kitty, what intelligence from the land of intrigue? What says the little frost-piece Julia?

Kitty. Oh, nothing new, my lord! She's as insensible as ever.—I makes orations all day long of your lordship's merit, and goodness, and fondness, and——

Spark. [*Staring.*] Merit, and goodness, and fondness! And don't you give a parenthesis to my sobriety, and my neatness too! Ha! ha! ha! you foolish little devil, I thought you knew better !—Tell her of my fashion, my extravagance ; that I play deepest at Weltjie's, am the best drest at the opera, and have half ruined myself by granting annuities to pretty girls.—Goodness and fondness are baits to catch old prudes, not blooming misses.

Kitty. What, my lord! is spreading out your faults the way to win a fair lady ?

Spark. Faults ! Thine is chambermaid's morality with a vengeance !—What have all my past lessons been thrown away upon thee, Innocence !—Have I not told thee, that the governing passion of the female mind is the rage of being envied? The most generous of them would like to break the hearts of

half a dozen of their friends by the preference given
to themselves. Go home again, good Kitty, and
con your lesson afresh : if you can pick up any sto-
ries of extravagance and gallantry, affix my name to
'em, and repeat them to your mistress.

Kitty. Then she'll tell 'em to Lady Bell, perhaps,
for a warning——

Spark. [*Drawling.*] For a warning, quotha!—My
devoirs to Lady Bell are of a different kind, and we
understand each other. I address her for a wife,
because she's the fashion ; and I address Julia for a
mistress, because 'tis the fashion to have mistresses
from higher orders than sempstresses and mantua-
makers.

Kitty. And is that your only reason, my lord, for
bribing me so high ?

Spark. Not absolutely. I have a pique against her
guardian, who, though he has the honour to be related to me, will not suffer me to draw on his banker
for a single guinea. His estates, indeed, he can't
deprive me of ; so as it can do no harm, I'll have
the *eclat* of affronting him with spirit.

Kitty. Oh Gemini ! I am glad to hear that ! I'd
do any thing to plague Mr. Fitzherbert, and can go
on now with a safe conscience.—He had like to have
lost me my place once, because he thought I was
flighty ; but I'll be up with him now.

Enter Servant.

Serv. Mr. Belville.   [*Exit.*

Enter BELVILLE.

Spark. My dear Belville ! [*Apart.*] Go, Kitty,
into that room, I'll speak to you presently.
                                   [*Exit* KITTY.
Welcome once more to the region of business and
pleasure !

Belv. I thank you. But pray, my lord, don't dismiss the lady.

Spark. The lady! Ha! ha! ha! That lady, sir, is a lady's gentlewoman, a'n't please ye. I suppose you have heard that I am going to marry Lady Bell Bloomer; we are the two most fashionable people in town, and in course must come together.

Belv. A clear deduction.

Spark. Now she has a friend, whom I mean at the same time to take for a mistress: won't that be a stroke, eh!

Belv. Decidedly. Your life is made up of strokes! Every thing with you, my lord, is a hit.

Spark. True, true! I detest a regular mechanical mode of doing things. Men of sense have one way of getting through life ; men of genius another.

Belv. Doubtless ; and the advantage lies with the men of genius, for to their genius are all their faults imputed ; nay, their faults are considered as the graceful meanderings of a mind too ethereal to be confined to the rules of common sense and decorum; —a mighty easy way of building reputation! ha! ha! ha! You are drest with infinite malice to-day, my lord.

Spark. Malice! not at all. The women now-a-days are neither caught by finery or person!—I am drest for court.—I was going to Westminster ; but I hear there is to be a presentation of misses to-day, and I would not for the world lose the dear creatures blushes on their first appearance ; for, faith, most of them will never blush again.—Will you go?

Belv. 'Tis too late to dress : besides, I have devoted this day to adventure. I am rambling through the town, discovering what new stars have appeared in the galaxy of beauty during my absence, and a dangerous progress it is! The rays of a pair of black eyes from a chariot in Pall-mall would have annihilated me, had not at the same instant two

beautiful blue ones from a window given a fillip to
my sinking spirits. A fine-turned ancle, whose polish shone through its neat silk stocking, encountered
me in St. James's-street ; but I was luckily relieved
by a little rosy mouth, that betrayed, with a deceitful smile, teeth most murderously white. A Gala-
tea darted by me on the right, whilst a Helen swam
along on the left :—in short, from such sweet be-
siegers nothing could have preserved me but the
sweeter charms of a beloved though absent fair one.
                                            [*Sighing.*

Spark. Now I never trouble my head about ab-
sentees!—I love beauty as well as any man ; but it
must be all in the present tense. Shall I set you
down any where? I must go.

Belv. No; but I see your writing things are here.
If you'll permit me, I'll pen a short note to Beauchamp on business I had forgot this morning, and
despatch it by a chairman.

Spark. To be sure. I penned a note ten minutes
since to my steward, to raise the poor devils' rents.
Upon my soul I pity 'em ! But how can it be otherwise, whilst one is obliged to wear fifty acres in a
suit, and the produce of a whole farm in a pair of
buckles? Adieu !   [*Exit singing.*

[*Whilst* SPARKLE *is speaking,* BELVILLE *seats himself,
and begins to write.*

Belv. [*Writing.*] Good morning!—My compliments to the ladies' blushes.

Enter KITTY; *passes* BELVILLE *in the front of the
stage.*

Kitty. So, so, his lordship has forgot me ! I must
go after him.

Belv. [*Coming forward.*] Hah! that's the confidante !—So, pretty one, whose chattels are you?

Kitty. My mistress's, sir.

Belv. And who is your mistress?

Kitty. A lady, sir.

Belv. And her name?

Kitty. That of her father, I take it.

Belv. Upon my word, your lady has a very brilliant servant !—Is she as clever as you are?

Kitty. Why, not quite, I think, or she would not keep me to eclipse her.

Belv. Bravo ! I wish I knew her. Will you tell me her name?

Kitty. Can you spell?

Belv. Yes.

Kitty. Why then you'll find it in the four and twenty letters.   [*Going.*

Belv. [*Catching her.*] Nay, by Heaven, you have raised my curiosity !

Kitty. Poh ! what signifies asking me? You know well enough who she is.—I heard you and Lord Sparkle talking about her. Let me go ; for I am going to carry a message to Mr. Fitzherbert.

Belv. Mr. Fitzherbert !

Kitty. Aye, her guardian.

Belv. Her guardian ! What, Fitzherbert, of Cambridgeshire?

Kitty. Yes ; and if you want to know more, he's the crossest old wretch that ever breathed. You'll find him out by that description ; and so your servant !   [*Exit* KITTY.

Belv. Fitzherbert's ward ! and this creature her servant ! and Lord Sparkle plotting to get her for a mistress!—I am astonish'd !—the very lady he this morning offered for my bride!—Well,—I must find Fitzherbert immediately.——Lord Sparkle will perhaps think me guilty of a breach of honour.—The imputation I must incur, that I may not be really guilty of a breach of humanity and of gratitude.

[*Exit* BELVILLE.

SCENE II.—*Lady* BELL BLOOMER'S.

Enter FITZHERBERT, *followed by a Servant.*

Fitz. Tell Miss Manners I am here. [*Exit Servant.*]—I cannot, perhaps, be seriously angry with Julia; but I must take some revenge on her disobedience, before I acquaint her with the felicity that attends her. Come in, young Cornish, pray!

Enter PENDRAGON.

Pen. What, does the lady live in this fine house?

Fitz. Yes:—but pray observe that I don't engage she shall be smitten with you. I can go no farther than to introduce you; the rest must depend on the brilliancy of your manners.

Pen. Oh leave me alone for that!—I knew how 'twould be, if I once shewed myself in London. If she has a long purse I'll whisk her down to Cornwall, jockey Lord Sparkle, and have the borough myself.

Fitz. A man of spirit, I see!

Pen. Oh, as to my spirit, that nobody ever doubted!—I have beat our exciseman, and gone to law with the parson; and to shew you that I did not leave my spirit in the country, since I came to London I have fined a hackney coachman for abuse.

Fitz. Very commendable!—But here comes the lady!

Enter JULIA.

Mr. Pendragon, this is my ward, who, I am sure, will give your addresses all the encouragement I wish them.

Pen. Servant, ma'am! [*Aside.*]—She looks plaguy glum!

Julia. I can scarcely support myself! [*Aside.*

Fitz. Pray, my dear, speak to Mr. Pendragon!—
You seem greatly confused.

Pen. Oh, sir, I understand it! Young ladies will
look confused and embarrassed, and all that sort of
thing, on these occasions; but we men of the world
are up to all that.

Julia. Heavens! is it to such a being I should
have been sacrificed!   [*Aside.*

Pen. I see your ward is one of the modest diffident
ones: I am surprised at that—bred in high life.

Fitz. Oh, now and then you find a person of that
cast in the best company!—but they soon get over
it.

Pen. Yes, formerly I used to blush, and be modest, and all that sort of thing; but if any one
ever catches me modest again, I'll give 'em my
estate for a pilchard.

Julia. Then it seems impossible———pardon me,
sir! [*to* FITZHERBERT] that a union can take place
between you and me; for I place modesty amongst
the elegancies of manners, and think it absolutely
necessary to the character of a gentleman.

Fitz. Well done, Julia! [*Aside.*]—Fie upon you,
to treat my friend with such asperity!

Pen. O leave her to me, sir; she's ignorant, but
I shall teach her. There are three things, miss, only
necessary to the character of a gentleman: a good
air, good assurance, and good teeth.   [*Grinning.*

Julia. [*To* FITZHERBERT.] Doesn't his list want
good manners, sir?

Pen. Oh, no, ma'am! If you had said good
taste, it would have been nearer the thing; but even
that is unnecessary.—A gentleman's friends can
furnish his house and choose his books, and his pictures, and he can learn to criticise them by heart.—
Nothing is so easy as to criticise;—people do it
continually.

Fitz. You see, Mr. Pendragon has information,

Julia.—I'll leave you a few moments, that he may unfold himself to advantage ; and remember, if you refuse the man I design for your husband you lose me. Keep it up with spirit ! I'll wait for you below. [*To* PENDRAGON.]——Now shall impertinence and disobedience correct each other !

[*Exit* FITZHERBERT.

Pen. Now to strike her with my superior ease ! [*Aside*]—So, miss, your guardian, I think, has a mind that we shall—in the vulgar speech—marry!

Julia. Well, sir ; but are you not frightened at your approach to such a state !—Do you know what belongs to the character of a husband ?

Pen. What belongs to it ? Aye ! Do you know what belongs to being a wife ?

Julia. Yes ; I guess that to your wife will belong ill-humour with you at home—shame with you abroad ;—in her face forced smiles—in her heart hidden thorns.

Pen. The devil ! What, you have found your tongue, ma'am ! Oh, oh, I shall have a fine time on't, I guess, when our connection begins !

Julia. Our connection !—Pray, sir, drop the idea !—I protest to you, that were it possible for me to become your wife I should be the most wretched of women.

Pen. O no, you wou'dn't ! I hardly know a wife who is not wretched.

Julia. Unfeeling man ! Would you presume to enter into a state, to the happiness of which, union of soul, delicacy of sentiment, and all the elegant attention of polished manners are necessary and indispensable ?

Pen. What's all that ? Union of soul ! sentiment ! attentions !—That's not life, I'm sure.

Julia. I am not able to conceive by what witchcraft Mr. Fitzherbert has been blinded to the weakness of your head and the turpitude of your heart.

—Tell him, sir, there is not a fate I would not prefer to that of being united to a man whose vice is
the effect of folly, and whose folly is as hateful even
as his vice.   [*Exit* JULIA.

Pen. Yes, yes, I'll tell, depend on't!—Egad, she's
a spirit!—So much the better, more pleasure in
taming her!—A meek wife cheats a man of his
rights, and deprives him of the pleasure of exacting
her obedience.——Let me see!——Vice—folly—
impudence—ignorance.—Ignorance too!
                              [*Exit* PENDRAGON.

Re-enter JULIA.

Julia. What have I done?   I dare not now see my
guardian!   His displeasure will kill me.   Oh, Belville, where art thou?   Come and shield thy unhappy bride!—What steps can I take?

Enter KITTY.

Kitty. Dear ma'am, I'm so grieved to see you so
unhappy!   If I had such a cross old guardian I'd
run away from him.

Julia. The very thought which that instant presented itself to my mind!—Have you not told me
that some relation of yours has lodgings?

Kitty. Yes, ma'am; the most elegantest in London.

Julia. I don't want elegant apartments; but I wish
for a short time to be concealed in some family of
reputation.

Kitty. To be sure, ma'am, 'tis the most prudent
thing you can do.

Julia. And yet my heart fails me.

Kitty. Oh, ma'am, don't hesitate!   I'll go and
pack up a few things, and call a coach and be off, before Lady Bell comes from court.

Julia. I fear 'tis a wrong step; and yet what other
can I take?   I dare not reveal my marriage without

the permission of my husband; and till his arrival I must avoid both a guardian's anger and the addresses of a lover.——The honour of Belville would be insulted, should I permit them to be repeated. [*Aside.*] [*Exit* JULIA.

Kitty. I know not what she means, but there is some mystery I find. So there should be!——If ladies had not mysteries a chambermaid's place would be hardly worth keeping.—I have mysteries too, and she shall have their explanation from Lord Sparkle. [*Exit.*

SCENE III.—CLARINDA'S *House.*

Enter Lady BELL *meeting* CLARINDA.

Lady Bell. Ha! ha! ha! my dear creature, what an *embarras!* Driving swiftly through the streets, Lady Whipcord dashed upon us in her flaming phaeton and six, gave a monstrous big Newmarket word to my poor fellows, and with infinite dexterity entangled the traces. It happened near your door; so I have taken shelter with you, and left her ladyship to settle the dispute with my coachman, ha! ha! ha! But why were you not at court to-day?

Cla. I had a teazing head-ach: but pray, tell me what happened there.—[*Aside.*] Deuce take her, she looks as well as ever!

Lady Bell. Oh, the ladies, as usual, brilliant—nothing so flat as the men! The horrid English custom ruins them for conversation. They make themselves members of clubs in the way of business, and members of parliament in the way of amusement: all their passions are reserved for the first, and all their wit for the last.

Cla. 'Tis better in Paris.

Lady Bell. Oh, 'tis quite another thing! Whilst we awkwardly copy the follies of the Parisians, we absurdly omit the charming part of their character.

Devoted to elegance, they catch their opinions, their wit, and their *bon mots* from the mouths of the ladies. 'Tis in the drawing-room of madame the duchess the marquis learns his politics ; whilst the sprightly countess dispenses taste and philosophy to a circle of bishops, generals, and abbés.

Cla. All that may be just; yet I am mistaken if you have not found one Englishman to reconcile you to the manners of the rest.   Lord Sparkle, for in-stance—your ladyship thinks, I'm sure, that he has wit at will.

Lady Bell. Oh yes, quite at will!——His wit, like his essence bottle, is a collection of all that is poignant in a thousand flowers ; and like that, is most useful when he himself is most insipidly vacant.

Cla. With such sentiments I wonder you can suf-fer his addresses.

Lady Bell. What can I do?   The man is so much the fashion, and I shall be so much envied.——Why you know, my dear, for instance—you'd be inclined to stick a poisoned nosegay in my bosom if I should take him.

Cla. Ha! ha! ha! ridiculous!   Believe me, ma-dam, I shall neither prepare a bouquet, nor invoke a fiery shower to grace your nuptials.

Lady Bell. [*Aside.*] No, your showers would be tears, I fancy.——Here he comes !

Cla. Hah! Lord Sparkle!   Your ladyship's ac-cident was fortunate.   [*Sneering.*

Enter Lord SPARKLE.

Spark. Heavens! Lady Bell! your horses fly like the doves of Venus.   I followed you from St. James's ;—but my poor earth-born cattle wou'dn't keep pace with yours.

Cla. Oh, don't complain!   If her ladyship won the race, you see she stopped for you at the goal.

Spark. Charming Miss Belmour, what an enlivening intimation ! Where was your ladyship on Thursday ? You would have found excellent food for your satire at Mrs. Olio's : We had all the law ladies from Lincoln's-inn, a dozen gold velvets from Bishopsgate, with the wives and daughters of half the M. D.'s and LL. D.'s in town.

Lady Bell. Oh, my entertainment was quite as good as yours ! We were in Brook-street, at Lady Laurel's, and found her surrounded by her literati of all denominations.——We had masters of art and misses of science :——on one hand an essayist, on the other a moralist :—— there a poetaster, here a translator ;—— in that corner a philosopher, in the other a compiler of magazines.——Tropes, epigrams, and syllogisms flew like sky-rockets in every direction, till the ambition of pre-eminence lighted the flame of controversy, when they gave each other the lie literary with infinite spirit and decorum.

Spark. Excellent ; I'll repeat every word in a place where it will be remembered, and the satire enjoyed.

Cla. In that hope your lordship may safely knock at every door in the street:—satire is welcome every where.

Lady Bell. Yes, if it will bear a laugh—that's the grand art of conversation. They pretend we are fond of slander ; but rob scandal of its laugh, and 'twould soon be banished to the second table, for the amusement of butlers and chambermaids.

Spark. Indeed ! Then I believe half our acquaintance would go down stairs to the second table too !—they'd think their servants had the best of the dish. [*Enter a Servant, gives Lord* SPARKLE *a letter, and exit.*

Spark. [*Reads it aside.*] Julia ! astonishing !—So sudden in your movements, Mrs. Kitty ?—[*Turning to the ladies.*] This vulgar thing called business is the greatest evil in life ! It destroys our most brilliant hours, and is fit only for younger brothers and humble cousins.—Miss Belmour, I must tear myself away. Shall I attend your ladyship to your carriage?

Lady Bell. If you please!—Miss Belmour, " I must tear myself away;"—but you'll shine upon us at night.   [*Exeunt Lord* SPARKLE *and Lady* BELL.

Cla. Shine upon you at night!—That, I know, you are insolent enough to believe impossible.—— What can I think of her sentiments for Lord Sparkle?   Sometimes I believe 'tis a mere attachment of vanity on both sides.—That reserved creature, Bèauchamp, is in his confidence; but he leaves town this very day, and I shall have no opportunity of conversing with him. [*Muses.*] There is but one chance—going to visit him.——But how can I possibly do that? Deuce take him! If he had a library, one might go to look at his books.   Well, I don't care, go I will; and if I can't invent an excuse, I'll put a good face upon the matter, and go without one.—[*Going.*] I should expire if my visit should be discovered.   Poh! I must risque every thing!—To be bold, is sometimes to be right. [*Exit.*

ACT IV.

SCENE I.—*An Apartment at Lady* BELL'S.

Enter Lady BELL, *followed by her Maid.*

Lady Bell. Miss Manners gone out in a hackney-coach, and no message left!

Maid. No, madam.

Lady Bell. Very strange!

Maid. Mr. Beauchamp has been waiting almost an hour for your ladyship's return.

Lady Bell. Mr. Beauchamp!—Here, go and put

some otto of roses in that handkerchief. [*Exit Maid.*] Now, shall I admit him, or not? This formal waiting looks very like formal business. Poh, I hate that!—I suppose he has at length vanquished his modesty, and is come to tell me that—that—Well, I vow I won't hear him.—Yes, I will. I long to know the style in which these reserv'd men make love.—To what imprudence would my heart betray me? Yet I may surely indulge myself in hearing him speak of love; in hearing, probably for the first time, its genuine language. [*Enter Maid, and presents the handkerchief.*] Tell Mr. Beauchamp I am here. [*Exit Maid.*] Now, how shall I receive him? It will be intolerable to be formal.—[*Takes her fan from her pocket and traverses the stage, humming a tune.—Enter* BEAUCHAMP.] Oh, Mr. Beauchamp, this is the luckiest thing!—I have had ten disputes to-day about the figures in my fan; and you shall decide 'em. Is that beautiful nymph a flying Daphne, or an Atalanta?

Beauch. [*Looking at her fan.*] From the terror of the eye, madam, and the swiftness of her step, it must be a Daphne. I think Atalanta's head would be more at variance with her feet; and, whilst she flies, her eye would be invitingly turn'd on her pursuers.

Lady Bell. I think you are right!——Yes—there does want the kind, inviting glance, to be sure.

Beauch. What a misfortune to a lover! I know one to whom your ladyship appears the disdainful Daphne.——How happy! could he behold in your eye the encouragement of Atalanta's!

Lady Bell. [*Aside.*] Mercy! for so bashful a man that's pretty plain.

Beauch. This is probably the last visit I can make you before I leave England:—will your ladyship permit me, before I leave it, to acquaint you that there is a man whose happiness depends on your favour? [*Agitated.*

Lady Bell. So, now he's going to be perplexing again! [*Aside.*]—A man whose happiness depends on me, Mr. Beauchamp? [*Looking on her fan.*

Beauch. Yes, madam!—and—and—[*aside.*] I cannot go on—Why did I accept a commission in which success would destroy me?

Lady Bell. How evidently this is the first time he ever made love! [*Aside.*]—The man seems to have chosen a very diffident advocate in you, sir.

Beauch. 'Tis more than diffidence, madam, my task is painful.

Lady Bell. Ay, I thought so! You have taken a brief in a cause you don't like; I could plead it better myself.

Beauch. I feel the reproach.

Lady Bell. 'Tis difficult for you, perhaps, to speak in the third person?——Try it in the first. Suppose, now, ha! ha! only suppose, I say! for the jest's sake, that you yourself have a passion for me, and then try—how you can plead it.

Beauch. [*Kneeling.*] Thus—thus would I plead it, and swear, that thou art dear to my heart as fame, and honour!—To look at thee is rapture; to love thee, though without hope,—felicity!

Lady Bell. Oh, I thought I should bring him to the point at last! [*Aside.*

Beauch. [*Rising, aside.*] To what dishonesty have I been betray'd!—Thus, madam, speaks my friend, through my lips;—'tis thus he pleads his passion.

Lady Bell. Provoking! [*Aside.*]—What friend is this, sir, who is weak enough to use the language of another to explain his heart?

Beauch. Lord Sparkle.

Lady Bell. Lord Sparkle! Was it for him you knelt? [*He bows to her.*]—Then, sir, I must inform you, that the liberty you have taken——[*Aside.*]

Heavens, how do I betray myself!—Tell me, sir, on
your honour, do you wish to succeed in pleading
the passion of Lord Sparkle?

Beauch. [*Hesitating.*] My obligations to his lordship—our relationship—the confidence he has re-
pos'd in me—

Lady Bell. Stop, sir! I, too, will repose confidence in you, and confess that there is a man whom
I sometimes suspect not to be indifferent to me ;—
but 'tis not Lord Sparkle! Tell him so ;—and tell
him that—that—tell him what you will.

Beauch. Heavens, what does she mean! What
language is this her eye speaks ? [*Aside.*

Lady Bell. Do you visit me this evening? Here
will be many of my friends ; and you shall then see
me in the presence of the man my heart prefers.

> [BEAUCHAMP *bows, and goes to the door; then
> returns, advances towards Lady* BELL, *makes
> an effort to speak; finds it impossible, then bows,
> and exit.*

Heavens! what necessity have lovers for words?
What persuasion in that bashful irresolution! Now,
shall I let him quit England, or not?—What! give
up a coronet and Lord Sparkle for a cockade and
Beauchamp! Preposterous! says Vanity.—But what
says Love? I don't exactly know; but I'll examine
their separate claims, and settle them with all the
casuistry of four and twenty. [*Exit.*

SCENE II.—*Lord* SPARKLE'S *House.*

Enter JULIA *and* KITTY.

Julia. I am so agitated with this rash step, that
I can hardly breathe! [*throwing herself into a chair.*]
Why did you confirm me in my imprudent resolu-
tion?

Kitty. Imprudent! I'm sure, ma'am, 'tis very

prudent, and very right, that a young lady like you should not be snubb'd, and have her inclination thwarted by an ill-natur'd positive old guardian.

Julia. [*Looking round.*] What apartments! and the hall we came through had an air much beyond a lodging-house! 'Tis all too fine for my purpose; I want to be private.

Kitty. Oh dear ma'am, you may be as private here as you please! [*A rapping at the door.*] There's my cousin come home, I dare say; I'll send her to you, and then you may settle terms.   [*Exit.*

Julia. I feel I have done wrong, and yet I am so distracted, I know not how I could have done otherwise. [*Enter Lord* SPARKLE.] Heavens! Lord Sparkle here!

Spark. Yes, my lovely Julia, here I am; and upon my soul, if you knew the engagements I have broke for the happiness, you would be gratified.

Julia. Gratified! I am astonish'd! equally astonish'd at your being here, and at your strange address.

Spark. Astonish'd at my being here! Why, to be sure, it is not usual to find a man of fashion in his own house; but when I heard that you were in my house, how could I do less than fly home?

Julia. Home! Your own house! What can all this mean?—

Spark. Mean! Love—gallantry—joy, and ever-new delights.

Julia. Oh! I am betray'd! Where is my wicked servant?

Spark. Poh, never think of her:—Why all this flutter, my sweet girl? You have only chang'd guardians; and you shall find, that being ward to a young man of fashion and spirit, is a very different thing from——

Julia. Oh Heavens! what will become of me?

Spark. Nay, this is quite ridiculous, after having

R

fled to my protection. I feel myself highly honoured by your confidence, and will take care to
deserve it.

Julia. Why do I remain here an instant?

[*Going towards the door.*

Spark. [*Holding her.*] This is downright rudeness!
But you young ladies are so fickle in your resolutions—But, be assured, after having chosen my
house for your asylum, I shall not be so impolite as
to suffer you to seek another.

Julia. Oh wretched artifice! You know, sir,
that your house and you I would have fled from to
the farthest corner of——[*Enter* BEAUCHAMP.]—
Oh, Mr. Beauchamp, save me!—I have been basely
betrayed!—

Beauch. [*Astonished.*] Betrayed!—Miss Manners!
Yes, madam, I will protect you at every hazard.

Spark. Come, none of your antique virtues,
George, pray! This is a piece of *badinage* of the
eighteenth century, and you can't possibly understand it!—Miss Manners chose to pay me a visit,
and I desire you'll leave us.

Julia. My lord, how dare you thus trifle with a
woman's honour?

Beauch. Be not alarm'd, madam, I will defend
you.

Spark. [*Taking him aside.*] Poh, prithee, George,
be discreet: This is all female artifice.—You popp'd
upon us, and this is a salver for her reputation.

Beauch. Pardon me, my lord! In believing you,
in opposition to the evidence of this young lady's
terrors, I may be guilty of an irremeable error.

Spark. Nay, if you are serious, sir, how dare you
break in upon my privacy?

Beauch. This is not a time to answer you, my
lord! The business that brought me here, I am indebted to; I should not else have prevented your
base designs.

Spark. Base designs, Mr. Beauchamp!

Beauch. Yes, Lord Sparkle.—Shall I attend you home, madam?

Julia. Oh, sir, I dare not go there! I fled from Lady Bell's, when I was betrayed into this inhuman man's power.—Convey me to some place where I may have leisure to reflect.

Spark. And do you think, Mr. Beauchamp, I shall put up with this!—Remember, sir——

Beauch. [*Interrupting.*] Yes, my lord, that, as a man, it is my duty to protect endanger'd innocence; that, as a soldier, it is part of the essence of my character; and, whilst I am grateful to you for the commission I have the honour to bear, I will not disgrace it, in suffering myself to be intimidated by your frowns.   [*Exit* BEAUCHAMP, *leading* JULIA.

Spark. So!—so!—so!—an ancient hero in the house of a modern man of fashion!—Alexander in the tent of Darius!—Scipio and the fair Parthenia! The fellow has not an idea of any morals but those in use during the Olympiads.

Enter Servant.

Serv. Mr. Pendragon and his sister, my lord.

Spark. Who?   [*With an air of disgust.*

Serv. Mr. and Miss Pendragon.

Spark. Then carry 'em to the housekeeper's room!——Give 'em jellies and plum-cake, and tell 'em—[*Enter* PENDRAGON, *leading* SOPHY.] Oh, my dear Miss Pendragon, you honour me.—But I am the most unlucky man on earth!—I am obliged, upon business of infinite consequence, to be at Whitehall within five minutes.

Pen. But, first, my lord, you must settle a little business here with Miss Pendragon.

Sophy. I tell you, Bobby, I'll speak myself;—and as few words are best, pray, my lord, what do you mean by treating me in this manner?

Spark. I shall be miserable beyond bearing, if any treatment of mine has incurred your displeasure.

Sophy. Well, now you talk of being miserable, you have softened my heart at once: but pray, my lord, is it fashionable for people on the terms you and I are to keep asunder?

Spark. What the devil can the girl mean? [*Aside.*

Sophy. Never even write!—no billets!—no bribing the maid to slip notes into my hand!——Why you don't even complain, though 'tis five days since you saw me.

Spark. Complain! I am sure I have been exceedingly wretched.

Sophy. Then why did you not tell me so? Why, that's the very thing I wanted: if I had known you had been wretched, I should have been happy.

Pen. Well, I see I shall lose an opportunity here! —I came to challenge you, my lord.

Spark. Challenge me!

Pen. Yes:—Miss Pendragon told me she was dissatisfied:——then, says I, I'll demand satisfaction: ——and I didn't care if things had gone a little farther; for to call out a lord would be a feather in my cap as long as I live.——However, you are agreed.

Sophy. Do be quiet, Bobby:—we are not agreed: —I have heard nothing of settlements yet; nothing of jewels.

Spark. My dear ma'am, you are pleased to amuse yourself.

Sophy. Why, my lord, those things must be all settled before-hand, you know.

Spark. Before what?

Sophy. What! before our marriage, my lord.

Spark. Marriage! ha! ha! ha!

Sophy. Hey-day! Will you pretend that you did not intend to marry me, when I can prove that you have courted me from twenty instances?

Spark. Indeed!

Pen. Ay, that she can: instances as striking as your lordship's red heels.—Come, Miss Pendragon, your proofs? I'll support 'em.

Sophy. Why, in the first place, my lord, you once placed a nosegay in my bosom, and said, " Oh! I wish I were these happy roses!"—the very speech that Sir Harry Hargrave made to Miss Woodville.—Another time you said, " I was a most bewitching and adorable girl!"—exactly what Colonel Finch said to Lady Lucy Lustre.—Another time you said, " How would a coronet become those shining tresses!"—the very speech of Lord Rosehill to Miss Danvers; and these couples were every one married.

Spark. Married! I never heard of 'em.—Who are they? Where the devil do they live?

Pen. [*Strutting up to him.*] Live!—Why, in our county, to be sure.

Sophy. No, no, Bobby; in The Reclaim'd Rake, and The Constant Lovers, and Sir Charles Grandison, and Roderick Random, and——

Pen. Yes, sir; they live at Random, with Sir Charles Grandison.—Now d'ye know 'em?

Spark. Ha! ha! ha! you are a charming little lawyer; [*to* SOPHY.] and might, perhaps, establish your proofs for precedents, if Sir Charles Grandison was on the bench: yet I never heard of his being made Chief-Justice, though I never thought him fit for any thing else.

Pen. What the devil's this?——What, did not you bring all those fine proofs from fashionable life? —And are you such a fool as not to understand what we call common-place?

Sophy. Common-place!

Pen. Yes; we persons of elegant life use the figure hyperbole.——

Sophy. Hyperbole! What's that?

Pen. Why, that's as much as to say, a stretch.

Sophy. A stretch! What, then, you have been mocking me, my lord?

Spark. Not in the least; I shall be the happiest man existing to, to—[*aside.*] Egad, I must take care of my phrases:——I mean that I shall be always, and upon all occasions, your most devoted, *tres humblement serviteur.*——Were there ever two such bumpkins!   [*Exit.*

Sophy. What's he gone? Oh! Villain! Monster! I am forsaken! Oh! I am rejected!——All Cornwall will know it!   [*Crying.*

Pen. Tin-mines and all. But don't ye cry, Miss Pendragon—don't ye cry!   [*Sobbing.*

Sophy. Oh! I am rejected!

Pen. I am glad on't, with all my heart. I'll challenge him yet, and they won't know in Cornwall exactly how it was.—They'll hear that a lord fought about ye, and all that sort of thing; and whether for ye, or against ye, 'twill be much the same.

Sophy. But will you challenge him, really, Bobby?

Pen. Upon honour!——I admire the claw of the thing. Egad, Sophy, I'm glad he's forsaken thee: now my character will be finished. A man can't shew his face in company, till he has stood shot, and fired his pistol in the air.

Sophy. In the air! If you don't fire it through him——

Pen. Oh, never fear! I'll do all that sort of thing. Come along! I'll go home directly, and practise at the hen-coop in the yard. I'll fire through one end, and you shall hold your calash against the other; and if I don't hit it, say I'm no marksman.

[*Exit* Pendragon, *with* Sophy *under his arm.*

SCENE III.—Beauchamp's *Lodgings.*

Enter Beauchamp *and* Julia.

Beauch. I intreat your pardon for conducting you to my own lodgings;—but here, madam, you will be safe, 'till you determine how to act.—What are your commands for me?

Julia. Oh, Mr. Beauchamp, I have no commands—I have no designs!—I have been very imprudent; I am still more unhappy.

Beauch. Shall I acquaint Mr. Fitzherbert?

Julia. It was to avoid him that I left Lady Bell.—I have reasons that make it impossible to see Mr. Fitzherbert now.

Beauch. Is there no other friend?

Julia. O yes, I have one friend:—were he here, all my difficulties would vanish!—It may seem strange, Mr. Beauchamp, but I expect that you believe—Heavens! here's company! [*looking at the wing.*] 'Tis Miss Belmour—the last woman on earth whom I would trust!—Where can I go?

Beauch. Miss Belmour! Very odd!—But pray be not uneasy.—That room, madam, if you will condescend—   [*She rushes through the door.*

Enter Clarinda, *laughing.*

Cla. Ha! ha! ha! I expect your gravity to be amazingly discomposed at so hardy a visit; but I took it very ill that you did not design to call upon me before your departure; and so, as I was passing your door, I stopped, in mere frolic, to inquire the cause.

Beauch. You do me infinite honour, madam: I am thankful that I fail'd in my attention, since it has procur'd me so distinguish'd a favour.

Cla. Oh, your most obedient:—You are going to leave England for a long while. You'll find us all in different situations, probably, on your return.—

Your friend, Lord Sparkle, for instance—I am inform'd that he is really to marry Lady Bell Bloomer;
but I don't believe it—do you?

Beauch. 'Tis impossible, madam, for me——

Cla. Poh! poh! impossible! Such friends as you
are, I suppose, keep nothing from one another.—
We women can't exist without a confidante: and, I
dare say, you men are full as communicative. Not
that it is any thing to me; but as I have a prodigious regard for Lady Bell—

Belv. [*Behnd.*] Beauchamp! Beauchamp!

Cla. Heaven and earth, how unlucky! Here's
some man! I am the nicest creature breathing in
my reputation: what will he think? I'll run into
this room.   [*Runs toward the door.*

Beauch. [*Preventing her.*] Pardon me, madam, you
cannot enter there.

Cla. [*Pushing at the door*] I must—Oh—oh! the
door is held, sir.

Beauch. My dear madam, I am infinitely sorry
for the accident; but suppose——suppose, I say,
ma'am, that a friend of mine has been in a duel, and
conceal'd in that room.

Cla. Ridiculous! I saw the corner of a hoop and
a white sattin petticoat:—is that the dress of your
duelling friends? I will go in.—[*struggling.*] So!
[*flinging away spitefully.*] 'tis too late!

Enter BELVILLE.

Belv. So! so! so! I beg your pardon. How could
you be so indiscreet, Beauchamp? Though a young
soldier, I thought you knew enough of generalship
to be prepar'd for a surprise.

Cla. Oh, so he was; but not for two surprises.—
One has happened already, and a hasty retreat the
consequence.

Beauch. Believe me, Belville—I am infinitely concerned—[*to* CLARINDA.]

Cla. Oh! I detest your impertinent concern! Keep it for the lady in the other room.

Belv. A lady in the other room too! Hey-day! Beauchamp, who would have suspected—

Beauch. 'Tis all a mistake! The lady in the next room—But, prithee, go.—

Belv. Only tell me if you have seen Fitzherbert. I have been seeking him this hour, on business of the utmost consequence.

Beauch. I have not; but, about this time, you'll find him at home.

Belv. Enough: Miss Belmour, pray suffer no concern; depend on my honour.—Beauchamp [*taking him aside*], who is the lady in the other room?

Beauch. Had I meant you to have known, that room would have been unnecessary.

[BELVILLE *seems still inquisitive;* BEAUCHAMP *draws him towards the wing.*

Cla. Now do I die to know who it can be. Indeed, 'tis necessary for my own sake.—Whilst she has been hid, I have been exposed; and who knows what the creature may say? I'll try once more. She has my secret, and I'll have hers.

[*Forces open the door.*

Julia. [*Rushes out.*] Belville! [*running towards him.*

Belv. [*Starting back.*] Julia!

Cla. Miss Manners!—Ha! ha! ha!

Julia. Oh, Belville, throw me not from you!

Belv. Astonishing!

Cla. Oh, charming! The modest Julia, and the reserv'd Beauchamp! Ha! ha! ha!—But, Mr. Belville, how came you of this sober party? ha! ha! ha!

Julia. Speak to me!

Cla. Now, Mr. Beauchamp, you know the purport of my visit.——I had heard that Miss Manners has been seen to visit you, and, not being willing to trust to such a report, was resolved, if possible, to discover the truth.

Belv. [*To* JULIA.] Wretched woman!

Julia. [*To* CLARINDA.] Barbarous creature! Oh hear me, I conjure you!

Belv. Hear you!—No, madam;—and if my contempt, my hatred, my——oh!——You, sir, I must speak to in another place;—yet, perhaps, you were not acquainted that——What would I say!——The word which I have pronounced with rapture, choaks me. From this moment farewell! [*To* JULIA.]
                                        [*Exit* BELVILLE.

Beauch. What can I think of all this?

Julia. Oh sir!

Beauch. Permit me, madam, to ask if you have long known Mr. Belville?

Julia. Yes, too long.

Cla. Oh, oh, too long!—Aye, young ladies should be cautious how they form acquaintance. For my part—But you look ill, child!—[*taking her by the hand.*] Well, I have no hard heart; I can pity your weakness, Miss;—I won't upbraid you now.—My coach waits;—shall I conduct you home?

Julia. Yes, to Lady Bell——to Lady Bell——I am very ill!

Cla. Adieu, Mr. Beauchamp! This has been an unlucky frolic.—'Tis amazing, you grave people can be so careless. [*Exit* JULIA *and* CLARINDA.

Beauch. An unlucky frolic, indeed! And I am so thoroughly confounded, that I know not what judgment to form of the adventure.—I always considered Miss Manners as a pattern of delicacy and virtue; nor dare I now, spite of circumstances, think otherwise.

Enter Lord SPARKLE.

Spark. So, so, Signor Quixote! What so soon lost your prize! Aye, you see quarrelling for these virtuous women is as unprofitable as the assault of the windmills.—Have you seen Lady Bell in my behalf?

Beauch. Lady Bell, my lord! Why, sure, 'tis impossible after your attempt on Miss Manners—

Spark. Psha! that is a stroke in my favour. Women like to receive the devoirs of those whom others of their sex have found so dangerous. What did you discover of Lady Bell's sentiment towards me?

Beauch. I meant to have given the intelligence softened, but the agitations of my mind make it impracticable; I must, therefore, inform you in one word, Lady Bell Bloomer's choice is made, and that choice has not fallen upon your lordship.

Spark. Then I must inform you in two words, that I am convinced you are mistaken. But your reasons, sir, your reasons?

Beauch. Her ladyship furnished me with a decisive one: she acknowledged a pre-engagement; and added, if I visited her this evening, I should see her in the presence of the man her heart prefers.

Spark. [*Laughing violently.*] Excellent! charming ingenuity! Ha! ha! ha! the kindest, softest message that ever woman fram'd; and you, like the sheep loaden with the golden fleece, bore it, insensible of its value.—Ha! ha! ha! you can't see through the pretty artifice?

Beauch. No, really.

Spark. Why, 'tis I who am to be there; there by particular invitation. You'll see her in my presence; and this was her pretty mysterious way of informing me that I am the object of her choice.

Beauch. Indeed!

Spark. Without a doubt: but you deep people are the dullest fellows at a hint; a man of half your parts would have seen it.—But I am satisfied, and shall go to her rout in brilliant spirits.—You shall come, and see my triumph confirmed.—Come, you rogue, and see the lovely widow in the presence of the man her heart prefers.—Poor George! You must have been cursedly stupid, not to have conceiv'd that I was the person.   [*Exit.*

Beauch. Yes, I will come.—Oh vanity! I had dared to explain—Yes, I construed the sweet confusion—Oh, I blush at my own arrogance! Lord Sparkle must be right.—Well, this night decides it. —Narrowly will I watch each tone and look, to discover——Oh!—ever blest!—he whom her heart prefers!   [*Exit.*

ACT V.

SCENE I.—*An Apartment at Lady* BELL'S. *A Table, with Candles.*

Enter Lady BELL *and Servant.*

Lady Bell. Are the tables placed in the outer room?

Serv. Yes, ma'am, all but the Pharaoh-table.

Lady Bell. Then carry that there too.——I positively will not have a table in the drawing-room. ——[*Exit Servant.*] Those who play don't visit me, but the card-tables; and where they find them is very immaterial.—Let me see! For whist, Sir James Jennet—Lady Ponto—Mrs. Lurchem, and Lady Carmine.——For Pharaoh, Mrs. Evergreen, Lord Dangle, Sir Harry—Hey-dey!

Enter CLARINDA *and* JULIA.

Cla. Come, child, don't faint!—You had more cause for terror half an hour ago.

Lady Bell. Heavens, Julia! where have you been?

Cla. Ay, that's a circumstance you would not have known, but for an accident; and I am very sorry it fell to my lot to make the discovery.

Lady Bell. [*Taking* JULIA's *hand.*] Speak, my love.

Julia. Miss Belmour will tell you all she knows.—
I am too wretched!

Cla. Nay, as to what I know,—I know very little.
—I can tell what I saw, indeed.—Having received
intimations not quite consonant to one's notions of
decorum, I pretended a frolic, and called on Mr.
Beauchamp, and there I found this lady concealed.

Lady Bell. Heavens, Julia! 'Tis impossible.

Cla. Nay, she can't attempt to deny what I myself
saw.—Other discoveries had liked to have been
made too; but Miss Manners may explain them
herself; for I see your rooms begin to fill.—I shall
report that your ladyship is a little indisposed, as an
excuse for your not immediately appearing.

[*Exit* CLARINDA.

Lady Bell. [*With a countenance of terror.*] Julia!
You at Mr. Beauchamp's!

Julia. Lady Bell, though I have acted rashly, and
was indeed found there, I am not the guilty creature
you imagine.—I am married!—I will no longer conceal it!   [*Bursting into tears.*

Lady Bell. Married! Oh Heavens!

[*Throws herself in a chair, with her back to* JULIA.

Julia. I dared not reveal it to my guardian, and
for that reason fled from your house.

Lady Bell. O Julia, and you are married! What
a serpent have I nourished!—But forgive me!—
You knew not——alas! I knew not myself, till this
moment, how much——

Julia. My dearest madam, do not add to my afflictions!—for indeed they are severe.

Lady Bell. Ungenerous girl! why did you conceal from me your situation?

Julia. Good heavens! is it destin'd that one imprudent step is to lose me every blessing! In the
agonies of my heart I flew to your friendship, and
you kill me with reproaches.

s

Lady Bell. And you have killed me by your want of confidence! Oh, Julia! had you revealed to me——

Julia. I dared not; for when Mr. Belville prevailed on me to give him my hand——

Lady Bell. [*Eagerly.*] Mr. Belville! Mr. Belville, say you?

Julia. Yes; it was in Paris we were married.

Lady Bell. [*Aside.*] So, so, so; what a pretty mistake I made!—But it was a mistake.———And so my sweet Julia is married! married in Paris! Sly thing! But how came you at Mr. Beauchamp's, my love?

Julia. In my rash flight this morning, my wicked maid betrayed me into Lord Sparkle's house.— There Mr. Beauchamp snatched me from ruin, and gave me a momentary asylum in his lodgings.

Lady Bell. Did Beauchamp!—But what is his worth and his gallantry to me?—Can't he do a right thing, but my heart must triumph?   [*Aside.*

Julia. At Mr. Beauchamp's my husband found me—and found me hid with so suspicious a secrecy! ——Hah! Here comes Mr. Fitzherbert! How can I see him!

Enter FITZHERBERT.

Fitz. My Julia!—My dear Julia!

Julia. Oh sir!——

Fitz. Come, I know all; and to relieve one cause of your distress, will tell you that the lover I shocked you with to-day was only my agent in the little revenge I had resolved to take for your having married, without my consent, the very man for whom all my cares designed you.

Julia. [*Clasping his hands.*] Is it possible!

Fitz. At the moment he left Paris for Florence, you received my directions to return home: thus

Belville's letters missed you, and he remained ignorant that you were in London.

Julia. Oh sir! had you revealed this to me this
morning, what evils should I have escaped!

Fitz. My dear girl, I decreed you a little punishment; but your own rashness has occasioned you a
severer portion than you deserved.

Lady Bell. But where is the bridegroom ! I long
to see the necromancer, whose spells can thaw the
vestal's heart, and light up flames in the cold region of a monastery.

Fitz. He is without, satisfied from the mouth of
Beauchamp of your conduct, [*to* JULIA] and impatient to fold his Julia to his heart.

Julia. Oh sir, lead me to him !—To find my husband, and to be forgiven by you, are felicities too
great.   [*Exit, led by* FITZHERBERT.

Lady Bell. What a discovery has Julia's marriage
made to me of my own heart! I have persuaded
myself it knew no passion but the desire of conquest ; that it knew no motive to admiration but vanity ; but the pangs of jealousy proved to me in one
moment that all its sense is love. [*Exit Lady* BELL.

An elegant Apartment, lighted up, Card-parties seen.—
Two Servants carrying Refreshments.—A Lady en-
ters from the Top of the Stage, and comes down in a
Hurry.

Lady. I protest I have been three quarters of an
hour getting from the top of the street to the door!
—I really believe, when people give routs, they
think more of the bustle they occasion without
doors than the company they have within.

Cla. Oh yes! I am quite of that opinion.—The
noise and racket in the streets are frequently the
pleasantest part of the entertainment ; and to plague
one's sober neighbours is delightful ! Ha! ha! ha!
My next-door friend, Mrs. Saffron, always wheels
into the country on my public nights,—on pretence

of her delicate nerves; but the truth is, her rooms
will hold but six card-tables and mine thirteen.

1st Gent. Well, I protest I wish the ladies would
banish cards from their assemblies, and give us
something in the style of the *conversazioncs*.

2d Gent. Oh no, Sir Charles, that won't do on
this side the Alps;—we have no knack at conversation:—we think too much to be able to talk. Good
talkers never think. Sir Harry Glare, full of *bon
mots*, never thinks.—I myself am allowed to be tolerable, yet I never think.

Cla. Oh, that I believe all your friends will allow.
—Hey-day! here comes Lord Sparkle's borough acquaintance, Mr. Pendragon.

Enter PENDRAGON.

Pen. Bobs, Miss Belmour, how d'ye do? I didn't
think to see you.—Mr. Fitzherbert brought me
here, and I have been examining every face, to see if
I knew any body; but fine ladies are so alike, that
one must have long intimacy to know one's acquaintance!—Red cheeks, white necks, and smiling
lips, crowd every room.

Lady. Hey-day! a natural curiosity!—Pray, sir,
how long have you been in the world?

Pen. How long! Just twenty years last Lammas.

Lady. Poh, I don't inquire into your age! How
long is it since you left your native woods? Was
you ever at a rout before?

Pen. Aye, that I was, last week!—It beat this all
to nothing.—'Twas at our neighbour's the wine-
merchant's, at his country house at Kentish-town.

2d Lady. Oh lud! I wish I had been of your party!
I should have enjoyed a Kentish-town rout.

Pen. Oh, you must have been pleased; for the
rooms were so little, and the company so large, that
every thing was done with one consent. We were
pack'd so close, that if one party moved all the rest
were obliged to obey the motion.

Lady. Delightful!—Well, sir——

Pen. We had all the fat widows, notable misses, and managing wives of the parish ; so there was no scandal, for they were all there.—At length the assembly broke up.—Such clattering, and squeedging down the gangway staircase, whilst the little footboy bawl'd from the passage, " Miss Bobbin's bonnet is ready !"—" Mrs. Sugar-plum's lanthorn waits!"—"Mrs. Peppercorn's pattens stop the way!"
                    [*Imitating.*

Cla. Oh, you creature, come with me! I must exhibit him in the next room.
          [*Exit* CLARINDA *and* PENDRAGON.

Lady. Oh, stay!—Take my card.—I shall have company next Wednesday, and I insist on yours.— He is really amusing ! [*Enter Lord* SPARKLE *from the top.*] But hide your diminished heads, ye beaus and witlings! for here comes Lord Sparkle.

Spark. [*Speaking as he comes down.*] I hope the belles won't hide theirs; for in an age where the head is so large a part of the lady, one should look about for the sex.

1st Gent. Well, my lord, you see I have obey'd your summons! I should not have been here, not-withstanding Lady Bell's invitation, had you not press'd it.

2d Gent. Nor I ! —I promised to meet a certain lady in the gallery at the opera to-night,—and I regret that I did not, for I see her husband is here.— Why did you press us so earnestly to come ?

Spark. Why, 'faith, to have as many witnesses as I could to my glory !—This night is given by Lady Bell to ME.—I am the hero of the fête, and expect your gratulations.   Here the dear creature comes!

Lady BELL *comes down from the top, addressing the company.*

Lady Bell. How do you do?—how do you do ? [*on*
                    s 3

each side.] You wicked creature, why did you disappoint me last night? Lady Harriet, I have not seen you this age! Oh, Lord Sparkle! I have been detained from my company by Mr. Fitzherbert, planning a scheme for your amusement.

Spark. Indeed! I did not expect that attention from him; though I acknowledge my obligations to your ladyship's politeness.

Lady Bell. [*Aside.*] That air of self-possession, I fancy, would be incommoded, if you guessed at the entertainment.—Have you seen Mr. Beauchamp?

Spark. For a moment.—But, charming Lady Bell, [*taking her hand*] I shall make you expire with laughing. I really believe the poor fellow explained your message in his own favour, ha! ha! ha!

Lady Bell. Ridiculous! ha! ha! ha!

Enter BEAUCHAMP.

Beauch. Ha! 'tis true! There they are, retired from the crowd, and enjoying the privacy of lovers.

Lady Bell. See there he is! I long to have a little *badinage* on the subject.—Let us teaze him.

Spark. Oh, nothing can be more delightful!—
" Hither, sighing shepherd, come!"—Come, Beauchamp, take one last, one lingering look!—sha'n't he, Lady Bell?

Lady Bell. Doubtless,—if he has your lordship's leave.

Spark. He seems astonished!—Ha! ha! ha!—Nay, it is cruel!—If the poor youth has the misfortune to be stricken, you know, he can't resist fate.—Ixion sighed for Juno.

Lady Bell. Yes, and he was punished too. What punishment, Mr. Beauchamp, shall we decree for you?

Beauch. I am astonished! Was it for this your ladyship commanded me to attend you?

Lady Bell. How did I command you? Do you remember the words?

Beauch. I do, madam.—You bid me come this evening, that I might behold you in the presence of the man your heart prefers.

Lady Bell. Well, sir, and now—now you see me!—

Spark. Oh, the sweet confusion of the sweet confession!   [*Kissing her hand.*

Beauch. [*Aside.*] 'Sdeath! this ostentation of felicity, madam, is ungenerous, since you know my heart; 'tis unworthy you! But I thank you for it—I have a pang the less.   [*Going.*

Lady Bell. Hold, sir, are you going?

Beauch. This instant, madam.—I came in obedience to your commands; but my chaise is at your door, and before your gay assembly breaks up, I shall be far from London, and in a day or two from England. I probably now see your ladyship for the last time.—Adieu!

Lady Bell. Stay, Mr. Beauchamp!   [*Agitated.*

Spark. Ay, prithee stay! I believe Lady Bell has a mind to make you her conjugal father at the wedding.

Beauch. I forgive you, my lord.—Excess of happiness frequently overflows into insolence, and it is the privilege of felicity to be unfeeling.—But how, madam, has the humble passion which has so long consumed my life rendered me so hateful to you as to prompt you to this barbarity? I have not insulted you with my love; I have scarcely dared whisper it to myself: how then have I deserved——

Lady Bell. O mercy, don't be so grave! I am not insensible to your merit, nor have I beheld your passion with disdain—But what can I do! Lord Sparkle has so much fashion, so much elegance—so much—

Spark. My dearest Lady Bell, you justify my ideas of your discernment; and thus I thank you for the distinguished honour. [*Kneeling to kiss her hand.*

Enter SOPHY *from the Wing.*

Sophy. Oh you false-hearted man! [*Crying.*

Spark. [*starting up.*] Hey-day!

Sophy. Don't believe a word he says, for all you are so fine a lady. He'll tell you of happiness and misery, and this, and that, and the other, but 'tis all common-place and hyperbole, and all that sort of thing.

Lady Bell. Indeed! What has this young lady claims on your lordship?

Spark. Claims! Ha! ha! ha! Surely your lady-ship can answer that in a single glance. Claims! Ha! ha! ha! Is it my fault that a little rustic does not know the language of the day? Compliments are the ready coin of conversation, and 'tis every one's business to understand their value.

Enter PENDRAGON.

Pen. [*Clapping him on the shoulder.*] True, my lord, true;—and pray instruct me what was the va-lue of the compliment, when you told me I should make a figure in the Guards, and that you would speak to your great friends to make me a colonel?

Spark. Value! Why, of just as much as it would bring! You thought it so valuable then, that you got me a hundred extra votes on the strength of it; and you are now a little ungrateful wretch to pre-tend 'twas worth nothing.

Enter FITZHERBERT, *leading* JULIA.

Fitz. But here, Lord Sparkle, is a lady who claims a right on a different foundation. She had no election interest to provoke your flatteries, yet you have not scrupled to profess love to her whilst under the roof of her friend, whose hand you was soliciting in marriage.

Julia. Yes, I intreat your ladyship not to fancy

that you are not to break the hearts of half our sex
by binding Lord Sparkle in the adamantine chains
of marriage.—I boast an equal right with you, and
don't flatter yourself I shall resign him.

Spark. Mere malice, Lady Bell! Fitzherbert's
malice!——I never had a serious thought of Miss
Manners in my life.

Enter BELVILLE.

Belv. What, my lord! and have you dared talk
of love to that lady without a serious thought?

Spark. Hey-day! what right have you——

Belv. Oh, very trifling! only the right of a husband—The lady so honoured by your love-making
in jest is my wife; in course, all obligations to her
devolve on me.

Spark. Your wife! My dear Belville, I give you
joy with all my soul! You see 'tis always dangerous to keep secrets from your friends. But is any
body else coming? Have I any new crimes to be
accused of? Any more witnesses coming to the bar?

Belv. No; but I am a witness in a new cause, and
accuse you of loading the mind of my friend Beauchamp with a sense of obligation you had neither
spirit nor justice to confer.

Lady Bell. A commission, my lord, which was
sent Mr. Beauchamp under a blank cover, by one
who could not bear to see his noble spirit dependent
on your caprices.

Belv. And when his sentiments pointed out your
lordship as his benefactor, you accepted the honour,
and have laid heavy taxes on his gratitude.

Spark. Well, and what was there in all that!
Beauchamp did not know to whom he was obliged;
and wou'dn't it have been a most unchristian thing
to let a good action run about the world belonging
to nobody?—I found it a stray orphan, and so fa-
thered it.——But you, Fitzherbert, I see are the

lawful owner of the brat; so prithee take it back, and thank me for the honour of my patronage.

Fitz. Your affected pleasantry, Lord Sparkle, may shield you from resentment, but it will not from contempt.   Your effrontery——

Spark. Effrontery ! Prithee make distinctions !—— What in certain lines would be effrontery, in me is only the ease of fashion; that delightful thing, which enables me at this moment to stand serene amidst your meditated storm.——Come, my dear Lady Bell, let us leave these good gentry, and love ourselv s amidst the delights of fashion, and the charms of *bon ton.*

Lady Bell. Pardon me, my lord ! As caprice is absolutely necessary to the character of a fine lady, you will not be surprised if I give an instance of it now ; and, spite of your elegance, your fashion, and your wit, present my hand to this poor soldier, who boasts only worth, spirit, honour, and love.

Beauch. Have a care, madam !—Feelings like mine are not to be trifled with !—Once already the hopes you have inspired——

Lady Bell. The hour of trifling is past ; and surely it cannot appear extraordinary, that I prefer the internal worth of an uncorrupted heart to the outward polish of a mind too feeble to support itself against vice, in the seductive forms of fashionable dissipation.

Spark. Hey-day ! what, is your ladyship in the plot ?

Fitz. The plot has been deeper laid than you, my lord, have been able to conceive. As I have the misfortune to be related to you, I thought it my duty to watch over your conduct. I have seen your plans, which generally tended to your confusion and disgrace ; and many of them have been defeated, though you knew not by what means. But what fate does your lordship design for these young people, decoyed by you from their native ignorance and home?

Spark. Let them return to their native ignorance and home as fast as they can.

Pen. No, no; hang me if I do that!—I know life now, and life I'll have—Hyde-park, plays, operas, and all that sort of thing.—But, old gentleman, as you promised to do something for me, what think ye of a commission?—The captain there can't want his now; suppose you turn it over to me?

Fitz. No, young man, you shall be taken care of; but the requisites of a soldier are not those of pertness and assurance. Intrepid spirit, nice honour, generosity, and understanding, all unite to form him. —It is these which will make a British soldier once again the first character in Europe.—It is such soldiers who must make England once again invincible, and her glittering arms triumphant in every quarter of the globe.

Sophy. Well, Bobby may do as he will—I'll go back to Cornwall directly, and warn all my neighbours to take special care how they trust to a lord's promises at an election again.

Spark. Well, great attempts and great failings mark the life of a man of spirit!—There is *eclat* even in my disappointment to-night; and I am ready for a fresh set of adventures to-morrow.

Fitz. Incorrigible man!—But I have done with you.—Beauchamp has answered all my hopes, and the discernment of this charming woman in rewarding him, merits the happiness that awaits her; and that I may give the fullest sanction to her choice, I declare him heir to my estate. This, I know, is a stroke your lordship did not expect.

Beauch. And was it then to you, sir!—The tumults of my gratitude——

Fitz. Your conduct has completely rewarded me; and in adopting you——

Lady Bell. [*Interrupting.*] Oh, I protest against that!—Our union would then appear a prudent, sober business, and I should lose the credit of having done a mad thing for the sake of the man—my heart prefers.

Fitz. To you I resign him with pleasure : his fate is in your hands.

Lady Bell. Then he shall continue a soldier—one of those whom love and his country detain to guard her dearest, last possessions.

Beauch. Love and my country! Yes, ye shall divide my heart.——Animated by such passions, our forefathers were invincible; and if we would preserve the freedom and independence they obtained for us, we must imitate their virtues.

WHAT IS SHE?

A COMEDY,

IN FIVE ACTS,

AS PERFORMED AT THE

THEATRE ROYAL, COVENT-GARDEN.

VOL. X.

DEDICATION.

TO THOMAS HARRIS, Esq.

SIR,

THE formal dedication of so trifling a perform-
ance, may, I fear, have the appearance of vanity;
and I am perfectly aware, that the suffrage of an
anonymous author is of small value, where the
esteem of the world has already been so amply and
so justly bestowed: but my object in this address
is, I trust, more laudable than the indulgence of
literary egotism, and more reasonable than the hope
that such praise as mine can be of consequence. I
wish to persuade writers of better talents, who have
a turn for dramatic composition, that the formidable
and repulsive tales of delay and difficulty, incident
to a communication with managers, are not always
to be credited; and that, judging from my own experience, I venture to assure them, they will, in
you, sir, find an encouraging candour and politeness, which the timid and inexperienced dramatist
will feel how to appreciate, better than any language
can suggest. Such a motive will, I hope, plead
my excuse; and however I may fail in being useful
to others, I have the highest gratification, myself,
in an opportunity of expressing those sentiments of
respect and esteem, with which I am,

Sir,

Your most obedient,

And very humble servant.

THE AUTHOR.

May 17th, 1799.

CHARACTERS.

Sir CAUSTIC OLDSTYLE,	*Mr Munden.*
BELFORD (Lord ORTON),	*Mr Holman.*
BEWLEY,	*Mr H. Johnston.*
PERIOD,	*Mr Lewis.*
JARGON,	*Mr Fawcett.*
AP-GRIFFIN,	*Mr Townsend.*
GURNET,	*Mr Emery.*
GLIB,	*Mr Farley.*

Servant.

Mrs DERVILLE,	*Mrs Pope.*
Lady ZEPHYRINE MUTABLE,	*Miss Betterton.*
Mrs GURNET,	*Mrs Davenport.*
WINIFRED,	*Mrs Litchfield.*

SCENE—Caernarvonshire.

*The TIME—From the Morning of one Day, till the
Evening of the next.*

WHAT IS SHE?

===

ACT I.

SCENE I.—*A small House, with a Garden before it, and a Seat, on which* WINIFRED *is discovered spinning.—In the Front of the Stage a River and a Bridge.—In the back Ground the Abbey, Mansion-House, and a distant View of the Welsh Mountains.*

WINIFRED. [*Singing*]

" *She thank'd him, and said, she could very well walk,*
For, should she keep a coach, how the neighbours would talk."

HEIGHO! I believe the dismal buz, buzzing of this wheel gets from my ears to my heart. Perhaps, after all, 'tis Mrs. Derville's fault—She is too good, or, at least, too silent for one to be comfortable with her. What signifies her good humour, if she never talks enough to shew it? Ah! if she was but like my poor dear late mistress, Mrs. Everclack! to be sure, she died of a consumption; but, while she did live, it did one good to hear her—so lively, such a charming larum from morning till night.

T 3

Enter Lord ORTON [*as Mr.* BELFORD.]

Well, my lord, I'm glad you're returned.

Belf. Hush, hush, good Winifred! You will certainly forget yourself, and call me by this title in Mrs. Derville's presence. But tell me, how has she been in my absence?

Win. Bad enough, I can assure your lordship— Mr. Belford, I mean.

Belf. You make one miserable, Winifred. What has happened? is she ill? is she unhappy?

[*Anxiously.*

Win. Oh, worse! there are remedies for bad health and bad spirits; but that sort of neither one thing or other like feel, I believe the first doctors, or the merriest bells in Caernarvonshire, can't cure it. Lord, we've been as dull as the black mountains.

Belf. You surprise me. Why, I thought Mrs. Derville had been elegant cheerfulness personified; every smile on her countenance seems to declare war against melancholy.

Win. Mrs. Derville, cheerful! Good lack, good lack, what hypocrites we women are!

Belf. Surely, Winifred, you cannot mean Mrs. Derville, she is not—

[*In an accent of alarm and suspicion.*

Win. Yes, but I say she is; and no more like what she seems, than I am to Edward the Black Prince.

Belf. You distract me—Have you perceived any thing improper in Mrs. Derville's conduct?

[*Still in a tone of interest.*

Win. To be sure I have; every moment she passes alone, she grieves, and pines, and sings such woebegone ditties, 'twou'd make a Turk yearn to hear her Yet, when she leaves her room, she is as sprightly as the river Dee; smiles like the vale of Glamorgan—in short, she is just what your lordship has been pleased to fall in love with, and to woo in masquerade.

Belf. Extraordinary! And has she always been thus?

Win. Always—from the moment I entered her service, on the death of my late mistress at Leghorn, till this blessed morning, I have never seen her wear a smile, but as a mere holiday dress to meet the world in.

Belf. Incomprehensible woman! Her situation, her mind, every thing about her, is mysterious. Yet my heart mocks at the doubts of my reason, and I have scarcely courage to wish them satisfied—yet I must know more of her, or endeavour to forget that I have known her at all.

Win. Aye, my lord, you're quite right—one can bear to see one's friends miserable; but not to know why, is too much for christian patience. Dear me, how I stand talking here, and have forgot to tell your lordship the news.

Belf. What news? does it concern me? does it relate to Mrs. Derville?

Win. Why, as to concerning my mistress, I can't say; but I'm sure it concerns your lordship to know, that, since you left the village, your sister Lady Zephyrine Mutable, Mr. Deputy Gurnet, her guardian, and a mort of company are arrived at the Abbey.

Belf. Arrived at the Abbey! This is, indeed, unlucky: 'tis impossible, then, I can remain long undiscovered. Yet hold—You are certain you never communicated my secret to any one, and that I am not suspected in the village?

Win. Oh, quite sure—I can keep a secret myself, though, I own, I do like to know other people's. Not a doubt is entertained of your being any thing more than what I have introduced you for to my mistress; that is, as Mr. Belford, a relation of my own, who has met with misfortunes in trade, and is come here to live cheap, and to seek employment.

Belf. I may yet, then, remain till I can satisfy my doubts, and come to some explanation with your charming mistress. My sister, Lady Zephyrine, was brought up here, in Wales, with her grandmother; and I have been so much abroad, that we have not met since we were children, and should now scarcely recollect each other.

Win. Yes; but then her guardian, Mr. Deputy Gurnet.

Belf. I know he used to transact money-matters for my father, but I have never seen him; and then as for tenants, or servants, you know this estate has lately descended to me; and I have never seen it but in the assumed character of Mr. Belford. But tell me, have you observed nothing which can lead to a discovery of Mrs. Derville's real situation?

Win. No; nor do I know why you persist in believing her higher born than she says she is. I'm sure, now, my mistress isn't half so smart as farmer Gloom, or farmer Hoard-grain's daughters.

Belf. 'Tis the simplicity of Mrs. Derville's dress and manners which distinguishes her from the vulgar. Then such active, and yet discriminating benevolence—such unobtrusive sorrow, such a love of retirement—all mark, at least, an elegant and cultivated mind, if not a noble birth. Unaccountable woman! Then her aversion to marriage, her hatred to mankind——

Win. Why, to be sure, my lord, as I tell her, that's the most unnatural thing—Indeed, I know of nothing more so, except your lordship's expecting my mistress to fall in love with you, under the character of my relation.

Belf. This reserve and mystery of Mrs. Derville, and her avowed hatred of men and marriage, made it impossible to assail her heart in any way but by interesting her benevolence. She would have feared and avoided me as Lord Orton; but to the poor and unfortunate Belford she listens with kindness.

Win. Yes; with kindness enough to satisfy any reasonable man; and I don't see why your lordship should persist in this project of trying my mistress's sentiments—Love and a cottage against a coach and a coronet. Oh! 'tis too much for poor woman's frailty; and, I declare, nothing but the gratitude I owe your lordship for saving my father's life, would persuade me to become your accomplice. But I hear my mistress. Pray retire a minute.

[BELFORD *retires.*

Mrs. DERVILLE *enters, musing and disturbed.*

Mrs. Derv. [*as she enters.*] Yes, marry—be as miserable as you please—but I will neither be accessary to your folly, nor witness to your repentance. You shall leave me.

Win. What can be the matter? You seem angry, madam.

Mrs. Derv. Oh! nothing unusual—only a pair of idiots conspiring against the peace of their whole lives.—There's Alice says she's going to marry.

[*With painful recollection.*

Win. Lord, ma'am, and if she does, why should that make you angry? I'm sure its quite natural.

Mrs. Derv. So the vicious will tell you are their vices; but our reason was given us to correct them.

Win. I'm sure, ma'am, I never heard that people's reason was given them to prevent their marrying, though it might assist them to repent.

Mrs. Derv. Once more; I'll have no marrying in my house.

Win. Was ever any thing so barbarous!

Mrs. Derv. I'll not have my rest disturbed by the eves-dropping of your amorous clowns, who will

swear and deceive you as systematically as a rake
of quality.—But I wonder Belford does not return
—Heigho!

Win. I'm glad, ma'am, you make some distinction
in your hatred of the sex, however.

Mrs. Derv. Belford, you know, is useful to us;
besides, he is your relation, and unfortunate; and I
invent little services as a plea for assisting, without
wounding him. [*In a tender, melancholy accent.*]
Poor Belford has every claim—his manners are superior to his condition; and what is yet more rare,
his mind is superior to adversity. [*While speaking,*
WINIFRED *goes into the house, and*

BELFORD *enters.*

Well, sir, may I congratulate you? Have you
succeeded in obtaining the employment you went
in search of? or, if you have not found fortune in
quitting our village, I hope, at least, you have found
amusement.   [*Recovering her gaiety.*

Belf. I am indebted to you, ma'am, for your good
wishes; but I return with the unwilling independence of poverty; and, for amusement, surely it is
not a pursuit for the unhappy.

[*In an humble and dependent tone.*
Mrs. Derv. [*Gaily.*] Ah! there, sir, you mistake.
What fills the haunts of dissipation, routs, balls,
theatres? What crowds auctions with those who
have no money, or exhibitions with those who have
no taste? What are the overflowing audiences of
speaking puppets, and dumb-show dramas, what but
refugees from the misery of their own reflections?

Belf. Yes, madam; and, I believe, amusement is
as often furnished by the unhappy, as sought by
them. Lord Cornuto's last *fête*, now, was given
only to convince the world, that the honours of his
head did not make his heart ache: and Mrs. Fore-
stall's great public breakfast by moon-light, was

merely to ward off the crash of an unlucky mono-
poly.—Yes, ma'am, the great secret of modern life
is appearance—there would be no living without
concealing our miseries more cautiously than our
vices. [*Forgetting his disguise, and assuming an easy
gaiety.*

Mrs. Derv. I fear, sir, your severity is no more
than justice: yet, for a person who has not been in
an elevated station, you are well acquainted with
the follies of one.

Belf. [*Recollecting himself.*] Who so likely, madam, to see the follies of the great, as the tradesman, who makes a fortune by their profusion, or is
ruined by trusting them?—Oh! there is a great
deal of fashionable knowledge to be acquired between the first humble solicitation for the honour
of giving credit, and putting an execution in the
house to recover the debt.

Enter GLIB.

What a rencontre! By all that's unlucky, a servant
of my father's, who must recollect me.

Glib. Good morning to you, Mrs. Winifred. [*Seeing Mrs.* DERVILLE.] I beg pardon, ma'am; but,
hearing the ladies at the Abbey talk of rambling this
way, I thought you would like to have notice. Lady
Zephyrine, ma'am, and [*seeing* BELFORD] Lord
Orton!

Mrs. Derv. I understood his lordship was abroad.
[*Not perceiving* GLIB's *surprise.*

Glib. Hem! I thought so, too. [*To* WINIFRED.]
But, if I may believe my eyes, I see——

Win. Well, and what do you see? My brother's
wife's first cousin, Mr. Belford. Is that any thing
to gape at?

Belf. And now, I recollect, this is Mr. Glib. Nothing can be more lucky. Your mother's brother's
wife, at her death, left you a trifling legacy, [*giving*

GLIB *a purse*] which I am very happy in having the
honour to remit to you, Mr. Glib.

Glib. 'Faith, I'm my dead cousin's very humble
servant, [*aside*] and my gratitude——

Belf. Oh, pray let your gratitude be silent. [*Significantly.*]

  [*Mrs.* DERVILLE *goes to another part of the stage,
   so as to hear, without joining the conversation.*

Win. Well; but what company are arrived at the
Abbey? I find there's to be great doings to-morrow
on Lady Zephyrine's coming of age.

Glib. Why, at present, there's only Mrs. Gurnet;
and the deputy, come down to enjoy himself, as he
calls it, though he's more tired of the country
already than ever he was of 'Change after dinner-
time. Then he fancies, because he's a citizen, that
every man who lives west of Temple Bar has designs
on his wife; and that all the morality in the kingdom
centres in the city. 'Twas but yesterday he quar-
relled with Mr. Jargon for picking up Mrs. Gurnet's
glove.

Win. Why, I thought he was an admirer of Lady
Zephyrine's.

Belf. [*With impatience.*] Is it possible Lady Zephyrine can admit such an admirer? Surely her
birth——

Glib. Her birth!—Lord, sir, you talk like one of
Queen Elizabeth's maids of honour! Nobody minds
these distinctions now. Money—money's your
only master of the ceremonies, your usher of black
rods and white wands: the Stock Exchange is the
Herald's-office.—A well-timbered estate supersedes
all the genealogical trees in the principality; and a
French cook and a turtle shall bring together the
peer of sixteen quarterings and his own shoemaker. It has, however, been reported, her ladyship's complaisance in admitting Mr. Jargon's visits

arises from her having lost a considerable sum to him at play.

Belf. [*With suppressed agitation.*] Distraction!—that my sister—[*aside*] and that the necessity of this fellow's secrecy should oblige me to hear his impertinence. [*Turning to* GLIB.] I thank you, sir, for your very agreeable communications. But, pray, don't let us detain you.

Glib. Oh! I shall vanish.—Has your lordship any commands for the Abbey?
[*Aside, but with a tone of impertinence.*

Belf. [*Aside to* GLIB.] Yes, sir—Silence and a place in my service, or the indulgence of your tongue, and a tour through the horse-pond. You understand me?

Glib. [*Turning to* WINIFRED.] Oh dear! yes—I have the readiest comprehension.—And you, my fair manufacturer of goat's whey, have you any commands?

Win. Yes—silence, and my hand at the parish-church; or a box on the ear—You understand me?

Glib. Oh, yes—But——

Win. What are you debating between then—my lord's service and the horse-pond?

Glib. No, no—certainly not.

Win. What between matrimony and the box o' the ear?

Glib. Well, well—matrimony first, and the rest will follow of course.—But meet me by and by at the next stile, and we'll deliberate on the choice of evils. [*Exeunt* WINIFRED *and* GLIB, *separately.*

Mrs. DERVILLE, *who, during the last part of the scene has sat down, comes forward.*

Mrs. Derv. This man's freedom seems to distress you, Mr. Belford.

Belf. No, madam; I was only reflecting, that, probably, the lady at the Abbey was not very un-

U

justly pourtrayed by this smart gentleman: for this
is one of the cases, where the manners of the artist
vouch for the likeness of the picture.

Mrs. Derv. [*With guiety and spirit.*] Perhaps not,
altogether. Lady Zephyrine has beauty, vivacity,
and elegance. Yet a votary to whatever is fashionable, anxious for the reputation of singularity;
placing her vanity, not in being admired, but in
being stared at; and wanting courage to avoid the
follies herself, which she laughs at in others. But,
with all this, generous and amiable, when she suffers her natural character to prevail over her assumed one.

Belf. She is fortunate, madam, in an apologist:
would it were possible to render you as favourable
to our sex as you are to your own.

Mrs. Derv. [*Seriously, and then assuming an air of
melancholy.*] Be satisfied, Mr. Belford, that I do
justice to your worth as an individual; but do not
expect me to become the panegyrist of your whole
sex—Alas! does the wrecked mariner describe,
with a flattering pencil, the rock where his hopes
perished?

Belf. [*With warmth and interest.*] Wrecked at the
very beginning of life's voyage!—Oh! Eugenia!
[*Correcting himself.*] Madam!—Mrs. Derville!—
would you but deign to confirm your good opinion
of me by explaining the mystery which hangs about
you, perhaps the friendship that would participate
your sorrows, might alleviate them.

Mrs. Derv. 'Tis mere vulgar affliction which is
relieved by communication: but you take this too
seriously. [*Resuming her gaiety.*] Come, you know
you promised me to superintend our little harvest—
I am, as yet, but a novice, and could as soon navi-
gate a ship as regulate a farm.

Belf. [*With embarrassed earnestness.*] I wish my
time were of more value, that I might have more
merit in devoting it to your service. Tell me,

may I, in return, ask one hour's serious conversation?

Mrs. Derv. An hour!—impossible!—unconscionable! Have I not too many serious hours already? —So, call our reapers together—scold the clowns— and, pray, do not take it into your head that I am some princess tending goats incognita.

[*Exit, singing.*

" *Venus, now, no more behold me.*"

Belf. 'Tis thus she ever eludes any discovery of her real situation; and all I gain by the attempt is a confirmation of that mystery which fills me with doubt and apprehension. I wish Period were arrived—our stratagem will at least assure me of her disinterestedness. Yet he is so whimsical with his double profession of lawyer and author, that I almost fear he may defeat the purpose of his disguise by his absurdities. Yet if Mrs. Derville's mind is vain or interested, the temptations of title and fortune will not be diminished by a little of the ridiculous in the possessor of them. [*Exit.*

ACT II.

SCENE I.—*A Saloon.*

Lady ZEPHYRINE MUTABLE, GURNET, *and Mrs.* GURNET.

Lady Zeph. 'Twas delightful!—scoured the road, forded a river, took two hedges and a garden-gate, while all the male animals were left behind, gaping, as though they had seen a centaur.

Gurnet. Aye, you make my bones ache with the thoughts on't. I warrant your ladyship shall never get me on a hunter again. Lost my wig, frightened

away my appetite—dogs yelping, puppies sneering
—A plague of such sport, where all the glory is, who
shall break their necks first.

Lady Zeph. Why, I thought, Mr. Deputy, you
told me you had hunted before.

Gurnet. So I have, but not o'horseback. I have
been twice at the Bald-fac'd Stag on Easter Monday.

Lady Zeph. What, in a gig, I suppose, crammed
with Mrs. Gurnet, all the children, and a plentiful
provision of cold ham and cheesecakes.

Gurnet. And very snug too. And let me tell your
ladyship, much more becoming than your mettle-
some horse, dragoon caps, and rivalship with your
grooms.

Mrs. Gur. I beg, Mr. Gurnet, you won't expose
us by your vulgarity. The Bald-fac'd Stag in Ep-
ping Forest indeed! 'Tis a martyrdom to a person
of sentiment to hear you.

Gurnet. And yet I remember, my dear, when you
used to make one of five stuffed in a little old chariot of the shape and dimensions of your father's till
—and when the hunt was over, you would squeeze
down country dances at the Mansion-house, till your
face was hardly distinguishable from your best red
sattin gown.

Lady Zeph. Now, really, Mr. Gurnet, you have
the most uncivil memory. Nobody remembers any
thing now, further back than the last year's almanack. Nothing makes more confusion in society
than a retrospective head.

Mrs. Gur. Ah! Lady Zephyrine, my nerves were
very robust then; but poetry, and the Minerva
press, refine the nervous system more than the
whole college.—I'm become a mere sensitive plant
—pure æther.

Gurnet. Like enough; but if your nerves have kept
pace with your size or years, they're not much of the

cobweb kind now; and as for æther—in my mind
you partake more of the Dutch fog.

Mrs. Gur. Dutch fog!—Heavens! Mr. Gurnet,
will nothing purify the grossness of your ideas?—
Was it for this that I addressed my ode to ignorance,
to you, in one of the morning papers? And didn't I
strive to correct you, by drawing your character as
a jealous German baron in my romance of " The
Horrid Concavity," or " The Subterraneous Phantoms?" But all my refinement is lost in you, Mr.
Gurnet.

Gurnet. No, no! I wish it was, Mrs. Gurnet, I
shou'dn't care who found it. But I tell you, Mrs.
Gurnet, I'm come here with my ward to enjoy the
country and to breathe the fresh air; and it's enough
to be awoke in the night with your starting up to
scrawl your ideas, as you call 'em, without having
my head stunned with your flights by day. 'Slife!
one might as well be in the Stock Exchange.

Lady Zeph. Come, come, you must consider the
sublimity of Mrs. Gurnet's genius.

Gurnet. What business have women with any genius at all? Have I any genius at all? Let her
consider my poor head. I am sure I never argue
with her, but I have a whizzing in my ears for four
and twenty hours after, as though I had been in the
heat of a battle. But now I think on't, how came
your spark, Mr. Jargon, not to dine with us to-day?

Lady Zeph. Oh fie!—he has, indeed, under pre-
text of visiting his uncle, followed me here; but we
don't ask such people to our tables.

Gurnet. Not to ask one to your dining-table,
whom you admit every night to your card-table?—
Gad, that's comical enough!

Lady Zeph. If you had never regarded my instructions, Mr. Gurnet, you would have known that persons of fashion play cards with people at night, they
are ashamed to speak to in the morning.

Gurnet. Then I say they're people of bad fashion. In the city, now, we eat with any body, but we play at cards only with our friends.

Lady Zeph. Oh! mere Bank and 'Change notions. People of fine feelings are delicate in their society; but there's no society in a card-table; and the *rouleau* of his grace is neither brighter nor heavier than that of a gambler, or——

Gurnet. Or a swindler. And let me tell your ladyship, that your people of fine feelings are people of coarse morals. And I hope I shall never win a guinea that wasn't honestly got, or elbow a man round a table, whom I cannot shake by the hand in the street.

Lady Zeph. [*Archly.*] Why, really then, your card-parties must be on a small scale.—No gambling; only now and then a snug job in the Alley. No gambling there, guardian, eh?

Gurnet. Your ladyship's a wag—we only speculate; that's not gambling, you know.

Enter JARGON.

Jargon. Ladies, your devoted—I should have darted in upon you earlier—if I had supposed your ladyship ventured to encounter the horrors of the morning's sun.

Lady Zeph. Then you must have darted very soon, for we were out with the hounds before seven—wer'n't we, Mr. Gurnet?

Gurnet. Yes! oh yes! we were out. [*To* JARGON.]—Do you understand any thing of surgery? Can you set a few limbs?

Jargon. What, hunter a little too sprightly?—None of your bowling-green work—Faith! your ladyship's a wonder. Every thing in every place. Why, I have seen you tremble at a bit of a gale in the Park, and swoon after a walk from the auction-

room in Bond-street to Mrs. Puffabout's, your milliners.

Lady Zeph. Why, you wou'dn't have one bring
one's opera-house languishing to Caernarvonshire:
besides, 'tis gothic to be delicate in the country.—
Lady Amazonia Suremark, who would go into hysterics at the sight of a lame sparrow in Hanover-
square, will kill you a couple of brace of birds before
breakfast in Yorkshire.

Mrs. Gur. Elegant! What a subject for a sonnet
in the manner of Petrarch!

Jargon. Gad, I like the idea! We'll adopt it,
we'll propagate it. It shall be a system, and we'll
call it localism.

Lady Zeph. Do you know, Mr. Jargon, when you
came in we were discussing two of the most interesting topics——

Jargon. Afflict me with stupidity, but they must
be eating or money.

Lady Zeph. You are very near it. Eating and
cards.

Gurnet. Yes; and I was saying, that eating's the
bond of society, and cards the bane of it.

Jargon. Yes; but does your ladyship know we
begin not to countenance eating—don't patronize
eating much now—we don't feed voraciously—'tis
out.

Gurnet. Here's a fellow! Eating out!—Pray,
sir, do you eat in partnership? for I observe you
seem to speak in the firm of the house.

Lady Zeph. Oh! don't you know—Mr. Jargon
belongs to the order of ridicules?

Gurnet. What! is there more of them? Faith, I
thought he'd been the only one of the sort.

Jargon. No—we're very numerous—I'll introduce
you.

Gurnet. Introduce me to a society where eating's
out! I'd as soon be a capuchin.

Jargon. Our business is to push fashions, oaths, phrases, shrugs, and gestures. Let a mode be ever so ridiculous, stamp it with the name of one of our order, and it passes current. Absurdity, absurdity is the grand secret to which we owe our success.— The first three weeks we sport a thing, it's laughed at ; the fourth it's abused, and the fifth becomes general.

Gurnet. But are you never, now, subject to little accidents, such as hooting, pelting, and such sort of familiarities ?

Jargon. Why they do quiz us now and then ; but assurance does our business. If we were penetrable only five minutes, we should be scouted. So, we never trust dashing a new thing to a member who is not stare-proof. Our propagandists are all bronzed. Face—face is our motto—it's your only system.

Gurnet. Aye, and a very proper one too ; for, egad, I believe you're all face, and have neither brains nor hearts. But, odso, Lady Zephyrine, what's become of the young man your father used to praise so ? Why, he hasn't been here yet. Is he of the order of ridicules too ?

Lady Zeph. You mean Mr. Bewley. [*Aside, and sighing.*] Alas! poor Bewley ! That, sir, has been over long since. [*Affecting to recover her gaiety.*] Oh ! it's ridiculous enough. You must know, when I first left Caernarvonshire, at my grandmother's death, the gentle swain followed me to town ; and, for the first fortnight, we were the Damon and Pastora of all our acquaintance : but I grew ashamed of being laughed at, and the gentleman grew angry with me for being so. And because I happened to go two nights in a week to Lady Rook's, he scolded, pouted, and set off for the country, to weave willows and sigh to the winds.

Gurnet. Nay, I don't wonder he shou'dn't like to trust his dove in Lady Rook's nest.

Jargon. Sighs and winds—tears and streams—

Gad, 'tis quite new—it won't take though. Your
great passions are not the system now. We don't
patronize the violent passions. [*Sings*] " To the
winds, to the waves"——But we must see this Damon of yours—a famous subject for quizzing.

Lady Zeph. [*With a tone of tenderness and dignity.*]
I doubt, sir, if Mr. Bewley will renew his visits
here. If he does, perhaps it may be charity to warn
you that he has courage enough to make his virtues
respected, even by those who are too vicious to appreciate them.

Jargon. [*Aside.*] Whew! what, comedy on the
stilts of sublime sentiments ! All in the wrong system here.

Lady Zeph. [*To* GURNET.] Come, sir, you know
you were to attend us on a ramble to the pretty
cottagers.

Gurnet. Aye, perhaps I may just step in and take
a syllabub.

Mrs. Gur. Well, now I think there's something
most romantically interesting in a young woman's
living in a farm here by herself, and nobody to know
who she is or whence she came. I'm sure there's
some mystery.

Lady Zeph. 'Tis vulgar to be curious—and I really
know no more than that she is very young, very
pretty, and very prudent, and doesn't seem accustomed to the state she is in.

Jargon. What ! some farm-yard beauty, fresh
from Marybone, come to retrieve. I'll wait on you,
ladies, though gallantry's not the existing system—
But I love to scamper the rustics.

[*Exeunt Lady* ZEPHYRINE, *Mrs.* GURNET, *and*
        JARGON.

Gurnet. If I had the making of laws, I think I
could twist a system that should scamper you and
your fraternity from old North Wales to New South
Wales, Mr. Jargon.—[*Yawns*]. Well, 'tis vastly pretty and rural here. Rooks cawing, and lambs bleat-

ing—[*Yawns.*]—I don't know how 'tis, though, but
the stillness of the night here prevents me from
sleeping. Somehow, when one's in London, the
rumbling of the late hackney coaches and early
stages, the jingling of the clocks, and the bawling of
watchmen, does so lull one, as it were!—[*Looks up.*]
Yes, wind's fair for the West-India fleet——hope
sugars won't fall though. Bad place for business
this too.—[*Looks at his watch.*] But when one's
come into the country to enjoy one's self, one
shou'dn't be thinking of business. No, I'll have
done with Garlic-hill—I'll retire, and end my days
in the calm delights of a farm and a dairy. [*Yawns.*]
Now, if Alderman Credulous would but pop in, and
let one know how things go on in the Alley.—
[*Yawns.*] Nothing like rural retirement.

[*Exit, yawning.*

SCENE II.—*A Room at* AP-GRIFFIN'S *House.*

Enter AP-GRIFFIN, *with a Letter in his Hand.*

Ap-Grif. Here's a pretty spark for you! His father mortgaged his estate twenty years ago, and now
the law gives me possession, he writes to me about
generosity. Aye, aye, when a man gets poor, he
always talks a great deal about generosity. But
would generosity have built me this house? Would
generosity have raised me from sweeping an office
to be the master of one? Would generosity have
rained a shower of diamonds on my head? [*Takes
out a case of diamonds.*]—There, now, was a lucky
stroke! Comes an old fellow from the world's end,
and before a soul could know who he was or what
was his business, dies suddenly in my house with
these glitters in his pocket. Now, if I could get rid
of them!—Were either of my nephews honest, like
myself——But no! Jargon's a rogue, and will cheat
me; and Tim Period's an author and a fool, and

will let others cheat him.—Ah! here comes Mr. Generosity.

Enter BEWLEY.

Bew. I have called once more, sir, to request I may remain in Bewley Hall a month longer.

Ap-Grif. It can't be, sir!—law must have its course. Zounds! hav'n't you had time enough?—Hav'n't you appealed, replied, demurred, rebutted? Why, you're the first man that ever thought a Chancery suit too short.

Bew. And you are the first attorney that ever thought one long enough. But you know I have for some time been in expectation of hearing from my uncle in India; and I still hope, through the kindness of my relations there, to be able to redeem my estate.

Ap-Grif. Why you don't want to redeem your estate contrary to law? Hav'n't we a decree in our favour? Besides, one great estate always requires another to keep it up; and if we hadn't foreclosed, possession would have ruined you. So the law only turns you out a little sooner than you'd have turned out yourself. I'm for the just thing—always respect the law.

Bew. Hark you, sir—I'm no more bound by the law to tolerate your impertinence, than you are to possess gratitude or humanity—therefore——

Ap-Grif. I'm gone, sir—off the premises in an instant, though they're my own. So, sir, to avoid ceremony about precedence, here's one door for me, and there's another for you.   [*Exit.*

Bew. Well said, old Quitam. This fellow, now, was the son of my father's coachman, and used to crop the terriers, catch moles, and scare the crows off the corn. But hang him, he's beneath contempt! Heigho! what avails wealth to one who has lost the hope of happiness? Oh, Zephyrine!—But I lose

time : I will at least make one effort to preserve her,
if not for myself. With her lofty and volatile spirit,
expostulation will be useless. No, I'll pique her—
alarm her pride by impertinence—excite her jealousy by neglect—and who knows but she, who
abandoned me as a rational and tender lover, may
take a fancy to me as a rake and a coxcomb ?—"*Allons! La feinte par amour.*"   [*Exit.*

SCENE III.—*Before Mrs.* DERVILLE'S *House.*

Enter Lady ZEPHYRINE, *Mrs.* GURNET, *and* JARGON.

Jargon. Really, now, 'twas atrocious and abominable in your ladyship to quit Cheltenham so early.

Lady Zeph. I can assure you, neither the atrocity
nor abomination of quitting Cheltenham [*in a ludi-
crous tone, in imitation, but not absolutely mimicking*
JARGON] is imputable to my inclination But you
know my rich uncle, Sir Caustic Oldstyle, after a
family quarrel of twenty years standing, has just
emerged from his Cornish estate, and is coming to
visit us. My father and Sir Caustic, though nearly
of the same age, had the difference of a century in
their manners. Lord Orton lived like his cotempo-
raries—my uncle like his ancestors; and I believe
nothing but the death of Sir Caustic's only son
would ever have reconciled him to relations who are
so degenerate as to think and act like other people.

Jargon. What a loss he has inflicted on the fashionable world !—Why, your ladyship has scarce
time to systemize the summer costume.

Lady Zeph. Oh, yes !—As soon as the dog-days
began, I took care to introduce the Kamschatka
robe, the Siberian wrapper, and the Lapland scratch.

Mrs. Gur. Well, I declare your ladyship has the
most elegant imagination ; though it is sometimes
a little at variance with our climate.

Jargon. O, no woman of spirit ever thinks about

climate or seasons—gauzes, muslins, cobwebs, in winter—furs, gold lace, and velvets in summer—'tis the system.

Lady Zeph. Ha, ha!—don't you remember how poor old Mrs. Parchment [*mimicking the appearance of a person cold*] used to be shivering through a frosty night and a thin opera, in a silver muslin, with her arms squeezed to her sides, and the natural crabbedness of her features improved by angular contractions, till she gave one the idea of a petrified mummy?

Jargon. Yes; and when the cold drew tears from her eyes she pretended it was the effect of music on her sensibility.

Lady Zeph. Then, there was poor Lady Lovemode got a quinzy by going to see the skaters in Hyde-Park in an Otaheite chemise.

Jargon. But where's this queen of curds and whey? This is the door, I suppose. Come, let's scatter the country folks. I love to make the hobnails stare. [*Knocks at Mrs.* DERVILLE'S *door.*] Holloa! here—Cuddy—Bumpkin! Is nobody at home?

Mrs. DERVILLE *comes out.*

Mrs. Derv. Lady Zephyrine, I hope nothing's the matter—your servant has so alarmed me——

Jargon. Servant! Faith, that's queer enough. Why, what the devil ails me? I hope I'm not such a quiz as to be ashamed.   [*Apart.*

Lady Zeph. You must excuse my friend, Mr. Jargon, here; he's a little rude; but it's his system.

Mrs. Derv. At least, madam, 'tis systematic; for when gentlemen adopt the dress of their grooms, 'tis very natural the manners of the stable should accompany the wardrobe.

Jargon. [*Aside, while Mrs.* DERVILLE *talks to Lady* ZEPHYRINE.] Severe enough that! Bright eyes, sar-

x

castic style—just the thing for a Faro-table. Now, if I could but take her to town, puff her, patronize her, she'll make me famous in a week.

Mrs. Gur. [*To* Mrs. DERVILLE, *in a romantic tone.*] Well, but really, young woman, I can't think you were born for the station you appear in. I should like to hear your history. Nay, if you will, I'll write—four volumes, interspersed with pieces of poetry—call it translated from the German—'twill be delightful. I have a moonlight scene, a dungeon, and a jealous husband—all ready done.

Mrs. Derv. [*Gaily.*] Oh! my history, madam, is the history of every body; and for that reason, nobody would read it. [*Ironically.*] 'Tis so common for men to be base, and women weak, that the vices of one sex, and the follies of the other, are subjects for jests and *bon mots* rather than history.

Jargon. Faith, this girl's an original. I'll negociate with her, take her to town, and bring her into fashion.

Lady Zeph. Hush! what young man's that crossing the field?

Mrs. Derv. 'Tis Mr. Bewley, ma'am.

Jargon. By all that's queer, the weeping lover, the willow-weaver!—Come, Lady Zephyrine, a compassionate glance at least. [*Sings.*]

" *Ah, well a-day, my poor heart!*"

Mrs. Gur. I shall like to see him of all things. I do so doat on a melancholy lover.

Lady Zeph. Poor Bewley! how shall I sustain his sighs, his reproachful looks, his despair?—Would I could avoid him.

Enter BEWLEY, *singing negligently, as if he did not perceive Lady* ZEPHYRINE.

Bew. " Merrily, merrily shall I live now!"——
[*To* Mrs. DERVILLE, *with an airy volubility, and an affectation of fashionable ease.*] What! my charming

neighbour!—*La belle voisine!*—Ah! Lady Zephyrine!—I beg pardon—I didn't see you. The sun, you know, is apt to dazzle one's vision. I fear I am not *en regle.* I ought to have left my card at the Abbey; but the very morning your ladyship arrived I had promised to give the Miss Strongbows a lesson on the kettle-drum, and they have kept me at the lodge ever since. 'Tis the very palace of Armida, the grotto of Calypso—no escaping.

Jargon. [*Aside.*] Psha! here's pining and willow-weaving! Lucky enough though—clenches my business with her ladyship.

Lady Zeph. [*With an air of pique.*] I confess, sir, the Abbey would have been a gloomy exchange for an enchantress's palace.

Bew. Nay, 'pon honour now, you wrong me. I was absolutely dying to leave my name with your ladyship's porter; but these country belles, when they get hold of a man that's a little followed—[*conceitedly.*]—not that I pretend—they're quite unconscionable.

Jargon. What, you are a favourite here! a sylvan deity! and all the Welsh Daphnes pulling caps for hur, look you!—[*Mimicking the Welsh dialect*].—This is better than sighing to the winds, Lady Zephyrine.—Come, Mrs. Gurnet, you doat upon a melancholy lover—Here's your man.

Bew. Fie! fie! shou'dn't boast—for its no sooner known that a couple of dear creatures are civil to one, than one's besieged by a whole bevy.—Apropos! did you see my little marquise at Cheltenham? I'm a downright inconstant there.—Lady Zephyrine, you must make my peace for me. You know a little inconstancy is but venial in the code of gallantry.

Lady Zeph. [*Apparently mortified.*] Oh, sir! I'm too much a stranger, both to your gallantries and yourself, to be a competent mediator.

Bew. A stranger! your ladyship's pleasant. I thought we had been old acquaintance.

Lady Zeph. [*Coldly.*] Sir, you are so unlike the Mr. Bewley I once knew——

Bew. As your ladyship is to your former self; but you're quite right—nothing so stupid as the sameness and constancy of an old-fashioned lover. Why, there's more variety in the imagination of a Dutch poet.

Jargon. Gad, you're correct—exactly correct— we scout it—it's quite out.

Bew. Yet, here's Mrs. Derville would tempt one to forego the doctrine. One might be her slave till constancy became the mode.

Lady Zeph. [*Aside.*] I can support this no longer. Mrs. Derville, it grows cool—we'll bid you good evening—Mrs. Gurnet, Mr. Jargon, will you accompany me?

Mrs. Gur. I'll glide after you in an instant—I have just finished a sonnet to the screech-owl, and 'tis the most pathetic thing——

[*Exeunt all but* BEWLEY, *Mrs.* DERVILLE *attending them.*

Bew. [*Alone.*] Thank Heaven, the task is so far over. But Mrs. Derville is too amiable to be trifled with. I'll after her, and explain my conduct.— Oh, Zephyrine! how much has it cost me to wound even your pride? Yet if I can, by this innocent artifice, awaken her to a sense of her own dignity, and snatch her from the abyss of this ruinous dissipation, whatever fate awaits myself, I will meet it without repining.   [*Exit.*

ACT III.

SCENE.—*Lady* ZEPHYRINE'S *Dressing-Room.*

Lady ZEPHYRINE *and* MIRROR *discovered.*

Mrs. Mir. It is very lucky your cousin left these clothes here ; they fit your ladyship exactly.

Lady Zeph. You think, then, Mrs. Derville will not discover me.

Mrs. Mir. That she won't, if your ladyship does but talk loud, stare at people, yet pretend not to see them, and behave rude ; there's no fear but she'll take you for a modern fine gentleman.

Lady Zeph. Yes, I cannot doubt but this village wonder, this Mrs. Derville, is some adventurer, perhaps placed here by Mr. Bewley, at any rate the object of his attention ; and under this disguise, and the assumed title of my brother Lord Orton, I hope, by professing a passion for her, at least to ascertain her sentiments with regard to him.

Mrs. Mir. Ah, my lady ! I remember when poor Mr. Bewley began courting your ladyship in the nursery, by teaching your birds to sing ; and though your ladyship being rich has a right to be fickle-minded, I can't think that Mr. Bewley——

Lady Zeph. Yet his visit last night was plainly intended for Mrs. Derville—he hung on her looks while he scarcely deigned to regard mine.—But have I not deserved this, and is not my present meanness less excusable than my past folly ?—Oh, Bewley ! how easily might I have avoided the errors I find it so difficult to retrieve.   [*Exit.*

SCENE II.—*Mrs.* DERVILLE's *House.*

Mrs. DERVILLE *at a Table, drawing.—On one Side of the Stage a Closet, with a Door, and a Window projecting into the Room.*

Mrs. Derv. [*Throwing down the pencil*] It doesn't signify—'tis in vain to attempt any thing new—this obstinate pencil of mine is continually multiplying the same resemblance—profile—three-quarter full-face—still the same features—yet 'tis singular—such animation—such sensibilit —a poor relation of Winifred's too——Heigho ! —I believe the house is now quiet, and I may venture to try the effect of my harp in dissipating a melancholy of which I dare not ask myself the cause.   [*Enters the closet.*

SONG.—[*Written to a French Air.*]

" Je crus tous mes beau jours."

Heart, I thought thy peace was flown,
Joy and hope for ever gone;
Reason's help I ask'd in vain ;
Time, friendly healing,
Softens each feeling,
And peace and hope return again.

Tranquil hours! how short your stay !
Sorrow still hung o'er your way;
Time his aid but lent in vain :
Love softly stealing,
Points new each feeling,
And sighs and tears return again.

While Mrs. DERVILLE *is singing,* BELFORD *enters with Papers in his Hand.*

Belf. Enchanting woman ! Still do I hover about her; still live but in her presence, who, perhaps, be-

holds me with indifference, or confounds me with
the objects of her hatred. Yet, no; she who inspires
a passion like mine cannot herself be insensible—
Oh, Eugenia! if I am not deceived—if I am happy
enough to have created an interest in your heart, I
swear, whatever your fate, nothing shall separate it
from mine—my hand—my rank—but she comes.
[*To Mrs.* DERVILLE.] I have executed your little
commission, madam, and have brought you the papers you desired.

Mrs. Derv. You are very exact, Mr. Belford.—
[*Gives* BELFORD *some papers; he appears agitated.*]
Shall I trouble you, sir, to look over these accounts
—I am so ignorant of business—Heavens! what's
the matter! You seem ill—you seem disordered.

Belf. I confess it—I am at this moment so agitated,
that I own I am incapable of obeying you.

Mrs. Derv. [*In an accent of kindness.*] Nay, 'tis of
no consequence—compose yourself, Mr. Belford, I
intreat you—I asked your assistance as a friend, and
surely didn't mean to impose a task on you—Speak,
sir, you alarm me!

Belf. [*Still agitated.*] Madam—Eugenia.

Mrs. Derv. Tell me—what means this agitation?
Have you any thing to impart to me?

Belf. Oh, I have indeed, if——

Mrs. Derv. [*With eagerness.*] Speak, then—am I
not—your friend?

Belf. [*Aside.*] How shall I begin?

Mrs. Derv. [*To herself.*] Oh, my fluttering heart!

Belf. [*Aside.*] Yet, should I be deceived—Let me
dissemble a moment if it be possible. [*Recovering
himself.*] I wished, madam, to consult you on a subject which distresses me more than I can describe.
You have been so kind, have appeared to take such
an interest in my fate, that I venture to intrude on
you a confidence——

Mrs. Derv. [*Anxiously.*] Go on, I intreat you.

Belf. The old relation you have heard me speak of, and on whom I depend to retrieve my affairs——

Mrs. Derv. Well, and——

Belf. Has persecuted me to marry.

Mrs. Derv. [*Tremulously.*] To marry! You to marry!

Belf. Yes, madam ; me.

Mrs. Derv. [*With an air of pique.*] And so you are come to consult me about it?

Belf. Yes, madam ; I thought, perhaps—

Mrs. Derv. [*Resentfully, yet affecting indifference.*] Oh, Heavens! in these cases people have nothing to do but to take their own counsel. [*With volubility and assumed pleasantry.*] I dare say now your uncle has discovered you have a fancy for some farmer's daughter—very young, very blooming, very silly, and very credulous, whom you will adore the first month, neglect the second, and abandon the third. —'Tis all in the usual course of things—nothing extraordinary in it ; and I wonder you should come to consult me about such trifles.

Belf. Yet hear me.

Mrs. Derv. [*Rapidly, with a tone of irritation.*]— Oh! it seems the very dæmon of matrimony possesses the whole principality—Every body talks of marrying. Marry, marry then, I beg you, sir, and leave me in peace.

Belf. Reflect a little, madam, that if I were so entirely decided, I should not consult you. Believe me far from desiring such a marriage, I have ever opposed it, and my unwillingness originates in a passion which is at once the delight and torment of my life—a passion I have never yet dared to disclose.

Mrs. Derv. [*More composed.*] That, indeed, is different—You love, then, my friend?

Belf. [*Passionately.*] Yes, I love, madam ; ardently love a woman that I do not yet know ; but who, by being known, can only be more adored. [*Mrs.*

DERVILLE *listens with agitation.*] A woman whose
sense and sweetness would have captivated my heart,
though it had not already been subdued by her personal attractions—A woman, all charming, in whom
there is nothing to regret, but the profound mystery
which envelopes her—A mystery, which might appear suspicious, did not the circumspection of her
conduct bid defiance to calumny—did she not nourish a prejudice against mankind, which, while it
guards her own reputation, is the despair of those
who aspire to touch her heart—a prejudice, of which
I am myself the first and most unfortunate victim.

Mrs. Derv. [*Half gaily.*] Do you know, sir, that
you are an orator? absolutely eloquent.

Belf. Oh! I could speak still better, would the
woman I love but deign to answer me.

Mrs. Derv. [*Confused.*] Perhaps the answers which
reach the ear are not always the most expressive.

Belf. [*Taking her hand.*] Doubtless not—and if I
dared to believe—to hope——

Mrs. Derv. [*Half archly.*] Come, release my hand,
and tell me—Is this fair one that won't answer rich?

Belf. She is for me—and it is this consideration
which restrains me—Alas! my ruined fortunes are
unworthy of her.

Mrs. Derv. [*Feelingly.*] You deceive yourself.
Our sex are naturally tender and generous.—And I
know those, to whom a lover sincere and affectionate, and unhappy, would be more formidable than
the splendid homage of the first prince in the world
—But alas!

Belf. Proceed, I conjure you.

Mrs. Derv. [*With an accent of depression.*] But
where find such a lover, such sincerity? Where is
the man that has not to reproach himself with the
misery of woman? Is there a female, who has not,
some time in her life, been the victim of her sensibility?—[*Becomes impassioned as she proceeds, and ends*

almost in tears.]—Yet, you wonder that we become false, dissipated coquettes, and sometimes worse. Warm, enthusiastic, we fancy life a path strewed with roses. We expect to find nothing but happiness and integrity.—At an age when our hearts are tender, and our reason weak, we make that choice which is to fix our destiny for ever—and she who, perhaps, might have lived in the bosom of peace and virtue, had she been fortunate in her first affections, irritated and degraded by the conduct of a seducer, devotes herself to all the vices which his example has taught her—and thus revenges her own wretchedness wherever her charms procure her dupes or victims.

Belf. [*Alarmed.*] Oh, misery! is it possible you can have been exposed to these horrors?—

Mrs. Derv. [*With dignity.*] No, sir; I have nothing to reproach myself with. 'Tis this consoling idea of my own innocence, which has supported and still supports me under my misfortunes. [*Feelingly.*] Yet the deceit, neglect, ingratitude I have experienced—Oh, sir! you know not what I have suffered.

Belf. Speak, then—deposit in the bosom of friendship this sorrow, so inconceivable to all the world. Never will I——

Mrs. Derv. I believe you; this dislike to society —this gay misanthropy, to which, however, I owe the little repose I have long felt, yields to the tender interest you have inspired. Learn, then, I am not what I appear—I was once——

Enter WINIFRED.

Belf. Cursed interruption! at such a moment too!

Win. Dear ma'am, here is Lord Orton just arrived from abroad; he's been strolling about among the tenants, and desires to see you. [*Aside to* BELFORD.] It's your friend Counsellor Period, I suppose, in masquerade.

Mrs. Derv. Surely, there's no necessity for my admitting him. What can his business be here?— am I ever to be persecuted?

Win. Oh, he's your landlord, you know, ma'am, and Lady Zephyrine's brother. I must ask him in.

Mrs. Derv. Well, well, if I must——

[*Exit* WINIFRED.

But pray, Mr. Belford, do you entertain his lordship while I compose myself a little, our conversation has so agitated me. [*Exit.*

Belf. [*Alone.*] How unlucky that Period should come at this juncture, and without apprizing me of his arrival. Our stratagem, too, now seems unnecessary, [*doubtfully*] I am—at least, I think I am, nay, I ought to be satisfied—Mrs. Derville—is every [*with the air of the man endeavouring to believe what he wishes*] thing I can desire—Why, then—Yet, as Period is here, he shall make this one trial, and then— I bid adieu to doubt for ever.

Enter Lady ZEPHYRINE *as Lord* ORTON.

Confusion! [*With a gesture of surprise.*] Why— What! this is not Period—'Sdeath! what can it mean? Oh! I have it—Some friend, I suppose, whom he thinks will act the part better than himself. Yes, yes, it must be so; Mrs. Derville, sir, will be here in an instant.

Lady Zeph. [*Confused.*] Sir, I—I—

Belf. I say, sir, Mrs. Derville will wait on you immediately. [*With a tone of intelligence.*] But how is it that Mr. Period has entrusted our scheme to you? Is he arrived? Is he in the village?

Lady Zeph. [*Perplexed.*] Really, sir, I don't understand you. A scheme—a Mr. Period—Upon my word I know no such person—I presume you are informed my name is Orton?

Belf. Yes, yes; a peer of my friend Period's making. You see I know the whole plot.—However, I

find you can keep a secret; but there's no occasion
to keep a man's secrets from himself. You understand what I mean?

Lady Zeph. [*Surprised.*] How the deuce shou'd I?
What do you take me for a necromancer, a con-
juror?

Belf. Why, I tell you, I know the whole story.
You have assumed the title of Lord Orton, and are
come in this disguise to discover Mrs. Derville's real
character and sentiments.—Now are you satisfied?

Lady Zeph. [*Alarmed and confused.*] Heavens! I
am discovered. Well, sir, as you seem acquainted
with my disguise, you, perhaps, would not advise me
to proceed. Shall I?—ought I?

Belf. By all means.—As you've gone so far, make
this one trial. But are you sure you have all the
story? Remember, you fell in love with her at
Florence, followed her to Leghorn, surprised to find
her here—Be sure you act your part well.

Lady Zeph. Why, the man's certainly mad—
Either a poet or a speculator—But I'll e'en profit
by his instructions. Oh, don't fear—nothing so
easy to imitate as a modern beau. You know it requires no talents.

Belf. Take care though not to shew we have any
intelligence together.

Lady Zeph. [*Archly.*] Certainly—certainly—She
shall not suspect any intelligence between us.—Besides you may contrive to quarrel with me.

Belf. Hush! here she comes.—Now don't forget
Florence, Leghorn, and the little marquis.

Enter Mrs. DERVILLE.

BELFORD *retires a little in the back ground.*

Mrs. Derv. [*With a serious but easy manner.*] To
what, my lord, am I indebted for the honour of this
visit? Has your lordship any directions to give
concerning the farm?

Lady Zeph. [*Affecting surprise.*] Excuse me, ma-

dam, this rencontre is so unexpected, so transporting, so superlatively fortunate; so, so surprising,
that I am unable to explain, but another time, a
more favourable moment——

Mrs. Derv. [*Looking attentively at Lady* ZEPHYR-
INE, *discovers her.*] Yes—the voice, the features—I
can't be mistaken—This is some trick of Lady Zephyrine's—Nay, then, her ladyship shall, for once in
her life, hear a little truth. [*Turning to Lady* ZE-
PHYRINE.] I can assure your lordship I am not a
little surprised myself at your sudden arrival—I believe it was quite unexpected, though long, very long
necessary.

Lady Zeph. How, madam! I hav'n't heard of any
accident.

Mrs. Derv. [*Seriously.*] Yes, my lord, the worst
of accidents. The peace, the reputation of a sister
is in danger.

Lady Zeph. In danger! I thought the character
of Lady Zephyrine——

Mrs. Derv. Yes; perhaps the same rank which
renders her imprudence conspicuous, may protect
her reputation; but what shall secure her peace?—
A worthy youth deserted—her fortune the prey of
a gambler, or fatally redeemed by her hand. Oh!
Lord Orton, what have you not to answer for, in
having selfishly sought your own amusement, while
destruction has hovered over those most dear to
you.

Lady Zeph. Yes; I confess the conduct of Lady
Zephyrine has been culpable—Oh, how much so!
But surely the character of her brother, Lord Orton, [*confused, as forgetting herself*] that—that is, of
myself, is without reproach.

Mrs. Derv. It is not enough, my lord, for the great
to be without reproach, they should deserve praise.
Fortune has given the world a claim on them; and
the very virtues of the indolent are pernicious.

Lady Zeph. You preach so charmingly, that I believe you'll make me a convert—And I'll engage
that whenever I reform, Lady Zephyrine will do so
too. [*Gaily.*] Heaven knows she needs it.

Belf. [*Comes forward.*] Of the actions of Lord
Orton I am not qualified to judge; but Lady Zephyrine shall not be attacked by a male slanderer,
though he were her brother.

Lady Zeph. [*Aside, as supposing his anger to be
feigned, to promote the deception.*] Very well indeed!
You act passion admirably.

Belf. 'Sdeath, sir, I am serious. Another time
your calumnies shall not pass.

Lady Zeph. [*Still supposing his passion affected.*]
When you please, sir—Sword or pistol—I'm your
man—hit you a side curl at fifty yards.

Belf. [*Aside.*] A few hours hence, and nothing
shall restrain me. [*To Lady* ZEPHYRINE.] Sir, you
shall repent this.

Lady Zeph. [*Aside to* BELFORD.] Admirable!—
never saw passion better acted—Now an oath or
two.

Mrs. Derv. [*With an air of pique.*] Belford so
zealous a champion for her ladyship—nay, then, I'll
punish him—There's no consistency in man. [*In a
coquettish manner.*] Come, my lord, I entreat you,
drop the matter. Your lordship's existence is too
valuable to be risked for or against trifles.

Belf. Furies! she's coquetting with him! [*To
Mrs.* DERVILLE.] I'll endure this no farther.—
[*Formally.*] Madam, have you any farther com-
mands?

Mrs. Derv. No, sir: and really his lordship is so
pleasant——

Belf. That you wish for no additional society.
I'm gone, madam. [*At the side of the stage, while going off.*] Sorceress! But an hour ago such fascinating tenderness! such angelic candour! and now co-

quetting with a coxcomb before my face. Yes, I
rejoice that I did not discover myself—Oh, woman!
woman!   [*Exit* BELFORD.

Lady Zeph. [*In a romantic tone.*] Ah, madam,
you see before you the most miserable of mankind!
the most faithful, the most ardent, the most sentimental, the most——

Mrs. Derv. [*Aside.*] Ridiculous! how shall I contain myself?

Lady Zeph. [*Kneels.*] Madam, I have so long
adored you, [*aside*] bless me, I forgot to ask how
long—Then, hav'n't I pursued you from—[*aside*]
[Heavens! I have forgot where] Oh! from Florence to Leghorn—from Leghorn to England, and
from—

Mrs. Derv. [*Agitated.*] Alas! then I am betray'd!

Lady Zeph. Oh, no, ma'am—indeed I'll never
betray you.

Mrs. Derv. But, by what means came you acquainted?——

Lady Zeph. Oh! I'm acquainted with all—not
forgetting the little marquis—[*Archly.*]

Mrs. Derv. I conjure you, my lord, in pity, tell
me who informed you of all this?

Lady Zeph. [*Aside*] Truly, that's more than I
know myself. How shall I get off? [*Turning to Mrs.*
DERVILLE.] Excuse me—I dare not enter into ex-
planations at present. I have the most powerful
reasons for avoiding it. But meet me near the
hermitage, about seven, and you shall be satisfied.
In the mean while, tell me, I conjure you, have I
not a rival? Is not Mr. Bewley a favourite rival?

Mrs. Derv. [*Aside.*] Ah! now the mystery of her
ladyship's visit is out. [*To Lady* ZEPHYRINE.] No,
my lord—Mr. Bewley is, I fear, too, too firmly attached to one who, having deserved to lose his heart

by her folly, may, perhaps, expect to regain it by unworthy artifices, and——

    [*A noise and voices are heard without.*

Lady Zeph. [*To* Mrs. DERVILLE.] I hear voices at the door—Permit me to escape on this side the village. I have particular reasons.

Mrs. Derv. This way, then, my lord.

   [*Mrs.* DERVILLE *goes out with Lady* ZEPHYRINE.

SCENE III.—*Near Mrs.* DERVILLE'S *House.*

Enter Sir CAUSTIC OLDSTYLE *and* PERIOD, *in travelling Dresses.*—PERIOD *with a Port-folio.*

Period. Why, I tell you, sir, it's the luckiest event of my whole tour between London and Caernarvonshire.

Sir Caustic. Lucky, you verbose coxcomb. [*Petulantly.*] Hav'n't we been overturn'd? wasn't I jamm'd under you and your port-folio, and your bag of briefs, till I can't feel the difference between my flesh and my bones? [*Mimicking.*] And now you tell me it's lucky—it's the very thing you wished.

Period. And so I did, to be sure. Here I'm come on a tour from London to North Wales, and hav'n't yet met with a single anecdote, not even one accident; no, not so much as a spoil'd dinner, or a sprained ankle—Nothing to describe, but turnpikes and sign-posts—Hav'n't I a hundred pages, all as dull as a great dinner? Then, you know, we may indict the road.

Sir Caustic. No, puppy, we can't—The road was good enough—Wasn't it Molasses the great West-Indian's chaise and four overset us, as he was scowering along to bid for the estate that Sir Plinlimmon Pedigree lost last week at the hazard table?

Period. And what signifies? You were only overturn'd a quarter of a mile on this side the Abbey, instead of driving up to the door—Then, 'twill make such a figure in my travels back again. Why, here's a farm-house; nothing ever was so fortunate —we go in, sit down to dinner—eggs and bacon— barn-door fowl and greens just ready; coarse but clean cloth; sentimental farmer's wife; tears of sensibility on our part; curtsies and sympathy on hers. —Where's my pencil? Such language, such style! Thank ye, Mr. Molasses—'tis the luckiest circumstance for a travelling author to be overturned.

Sir Caustic. Here's a flourishing rascal! There happened to be but one pair of horses at the last stage, and finding we were going the same road, I offer him a place in my chaise without knowing even his name; and, now we've nearly got our necks broke, he tells me 'tis the luckiest circumstance. Aye, aye; this comes of your modern improvements —in my time people travelled with dignity and sobriety—none of your nick-nack springs and prancing steeds.

Period. Yes; then the vehicle resembled the lac'd waistcoat of the owner, large, rich, and heavy; while the very horses seemed to feel their importance, and moved like elephants in a procession. But then there were no tours or tourists, nothing but poor stupid selfish people, who only travell'd about their business, instead of being philanthropists like myself, and travelling to amuse the whole world.—Ah! yonder's my friend Belford—I'll just speak to him, look to the baggage, and be with you in an instant. In the mean while repose yourself at this farm-house, and don't forget the barn-door fowl, and the sentimental hostess. Oh! I'll describe them in such a style!   [*Exit.*

Sir Caustic. [*Always in a tone of petulance.*] And what should they travel for; to write nonsense, and

Y 3

set other blockheads a gadding after them.—A
plague of your new-fangled notions and refinements!
A fellow, now, that ought to be nail'd to his count-
ing-house, from one year to another, like a sheet
almanack, jumps into a carriage, kills horses, and
breaks people's necks, that he may get in an hour
sooner to an opera dancer, or a gaming table.

[*Exit into Mrs.* DERVILLE'S.

SCENE IV.—*A Room in Mrs.* DERVILLE'S *House.*

Enter Sir CAUSTIC, *Mrs.* DERVILLE, *and* WINI-
FRED.

Mrs. Derv. I hope you're not hurt, sir——
Sir Caustic. Why, no; I believe the trunk and
limbs of the old tree have escaped safely; and I have
been weather-beaten about the world too long to
mind a little scratching on the bark.
Mrs. Derv. I'm sure, sir, you must have been
greatly alarmed; let me prevail on you to take some
refreshment.
Sir Caustic. [*Looking at her attentively.*] I thank
you—I thank you—I hav'n't had so much civility
without paying for it, since I left Cornwall.
Mrs. Derv. [*With warmth.*] Then, I'm sure, sir,
you have not before had occasion for it—Never did
misfortune appeal in vain to the hearts of my coun-
trymen.—If you are rich and prosperous, perhaps
you may have met with imposition, flattery, or self-
ishness; but had you been a poor and friendless
stranger, a thousand hands had open'd to relieve
you—a thousand hearts have given you the tribute
of sympathy and compassion.
Sir Caustic. Well, I'm glad to hear you say so:
I know, in my time, we were a generous nation; but
I see such changes, such carving and gilding, such

polish and ornament, that I hav'n't yet been able to examine whether the good old oak remains sound at heart.—I'm not, you see, of the newest cut, either inside or out, and I can only tell you I love kindness, and not the less for being set off by a pretty face.— Surely, I think, I have seen you before; were you ever in Cornwall?

Mrs. Derv. No, sir.

Sir Caustic. Then I'm mistaken—for you are too young even to have been born before I retir'd there. —May I ask your name, young gentlewoman?

Mrs. Derv. Derville, sir.

Sir Caustic. And your situation.

Mrs. Derv. Not affluent, sir; but equal to my wishes.—I rent this small farm under Lord Orton.

Sir Caustic. Why, then, you can tell me a little about my niece; is she worth an old man's travelling from the land's end to see?

Win. Lord, sir, she is——

Mrs. Derv. Hush!——Lady Zephyrine, sir, is young, gay, and elegant—a little lively, but I'll answer for the goodness of her heart.

Sir Caustic. [*With warmth and severity.*] Yes, but do you mean a good heart, as good hearts us'd to be fifty years ago—now women may betray their husbands, abandon their children—yet have delicate feelings; shrink from the name of vice, and have the best hearts in the world.

Mrs. Derv. You mistake me, sir—Lady Zephyrine——

Sir Caustic. Yes, yes; I know your modern ethics, your splendid vices—your good hearts that ruin more tradesmen than all the swindlers between Hyde Park and Whitechapel—They won't do for me, I tell you.

Mrs. Derv. Do not let your prejudices make you unjust, sir—in spite of the gaiety of Lady Zephyrine's manners—her feelings—her sensibility——

Sir Caustic. There again—her feelings—her sensibility—[*In a tone of petulance.*]—What, I suppose she sighs over the distresses of a novel—wipes her eyes while a ghost in an opera comes out of his tomb to accompany the orchestra; but is shock'd too much at real misery to suffer its approach, and avoids sickness and poverty as though she herself were not human. These fine feelings won't do for me—has my niece benevolence and common sense? I want none of your foil and tinsel qualities.

Mrs. Derv. Indeed, sir, you'll find her very amiable.

Sir Caustic. Nay, I own I have seen a picture of her, and have left her half my fortune, merely on the credit of her simple dress and modest countenance—her grandmother wrote me word two years ago, that she was the only young woman in the principality uncorrupted by modern modes, and London manners.—But come, I'm now sufficiently recovered, and if you'll let your damsel shew me the way, I can reach the Abbey—thank you, fair lady, for your kindness; and if you'll permit an old man's visits—

Mrs. Derv. I do not often mix in society, sir, but the respect I feel for you—This way, sir, let us assist you.

[*Exeunt Mrs.* DERVILLE *and* WINIFRED, *shewing Sir* CAUSTIC *out.*

SCENE V.—*In the Country, near the Village.* BELFORD *and* PERIOD *in Conversation.*

Belf. And you absolutely know nothing of this coxcomb, who personated me at Mrs. Derville's?

Period. Not a syllable, my lord, nor did I intend any coxcomb but myself should have that honour. Why, an action will lie at common law, and I'll so exhibit the fellow in my tour——

Belf. A truce with your law and your literature, and devise what's to be done. I dare not think of it; yet is there too great cause for suspecting that Mrs. Derville is herself in concert with the impostor, and that he is a favour'd rival.

Period. If she has promised you marriage, you may bring an action against her as soon as the wedding is over—or you may be revenged by a satire—and in either case, the Court of Common Pleas, or the Court of Parnassus—I'm your man.

Belf. Torment and furies! Will you be serious for a moment?

Period. Hav'n't I been serious my whole tour? Hav'n't I been reduced to transcribe doggrel from the country church-yards, and dates from the doors of alms-houses? and now you tell me I'm not serious.

Belf. I wish, then, your tongue were as barren of words as your head of ideas. Once more, can you suggest how we may discover this adventurer, this pretended Lord Orton?

Period. Really I can think of no better plan than for me to personate his lordship, as we first proposed. Say that my letters and baggage have been stolen, and insist upon it that the thief must be the impostor she received at her house.

Belf. But what purpose will this answer?

Period. Why, I shall judge by her manner if she is really privy to the deception.

Belf. You are right. Nay, you shall get yourself installed at the Abbey—pretend a passion for her as we originally plann'd, and if she stands the test, and clears up the mystery of her conduct, I will offer her my hand, and throw aside my doubts for ever.

Period. And I'll draw up the marriage articles, and relate the whole history in my travels. For if you know any little secret history of a friend, always publish it; nothing sells like private anecdote.

Belf. O, sell as many anecdotes as you will; all I desire is, not to be favoured with them gratis—So, meet me at my lodgings an hour hence, and I'll give you farther instructions for your reception at the Abbey.

Period. Yes; but will it be possible to impose on Lady Zephyrine and Sir Caustic?

Belf. On Lady Zephyrine perhaps not—but I'll give you letters, in which, without explaining my reasons, I shall apprize her of my return, and en-gage her for a few hours to favour the deception. You must, however, take care to see her alone on your first arrival—As for Sir Caustic, as I have never seen him, with her ladyship's assistance, it will be very easy to prevent any suspicion on his part.

Period. There's one thing, my lord, I had forgot. I've an old uncle in the next village, and if I meet him we shall be discovered.

Belf. Oh! your peerage will not last so long as you might be making your maiden speech—and it's not likely he will see you at the Abbey, still less at Mrs. Derville's. Yet stay; a thought has just struck me, but 'tis mean, detestable.—But then does not the mystery, nay, the conduct of Mrs. Derville jus-tify me.—No matter—if she loves me, love will plead my pardon; if not, even her anger will scarcely add to my wretchedness. By means of my intelligence with Winifred, I can get concealed during your first interview.

Period. 'Tis eaves-dropping, my lord, and liable to an action. However, as you please; and I think your lordship is authorised to take down the evi-dence in short-hand.

Belf. Adieu! In an hour I shall expect you. My doubts and anxiety are worse than conviction: and I can endure this suspense no longer.   [*Exit.*

Period. [*Taking papers out of his port-folio.*] And

now for my notes—Saw—yes—saw trees by the
road side; whether oaks or apples, not quite sure.—
Saw between—Zounds! 'tis very hard, when a man
travels on purpose to write, that he can see nothing
but what other people have seen before him! Hold,
though—[AP-GRIFFIN *enters and listens behind.*]—
Saw between Cum Gumfred and Aberkilliguen,
young goats, an old fox, and a Welsh ass.

Ap-Grif. Eh! my nephew Period! How the
devil came you to be ass hunting in Wales, when
you should have been braying yourself at Westminster Hall? What business have you to be engross-
ing here by the road side, when you should be
taking notes at the Old Bailey.

Period. Why, now, don't be choleric, uncle; don't
irritate the blood of the Ap-Griffins—I'm only
[*aside*] 'Slife! what shall I say? I'm on the circuit—I'm on a tour—I'm going to publish "Travels in North Wales," and I thought [though it
isn't absolutely necessary] I might just as well take
a peep at the country, before I gave an account
of it.

Ap-Grif. Zooks! hav'n't you done with your
nonsense yet? Why, when I was in London, your
chambers were beset with printer's devils, bringing
proof sheets, as you call'd them, of your "Tour to
Wandsworth; with Remarks during a Voyage to
Battersea." Ads-death! is this the way to rise at
the bar? to advertise yourself running about on a
Tom fool's errand, as if nobody could see mile-stones
and church steeples but yourself.

Period. Why, if I have but a name, what signifies
how?

Ap-Grif. Yes, yes; I see you're incorrigible—
just as you were when you carried your briefs and
your tours in the same bag to the Old Bailey, and
astonished the court by beginning a flowery descrip-

tion of Botany Bay, instead of a defence of petty larceny.

Period. I tell you, a professional man's nothing if he doesn't write—Don't all the physicians who have nothing to do at home travel abroad, and write themselves into practice? Don't the clergy write themselves into livings? and don't the lawyers write plays and pamphlets till they get briefs?

Ap-Grif. Eh, jackanapes! Did Hale ever rise by scribbling farces and tours, eh?

Period. Hale! dry—dry; dull as the *bon mots* of a newspaper. Language, sir—nothing will do now but style. Only—only let me be Lord Chancellor, and you shall see Hale, and Bacon, and Littleton, and Coke, as much out of fashion as their own wigs and whiskers.

Ap-Grif. You reprobate, I shall see you hangman first.

Period. Oh! I'll so reform the dissonant language of the law—then you shall see reports measured into blank verse—Briefs like the descriptions of the moon in modern romance, and chancery suits in the style of Gibbon.

Ap-Grif. Here's an unnatural coxcomb! Here's a profane rascal! wants to violate the venerable obscurity of the law.

Period. Then I'll have none of your John Does and Richard Roes—your Nokes and your Styles. Law shall be a comment on history and poetry As thus—" Brutus *versus* Cæsar"—" Pan *versus* Apollo"—or in a conspiracy, " Menelaus, and others, *versus* Paris."—I'll explain the rest another time.— Bye, uncle.

Ap-Grif. How I could twist the profligate's neck! Why, sirrah, you're not leaving the country without letting me know how you came, and where you are going, and——

Period. [*Aside.*] An inquisitive old blockhead, plague of him! If I tell him I'm going to the Abbey, he'll follow me, and spoil our scheme. I won't hear him.   [*Going.*

Ap-Grif. Why, sirrah, I say, how came you here? Where are you going?

Period. I hav'n't time to tell you, now. I'm in haste. I must be brief—Good bye, uncle, good bye!

Ap-Grif. What, you keep me here an hour, prating with your Pans and your Cæsars, and now you're in haste—I must be brief, uncle, [*mimicking him*] I must be brief—Answer me, I say, or I'll crack—No, your skull's crack'd already—but I'll beat you, till you shall be of as many colours as a mildew'd parchment.

Period. Psha!—tiresome! You must know, then, that I came here with an old gentleman that's rich enough to buy the principality. I'm now going to dine with him at the next town, and then we set off in a chaise and four, for—for—for the Chester assizes.

Ap-Grif. Rich, did you say? And do you know him?

Period. Oh, yes! We've been hand and glove these three, ay, these seven years. He's the most comical old fellow—continually in a passion through pure benevolence; and is out of humour with all the world, merely because he thinks it neither so good nor so happy as it was fifty years ago.

[AP-GRIFFIN *debating with himself, and standing between* PERIOD *and the way he was going.*

Ap-Grif. Gad, a notion is just come into my head—Now, if I could but trust him, perhaps this rich stranger would buy the diamonds; and I do so long to get rid of them. Then, if this fellow here should cheat me—but no; the whelp's honest—A little wrong above, [*pointing to his head*] but sound

z

enough below [*pointing to his heart.*] Nay! I'll e'en
trust him. [*Altering his tone.*] Well, Tim, I believe
I must forgive thee, thy tours, and thy whims. I'm
sure thee art an honest lad after all.

Period. What does the old crocodile mean now?

Ap-Grif. Dear Tim, it's just come into my head
that you can do a little job for me—can you be
secret?

Period. As a chamber counsel.

Ap-Grif. Can you be honest?

Period. Ah! thank ye; am I not your nephew?

Ap-Grif. Hum—Nay, I don't doubt your honesty
—even a lawyer, you know, shou'dn't cheat his own
flesh and blood. Always do the just thing, Tim,
when it's not against the law. Why, I've got some
jewels here to dispose of for a client—Mind, they're
not my own—Now, don't you think your rich fellow-traveller might purchase them? Here they are.

[*Takes out the jewels, and gives them to* PERIOD.

Period. They're rich enough for the great Mogul. The gentleman's old, and, perhaps, may not
care for them; but I'll try, if you will——

Ap-Grif. Do, then, my good lad [*in a doubtful
wheedling tone.*] I know, Tim, thou'lt be honest.

Period. Oh, if you doubt it!

Ap-Grif. No, no; I don't doubt. But I may as
well go along with you to the gentleman.

Period. 'Twill be too far, sir—Pray don't attempt
it.

Ap-Grif. No, no, it won't—I can walk, Timmy, I
can walk.

Period. [*Aside.*] Zounds! what an old torment it
is! Indeed, sir, 'tis too far; so, if you can't trust me,
take the diamonds again.

Ap-Grif. Why the deuce can't you let me go with
you? If you won't, I'll follow you, and offer them
to a gentleman myself.

Period. 'Sdeath! what shall I do? I must even
tell him partly the truth—only, instead of an inno-

cent frolic, I'll say I'm engaged in a bit of roguery, and then he'll be sure to keep my secret.

Ap-Grif. What are you muttering? Come, let's set out. I thought you were in a hurry.

Period. So I am; but——

Ap-Grif. But what!

Period. Ha ha! its comical enough too—it will make you laugh. Why, you must know, I'm going to the Abbey with the gentleman I have been telling you of, and I have pass'd myself upon him for Lord Orton. Nobody here knows his lordship's person; so I'm to marry, in his name, a great heiress that's just come down on a visit. Isn't it a special project? Isn't it a good thing?

Ap-Grif. [*Alarmed.*] Oh, yes; a devilish good thing. [*Aside.*] I wish I had my diamonds again, though, honest Tim.—[*To* PERIOD.] Udso, I had forgot—give me the case—there's a ring wanting.

Period. Give it me, then, and I'll wear it—as I am to personate a lord, you know.

Ap-Grif. But, now I think on't, I don't know what to ask: so I'll stay till Ephraim Lacker, the Jew, comes this way.

Period. No, uncle, no ; I understand diamonds, and understand you—You're afraid to trust me; but I'm a very honest fellow, though I'm your nephew. I shan't, however, part with the jewels; for, now you have my secret, I'll keep them as hostages for your secrecy; so come to the Abbey this evening, inquire for Lord Orton, and you shall have either the diamonds, or the value of them.

Ap-Grif. Well, then, I'll keep your secret—but, remember now, Tim, honesty's the best policy—always do the just thing. Hark ye, though, what new freak's this? I see you've got a cockade in your hat.

Period. To be sure—why, I'm in the volunteers.

Who so fit to fight for the laws as those who live by them?   [*Exit* PERIOD.

Ap-Grif. If I had known, though, that this fool had improv'd so much by my counsels as to be such a proficient in knavery, I wou'dn't have trusted him.—A little roguery's a very good engine to employ against others; but we always view it with virtuous indignation when it may be turn'd against ourselves.   [*Exit.*

ACT IV.

SCENE I.—*A Music-Room at the Abbey.*

Through Doors. PERIOD *as Lord* ORTON, *Sir* CAUSTIC OLDSTYLE.

Sir Caustic. And why the deuce didn't you tell me on the road, that you were my nephew?

Period. And how shou'd I know I was your nephew, unless you had told me you were my uncle?—To say truth, however, I did suspect it, and only had a mind to surprise you agreeably.

Sir Caustic. [*Ironically.*] Yes, yes——I'm very agreeably surpris'd. I wish I was in Cornwall again, though 'twere at the bottom of a tin-mine. The transition from soft sea breezes to the keen air of these Welsh mountains would throw some people in a consumption; now, I plainly perceive, it will give me the jaundice—I hadn't been here an hour before one begins ringing rhymes in my ear, till she's as hoarse as a drill serjeant. Another stuns me with inquiries, about the price of turtle and consols. Yet my own niece is not visible, as they call it.

Period. Sir, it's the custom amongst people of rank to——

Sir Caustic What, to be visible every where, and to every body, but at home, and to their own relations? A plague o' such customs.

Period. They're very necessary, sir, for people in a certain style—myself, for example. Were husband and wife, father and son, uncles and nephews, to have free access to each other, 'twou'd occasion more practice than we shou'd get through, if courts of justice were as numerous as gaming-houses, and term to last all the year.

Sir Caustic. Get through in the courts, I don't understand you.

Period. For instance now—there was a Crim. Con. cause, where I pleaded for defendant.

Sir Caustic. You pleaded!

Period. Yes—[*recollecting himself*]—in the house, you know, as a peer.

Sir Caustic. Plead for the defendant in a Crim. Con. cause! Here's morality!

Period. But hold—I had forgot my commission. You old-fashion'd people love magnificence more than convenience. Now, if you are fond of diamonds, and want to make a purchase, here are some. Do look at 'em—they're the prettiest rings.

Sir Caustic. Not I—A man should be asham'd to wear a diamond on his finger, while there's an industrious hand wants employment, or a disabled one, relief. But let's see 'em; perhaps my niece may have a fancy to some baubles. [*Taking them.*] Why, sure—No, it can't. Why, yes—They are the very family jewels lately sent me by one of my friends, now abroad, for his nephew, young Bewley. Tell me how you came by them.

Period. [*Aside.*] Here's an anecdote! What the devil shall I do? Old nunc has certainly stole them. [*To* OLDSTYLE.] Sir, 'tis a commission of delicacy; and we never betray a client's, that is, a friend's secrets.

Sir Caustic. Yes, but I must know—there's some villany in this business.

Period. I'll warrant there is.

Sir Caustic. These diamonds were certainly consigned to me by my old friend, as a present to his
nephew, and for the purpose of redeeming a family
estate out of the claws of an old rogue of an attorney.

Period. [*Aside.*] Aye, aye, that's uncle sure
enough.

Sir Caustic. When I left Cornwall, having some
inquiries to make in London about my deceased
son, and the case being urgent, I dispatch'd a
trusty agent with the diamonds; but, notwithstanding my repeated inquiries, I have never heard of
either diamonds or messenger. All that I know is,
that the young man, who was then from home,
never received them.

Period. I assure you, sir, they came fairly into my
hands, whatever roguery they may have encountered before; but do you keep them, and——

Sir Caustic. Yes, but the person who entrusted
them to you!

Period. He'll be here this evening, and you shall
see him. [*Aside.*] Get the old shark off though, if
I can.

Enter Lady ZEPHYRINE *and* GURNET [*through
Doors.*]

Lady ZEPHYRINE *dressed in the Extreme of the Fashion.*

Lady Zeph. You're welcome to the Abbey, sir.
Believe me, I am rejoiced to see you well, and in
this country.

Sir Caustic. Thank you, thank you, ma'am. I
suppose my niece will be here by and by—though,
methinks, she's not over civil.

Gurnet. Why, this is my ward.

Period. Yes, sir, this is my sister.

Sir Caustic. It isn't, nor it can't, nor it shan't be.

You, my niece Zephyrine Mutable!   What! this, I
suppose, is one of your agreeable surprises, too?

[*To* PERIOD.

Lady Zeph. Really, sir, this is so strange!

Sir Caustic. Strange!   Aye, strange indeed.   Let
me see. [*Looking in his pocket, takes out a picture,
returns it, and takes out another.*] No! that's not it—
Oh! Here it is—Here's a picture of my niece, done
only two years ago; and you're no more like her
than I am to Tippoo Saib.

Lady Zeph. The miniature, I presume, sir, which
was sent you to Cornwall before my grandmother's
death?

Period. Oh, the want of likeness, sir, is nothing.
These cursed painters only think of making what
they call a good picture ; and whether it resembles
you or your horse, is no concern of theirs.   Why,
you might have had what they call a portrait of
Lord Orton only three months ago, and it mightn't
be like me the least in the world—I appeal to Lady
Zephyrine.

Sir Caustic. Zooks, sir, but did you ever know
black ringlets change to auburn?   Then, instead of
the clear brown lively complexion of my niece, a
dead white stucco; [*looking at the picture*] and, for
the cheeks, egad the amateur has outdone the artist,
and the rosebud is become a downright piony.

Lady Zeph. Perhaps, sir, my exterior may deserve
this censure; yet, I trust, I have a heart which will
not be found unworthy of your affection.

Sir Caustic. Why then, I wish pretty women with
worthy hearts wou'dn't deform the index to them.

Lady Zeph. But fashion, sir—

Sir Caustic. Don't talk to me of fashion.   Will
you, or any woman in these days, ever be as handsome as your grandmother?   And did she rouge,
and varnish, or wear a red wig?   I detest your
modern whim whams.

Period. Modern, sir! Why the ladies all dress now *à l'antique*—Gone back two thousand years at least. Nothing but Portias and Lucretias, from St. James's Square to St. George's Fields.

Sir Caustic. Aye, aye; as absurd as they are licentious, and they hav'n't even discernment to see that their follies are a satire on their vices. There's Mrs. Gadfly, who gets rid of her children to a nurse as soon as they're born, and to a boarding-school as soon as they can speak, trusses and twists her head up to imitate the mother of the Gracchi!

Period. 'Faith, it's very true—Then, there's the fat, giggling widow, who married her butler three weeks after her husband's death, wears a black wig *à la Niobe.*

Lady Zeph. Come, sir, forgive me for not being so old or so handsome as my grandmother; and let me shew you our improvements.

Sir Caustic. I've seen too many of your improvements already; however, I'll accompany you, because, in my time, attention to women was the fashion.

Period. [*Aside.*] Now, if I could borrow this miniature of Lady Zephyrine, it would certainly convince Mrs. Derville of my being the real Lord Orton. Sir Caustic, will you oblige me with Lady Zephyrine's picture for a few hours? I've a friend hard by, who copies admirably.

Sir Caustic. [*Gives the picture.*] Here—But hark ye. Hadn't your friend better just take a peep at the red wig? [*Going.*]

Period. Stay, Sir Caustic, you have lately received letters from India. Cou'dn't you now assist me with some little domestic anecdote of the Bengal tyger, or the amours of Tippoo Saib, or some secret history of a nabob, just to embellish my tour?

Sir Caustic. Tippoo Saib, nabobs, and Bengal

tygers, in a tour to Caernarvonshire! Why what the
devil shou'd they do here?

Period. Introduce them—perfectly apropos. I see
a palace by the road side newly built—half a dozen
farms turn'd into a park—immorality plenty; provi-
sions scarce. I conclude, of course, I am in the
vicinage of a nabob: then pop comes in the secret
history, and Tippoo Saib, and the Bengal tyger, by
way of episode.

Sir Caustic. Why, if you could make this rambling
mania serve to expose the danger of over-grown,
ill-spent fortunes, perhaps I might be tempted to
take a frolic with you myself.

        [*Exit, leading Lady* ZEPHYRINE.

Period. And now for my attack on the fair cottager. Sorry to leave you, deputy; but if you want
amusement, I'll lend you my manuscript, or my
Tour to Wandsworth.

Gurnet. No, I thank your lordship; I'm just going
to take a peep in the butler's pantry, and I can't
say I'm much of a reader—never buy any books.
I gave sixpence once for a Treatise on Corn Cutting;
and instead of finding any thing to the purpose,
there were politics enough to crack the clearest
head in Lombard-street.

Period. Yes, it's our way. When we want to
push a subject, we give it a taking title; no matter
whether the book contains a word that answers to
it, or not.   [*Exit* PERIOD.

Gurnet. A pretty sample of nobility, this: begins
making love to my wife, before he'd got his boots
off; and I've already found 'em twice closetted together from poetical sympathy, as Mrs. Gurnet
calls it. Just now, too, I overheard them make an
appointment, under pretence of reading their pro-
ductions in the Park; but I'll after them—prevention
is better than remedy. These whirligig chaps think
if a man lives east of Charing-Cross, he's made for

nothing but cuckoldom and gluttony, though egad
the line of demarcation has long been past, and I
don't see but horns and turtle are as much the fashion in the west as in the east.   [*Exit.*

SCENE II.—*A Parlour at Mrs.* DERVILLE'S.—
WINIFRED *pushing* BELFORD *into a Closet at the
Extremity of the Scene.*

Win. There, there, you'll be safe enough; my
mistress never uses this closet; and, to make sure,
I'll lock it, and take the key—I wish though my
lord had done with his trials and disguises; he'll
certainly get me into some scrape at last. Oh! how
your people of fine notions torment themselves.
                                          [*Exit.*

Enter PERIOD *as Lord* ORTON, *and Mrs.* DERVILLE.

Mrs. Derv. Nay, then, I acknowledge, my lord,
that I do know the person who assumed your name;
but, as I am certain he could have no concern in the
theft of your letters and baggage, you must excuse
my betraying him.
Period. [*Affecting passion.*] Alas! madam, these
are trifling considerations; but if you knew how
deeply I am interested in discovering an impostor,
who, I fear, is a fortunate rival——
Mrs. Derv. Rival, my lord! If you have no further commands, permit me——
Period. Commands, madam! No! I have to supplicate, to tell you, that I have long admir'd, long
ador'd you.   Did you but know how I have pursued
you; from Florence to Leghorn; from Leghorn to
London; and from London to Caernarvon; but you'll
know it all when you read my tour, and I'm sure
you'll admire the style, and pity the author.
Mrs. Derv. [*Ironically.*] Why, I must confess,

your lordship seems in a state deserving of pity. How you became acquainted with these circumstances, I am at a loss to guess; but if this is not some now artifice, and you are really Lord Orton, I trust you will not avail yourself of a situation, you perhaps know, is unfortunate, to insult me.

Period. I insult you, ma'am! I never insulted any one in my life, except a coffee-house critic. Surely you cannot suspect my honour, or doubt my rank. I have this moment left the Abbey. Then there's my sister's picture. [*Giving her the picture.*] Let that convince you—have compassion on my sufferings, madam—I'll draw you up such a settlement— I'll dedicate my work to you—I'll——

[*Mrs.* DERVILLE *takes the picture carelessly; but on looking at it, nearly faints.*

Mrs. Derv. Tell me, my lord—I conjure you by your dearest hopes. Tell me how you came by this picture?

Period. 'Sdeath! what's all this? That picture, ma'am—that picture—Why, ma'am, to say the truth, it's not mine; it's my uncle's, who is now at the Abbey.

Mrs. Derv. Permit me to keep it a few hours. It was once mine, and is not the portrait of Lady Zephyrine. Look at it, [*shewing the picture*] it's of the utmost importance that I should see the owner.

Period. Now I recollect, I saw the old gentleman with two pictures, and he has, by mistake, given me the wrong one. [*Looking at the miniature.*] No, no; this is certainly not the lady with the red wig, and——

Enter WINIFRED.

Win. Ma'am, here's Mr. Jargon, Lady Zephyrine's suitor, at the door, and he's so rude, he protests he must see you, and have an answer to his letter.

Period. [*Aside.*] Zounds, what that rascal, my

cousin Jargon! Nay, then, I must vanish. Will
you give me leave, ma'am, just to slip up the chimney, or out at the house top, or into the clock-case,
or under a cheese-press? I have such reasons,
'sdeath, I wou'dn't, for my peerage, be seen by this
fellow.

Mrs. Derv. Well, you may go this way, my lord;
I shall be releas'd from him at any rate. [*Shews*
Period.] Yes, this Jargon sent me an impertinent
letter this morning, and I'll see him; for, though
Lady Zephyrine's conduct towards me has been unworthy, yet, if I can, by convincing her of the baseness of her pretended lover, save her from the ruin
of such an union, it will repay me for the momentary
indignity of his addresses. Winifred, you may shew
Mr. Jargon in. [*Exit* Winifred.] Alas! I had
hoped the situation I have chosen would have
serv'd me from being thus persecuted. Belford,
too, so warm an advocate for Lady Zephyrine, and
so long absent—Heigho!

Enter Jargon *and* Winifred.

Jargon. Faith, ma'am, you're so snug, and as
difficult of access as a poet in debt; I've been
arguing with the tongue and the claws of your
Welsh dragon here this half hour.

Win. Dragon, indeed! A conceited, ugly fel-
low.   [*Exit.*

Jargon. Well, what say you, my little original?
What do you think of my proposal? A house in
Marybone, a black boy, and a curricle—None of
your old-fashion'd, mysterious work; nobody now
do any thing they're ashamed of, or at least are not
asham'd of any thing they do—an opera-box next my
wife [that is to be] Lady Zephyrine—a Faro-table—
then our whole order in your train—puff you in the papers—[*takes out a glass*] stare you into notice at
the theatre, you'll make such a blaze.

Mrs. Derv. [*Aside.*] Oh! patience—But I'll have

my revenge, and for Lady Zephyrine's sake. 'Tis impossible, sir, for me to treat your generosity as it deserves, till I have had a little time to reflect. But if you'll meet me at eight this evening in the Hermitage, you shall receive my answer. This key, which the steward lends me during the absence of the family, will admit you. At present I must intreat you to depart.

Jargon. Oh, oh! she parleys—Yes, yes, ma'am, —give you time—all fair, that I see you understand business. No Philandering—'tis not our way. Negociate—dispute term—offer our ultimatum—sign the treaty, and heigh for the black boy and curricle!

Mrs. Derv. I must beg, sir, at present, that you'll retire.

Jargon. I'm gone. Won't interrupt your reflections. Oh! I'm a made, a complete made man. Such a decoy for a Faro-bank!   [*Exit.*

Enter *Mrs.* GURNET.

Mrs. Gur. [*In a flippant familiar manner.*] Pray excuse this intrusion, my dear. A countryman told me just now I should find Lord Orton here, and we are going to have the most delightful literary ramble in the Park.

GURNET *entering with* WINIFRED.

Gurnet. I tell you they're both here; I watched 'em in. Why, you rural go-between, I'll have you put in the stocks—sent to the house of correction. So, so, Mrs. Muse, I've found you, have I? This comes of your sentiments—your odes—your pastorals—But I'll search out your Apollo—I'll have a divorce, if it's only to warn other men of the danger of rhyming wives, and the iniquity of travelling authors and tour-mongers.

Mrs. Gur. Mr. Gurnet, you make me blush for

A A

the coarseness of your ideas. You ought to know, that the little platonic attachment between me and Lord Orton does you honour.

Gurnet. Oh! what assurance reading and writing gives a woman! If you hadn't been a poet and an author, you'd have had some shame—Shan't escape though. I'll ferret out your platonic Apollo, I warrant. [*Looks about, and stops before the closet where* BELFORD *is.*]—Aye, I have him—here he is. Open the door, I say!

Mrs. Derv. Sir, this violence——

Gurnet. Out of the way, thou village handmaid of iniquity! Where's the key? I'll have him out!

Mrs. Derv. Open the door, Winifred, that I may be released from these insults. I assure you, sir—

Win. [*Aside.*] Blessed St. David! what shall I do? Lord, ma'am, I can't find the key! and the gentleman ought to be ashamed to make such an outcry in a modest house. Why, there's nothing in the closet but wool.

Gurnet. [*Shews a part of* BELFORD's *coat.*] Then the wool has manufactured itself into cloth; for I'll swear here's a piece of a man's coat between the door. Now what say you, Mrs. Modesty?

Win. Then I'm sure the fairies have been here.

Mrs. Derv. What can this mean? Let the door be opened this instant.

Win. Well, if I must—I believe, for my part, the house is haunted. [WINIFRED *opens the closet door, and discovers* BELFORD.

Enter Sir CAUSTIC OLDSTYLE, *who speaks from within.*

[*The surprise and confusion of Mrs.* DERVILLE *should appear as the effect of shame at detection.* BELFORD *turns against the scene in agitation.*

Mrs. Derv. Heavens! Mr. Belford!

Mrs. Gur. Why, this is the most mysterious event!

Gurnet. What's this one of your Welsh fairies? or is it another of your platonic attachments, Mrs. Gurnet?

Mrs. Derv. Cruel, ungenerous Belford!

Sir Caustic. What, a man hid in my pretty cottager's closet! I came here to thank you for your kindness this morning, and to escape for a moment the dissipation of a fashionable family in retirement; but I see licentiousness is not confined to the mansions of wealth. Adieu, young woman. I had hoped to find in you one who had preserved, with modern elegance of manners, a simple and uncorrupted heart. Perhaps the time may come when you may grow tired of that vice for which you do not seem intended; and in the hours of sorrow and the pangs of repentance—remember—you have a friend.   [*Exit.*

Mrs. Derv. Stop, sir!—Oh, how shall I survive this humiliation!—[*To* GURNET.]—For you, sir——

Mrs. Gur. Yes, you indelicate monster!—This comes of your gross suspicions. But I'll write a romance on purpose to expose you. I'll make you an epitome of all the German barons and Italian counts. I'll——   [*Exit.*

Gurnet. And I'll secure myself from a platonic cuckoldom in future. I'll take you to Garlic-hill, and there you shall fast from pens, ink, and paper as long as you live. So, come along, and let's get out of rural felicity and the delights of retirement.
     [*Exit Mrs.* GURNET.

Belf. Before you go, sir, let me exculpate— 'Sdeath! they're gone, madam! I feel too much the cause you have for resentment to attempt any justification. Yet, be assured the conduct to which I have descended is punished, cruelly punished, by this fatal conviction, that I am doomed to love where I cannot esteem.   [*Exit.*

Mrs. Derv. [*After a moment of agitation, turns to* WINIFRED.] Treacherous, ungrateful girl! you who have witnessed my hours of sorrow and seclusion, have seen with what solicitude I have avoided mankind. If your heart is not entirely corrupted, you will feel with remorse the complicated disgrace and wretchedness in which you have involved me.

Win. I'm sure, ma'am, I didn't mean——

Mrs. Derv. Well, I shall not reproach you: but my resolution is taken. The only further service I require of you is to prepare for my leaving this place to-morrow morning.

Win. Oh, ma'am! surely you won't leave the farm, and the stock, and the cows, and the poultry?

Mrs. Derv. Argue not, but obey me. I'll now keep my appointment with Lady Zephyrine, that I may at least explain my own conduct, if not reform hers. Did you send my note to Mr. Bewley?

Win. Yes, madam—he received it two hours ago.

Mrs. Derv. Then this picture.—I'll see the stranger at the Abbey, learn how it came into his possession, and then bid adieu for ever to a scene in which my innocence could not protect me from shame and misery. Oh! never let the humble votary of retirement seek it near the contagious abode of riches and dissipation.   [*Exeunt.*

ACT V.

SCENE I.—*A Park or Pleasure-Ground.*

Enter BELFORD.

Belf. Yes, this is the place—I can't have mistaken. Jargon must pass this way to the hermitage; and if he is not as cowardly as he is base, I shall at once revenge the perfidy of Mrs. Derville, and prevent his designs on my sister. Oh! Eugenia, thou hast made my life of so little value, that I do not hesitate to risk it, even against that of a coxcomb—But I hear footsteps.

[*Retires as behind the trees.*

Enter Lady ZEPHYRINE.

Lady Zeph. Well, if she does but come, I shall enjoy her confusion at finding her gallant peer dwindled into a spinster; she's here—And now for my triumph over this little prude with her heroic sentiments and her closetted heroes.

Enter Mrs. DERVILLE.

You seem in search of somebody, ma'am.

Mrs. Derv. [*Distinctly, and with dignity.*] I am, madam; I came in search of a female, who was once a model of feminine excellence—As lovely in her mind as her person; but who, seduced by dissipation, dazzled by splendour, and perverted by vanity, abandoned the object of her first affections, degrades her family, and sullies her reputation by becoming the dupe and the victim of a—gambler.

Lady Zeph. [*Confused.*] Enough, madam—Hold! I——

Mrs. Derv. Nay, this is not all. In the wanton-

A A 3

ness of an unfeeling prosperity, either curious or
jealous, forgetting the dignity of her rank and the
delicacy of her sex, she came, in a mean disguise,
to assail with the temptations of affluence and vice
the integrity of an—inferior.

Lady Zeph. [*Mortified.*] Oh! spare me, spare me!
I intreat you.

Mrs. Derv. And if unaware of the artifice, dazzled by the title she assumed, or allured by the
offered prospect of wealth and pleasure, the rectitude she attacked had proved too weak for the
combat—O ungenerous, unworthy triumph! to have
found that a poor, friendless, unprotected woman
had yielded to the same temptations which, under
all the advantages of birth, fortune, and surrounding friends, have alienated the affections and corrupted the heart of Lady Zephyrine Mutable——

Lady Zeph. Forgive me, you have taught me a
lesson which that heart will never forget. From
this moment I relinquish my assumed follies, and
dare to be myself.

Mrs. Derv. Yes, Lady Zephyrine, I'm persuaded
you were designed by nature for something better
than a fashionable coquette.

Lady Zeph. [*Gaily.*] I dare say I was; for I feel
already as if I had just put off my great grandfather's
coat of armour : why, do you know, that though I
play on the tambourine, I hate the sound of it; and
though I boast of being a good shot, the touch of
fire-arms gives me an ague; and as for cards, in my
grandmother's time, I have gone to sleep with three
honours in my hand at the most critical point of a rubber.   But fashion, my dear Mrs. Derville, fashion!
—one doesn't like to be different from other people.

Mrs. Derv. Ah, Lady Zephyrine, don't deceive
yourself.   It is not the desire of resembling other
people, but that of being distinguished from them, is
the source of your errors.   Believe me, the trifling

and vicious characters whom you have been so zealous to imitate are few compared to those, among
your own rank, who behold a conduct like yours
with regret and censure——

Lady Zeph. Nay, I am sure I would never have
endured the labour of making myself ridiculous, if
I hadn't thought it fashionable.

Mrs. Derv. No, no, thank Heaven, neither vice
nor folly are yet fashionable. And though both
are too much tolerated, the example of domestic
virtues, conspicuous in the highest station of the
kingdom, will, I trust, long preserve our national
manners from that last state of depravation which
erects vice into a model.

Lady Zeph. [*Archly.*] You preach charmingly.—
Pray, was all this eloquence taught you by the closet orator?

Mrs. Derv. I understand your raillery; and when
I acknowledge that this young man is the secret object of my affections, I hope you will credit me, when
I assure you I am yet to learn the motives of his con-
cealment. But no matter. To-morrow, Lady Zephyrine, I quit this country for ever.

Lady Zeph. For ever?

Mrs. Derv. Yes; but before I go, I have a communication to make, which, if you do not love Mr.
Jargon——

Lady Zeph. Love him! I won't say I hate him,
because he's too contemptible for hatred; but I
hate myself for the folly which obliges me to listen
to him.

Mrs. Derv. How has your ladyship forfeited the
best privilege of rank? that of repelling impertinence?

Lady Zeph. Why, as I have confided my follies to
you, you may as well know the consequences of them.
This vile Jargon has won of me impossible sums;
I am no arithmetician, I can't recollect and mul-

tiply the items; but I have been obliged to give him a note for—four of the six thousands which are my whole fortune, independent of my brother.

Mrs. Derv. Fatal imprudence! read this letter.

Lady Zephyrine reads—at first to herself.

Lady Zeph. [*Reading.*] " Accept my terms—my marriage with the little idol of the Abbey shall not prevent my adoring you with the most perfect and unimaginable devotion—　　　JARGON."
Well, the wretch is no hypocrite; for he scarcely takes the trouble of professing a passion for me.— However, if you'll give me this letter, though I don't expect a cold, systematic coxcomb should be susceptible of shame for the commission of a base action, he may of the ridicule to which he is exposed by detection. He'll be at the Abbey this evening.

Mrs. Derv. I fancy we shall find him without going so far. Come this way, and I'll explain to you as we go along.

Lady Zeph. [*Taking her hand.*] My fair monitress, I came here in expectation of a triumph, which, I trust, my heart would hereafter have reproached me for; but to you I am indebted for the best of triumphs, the triumph over my own follies. [*Exeunt.*

SCENE II.—*Before the Door of the Hermitage.*

Lady ZEPHYRINE *and Mrs.* DERVILLE, *following each other cautiously.*

Mrs. Derv. I've exceeded my time, and perhaps my spark's patience. He's not here.

Lady Zeph. [*Softly.*] I'll just peep in at the hermitage window. [*Looks in.*] Well, my dear, if you are not the object of his waking thoughts, I dare say you are of his dreams, for there he is, fast asleep.

Mrs. Derv. I suppose he has sacrificed so freely to your ladyship's birth-day, that he has forgotten both me and himself.

Lady Zeph. O, don't suppose a gamester ever forgets himself. [*Looks in at the window.*] I dare say now, he has been calculating chances. Look, there's his pocket-book and pencil down by him.

Mrs. Derv. I wish we could take it without waking him, and write both our names in it—if he is yet susceptible of shame.

Lady Zeph. A gamester susceptible of shame! O, you know nothing of the world.

Mrs. Derv. Have you the master key of the grounds?

Lady Zeph. Luckily I have—here it is—but——

Mrs. Derv. Hush! stay! [*Goes in cautiously, and brings out the book.*] Here's the book—will your ladyship write your name first—quick!—I tremble so.

[*Lady* ZEPHYRINE *taking the book from Mrs.*
DERVILLE, *a paper drops out of it.*

Lady Zeph. Heavens! what's this? My note, which, through fear of being exposed to my uncle, I renewed on my coming of age this morning.

Mrs. Derv. Surely, what has been so basely obtained, might, without blame, be cancelled. Decide—perhaps a moment——

Lady Zeph. [*After some agitation.*] No, though this wretch has no honour, mine shall be sacred. The loss of my fortune is the just punishment of my folly, and I will abide by it. Replace the book.

Mrs. Derv. As you please. [*Aside, takes the note unperceived by Lady* ZEPHYRINE, *and returns with the book cautiously.*] But, by your ladyship's leave, the point of honour shall be determined by your uncle; in the mean while I'll secure the point of law. You seem agitated.

Lady Zeph. I am—I have had a little struggle between love and integrity.—Ah! Eugenia! with that little sum I could have retired with Bewley, but now——

Enter BEWLEY, *gaily.*

Bew. What, again, Lady Zephyrine. Why, I am become the very favourite of fortune. Let her throw her acres to fools, and her dross to knaves—here's metal more attractive!

Lady Zeph. You are gay, sir!

Bew. Yes, gay as your ladyship's smiles. Why not? Why shou'dn't a man without a care left be gay? Others are the slaves of fortune or of love; but for me, I'm a free man—I've lost my estate by the folly of my ancestors, and I've lost my mistress by——

Lady Zeph. [*Archly.*] By her own, eh?

Bew. Hem—no matter—One smile from Lady Zephyrine to-night, one adieu to-morrow, and heigh for London.

Lady Zeph. [*Timidly.*] For London, sir?

Bew. Yes. Isn't London the place for a man of spirit without sixpence? Are there not hazard tables and Faro banks, where those who have nothing become rich, and those who are rich become nothing? So, Cupid, take wing—honesty, avaunt, and heigh for London!

Lady Zeph. [*With volubility and spirit.*] I commend your resolution. Ah, the bewitching joys of the gaming-table, and the society of dear friends impatient to ruin you! the animating suspense between hope and fear, while Avarice, with sanguine eye and dilated palm, seizes in imagination its devoted sacrifice.—Oh—glorious! heigh for London! [*Turning suddenly to* BEWLEY.] Will you draw straws with me for a couple of thousands?

Bew. No, madam—your stake's too high for a ruin'd man.

Lady Zeph. Just the contrary—why, if you're ruin'd already, you know you can't lose. But, come, if you won't draw straws for the two thousands, will you take them without?

Bew. No, madam.   I—I—[*Surprised.*

Lady Zeph. Why, what an untractable mortal it is !   Then, will you take me and the two thousand together ?—[*She stops short, and then lays her hand on his arm with a tender frankness.*]—Oh, Bewley! this levity of yours is assumed—'tis in vain to deny it.   I know you love me.   My heart is yet—nay, it ever has been yours.   Will you accept my hand along with it ?

Bew. [*After some agitation.*]   Believe me, Lady Zephyrine, were that heart what I once thought it, the gift you offer, though it were accompanied by slavery, poverty, and a thousand ills, should be received with transport.   But now, forgive me, had I been rich, love might have tempted me to forget the conduct I have so long deplored: as it is, it shall not be said that I was bribed by the fortune of the wife to overlook the errors of the mistress.

[*Exit in disorder.*

Lady Zeph. Here's an obstinate wretch !   But he shall take me, errors and all, yet.

[*During the foregoing scene,* BELFORD *enters, and talks in the back ground with* Mrs. DERVILLE *in an air of supplication.*

Mrs. DERVILLE *coming forward with* BELFORD.

Mrs. Derv. The passion you profess, sir, is no excuse for your degrading its object.   From this moment we part; and let our separation be accompanied by this remembrance, that your misfortunes have not prevented your creating the tenderest interest in that heart which you have overwhelmed with shame and affliction.

[*Exeunt Mrs.* DERVILLE *and Lady* ZEPHYRINE.

Belf. Dear, generous Eugenia!   Yet still the mystery of her appearance—But away with suspicion.   I'll now to the Abbey, discover myself to Sir

Caustic Oldstyle, and by a candid explanation of
my conduct to Mrs. Derville, plead my pardon :

For doubts caus'd by passion she never can blame;
They are not ill-founded, or she feels the same.

[*Exit.*

SCENE III.—*A Room at the Abbey.*

Sir CAUSTIC OLDSTYLE *and* PERIOD.

Period. Then we've hung the cloisters and statues with artificial flowers. The space between is
made into a temporary room, in imitation of a grotto. How I shall shine in describing it.

Sir Caustic. I hate your paltry imitations of nature,
while nature herself is neglected. You'll run from
the shade of your villas to see a canvas grove at the
Opera-house—or only advertise that the Pantheon
is converted into an Esquimeaux hut, and all the
drawing-rooms shall be deserted.

Period. A proof, sir, of our love of simplicity.

Sir Caustic. Yes, as you eat dry biscuits after a
luxurious dinner. No, it's mere wantonness, and
rage for novelty. 'Twas but just now I met a fellow with a rule and pencil, estimating how much
'twould cost to pull down this venerable pile, and
erect some Italian gimcrack on the scite.

Period. What, Mr. Stucco, the great architect,
you mean? Yes, he's to run up a smart villa, convert the chapel into a private theatre, the kitchen
into an ice-house, and then he's to make the com-
pletest ruin in the Park.

Sir Caustic. Yes, yes; I dare say you'll not want
for ruins, if you've sent for a great architect. But,
mark me, I'll have nothing to do with your extra-
vagances. I never obtained my wealth by disgrac-
ing my country, nor shall it be spent in corrupting
it. No—I'll adopt the first blockhead that comes
in my way, provided he's not one of our own family.

Period. [*Aside.*] Now, if the old gentleman would but keep his word, then how I would write—such paper, such a type !—Ah ! didn't you say, sir, you were looking out for a blockhead of an heir? There's a very honest fellow, a friend of mine, Tim Period, a sort of a crackbrain—he's your man, sir—Adso, you'll have the merriest heir in christendom.—
                    [*Takes down a tamborine, and plays.*

Sir Caustic. Ah ! what you're going to have a dance ? Well, as 'tis my niece's birth-day, egad, if old Twang, the harper, were alive, I don't know but I might foot it a bit myself.

Period. I dare say, sir, Lady Zephyrine will, to oblige you, just—— [*Imitates the action of playing.*

Sir Caustic. Zounds, sirrah !—why, she's not turned drummer.

Period. Not absolutely beat the drum, sir; but this little elegant instrument—[*still imitating*]—Such grace ! such attitudes !

Sir Caustic. Mercy on us ! what has a modest woman to do with attitudes ? Does she dance on the rope too ? But I'll have done with her—I'll cut a passage through Snowdon, make a tunnel under the Irish channel, build churches of porcelain, and erect bridges of pearl—I'll die a beggar.

Enter a Servant.

Serv. Here's young Squire Bewley, my lord; he says your lordship desired to see him.

Period. Shew him into my office—[*Recollecting himself.*]—Psha ! my dressing-room, I mean.—Will you go with me, sir? You know you sent for him about the diamonds.

Sir Caustic. Aye, I'll follow you.
                    [*Exeunt* PERIOD *and Servant.*

This Bewley, too, I suppose, is some puppy, who has been running a match between his fortune and his constitution, and the latter happens to have held out

longest. Aye, aye, his uncle's prodigality to him
will be the only means of his starting again on the
same course. But this is the way—a man scorches five
and twenty years abroad, or abridges all the comforts of his life at home, as I have done, only to acquire a fortune for a son who turns jockey, and breaks
his neck; or a nephew, who turns author, and loses
his wits ; or a niece, who beats the drum, and wears
a red wig. But I'll game, build, die a beggar.——

Enter a Servant, shewing in Mrs. DERVILLE.

Well, young gentlewoman !—There's another disappointment too—Who would have thought—But the
whole sex are syrens—crocodiles !—I presume your
business isn't with me—You want the young spark
within, I suppose?

Mrs. Derv. Your pardon, sir ; but if you are the
uncle of Lord Orton——

Sir Caustic. Not I—I am uncle to nobody in the
world. I have neither nephews nor nieces. No, no
—thank Heaven, I have done with them.—There's
a couple of modern youngsters within, indeed, who
write tours and beat the drum—But mind, they
don't belong to me.

Mrs. Derv. I thought, sir, you had been the gentleman from whom Lord Orton received a miniature, that——

Sir Caustic. Aye, 'twas a fancy picture—not like
any body in the world—never had an original. If
you want to inquire about the painter, Lady Zephyrine will tell you ; and if you don't want to put me
in a passion, don't say another word about it.

Mrs. Derv. This is the strangest old gentleman !
—I will not, then, trouble you, sir, with this inquiry; yet, as I leave this country to-morrow, never
to return, give me leave to justify myself from the
suspicions which the extraordinary scene you were
witness to——

Sir Caustic. What, the closet scene! But I'll not hear a word—I'll not believe a syllable. There has been neither truth nor simplicity in any woman these fifty years.

Mrs. Derv. It is not, then, for an unhappy stranger, like myself, to contend against your prejudices; and I must, though with regret, depart unjustified in your opinion.

Sir Caustic. Eh! what! who told you to depart? How should I know you were unhappy? Who are you? Where are you going?

Mrs. Derv. Alas, sir! I can scarcely tell—If possible, where I shall be no longer liable to the persecution of man.

Sir Caustic. Then you'll travel far enough. But what the deuce, don't you know where you are going? You belong to somebody—you came from somewhere—you didn't drop from the clouds—ride through the air in a whirlwind, or pop out of the sea on a wave. Then there's that addle-brain, Lord Orton, in love with you—why, if you could explain the spark in the closet, and were not of mean birth, why, as women go——

Mrs. Derv. [*With dignity.*] My birth, sir, could not be the obstacle, were there not other reasons.—It is at least equal to his own—a distinguished name, a fortune.—But why do I dwell on past misery? Why suffer——

Sir Caustic. [*Looking earnestly at her.*] If, after searching so long in vain, I should have stumbled at once—Yes, the very features—you interest me, young woman. You are too pretty to be wandering about the world without protection. Confide in me —I'm no gallant—no seducer. Thank Heaven, I'm not old enough yet to run away with a girl of twenty.

Mrs. Derv. Your frankness is to me, sir, more

valuable than compliment ; and if the relation of my
misfortunes will gratify you——

Sir Caustic. Proceed—proceed. You women allow nobody to have any curiosity but yourselves.—
Go on.

Mrs. Derv. I have already confessed, sir, that my
birth was elevated, my fortune large. At an early
age I was deprived of my parents, and left to the
guardianship of an uncle, whose bigotry and avarice suggested to him the design of burying the
claimant of a fortune, to which he was next kin, in
a convent. Aware of his design—averse to a cloister, and irritated by persecution, I accepted of the
assistance of a young Englishman, whom chance
threw in my way, and eloped from the convent
where I was placed.

Sir Caustic. An Englishman!—the convent!—Oh!
go on.

Mrs. Derv. My deliverer, I found, was poor ; and
ere I had time to consult my heart, with all the
enthusiasm of gratitude at sixteen, I gave him my
hand.

Sir Caustic. It is—it must be! Conclude, I beseech you !

Mrs. Derv. My fortune being left me on the day
of marriage, for some months we lived in a constant
round of gaiety and expense. But, ere two years
were past, my husband's unbounded dissipation first
corrupted, and at length hardened his heart. Deprived of his affection, abandoned, neglected, I
lived, scarcely certain even of his existence ; till, at
the end of the third year after our marriage, he was
brought to me, mangled by a fall from his horse,
senseless and expiring.

Sir Caustic. Unfortunate girl !

Mrs. Derv. My fortune dissipated, alone, unprotected, awakened to a sense of my early imprudence,

and weaned from an attachment which I had in a
thoughtless moment rendered a duty, I now felt all
the horrors of my situation—My heart wounded by
injuries, my spirit embittered by ingratitude, I beheld the world with disgust, mankind with horror,
and at nineteen I fancied myself a misanthropist.
With the scattered remains of my fortune I retired,
under a borrowed name, to a convent; but the disappointed avarice of my guardian pursued me to my
retreat, and obliged me to escape from Florence to
Leghorn. Public events again removed me to England ; and by the assistance of an English servant, I
at length settled in my present situation.

Sir Caustic. And your name is Harcourt, the wife,
the generous wife of my unhappy boy. Oh, Eugenia! how shall I reward you for the miseries you
have suffered!

Mrs. Derv. The father of Harcourt! Then this
picture is——

Sir Caustic. Is mine. It was sent me by my son
on his marriage; and while he was soliciting pardon
for errors, which had occasioned his banishment
from his family.

Mrs. Derv. Ah, dear sir! had I known—but the
name of Oldstyle, of Orton, had never been mentioned to me.

Sir Caustic. The title is recently descended to my
nephew, and the name of Oldstyle I adopted on an
acquisition of fortune from my late wife's father. But
come, retire to a less public apartment, keep this
discovery secret a few minutes, and in the mean
while, dear, injured girl, remember you have found a
parent.   [*Exit, leading Mrs.* DERVILLE.

SCENE IV.—*Cloisters on each Side of the Stage, il-
luminated and ornamented with Flowers at the Extremity.—Statues and Trees ornamented in the same
Manner.—Music.*

Enter Mr. and Mrs. GURNET, *and Lady* ZEPHYRINE
*after.—*JARGON.—*Then* BEWLEY *from a different
Side of the Stage; and at last, Sir* CAUSTIC, BEL-
FORD, *and* PERIOD, *as in Conversation.—Music
ceases. Lady* ZEPHYRINE *approaches Sir* CAUSTIC,
*and he addresses her.—*BELFORD *and* PERIOD *appear to talk together till the Denouement.*

Sir Caustic. Aye, aye, I forgive the drum and the
wig. I'm in so good a humour I could forgive any
thing. Come, niece, as this is your birth-day, and
as young women of one and twenty begin to look
about 'em, I ought to inform you, that the bulk of
my fortune is only at my disposal, in case my late
son's wife should never appear; but, subject to
this proviso, why I think a few score thousands for a
wedding gown won't hurt me.

Lady Zeph. Believe me, sir, if the discovery of
the claimant you mention contributes to your happiness, I shall not regret the retraction of your
bounty.

Sir Caustic. Why, that's noble; that's an old sentiment, which even a new-fashioned outside cannot
diminish the value of. I'm glad to see you are capable of receiving generously the daughter whom
my good fortune has restored to me. [*Goes on one
side of the scene, and leads in Mrs.* DERVILLE.

All. Mrs. Derville!

Sir Caustic. Come, no sentimental overflowings
now. Eugenia, my poor boy, was but a sorry help-
mate. You chose ill for yourself. What say you
to a husband of my fancy, to my nephew, Lord
Orton?   [*Pointing to* PERIOD.

Mrs. Derv. Ah, pardon me, sir, if I decline. There is——

Sir Caustic. What! the closet spark, I suppose.—I know the whole business; but I must have you a countess—Perhaps, in a more humble rank, you might yourself be equally happy; but the distinctions of society, which render virtue conspicuous, are a benefit to the world. So if you won't have my old fellow-traveller, honest Tim Period, why you must even take a peer of my creation. Come, nephew, is your delicacy satisfied now, or has your lordship any more disguises and experiments?

Mrs. Derv. What! Belford?

Lady Zeph. Yes, this is, indeed, my brother.

Belf. [*Embracing her.*] Dear Zephyrine! Eugenia! [*taking her hand*] my beloved Eugenia! Can you, will you pardon the deception?

Sir Caustic. No, I warrant she won't. Women never pardon any deceptions except their own. But I am too old to wait the usual fopperies of your penitence and her coquetry; and as this is one of the few deceptions which explanation will not make worse, why, you shall marry first, and you'll have time enough to explain hereafter.—And now, my pretty rake, if some sober subject of the old school would take you off my hands—Your fortune, indeed, is reduced, but then you can shoot flying, and beat the drum, you know.

Gurnet. Aye, and a wife may make worse noises than that. Isn't the sound of a drum better than the rumbling of an ode?—What say you, Mr. Jargon, to my ward and her six thousand? There, 'tis all right and fair—India, Bank, Consols—I've turn'd it for her.

Sir Caustic. Hey! why, here's a lover for you, humming and lounging—that's modern too, I suppose.

Jargon. Lady Zephyrine's accomplishments, sir, are too brilliant to be set in any thing but gold;

and six thousand isn't a month's pin-money (powder
and shot money I should say) for a woman of spirit.
So, sir, with your permission, I limit my claim to
four only of the six thousand.

Lady Zeph. What relinquish " the little idol of the
Abbey?"

Mrs. Derv. And disappoint me of the black boy
and curricle?

Jargon. 'Sdeath! I've lost the note! I see, ladies, you're inclined to be merry; and as mirth is
vulgar, and I hate family parties, why, I leave you
to the reigning system. [*Going.*]

Period. Hark ye, my honest cousin, don't depend
much on your four thousand—or a note obtained by
a little dexterity at the gaming table; take the thing
snugly.—Magistrates in town are active—judges uncivil—and the toleration of artists of your description
tion is no longer the—reigning system. So, snug's
the word.   [*Exit* JARGON.

Lady Zeph. So, you see, good folks, I'm abandoned by one swain, and it isn't two hours ago since
I was rejected by another; but as you are determined, sir, not to be troubled with me, perhaps Mr.
Bewley here, to oblige you, not on my account
though, I declare.

Bew. When I refused your offered hand, dear
Lady Zephyrine, I was a beggar.—The bounty of
my uncle, and Mr. Period's integrity, have now enabled me to accept with honour a gift it cost me so
much pain to refuse.—Will you again renew——

Lady Zeph. Well, if I do condescend to forgive
you, mind, 'tis purely to oblige my uncle.

Sir Caustic. Come, I think we shall be able to add
enough to the six thousand for a sober pair of bays
and a chariot—but none of your wildfire equipages
to run over quiet people, and make anecdotes for
my friend Period's travels.

AP-GRIFFIN (*within.*)

Ap-Grif. I say I must see him.—Eh, Timmy! Hast sold the diamonds? got the cash!

Period. Yes, I've disposed of 'em.—Won't cheat my own relations. [*Gives him a paper.*] I'll give you all I received.

Ap-Grif. [*Reads.*] " Received of Humphrey Ap-Griffin, by the hands of Mr. Timothy Period, the under-mentioned diamonds, entrusted to the care of the said Ap-Griffin.—Edward Mansel." Why, you rascal, you unnatural rogue, I'll hang, I'll quarter you!

Period. Hush! hush! uncle—Honesty, you know, is the best policy—always do the just thing.

Ap-Grif. A plague of your memory—But I'll be reveng'd; I'll take out a statute of lunacy against you, and you shall scribble tours on the walls of Bedlam as long as you live.   [*Exit.*

Period. And now, my lord, I resign my peerage for a character, I hope ever to maintain, that of your friend, honest Tim Period.

Belf. We shall not forget your services ; you shall be retained in all the family suits of the whole principality. We'll purchase a dozen editions of your tour.

Period. Ah! my lord, I'd rather you'd praise it. And if this good company should but approve the first edition, my gratitude will last till I travel to that " bourne, from whence no tourist returns."— But as I'm in no hurry to go there at present, let me hope, in the mean while, for permission to travel this way again.

LIE OF A DAY:

A COMEDY,

IN THREE ACTS,

AS PERFORMED AT THE

THEATRE ROYAL, COVENT-GARDEN

———

BY JOHN O'KEEFFE, Esq.

CHARACTERS.

Sir CARROL O'DONOVAN,	*Mr Waddy.*
Young O'DONOVAN,	*Mr Clarke.*
AIRCOURT,	*Mr Lewis.*
LARRY KAVANAGH,	*Mr Knight.*
ALIBI,	*Mr Quick.*
METHEGLIN,	*Mr Fawcett.*
POVOT,	*Mr Simmonds.*
WAITER,	
FOOTMAN,	*Mr Blurton.*
BOY,	

Lady ARABLE,	*Miss Chapman.*
SOPHIA,	*Mrs Knight.*
KATTY KAVANAGH,	*Mrs Davenport.*
FIB,	*Mrs Watts.*

SCENE—Hampton Court.

LIE OF A DAY.

ACT I.

SCENE I.—*A Room at the Toy.*

Enter AIRCOURT *and Waiter.*

Airc. ANY of our lads up here at the Toy since, Ned?

Wait. Yes, your honour; the crew of your cutter dined with us last Sunday.

Airc. Is old Alibi, the attorney, down here much?

Wait. Yes, sir; he's over at his house.

Airc. Have you seen his ward, Miss Sophia Seymour, lately?

Wait. Ah! poor young lady! he seldom lets her go out but to church—A charity for some gentleman, like your honour, to whip off to church with her.

Airc. Why, Ned, I have some notion—but to give you a simile in your own way—the old black rascal keeps her as close as a cork in a bottle; which, to get out, I mustn't bolt inward, but turn screw round and round, and then cluck's the word. Get me a

c c

room, and put my things in it. [*Exit Waiter.*]
How shall I get to see her? My new rival too!
Who can he be?—Let's see—Where did Sophia
say she first saw him? [*Peruses a letter.*] " Noticed
his watching me at the gate of Sir Ashton Lever's
Museum——heavy shower at Chelsea——brought
guardian and I to town in his hackney-coach—A
monstrous fool!"—Yes; but if this monstrous fool
should prove an over-match for all my wit—If I
could only contrive to see her.

Enter LARRY KAVANAGH *and Waiter.*

Wait. Please, sir, to walk into this room. [*Exit.*
Airc. O'Donovan!
Larry. Aircourt! Who'd have thought of meet-
ing you here at Hampton-Court?
Airc. Why, but what the deuce brought you
here?
Larry. I'm here upon a love-scheme—incog.—
hush! you remember I told you over the last bottle
we crack'd together at the Bedford——
Airc. True; our candles went out, and your story
set me asleep. [*Yawns.*]
Larry. Well, rouse now—You know Alibi, the at-
torney——he's guardian to the most lovely——the
sweetest——
Airc. Zounds, my Sophia! [*Aside.*]
Larry. I'll have her.
Airc. Will you, faith? [*Aside.*] What, then, you're
acquainted with her?
Larry. The first time I saw my charmer, she was
engaged in a wrangle with her guardian at the gate
of the—Museum—in—a—Leicester-fields.
Airc. Leicester-fields! Oh, ho! [*Aside.*]
Larry. She would see the butterflies, ha, ha, ha!
He, in a rage, slapping his cane on a show-glass of
watch-strings, seals, and sleeve-buttons——cries,
" Zounds! it's half-a-crown"——" The exact price

of that pane," says the man of the shop—" Jack,
fetch the glazier"—The expence of this accident
determined the affair; and the generous attorney,
instead of Sir Ashton's, proposing a trudge to Don
Saltero's, I whip'd in a hack before them to Chelsea
—Returning home, down comes an auspicious
shower, and, to save eighteen-pence, Alibi accepts
of part of my coach.

Airc. What, your own hack, ha, ha, ha!—Yes,
this is Sophia's monstrous fool. [*Aside.*]

Larry. I throw a tender glance—Sophia blushes,
and we exchange hearts through our eyes—Such
ogles!

Airc. Damn your ogles! [*Surly.*]

Larry. What!

Airc. That is, I want to know your scheme.

Larry. Will you help?

Airc. With pleasure—to cut your throat. [*Aside.*]

Larry. Vastly good! That letter——[*Gives it.*]

Airc. " To Capias Alibi, Esquire—Dear sir, the
bearer is a young man from Yorkshire, being desirous to improve himself in the profession of an
attorney, I recommend him to you; and think a
dealing in this case will be to the advantage of both.
Yours, Nol Pross."——Well, what of this?

Larry. Ha, ha, ha! Can't you see? That I procured for a little cash, of a brother rogue of Alibi's
—I deliver it—it gains me free access to Sophia; of
which, if I don't avail myself——

Airc. Must turn him off from this. [*Aside.*] Won't
Alibi remember you in the Chelsea shower? Ha, ha,
ha! won't he?

Larry. No, he won't; ha, ha, ha! [*mimicking.*]
For, to get the worth of his money in gaping about,
he scarce look'd at me at Don Saltero's—And then,
to face my charming Sophia, I sat beside him in the
coach; besides, I shall change my voice; and, to
provide for that, I've made Nol say I am from

Yorkshire—Oh, you'd laugh to see—I shall be clerkified all over.   [*Displays his dress.*

Airc. But really now, do you think old Alibi is such a blockhead as not to perceive from your air, person, address—the fashion that is in your manner altogether! What! take you for a sordid, shabby Cursitor-street ramskin scribbler? Ha, ha, ha! never! The gentleman in your coat would belie Nol Pross's letter, and get you and it kicked out of the house, to the eternal disgrace of St. James's, and the triumph of Chancery-lane.

Larry. Egad, Aircourt, I believe you're right.

Airc. Depend upon't, the old attorney would perceive the diamond, though set in copper.

Larry. Hang it! this air of travel which we acquire abroad—I wish I wasn't so—elegant in my *manière*—I wish I had a little of the common—vulgar——Now you, Aircourt, how natural you'd look the ramskin scribbler!

Airc. D'ye think so? you flatter me.

Larry. O, you'd top the character!

Airc. Then, dem'me, I'll appear in it. I will secure this letter—that will do—and for change of dress, Ned the waiter will equip me! [*Aside.*] Zounds, it is two o'clock! but I can get to Drury-lane by the second act.

Larry. 'Sdeath! don't think of town or play-houses to-night!

Airc. Her Calista is one of the most capital—— When she tears the letter—" To atoms thus let me tear the wicked, lying evidence of shame"—[*having, unseen, put* LARRY's *letter in his pocket, tears another.*

Larry. Why, zounds, you've torn my letter!

Airc. And then her smile of contempt upon Horatio, after——

Larry. Damn you and Horatio, sir! D'ye see what you've done? Knock'd up my whole affair!

Airc. 'Pon my soul I ask pardon—I did not think what I was about.

Larry. The devil! What am I to do now? This is cruel of you, Aircourt.

Airc. Come, O'Donovan, though I've destroyed your passport, no harm done. For any project to gain Sophia, I'm yours—from a spank to Scotland, burning old Alibi's house, or any mischief of that sort.

Larry. My dear Aircourt, I thank you heartily—I'll go dress, and then for Lady Arable's, a charming young widow here at Hampton Court—Has been over in Ireland to view some of her estates there, and my father has squir'd her back again—Designs her as a match for me—Ha, ha, ha! Rather a nice thing to match me, Eh, Aircourt?

Airc. Yes; but I think I'll match you, ha, ha, ha!

Larry. My father don't know I have been five months diverting myself in England under an assumed name—Dad thinks I'm still on my Italian travels—my bills will come pelting in upon him rarely—An't I right, my boy? Lovely Sophia!—Love, fire, and frolic, that's my motto!

Airc. Plague of your frolics! [*Aside.*]—Sophia, perhaps, is at home, now?—That is—he keeps her close.

Larry. Close! she saves him the expense of a clerk. But, Aircourt, don't think of London tonight.

Airc. Well, I won't.

Larry. [*Looking at fragments.*] Honest Nol Pross's letter—What the devil's to be done?

Airc. Oh, Nol Pross's letter [*looking at him*]; it will do something yet, ha, ha, ha!   [*Exeunt.*

SCENE II.—*An Office in* ALIBI'S *House.*

SOPHIA *discovered writing at a high Desk.*

Sophia. [*Dashes the pen away.*] I will not write any more of his law-gibberish! Was ever poor girl so used as I am by this wicked old attorney! Cruel mamma! to make such a wretch her executor; and condemn me to the guardianship of one who will never suffer me to be united to the man I love, whilst it's his interest to keep my fortune in his hands. O, my beloved Aircourt! [*Sings.*] " Young Harry's the lad for me!"

Alibi. [*Without.*] Yes, the very thing I wanted.

Enter ALIBI.

Sophy, look at my forehead—any blood come? I only wish it would! I've been endeavouring to provoke the exciseman, and abusing him these six weeks; but at last he has given me a choice knock on the pate—The rogue's worth money, and I'll having swinging damages!

Sophia. Lord, sir! Do you go out to quarrel with the people only on purpose that they may beat you?

Alibi. To be sure! Beat! Why, I have made fifty pounds out of the wag of a finger, and have earned a hundred guineas of a morning, only by single tweaks by the nose.—Now, miss, have you drawn up the bill of indictment? Egad, child, you'll have no use for your fortune! By the Lord! you'll make a choice chamber counsel.—[*Reads*] " Parish aforesaid—county aforesaid—did make an assault upon one——and did then and there beat, wound, and cruelly ill-treat——against the peace of our sovereign lord the king——But of all the fine wrestlers that dance on the green, young Harry's the lad for me!"—Oh, the devil! here's a bill of in-

dictment to come before a grand jury!—So, the exciseman breaks my head with his gauging-stick, and
then " Young Harry's the lad for me!"

Sophia. Well; and so Harry Aircourt is the lad
for me, in spite of you, or all Westminster-hall, with
Lord Chief Justice at your head.

Alibi. I wish I could but once see this fine Mr.
Harry Aircourt in the street, though, only to see
if he's such a prime serjeant as you make him.

Sophia. He a prime serjeant! No! heaven made
my Aircourt handsome, witty, gay, elegant, generous, and good natur'd.

Alibi. It's his good nature that shoves him on to
make ballads about me, and set all his drunken com-
panions at the Anacreontic roaring out in chorus
" O rare old Alibi!"—But if he comes, if I don't
set my bull dog at him—

Sophia. O, then, from your bull dog Heaven defend me—ha, ha, ha!

Enter AIRCOURT, *disguised as a country lad.*

Alibi. [*Sees* AIRCOURT, *puts* SOPHIA *out.*] Who
are you? What do you want?

Airc. I want to larn the laa.

Alibi. You want to larn the laa! I wish you'd larn
manners.

Airc. Oh, I have—for I daunce mortishly weel.

Alibi. You daunce! Then, perhaps, you come
here for a partner. [*Looking after* SOPHIA.]

Airc. Yez.

Alibi. What do you want?

Airc. I want—that letter——[*Gives one.*]

Alibi. You want—this letter?—then what the
devil do you give it me for?

Airc. Look at the outside.

Alibi. " Capias Alibi——Bearer—from Yorkshire
—attorney—recommend—dealing—this case—advantage—Yours, Nol Pross."—Well, Yorkshire's

a good country to produce an attorney.   My friend
Nol Pross gives you a good character.[4]

Airc. Oh yez, sir—I'm a very honest lad.

Alibi. Honest! and want to be an attorney!
Hem! I don't think I can do any thing with you.

Airc. No! Then what am I to do with the money
feyther sent up wi' me for it?

Alibi. You have money! Now I look at you again,
you're a very promising lad.

Airc. Cousin Nol said I might larn, board, and
sleep here.

Alibi. Ecod! if you sleep here, you must board;
for I've no bed for you. [*Aside.*]

Airc. You see my money is ready; so I hope
you'll afford me a good bed.

Alibi. Why, you dog!—your ready money shews
you don't want to lie upon tick, ha, ha, ha! Hark
ye! Perhaps I sha'n't beat you above once before
you commit a fault.

Airc. Before!

Alibi. Yes; I may thresh you out of pure good
nature, only to shew you what you are to expect if
you deserve it.

Airc. Oh, then I'm to be beat to save me from a
threshing! Good natur'd indeed, he, he, he!

Alibi. You're not given to girls, are you?

Airc. I sometimes play in the meads a wi' bit.

Alibi. Well said, Yorkshire! But you won't dare
to speak to a young lady?

Airc. Not for the vorld! I'd blush so hugely.

Alibi. That's right—I like a modest youth—because I have a young miss within here.

Airc. Lack-a-daisy! do you keep a miss?

Alibi. Ha, ha, ha! What a simpleton! Before I
determine to retain him, I'll first see their behaviour together—Miss Sophy!

Enter SOPHIA.

Airc. My beloved girl! I hope she'll know me.

[*Aside.*

Alibi. Well, Sophy, I've got a new clerk.

Sophia. This must be the fop that followed me to Chelsea—He said he'd visit me in some disguise; but I'll discourage his impertinence in time. [*Aside.*] Ha, ha, ha! my very wise, vigilant, shrewd, sagacious guardian! A clerk! ha, ha, ha! This is a very facetious gentleman, that's come hither on a scheme to run away with me! ha, ha, ha!

Airc. 'Sdeath! what can she mean? [*Aside.*]

Alibi. How! an impostor!

Sophia. Look! You can't know the polite Strephon that brought us from Chelsea in his hackney-coach?

Alibi. This!

Airc. What! I!—he, he, he!

Sophia. Bless me! it's my Aircourt himself.

[*Aside.*

Alibi. Why, Sophy, you're the most conceited—When, neither you nor I ever saw this young man before. That coxcomb Aircourt has blown you up so with his love nonsense, that you imagine all the young men in the town are laying plans and stratagems, ha, ha, ha! You are welcome, my lad, and so is your money! [*Takes it.*]

Sophia. Now I look at him again, he's vastly like Aircourt.

Alibi. She only says this to vex me. He shall be my clerk above all the clerks in Christendom.

Airc. He, he, he! Thank you, sir. [*Bows.*]

Sophia. " He, he, he ! thank you, sir"—Oh, you shock!

Alibi. He's no shock! he's a pretty boy, and will be Lord Chancellor, won't you, Robin?

Airc. Ecod, that's my name, sure enough.

Sophia. Well, mind, Jack Robin—since guardian

will keep you, you shall be my beau, and make love
to me.

Airc. Love! Oh, miss!

Alibi. Get you in.

Sophia. Now, pray——

Alibi. Go—[*puts her in.*] Don't mind her, Robin
—Her heart's so full of this Aircourt, that I believe
she'd despise even a judge upon the bench.

Airc. What, then she loves one Aircourt?

Alibi. But, my young clerk, by way of beginning,
I'll set you a task—Step into that room there, and
ingross this deed [*gives him papers.*—AIRCOURT *going towards the door where* SOPHIA *went off.*]—Stop
—that door. [*Pointing to the centre door.*]

Airc. I thought I was to ingross there, he, he, he!

Alibi. Robin, you're a good lad; but for a lawyer, heaven save us!

Airc. Then you think my coming here answers
the purpose.

Alibi. Oh, yes, your coming here answers the
purpose! [*Clinking the money.*]

Airc. And that by this means I shall get all I
want. [*Steals the key out of* SOPHIA's *door.*]

Alibi. [*Counting the money.*] Yes; by this means
we get all we want—Go yonder.

Airc. Dear, how much I am obliged to Mr. Nol
Pross!   [*Exit at centre door.*

Alibi. Write away, my boy! and I warrant you'll
be Lord Chief Baron some Sunday or other—
Dam'me, I'll dress my wig on your pate next Sa-
turday evening. As I am going out, no harm to
lock up my ward—The key gone! How's this?
Soft! [*Locks the centre door, and takes the key.*] One
key is as good as another. Good bye, Robin.

                                              [*Exit.*

SCENE III.—*The Coffee Room at the Toy.*

Enter Sir CARROL *and Waiter.*

Sir Car. Never mind, young man! I don't want any refreshment—I've set Lady Arable down at her house, and am only walking about to see your town and palace. And, Joy, so this is your coffee-room? Oh, newspapers! Let's peep at the " Lie of the Day." [*Reads.*]   [*Exit Waiter.*

Enter Young O'DONOVAN *with a small bundle on a stick over his shoulder—weary, sits.*

This poor young man seems to have had a long walk of it.

O'DONOVAN *rings—Enter Waiter.*

Wait. Did your honour call? [*To Sir* CARROL.]
O'Don. 'Twas I that rung—A little wine and water.
Wait. [*Surveys him contemptuously.*] Coming, sir.
O'Don. I spoke to you.
Wait. This room is only for gentlemen—— Coming.
O'Don. [*Looks sternly at Waiter.*] Sir, I ask pardon.
    [*Bows to Sir* CARROL, *and is retiring.*
Sir Car. Stop, sir.—[*Turns to Waiter.*] Hark ye, friend! remember, as you live by the public liberality, your guest, be his appearance what it may, has a claim, at least, to your civility. You say this room is appropriated to gentlemen—I am one, and master of a parlour in Ireland to the full as good as this: and, by my soul, I could never think it more highly honour'd than by giving a welcome to the weary traveller. Go. [*Exit Waiter.*] I ask pardon, sir—whence are you?

O'Don. Sir, I came from London now, and got
there only last night from Ireland.

Sir Car. Then you're Irish?

O'Don. Sir, I have that honour.

Sir Car. And pray, my young traveller—excuse
my question; but I feel myself interested in your
concerns, though a stranger to them. Tell me,
what are your views?

O'Don. In my infancy, my father, sir, (I never
knew the cause,) came over to England, and thus
destitute, Providence raised a friend, who placed
me at Dublin College. The death of this benefactor stopping my resources, obliged me to quit
my studies; and I have been drawn to Hampton-
Court on the credit of a disjointed kind of story,
that my father had retired here in the enjoyment of
an ample fortune, which he had acquired by the
practice of an attorney: but after a long journey,
and every possible inquiry, I can hear of no such
person.

Enter LARRY KAVANAGH, *dressed.*

Larry. Povot! bring a glass—Such an abominable room to dress in! For a glass you thought, I
suppose, Narcissus-like, I was to set my face in a
bason of water.

Enter Servant with a glass, powder puff, &c.

Hah! this is something! [*adjusts himself before a
glass.*] There you are, from toupee to shoe-string—
As this lady's house is so near—Povot, another
volley from your powder-puff.

Sir Car. Why, you scoundrel! what, do you mean
to make a barber's shop of a coffee-room?

Larry. A little more on this curl, Povot.

Sir Car. Take that, sirrah! [*Strikes* POVOT.]

Povot. Ventre bleu!

Sir Car. And your master's a puppy, whoever he is.

Larry. Can you fence, old Touchwood?

O'Don. [*Interposing.*] I can, a little, sir.

Larry. You!—ah! [*contemptuously.*] Tol, lol, lol!

[*Exeunt* LARRY *and* POVOT.

Sir Car. [*Looks after* LARRY, *then at* O'DONO-VAN.] Oh, what a bitter mistake has fortune made! Now that thing, void of manners and humanity, may have a worthy father, who, while he supplies with a liberal hand, little thinks he's throwing his money away upon a rascal! Ah, this is your home education! I have a son abroad that I expect in a few days, stay till you see him, my generous lad— he shall thank you for your spirited politeness to me.—Since you have lost your friend, and can't find your father, inquire for me at Lady Arable's— Something may be done—Hold!—I'll perform first, and that saves the trouble of a promise, and pre-cludes even a chance of disappointment. [*Offers money.*]

O'Don. I thank you, sir; but it's too soon to accept of favours, even when we stand in need of them. [*Declines.*]

Sir Car. Well, well, my boy—I—I—like your—spirit—I was abrupt—I ask your pardon.

Enter Waiter.

Wait. Sir, Lady Arable has sent over.

Sir Car. Very well. Ask for Sir Carrol O'Do-novan—(a fine young man!) What an unhappy father must he be, that could abandon such a son.

[*Exit Sir* CARROL *and Waiter.*

O'Don. Sir Carrol O'Donovan! Then the son that he speaks of must be the child my mother nursed—Now I shall know if she's yet living.—But alienated by her neglect, as I never knew the tender care of a parent, I don't feel that impulse of filial affection—Sir Carrol sha'n't know who I am—The meanness of my birth might add contempt to the compassion that my poverty has already excited.

[*Exit.*

ACT II.

A Room at Lady ARABLE'S.

Enter Sir CARROL, *leading in Lady* ARABLE.

Lady Arable. Now, Sir Carrol, with thanks for your hospitality to me at your house in Ireland, I bid you welcome to my house in England.

Sir Car. Well, Lady Arable, recollect that your wise, old, and very good friends advised you to put yourself and fortune under the protection of an husband—I am entirely of their opinion; besides wasting the charming bloom of life in lonely widowhood, your property requires an hearted solicitude to manage it—If on sight (as you promised your relations) you should like my son well enough to bless him with your fair hand—Oh, you will make me happy! I have never seen Edward no more than you, my lady, as 'twas my father sent him abroad for education; but I expect you'll soon behold in my boy an accomplished gentleman.

Enter Footman.

Footm. Sir, a young man inquires for you.

Sir Car. Shew him up—With your permission, madam.   [*Exit Footman.*

Enter O'DONOVAN *clean—he and Lady* ARABLE *look with surprise and embarrassment at each other.*

O'Don. Sir, in obedience to your commands—

Sir Car. Lady Arable, a boon. As you'll have a good deal of stewardship and settling your affairs with old Alibi your attorney, some employment may be found for this young man.—Till I can do something for him, you'll oblige me by taking him under your protection: though he's a stranger, I'll stake my fortune on his honesty. [O'DONOVAN *bows.*]

Lady Arable. The very young man! Can he forget me? He come to England! [*Aside.*]

O'Don. She's ashamed to recollect me: but she's right. [*Aside.*]

Enter Footman.

Footm. Sir, Mr. O'Donovan is arrived. [*Exit.*
Sir Car. [*Joyful.*] Hah! my son!

Enter LARRY KAVANAGH *dressed.*

Larry. As I never had the honour of paying my duty to a father, I presume, sir, you are——How! [*Surprised.*]

Sir Car. [*Surprised.*] Edward! this!——My lady, my son has paid his duty to me before in a powder puff!

Larry. I'm shock'd, sir—with—such awe——

Sir Car. Pray, can you fence, old Touchwood?

Larry. Sir—I—I—[*Sees* O'DONOVAN.] He can, a little.

O'Don. Then this is my foster brother. [*Aside.*]

Larry. I ask pardon, sir; but at the first transient glance, I mistook you for a—some mechanic.

Sir Car. Did you, faith?—Ah, then at my first glance, I protest I mistook you for a—gentleman— So we were both mistaken [*mortified.*] Son, this is Lady Arable, whom I so often mentioned in my letters. [*Introduces them.*]

Lady Arable. Sir, you are welcome.

Sir Car. Edward, though your marriage with this

lady is rather to be hoped than expected, try if you can win her heart; for, sir, the affection of an amiable woman is the first supreme delight that can possess the soul of man.—With all the shining, foreign education, a few home-spun documents are wanting here [*aside.*]—A few words with you, sir.

[*Exit.*

Larry. [*Looking at Lady* ARABLE.] This still life! no dem it, the sprightly Sophia for me [*aside.*] Tol, lol. lol.   [*Exit.*

Lady Arable. Pray, sir, how have you left our amiable friend?

O'Don. Madam!

Lady Arable. Then you don't recollect ever having seen me in an agreeable party one evening?

O'Don. I hadn't a thought that the pleasure of that honour could be succeeded by the honour of this!

Lady Arable. Excuse me—but do you know any thing of this Mr. O'Donovan?

O'Don. Only, madam, that he's the happiest of mankind.

Lady Arable. Oh, if married to me!—Vastly obliging!—But I am apprehensive, that where a mistress is the object, your judgment of happiness is not very extensive. Devoted to the muses, you are, I presume, only their humble admirer.

O'Don. Madam, was there a muse for every star, and that star like Lady Arable, the odds would still be in her favour. [*Bows.*]

Enter FIB *hastily.*

Fib. Oh, ma'am! ma'am!

[O'DONOVAN *bows and exit.*

Lady Arable. Well? [*Peevish.*]

Fib. Lord, that's a very handsome young man! but they're all deceitful creatures!

Lady Arable. I'm in no humour now——

Fib, Ma'am, only think of Mr. O'Donovan's pretending to his father that he will marry you, and yet all the while going on with an underhand scheme to carry off a young lady in the neighbourhood.

Lady Arable. Paying his addresses to another! O, if I can but bring this to a proof, it will justify to Sir Carrol a refusal that I'm now determined upon. [*Aside.*]

Fib. Ay, and I can tell you more of his scandalous goings-on my lady.

Lady Arable. Sophia knows every body; I may hear from her who my rival is—But to employ this dear stranger as Sir Carrol requested. My steward Metheglin's neglecting my affairs, and gallanting about with this fine Irish belle that he has brought over, gives a colour for taking some of my papers out of his hands. Send Metheglin to me, and fetch my cloak.   [*Exeunt severally.*

Enter METHEGLIN *and* KATTY.

Meth. Come in, I tell you, Mrs. Katty; this room and furniture is worth your seeing above all the rest.

Katty. Yes, Mr. Metheglin; but if your lady should catch you bringing folks all about her house, I should die with shame.

Meth. My lady! ah, my dear, when ladies have taste, and butlers have—[*Conceitedly.*]

Katty. Certainly, Mr. Metheglin, you are a very comely man, to give the devil his due.

Meth. My lady's going to be married to another—therefore—honour—if she wasn't quite in love with me, she'd have turned me out of the house long ago, I'm grown so idle—Cou'dn't part with me, so took me over to Ireland with her, where I met you, my dearest Katty!

Katty. But, Mr. Metheglin, as I have had one

bad husband already, the trifle I bring you you must settle upon me in case I should outlive you, honey.

Meth. I hope there's no fear of that, my sweetest.

Fib. [*Without.*] Mr. Metheglin!

Meth. Do you hear? these women won't let me alone.

Enter FIB.

Fib. Pray come, my lady wants you.

Meth. Oh this jealousy!—So here my Katty says, " Sit with me, my comfort"—and my lady sends word that she wants me.—If we're ordinary, we're ugly fellows; if beautiful, we are cruel souls and barbarous gentlemen—and from the lady in the drawing-room to the maids in the garret, they buz about us like flies round a honey-pot.

Fib. My lady sent me to——

Meth. Yes, your lady sent you to me ; I send you to my lady, and so return the compliment.

Fib. Ah, if you go on this way, you'll get the wrong side of the door.

Meth. The side of the door, Madam Fib?—— here's my thanks for not telling when I caught you daubing my lady's tooth-powder on your cheeks, and cribbing her imperial tea.

Fib. Upon my word, you take an immense many airs upon you since you have brought over your bog-trotter.   Ha, ha, ha!   [*Exit.*

Katty. Bog-trotter! only stop a moment, Mrs. Minikin, and I'll give you a mighty handsome slap on the forehead.

Meth. She wou'dn't stop, Katty, if you'd even give her two.

Katty. Bog-trotter, indeed! I'll soon shew the proudest of them all—Oh, stay till they see my son Larry master of Sir Carrol's estate!

Meth. A son of yours master of Sir Carrol O'Do-novan's estate!

Katty. Since you and I are so soon to be one, you shall know all about it—I'll soon shew them who I am, and who my son Larry is.

Meth. Who is he, pray?

Katty. You all think I only nursed this fine young gentleman that arrived an hour ago, but that's my own child.

Meth. Yours! the devil he is!

Katty. Mine. Sir Carrol making a stolen match, his father, on hearing it, sent him abroad, and the poor young lady, his wife, lying in privately at my house, died in child-birth; so faith my husband, (poor man,) who was a little bit of a lawyer, made me send our own infant to the grandpapa instead of Sir Carrol's baby, and by this my son Lawrence is bred up like a fine gentleman; and t'other poor fellow was placed at the college of Dublin as a sizer, or something of that sort.

Meth. How! shall I be master of Sir Carrol's great estate? see, Katty, if I don't manage it tightly for him. Steward, agent, and bailiff—encourage him to run out—lend him his own money—borrow myself of every body—get into parliament, and—[*suddenly claps his hand to his mouth.*] Lord a mercy! what was I going to say? [*Exeunt.*

SCENE II.—Alibi's *Office.*

Enter Sophia—*speaks at centre Door.*

Sophia. Mr. Aircourt! my guardian's gone out.

Airc. [*Within.*] But how shall I get out?

Sophia. What a malicious old creature to lock you in. Can't you push back the lock?

Airc. I have already broke his penknife attempting it.

Sophia. Try my scissars [*puts them under the door.*] There, take them—Lord! man! try. What the

deuce, have you fallen asleep? how provoking!
Aircourt!

Enter AIRCOURT *at the side unperceived.*

Ah! you're a pretty Pyramus! Why don't you try
my scissars?

Airc. What, to cut love or to kill the lion, my
Thisbe!

Sophia. Ah! how the deuce did you get there?

Airc. Popped out of the back window—perched
upon a cucumber frame—hopped up stairs—-and
here I am your own poor Robin!

Sophia. Ah, " You foolish fluttering thing"
[*sings*] " Sweet Robin, sweet Robin!"

Enter ALIBI.

Alibi. Now do I suspect this Robin to be a ca-
nary. [*Aside.*]

Airc. [*Seeing* ALIBI.] The old one! but mind
me [*apart.*] Yes, miss, I think I could teach you
to play at cribbage after dinner, for I was counted
a dab at it in our parts.

Sophia. Thank you, Robin.

Alibi. Now this must be Robin Goodfellow! and
has whipped through the key-hole. I won't seem
to know he's got out, only to try how he'll carry it
off [*aside—unlocks the door and calls.*] Well, Robin,
have you engrossed that? Come here, my lad!

[AIRCOURT *walks by him in at the door, and in-*
stantly returns.]

Sophia. Ha, ha, ha!

Alibi. Eh! that's one way of coming out.

Airc. The Yorkshire way; whenever we'd come
out of a room, we always go in first.

Alibi. Your hand; you'll make a damned good
lawyer! But I left you in that room, and I locked
the door.

Airc. Yes, sir; but you didn't lock the window!

Alibi. He'll do.   A queer beginning though! no doing without application, my friend!   I set you about an affair of consequence within there, and I find you with my ward without here

Sophia. O, my poor guardian! so when you thought you had Robin in crib, here was he teaching me to play cribbage—He, he, he!

Alibi. How dare you quit your station?

Airc. Oh, sir, I thought it was dinner-time.

Alibi. No danger from this fellow—I never heard or read of a lover that was hungry. [*Aside.*]

Airc. Sir, I'd have you take care of one Aircourt, her head runs on nothing but him—he'll certainly carry her off.

Sophia. Oh, that nothing may hinder him!

Alibi. Yes, but something shall hinder him—my wit, my vigilance shall.

Airc. But what's your wit to a young fellow with strength in his arm, and the devil in his head?

Alibi. What do you mean—to talk so, boy?

Sophia. Guardian! in spite of all your art and cunning, if my Aircourt, inspired by love and superior wit, had by an ingenuity of stratagem got in here, what would you do?

Airc. Aye, sir, what would you do?

Sophia. Cou'dn't he push a little feeble old quizby like you down into a—chair?

Alibi. How, pray?

Sophia. Shew him how, Robin.

Airc. Why, there. [*Shoves him into a chair.*]

Alibi. Well, now what would he do then?

Airc. Why he'd carry the girl off.

Alibi. If these are your notions, your friends did well to have you " larn the laa," if only to save you from being hanged some time or other!   A good occasion this to give him his first lesson [*aside.*]—Well, honest Robin, you suppose it a very easy

pleasant thing for a young fellow to run away with
a lady from her guardian?

Airc. Quite easy, and vastly pleasant mayhap.

Alibi. Then I'll shew you how, for such a pleasant
trick, you may hop and dance too. Sophy, hand
me down that Coke yonder.

Airc. Stop, miss, I'm taller nor yow [*helping her,
the book falls.*]

Alibi. Why, you dog, do you want to kill the girl?

Sophia. Yes, he's quite a killing creature.

Alibi. Now, my boy, I've something here under
my thumb, that will open your eyes to the danger
of breaking the laws of your country!

Sophia. But a true lover despises law and danger.

Alibi. Despise law! that's a decent word out of
your mouth, miss, before my pupil [*apart.*]—Now,
Robin, for argument's sake, we'll suppose that this
young lady has 30,000*l.*—I don't say she has, only
putting a case—and here I am her guardian; and
we'll say, still for argument's sake, you are Aircourt.

Sophia. Aye, you are my Aircourt.

Airc. And you my Sophia; and there sits your
gentle old quizby with Lord Coke under his thumb.

Alibi. Now, Robin—I beg your pardon, Mr. Aircourt—only just take that lady out of that door,
and if you can read I'll after that shew you a few
lines here that will convince you what a hopeful
hobble one of us will be in.

Airc. But let's understand—Oh! I'm to make
believe to run away with her, and we're to leave
you in a hobble.

Alibi. What a stupid—he, he, he!—Sophy, carry
it on with him.

Sophia. Me go out with him! Silly! indeed I
shan't.

Alibi. Why, you perverse girl! mustn't I give the

lad some insight of the profession since I've touched
his money? and no conviction like example—do
it [*apart.*] Take Sophy away.

Airc. I woll, I woll. But, sir, if Aircourt even
had carried off miss in the manner I'm going to do,
nobody would believe it—it's so comical—he, he,
he!—They'd only think it the " Lie of the Day."

Alibi. Aye, Robin! the " Lie of the Day!"—
There, go.

Airc. Well then, good bye—till we see you
again.   [*Exit whistling with* SOPHIA.

Alibi. Ha, ha, ha! Oh, you ignoramus!—the fool
little thinks that a man can't even run away with
his own wife without being punished for it.—Now,
where is the chapter?—don't come in yet—I'll shew
him that he may get hanged for what he now
whistles at—Oh, here it is—Robin!—Sophy!—
Come, don't stand grinning out there at each other
—Robin! Zounds! come in [*goes to the door.*] Eh!
the door bolted!—Treachery!—Sophy!—Murder!
—I'm robbed—Plague of Lord Coke—I'm non-
suited—that villain Nol Pross—Oh! damn Yorkshire!   [*Exit at centre door.*

SCENE III.—*A Room at the Toy.*

Enter SOPHIA *hastily, speaking off.*

Sophia. My dear Aircourt! make haste; get us a
good chaise and fine horses!—By this my guardian's
in a precious fury—Heigho! Eh! Isn't that Lady
Arable? [*calls.*] Dear! I'm like a poor bird just got
loose, can scarce believe my own happiness.

Enter Lady ARABLE.

Lady Arable. Sophia! what can have brought you
to such a house as this? I could scarce believe it
was you.

Sophia. O, Lady Arable! I've done the maddest thing—I've eloped from my guardy.

Lady Arable. Eloped! but with who, and what, and how?

Sophia. As to your who, it is with Mr. Aircourt; your how, he came and got me off disguised like a Yorkshire clerk; the what, we'll be married directly.

Lady Arable. Disguised like a clerk! the very circumstance Fib told me! Are you sure your lover's name is—What do you call him?

Sophia. Aircourt.

Lady Arable. Don't be surprised, my dear, if I assure you that your very Mr. Aircourt is no other than my Mr. O'Donovan, that was to have been married to me directly.

Sophia. Dear Lady Arable, how can such a thing come into your head?

Lady Arable. Wasn't his letter of introduction from a Mr. Nol Pross?

Sophia. The very same.

Lady Arable. Believe me, it's beyond a doubt; yet when you beckoned me I hadn't an idea that you were my triumphant rival, ha, ha, ha!

Sophia. No, but seriously, can this be true?

Lady Arable. Most indubitable!—Fib got the whole affair from Povot his valet, ha, ha, ha!

Sophia. Nay, but don't laugh at me, Lady Arable, for I'm exceedingly hurt.

Lady Arable. Pray, what introduction? how came you acquainted?

Sophia. Mere accident; at the dancing master's ball at the London tavern—happened to be my partner.

Lady Arable. Yes; his man told Fib that he had been dancing about London under a fictitious name, and his father Sir Carrol thinks he is just arrived from Paris.

Sophia. Oh, he's one of the most dissembling, cruellest—— [*Cries.*]

Lady Arable. I request my dear Sophia won't imagine that I made the discovery out of jealousy, envy, or any other pretty little female principle of good nature.

Sophia. I'll never see him more—I despise—I'll try to hate him—[*cries.*] Cruel Aircourt! he's gone for a chaise—but let him go by himself for a traitor —I'll go directly back to my prison—I'm so vexed!

[*Exit crying.*

Lady Arable. I'll meet Mr. O'Donovan, and bring conviction to his face.

Airc. [*Without.*] Come, my love! the chaise is ready.—[*Enters.*]

Lady Arable. I'm glad to hear it, sir [*turns.*] Sir, I beg ten thousand pardons—I expected another gentleman.

Airc. And I, madam, expected another lady.

Lady Arable. Pray, sir, is your name Aircourt?

Airc. At your service, madam.

Lady Arable. O! what an egregious blunder have I made! my poor Sophia! Sir, I can't wait now for an explanation—As I was the cause, though innocently, of your losing the lady, you shall command every effort of mine to regain her.   [*Exit.*

Airc. What magic could have transformed Sophia to Lady Arable?—Here comes this fool!

Enter LARRY KAVANAGH.

Larry. Aircourt, I've been affronted so by Lady Arable—Do you know that she laughed at me this moment as I passed her?

Airc. No!

Larry. She did!—think of laughing at me! Damn me, I'll give her up—with all her beauty and fortune, she is only a widow!

Airc. Aye, a second-hand wife. You're a fine fellow, O'Donovan, and should have a new one.

Larry. I will—I'll make formal proposals for Sophia. I had the sweetest smile from her window just now.

Airc. Gone home? [*aside.*] Was ever such a little twirlabout tee-to-tum.

Larry. I have sent my man to Alibi's to request an interview—but, Aircourt, you told me you were on a love scheme here? What are you about with your girl?

Airc. I don't know. [*Peevish.*]

Larry. Don't know! don't bite me, ha, ha, ha! I see it, you've a puppy rival in the way.

Airc. I have; and a damned troublesome puppy he is—Just as you intend to Sophia, I am told he designs to make proposals for my mistress to her guardian.

Larry. But what objection has this guardian to you?

Airc. Why, I don't know: some busy body has been chattering that I wrote a song upon him, or I intended to have him caricatured in the print-shops; the thing above all others it seems he's most afraid of.

Larry. Gad! I have it—Send an anonymous line to the guardian, that a most notorious hummer has laid a plan to come as a suitor to his ward, but his real purpose to get his person and manner for a caricature print, or song, to turn him into ridicule; and if he is such an unique, he'll take the alarm at once —I warrant your rival trundled out of the house without a hearing, ha, ha, ha!

Airc. And so, O'Donovan, this is your comfortable advice?

Larry. I only wish I had a rival with my Sophia that I might put the joke in practice. What a cursed foolish figure he'd cut!

Airc. You really think he would?

Larry. Oh, by Heaven! it would be the highest —only do try it.

Airc. Well, perhaps I may—You've sent your man, you say, to Alibi?

Larry. Yes; and in three minutes time I shall be there myself and make proposals. But never mind me, Aircourt; do send the letter to your old lad; you may sign yourself " unknown friend," or " Q. in the corner."—Ha! ha! ha! 'twill make a screeching laugh.

Airc. Gad! I think it will—I'll try it however.

[*Exeunt laughing.*

SCENE IV.—Alibi's *House.*

Enter Alibi *and* Sophia.

Sophia. Don't mention him; I hate him now as much as ever I loved him.

Alibi. I thought you'd repent of your fondness for your charming Aircourt.

Sophia. Do now let's hear no more of him; and upon my honour I won't run away again.

Alibi. 'Pon my honour, I don't think you will, my little Soph! if a wise brain, brick wall, strong bolt, and double lock can prevent it.

Sophia. Ah! guardian, if a woman's mind is set upon a young fellow with a true heart, handsome face, and elegant person, your wall's a cobweb— bolt, straw—lock, pie-crust—and your brain syllabub!

Alibi. Don't tell me of cobweb—pie-crusts!—You shall find me a spider, Mrs. Lady-bird. [*Puts on his gown and cap.*]

Sophia. Oh that somebody was to see you, ha! ha! ha! I'd have you taken off just as you are now.

Alibi. Take me off! If they gibbet me in their

print-shops, I'll bring my action for a libel! their
windows are a nuisance, exhibitions of scandal and
indecency, to block up the footpaths and make a
harvest for pickpockets.

Enter LARRY KAVANAGH.

Larry. Mr. Alibi—Ma'am, your most——Ha!
charming, by heaven! [*Aside.*]
Alibi. Sir!
Sophia. This Chelsea fop to plague me! [*Aside.*]
Larry. I have taken the liberty to wait upon you,
in hopes that my addresses to this lady may prove
agreeable to her tender inclination and your sage
opinion. [*Bows.*]
Alibi. Why, sir, as to the tenderness of that lady's
inclinations, that's a matter with me of just—about
three halfpence. [*Mimicking* LARRY.]
Sophia. And, sir, the sagacity of that gentleman's
opinion with me just—about—a penny farthing under that sum. [*Mimicking* ALIBI.]
Larry. As I have totally forgot the multiplication
table, Gad curse me! if I can strike a balance upon
this business—But, sir, I love, and will marry this
lady; that's my sum total.

Enter BOY.

Boy. [*Giving a letter to* ALIBI.] A man left that
for you, sir.   [*Exit.*

LARRY *and* SOPHIA *walk up.*

Alibi. [*Reads.*] " An unknown friend warns you
against a design to turn you into ridicule by carica-
turing you for the print-shops: the person is a noted
hummer, and introduced himself to you at Chelsea."
—Chelsea! the very fellow! [*Reads.*]—" And to finish
his *outre* picture, he's to obtain an interview as a
man of fortune in love with your ward Miss Sophia!"

—Oh, oh, my friend!—" Take this hint from yours
—Q. in the Corner."

[*Puts the letter up, and holds his face up to* LARRY.

Well, look! have you got a likeness?

Larry. Eh!

Alibi. I've a striking phiz, an't I?

Larry. You have a very good phiz, indeed, sir.

Alibi. But when I've the pipe——

Larry. What the devil has he got at now?

Alibi. The tune of the ballad, I suppose, will be
bow wow!—or, stop—Derry down's a good tune.

Larry. Sir, I don't know what you mean by derry
downs.

Alibi. Don't you? then I'll speak plainer—there's
the stairs, and pray, sir, do you walk down, down,
down derry, derry down! [*Sings.*]

Sophia. Ha! ha! ha! this is the very thing I was
wishing for—I guess how it is—ha! ha! ha!

Larry. The laugh is against somebody, but
dam'me if I can tell who.

Sophia. There, sir, you see the attorney to advantage. Guardian, make a face for the gentleman.

Alibi. Ma'am, do you step in [*puts* SOPHIA *in*];
and, sir, do you step out.

Larry. Sir, I'm a person of rank and consequence,
and must desire——

Alibi. And I desire you'll pack up your consequence, be your own porter, and carry it out of my
house.

Metheglin. [*Without.*] Are you above, Master
Alibi?

Larry. Oh, Lady Arable's butler! he can tell you
that I'm a person of fashion.

Enter METHEGLIN.

Meth. Ah! what are you here, Larry?—Gad, I
forgot.

Alibi. So then, Larry, you're a man of fashion?

E E 3

Larry. Fellow! I'll see if your lady authorises this insolence to her guests; and as for you, I'll carry your ward by all the powers of love and stratagem. [*Exit.*

Alibi. A goose quill for your stratagem—Damn the fellow! Did you ever see such a puff-crack?— Who is he, Metheglin?

Meth. Can't reveal that without my wife's leave.

Alibi. Wife! Zounds! you hav'n't married her yet?

Meth. No.

Alibi. Where is she?

Meth. So eager to have her little penny settled upon her before our marriage, that she would come with me—she's in the next room.

Katty. [*Without.*] Mr. Metheglin!

Alibi. Her very voice! It is my dear wife! [*Aside.*] Has she much money?

Meth. A power!

Alibi. I feel all my conjugal tenderness revive. Metheglin, reach the ink-stand off the desk yonder.

Meth. She's a jolly body! be civil to her—the pen and ink! ay, ay! [*Exit.*

Alibi. It is she—I gave her time to roll; and the prudent creature in purse and person has gathered like a snow-ball.

Enter KATTY.

Katty. Pray, Mr. Counsellor, do you know much of this husband I am going to marry?

Alibi. I know a husband you did marry. [*With solemnity.*]

Katty. And is it! are you alive, my Bryan! my own honey?

Alibi. Kate! Katty! O my Catherine! [*Embrace.*]

Enter METHEGLIN *with ink-stand.*

Katty. Mr. Metheglin, though now you and I are two, I believe you're an honest man.

Alibi. Mr. Metheglin, your wife turns out to be my wife !   [*Exeunt* ALIBI *and* KATTY.

Meth. Is the world at an end ? am I myself ? Quit me in a half a minute for this big little villain ! because he has money—for this false woman to reject my lady !—I'll—I'll lay my heart at her feet and make her happy !—Yes, I'll go to the drawing-room —No—first to the wine cellar !—Cruel Katty! barbarous—hem !   [*Exit.*

SCENE.—*Outside of the Toy.*

Enter AIRCOURT *and* LARRY KAVANAGH.

Airc. Ha! ha! ha! what trundled you down without a hearing?

Larry. Gad! as you say, trundled me down without a hearing; but held up his phiz as he called it, and in the most rude and ill-bred manner fairly derry-down'd and bow-wow'd me out of his house.

Airc. Well said, Q. in the corner. [*Aside.*]

Larry. And yet in my vexation I can scarce help laughing—for—brushing through Alibi's hall in my fury, who should I see sitting in the parlour very stately, but my Irish nurse. Prompted by curiosity and another peep at Sophy——

Airc. Sophy ! well—

Larry. I popped into the adjoining room, and overheard—Why she's Alibi's wife ! and old pettifog is in horrid dread of a most tremendous Irish admirer, who paid his addresses on the supposition of her being a rich widow.

Airc. Ay, well!

Larry. Alibi fears he'll follow her from Ireland

and cut his throat, ha! ha! ha!—he is called Captain Kilmeinham O'Squramough!

Airc. Psha! Damn your grinning, let's hear.

Larry. Why this hero is really it seems a devil of
a wicked fellow—has been in the German service,
and in some of the most dangerous actions on the
Turkish frontiers.

Airc. Alibi in dread of this formidable Hibernian
Hector! this may prove a *coup-de-main.* [*Aside.*]

Larry. But, Aircourt, about your mistress—
What have you done with your fool of a rival?

Airc. As great a fool as ever—he has been just
now communicating a circumstance to me that I
hope will put it into my power to jockey him once
for all, ha! ha! ha!

Larry. Why, what a cursed blockhead must he
be, to make you of all men his confidante!

Airc. A cursed blockhead!

Larry. Jockey him.

Airc. I will—ha! ha! ha!

Larry. But you promis'd to assist me in getting
Sophia out.

Airc. If I don't get her out may I be——Well,
good bye! when next we meet, you shall hear something of your girl that will astonish you.

Larry. Thank ye—Adieu!

Airc. I'll about it, my boy—I'll jockey him, ha!
ha! ha!   [*Exeunt.*

ACT III.

SCENE I.—*A Room at Lady* ARABLE'S.

Enter METHEGLIN *with Wine.*

Meth. Perfidious Katty! But let her go to the ——
Indeed the black gentleman has got her already.—

Ah, for—[*fills and drinks*] sweet revenge—I could quaff aquafortis.—My lovely mistress, Lady Arable, I'm now all yours—I'll return your smiles with ogles, your leers with kisses, your money with—myself. But Sir Carrol seems so bent upon his son's marrying her—How to ward that! If I discover to Sir Carrol that Larry's not his son—But Katty told me that under the seal of secrecy—Honour—honour —honour! As I'm sure of my lady's heart, what if I start this young stranger at her—Sir Carrol perceives it; his proud Irish blood is up, and he commands his son to think no more of her. In steps I, and all's my own. Oh, the beagle! Hip, boy, holloa!

Enter Young O'DONOVAN *with papers in his hand.*

I've a secret for you: take a drop out of the bottom of that glass.

O'Don. I thank you; but you see I'm in a hurry. [*Going.*]

Meth. Stop—A false woman's worse than—an empty glass—Adieu to the cellar delights!——As I've made up my mind to marry my mistress, I must hire a butler of my own.

O'Don. You marry your lady! Very good indeed! ha! ha! ha! Pray, isn't the match concluded between Lady Arable and Mr. O'Donovan?

Meth. Yes; it's at an end, if that's a conclusion. [*Bell rings.*]—Aye, pull away now, my lady; but presently, when I'm your lord and master, I'll teach you to knock my bells about in that manner.

O'Don. If Lady Arable's refusal of Sir Carrol's son is true, though I cou'dn't rejoice at her union with O'Donovan, yet I most sensibly feel at every cause of uneasiness to his worthy father. [*Aside.*]

Meth. It's not birth; beauty is the mark women look at—it is not pedigree—not for the root, but the

fruit of the tree their mouths water.—Lady Arable
has cast an eye upon you—and two upon me. [*Aside.*

O'Don. How!

Meth. Fib told me that her ladyship swore this
morning you were the prettiest man in the house—
except me. [*Aside.*] I'll bring you together—you
shall jink Larry——Hem! I mean 'Squire O'Donovan.

O'Don. But, Metheglin, just now you were going
to marry your mistress, ha! ha! ha!

Meth. Never mind—I'll tell her how you love
her.

O'Don. [*Surprised and angry.*] Me!—I don't—
Did I ever tell you any such thing? Lady Arable
lose a thought upon me!—If I could think it possible, sooner than distress the worthy Sir Carrol, by
being the cause that she rejects his son, I'd quit the
house immediately. [*Aside.*]   [*Bell rings.*

Meth. Go to her! go, go! [*Pushes* O'DONOVAN
off.] Now I've primed him with love, he'll be talking
soft: then I'll send Sir Carrol in upon them; but if
the beagle shou'd jink me in this affair. [*Bell rings*].
—There, she can't do without Metheglin!—How
do I look? [*Looks in a glass.*] That glass of red
mantles in my cheek and sparkles in my eye—Smile,
you monkey! [*Grimaces.*] The other corner—the
other eye—Oh bravo! I'll put on my wedding
clothes, white fring'd gloves, bag wig, and clap my
head in a new brigadier—then have at her noble
countenance—I'll go to Alibi's, and see that the
marriage articles are drawn up—Soon shall I be
lord of all her houses, consuls, hogsheads, jointures,
mills, meadows, plate, and puncheons.   [*Exit.*

Enter SOPHIA *running.*

Sophia. Lady Arable! [*calling.*] Where can she
be?

Enter FIB.

Fib, where's your lady?

Fib. I'm looking for her, ma'am.—The jeweller has brought home her picture—I believe 'twas inended for Sir Carrol to give to Mr. O'Donovan.

Sophia. What! the flashy fool that's teazing me? [*Opens the case.*] Dear! it's very like Lady Arable. —Oh! here she is.—Fib, go; I want to consult your lady about my love affairs.

Fib. Ah, my poor lady, I fancy, has love affairs of her own!   [*Exit.*

Enter Lady ARABLE.

Lady Arable. Sophia! why you fly in and out like a bird from the nest!

Sophia. Lord, my guardian has got a new wife!— She let me escape—I told her I knew where there was real genuine Irish snuff to be sold, and that I'd go and buy her some—But, dear, it wou'd be very wicked in me to set the poor old soul sneezing, he! he! he!—Lady Arable, I came to ask about Aircourt—I suppose you think me very forward?

Lady Arable. We must be blameless ourselves before we censure others.—But, Sophia, you found I was wrong; that your Aircourt and Mr. O'Donovan are distinct persons.

Sophia. Yes, yes: oh, such a trick as Aircourt served him, ha! ha! But yet I fear my lover, from thinking himself sure of my heart, will grow careless.—If I cou'd but make him jealous—He despises his present rival too much for that—Lord! Lady Arable, if that handsome young man you've here would walk before my windows, sighing and kissing his handkerchief, it would be such a spur to Aircourt—Oh, he'd whip me off to Gretna Green at once.

Lady Arable. But, Sophia, what if that handsome young man should not be quite indifferent to me.

Sophia. You're in love with him; I see it in your face—Lord, never mind his being poor!—have him, and we'll all four run away together.

Lady Arable. Though I flatter myself he's touch'd with mutual tenderness, yet the disparity of our situation can't suffer him to disclose it.

Sophia. O the fate of us poor women! We must walk round about the dear object, and, like a troubled ghost, never speak till we're spoken to; whilst the men can spout away—" Oh, never, my most adorable creature!"—"I die for you!"—" My angel!"—" I languish!"—" 'Pon my honour!"—" My love!"—" Oh! oh!" [*Mimicks.*]

Lady Arable. Ha! ha! ha! As you say, Sophia, it never can come from me, therefore we must both pine in thought.

Sophia. It shall come from you though; you're a friend to my love, and I'll be a friend to yours, he! he! he!—Lady Arable, since you're out of all hope with this young man, tell him I have a *penchant* for him—it will make Aircourt so jealous.

Lady Arable. Well, Sophia, I will—It may at least be a trial how his heart is really affected towards myself.

Sophia. Lady Arable, shew him this; it's my picture. [*Gives it.*]

[*Lady* ARABLE *going to open it,* SOPHIA *prevents her.*

Lord, you've seen it a thousand times! Tell him that's a strong likeness of a lady that admires him. —Here he is—Now, now! [*Runs off.*

Enter O'DONOVAN.

O'Don. Madam, as Sir Carrol desired, I have looked over those papers.

Lady Arable. Well, well.—I'm entrusted, sir, with

a strange kind of commission—You'll not be very
surprised ; for these things are more common than
they should be.—There is a certain lady, who, if
your heart is quite disengaged, is inclined to enter
into some ideas in your favour.

O'Don. Madam ! [*Surprised and hurt.*]

Lady Arable. The lady is a very particular friend
of mine, and will have a very ample fortune.—Now,
if that and Sophia's pretty features captivate him,
farewell my silly hopes ! [*Aside.*]

O'Don. Your ladyship is inclined to amuse yourself at the expence of my vanity.

Lady Arable. I assure you she is not a mean conquest.—You may judge of her charms from this her
picture ; with which, to spare her the indelicacy of
a declaration, she desired me to present you. [*Gives
the picture.*]

O'Don. [*Opens it indifferently.*] How ! [*surprised*]
Impossible ! Oh, Lady Arable ! my heart, while I
confess it sensibly awake to each perfection, never
harboured a thought of the divine original. [*Kisses it.*

Lady Arable. Then he knows Sophia ! Her money
must have been his first attraction, and doubtless
brought him to this neighbourhood.——Divine !
[*Walks angry.*]

O'Don. She's offended.—First try, and then punish my presumption ! Cruel of you, madam, to
betray me into a confession, that before I could make
I'd have perish'd.—Pardon my audacity—I return
you your picture, and relinquish every hope—I can
never shew my face again—to you—or my benefactor—Heaven protect !—— my heart is full !——
Adieu, most honoured lady !   [*Exit.*

Lady Arable. [*Looks at the picture.*] Heavens ! my
own picture ! What a prank has Sophia played me !
—What must he think of me ? And I to wrong his
purity by my doubts—Yes, I have blasphemed the
god of my idolatry—but was I quite certain that he

F F

entertained one tender thought for me, for the first
time in my life I'd rejoice at being born to a splendid fortune.   [*Exit.*

SCENE II.—*A Hall with several Doors at* ALIBI'S.
—*Wine and Tea.*

Enter KATTY.

Katty. Lord, what I fool was I to let that young
creature go out and buy me snuff, and it already to
cause a quarrel between me and my little old husband!—He said " The devil's in your nose, Katty!"
and that's what he said, sure enough.

Alibi. [*Without.*] Go in, I say!

Enter ALIBI *with* SOPHIA.

She run out to buy snuff, indeed! And there I find
her walking about the palace gardens.—Zounds! I
never knew they sold snuff in the palace gardens.

Sophia. Let me peep at this letter the man slipt
me—I'm sure he was a waiter at the Toy [*opens it.*]
It is from my dear Aircourt.

Katty. But my pretty soul, where's the Irish
snuff?

Sophia. Get along, you old fool. [*Peruses letter.*]

Alibi. Running about after you has made me so
thirsty. [*Drinks.*]   [*They all sit.*
Oh, Sophy! Oh, Katty! here had I retired after all
my turmoils to enjoy the snug chimney corner of
life; yet, on a sudden, I'm wound up in cares like a
silk-worm in his woof—all of my own spinning too
—In this country I'm sure I can't stay long; and if
I were to venture back to Ireland, there I have ready
before me that damn'd terrible Irish cossack.——
Katty, my love, what is that hector's name, the captain that loved you so much in Ireland?

Katty. Captain Kilmeinham O'Squramough!—

Faith, and he did love me! If he was to come over
he'd shoot me in your arms.

Alibi. I'd as lief he would shoot you anywhere
else.

Airc. [*Without.*] Tell her it's her friend Captain
Kilmeinham O'Squramough! just come from Dublin. [*With the brogue, very loud.*]

Alibi. What! [*Terrified.*]

Sophia. My dear Aircourt keeps his promise to
free me. [*Aside.*]

Katty. Oh, husband! 'tis Captain Kilmeinham
O'Squramough, and seems to have been at his bottle—Here will be cutting and shooting!

Alibi. Cutting and shooting!

Sophia. A captain! Perhaps he will take a dish of
tea with us, ha! ha! ha!

Alibi. Tea! give him some aquafortis!

　　　　　　　　　　　　　[*Glass broke without.*
Zounds! if he hasn't broke the lamp in the hall!—
Who's there? [*Trembling.*]

　　　　　　　　[KATTY *and* SOPHIA *exeunt.*

　　　　Enter AIRCOURT *disguised.*

Airc. Sir, as I am a gentleman, I think it rudeness to force into any man's house.

Alibi. Really, sir, I am somewhat of your way of
thinking.

Airc. I find you are, sir: as we both think of having the same woman.—With submission, I think
that's damn'd impudent in one of us.

Alibi. I think so too, sir; but pray, to whom am
I indebted for the honour of this visit?

Airc. To that amiable inconstant, the widow Kavanagh.

Alibi. The very desperado! Sir, I imagine you
design to affront me.

Airc. I came on purpose.

Alibi. Civil creature! [*Aside.*]

Airc. Look you, sir; I have had the honour to serve at home and abroad—Oczakow and Balbriggin—the Danube and the Liffey—Volunteer reviews and Belgrade sieges—all one to Kilmeinham O'Squramough—And I have learnt in Ireland and Germany by tactic, theoretic and practic, that there are two ways of doing things. The first is [*fills*]—health [*drinks*]—that's one way! The second is [*fills*]—Sir, your health [*drinks*]—that's another way.

Alibi. Now, sir, with deference to your tactics, those two ways seem to me but one.

Airc. Right, sir ; [*fills*]—two and one make three [*drinks*]—You see, sir, how I love my bottle.

Alibi. I see how you love my bottle ! The greatest marauder I ever saw. [*Aside.*]

Airc. How can you keep such wine ?

Alibi. It's very difficult.—I wish I had a constable. [*Aside.*]

Airc. Now, our Irish claret glides down like new milk—makes a man sprightly and good-natur'd ; but your damn'd gunpowder port sets my kiln afire [*strikes his forehead*], and makes me as hot and as wicked—It has just primed me for business ; and now for the business that brought me before your citadel.—Hark'e, friend, as I doat on Mrs. Kavanagh, the man that loves her is a scoundrel!

Alibi. Sir, we still agree in opinion ; but this widow happens to be my wife.

Airc. What ! then you've married her, hah ! O you most outrageous——

Alibi. But, sir, long before you ever saw her.

Airc. Then you didn't give me fair chance—election or rejection, that's the word ! But it can't be ! She was never before in England.

Alibi. But I was in Ireland.

Airc. Sir, I have done—I ask pardon for all favours ! [*Bows low.*]

Alibi. [*Bows low.*] Now you're cool, sir—if I shou'd thrust myself into your house, break your glass lantern, and make all this uproar, what wou'd you say?

Airc. Faith, sir, I'd say nothing at all at all ; but I'd like a crow have the honour to take you up to the garret window, decently drop you down upon the flags, and crack you like a cockle.—Oh, I'd knock your head against the walls of Bender, as Charles the XIIth did the Janissaries!—I'd kick you just so [*throws down the table and breaks the china.*]— I'd turn you out of my house just so—Get along, you scoundrel!——I'd demolish all your aiders and abetters——

Enter METHEGLIN, *drest as a bridegroom*—AIRCOURT *shoves him.*

I'd slay you and every scoundrel who'd take a lady from Captain Kilmeinham O'Squramough!   [*Exit.*

Alibi. Sophia! The marauder's gone kown the road—Stop him, and I'll give you a hundred guineas!

Meth. Me! Wou'dn't stop a man on the king's highway for five thousand!

Alibi. O my ward!—Get along, you muzzy-headed fool—If you won't help to recover Sophia, get home to your sideboard—Furies! if she meets Aircourt, she's irrecoverably lost!—Sophy! [*Exit.*

Meth. Muzzy-headed!—Fool!—Sideboard!—— Very well.—Yes, I think I'll introduce one Sir Carrol O'Donovan into this house.—Yes, he may be listen'd to, though I can't—I will—Master Larry.— Oh, ho!—Ay, ay—Master Alibi—I'll discover—— Aye—aye—   [*Exit.*

SCENE—*As before.*

Enter O'DONOVAN.

O'Don. How unlucky this mischievous foolMethe-
glin to acquaint Sir Carrol of my passion for Lady
Arable ; hers for me I have proved was entirely his
own fancy. My benefactor must think me presumptuous and ungrateful.   No; I'll return no more—
This lawyer may afford me at least a temporary employment—if not, I'll directly for London.   Sir
Carrol seems disturbed.   [*Retires.*

Enter Sir CARROL.

Sir Car. May I believe Metheglin's story—this
young Larry, as he calls him, whom I considered
my son, really Alibi's !—Would they graft their ras-
cally bramble on the noble stock of the O'Donovan's ?   Then, my poor unhappy child, whoever he
is, must go by their name—Lawrence Kavanagh !
Perhaps they have abandoned him, and he now lan-
guishes in penury—perhaps—dead !

O'DONOVAN *advances.*

Ha ! my lad, we were all surprised at your abrupt
departure.

O'Don. Sir Carrol, though I confess myself unworthy of your bounty, I'm not yet so base as to accept obligations from the person I have injured.

Sir Car. Why, Metheglin has been telling us—

O'Don. Truth !   By insidiously cherishing a passion for your son's intended lady, I fear I have frustrated your favourite wish.

Sir Car. So a point of gratitude impelled him to
relinquish the affluence that probably offered a reward to his merit—a noble-minded youth [*aside.*]—
How you first became acquainted with Lady Arable
I do not ask; but had she been more candid, you

should not have been hurt, nor her ladyship troubled by my proposals for my son.   The opinion I conceived of you at first sight has not deceived me.   You have interested me to a more particular inquiry ; and first tell me what is your name ?

O'Don. Kavanagh.

Sir Car. How ! your christian name !

O'Don. Lawrence.

Sir Car. Who are your parents? [*Quick, and with great emotion.*]

O'Don. Sir, I have just now seen my mother in this house, but I think she did not know me.

Sir Car. She nursed my son!

O'Don. [*Bows.*]

Sir Car. It is—my Edward !—my generous boy ! [*embraces him*]—so long the forlorn child of indigence—alike an unhappy subject for the scorn of pride and the tear of pity. [*Puts his handkerchief to his eyes.*]

O'Don. Can this be ?

Alibi. [*Without.*] No, wife, you shan't prevail upon me to connive at your imposition.

Enter ALIBI.

Since Katty has squeaked, I'll slip my own neck out of the noose. [*Aside.*]

Sir Car. Well, Mr. Alibi, alias Kavanagh ! [ALIBI *surprised.*]   I left you in Ireland twenty years ago a profligate young man, and now I find you in England a hardened old knave.

Alibi. Sir !

Sir Car. In youth, when the passions take the rein, vice may be the effect of folly ; but when judgment is matured by age, a vicious man is a confirmed scoundrel.   Where's my son, rascal ?

Alibi. [*Trembling.*] Indeed, Sir Carrol, I'd myself give a thousand pounds to find him.

Sir Car. Look, honour—and ask his pardon.

Enter Lady ARABLE.

O'Don. Merciful heaven! I came hither to seek
—but to find such a father! [*Kneels.*]

Sir Car. Rise, my dear son; I'm not more rejoiced
at finding you, than by fortune's knocking at the
door of poverty to see it opened by an honest man.

Enter METHEGLIN.

Lady Arable. This gentleman your son, Sir Carrol! This, I hope, may in some measure justify
what I dreaded would prove the inexcusable error
of my heart.

Meth. Your choice of me, error, my lady! [*All
stare.*]

Sir Car. Ha! ha! ha! Mr. Metheglin, I fear
you've been in a little mistake here; but as it has
discovered your perfidious Katty and her husband's
imposture upon me, you shan't lose your place at
the sideboard.

Meth. Sideboard! My wedding suit, new white
gloves and brigadier wig!—Ah! you'll be yet Sir
Edward! Title turns it—Oh, woman! sacrifice
happiness to vanity!

Enter LARRY.

Larry. Ah, my haughty goddess! your consent
comes now too late.—Upon my honour, you cannot
have me!

Meth. Well said, Larry!

Larry. Larry!

Sir Car. Thank Heaven, you are no son of mine!
There is your father! [*Pointing to* ALIBI.]

Alibi. Sir Carrol's right. This is his young gentleman, and you are mine.

Meth. How do you do, Larry?

Larry. Larry! what the devil do you Larry me

for?—Your son! Eh?—Old Alibi's son! [*Noise without.*]—What is the meaning of all this?

Alibi. The captain again! Hide that bottle, and lock the china cupboard.

Meth. Give me the bottle, and lock us up together.
[*Retires.*

Enter AIRCOURT *and* SOPHIA.

Airc. Be it known from Belgrade to Balbriggin that old gentlemen may keep their widows! for this lady is now the wife of Captain Kilmeinham O'Squramough.

Alibi. Your wife! And who are you?

Airc. Mr. Alibi; I supposed from the known venality of your character, had I asked your consent fairly and openly I never should have gained it; but instead of a needy adventurer, my Sophia shall prove, that to obtain her charming self was the sole object of her affectionate Aircourt.

Larry. No, my dear fellow, you took her off for me!

Airc. No, my dear fellow, I took her off for myself!

Larry. But you said for me.

Airc. Pho! 'twas only the " Lie of the Day!"— With any other motive I'd scorn to circumvent a friend; but in love all stratagem is allowable.

Meth. Ha! ha! ha! how do you do, Larry? [*Exit.*

Alibi. This Aircourt!

Airc. Aye, poor clerk Robin! who used to play with the maids.

Alibi. Mind, her fortune is still in my hands—I'm her guardian.

Sophia. No, sir, you are not. The name for executor in my mother's will is Alibi: now, as I understand that yours is Kavanagh, we shall make your part in the trust void by the misnomer!

Alibi. Here's petticoat pleading ! I must make her a chamber council, and be curst to me !

Sophia. He! he! he! How did you like my picture, sir ?

Lady Arable. Ah, you arch one !

Sir Car. Reimburse the four thousand it has cost me in the training of your son Lawrence! and give this lady her fortune, or for your fraud on me I'll prosecute you to beggary ! To acquire riches was the cause of your crime ; the loss of them now be your punishment. The events of this day have proved, that the Eye which sees all directs an unerring hand, to give vice the lash, and drop on the brow of honour the blooming wreath of unfading happiness.

THE END.